DATE DUE

DEC 0 8 1998		
JUN 1 7 2002		
JUL 01 1999		

A FINE WILL BE CHARGED
FOR EACH OVERDUE BOOK

HIGHSMITH #45115

D1478488

Francis Bacon

FRANCISCVS BACON BARO DE VERVLAM, S. ALBANI VIC.
SEV NOTIORIBVS TITVLIS
SCIENTIARVM LVMEN, FACVNDIÆ LEX.
SIC SEDEBAT

Francis Bacon

The History of a Character Assassination

Nieves Mathews

Yale University Press
New Haven and London

Set in Meridien by Best-set Typesetter Ltd, Hong Kong
Printed and bound in Great Britain by St Edmundsbury Press

Library of Congress Catalog Card Number 96-60105

ISBN 0–300–06441–1

A catalogue record for this book is available from the British Library.

Frontispiece: Engraving of the monument put up for Bacon by his secretary – later his great-nephew by marriage – Sir Thomas Meautys, with the Latin inscription: *Sic sedebat . . . Tanti viri mem. Superstitis cultor, defuncti admirator, H.P.* (So he sat . . . In memory of so great a man, one who in life served him and in death admires him, set up this monument.)

The engraving was made by the Bohemian artist, Wenceslas Hollar, who also designed the frontispiece of Sprat's *History of the Royal Society*, in which Bacon appears with its first President. It was prefixed to the *Resuscitatio*, the *Works* of Bacon edited by William Rawley, his chaplain and secretary, in 1657. John Carteret described it in *Biographia Britannica*, in 1747, as 'an excellent plate of the monument erected by the masterly hand of W. Hollar'.

The statue has been placed out of easy reach, but anyone willing to take a ladder into St Michael's Church, St Albans, and climb high enough will note that Hollar's engraving is a quite faithful reproduction, with perhaps an added touch in the eyes of that 'aspect as if he pitied men' which Bacon attributed to philosophers, and to the fathers of the New Atlantis.

The slander of a dead man is a living fault

Edward Coke, in
*Wraynham's Case or A Vindication
of the Lord Chancellor Bacon,*
1618

Contents

Contents

Dedication and Acknowledgements

This book is dedicated to four continuing presences: my mother, C.H.M.A., whose lively interest in Bacon first kindled mine; my father, S. de M., whose mind, like Bacon's crossed all the frontiers, and who died, as he did, 'in earnest pursuit'; my friend, E. de R., who persuaded me to stop talking and begin to write; and my teacher, Osho, who thought highly of Francis Bacon, and gave the book his blessing. Finally it is dedicated to the memory of Professor Benjamin Farrington, whose intention of contributing, on his retirement, 'to the extinction of the pestilent habit of abusing Bacon' is recorded on the dust jacket of his *Philosophy of Francis Bacon*, often resorted to here. He did not live to do so, but he was happy with the first outline of my book, and I am confident that he would have welcomed the fuller version presented here.

Among the many friends and relations who have helped me, I owe particular thanks to Professors Raymond Klibansky and Paolo Vivante for assistance with Latin allusions, and to Geoffrey Plowden for advice on Alexander Pope (usually heeded); to Christopher, Beatrice and Marianne Mathews and Professor Isabel de Madariaga, and to Professor Elemire Zolla, John Sligo and John Cairncross, for perseverant critical reading of the text; to Sheila, Countess Powerscourt, and to Eric Sams and Christopher Nupen for sharp sword-thrusts and lightning ideas; and last but not least to Professor Brian Vickers for painstaking, ruthless, but essential criticism, numerous helpful suggestions and unstinted encouragement.

I am grateful to Sylvia England and Paul Cross for their help in searching for clues in the British Library; to Rakhi Punjabi and Rosemary Torigian, who assisted me with typing in the early stages; to Candida Brazil and Ann Bone for their attentive and responsive editing; to the Francis Bacon Society, and to Mrs Elizabeth Wrigley, until recently Librarian of the Francis Bacon Library in Claremont, California, for their answers to many questions; and above all to the Librarian and staff of the London Library, without whose assistance and forbearance this book could not have been written.

Significant Dates in Bacon's Life

Born	22 January 1561
Matriculated at Trinity College, Cambridge	10 June 1573
Left for France	25 September 1576
Admitted at Gray's Inn during his absence	21 November 1576
Death of his father, Sir Nicholas	17 February 1579
Returned to England	20 March 1579
First sat in the House of Commons as Member for Bossiney, Cornwall	January 1581
Called to the Bar	7 June 1583
Granted a Reader's privileges at Gray's Inn	10 February 1587
Elected Reader with chambers at the Inn for life	21 November 1588
On the defeat of the Armada, appointed to a commission to examine recusants	August 1588
Appointed to a board of twenty legal advisers set up to reform the Statutes	27 December 1588
Return of Anthony Bacon from France	4 February 1592
Queen's Counsel Extraordinary (unpaid)	Michaelmas 1594
Proposed to Lady Hatton	June 1597
Departure of Essex for Ireland	17 March 1599
Essex's unwarranted return	28 September 1599
Essex admonished in the Star Chamber	29 November 1599
York House Proceedings against Essex	5 June 1600
Rebellion, trial and execution of Essex	8–25 February 1601
Funeral of Anthony Bacon	17 May 1601
Death of Elizabeth and accession of James I	24 March 1603
Knighted	23 July 1603
King's Counsel Learned	25 August 1604
Married Alice Barnham	10 May 1606
Solicitor General	25 June 1607
Treasurer at Gray's Inn	17 October 1608
Death of Sir Robert Cecil	24 May 1612
Death of Prince Henry	6 November 1612
Attorney General	26 October 1613
Privy Councillor	9 June 1615
Lord Keeper	3 March 1617

Lord Chancellor	4 January 1618
Baron Verulam	12 July 1618
Viscount St Alban	20 January 1621
Accused of corruption in the Commons	14 March 1621
Sentenced by the House of Lords	3 May 1621
Death of James and accession of Charles I	27 March 1625
Died	9 April 1626

For the dates of his interventions in Parliament, see chapter 20

Principal Writings of Bacon Referred to Here

Unless otherwise stated, references are to the English texts in the edition of Bacon's works by Spedding, Ellis and Heath, cited by volume (in bold) and page number only.

INTRODUCTION

1

'The Peremptory Tides of Reputation'

'To the Present and Future Ages, Greeting.' With these words, in 1623, Francis Bacon addressed the *History of Life and Death* to his spiritual heirs in centuries to come. In the same year he concluded another work saying, 'It is enough for me that I have sown unto posterity and the Immortal God.' It was Bacon's vocation to sow 'for future ages the seeds of a purer truth'. Meanwhile he could also expect that 'immortality or continuance . . . whereunto man's nature doth most aspire'. Indeed he was confident, as he told James I, that he would be the means of making his age famous to posterity.[1] But it was of his personal character Bacon was thinking when in his last will he bequeathed his name and memory 'to men's charitable speeches, and to foreign nations, and the next ages'.[2] The aim of the present study is to look into what we, the next ages, have done with his bequest.

Regarding what he called 'that durable part of memory' – his writings – Bacon left detailed instructions in his will. Like many of his contemporaries, and perhaps more sincerely than some, he did not 'court the present time'. He accounted 'the use that a man should seek of publishing his own writings before his death, to be but an untimely anticipation of that which is proper to follow a man, and not to go along with him'.[3] The immortality Bacon sought was not literary fame in the ordinary sense of the term. If anything, he did not care enough for it, and he has been criticized for leaving so many of his works unfinished. 'Both in what I now publish,' he could write, 'and in that which I plan for the future, I often consciously and purposely cast aside the dignity of my genius and my name (if such a thing be) while I serve the welfare of humanity.'[4] Bacon looked to 'the sons of the dawn', as he called the future generations, to continue the work he had hardly been able to begin. 'I have been content to tune the instruments of the muses, that they may play that have better hands' – this is the leitmotiv of his prefaces and letters. He was well aware that what he wanted to achieve could not be done 'within the hour-glass of a man's life': an age would be needed to prove his words, and many ages to perfect them. But he believed that, like other 'images of men's wits', they would 'continually generate and cast their seeds in the minds of others, provoking and causing infinite actions and opinions in succeeding ages'.[5]

The images of Bacon's wits did provoke infinite and valuable actions. As for opinions, what the succeeding ages have done with his philosophy, science and law, his principles of statesmanship, his psychology or 'science of man', his thoughts on 'poesy', has been looked into by many students of his works, from his day to ours. It can be summed up in the words of one of them, written in 1961: 'the volumes of disagreement' over Bacon's contribution to thought 'must be without parallel in literary history'.[6] In general terms the seventeenth century praised and imitated him, the eighteenth idolized him (for Leibniz he soared to the heavens, while Descartes grovelled on earth), and the nineteenth and early twentieth centuries devoted a large part of their energies to debunking him; so that the Secretary of Nature and all Learning, as his own time saw him, came to be despised as a charlatan and a quack, and was labelled the worst enemy science has ever known.[7] Throughout our century diametrically opposite judgements have been made about Bacon's thought. Dubbed an atheist and hailed as a religious thinker, he was pronounced a mediocre – and a brilliant – historian, acclaimed for his prophetic insights in natural history, his understanding of logic, his theory of forms, his powerful imagination – and decried at the same time for his ignorance of natural history and logic, his absurd notion of forms and his entire lack of imagination. In 1911 he was presented as the defender of a strong monarchy, in 1955 as the champion of constitutional Parliament.[8]

It is not surprising that a man whose mental net was cast so wide should have aroused a considerable variety of responses. 'Lord Keeper of the Great Seal of England and of the Great Seal of Nature both at once' was, as an early editor saw it, 'a mystery beyond the comprehension of his own times'.[9] Narrower minds, like Sir Edward Coke, were disconcerted, as shown by the well-known lines he scribbled in his copy of the *Novum Organum*, that it was fit only 'to be freighted in the ship of fools'; and King James, though he prided himself on his scholarship, remarked that 'like the peace of God, it passeth all understanding'.[10] Not so Ben Jonson, who foresaw that, though it was 'not penetrated, not understood' by 'the most superficial men', the *Novum Organum* would cross the seas and live 'as long as nature is'.[11] No one, however, was equipped to write the life of such a man, so a contemporary scholar remarked, and in the eighteenth century a writer – who had also found no man 'competent to embrace the vast extent of his genius' but Bacon himself – was criticized in his turn for embarking on the life of one whose genius he was 'not comprehensive enough to embrace'.[12]

No single person has yet been found comprehensive enough to embrace Bacon's many-sided writings. It took three specialized editors to assemble his works in the nineteenth century; in ours, as has been noted, it would take a team of full-time researchers to cover his influence.[13] 'Glance at the index', wrote a biographer in 1933, as he leafed through the histories 'of biology and music, of constitutional law and industrial developments, of economics and literature, of philosophy and architecture, of man's creeds and man's knowledge', and there is Bacon's name, with 'a paragraph, an allusion, deprecating comment, judicial summary, exquisite homage . . .'[14] In 1964 a historian pointed out that no successful synthesis of 'this immensely versatile man of genius' had ever been made, and in 1992 a student of his thought dwelt on the need to reintegrate the several unrelated Francis Bacons which Baconian scholarship has produced.[15] Those who could not comprehend, however, have felt free to attack, yet Bacon's diversity does not account for the unprecedented extremes of opinion which have been voiced about his work. We will have to look beyond the 'durable part' of his memory for an explanation.

As for its non-durable part, Bacon cared deeply for his good name as it is understood in the world. It was for him 'the purest gem' – as Shakespeare had called it, the 'immediate jewel' of man's soul.[16] When, towards the end of his life, he was accused of corruption and fell from the highest position in the land, whatever the pressure of his material needs, Bacon's reiterated appeal to King James was for the clearing of his name. 'I desire not from your Majesty means, nor place, nor employment,' he wrote three years after his disgrace, 'but only, after so long a time of expiation, a complete and total remission of the sentence of the Upper House, to the end that that blot of ignominy may be removed from me, and from my memory with posterity.' This request, 'granted, may make me live a year or two happily; and denied, will kill me quickly'.[17] A few months before his death he was still trying to procure the removal of that blot from Charles I, who was too much absorbed by then with the threat of a graver impeachment than Bacon's – that of Buckingham, the royal favourite – to remember his old servant and friend.

In an earlier will, written under the shock of the charges brought against him, Bacon had left his name to foreign nations, adding only afterwards, 'and to my own countrymen, after some time be past'.[18] The foreign nations, by and large, honoured this appeal, but his countrymen responded, after some time was past, with an even greater variety and contrast of opinion over his character than they were to express over his works. So great a contrast that it has become a practice among his biographers to devote a special chapter to Bacon's personal reputation, and the editor of his complete works in Italy has a section of bibliography on writers for and against him.[19] 'Has any man in history', asked a biographer in 1963, 'been so variously bespoken, so loved and hated, admired and despised, venerated and damned?'[20]

During the 1950s, when the damning was at its height, a new breath entered Baconian studies, and scholars were confident that they had laid it to rest. But they spoke too soon, for three decades later the damning was still going strong. 'Bacon? A crook if there was one!' – so I heard a distinguished poet exclaim in 1983.[21] This view of Bacon, widely held in Britain, is still being implanted in the minds of English students, obscuring the more universal idea of the great reformer who influenced the development of their country in practically every field of human endeavour and inspired many of the 'illuminations and inventions' they live by. We may remember, among the hundreds of now familiar subjects he suggested for scientists to work on, the 'scarlet oranges' which the sailors of New Atlantis were given long before the British Navy adopted them, as 'an assured remedy for sickness at sea'; the coastlines of Africa and America, which, he guessed, 'cannot have been by accident'; the bi-literal code he invented, which is the basis of the binary scale used today in electronic computers.[22] Students are still taught to despise the man who helped to forge the very language they are speaking, with metaphors as *crucial* – to use a Baconian term – and as modern today as they were in the seventeenth century. In Bacon's *History of Henry VII* the 'mole' was already undermining governments with his 'secret espials'.[23] And a vivid image, central to Bacon's philosophy, could still get Alexander Solzhenitsyn into trouble with the Soviet authorities when in 1967 he denounced some of their slogans as 'idols of the market-place'. Confusing these Baconian 'idols of the mind' with others he had called 'idols of the theatre', they interpreted Solzhenitsyn's words as a disparaging reference to a quite different idol, the monument to Karl Marx in Moscow's Theatre Square – now toppled.[24]

The time appears to be ripe for a new look at the dark view of Bacon's character, to find out if it is justified, and if not, why it is still so prevalent. I propose to examine here what Bacon's contemporaries believed, what his worst critics have contended, how far they were right, and – to the extent that they were not – how and why this legend grew up, and with it a controversy that has run into many thousands of pages for the prosecution and the defence.

2

'That Angel from Paradise'

To begin with, how did his own age see Bacon? What did his friends and colleagues, his patrons and servants think of him? The people who knew him in everyday life, at his worst and at his best; the scholars who were familiar with his thought? 'Daring example of how far the human mind may reach!', 'The very nerve of genius', 'thy darling, oh Nature and the world!': so did Cambridge University mourn 'the greatest philosopher since the fall of Greece'. Disregarding his condemnation for corruption in office, his scholarly admirers celebrated an unsullied 'despiser of wealth', who must now be administering justice 'among the angels'. 'Your life was resplendant!' cried one of them; another could find no man 'of loftier soul'.[1] Allowance must be made for the exaggeration of conventional eulogy in these 'tokens of love and sorrow', bearing in mind, however, that, as has been noted, such fashionable hyperbole often bore a genuine relation to the truth.[2] But we cannot fault the testimony of Ben Jonson, a severe judge of his fellow man, who knew Bacon well. He was, Jonson later recalled, 'one of the greatest men and most worthy of admiration that hath been in many ages. In his adversity I ever prayed that God would give him strength . . . knowing no accident could do harm to virtue, but rather help to make it manifest.'[3]

Most of the admirers of Bacon's 'parts', or mental qualities, dwelt also on his mild and upright character. Let us hear William Rawley, his personal chaplain and the first editor of his works. Some degree of partiality may be looked for in this witness, towards a master of whom he believed that 'if there were a beam of knowledge derived from God upon any man in these modern times, it was upon him'. Yet Rawley had lived for many years as a member of Bacon's household, and few could have known him better. The fifteen-page 'Life' of Bacon he has left us is the story of a compassionate public prosecutor and judge, an honourable counsellor, an inspired thinker and a practising believer; as also of an affectionate brother, a considerate husband, and – last but not least – a beloved friend and master.[4]

For a shorter outline of Bacon's life and character we can turn to David Lloyd's book on *State Worthies . . . their Advancements and Falls*, drawn directly from the testimony of Rawley and of others close to their subject; though here we must allow for the panegyrical mode then in favour among historians. In these pages we find the boy 'sucking in experience with his milk' and 'inured to policy as early as to his grammar'. Sent abroad at fifteen, in the suite of the English Ambassador, to allay 'the solidity of England with the air of France', he behaved with such discretion that he was employed soon afterwards as the Ambassador's agent to the Queen. After which he is found instilling 'wholesome precepts of prudence and honour' in the Earl of Essex – 'to whom he was more faithful than he to himself.' Though 'high in spirit', his inclination was 'moderate and temperate'. While in the House of Commons he was a popular, zealous and experienced patriot; in the House of Lords he proved 'successfully serviceable to the Crown'. Bacon's excellence in speech and action are lauded – 'so acute and ready his wit . . . so penetrating his judgement, so large and rational his soul'; as also his love, 'to relations tender, to friends faithful, to men universal, to his very enemies civil'. He fell principally because of one particular fault: 'he was above the age he lived in; above it in his bounties . . . above it in his kindness to servants, to whom he had been a better master if he had been a worse . . . Though indeed he rather trusted to their honesty, than connived at their falsehood, for he did impartial justice commonly to both parties.'[5]

We shall see later to what extent this rosy view corresponds to the reality. Meantime we may gain some idea of the man from his physical appearance. What did Bacon look like to his contemporaries? We have an early glimpse of him in a miniature, done in Paris by the master miniaturist Nicholas Hilliard when Bacon was eighteen, with the device: 'If only I could paint his mind!' Unfortunately readers of Bacon's 'Lives' are more likely to remember him from the portrait usually reproduced – a mediocre rendering of the full-length painting of him as Lord Chancellor by Paul van Somer, which gives the impression of a stiff, sad man, overburdened with cares of state – or perhaps simply tired of posing. An engraving after a more exact portrait by Simon Pass, painted around the same time, shows the humorous expression of the mouth, the wrinkles of laughter and the smile lurking in the eyes, as well as the general feeling of responsive alertness which we would expect from the descriptions that have come down to us.[6] We have here 'the presence grave and comely' recalled by the Queen's historian, William Camden; the 'lively hazel eye' described by the famous Dr Harvey, who was Bacon's personal physician; the 'spacious forehead and piercing eye' that John Evelyn, the diarist, had been told of 'by one who knew him well'.[7] But for a likeness chosen by one of those who knew him best, we should visit the monument put up over Bacon's tomb by his secretary, Sir Thomas Meautys, with the inscription 'so he would sit'. In an engraving of this statue (reproduced as frontispiece above), we will recognize the eye 'looking upward', as Evelyn described it, 'and the whole appearance venerably pleasing, so that the beholder was insensibly drawn to love before he knew how much reason there was to admire him'; the expression 'as if he pitied men', worn by Bacon's Fathers in the New Atlantis (an aspect of Bacon 'more often missed', as was recently noted by one of the students of his science, that of 'the dreamer and visionary').[8]

'Venerably pleasing,' wrote Evelyn. According to the satirist Francis Osborne, a younger contemporary of Bacon's, 'the knowledge of his universal genius, husbanded by his wit and dignified by so majestical a carriage . . . struck such awful reverence in those he questioned that they durst not conceal the most intricate part of their mysteries from him.' 'His language,' said Jonson, 'where he could pass by a jest, was nobly censorious.' But Bacon could not pass by a jest. Nor could he bear 'grave and solemn wits, with more dignity than felicity', and he appeared to his acquaintance as full of fun as he was imposing.[9] 'How well combinest thou merry wit with silent gravity!' exclaimed the poet Thomas Campion, a friend of his young days, in a poem addressed to him as Chancellor. For his lifelong friend Toby Matthew, 'there was no such company in the whole world.'[10] Nor did he fail to see the funny side of his own tragedy, as we gather from the remarks entered by John Aubrey – that tireless collector of reminiscences – in the 'brief life' he devoted to Bacon. This is not surprising in a man who collected witticisms in his youth ('hear me out – you were never in') and who, when lying ill in his old age, dictated some three hundred humorous anecdotes in one day – not excluding some against himself. Nor would he omit any that were vulgar, he said, 'for many vulgar ones are excellent good.'[11]

His playful humour stood him in good stead when dealing with royalty. As he pointed out, 'a jest is many times the vehicle of a truth which would not otherwise have been brought in.'[12] And one man may well have owed his life to a *bon mot* of Bacon's. This was the historian Dr Hayward, author of a book on the deposition of Richard II which he had dedicated in pointed terms to the Earl of Essex, when that Earl was hatching his rebellion against Queen Elizabeth. Hayward was committed to the Tower, and the incensed Queen 'asked Mr Bacon', being then of her learned counsel, *whether there were any treason contained in it.* Mr Bacon, intending to do him a pleasure, and to take off the Queen's bitterness with a merry conceit, answered, *No, Madam, for treason I cannot deliver opinion that there is any, but very much felony.* The Queen, apprehending it gladly, asked *How and wherein?* Mr Bacon answered, *Because he had stolen many of his sentences and conceits out of Cornelius Tacitus.* When later the Queen 'would not be persuaded that it was his writing whose name was to it, but that it had some more mischievous author, and said with great indignation that she would have Mr Hayward racked to produce his author', Bacon replied, *Nay Madam, he is a doctor, never rack his person but rack his style,* and undertook, if Hayward were set to continuing his story, 'by collating the styles, to judge whether he were the author or no'.[13]

In jest or in earnest, Bacon fascinated his public. The Earl of Dorset – his 'great admirer and friend', according to Aubrey – took a secretary with him to write his sayings down at table; and Jonson noted that 'when he spoke his hearers could not cough or look aside without loss . . . The fear of every man was lest he should make an end.' 'His most casual talk deserved to be written,' said the generally antagonistic Osborne; 'he treated every man in his respective profession, and what he was most versed in, so as I have heard him entertain a country lord in the proper terms relating to hawks and dogs, and at another time outcant a London surgeon.' Yet he did not, said Rawley, 'delight to outvie others', but would 'draw a man on and allure him to speak upon such a subject wherein he was peculiarly skilful and would delight to speak. And for himself he contemned no man's observations, but would light his torch at every man's candle.'[14]

No 'plodder upon books' (as Rawley also remarked), Bacon had his knowledge 'from some grounds and notions within himself'. He would (Aubrey had heard from a follower) 'drink a good draught of strong beer to bedwards, to lay his working fancy asleep, which would otherwise keep him from sleeping a great part of the night'. But more often (his mother complained) he would go 'untimely' to bed, and muse on she knew not what when he should sleep. Then he would dictate early in the morning (a secretary recalled) what he had invented and composed during the night. We see him through Aubrey's pages, 'in his delicate groves where he did meditate, and when a notion darted into his mind' straightaway dictating it to one of his gentlemen who attended him 'with pen and ink-horn'. He would 'many times have music in the next room', and he liked it at night (he himself tells us) 'when the general silence helpeth' – or better still when it came to him 'between sleeping and waking'.[15] Bacon's was a singularly nervous and excitable temperament. An ever-conciliating Member of Parliament, he could be overcome with emotion – as when, defending a bill for the relief of the poor which he had very much at heart, he 'kept such a quoil' and was 'so hot' (wrote a Parliamentary reporter) that the other bills under discussion were 'clean hushed up'.[16] And Rawley recalls a curious symptom of oversensitiveness: 'the moon was never in her passion, or eclipsed but he was surprised with a sudden fit of fainting.'[17]

A garden was for Bacon 'the purest of human pleasures' and 'the greatest refreshment to the spirits of man', and wherever he stayed, like God, he planted one. At Twickenham – 'my pleasure and my dwelling', and the refuge of his younger days – he planted 'gardens of Paradise', as another editor of his works, Archbishop Tenison, called them, including a herb garden, and a row of elder trees. At Gray's Inn – the law college where he kept rooms almost all his life – it was Bacon who planned the grove of elms he was later to walk in with Sir Walter Ralegh, and who first thought of turning 'our back field' into gardens that were to be celebrated for their beauty. The accounts of Gray's Inn show that he was paid £7 15s. to buy cherry trees, standard roses, pinks, violets and primroses – flowers that were still among his favourites thirty years later, when he wrote his essay 'Of Gardens'.[18] Some twenty-five years after his death, Aubrey visited what was left of the 'rarely planted garden', another 'paradise' which Bacon had laid out around his new house at Verulam. Aubrey devoted pages to its 'delicate walks and prospects . . . its diversity of greens on the side of the hill', the door which opened on to an oak wood, where 'his lordship much delighted himself,' having set under every tree 'some fine flower'. The lake was gone by then, with its 'arbour of musk-roses' in one island, 'set all about with double violets for scent in the autumn', and its music room on another; but the peonies and tulips were still there, under the 'very great shaded trees'.[19]

Bacon's friends included many scholars at home and abroad, courtiers of high repute, and not a few poets, who looked on him, in Campion's phrase, as 'one whom the sweet muse calls'. 'Thy notes are sweetest airs,' wrote John Davies of Hereford, in a sonnet for 'Sir Francis Bacon, embracing his Bellamour, the Muse'; and the dramatist Thomas Randolph addressed him as himself 'a singer'. Chapman dedicated his translation of Hesiod's *Georgics* to Sir Francis Bacon, as one of the few 'that live now combining honour and learning'; who, he grandly claimed, had renewed the belief that 'the love of all virtue and integrity' was 'the only parent and argument of all truth'. Beaumont, Sackville and the other John Davies, as well as Lord Herbert of Cherbury, were among Bacon's friends, and John Donne is mentioned by Aubrey as his admirer.[20] But closest of all was the young poet-parson George Herbert, who was to mourn the death of his 'chosen friend' with the most beautiful of all the elegies addressed to him:

> Thou needs must die in April, so they willed
> That here the flowers their tears might weep forlorn
> And there the nightingale melodious mourn . . .[21]

To his secretaries, followers and servants, whom Bacon looked on as his pupils, he was so good a master that, said Rawley, 'many young gentlemen of blood and quality sought to enlist themselves in his retinue'; and at Gray's Inn, 'to his dying day, he carried himself with such sweet comity and generosity that he was much revered and beloved by the readers and gentlemen of the house'.[22] His generosity was often excessive, and many of his contemporaries saw it as the cause of his downfall. Yet, perhaps because it made the overwhelming brilliance of his Chancellor more palatable to him, King James liked him the better for it. Once, on hearing that Bacon had given ten pounds to an underkeeper by whom he had sent him a buck, the King 'said merrily, *I and he shall both die beggars*'.[23] Bacon did.

In all this praise was there no dissonant voice? Not among those who knew him personally. Three voices were raised in the following generation, but they were bitterly attacking the Stuart regime with libels and lies, and, though their lives overlapped his, they had no inside information on Bacon. We shall hear them later.[24] There was one contemporary, however, who, observing him from a distance, tended to look on him with irony and suspicion. This was John Chamberlain, whose letters are the source of so much invaluable gossip during King James's reign. He did not meet Bacon until late in their lives, when, invited to dine with him as Lord Chancellor, he was impressed by his host's kindness and friendliness towards him.[25] Chamberlain was a great relayer of what 'the world' believed. Generally indulgent, he looked with a jaundiced eye on intellectuals such as Bacon and Sir Thomas Bodley, whose political opinions differed from his own, and whose ideas were alien to him. We will find him among those disdained by Jonson for their inability to understand the *Great Instauration*, when, having read 'no further than the bare title', he passed on a friend's remark that 'a fool could not have written such a work and a wise man would not.' He was more at home with worldlier minds, such as that of his good friend, Secretary Winwood – with whom Bacon once quarrelled for hitting a dog. (And of whom Bishop Goodwin adds, recalling the incident, that he did Bacon 'no good office'.)[26]

Throughout a correspondence that spanned some twenty years, Chamberlain rarely had a good word for Bacon. Of his generally appreciated first speech as Lord Keeper, Chamberlain remarked that 'he pleased himself much in flourishing of the law,' and that in any case he would never make 'a good Keeper' – an allusion to Bacon's extravagance, of which, unlike James, he disapproved. When the Keeper was made Lord Chancellor, it was with slackness that he reproached him, Bacon having kept away from Parliament for three days, not from 'any real indisposition', but because he feared 'the cold weather should pinch him'; which, added Chamberlain, had not stopped him from dining at Gray's Inn to 'give countenance to their Lord or Prince of Purpoole, and see their revels'. We may well believe that only severe indisposition would have kept Bacon from the Christmas revels at Gray's Inn, which he had more than once taken part in as a young man.[27]

Chamberlain also objected to Bacon's indulgence in ceremonial – in which the Dutch statesman, scientist and poet Constantijn Huygens agreed with him. Though a fervent admirer of the works of 'this divine Proteus', when, at the age of twenty-five, Huygens was received in state by the English Chancellor, he thought him 'the height of vanity, arrogance and affectation'. (He continued to revere him, however, having been told that among friends the Chancellor 'completely renounced his proud pomposity'.)[28] Like his contemporaries, Bacon looked on ceremonial as a necessary function of the dignity of office, and he may have enjoyed it up to a point, even if he could write, on his investiture as Lord Keeper, that 'this matter of pomp, which is heaven to some men' was hell, or at least purgatory to him.[29] In Chamberlain's opinion, however, he appeared on that occasion with 'a great deal more bravery and show of horse than was expected in the King's absence'; and when his fall was imminent, Chamberlain complained, he continued 'vain and idle in all his humours, as when he was at his highest'.[30] (Prince Charles, whose viewpoint was different, seeing the Chancellor go by around that time 'with a goodly troup of horsemen', admired the panache that irritated Chamberlain, and commended 'his undaunted spirit'.)[31]

But let us now hear someone who knew Bacon intimately, the attractive Toby Matthew (later Sir Toby), a Catholic convert, whose friendship with Bacon had stood the test of absence and adversity – and worse, of religious difference – since their young days, when they had acted together in one of Bacon's dramatic devices at Court. 'He was a bottomless mine,' Matthew declared in his preface to the Italian edition of the *Essays* (1618), 'where the fine gold of a good nature is found . . . A man so rare in knowledge', with a 'felicity of expressing it' in 'so choice and ravishing a way of words, of metaphors and allusions, as perhaps the world hath not seen since it was a world.' Here Matthew paused to disarm protest. 'I know this may seem a great hyperbole, but the best means of putting me to shame will be for you to place any other man of yours by this of mine.'

> Praise [he went on] is not confined to the qualities of his intellect, but applies as well to those which are matters of the heart, the will and the moral virtue; being a man both sweet in his conversation and ways, grave in his judgements, invariable in his fortunes, splendid in his expenses; a friend unalterable to his friends; an enemy to no man; a most indefatigable servant of the King and a most earnest lover of the public; having all the thoughts of that large heart of his set upon adorning the age in which he lives, and benefiting, as far as possible,

the whole human race. And I can truly say, having had the honour to know him for many years, as well when he was in his lesser fortunes as now that he stands at the top and on the full flower of his greatness, that I never yet saw any trace in him of a vindictive mind, whatever injury were done him, nor ever heard him utter a word to any man's disadvantage which seemed to proceed from personal feeling against the man, but only (and that too, very seldom) from judgement made of him in cold blood . . .

It is not his greatness I admire, but his virtue; it is not the favours I have received from him (infinite though they be) that have thus enthralled and enchained my heart, but his whole life and character.[32]

Toby Matthew spoke as warmly of his friend after he had fallen from power, and dealt as warmly with him, as when he was 'in the full flower of his greatness'. Bacon's confidant in good times and in bad, if anyone had an opportunity to hear him express ill-feeling towards his antagonists, Matthew was surely the man. Rawley, similarly situated, bears him out: 'He was free from malice, which he never bred nor fed. He was no avenger of injuries, which if he had minded, he had both opportunity and high place to have done it; he was no heaver of men out of their places, as delighting in their ruin and undoing; he was no defamer of any man to his prince.'[33] Another secretary of Bacon's, who had also been his personal apothecary, recalled his master as 'a noteworthy example and pattern for everyone, of all virtue, gentleness, peacefulness and patience'.[34]

The peacefulness and patience are reflected in the following anecdote. One day, when he was dictating to Rawley some experiments for his *Natural History*, the news reached him that a long-cherished project – that of ending his days, with a team of scientists, as Provost of Eton – had fallen through. '*Be it so*, said his lordship; he cheerfully thanked the friend who had brought the news and turned straight back to his dictation. *Well sir, yon business won't go on; let us get on with this, for this is in our power.* And then he dictated to him afresh for some hours, without the least hesitancy of speech or discernible interruption of thought.'[35] Bacon showed the same qualities in his professional dealings. 'When his office called him, as he was of the king's counsel learned, to charge any offenders,' said Rawley, 'he was never of an insulting and domineering nature over them, but always tender-hearted,' looking upon them 'with the eye of compassion'. Unlike his rival Edward Coke, who (as Aubrey noted) 'would play his case as a cat with a mouse', and who bullied prisoners shamelessly while passing sentence.[36]

In 1626 the illustrious Venetian scholar Fra Fulgentio Micanzio, who esteemed Bacon as 'one of the most capable spirits of the age', referred to him as 'that angel from Paradise'. The English parson George Herbert had seen him some years earlier as 'the only priest of the world and of men's souls'. Aubrey, who knew so many of them, was in no doubt about the views of Bacon's contemporaries. 'In short,' he concluded, 'all who were *great and good* loved and honoured him.'[37]

3

The 'Horrible Old Rascal'

Let us now skip three centuries, and have a look at our own. On 19 February 1995 the *Sunday Telegraph* published an article entitled 'Towering Genius that Hid the Coldest of Hearts', with a portrait of Francis Bacon as a 'wicked benefactor'. The paper's readers are reminded that 'some of mankind's greatest benefactors have been scoundrels,' and Bacon is cited as a revolutionary philosopher 'who committed monstrous crimes'. Looking back in time, we shall find the same contradictory denunciation of Bacon in articles and introductions to his works throughout the century. 'Lord Bacon was a horrible old rascal, but he wrote very charming essays.' This is *Blackwood's Magazine* in 1930. In 1933 an article distributed among the students of King's College, London, as part of a series aimed at encouraging them to read philosophy, was entitled 'Francis Bacon, a Wicked Man who Did Good'. Around this time an American reviewer described Bacon as 'one of the most polished scoundrels of his age' – thus echoing the words of a British scientist, in 1887: 'I will listen to nothing that would reflect the least credit upon that scoundrel.'[1]

Early twentieth-century textbooks dwelt almost exclusively on three episodes out of Bacon's rich and varied life, as they were to be spelled out in the *Telegraph* in 1995. They read like a brief for the prosecution. The first accusation appears in *A History of England for Family Use and the Upper Classes of Schools* (Burns and Oates, 1913), where an ambitious and avaricious Bacon is condemned for 'fraud and corruption altogether without a precedent'. In *A History of England* (Cassel, 1926), 'the House of Commons declared that he had over and over again been guilty of taking bribes, which were offered to him on condition that he would give unjust judgement. The charges were true, and proved beyond all doubt.'[2] *A Textbook of English Literature* (Wyatt and Collins, 1930) stressed the second principal charge. Bacon's dismissal for corrupt practices 'was not such a stain on his name as his treachery to Essex . . . A false friend and corrupt politician, such is the man whom Pope called "the wisest, brightest, meanest of mankind".' 'His work is noble, his life is ignoble,' wrote

Sidney Lee in *Great Englishmen of the Sixteenth Century* (1904, last in print in 1952); his moral perception 'blurred past recovery'. This critic took it on himself to answer Bacon's famous bequest of his name. 'When his personal career is surveyed it is impossible for men's charitable speeches or foreign nations or the next ages to apply to it the language of eulogy.' Lee did not: he devoted his twenty-page article to denigration, stressing yet another aspect of this new Bacon's depravity: 'self-advancement was the only principle which he understood' to govern affairs; and Bacon's 'tortuous mind' is seen here practising deceit and dissimulation 'wherever it can be made to pay'.[3]

The introductions to Bacon's more popular works dwell on the same episodes – his 'betrayal of Essex' and his 'ignominious fall' – and on the same 'undignified struggle for place', and mention little else. The World's Classics edition of the *Essays* by Geoffrey Grigson (1923, reprinted 1960) listed the usual iniquities, noting once again that the contrast in Bacon's character, 'too glaring to be missed', had been 'summed up by Pope in a single witty line, and elaborated by Macaulay in a famous article'. 'Seldom has legal corruption been so deep-seated, or so clearly revealed,' wrote a new editor of the *Essays* in 1959. A third and more sinister episode was highlighted in *A Preface to Bacon* (Hutchinson Educational, 1963). The editor of these selected works, after recapitulating the familiar charges, stated as an accepted historical fact that Bacon caused an elderly gentleman to be tortured in order that he should confess to sedition.

The dictionaries and encyclopedias of the twentieth century retailed the same charges with monotonous regularity. *Chambers Encyclopaedia* (1911) castigated Bacon for recognizing no moral obstacle on his path to success, and concluded that 'neither Macaulay's mingled contempt and admiration, nor Pope's popular epigram in his *Essay on Man* – "If parts allure thee, think how Bacon shin'd, / The wisest, brightest, meanest of mankind" – is an adequate summary of his character': the author would have used stronger language. *Chambers Biographical Dictionary* (1964) did so. In half a dozen sentences it succeeded in presenting every act of Bacon's life as a crime. By now, however, some of these writers had begun to moderate their language. *Chambers Encyclopaedia*, in 1955, replaced 'craving' for advancement with 'striving', and 'abject apology' with 'fulsome offer of his services'. In 1971, *Encyclopaedia Britannica*, while making the usual charges, attempted a few lame excuses for Bacon ('it was fair to remember' . . .). But the subject who emerged from these half-hearted corrections was hardly more likeable.

This toning down was the result of a revival of interest in Bacon launched from the late 1950s on by such scholars as Benjamin Farrington, Fulton Anderson and Brian Vickers, and in Italy by Paolo Rossi, a pioneer in the study of his science. Their fresh appraisal of Bacon, both as man and thinker, ushered in a few less biased biographies.[4] But on the whole the light cast on Bacon's works fell only dimly on his life. The students of Bacon who, on the tercentenary of his death, in 1926, had paid tribute to 'a mean and corrupt sycophant' and 'a damaged soul', on the fourth centenary of his birth celebrated a sordid 'son of Judas'.[5]

I can tell what one schoolboy was being taught in 1977. My grandson Nathaniel, aged ten, seeing me at work on Bacon, told me that he did not think much of him. He showed me the American history book from which he had drawn his opinion. It consisted of portraits of famous Elizabethans and Jacobeans, all sympathetically drawn but one. The four pages devoted to Francis Bacon were variations on a single theme. 'This thin face, with the pointed beard and sharp eyes is that of a most ambitious man, whose fame rests not upon his deeds but upon his words.' He was to be found 'at almost any hour of the day or night in his lonely lodgings at Gray's Inn . . . covering page after page with his nervous writing,' and 'nothing was heard but the continuous scratching of his quill'. The reason? He was producing 'yet another' book dedicated to King James, 'so ambitious was this man of words to prove himself worthy of advancement'. He wrote on every subject that he thought might please the King, until finally, 'bombarded with words', James gave way and 'improved his fortunes'. Queen Elizabeth had known better, for Bacon's uncle, Lord Burghley, had told her, it seems, that Bacon was 'an overly ambitious and dangerous man'.[6] Seven years later there was little change in Nathaniel's briefing. As a sixth-former at an English boarding school of repute, he was taught – so he wrote to me – that Bacon 'was a brain, but shifty as they come'.

Meanwhile the popular view of Bacon continued at worm's eye level. In 1982 the science column of the *Daily Telegraph* gave us a preview of the sentiments its author was to improve on in 1995. Alongside a villainous-looking portrait with the caption 'Francis Bacon, a squalid figure in political history and the father of modern science', we could read, among other familiar remarks, that he was in political life 'a crook . . . unscrupulous beyond the standards of his day'; that he 'laboured to send his best friend, the Earl of Essex, to the scaffold', and finally, as Chancellor, perpetrated the most 'spectacular' of his evil actions: he accepted 'secret payments from all parties', and awarded his cases 'to the highest payer'. Readers of *Encounter* in 1984 fared no better. They were presented with a disgraceful and sordid philosopher, getting off only too lightly for soiling his integrity – disgrace and dishonour not being a sufficient punishment for his misdeeds. In America most people will have known of Bacon, since 1985, not for his keen interest in 'that vast extension of the kingdom of man', as he called their future country, but as one of a trio of glum faces selected by *Time* magazine as typical examples of corrupt mankind. The caption: 'Bacon and Garsfield enjoyed beards and bribes'. The third face in the picture is Nixon's.[7]

The decline in incriminating biographies, hopefully noted in 1968, proved illusory. The late 1970s saw two low-level Bacons, one of whom devoted his faithless and corrupt 'life' to the 'planned production' of learned works as platforms from which he could 'air his hopes and frustrations' and 'urge his worthiness' on his royal masters. In the 1980s one preface to a paperback outline of his philosophy, dwelling on all the old charges, offered students a generally disliked and frustrated Bacon, who clearly deserved Pope's 'remarkably concise' couplet and Macaulay's essay; while another preface, to a new edition of the *Essays*, also in paperback, showed a dreary personage, toppling favourite after favourite, in trials that had been 'fixed' – presumably by a government as corrupt as himself. In 1992 Bacon's life was once again presented in a scholarly work in terms of the few main themes noted here: successful prosecution of his patron, frustrated ambition, torture, and self-confessed corruption.[8]

In reducing Bacon's varied existence to half a dozen highly damaging statements, these biographies exclude all the interests, aspirations, achievements and human contacts that make up any man's life, not to speak of a life like Bacon's, so 'resplendent' and varied, according to his contemporaries, that they thought no one capable of writing it. There is not a glimpse here of the man whom Ben Jonson, Thomas Hobbes, George Herbert and many others loved, whom Cardinal Richelieu admired and Coke envied, and about whom Chamberlain grumbled and Aubrey gossiped with such affectionate interest. The contrast between the bare bones of accusation and a fleshed-out existence is particularly evident when we compare Aubrey's vivid pages with the up-to-date biographical sketch that precedes each of his brief lives in their twentieth-century edition. In the text we have all the passages of Bacon's life that struck Aubrey as worth noting, just as they came, freshly to his pen: the glowing praises of his admirers, and his 'dearly beloved' and loving friends; the remarks with which he showed his sense of humour, his worldly – and his unworldly – attitudes, his likes and dislikes; glimpses of him at table, at work, in his garden; his poetic gifts, his archaeological interests; and the final judgement, that he always decreed 'as was just and good'. But we are armed against the attractions of this image by the editor's introduction, a rehash of all the time-worn accusations – including of course the time-worn couplet from Pope. This edition of the *Brief Lives* was published in 1949. The same introduction was reproduced practically verbatim in 1985, on the first page of the Penguin edition of the *Essays*, mentioned above.[9]

The habitual, almost systematic defamation of Bacon throughout the twentieth century will be examined more fully below.[10] Meantime what is finally striking about most of the brief biographies in circulation today is that in hardly one of them is there so much as an allusion to the fact that every charge brought against Bacon was thoroughly refuted over a century ago by his master biographer, James Spedding, editor of his complete works. Students are not referred to Spedding – or if they are, it is only to dismiss him, and to disregard everything he wrote. Instead they are given extracts from the hostile critics, in particular from *Elizabeth and Essex*, by Lytton Strachey, who made Bacon the villain of his piece. And, of course, from Macaulay's essay, as 'the best insight into Bacon's character'.[11] It is in one of the passages selected for students that, in 1928, Strachey spread to the four winds an epithet for Bacon which to this day few biographers have been able to resist: that of the 'creeping snake'. In 1963 A. L. Rowse bestowed on him another when he called Bacon 'the first rat to leave Essex's leaky vessel'.[12]

It is a long way from priest and angel of paradise, to snake and rat. Allowing for a difference of angle between contemporary biographers inclined to eulogy, and later historians with more documents at their disposal, the gap is still disproportionately wide. What happened between Bacon's age and ours? Two recurrent themes will have been noticed time and again in the textbooks and articles cited: Alexander Pope's famous couplet from the *Essay on Man*, published in 1734, in which Bacon was branded 'the wisest, brightest, meanest of mankind'; and the 'Essay on Bacon' by Thomas Babington, Lord Macaulay, in which, a century later, this celebrated historian poured contempt over him in masterly prose.[13] Pope's lightly spoken, though eminently quotable paradox – of which more later – would have had little effect on the reputation of such a man as Bacon had Macaulay not taken it up and amplified it in his brilliant, fatally effective essay in which, after vilifying Bacon the man for forty pages, he spent the next sixty praising his philosophy, as he understood it, to the skies.

All the accusations against Bacon still in vogue today, as well as countless minor insinuations, are founded on the widely read essay with which Macaulay turned the tide of history against the man he so greatly admired. Our first question must therefore be whether he is a reliable historian. The answer is a surprising one. No English historian has had so wide and deserved a renown as Macaulay, and no historian of any eminence has been found so completely untrustworthy. Early in our century, J. M. Robertson, editor of Bacon's philosophical works and author of a balanced appraisal of his reputation as it stood in 1907, denounced 'that masterpiece of injustice and impassioned untruth', Macaulay's 'Essay on Bacon', as 'a triumph of special pleading that is a scandal to literature'. In this review, he wrote,

> All the rhetorical powers and expository gifts of a first-rate platformer were bent to bluffing the jury, perverting the facts, gar-

bling the defence and dexterously playing the saddened censor of a great man's faults, till by a thousand cumulative touches of falsification, missing no opportunity for distorting incident or motive, there is wrought by wayward prejudice a comprehensive slander which wilful malice would hardly outgo.[14]

From Macaulay's time to ours, criticism, whether of his *Essays* or his *History of England* has been severe. The best historians found him shallow, inaccurate and prejudiced. 'He misread his authorities,' wrote a contemporary in 1869, 'or more frequently left out some essential point whose omission vitiated the whole statement,' and his essay on Bacon betrayed a radical ignorance of the subject. Another historian, in 1883, thought he showed his incompetence most particularly in his 'grossly unfair' review of Bacon. A third, in 1911, concluded that his methods were 'altogether destructive of real historical knowledge', and his influence on later generations 'little short of pernicious'.[15] In 1934 Winston Churchill, defending the Duke of Marlborough, his ancestor, against an attack as libellous as the 'Essay on Bacon', apostrophized Macaulay as 'the prince of literary rogues', who 'always preferred the tale to the truth, and smirched or glorified great men according as they affected his drama'; who deliberately falsified facts 'upon evidence which he knew, and in other connexions even admitted was worthless', for the sake of startling contrasts and colour; and who incorporated forgotten slanders in his 'stately pages' and 'set them rolling round the world'.[16]

In 1938 Charles Firth, in a book devoted to appraising Macaulay as a historian, drew attention to his many inexactitudes, omissions and misrepresentations, his partiality and narrowness of view, his lack of insight into men's motives, and his practice of making entirely unfounded charges against historical characters for purely subjective reasons; defects, as he pointed out, not so much of knowledge as of character.[17] Later historians and biographers have been no less rigorous in their criticism.[18] Clearly the consensus of opinion on Macaulay's untrustworthiness as a historian is such that it ought to be a waste of effort to disprove anything he or his followers have said. How is it then that almost every one of the false asseverations about Bacon originally put forward by Macaulay is still being presented to students as accepted fact? It is perhaps Rowse who best understood Macaulay's persistent influence over the first half of the twentieth century. Few works have been shown to have more serious errors than Macaulay's *Essays*, he remarked in 1944. Nevertheless very many people owed their first intellectual stimulus to them, and notions formed in one's youth are not easily given up. 'The pity is that Macaulay had such power, such unique vividness, that when he was wrong, as he often was, he has impressed his own version upon the English mind more firmly than the truth.' Did he not also impress it on the author of these remarks, who, in this same volume, found Bacon 'so impossible to like, so hard to explain'?[19]

An analysis of Macaulay's continuing influence until late in our century, long after his *Essays* had ceased to be generally read, will be attempted below.[20] It is all the more surprising when we consider that barely a decade after Macaulay had published his famous review, every charge he had brought against Bacon had been sifted with scrupulous attention, and proved baseless. *Evenings with a Reviewer*, the work Spedding devoted to the vindication of Bacon's character, though not published until 1881, had been privately printed and circulated in 1846. Its two 400-page volumes, as a contemporary noted, 'form an exhaustive accumulation of evidence, arranged and interpreted by the clearest of intellects with an honesty which is rarely shown in controversial discussion'.[21] Nevertheless it is little read. In 1957 Paolo Rossi was surprised to find that this 'fresh, pleasing and intelligent study' was still ignored in so many bibliographies, and neglected by most interpreters of Bacon.[22]

Spedding described Macaulay's 'faculty of conveying the greatest amount of false effect with the smallest amount of definite misstatement' as 'an unconscious felicity in him, more like genius than any other faculty he possesses'.[23] He was entitled to criticize, for his own methods were the exact opposite of Macaulay's. In 1907 Robertson rightly saw in his work a 'vigilance of scrutiny, a security of handling, that realizes every ideal Macaulay misses'. Spedding's confutation, he concluded, was complete. It was clear that Macaulay had 'merely suppressed truths and accumulated false facts'.[24]

The suppressed truths, however, were largely forgotten, and the false facts continued to circulate throughout the twentieth century. Since those who disagreed with Spedding's conclusions – or, more frequently, brushed them aside – did not examine the arguments on which they are based, any new attempt to get at the truth must start perforce with the refutations he presented with so much care; they must now be looked at again, in the light of a century and a half of research on the period Bacon lived in. Macaulay had written his famous essay as the review of a 'Life' of Bacon, published by Basil Montagu in 1825, with his edition of Bacon's collected works.[25] While approving the minute and accurate researches with which this biographer had collected his facts (and taking his own facts almost exclusively from them), Macaulay claimed that this 'Life' was presented in a far from Baconian manner, since it proceeded on the assumption that Bacon was an eminently virtuous man. He himself was to proceed on the opposite assumption; one which so radically changed the pre-existing concept of Bacon that since then most of Bacon's actions have automatically been ascribed to low motives. Following his own preformed view, Macaulay queried Montagu's statements at every step. 'Mr Montagu's notion that Bacon desired power in order to do good to mankind appears somewhat strange to us . . .';[26] so does every honest intention expressed by or attributed to Bacon.

Spedding did not set out to defend Montagu, whose partiality in favour of Bacon he conceded, but to discover the truth. It was now his turn to take Macaulay's review sentence by sentence, and show up all its dishonesties, dwelling principally on the three main accusations we have seen repeated in so many articles and textbooks, and the underlying assumptions they were based on. Over a century has passed since Spedding published his work in final form. It is time to take another look at the charges that were so thoroughly refuted, seemingly in vain. This will involve stirring up the mud of many ugly calumnies, but the calumnies are there, and the hidden reasons for so much mud-slinging must be faced. Bacon would have felt this need. ('For as the fable goeth with the Basilisk . . . if you see him first he dieth.')[27] It will also require a lengthy book. Defamation is brief, but vindication is long, and where a witty libel can make its mark in a single line, many pages may be needed to examine its historical background and set the record straight.

On taking up the charge that Bacon sent his patron to the block, we will find that his story ties in closely with the mythical story of Essex, still current among biographers today. Four chapters of the present book will be needed to unravel these threads – entangled on the one hand by Macaulay and his followers, on the other by Essex's own dreams, and those of his hero-worshipping biographers – in order to form a reliable estimate of the two men's dealings with each other. A longer section will be required to examine the only real charge brought up against Bacon in his lifetime, his impeachment for judicial corruption, so as to see it in perspective, against the background of Jacobean Court and parliamentary history, which has been well studied over the past few decades. It will then be possible to look into the two basic assumptions on which these accusations rested. The first – that Bacon was an ambitious schemer, working almost entirely for his own advancement – will require a new attempt to evaluate the part he played on the political stage of his time, long obscured by the anachronistic judgement of the Whig historians. The second, even more fundamental, and still widely believed, that Bacon was a cold, selfish and friendless man, will involve a thorough examination of the image which has haunted biographers for a century and a half – and is still freely improved on today – of a philosopher intent on torturing his fellows. We can then follow some of the strange vicissitudes of Bacon's legend in England and abroad, and look into the influence it has exerted on his reputation as scientist and philosopher; and finally draw a few conclusions about the process of legend-making, which may affect other myths that flourish in our time.

In order to stay close to Bacon himself, under a mountain of comment, and allow the reader to evaluate his sincerity, I shall let him speak with his own voice wherever I can; although because of the variety and subtlety of a mind which has fascinated accusers and defenders alike, it is not always easy to quote him in the round. He has too often been presented by his detractors – and by some of his more partial champions – in isolated fragments, removed from the context of his many-faceted thoughts, to suit a preconceived thesis. Any attempt at fairness, however, has before it a salutary example, that of Spedding himself. With a view to maintaining the highest possible standard of impartiality, Spedding presented the two volumes of his vindication in the form of a dialogue, in which A, acting as devil's advocate, made out a case for Macaulay's statements, and B, resorting to the relevant letter, parliamentary journal or other contemporary document, showed them up as inexact, and frequently in diametrical opposition to the truth. Spedding made no secret of his feeling in favour of his subject. He claimed impartiality, not indifference. But he may well be the only one of Bacon's biographers who never passed by an interpretation or omitted a scrap of information that could tell against his conclusions. In this also I shall try to keep him as my model.

PART I

THE FAITHLESS FOLLOWER

4

Who Abandoned his Patron

In the eyes of the moralizing historians of the nineteenth century and the popular biographers of the twentieth, nothing has damaged Bacon so much as the part he played in the prosecution of the Earl of Essex for high treason. As one biographer noted, it has probably been 'the subject of more vituperation than any other single act of any other single man'.[1] 'The lamentable truth must be told,' Macaulay had declared in 1837, 'the friend – so loved, so trusted – bore a principal part in ruining the Earl's fortunes, in shedding his blood and in blackening his memory.'[2] Nine years later, in a hundred pages of documented analysis, Spedding demonstrated that Essex had suffered nothing 'in purse, person or fame which he would not have suffered had Bacon never been born'.[3] But few heard him, and since then the glamorous Essex, washed to varying degrees of white, has become a mythical victim, while Bacon is still presented as a Judas. A new attempt will be made here to separate the reality from the myth in which almost every biographer of either man has to some extent been caught up.

The principal document in the case, which has served defenders and detractors alike, is the *Apology Concerning the Earl of Essex*, a letter written and published by Bacon in 1604, three years after the Earl's death, to counter the rumours circulated about him by Essex partisans, now in favour with the newly crowned King James I. He addressed it to his friend Lord Mountjoy, to whom he had dedicated a philosophical essay some years earlier.[4] Mountjoy had been an intimate of Essex – indeed, as the lover of Penelope Rich, he was his brother-in-law in all but name – and Bacon had chosen him, he said, first 'because you loved my Lord of Essex, and therefore will not be partial towards me'; next, because Mountjoy had always proved to Bacon 'an honourable friend'; and lastly, because, as an experienced government servant, 'grounded in the true rules and habits of duty' (unlike most of Essex's followers), he could understand better than most the meaning of service to Queen and state. Mountjoy, closely involved as he had been in all Essex's affairs, was also the last person Bacon could have deceived with false history, had he wished to. 'I will leave nothing untold that is truth,' he stated, 'for any enemy that I have to add.'[5] A man speaking, like Bacon, in his own defence might be suspected of errors, intentional or not. But the *Apology* nowhere contradicts other contemporary sources, as Spedding found after carefully checking each paragraph, and it is frequently borne out by letters written at the time.[6]

Neither the *Apology*, however, nor any other document was much use to Macaulay, who, writing in India without access to contemporary records, collections of letters or reports of the state trials, relied almost solely on the biography he was reviewing – meagre on Bacon and particularly vague about Essex – for his facts. Even this he did not read with care, so that many of his misjudgements may be attributed to gratuitous mistakes of dating that were not in Montagu. Noting, for example, that Bacon had spoken against a proposal made by his uncle, Burghley, the Lord Treasurer, in the Parliament of 1593, and that soon afterwards Essex began his campaign to launch him as Attorney General, Macaulay assumed that Bacon, in search of 'wealth, precedence, titles' and other advantages, had found his advancement blocked by his uncle, and transferred his allegiance from Burghley to Essex. There was no such transfer. Bacon's friendship with Essex, begun five years earlier, was flourishing when in 1589 Burghley obtained for his nephew the reversal of the prestigious and lucrative post of Clerk of the Star Chamber, when in 1592 Bacon wrote his spirited vindication of Burghley's character and policies, and when, in 1594, he made his first pleading in the King's Bench, to his uncle's considerable satisfaction.[7] Unaffected by Bacon's independent stance in the 1593 Parliament, much as it had irritated the Queen, Burghley continued to assist him in his career, and the nephew did not quarrel with his uncle. As for the much repeated story of Bacon's desertion of Essex as soon as Essex's fortunes began to decline – a decline variously placed by Macaulay in 1596 and in 1600 – it reposes on the latter's ignorance of the events of Essex's life throughout those years. The present chapter will deal with the first stage of this alleged desertion, the decade in which Bacon acted as political counsellor to Essex.

Had the advancement of his personal fortunes been his principal aim, Bacon would probably have had the sense to stay as close as he could to his experienced relative, sure of the Queen's ear to the last, rather than throw in his fortunes with an unsteady favourite, who was always putting his favour in jeopardy with his erratic behaviour. He knew that he owed his well-deserved, but still exceptionally rapid rise in Gray's Inn, in part at least, to Burghley, ever ready to assist his nephew in a safe legal career that did not cross the advancement of his own ambitious son, Robert Cecil.[8] But Bacon found no response to his higher aspirations in that aged Polonius. What could Burghley have made of his nephew's declaration to him, in 1592, that he had taken all knowledge to be his province and that the love of mankind was so fixed in his mind that it could not be removed? And what, we may wonder, had he made of that 'rare and unaccustomed request' submitted to him by his unpredictable nephew soon after his return from France, twelve years earlier – which, if granted, Bacon declared, would allow him to abandon the law for 'studies of more delight'?[9] It has been suggested that this unknown project, which puzzled Spedding, and which no one has yet been able to explain, could have been an attempt to establish a Crown-sponsored academy of arts and sciences, along the lines of the French Court's academies that, when Bacon visited France, were gathering 'good poets and the best minds of the day'.[10] Bacon's known programme, as we have it in 1594 – he had proclaimed it intrepidly in those years as 'The Greatest Birth of Time' – included laboratories, a research library, botanical gardens and a zoo, thus reflecting the many practical and scientific interests of the French poet-academicians. But if such was his proposal, Bacon was surely right in fearing that it would seem 'altogether undiscreet and unadvised' to Lord Burghley, for whom (as his nephew remarked many years later) 'the Frenchman, when he hath talked hath done'.[11]

When in September 1580 he made his 'not ordinary' request Bacon was not yet twenty, and his youth was naturally held against him. But the Queen, who was interested in French academies – and in the Duke of Anjou, the founder of one of them – had given Bacon 'exceeding comfort and encouragement' in his project. And when, a year later, Anjou came over to visit her, Bacon acted as interpreter for the royal couple.[12] He was to keep up his connection, formed on this occasion (in Paris), if not earlier, with Jean de la Jessée, Anjou's private secretary – 'a lone survivor', as he described himself, of that illustrious *Pléïade* of poets, the precursor of all the French academies.[13] Meanwhile Bacon could frequent an informal academy at home, known as the 'Areopagus', which met regularly at Leicester House, by Gray's Inn, under the auspices of Sir Francis Walsingham, Elizabeth's strongly Protestant Secretary of State, and of his son-in-law Sir Philip Sidney. It was in Leicester's interest that Bacon sat for the Parliaments of 1581 and 1583, and in all likelihood he shared in the debates on the purpose of knowledge, in which poetry was celebrated – under the banner of Sidney's *Defence of Poesie* – as the best incitement to virtuous action.[14] Probably recalling their association at this time, Edmund Waller was to celebrate Bacon and Sidney as two 'wise and worldly persons' for whom 'poetry had been the diversion of their youth'.[15] In August 1585 Bacon made one last appeal to Walsingham in favour of his 'poor suit' – so old by then, he pointed out, that 'the objections of my years' should have been quite 'worn away'. Sir Christopher Hatton, the Vice-Chamberlain, had promised 'his furtherance', but, said Bacon, if the Queen did not like it, he could no longer put off attending a course in legal practice. No more is heard of the project, and he went back to studies of less delight.[16]

After the death of Sidney and Leicester, however, and finally, in 1590, of Walsingham himself, Essex, who had inherited Sidney's highly symbolic sword, stepped naturally into the double role of defender of the Protestants and promoter of 'poesy' and learning. The generous, open-minded favourite of Elizabeth, who not so long before had declared himself more in love with knowledge than with fame, was the very man with whom Bacon could share his visions. And with whom, 'waxing somewhat ancient', at thirty-one, to Essex's twenty-five, he could take on a role he felt eminently qualified for, that of political mentor to a young man, able and willing, perhaps, to put some of his ideas into effect. He was to devote most of his time, as he later recalled, and his best endeavours over the next six years to making Essex 'the fittest instrument to do good to the State'; happy, he told his patron, in 'your singular affection towards me', and to have been 'chosen by you to set forth the excellency of your nature and mind'.[17]

For Essex the 'rarely qualified' Bacon, as he described him, was a godsend when, in 1592, tired of his military adventures in France, he was disposed to concentrate on civil greatness for a while. Bacon, as he told Mountjoy in his account, 'knit' to Essex's service his brother Anthony, just back from France after almost a decade as 'intelligencer' under Walsingham. The brothers set up a personal foreign affairs, information and intelligence service for the well-pleased Essex – newly made a Privy Councillor – and coached him as a potential Foreign Secretary. Not always an easy task, as we may assume from the letter of a trusted agent to Bacon: 'No other fault hath the Earl but he must continually be pulled by the ear, as a boy that learneth ut, re, mi, fa.' In return for Bacon's labours, political and literary, and his solicitous, almost maternal advice, Essex gave enthusiastic support, even on such matters as Bacon's aspiration to the hand of Burghley's granddaughter, Lady Hatton. 'If she were my sister or my daughter,' wrote Essex to her parents, 'I protest I would as confidently resolve myself to further it, as I now persuade you.'[18]

Bacon's letters bear witness to his thankfulness for the Earl's 'love, trust and favour' (as he put it in the *Apology*), and his desire to be worthy of them, and serve him the better; but he could have done with less enthusiasm. For Essex now staked his whole patronage on obtaining the post of Attorney General for his follower, over the head of the obvious candidate, Sir Edward Coke, who was nine years Bacon's senior, and if not more qualified, considerably more experienced in the law. If Elizabeth considered the young Bacon at all, it may have been because, knowing both men, she saw merits in Bacon – and above all defects in Coke – which gave her pause. As for Essex, his ardour sprang in part, no doubt, from an eager desire to assist the friend he so greatly admired – a man, he wrote, 'never destined for a private end' – so that 'his virtues might be active, which now lie as it were buried'; but also from his own urgent need for followers in high place, essential to his struggle for political supremacy. Accustomed to having his own way, he would not allow Bacon to apply for the more modest office of Solicitor General, for which Burghley was willing to support him. 'The Attorney Generalship is that I must have for Francis Bacon,' he told Robert Cecil, upbraiding him for not backing his cousin, 'and in that I will spend my uttermost credit, amity and authority against whomsoever; and whosoever getteth this office out of my hand for any other before he have it, it shall cost him the coming by.'[19]

Words hardly likely to please the Queen, on whom Essex urged his candidate in and out of season for a whole year, with little discretion and less psychology; convinced, when she disregarded his tantrums and sent him home to bed, or put him off with a kiss, that he knew 'women's minds' and that what she really wanted was to be overborne. When in April 1594 Coke was appointed Attorney General, a friend remarked that the Earl's failure to place his follower had considerably damaged his credit. Undeterred, Essex now pushed Bacon for the post of Solicitor General with equal forcefulness. 'Upon me must lie the labour of his establishment, and upon me the disgrace will light of his being refused,' he wrote to the Lord Keeper; and he succeeded so well in putting the Queen's back up that she said she would 'seek all England for a Solicitor' rather than take Essex's man.[20]

Bacon knew that her rejection had nothing to do with him. As he wrote to Anthony, 'my conceit is that I am the least part of my own matter . . . Against me she is never peremptory but to my Lord of Essex.' Others had noticed this, including his cousin Robert Cecil – and Essex himself, who wrote to Bacon that 'the Queen was not passionate against you till I grew passionate for you'.[21] It was to Essex (prompted quite possibly by her new Attorney General) that she said Bacon could make a considerable show in the law, but 'was not deep'; to Bacon's friend, Fulke Greville, she remarked soon afterwards that he had 'begun to frame very well'.[22] In vain did Bacon try to restrain his impetuous patron, and 'limit' his affection; until finally, after Essex had begged and bullied Elizabeth for eighteen months, she appointed another man her Solicitor General.[23] 'Her Majesty was too much pressed at first, which she liketh not' was Cecil's comment; and Lady Bacon remarked to her son Anthony that 'though the Earl showed great affection he marred all with violent courses'.[24]

These were the courses Bacon so often tried to steer his patron away from. 'Overcome her with yielding,' he urged, when Essex boasted of getting his will with the Queen by his forcefulness. Violent courses, 'like hot water, help at a pang', but they have to be made stronger and stronger, and in the end 'lose their operation'. They were already losing their operation with Elizabeth, who had seen through her favourite's passionate suit, and suspected his motives. It was dangerous in a factious age, a contemporary noted, 'to have my Lord of Essex his favour'. Bacon was not the first man Essex had tried to impose on her, and anyone placed by Essex increased the pressure on Elizabeth. As has been pointed out in our time, had she allowed such a man to pack the Government with his nominees, she would soon have become a puppet Queen.[25]

So far, rather than Bacon ruining Essex, it seems that Essex was well on the way to ruining Bacon. Nor was Essex unaware of the fact. 'My intercession hath rather hurt him than done him good,' he wrote to the Lord Keeper, while attempting yet another move in his friend's favour.[26] Both Bacon brothers were by now in need of assistance. Throughout their years of unrewarded service, with foreign agents to be paid, usually out of their own pockets, they had never been out of financial straits. Much as he wished to help them, Essex lived on the edge of bankruptcy. Resorting finally to payment in kind, he took Anthony to live with him at Essex House (to a damp room without coal, however, a doubtful benefit for his arthritic servant). And to Francis he offered, as a reward for his services, a piece of land, later valued at £1,800, near the lodge at Twickenham which Bacon leased from the Crown. We know of this offer, made in November 1595, soon after the appointment of Fleming as Solicitor General, from Bacon himself. 'You fare ill,' Essex told him, 'because you have chosen me for your mean and dependence . . . I die (these were his very words) if I do not something towards your fortune . . .'[27]

As touched by the manner of giving, 'with so kind and noble circumstances', said Bacon, as by the gift itself, he accepted it with gratitude, but with a reservation which he records in the *Apology*: 'I see I must be your homager, and hold the land of your gift; but do you know the manner of doing homage in law? Always it is with a saving of his faith [a proviso that he owed his first allegiance] to the King . . .' As he put it in a letter to Essex around that time, 'I reckon myself as a common . . . and as much as it is lawful to be enclosed of a common, so much your lordship shall be sure to have.' He was later to use this image in his most explicit declaration of his life's aims. 'Conceiving that I was born to be of use to mankind, and that the care of the Common Weal is a kind of common property which like the air or the water belongs to everybody . . .' Although to serve Essex, Bacon explained in the *Apology*, he had neglected 'the Queen's service, mine own fortune, and in a sort my vocation' – 'The Greatest Birth of Time' never far from his mind – at no stage of his life could he have been bound by vassalage to any man, 'more than stood with the public good'.[28] Yet 'all that was lawful to be enclosed' he promised and gave his friend.

Not least, his unremitting concern. The following summer, when back from the expedition to Cadiz with flying colours, Essex was at the height of success and favour, Bacon wrote him a long and impassioned letter of advice. Displeased with Court and Council over the distribution of the spoil – and of the glory, which he would share with no one – Essex had gone off to sulk in the country, following a now habitual pattern of quarrels and reconciliations with the Queen. Instead of dispensing the admiration and praise which everyone else, including Anthony, was showering on him, Bacon wrote in a vein of admonition and foreboding. He was 'infinitely glad', he began, that Essex's voyage was over. It was now high time for him to put a stop to military ascendancy, and concentrate on one thing only, 'winning the Queen'. Rather than seek the place of Earl Marshal or Master of the Ordnance, he urged, Essex should return to his bookish ways, look after his estate, give up all 'impression of a popular reputation', and aim at 'a fine honour and a quiet place', such as that of Lord Privy Seal ('it fits a favourite to carry her Majesty's image in seal who beareth it best expressed in his heart').

Finally, in order to set his Sovereign's mind at rest, he should bring some other military man into the Council, 'the fittest' being that same good friend Lord Mountjoy to whom Bacon's *Apology* was addressed. He went on to draw an eloquent picture of the favourite as he must appear to an anxious Queen:

> A man of a nature not to be ruled; that hath the advantage of my affection and knoweth it; of an estate not grounded to his greatness; of a popular reputation; of a military dependence: – I demand [said Bacon] whether there can be a more dangerous image than this represented to any monarch living, much more to a lady of her Majesty's apprehension?

While this impression continued 'in her Majesty's breast', what could he expect but 'crossing and disgracing your actions', and a long list of repulses, 'yea, and percase venturing you in perilous and desperate enterprises?'[29] Written almost five years before Essex's rebellion, these lines have an ominous sound.

It is at this point in time that Macaulay, influenced perhaps by the warning tone of this letter, placed the beginning of that decay of the Earl's fortunes which, he said, moved Bacon to abandon him. 'The person on whom, during the decline of his influence, he chiefly depended, to whom he confided his perplexities, whose advice he solicited, whose intercession he employed' now set out to ruin him.[30] In fact, Bacon's intercession – conceded to have been honest and zealous – did not reach its height until Essex's return from Ireland, three years after this date. As for the advice, 'generally most judicious', said Macaulay, Bacon continued to give it whenever Essex would let him, and there is no denying that, as he put it to Mountjoy, 'while I had most credit with him his fortune went on best.' But though usually 'very patient of the truth', Bacon tells us, Essex had stopped listening. The last thing he wanted was a quiet place. He was soon to take sole command of the military expedition against the Spanish Navy in the Azores, after which, by resorting to the usual 'violent courses', he won the very posts – Master of the Ordnance and Earl Marshal – which his mentor had so strenuously warned him not to apply for.

These differences of opinion, Bacon wrote to Mountjoy, 'bred in process of time a discontinuance of privateness (as is the manner of men seldom to communicate where they think their courses not approved) between his Lordship and myself'. In a letter written before Essex's ill-advised voyage to the Azores, in the summer of 1597, not knowing whether they would meet before it, a clearly anxious Bacon prayed for his preservation, and urged him to watch his actions – in vain, since jealousy of his captains' success would impel Essex to make the gravest blunders. Bacon had begun to fear, he frankly told his patron around this time, that he had been mistaken in taking him 'for a physician that desired to cure the disease of the State'.[31] And with good reason, it seems, for on his return from the islands, again in a huff with the Queen for his poor reception, Essex refused to attend Court or Council, and Bacon was no longer called in to advise him.

Instead the Earl spent such time as he was not brooding in the country, cultivating his popularity in City taverns, among the bankrupt nobles and down-at-heel knights of his acquaintance, and his less reputable military friends. His favourite companion now was his mother's third – and youngest – husband, Christopher Blount, a renegade Catholic who boasted of the part he had played as *agent provocateur* in Babington's project to assassinate the Queen, and who was soon to take part in conspiracy with his stepson. Blount introduced him to an assortment of discontented Catholics, among them Father Thomas Wright, a Jesuit in close touch with the Spanish Court, whom Essex had conveyed to him secretly at night from Bridewell prison; while for the good of his soul he assiduously attended the sermons in which Puritans preached their own variety of subversion.[32]

Whatever he may have heard, Bacon was not easily discouraged, nor, as he put it, would he 'judge of the whole play by the first act'; he continued to offer that 'devoted and careful counsel' by which, as he had once reminded his patron, Essex had never taken hurt, and, when he could, encouragement. On the occasion of one of Essex's reconciliations, he wrote him a warm letter of congratulation, expressing the hope that 'of your eclipses, as this hath been the longest it shall be the last', and that 'upon this experience may grow more perfect knowledge, and upon knowledge more true consent'. A reconciled Essex did indeed attend the Council, early in 1598, but, though he charmed the French Ambassador, he gave him the impression that he suffered from delusions of grandeur, and aspired only 'to greatness'.[33]

Bacon now made another effort. When, in the absence of Cecil in France during the spring, Essex took over some of the Secretary's duties at Court, he attempted to interest his patron in the 'much neglected' Irish causes. Peaceful 'plantation' in Ireland was one of the causes Bacon had most at heart. The plough and not the sword was his constant refrain, and he begged Essex, in two inspired letters, to 'have some large and serious conference' with those best informed on Irish questions, with a view to establishing a lasting treaty with the country's leader, the rebellious Earl of Tyrone, and planting 'a surer Government than heretofore'. This could be achieved by establishing a commission 'of peaceable men' to ensure 'a reform of abuses, extortions and injustices', and Essex could thereby 'win a great deal of honour gratis'.[34] In order to conclude such an agreement with the reluctant Irish leader, Bacon thought it might be necessary for him to 'be menaced with a strong war' – a policy to which Essex could 'lend his reputation' by threatening, if Tyrone refused to collaborate, that he would himself lead 'a full reconquest'. Bacon made it quite clear that he meant this as what we would call an act of brinkmanship, and he warned Essex against following up his threat, 'knowing your Lordship is too easy to pass in such cases from dissimulation to verity'.

Unfortunately by October 1598 war had become inevitable, and Essex rushed back to Court, after another quarrel with his royal mistress, in time to overturn a preliminary nomination of Mountjoy as Commander of the expedition to Ireland. He pressed his own claims so well that he was finally appointed to the post – entirely against his interests, Cecil's party being, as he well knew, only too happy to have him removed from the political scene. When Bacon heard of it, he protested against his going, 'with much vehemency and asseveration'; it would be 'ill for the Queen, ill for him, ill for the State,' he told Essex, as recorded in his *Apology*; and though there is no letter available to confirm his statement, it is entirely consonant with all he had been urging on his patron throughout the past years. 'I am sure I never in anything in my life-time dealt with him in like earnestness, by speech, by writing, and by all the means I could devise . . . But my Lord, howsoever his ear was open, yet his heart and resolution was shut against my advice.'[35] Only once after this, a few days before his departure, did Essex, uneasy about what he had taken on, turn to his old mentor for reassurance. Bacon wrote back all the encouragement he could muster, but his misgivings can be read in and between every line. Seek merit, he urged, rather than fame, keep within the limits of obedience, and above all 'be your own waking censor'. Remember, as Demosthenes did, that 'things go ill, not by accident but by errors'.[36]

Essex set forth on 17 March 1599, acclaimed by the populace but anxiously watched by the more thoughtful. Sir John Harington, the Queen's godson, who was attached to the expedition, received a confidential warning from a kinsman at Court: 'Observe the man who cammandeth, and yet is commanded himself; he goeth not forth to serve the Queen's realm, but to humour his own revenge . . . I sore fear what may happen hereafter.'[37] Disregarding his state of mind, however, Essex's biographers lay the blame for the failure of his Irish campaign on Ireland itself – that 'strange land, charming, savage, mythical', which 'lured him on with indulgent ease'; but Mountjoy's success, soon afterwards, points to other causes.[38] Causes that we will have to look at through a double glass, for there are two parallel stories – indeed more, if we take into account what Queen Elizabeth suspected, what Bacon, faithful to his image of a basically loyal servant, hoped against hope to the last, and what Essex was actually doing, which may not always have been entirely clear to himself.

'I have beaten Knollys and Mountjoy in the Council, and I will beat Tyrone in the field!' Essex boasted when he obtained the command. 'Petty undertaking' in any province in Ireland, he said, would be but loss of time, treasure and men, 'until Tyrone himself be first beaten'.[39] And he had himself originated the instructions he received: to go north at once and attack the rebel in his stronghold. On the assumption that he really meant to do so, no biographer has convincingly explained Essex's behaviour on his arrival in Ireland. After pressing for unheard-of powers and obtaining the largest army that had left England during Elizabeth's reign – and appointing his inexperienced companions, Southampton and Blount, against the Queen's express wishes, to assist him in commanding it – he marched back and forth all over the island, from April to August, except to Ulster; he made a fine show everywhere, gaining much popular applause, but consuming treasure and losing soldiers to skirmishes and illness at a great rate; and all the while sending back querulous reminders, having soon forgotten Bacon's warning that if things went wrong it would not be his fault. Whereupon, having demanded and obtained a reinforcement of two thousand men, he coolly reported to the Queen on 21 August that he could not safely undertake the journey north.[40]

Essex's biographers cannot explain why, on 7 September, as usual without waiting for her approval, he finally set off with his remaining forces to meet Tyrone; or why, having done so, instead of giving battle, he spent half an hour in private parley with 'the arch-traitor' (as he himself had called him, along with everyone else); and, though empowered only for outright submission, he undertook to transmit to the Queen Tyrone's verbal conditions for a truce more advantageous to the Irish chieftain than had ever been granted in Ireland before. The Queen's anger was all too justified. 'None of the four quarters of the year' were in season for him to engage the rebel, she exclaimed, in a letter he did not stop to read;

he had nothing to show for the unprecedented sum of £300,000 he had squandered and the twelve thousand men he had lost. At that rate she might well conclude that it had been 'superfluous to have sent over such a personage as yourself'. And when she heard that he had spoken for half an hour, without witnesses, to a traitor whose oath was not to be trusted, she wrote to him again, upbraiding him for not letting her know what passed 'but by divination', and commanding him once again not to make any peace without her authorization.[41]

Here, in the summer of 1599, begins a second stage in Bacon's relationship with Essex: from adviser to a potential statesman, he had now moved to mediator – a role he was to assume in almost every aspect of his life – between his patron and the Queen. It is possible to argue that in advising a Commander and Privy Councillor Bacon was working to advance his own fortunes – admittedly comprehended in those of Essex. But he knew that as mediator he would arouse the hostility of Essex's supporters, who suspected the Queen's Counsel (admitted to her presence while they were not) of murmuring against him, and would irritate the Queen. 'She had me in jealousy', he told Mountjoy, 'that I was not hers entirely,' and had more 'inward and deep respects to my Lord' than she liked; and on one occasion, when he had written with particular warmth about Essex, she told him 'she perceived that the old love would not easily be forgotten'; to which Bacon promptly replied that he hoped she meant it of her own love towards her favourite.[42] Meanwhile, disregarding her susceptibility, time and again he threw himself into the breach.

While Essex was in Ireland, and he himself had legal business on hand with the Queen, Bacon was able to watch for opportunities. He mentions one which occurred shortly before the Earl had written that he would not go north to fight Tyrone. The Queen had shown, to others besides himself, 'a passionate distaste of my Lord's proceedings in Ireland, as if they were unfortunate, without judgement, contemptuous, and not without some private end of his own'. Whereupon Bacon made the same suggestion to her as he had made to Essex three years earlier, when he had advised him to take his stepfather, the Earl of Leicester, for his model:

> I would think that if you had my Lord of Essex here with a white staff in his hand, as my Lord of Leicester had, and continued him still about you for society to yourself, and for an honour and adornment to your attendance and Court in the eyes of your people, and in the eyes of foreign Embassadors, then were he in his right element; for to discontent him as you do, and yet to put arms and power into his hands, may be a temptation to make him prove cumbersome and unruly . . . Which course your Lordship knoweth [Bacon added, addressing Mountjoy], if it had been taken, all had been well . . .[43]

Only ignorance of his consistently held views could have prompted Bacon's twentieth-century detractors to declare that with this advice he was poisoning the Queen's mind against his friend – as if she were not acquainted from long experience with his 'cumbersome' unruliness.[44]

The next Bacon heard was that Essex had returned unexpectedly at the end of September, and was confined to his room. Did he then turn his back on the patron who had failed to heed every one of his warnings? He at once dashed off a brief line of support, declaring himself 'more yours than any man's'; and followed it up, he tells us, with a visit to comfort and advise on ways of removing 'all umbrages and distastes from the Queen'. 'It is but a mist,' he wrote, and would soon clear, providing Essex appealed to her in the right spirit. He should make light of the peace with Tyrone as 'an unfortunate, shuffling affair', avoid any reference to his possible return to Ireland, and above all seek access – 'seriously, sportingly, every way'. However, Bacon added in his account, 'sure I am he did just the contrary to every one of these points.'[45]

We must now begin to hear the alto and the bass together, for throughout the year that followed, while Bacon was thinking up ever new ways of reconciling the Queen with her favourite, in the hope that he might remain in some civilian post at Court – and of keeping Essex in a submissive mood towards the Queen – Essex himself was playing a dangerous double game. Only after the insurrection, when he saw the freely given and fully attested confessions of the conspirators, did Bacon learn that the man he had been appealing for almost daily to the Queen had been considering rebellion against her for at least three years, had been engaged in treasonable actions throughout the Irish campaign, and had actually plotted his revolt in Court and City for three months before it took place. It was with this secret, though still wavering purpose in mind that Essex had insisted on taking command of the Irish expedition, had made his exorbitant demands for men and authority, including the unheard-of 'regal authority to pardon treasons and traitors', had appointed his personal friends to posts of high command, and had made his triumphant progress through southern Ireland. He was accumulating the power and popularity he needed for a march on England. With the same purpose in mind he had kept out of reach of the Queen's instructions until he could make his own private agreement with Tyrone.[46]

Bacon was also to learn from Essex's confession (which tallies on every point with those obtained independently from his confederates, Southampton and Blount) that when he had rushed off to cheer his newly returned patron, that patron was not merely in danger of 'distates' from the Queen, but of imprisonment in the Tower, should his original plan become known. He had planned, said Blount, to march on London, 'with as much of the army as he could conveniently transport' and 'make his conditions as he desired'. He would bring over 'a choice part of the army of Ireland, land them in Wales' and gather more forces on the way, as well as help from his 'many powerful friends'. Both Southampton and Blount declared that they had opposed the plan, warning that 'as it was most dangerous, so it would cost much blood', and arguing that Essex would lay on himself 'an irrecoverable blot, having been so deeply bound to her Majesty'. Essex had finally taken Blount's advice, which was 'to go over himself with a good train, and make sure of the Court, and then to make his own conditions'. He had brought out 'a great number of knights and captains, officers and soldiers', as a contemporary noted, 'that this town is full of them', and, leaving them to create unrest in the streets of London, repaired to the Palace with only six men, in a last bid to win the Queen by persuasion.[47] When he failed to do so, Essex had good cause to tremble. To the messengers he had sent secretly to treat with Tyrone he had given advance pardons in case the matter leaked out. There was no advance pardon for himself.

How much the Queen knew, or Bacon feared, is difficult to tell, particularly since, writing to Essex's closest friend after his death, Bacon did not like to dwell on treasons that were only too familiar to Mountjoy – who prompted by his desire to see the succession question settled on James, had played a part in the early stages of the conspiracy. Sinister rumours came in from Ireland, where Tyrone boasted that before their parley he had sent to Essex offering to make him 'the greatest man that ever was in England'; and, soon after it, had repeatedly sworn that 'the greatest and strangest of alterations' could be expected, by which he should have 'a good share in England'. 'The Earl is now in trouble for us,' said one of Tyrone's men, for not attacking the Irish leader in the North, 'which he never meant to do, for he is ours and we are his'. Tyrone, it later appeared, as the future Viceroy of Ireland, had promised him eight thousand men 'to aid him towards the conquest of England', a promise he could no longer fulfil, now that Essex had been apprehended. Still hesitating between outright rebellion and hopes of a return to favour, Essex must have fervently hoped that these declarations would not leak out. When hankering after the Queen's favour he could be convincing, which explains why she was sometimes willing to distrust rumour and believe in the sincerity of his appeals; and to hear his advocate, who was to spend the whole autumn pleading for him.[48]

'I was never so ambitious for anything in my lifetime,' Bacon recalled, 'as I was to have carried some token or favour from her Majesty to my Lord – myself to be the messenger' (which was also his only way of seeing Essex). He knew how personal was the Queen's feeling for her unmanageable protégé, and the good that could come of it 'if she once relented to send or visit'; and he played on her desire to believe in Essex's good faith towards her. 'I was never better welcome with the Queen,' he tells us, 'nor more made of than when I spoke fullest and boldest for him.' As, no doubt, he did when she crossed the river to dine with him at Twickenham, and he presented her with a sonnet which he had written 'directly tending and alluding' to a reconciliation. The sonnet is now lost, though we have a later appeal on Essex's behalf to the Queen's clemency ('that excellent balm that did continually distil from her fair hands').[49] Elizabeth emerges vividly from Bacon's pages, with her suspicions and her reluctant affection.

But Bacon's position was not enviable. 'A great many love me not,' he told the Queen, 'because they think I have been against my Lord of Essex; and you love me not because you know I have been for him; yet will I never repent me that I dealt in simplicity of heart towards you both.' This is what Essex could no longer do. So we now find Bacon aware, throughout those autumn months, of the 'dangerous hopes' of Essex's partisans, but confident (he writes to one of them) that Essex himself did not seriously entertain such hopes; and, convinced that the Queen and he could still 'wrap it up privately between themselves', advising her strongly against the public prosecution, which she sought 'for the satisfaction of the world'. After which, when she insisted on a public admonition in the Star Chamber, and convened it on 29 November, he offended her by staying away. Essex, meanwhile, having considered, and rejected, three different plans to escape from his predicament – a new attempt to possess the Court, a flight to Wales, where he could always count on supporters, and a private escape to France – had been pressing Mountjoy 'to think of some course to relieve him'. He was now anxiously awaiting replies from him, and from King James of Scotland, who had been invited to support Essex in exchange for a confirmation of his succession to the throne. There was no response from James, and Mountjoy, who had undertaken the Irish command in mid-November, was busy now with the realities of war. Finally in March 1600 he wrote back that matters of succession were best dealt with by those directly concerned in them. He had been prepared to intervene, he said,

> to deliver my Lord of Essex out of the danger he was in, yet now his life appeared to be safe, to restore his fortune only and to save himself from the danger which hung over him by discovery, and to satisfy my Lord of Essex's private ambition, he would not enter into an enterprise of that nature.[50]

Around this time Elizabeth again brought up the subject of legal proceedings against Essex, for mismanagement and disobedience, and once more Bacon demurred, saying they would 'strike too deep' into his fortune and reputation; so that 'she seemed again offended, and rose from me'. In the end, adopting his suggestion to treat these proceedings, if they must take place, as a mere 'Council-table matter', she set up a special commission to try Essex in a private room at York House. Bacon asked her to release him from attending – he would 'reckon it as one of her highest favours' – but she refused. Convinced that this would prove the end of all 'bitterness and harshness between the Queen and my Lord', and hoping also to keep his credit with her for Essex's sake (which he had lost for a while, after his refusal to attend at the Star Chamber), he did not insist. Which was lucky for Essex, since when this trial took place, on 5 June 1600, the aggressive Attorney General, Edward Coke, almost defeated its purpose by accusing him not only of disobedience but of outright disloyalty, or treason, thus provoking Essex to attempt a justification, instead of the humble admission of his offence which alone could obtain him a mild penalty. Bacon promptly spoke up and freed him of this charge in unmistakable terms, as a result of which Essex threw himself on the Queen's mercy, and was condemned to nothing worse than continuing a prisoner in his own house during her pleasure.[51] Her pleasure lasted only a few more weeks.

Coke was right, of course, about the Earl's disloyalty, and Bacon was wrong. Yet this is when Macaulay, ignoring Essex's subversive activities and telescoping three trials, along with the developments of a whole year, into a couple of sentences, decided that Bacon had finally read the signs of his patron's fall, 'shaped his course accordingly', and abandoned the friend who had relied on his intercession. Far from abandoning him, no sooner was the York House trial over than Bacon was at work again with the Queen, insisting that Essex had 'never in his life-time been more fit' for her favour, and begging her 'not to mar it by lingering', but 'receive him again with tenderness' ('whereat I remember she took exceeding great contentment,' and reminded him that her actions were for the Earl's reformation, not his ruin). Early in August 1600 Essex was a free man, and Bacon, the only counsellor at hand – for Mountjoy and Southampton had given up all thoughts of conspiracy and were both abroad – was at last in a position to communicate with him. He wrote at once, offering his patron every assistance that was compatible with the Queen's service and quiet, and, receiving, as he noted in the *Apology*, a courteous acceptance of his goodwill, followed this up with further interventions on Essex's behalf.[52]

Essex, however, was using his new freedom to keep open house for less reputable friends, and attempting to sow discontent in the hearts of his more able courtier acquaintances, in hopes of winning them to his cause. He was now in an increasingly schizophrenic condition. Despite his desperate efforts to seize power, if only enough to make himself too dangerous to be attacked, he was still trying to keep his way open for a return to the fold. It was not too late to follow the advice Mountjoy had given him a few months earlier – to 'recover by ordinary means the Queen's ordinary favour' (or if necessary 'be satisfied with less') and retire to a private life, as Bacon put it, 'out of want, out of peril, and out of manifest disgrace'; with in due course, when the rumours of his insubordination had died down, 'some addition of honour to take away discontent'.[53]

Did Essex ever seriously consider this alternative? During the weeks that followed, he asked Danvers to organize more armies out of Ireland, sent his steward, Gilly Meyrick, to recruit a contingent for him on his Welsh estates, and requested his secretary, Henry Cuffe, to procure a letter from Mountjoy complaining of the misgovernment of the state and calling on himself to 'do somewhat to redress it'.[54] And all the while he was penning wild love-letters to the Queen – 'Haste paper to the happy presence from whence only unhappy I am banished. Kiss that fair correcting hand . . .' – and crying to her, out of 'the passion of his soul', that until he could see her, time was 'a perpetual night' and 'the whole world a sepulchre'. Which did not stop him from ugly words when she failed to respond ('her conditions were as crooked as her carcase').[55] No wonder Harington wrote of him as a man whose soul 'seemeth tossed to and fro, like the waves of a troublesome sea', as he shifted 'from sorrow and repentance to rage and rebellion', and on one occasion 'uttered strange words bordering on such strange designs, that made me hasten forth and leave his presence' – an obvious attempt to sound out the Queen's godson as a potential conspirator, as Essex had recently done with Bacon's kinsman, Sir Henry Neville, the English Ambassador in France.[56]

Sometime in October 1600 the fair correcting hand refused to renew Essex's monopoly of sweet wines, his principal source of income. ('An unruly horse', Elizabeth is reported to have said, 'should be stinted of his provender, that he might be more easily managed.')[57] Essex, who had been awaiting this decision, took the plunge: before the end of the month he was meeting his fellow conspirators at Drury House – the home of his right-hand man, Southampton – and they had worked out a plan to surprise the Court and remove the principal Councillors by force. The Queen may have had wind of their gatherings. At any rate she had sensed a change in Essex's manner to her – 'some slackness on my Lord's part', was all Bacon said of it to Mountjoy. But for Elizabeth, by now, it was a question whether she or Essex should rule England. At that point, Bacon added, 'remembering belike the continual and incessant and confident speeches and courses that I held on my Lord's side', she 'became utterly alienated from me'.

It is typical of Bacon that he should have defended Essex to the last over those very sweet wines which had decided him to launch his revolt. When the Queen complained that Essex's 'dutiful letters' had been aimed merely at forwarding his suit for the monopoly, Bacon, taking his image from the wines, and projecting his own beliefs on to his friend, said, 'Madam you must distinguish.' Iron is drawn to the loadstone while the vine creeps towards a stake. 'My Lord's desire to do you service' is 'that which he thinks himself born for'; his suit 'is but for sustentation'.

For three months, while Essex was actively preparing his revolt, the Queen refused to see Bacon. Not until after New Year's Day 1601 was he admitted to her presence, and this was the last time he saw her before the insurrection.

> I dealt with her plainly and said, Madam, I see you withdraw your favour from me . . . I am not so simple but that I take a prospect of mine overthrow, only I thought I would tell you so much, that you may know that it was faith and not folly that brought me to it . . . Upon which speeches of mine, uttered with some passion, it is true Her Majesty was exceedingly moved, and accumulated a number of gracious . . . [and 'sensible and tender'] words upon me . . . but as touching my Lord of Essex, *ne verbum quidem.*[58]

Not a word. But perhaps it was not so much Bacon's situation that moved Elizabeth at this late hour, as his faith in Essex, which she would have liked to share.

5

And Betrayed Him

Essex's march on the City, on that memorable 8 February 1601, in hopes of raising an insurrection and forcing his way to the Palace, is a familiar story. Many will recall his anguished cavalcade through the streets, in a cold sweat, when the citizens shut their shutters and not one man would join him; his surrender to the Queen's men (his cousin Robert Sidney and his friend Fulke Greville among them) at Essex House, after burning his diary and other papers; his arraignment for high treason, and the sentence passed on him by his peers – nine earls and sixteen barons. Deservedly, for an attempt on the City by a man of his standing and popularity, though undertaken for purely personal reasons, might well have led to a civil war. As a contemporary remarked two days after the rising, it was 'a blessed thing that the Earl failed in judgement and attempted London first, for had he gone straight to Court, he would have surprised it unprovided of defence, and full of his well-wishers, before the world had notice of his treasons'.[1]

Light-heartedly underestimating the venture as an individual's 'rash' enterprise (in which nearly all Essex's biographers were to follow him), and quite out of touch with the Tudor scene, Macaulay drew a romantic picture of a 'high-minded' Bacon who would have stood by 'the unhappy young nobleman' at the trial, would have been 'a daily visitor at the cell' and would have 'received the last injunctions, and the last embrace upon the scaffold'. And he described Essex's trial as if the law against treason had been made not to protect the state against violence, ever present in Elizabeth's reign, but for the personal vengeance of queens.[2] It was of course for the protection of the state that Francis Bacon, the most skilful of the Queen's legal counsel, was called in four days after the revolt, along with the Attorney General (Edward Coke), the Solicitor General, the Queen's Serjeant, the Recorder of London and the two Serjeants-at-law. He was not asked to build up a case against Essex, whose condemnation, since he had been caught red-handed, was a foregone conclusion, but to examine witnesses in order to discover the extent of the plot. As all the interrogatories show, the Council, still completely in the dark, suspected that the sudden attempt might have 'a further reach than appeareth'. They did not get to the bottom of it until the tenth day of the trial, and a year after Essex's revolt had been crushed they were still looking for 'the roots and offshoots of conspiracy'.[3]

Some things were impossible in Elizabeth's reign. No one could visit a man imprisoned under the Queen's displeasure. Neither could a Queen's legal officer refuse to collaborate in the prosecution of a traitor without incurring serious reprisals from an irate Sovereign and Council. In a similar situation, a generation earlier, Burghley had known that he risked not only dismissal but prison.[4] Bacon had stayed away from the Star Chamber proceedings and Elizabeth had called him to account; he had asked to be excused from the York House trial and been commanded to take part in it. Heroic abstention is what Macaulay now had in mind – a withdrawal to Cambridge to write his books in seclusion. But this trial was not for indiscipline or disobedience, it was for high treason. He would more likely have had to write them in the Tower.

It has been suggested that in playing his allotted part at the trial Bacon was influenced by fear, either for himself or for his brother Anthony, who had been Essex's messenger to James in some early exchanges.[5] There would have been nothing surprising about it: others connected with Essex had panicked around this time, not excluding that very Mountjoy whom Bacon was now addressing. But there is no need to look for explanations. Bacon acted from conviction. 'Every honest man that hath his heart well planted', he told Mountjoy, expressing a lifelong credo, 'will forsake his King rather than forsake God, and foresake his friend rather than forsake his King; and yet he will forsake any earthly commodity, yea his own life in some cases rather than forsake his friend.'[6] And he did not forsake Essex now, though there could be no more reconciliation on the part of the Queen, only mercy.

But we must bear in mind the shock and revulsion Bacon will have suffered when the principal conspirators – Gorge, Blount, Danvers, Cuffe and Davis, who knew they were to die – confesssed without reserve, and the whole extent of his patron's guilt came to light.[7] It was not until the day before the trial that Bacon heard of the secret meetings they had held over the past three months, and learned that Essex had planned to return to England with an army, collecting all the malcontents he could muster on his way; that he had intended to call a new Parliament, appoint his own Speaker, name his own Council – condemning some of the present Councillors for misgovernment; and that all the while Bacon had been pleading for him, and he had been sending his pathetic love-letters to the Queen, he was plotting to overthrow her. Bacon had accepted the dangers of his prolonged defence of Essex with open eyes, 'from faith not folly'; but that faith was broken. Even Coke, prepared for the worst, was shocked, and as for Bacon's old friend, the Lord Keeper Egerton, who had most lovingly admonished Essex during his quarrels with the Queen, when addressing that 'arch-traitor', as he now called Essex, at the trial, overcome at the news of an attempt to free the prisoner by putting the Queen in fear of her life, 'he stopped up his speech with tears'.[8]

Taking into account not only his friendship for Essex, but the special regard he had for the Queen – feelings he had shown unmistakably in his many efforts to bring them closer together – Bacon must have been shattered. Like Burghley, and others about her, while he identified the Queen with the state, he had a warm affection for the woman who represented it, and whose life, for that reason, was constantly at risk. Already in 1584, on the failure of one of the many conspiracies against her, the young Bacon had written a paper proposing ways of avoiding such 'wicked and barbarous attempts', and in later years he had frequently been employed to examine plotters against her life. On the occasion of another conspiracy three years before this last uprising, he had dwelt at length on the dangers she was exposed to – 'by violence, by poisoning, by superstitious votaries, by ambitious undertakers, by singular con- spirators . . . beside a number no doubt of the like which have grovelled in the darkness'.[9] Now his own patron, so long watched over and cared for, was revealed as one of these same 'ambitious undertakers', as he had described them, whose conspiracy had all the time 'grovelled in the darkness'. Bacon did not live in times when revolution was hailed as a glorious cause. He was thoroughly in sympathy with the Elizabethan outlook on rebellion against a legitimate sovereign, as expressed by Sir Thomas More in the pages of the play attributed to Shakespeare:

> What do you then
> Rising 'gainst him that God himself installs
> But rise 'gainst God?[10]

'This late and horrible rebellion' – so he opened his brief speech at the trial – must indeed have been horrible to him.[11]

None the less he played no great part in Essex's trial. It was Coke who, as Attorney General, marshalled all the Government's evidence, includ- ing the depositions of the accused, and brought the witnesses for the prosecution into the box. Bacon was rather a witness than a prosecutor, and, as his notably fair-minded eighteenth-century historian John Carteret, Earl Granville, saw it in *Biographia Britannica*, he 'performed the functions of his office' – which he could not have avoided – with 'tender- ness and decency'.[12] Some nineteenth-century biographers, [13] admitting that he could not have declined to sift the evidence, report on the inquiry or be present at the trial, would still have liked him to have sat silent through the proceedings. Instead of employing, as Macaulay alleged, all his wit, his rhetoric, his learning, not to ensure a conviction – for circumstances were such that a conviction was inevitable – but to deprive the unhappy prisoner of all those excuses which, although legally of no value, yet tended to diminish the moral guilt of the crime, and . . . might incline the Queen to grant a pardon.

This quite unwarranted accusation is still repeated today, along with the graver, and equally unfounded, charge that he himself secured his patron's conviction.

Spedding, when collating the many different reports of Essex's trial, assumed nothing for a fact that was not corroborated by evidence independent of Government sources, and, aiming at maximum impartiality, he based most of his conclusions on the report of an Essex partisan.[14] This clearly showed what Macaulay, writing in India with little knowledge of the historical background of the trial, had failed to realize: that the principal aim, if not the whole purport of Bacon's two brief interventions was precisely to incline the Queen to grant a pardon – in the only way it could be done. Which was not, as Macaulay believed, by influencing her to accept Essex's flimsy excuses (the best of reasons would never excuse rebellion in her eyes), but by influencing him to throw himself on her mercy. This was the counsel Bacon had given his patron on many less perilous occasions. He was to be throughout his life an advocate of clemency, once the truth had been acknowledged. And it may well be because he knew this to be the Queen's view also that he played his part in the trial with so little unwillingness – 'with tenderness', as Carteret saw it. The contrite approach he hoped to foster in Essex, which alone could soften the verdict against him, would hardly have been achieved if the prosecution were left entirely in the hands of the rude, aggressive and pitiless Coke. Bacon cannot have forgotten the effect of Coke's bullying at the York House proceedings, which had altered Essex's tone from submission to a misplaced attempt at justification. In fact the same thing was happening again; Coke was taking every chance he could to quarrel with the accused.

Had Essex pleaded guilty would he have won a different verdict from the Queen? Some months after his execution she confessed to the Duc de Biron, sent over by Henri IV of France as his ambassador, that she would willingly have spared the 'perfidious ingrate's' life; adding, possibly with Bacon in mind, that if only the Earl had taken the advice of his wiser friends instead of 'obstinately disdaining to ask pardon', all might have been well. In reality she could not have pardoned him. She knew that 'reason of state, dignity of her Crown, and the repose and weal of her subjects required the course which she had taken, and admitted no mean'. Henri saw her position clearly, and admired her resolution: 'she only is a King!' he exclaimed.[15]

Bacon, however, still hoped she might be swayed, and he had prepared a speech, along the lines, we may presume, of those he was later to pronounce at the trials of repentant criminals, praising the 'generous mind' that by confession 'paves the way to clemency'.[16] But Essex never asked for clemency. He pleaded not guilty, and he justified his actions, declaring at first that he had launched his revolt in self-defence against a plot laid by his private enemies to assassinate him, and later, when he found the whole conspiracy had been discovered, that he had meant to present himself to the Queen as a suppliant only, in order to 'unfold his griefs' to her. Arguments in favour of deliberate rebellion were not excuses, nor were they, as Macaulay put it, 'a palliation of his frantic acts'; they were plain denials of his crime, and Bacon thought them damaging above all to Essex himself. 'I expected not', he said, 'that matter of defence should have been alleged for excuse, and therefore I must alter my speech from that I intended. To rebel in defence is a matter not to hear of.' The only way now open to Bacon was to block the dangerous avenue of excuses, and do his best to steer Essex back towards unconditional repentance. And we find him showing up those feeble attempts at explanation for what they were, and urging, almost begging his old friend: 'Oh my Lord, strive with yourself, and strip off all excuses . . . All that you have said, or can say in answer to these matters are but shadows. It were your best course to confess, and not to justify.'[17]

Essex's first pretext for rebellion was that 'an ambuscado of musketeers' had been 'placed upon the water by the desire of my Lord Cobham and Sir Walter Ralegh to have murdered him by the way as he passed'.[18] Even if this were true, could anyone have taken it seriously as a reason for insurrection? Did he call on the City for help because his three hundred friends were not enough to defend him, and did he mean to force his way to the Queen as a refuge from danger? If he was really afraid of being shot in the streets, said Bacon, what could have prevented him from accepting the Queen's fair offer when she had summoned him on the morning of his revolt? Had she not sent his old friend, the Lord Keeper Egerton, with three other lords of her Council – one his uncle, Sir William Knollys – to ask him the cause of the gathering in his house, and promised to hear any complaint he might wish to put before her? Instead, he had locked the lords up in his study, and set off on his march to the City.

But there was no such ambuscado; as one of his followers later confessed, the story had been circulated 'to colour other matters' – in other words to give the multitude an aim: they would be rescuing the Earl from danger.[19] On the following day, confronted by his chaplain with the fear of eternal damnation, Essex broke down and confessed. 'Yesterday at the bar, like a most sinful wretch, with countenance and words I imagined all falsehood.' His plea of enemies had been one of the falsehoods, and he later apologized to Cobham and Ralegh, of whom 'he knew no other than that they were true servants of the State'. The aggressive intentions had been all on Essex's side, as Blount admitted; his followers had planned to kill Ralegh, and Blount himself had 'sent four shot after him'. On the scaffold Blount too was to beg Ralegh's forgiveness – and obtain it – 'for the wrong done you and for my particular ill intent toward you'.[20]

When Bacon said at the trial that there were 'no such enemies, no such dangers', Essex interrupted him with a wonderfully inapposite remark, which none the less Macaulay, and others after him, have taken seriously. 'I call on Mr Bacon against Mr Bacon!' he exclaimed, and reminded him of two letters Bacon had written on his behalf, in which he 'did plead for me feelingly against those enemies and pointed them out as plainly as possible'. As anyone who reads them can see, Bacon had drafted what he called his 'framed letters' – 'with my Lord's privity and by his appointment' – to assist Essex in 'winning the Queen', to encourage him to believe in her goodwill, and also to strengthen that goodwill in herself when she saw them.[21] Both letters contained a reference to Essex's known ill-wishers at Court (described as 'tolling the bell of his fortunes in the Queen's mind'), to whom Bacon had drawn attention, so to speak, as her hard partners, in order to absolve the Queen herself of severity. He was convinced, as he later remarked, that Essex had 'but one enemy' – himself.[22] Better, however, that he should harbour suspicions of her courtiers than believe Elizabeth had turned against him, and resort to desperate solutions. But it is a far cry from ill-wishers at Court (who was without them?) to assassins threatening death. Bacon now replied briefly, without going into details which could not reflect well on Essex: 'Those letters of mine will not blush in the clearest light, for I ever laboured to have done you good, if it might have been; and what I intended was wished from my heart.' ('A shuffling answer', was Macaulay's comment.)[23]

So much for Essex's first excuse. The second – resorted to when the first one was belied – was that when attempting to raise help in the City he had only meant to 'unfold his griefs to the Queen'. Recalling the Duke of Guise's similar, but fatally successful attempt against Henri III of France, Bacon said: 'Grant that you meant only to go as a suppliant, shall petitions be presented by armed petitioners? It was not the company you carried with you, but the assistance you hoped for in the City.' Macaulay, seeing things as usual from the personal angle, objected strongly to this allusion for the impression it was bound to produce 'on the mind of the haughty and jealous princess on whose pleasure the Earl's fate depended'; and it is still presented by Bacon's detractors as his most dastardly action. But Elizabeth, as Bacon well knew, needed no reminding of the similarity of her situation to that of Henri III, faced by the domineering and popular Duke. In expressing himself so trenchantly, Bacon had other thoughts in mind. While still bent on bringing Essex to his senses, his less personal intention was clearly to bring the discussion – which, at the hands of Coke, had drifted so far from the present charges that they were almost forgotten – back to the point.

Trials for high treason in those times had one principal aim, besides convicting the traitor: to satisfy the public that justice was being done. From that point of view the case was badly mismanaged. Coke had so often allowed the accused to distract him from the main issue by provoking him into irrelevant disputes of detail – which he could not resist – that nobody knew any longer what the trial was really about. Thus it was that a case of treason proved up to the hilt came to be presented in such a confused way (the confessions of the conspirators not having yet been made public) that, as Camden, the Queen's historian, was to write, 'some called it a fear, others an error' or 'an obstinate impatience and desire of revenge' or 'an inconsiderate rashness'; and few saw it for what it was, 'a capital crime'.[24] This confusion contributed to the spread of Essex's legend and had consequences also for Bacon himself. It was to be regretted, as Carteret rightly put it a century later, that

> this affair was never truly stated by men of knowledge and capacity, but left to the pens of such as, for want of more authentic vouchers, had recourse to traditional memoirs, enlarged and pieced out by their own fancies, by which means this is become one of the most perplexed passages in history.[25]

The more astute contemporary observers were not deceived. Chamberlain, observing that Essex's defence was that of a man whose 'chief care was to leave a good opinion in the people's minds', deplored 'his many and loud protestations of his faith and loyalty to the Queen and State, which no doubt carried away a great part of his hearers', but which he could not believe 'against manifest proof'. Apparently, Chamberlain added, Essex had begun to be sorry for his arrogant behaviour at his arraignment, 'and, which is more, to lay open the whole plot and to appeach divers not yet called in question'.[26] He continued these confessions, and died calling himself 'the greatest, the most vilest and most unthankfullest traitor that was ever born'.[27]

'All treasons of rebellion did tend to the destruction of the King's person,' Essex had once remarked.[28] He himself had a remote claim to the throne, and no one knows to this day how far he would have gone had he been successful. 'For the Crown, I never affected it,' he told his chaplain, early in his confession, while he was still maintaining that he had rebelled to save the Queen from atheists, papists and 'other mortal enemies of the kingdom'.[29] But even if he meant it at the time, could he have resisted his followers, on whom he was soon to lay the blame for all his actions? And would they have stopped at a mere change of ministry?

They had cried 'kill, kill!' when he had locked the Councillors up in his study. And Blount admitted on the scaffold that 'rather than we should have failed our purpose, it would have cost much blood, and perhaps drawn some from her Majesty's own person.'[30] Would the chief plotters have insisted on the staging of the play 'of the killing of Richard the Second', as they called it (Shakespeare's play, now long out of date), on the eve of their revolt, if not to show such of their fellow conspirators who might have qualms how easily a sovereign could be deposed – and murdered?[31]

The use made by Essex of the long-standing parallel between Elizabeth and Richard II, with himself as the usurping Bolingbroke (later Henry IV) is a pointer to his real aims. The 1590s had seen a series of allusions to this theme in print, but none more suggestive than John Hayward's *Life of Henry IV*, dedicated to that 'great expectation of the future', the Earl of Essex, just as he was about to set forth for Ireland with a powerful army.[32] It was strongly biased in favour of the rebels, and so full of transparent allusions to the contemporary scene that Elizabeth suspected 'some more mischievous person' behind the offending historian. In June 1600 Hayward was sent to the Tower, and, having confessed that he had added many subversive speeches of his own invention, he was kept there until after Essex's death. The book was suppressed, though when reprinted without the offending passages, 'none ever sold better'.[33]

The Earl's 'giving occasion and countenance' to this allegedly 'seditious pamphlet' had been touched on by Bacon at the York House proceedings that same month (under instructions, and under protest, Bacon tells us, and it was probably around this time that he had tried to divert Elizabeth's suspicions away from Hayward's *History* with a joke).[34] It was not, however, given undue importance at that stage, when Bacon's intervention was seen as an 'admonition' to Essex rather than a charge. But at the trial of the conspirators, in February 1601, when Coke brought up the revival of the play setting forth 'the killing of a King upon a stage', Essex had come near to re-enacting it. 'Note but the precedents of former ages,' said Coke, 'how long lived Richard the Second after he was sur- prised in the same manner?'[35] The authors of a memorandum on both play and book, which was found among the trial documents, remarked on Essex's 'being so often present at the playing thereof' and 'with great applause giving countenance and liking to the same', adding that his intent of 'settling to himself the crown of England as well as that of the Kingdom of Ireland' was confirmed by 'his underhand permitting of that most dangerous book', in which it was 'plainly deciphered for whose behoof it was made'. And the parallel was still on the Queen's mind months later, when, looking over some records with William Lambarde, Keeper of the Rolls, she 'fell upon the reign of King Richard II saying, "I am Richard, know ye not that?"' Lambarde knew it of course. 'Such a wicked imagination', he replied, 'and attempted by a most unkind gentle-man, the most adorned creature your Majesty made.'[36]

Those who take Essex at his word as to his not affecting the Crown can hardly have looked closely at the play. Apart from associations that would have been obvious to the conspirators, such as Glendower's fierce Welsh fighters – when Meyrick's unruly recruits from Wales were all over London – there are verbal echoes which suggest that the rebels were directly inspired by it.[37] And Essex's tactics were the same as those which Shakespeare has depicted in Henry Bolingbroke. His intention, he declared at his trial, was 'to come to her Majesty's feet', and to have 'severed' some from her (Ralegh in particular) who 'by reasons of their potency with her, abused her ears with false information'. But 'without purpose of harm to her Highness, for I protest I do carry as reverent and as loyal duty to her Majesty as any man in the world.'[38]

Bolingbroke's protestations in the play are famous. 'The King is not himself, but basely led by flatterers . . . those caterpillars of the Common-wealth which I have sworn to weed and pluck away.' Like Essex, he had 'no purpose of harm'. Drawing blood was 'far off from the mind of Bolingbroke'. His mission once accomplished he would commend his arms to rust, 'his heart to faithful service of your majesty'.[39] In thus following what Bacon called 'the beaten path of traitors', the two great rebels may have believed in their own good intentions. Both men had a horror of rebellion and treason, which would cause them to repent bitterly – and meanwhile made it difficult for them to admit to themselves that they were on a road which had no issue but regicide. (With the same horror of rebellion in their hearts would the Parliamentarians claim to rescue Charles I from the evil counsellors who were leading him astray.) Bacon, of course, has no word of this in his account to Mountjoy, but we know from later references that he had not forgotten it.[40]

Did the possibility of becoming King arise in the mind of Essex when *Richard II* was first produced in 1595? Cecil averred at his trial that he 'had been devising five or six years to be King of England'.[41] All we have to go on is Essex's presence at a private showing of the play arranged for Cecil by his cousin – and Bacon's – Sir Edward Hoby in 1595, and another such showing in 1597, at which, sharing with Cecil and Ralegh an understand-ing of its political significance, Essex was 'wonderful merry'.[42] It was in 1597 that he first confided to Blount his 'dangerous discontent', tending to 'the alteration of the State'.[43] But rumours of his intention reach us from many quarters – from Ireland, in particular, where Tyrone's friends spoke of their joint plan 'that the Earl of Essex should be King of England and Tyrone of Ireland'; from the English Catholics, prepared to recognize Essex as King (on conditions); and from Spain, where Philip III had also considered supporting him.[44]

Although Essex was not accused at his trial of attempting to seize the Crown, Cecil, after much provocation, told him to his face that he had planned to be King, and Coke could not resist a sneer at him for thinking to be 'Robert the first'.[45] It would be interesting to know which of his correspondents James of Scotland believed: Ferdinand of Tuscany, who, already in 1594, had warned him that Essex was the man 'most able to hinder a pretender'. Or Essex's brother-in-law, Northumberland, who wrote to him soon after the execution that Essex 'wore the crown of England in his heart these many years, and was far from setting it upon your head'. Or Mountjoy, when, to help Essex, he offered James his support in securing the succession of the throne, assuring him 'that my Lord of Essex was free from those ambitious conceits which some of his enemies sought to possess the world withal'; yet, before doing so, had felt the need to make Southampton and Danvers join him in a solemn oath 'to defend with the uttermost of our lives her Majesty's person and Government'.[46]

Macaulay now made three unfounded allegations against Bacon. For the first of them – that Essex was convicted and Bacon made no effort to save him, though it would have been easy – there is no contemporary evidence in support of Bacon's story in the *Apology*. It is Bacon's word – his solemn declaration to Mountjoy, promising the truth – against Macaulay's, put forth as a fact, with no attempt at substantiation, and no reference to Bacon's *Apology*.

> I well remember [wrote Bacon], between the arraignment and my Lord's suffering I was but once with the Queen, at what time ... I commended her majesty's mercy, terming it to her as an excellent balm that did continually distil from her sovereign hands and make an excellent odour in the sense of her people; and not only so, but I took hardiness to extenuate not the fact, for that I durst not, but the danger; telling her that if some base or cruel-minded persons had entered into such an action, it might have caused much blood and combustion; but it appeared well they were such as knew not how to play the malefactors.[47]

Unfortunately, Bacon concluded, 'after that last fatal impatience there was not time to work for him'. There was more time for less guilty men, and his 'affection, when it could not work on the subject proper, went to the next' – the young Southampton, that is, for whom Cecil also pleaded, and who was spared. 'I have many honourable witnesses can tell that the day after my Lord's arraignment, by my diligence and information touching the quality and nature of the offenders, six of nine were stayed, which otherwise had been attainted.' 'A thing,' said Cecil's brother, Lord Burghley, 'the like was never read of in any chronicle.'[48] Coming from a convinced advocate of clemency, the story is not an unlikely one, and we may note that Sir John Davis, the only principal conspirator to be interrogated by Bacon, was the only one spared.

Bacon's conduct – so runs Macaulay's next allegation – 'excited at the time great and general disapprobation', and in the years that followed he was 'loudly condemned' by the multitude – and by his conscience, which 'told him that the multitude had but too much reason'. Bacon's conscience, as will be shown below, told him nothing of the kind.[49] As for the general disapprobation, it began in 1837, with the publication of Macaulay's essay. From the observers who recorded events in those years – Camden, Rowland Smith, Chamberlain and others, all with their ear to that hotbed of gossip, the Court – not a whisper has reached us. If, that is, we discount one improbable rumour to the effect that when the Queen considered annulling the seventy-five or so valueless knighthoods conferred by Essex on his untried captains in Ireland, Bacon was 'thought to be the man who moves her Majesty to it'. (She was dissuaded from this impolitic step, and Bacon, always on the side of moderation, is likely to have been among the dissuaders.)[50] There can be little doubt as to the source of any such rumours. Essex's more rowdy followers, many with secrets on their conscience and, like their leader, only too ready to conjure up enemies, finding the man who had most consistently opposed their counsels in frequent conversations with the Queen, would naturally jump to their own conclusions.

'While Elizabeth lived,' said Macaulay, 'this disapprobation, though deeply felt was not loudly expressed.' As far as we know, it was expressed only once, and that was in Elizabeth's lifetime, when at the end of 1599 Bacon was offending her by his persistent intercessions for Essex; and (he now told Mountjoy) he had been threatened with assassination because of a false rumour that he was 'one of those that incensed the Queen against my Lord of Essex'. It was thought that he had been advising her to bring Essex's case into the Star Chamber (when in fact he had argued persistently against her doing so). The rumour reached his cousin, Robert Cecil, who refused to believe it; and, wrote Bacon in his *Apology*, 'I satisfied him how far I was from such a mind.' His own letter at the time, indignantly denouncing 'the utter untruth of this report', whose improbability 'every man that hath wit more or less can conceive', bears out his account.[51] His even angrier letter on the same subject to one of Essex's less savoury friends, Henry Howard, Earl of Northampton, is worth quoting in full, as it sums up Bacon's whole attitude to his patron:

> There is shaped a tale in London's forge, that beateth apace at this time, that I should deliver opinion to the Queen in my Lord of Essex's cause . . . that it was high treason. But the truth of this fable God and my own sovereign [to whom he had also written] can

witness, and there I leave it, knowing no more remedy against lies than others do against libels . . . For my Lord of Essex, I am not servile to him, having regard to my superior duty. I have been much bound unto him. And on the other hand I have spent more time and more thoughts about his well doing than I ever did about my own . . . For my part I have deserved better than to have my name objected to envy, or my life to a ruffian's violence. I am sure these courses and bruits hurt my Lord more than all.[52]

We will recall that at the York House proceedings, six months later, it was Bacon who had refuted Coke's accusation that Essex was guilty of treason.

As for the 'loud condemnation of the multitude', after Elizabeth was gone and Essex's followers were back in favour with James, the only contemporary witness to any such disapprobation was Bacon himself, when in 1604 he gave Mountjoy his reasons for writing the *Apology*: 'I cannot be ignorant of the wrong I sustain in common speech, as if I had been false or unthankful to that noble but unfortunate Earl, the Earl of Essex.' Not that Bacon ever paid much heed to common speech, though he did value 'the good opinion of certain persons' – among them the man he was addressing in his *Apology*.[53] But hostile comment can hardly have spread beyond Essex's ill-disposed followers, for at this time, as many historians have noted, Bacon stood high in the estimation of his contemporaries. Officially appointed King's Counsel Learned that same year, he was also the most popular man in the House of Commons. Two different boroughs had elected him a Member of James's first Parliament, and he was so active in it – his name was on every one of its twenty-nine committees – that his health forced him to 'pray the House that at other times they would use some other, and not oppress him with their favours'.[54]

As far as we know only one person ever attributed ingratitude to Bacon in his lifetime, and that a person who was himself guilty of much ingratitude. Some sixteen years after Essex's uprising, while the King and his Court were in Scotland, Buckingham – James's favourite and Bacon's patron in later life – furious with Bacon for advising against the marriage of his brother, John Villiers, to the daughter of Edward Coke, accused him (so Bacon learned from a colleague) of being unfaithful to himself, by 'inveterate custom', as he had been to the Earl of Essex.[55] A predictable reaction on the part of the all-demanding, only too inconstant Buckingham, as a contemporary described him.[56] Coke, at that time in Scotland with the Court, was 'transported with passion' against Bacon (so wrote the colleague), for attempting to put a spoke in his wheel, and had not foreborne 'any engine' to heave at him; while Buckingham was setting the now triumphant Coke 'as close to him as his shirt – the Earl speaking in Sir Edward's phrase, and as it were menacing in his spirit'. Bacon, it seems, could well owe the myth of his inveterate ingratitude to an apt phrase, whispered by his lifelong ill-wisher in the favourite's ear.

Macaulay's third charge reads as follows: 'The faithless friend, who had assisted in taking the Earl's life, was now employed to murder the Earl's fame . . .'[57] He was referring to the *Declaration of the Treasons of Essex*, of which Bacon was the principal author, and we must now look into the history of that document. Alone with the Queen, Bacon could make light of the traitors' inefficiency, but the civil unrest was not over. The people had heard only a confused account of the trial. The confessions of the conspirators would have shown their favourite in his true colours, but in order to spare the reputations of men such as Mountjoy and Neville, only marginally involved, they were not made public at his trial, and false accounts of Essex's condemnation and execution were rife. Without either a professional army or a paid bureaucracy, the stability of the Elizabethan regime demanded a continuous and arduous wooing of the body politic, and after every major event, plot or trial, a declaration was put forth to inform the public. A clear, readable and authentic narrative of the whole proceeding against Essex was now essential. It was probably Bacon's misfortune, from the point of view of the legend, that he had inherited his uncle Burghley's talent – along with Burghley's care in checking and counterchecking the facts – as the expert writer of these declarations. The Queen chose the fittest man for the task: having, he said, 'taken a liking of my pen', she commanded him to write 'that book which was published for the satisfaction of the world'.[58]

'Could no hack-writer, without virtue or shame,' cried Macaulay, 'be found to exaggerate the errors, already dearly expiated, of a gentle and noble spirit?'[59] Bacon – who, for all we know, might have preferred to write the report himself, rather than have it bungled by a hack-writer – was only too well aware of the odium that the author of such a declaration would incur among Essex's vociferous supporters. Clearly he had other motives in writing it than to curry favour with the Government. We know his priorities: Queen and state before friend – and rebel. He had been called on in a time of emergency, not to justify a bad case, but to set forth what had actually happened in a trial he considered just and inevitable, attaching at every step the documentary evidence on which his information was based. Macaulay's strictures on the *Declaration* were drawn from the Whig tradition of anti-Stuart propaganda, which, in the generation that followed, had declared it – on no grounds but emotion – a 'pestilent libel'.[60] Thus encouraged, Macaulay gave free reign to denunciation of the man who could 'prostitute his intellect' with 'some slander invented by the dastardly malignity of Cobham' or 'the envy of Cecil', and not feel he was 'sinning against his friend's honour and his own'. But he could give no instance of any slander, false implication or exaggeration in this so-called 'abusive pamphlet', because there was none. Barring a frivolous and completely spurious charge brought up in the 1880s, which will be discussed below, no statement in the declaration has ever been challenged, and no inconsistency found in it. It is, as Spedding concluded, 'a luminous and coherent narrative', and nearer to the truth than any since put forth.[61]

At least as to the facts. As to the tone, opinions differ. Hepworth Dixon, always a defender of Bacon's good name, thought the whole declaration 'so mercifully worded that it saved the memory of Essex from public execration' and 'left the future open to his misguided followers and to his innocent son'; Macaulay saw it as 'a performance abounding in expressions which no generous enemy would have employed respecting a man who had so dearly expiated his offences'.[62] As Bacon reminds us, however, the published text could hardly be called his own. It was penned 'so as never secretary had more particular or express directions in every point', but after he had handed over his draft, while it remained impeccably accurate – for, like himself, 'their Lordships' were 'religious and curious of the truth' – it had been so 'perused, weighed, censored, altered' by the Queen and her Councillors as to make it 'almost a new writing'.[63] (The Queen, for example, had not thought it fitting that, following 'his ancient respect', Bacon should refer to 'my Lord of Essex', on every page, but 'would have it made Essex', and it was reprinted accordingly, and the first copies suppressed.)

We may form some idea of Bacon's original version by comparing the cold formality of the official *Declaration of Treasons* with his report on the York House proceedings – unhampered by instructions, and unedited – in which, skating gently over thin ice, he had presented an exemplary, merciful Queen, and, with undisguised sympathy, a contrite Essex, 'beseeching that that bitter cup of justice mought pass from him'.[64] Or we may turn to that quiet statement of the facts, without rhetoric or special pleading, the *Apology* itself, which has been followed throughout these chapters. True, at the time of writing, Essex was no longer a danger, and his friends were back in favour, but the impression given here is that the change of political climate allowed Bacon to express in his own language what had been in his mind all along. His story flows in one clear, vivid stream from beginning to end, and the author's feelings are often near the surface. Impatience, distress, relief, humour, the excitement of past speeches relived in the same phrases, his pleasure at the Queen's 'sensible and tender words' – these things are everywhere in and between the lines.[65]

Bacon's services to Essex are mentioned, but not emphasized; his obligations recorded with warmth. We miss one thing only: there is no vindication of the part played by Bacon himself at the trial and after it. Neither is there a word in justification of the trial and sentence. The heavier Essex's fault, the less blame could be laid on Bacon by his partisans. But here, where it would have suited him to inculpate Essex, Bacon is silent. Spedding – moved by the 'unstudied simplicity and subdued earnestness' of these pages – explained Bacon's silence, saying 'he would not, out of regard for his own reputation, keep alive for one day more the memory of his benefactor's guilt.'[66] Bacon's affectionate tone when speaking of his old patron, 'whose fortune I cannot remember without much grief', is manifest. Everything that could be argued in Essex's favour is mentioned. Essex's expressions of disloyalty are passed over or hinted at only as 'some slackness' towards the Queen, his rebellion is referred to as his 'last fatal impatience', and the day it took place as 'the day of my Lord of Essex his misfortune'. The story ends with Bacon's above-quoted appeal to the Queen's mercy, suggesting that Essex and his fellows 'were such as knew not how to play the malefactors'.

Bacon felt a particular sympathy for 'the generous sins of youth'. When writing to Essex after the York House trial, he had compared him with Icarus, who flew with waxen wings too near the sun, and he may have remembered his friend when, in his study of myths a few years later, he described Icarus as the hero who, 'in the pride of youthful alacrity, naturally fell a victim to excess'. It must be admitted, he said,

> that of two paths, both bad and mischievous, he chose the better. For the sins of defect are justly accounted worse than the sins of excess, because in excess there is something like the flight of a bird, that holds kindred with heaven, whereas defect creeps on the ground, like a reptile.[67]

There was in Essex a strain which aroused in some of his critics 'a troubled compassion', and Bacon certainly felt it.[68]

His expressions in the *Apology*, as well as his silences, were to have a considerable effect on the reputation of both men, and Spedding was right to conclude that his chariness in throwing the blame on Essex has helped mankind to forget how much the Earl was actually to blame.[69] This from the so-called faithless friend, and for one who, noble and unfortunate as he may have been, before he died betrayed all his accomplices, denouncing even some who were guilty only of keeping his sinister secrets; who accused his most devoted followers of having 'more malicious and dangerous ends' than his own, and laid the whole blame of his rebellion upon them; who charged his follower, Henry Cuffe, to his face with being his principal instigator, and declared that his own sister had urged him to revolt – 'She must be looked to, for she hath a proud spirit.'[70] 'Passing strange', wrote a contemporary, that these 'noble and resolute men . . . combined together by firm oaths', and now facing their deaths, should strive which of them could draw the other in deepest, as 'first movers and contrivers of these confessed treasonable plots'; but 'the Earl himself exceeded all, to all men's wonder.'[71]

Bacon ended his *Apology* with the following words: 'Your Lordship [I now hope] will vouchsafe to hold me in your good opinion, till you know I have deserved, or find I shall deserve to the contrary.' If at this point we, to whom the work is also dedicated, can accede to this request, we will appreciate the summing up of these events by the historian Thomas Fuller – born four years after the *Apology* was published. Sir Francis Bacon, wrote Fuller, was

> favourite to a favourite, I mean the Earl of Essex, and more true to him than the Earl was true to himself; for finding him to prefer destructive before displeasing counsel, Sir Francis fairly forsook not his person (whom his pity attended to the grave) but practices; and herein was not the worse friend for being the better subject.[72]

6

Essex, Hero and Martyr

The foregoing chapters will have shown that it is not possible to make a reliable estimate of Bacon's attitude and actions towards Essex if we cannot see Essex's own motives in a clear light. The innocence of the one depends to a considerable degree on the guilt of the other. As Elizabeth Bennet said of the seemingly innocent Wickham and the apparently guilty Darcy, in a somewhat different context: 'Take your choice, but you must be satisfied with only one. There is but such a quantity of merit between them.'[1] The myth of Essex as a 'gentle and noble spirit', more sinned against than sinning, which, at the expense of his own reputation Bacon himself did much to promote, runs parallel with the legend of a vicious Bacon plotting his patron's death.

The most dependable historians, Spedding among them, have shown us a spoilt favourite, harbouring rebellious intentions for at least five years, prepared, for no other reason than to gratify his personal ambition, to plunge the country into civil war and to bring about the deposition of his sovereign – with its inevitable corollary, her murder. If, instead, Essex can be presented as a simple-hearted, impulsive soldier, harried and finally driven to desperate measures by the persecutions of a hysterical Queen and the machinations of her hunchbacked secretary, then indeed Bacon must appear as a pawn – if not one of the prime movers – in a conspiracy to condemn his friend and to denounce him falsely before the world as a traitor. This is actually what has been attempted, not once but many times. Spedding's analysis of Essex's actions, from the Irish campaign until his execution, has not been invalidated by twentieth-century research. On the contrary, a number of mid twentieth-century studies, based on a broader range of sources, with richer, subtler interpretations – essays on patronage and clientage, and on the concealed debate over the succession to the throne – have all tended to confirm Spedding's coherent view of Essex's dealings with the Government, and the Government's with him.[2] New works on Tyrone, Elizabeth and Burghley bear him out, and in particular they confirm the truth of the *Declaration of Treasons*. They give no support to the alternative version. Yet that version has thrived in the face of all evidence. We must now trace its growth, and attempt to discover the reasons for its prevalence.

Throughout his short life – he died at thirty-three – Essex sought, and enjoyed to the full, what he was most addicted to: popularity. He was warned against this addiction by his friends, satirized for it by his enemies, accused of it at his trial, and remembered for it by the historians of his day as the main cause of his misfortunes.[3] It lost him his life, and it gained him his particular form of immortality. Popularity, Bacon had written to him, 'is one of the best flowers of your greatness', provided it is obtained fairly (*bonis artibus*) and 'handled tenderly', by which he meant that Essex should cultivate the approval of his peers, and achieve successes in Parliament that would assist the Queen in obtaining funds for the war.[4]

But for Essex, who belonged to the old nobility, popularity was a headier drink. He was 'hurried and transported', as James's Secretary, Robert Naunton, later described him, 'with an over desire and thirstiness after fame' – particularly 'the deceitful fame of popularity and applause'. In his *Annales*, John Stowe placed 'affection of popularity' before 'desire of revenge' or of power as the 'main cause of his misadventure'. 'No man was more ambitious of glory,' he noted, 'or more careless of all things else.' Unfit as Essex was for military command, he saw himself – and was seen – as 'the English Achilles', and that role was life to him. 'Tell them that are sorry at my going', he wrote to Anthony Bacon before embarking for Cadiz, 'they would not wish me diverted from this army if they saw the beauty of it.' He was never more at ease than among his men. 'I find a sweetness in their conversation,' he wrote elsewhere, 'strong assistance in their employment with me, and happiness in their friendship.'[5]

The 'strong assistance' was of course the backbone of all his efforts to achieve predominance, and he lost no opportunity of attaching his men with links of personal gratitude and hopes of reward – principal among them being those indiscriminate knighthoods he awarded 'by the half hundreds' (as one observer noted) to 'tag, rag, cut and longtail', not excluding (said another) menial servants, base captains and rascals, cut-purses and convicted thieves – before they had even begun to show their mettle, in Ireland or elsewhere.[6] High and low were attracted to Essex's service, and not only in hopes of gain. The very qualites that made him incompetent as a war commander, those deeds of defiance and extrava-gant bravery, carried off with all the panache of the old-style warrior, acted like a spell on officers and men, as they did on the people who flocked in their thousands to see his shooting matches, and acclaim him on his return from the wars.[7] Kissing the blade of his sword at the close of the French campaign, or, as he entered Cadiz harbour, throwing his hat into the sea; challenging his counterpart, the French Marshall Biron, both in white plumed hats, to a leaping match, where Essex 'did overleap them all'; or offering Tyrone, who was twenty years older than himself, and far too wily to accept, a chance of settling the Irish question between them in single combat – these things made him a hero in the people's eyes.[8]

They also exposed him to absurd risks for the Commander-in-Chief of an expedition, as when, reconnoitring in a boat near the enemy coast, he refused to wear armour because the waterman who carried him went unprotected. In France one such act of bravado cost him his brother.[9] Vainly did Bacon point out to him before his departure for Ireland that 'designing to fame and glory may make your Lordship in the adventure of your person to be as valiant as a private soldier, rather than a general.'[10] It was to the image of himself he saw in that waterman's eyes that Essex paid homage. Both before his revolt and after his death, his assiduous courtship of the common people was compared to Bolingbroke's in the play of *Henry IV*, and he appeared, in satirical verses full of Shakespearian echoes, doffing 'his bonnet to an oyster-wench', to a craftsman, a 'broom-man' – to any of 'the vulgar sort that did admire his life'.[11]

He did not win them all, as we assume from an amusing encounter in the streets of London in March 1600 – between a night-watch of law-abiding blacksmiths, haberdashers and cloth-workers, and a band of his captains 'in the distemperature of drink' (so runs the deposition on their arrest). 'Good gentlemen, be quiet,' ventured one of the watch. 'God's wounds!' cried Sir Edward Bainham, recently knighted, 'dost thou make a gentleman of me? I am a knight!' And, when quietly overpowered, 'I will live to be revenged on thee, Briggs, if thy name be Briggs. I will fire this city!' 'The constable is an arrogant rogue,' exclaimed another captain, 'I hope to be at the cutting of a hundred thousand better men's throats than his within this city!' And Bainham, 'If I had but fifty horse I could overcome the city!'[12]

It was to this notorious 'rakehell' in particular, among the desperate characters whom the Earl was now freely entertaining, that the son of Buckhurst, the Lord Treasurer, objected when he visited Essex on the Queen's behalf a month before the uprising. Nor had the Government seen the last of Bainham. Condemned to death after conspiring with Essex, he was reprieved, bought his pardon from Ralegh, was 'clapt up' for desperate speeches against the newly crowned James, turned up again in the Gunpowder Plot, and lived to stir up more trouble for the Lord Chancellor Bacon in later years.[13] Meanwhile there must have been quite a few similar collisions between the 'poor craftsmen', wooed by Essex, and Bainham's fellows, those rashly knighted officers who thronged the streets on their leader's return from Ireland, drinking damnation to his enemies, spreading seditious pamphlets and scrawling libels on the City walls. If, none the less, the London tradesmen did not rise for Essex, it can still be said of him that, like Hamlet, he won the love of 'the distracted multitude' ('Who like not in their judgement but their eyes. And where 'tis so, the offender's scourge is weighed, but never the offence').[14]

It is in this multitude, responding to the clamour of Essex's followers, that the legend of the 'Valiant Knight of Chivalry' seeded and produced its crop of myths. Among these was a hoax letter purporting to be from the French Ambassador to his son – but disclaimed to Elizabeth's full satisfaction – which, while mistaking everything about the trial, described it as a farce. Essex's peers, it was alleged, drunk with beer, sweetmeats and tobacco, had condemned to be hanged, drawn and quartered 'of all Englishmen the one with the most virtues . . . a man so noble and brave, and entirely innocent of what he was accused of'.[15] Other myths claimed that on the day of his death some of the multitude tried to kill the executioner, and soon afterwards three rainbows were seen over the Tower, and a spectre appeared in the place where he was beheaded (not hanged); while some told of 'a bloody block, seen by the guards, falling from heaven to earth upon that spot'.[16] 'Sweet England's pride is gone,' sang the ballad-makers. 'He ne'er did deed of ill, but envy, that foul fiend, hath brought true virtue's friend unto his thrall.'[17]

One of the longest-lived myths woven around Essex – a new version of an age-old legend – is the story of the Queen's ring, bestowed on her favourite with the promise that it would secure forgiveness from her at any time, and sent to her by Essex from the Tower, but witheld by Lady Nottingham, to whom he had entrusted it – and who, on her death-bed, confessed her misdeed. 'God may forgive you Madam,' cried Elizabeth in one of the variants of the story, 'but I never!' – and died, not long after, of remorse. In reality Elizabeth lovingly attended Lady Nottingham's last hours and bitterly mourned her old friend.[18] The principal source of the perennial myth of Essex, however, was his resuscitation, a generation later, in a political tract entitled 'Robert, Earl of Essex, his Ghost sent from Elizium to the Nobility, Gentry and Commonaltie of England'. The occasion was the return of Prince Charles with James's favourite, Buckingham, from their unsuccessful trip to Spain, when Buckingham was denouncing the marriage they had set out to negotiate, along with all things Spanish. Although Essex had no political programme, he stood for war, which, despite his secret promises to certain Catholics, meant war with Catholic Spain. In the tract he was invoked as the vanquisher of that wicked country – and, of course, as the real subduer of Ireland – who, by means of intrigue and false accusations, while others took the credit for his action, had been hounded to his death.[19]

Thus, as Spedding observed, a fiction based on popular emotion, without the slightest foundation in fact, was accepted as truth brought to light by time, while the studiously accurate *Declaration*, guarded with attested depositions and resting on the personal credit of responsible statesmen, was denounced as a libel.[20] On the advent of the Civil War, embittered and highly partisan writers took Essex for their emblem against the Stuart kings; and the rebellion of a man with no aim but to gain power for himself was interpreted by those of a new age as of a piece with their own struggle against tyranny.[21] The times had changed, but some of the names had not. Essex's son, brought up in Charles's Court, turned Parliamentary general and fought against the King, with Sir John Meyrick, a nephew of his father's fellow conspirator, as his adjutant; and Oliver Cromwell was related to the rowdy and bankrupt noble, Lord Edward Cromwell, who had taken part in Essex's rising. It was natural for these men to interpret the previous generation's motives in the light of their own.

By the middle of the eighteenth century, the myth, furthered by Coke's confused handling of the trial and the Government's well-meant hesitation in publishing the confessions of the conspirators, kept alive by Bacon's reticence in telling the story, and firmly rooted all along in the popular mind, had been adopted by quite a few historians. Essex, so clearly seen for what he was by those of his own time, now became the great favourite who, like many such favourites, 'fell into deep misfortunes', and whose 'last unfortunate act' ('his last fatal impatience', Bacon had called it) was no better than an act of madness. Still more rosily, he became 'the brave and generous young man . . . who abandoned himself to all the impetuosity of his temper, or rather to the pernicious suggestions of his followers', and who, though 'embarked in a kind of rebellion . . . knew not how to be a rebel' (Bacon again, who had said he 'knew not how to play the malefactor').[22]

Throughout the nineteenth and twentieth centuries, while scholarly historians filled in the outlines of Essex's story as it has been told here, others perpetuated the legend of the Valiant Knight – no mean feat, for in order to present Essex's rebellion and death as mere phases in the love affair between Earl and Queen, the political realities of war and government had to be removed to a hazy dreamland, and major events in his saga left unexplained, or passed over in silence. How great was the romantic appeal of these famous lovers may appear from a glance at the Hollywood production of a play on the private lives of Elizabeth and Essex, produced in 1939.[23] In brilliant technicolour, a hysterical Queen (Bette Davis) confesses her passion for a truant Essex (Errol Flynn) to Lord Burghley – resuscitated for the occasion – and to that 'weathervane, always riding whatever wind is fairest', Sir Francis Bacon, knighted also for the occasion. 'I'm only a woman, Bacon, must I carry the weight of the world alone?' 'Not alone, your Majesty,' Sir Francis replies, 'you will need a leader for Ireland.' No sooner has Essex left for Ireland, however, than the dead Burghley, with two other plotters, Cecil and Ralegh, and Essex's sister Penelope – here his jealous girl-friend – conspire to suppress all correspondence between the Queen and her General. Left without the men, arms and supplies with which Essex knows he could have beaten Tyrone in a month, he is forced to surrender. 'Tell your Queen I thank her for my victory,' says Tyrone, patting him on the back, 'if she'd given you the support your campaign deserved, it would be me surrendering this day.'

Meanwhile the harrowed Queen confesses to Bacon that she has written Essex her love time and again and received no reply from the traitor. What to do? Bacon, who knows about the intercepted letters, keeps a self-serving silence. Essex on his way home gathers a new army and surrounds the palace, but though Burghley warns Elizabeth that the whole town is behind him (Burghley has himself forbidden a performance of that dangerous play, *Richard II*), she refuses to defend herself. Essex-Flynn marches up in irresistible splendour to kneel before the Queen. The plot is uncovered. 'Heads will fall!' cries Elizabeth-Bette, and dismisses the Court to embrace her dear rebel. 'You shall stand behind my throne, together we will build an England, the wonder of the world!' But Essex, confessing that his thirst for power is even greater than his love, insists that he must be King. Elizabeth, realizing how unfit he is to rule, agrees to share her throne with him, but as soon as he has trustfully disbanded his men, orders his arrest. Fade to the Tower, where the Queen sits waiting – in vain – for him to send her the ring. Finally, while outside the people clamour against his death, Essex comes up through a trap-door and the lovers fall into each others' arms. Loving England more than Essex, Elizabeth still refuses to give up her throne. 'You're right,' says Essex, 'I'd make a sorry King. I would be your death,' and disappears through the floor, while the Queen calls after him, 'take my throne, take England!' – too late – and remains quivering in her chair as, in the courtyard, the axe falls.

What had playwrights and producers to go on? In 1934, five years before their presentation of Essex's life in a manner which is hardly more far-fetched than some of the historians' versions, the facts had been set forth by an expert student of Elizabethan history, J. E. Neale, in terms substantially the same as Spedding's. Neale correctly depicted Essex as a conscious if reckless traitor, already in his earliest military engagements enrolling a potentially dangerous personal band; tempted by Tyrone's proposal to make him the greatest man in England, and probably letting Tyrone into the secret of his own desperate projects; behaving with arrogant impudence at his trial, and when it was over denouncing all his friends.[24] Neale's account is written from Elizabeth's viewpoint, but nothing is left out or glossed over on either side.

The same cannot be said of J. B. Black's *Story of the Reign of Elizabeth*, published two years later. Essex is presented here, in his own words, as 'the victim of unscrupulous rivals, who waylaid him at every turn, and of a jealous queen, whose surrender to a sadistic impulse subsequently brought her hours of remorse'.[25] He is 'jockeyed' into the Irish command, regardless of his prolonged struggle to gain it and his triumphant cry that he had beaten Knollys and Mountjoy to it.[26] His inefficiency is a picture 'built up in the royal mind', his long tête-à-tête with Tyrone no more than a 'capital mistake', his 'madcap irruption into the city' the inevitable result of the Queen's enraged persecution, which made him 'turn plotter to destroy a plot'. His professions of innocence are taken at face value – his intention being clearly none other than to warn the Queen of the danger that threatened the country – and the whole episode, 'one of the most pathetic in the reign', is dismissed as the outcome of a generation gap. No reference at all is made to Essex's plans for leading a rebellious army into England, or to the full confession he made to his personal chaplain after the trial, and wrote out in his own hand. A letter written by Essex's ever-protective uncle, Knollys, allegedly advising the Council to betray him – which Black adduces to prove that the Cecilian party was attempting to sabotage the Irish expedition – when quoted in full turns out to be an appeal to the Council to supply all the aid they had promised him.[27]

The film-makers had another truncated account to hand, this time from a popular Catholic viewpoint, in Hilaire Belloc's *History of England* (1931), where Essex is 'forced' by Government intrigues against him to plan a violent return from Ireland, and is so 'shaken by the old terror of assassination' that 'the inevitable' – his rebellion – happens.[28] But their best jumping-off ground for an amorous dialogue between the valiant knight and his apprehensive and jealous Queen is without doubt that published in 1928 by their famous – and notorious – biographer, Lytton Strachey, past-master at making his largely fictitious characters come alive. His *Elizabeth and Essex* is the tale of a hapless hero, convinced of his own high purposes, who dreamed a bloodless revolution that would allow 'the Queen to be his, and he the Queen's, for ever and ever'. Egged on by his fellows, delicately prodded by Cecil, he embarks on revolt, determined – 'who could be so base, or so mad as to doubt it?' – that the Queen should remain inviolate. Elizabeth, of course, has known all along that the revolt was a mere act of folly. Could she, by a royal pardon, regain 'with new rapture the old happiness'? No, she remains deaf to her heart, and her inordinate triumph ends in solitude and ruin.

So widespread was the myth by now that, later in our century, when it was no longer possible to ignore the discoveries and reinterpretations of Tudor history, it lived on unperceived in some historians' minds. When depicting Essex (with Bacon's image) as the 'Elizabethan Icarus' in 1971, Robert Lacey faced the facts. Essex's wooing became 'a calculated exercise in financial survival', Elizabeth's response a 'wilful infatuation'. But the coldly ambitious rebel still failed to realize what he was doing, and his absurd fears of assassination remained an inexplicable pretext for a rising which, once again, 'just happened'. In some of Lacey's pages this pretext was seen in the old romantic way as the 'tragic product of a deluded mind', while in others it was presented in a colder light, as a rationalization covering 'the rough, greedy, insensitive ambition' of his 'flawed' personality. He was 'at worst a traitor, at best a fool', Lacey concluded – or rather, failed to conclude, because, while his mind accepted the realities of history, his heart had decided otherwise. Already on his third page he had joined those who 'mourned the foolishness that had brought an over-impulsive friend to the block'.[29]

An invariable constant runs through the idealized biographies of Essex. The noble, innocent, misguided hero – the product of a series of significant omissions – is dogged at every step by a shadow Bacon, sketched out in degrees of blackness that vary from the villainy of Machiavelli to that of Iago. There is one honourable exception to this practice: G. B. Harrison, in a sympathetic account published in 1934, omits no important fact, and says not a word against Essex's mentor and follower.[30] In Belloc, Bacon is principal plotter, bullying Essex at his trial and loading him with abuse; in Black, he delivers 'venomous onslaughts' against his master; and we will find him backstage in all the other biographies of Essex, working out his sinister designs. In Strachey, a heartless, self-seeking Bacon is very much in evidence, taking his patron's misfortunes as 'a heaven-sent opportunity' of acquiring the confidence of the Queen, seizing the chance to fan her smouldering suspicions of her favourite to red heat, and delivering the death blow to him with supreme subtlety.[31] In Lacey, alongside a hero only partially revised, the same villain 'abjectly' pursues his way to official power,'unctuously' recalls his own words as he turns his past efforts for Essex to his own credit, 'craftily' insinuates malicious motives at the trial, and is duly 'treated as a pariah' by all his friends.[32] The romantic myth and the black legend remain inextricably intertwined.

Bacon did not appear alone on the reverse side of Essex's coin. All the historians attached to the partial image of Essex have had to make out that the Queen and her Secretary acted towards him in bad faith – Cecil to destroy a rival, Elizabeth to wreak a personal revenge. In order to prove this contention, it became necessary to cast doubt on the documents, in particular the confessions in which the prisoners freely denounced each other – to the dismay of contemporary letter-writers, as we have seen.[33] Thus in the 1880s E. A. Abbott, one of Bacon's most enthusiastic detractors, launched a campaign to show them up as forgeries.[34] These confessions, however, are no 'casket letters', like the Queen of Scots' private correspondence – spied on and manipulated in secret, and the originals lost – but publicly attested declarations. No serious historian has ever questioned their authenticity, and only the strong pull of the romantic image, along with its accompanying shadow, can explain why they were ever doubted at all. Commenting in 1901 on the curiously inconsistent 'shifts of criticism' resorted to in order to get rid of these men's testimony, John Nichol, a distinguished exponent of Bacon's philosophy, remarked:

> at one time it is insinuated that the witnesses themselves were perjured, as if men would conspire for their own death; at another that the evidences were forged by the Government after the execution of Essex, and in the same breath, because for State reasons certain portions of the truth were withheld, that they did not dare to justify it . . . [If however] these evidences were forged or altered, it must have been done so ingeniously, by a perjury so unanimous on the part of so many otherwise unimpeachable authorities, on so grand a scale, and with so little purpose, that we can never again allow any weight to evidences of any State trial whatsoever.[35]

Abbott made a similar effort to cast doubt on the authenticity of Tyrone's peace propositions, of which, since they were given verbally, the only record we have is a memorandum thought to have been forwarded by Cecil to France.[36] It is not known whether this text (allegedly concocted by the Government to circulate their own unfavourable view of the treaty) was an early draft that had reached the Queen before Essex's return, or a list of the clauses he had laid before her, or possibly a note of those he had failed to mention. The attempt to invalidate it, however, is relevant to the present study only in that it shows the lengths to which the promoters of the myth will go. A letter from the Queen herself to General Fenton in Ireland leaves us in no doubt about the terms Essex had provisionally agreed to on her behalf – principal among them, as she complained, 'that all the ancient exiled rebels be restored to all that our laws and hereditary succession have bestowed on us'.[37] In other words, the Queen's subjects 'displanted' and Ireland for the Irish, which, as terms agreed on by a commander sent to put down a rebellion (and whatever we might think of them with hindsight today) were downright treason, and, as Elizabeth put it, 'full of scandal to our realm and future peril to the State'. But are we now to mistrust Elizabeth herself?

We have seen something of the kind of Queen required to support the notion of a misled and persecuted Essex: Black's cold, unheroic and unmagnanimous Elizabeth, exacting the last ounce of punishment from her old love out of personal pique; Strachey's, great, at least, but 'with a sinister touch about her' and with rage and hatred in her heart; Lacey's nasty, vicious and selfish Queen, a 'toothless, bewigged old harridan' without genuine feeling, who looked upon Essex as a toy.[38] The view of Elizabeth as one whose vices 'were such as could not exist with a good heart, nor her weaknesses with a good head' – as presented by one of its anti-royalist propounders in the eighteenth century – was also Macaulay's.[39] Abbott, in 1885, depicted her as 'almost destitute of all spiritual and moral sense'; pursuing her policies 'not because it was best for the nation, but because it was best for herself'. 'Such an idol as this,' he concluded, 'it was not possible to serve and at the same time maintain one's own self-respect.'[40]

A different Elizabeth emerges from the research of mid-twentieth-century historians, concerned mainly with the working of her Government and Parliaments. In the course of their special studies they discovered, as one of them explained, with a 'deep and growing respect', the significant part she had played in shaping policy, both at home and abroad. She had encouraged the 'pseudo-romantic' cult of herself with 'a purposeful and calculated artistry', and, while guided in part by expediency, had stood firm on matters of principle.[41] If this image, carried at the time on a wave of national idealization, involved some underestimation of her ministers' contributions, it did not greatly overestimate hers.[42] This was once more the Queen of contemporary record, ready to face her kinsman and see which of the two of them should reign; admired by Henri IV of France for her resolution in handling his revolt; working for Essex's reformation, not his ruin, and relenting again and again towards him – never so happy as when Bacon spoke for him most boldly; yet, when there was no more hope of his reformation, telling the French Ambassador – who saw the tears in her eyes – that, where the welfare of her state was concerned, she dared not indulge her own inclinations.[43]

Elizabeth's famous delays and hesitations, denounced by Essex's biographers as signs of her capricious nature – her way of leaving open the posts which her overbearing suitor was pressing her to fill, until, in his absence, she could place the candidate she thought fittest (afterwards offering the incensed Essex a compensation prize to satisfy his pride) – were now seen as the tactical moves of a Queen dealing with a dangerously powerful subject. It became clear that when she failed to give him the much coveted Mastership of the Wards, or to renew his licence for sweet wines, she had other considerations in mind than the indulgence or punishment of a favourite. As was pointed out by Joel Hurstfield in his study of the Wards, had Elizabeth made him Master of that office, with its unlimited opportunities for wealth and patronage, the ever bankrupt Essex would have become the power behind the throne, destroyed his rivals and fundamentally changed the history of the century that was just opening.[44]

Unlike James, so thoroughly infatuated with Buckingham that he all but surrendered the kingdom into his hands, Elizabeth never allowed her favourites to influence her in matters of state, and in her last years, as Hurstfield observed, she 'destroyed an aspiring Buckingham in the person of the Earl of Essex'.[45] Bacon had seen her in a true light when in his disourse 'in happy memory of Elizabeth', after dwelling on various praiseworthy aspects of her character, he remarked that, as for allowing herself 'to be wooed and courted and even to have love made to her', and liking it, these things, whatever 'the sadder [graver] sort of persons' might say, were to be admired.

> For, if viewed indulgently, they are much like the accounts we find in romances, of the Queen in the blessed islands . . . who allows of amorous admiration but prohibits desire. But if you take them seriously, they challenge admiration of another kind and of a very high order; for certain it is that these dalliances detracted but very little from her fame and nothing at all from her majesty, and neither weakened her power nor sensibly hindered her business.[46]

To a jealous and hysterical Queen corresponds a silently venomous Secretary who worked for Essex's death by making a show of defending him (Belloc), and gained his ends (Strachey) by 'infecting' the royal mind – 'What could his shameful crooked posture really betoken?'[47] An actively hostile Cecil was essential to the supporters of Essex's claim that his enemies were after his life, though, as often happens with this kind of psychological projection, the exact reverse was the case. It was Essex who plotted to replace Cecil with his own nominee, and it was his more turbulent followers who manifested towards Cecil, and other members of the Government – including Bacon, as we have seen – murderous designs that were without precedent in that reign. After his return from Ireland, on his way to the Queen, Essex had turned down the offer of one follower to kill Lord Grey, and Cecil after him. But as his young fellow conspirator, the Earl of Rutland, declared, it was 'to enable himself to revenge him on his enemies' – Cobham, Cecil and Ralegh – that he had planned 'to possess himself of the City'.[48] None the less, a cluster of Cecil myths now grew up alongside those of Essex, of which one will give us a taste. Advanced in 1922 by a biographer of Southampton, it explains the rebellion as the outcome of a secret plan of Cecil's to instal the Spanish Infanta in England as the Queen's successor – the Earl's contacts with English and Spanish Catholics to back his seizure of power being conveniently forgotten. In fear of Essex, who had warned James of the supposed plan, Cecil trapped his rival into 'accepting the impossible task of subjugating Ireland', and 'completed the manoeuvre by sabotaging the Irish campaign'. Well did Hurstfield describe this tale as 'a speculation of the most fantastical kind'.[49]

The notion of Cecil as the real author of Essex's rebellion, although defended among others by the Catholic Hilaire Belloc, originated with the Puritan chroniclers whom Macaulay was to draw on for his Bacon. These writers, to whom all things royal were anathema, cared little for the truth about the men they decried. The destruction of Essex, wrote one of them, was 'encompassed by his more subtle enemies' at Court. They inveigled him away to Ireland by the only possible means: 'accumulating upon him such high favours and honours as they observed more suitable to his humours'; so that with his rebellion he was merely 'exceeding' them in their 'highest and most extraordinary plots'. This is from the *Historical Memoires* of Francis Osborne, a fertile spinner of Essex myths. In his version of the story of the ring, which he was the first to tell, it was of course a villainous Cecil who prevented the Countess of Nottingham from delivering it to the Queen. Another of his fabrications, probably picked up from some old Essex partisan attempting to explain his lord's unexpected return from Ireland (it was later to be repeated by other tellers of tales), runs as follows. Cecil, in order to entrap Essex into confirming 'the dismal whisper' that he was bringing an army over from Ireland, with which that infamous minister was 'hourly inspiring' the Queen, sent word to him that she was dead, 'stopping in the meantime all ships else but what came loaden with the fatal intelligence'. Whereupon, rushing over hot-foot 'with some few gentlemen', and 'finding the report false', Essex cast himself at the feet of his royal mistress.[50]

'Robin the devil never did good,' sang the popular poets at Cecil's death – the same who had celebrated Essex as 'sweet England's pride', who 'ne'er did deed of ill'. And in fact the devious, secretive and deformed Secretary (a chord which, as we saw, Strachey did not fail to touch) was as unpopular in his day as ever handsome Essex was acclaimed.[51] Of Cecil it cannot be denied that despite sincere efforts to serve his country, and a probably sincere remorse for some of his worst exploitations, he deserved the hatred of his contemporaries. He had spent too many years extending the Government's profiteering racket far beyond the modest limits his father had kept it to, enforcing enclosures of common land on reluctant tenants to run his lucrative sheep farms, and effecting shady transactions in the City, to his enormous gain and others' loss. But if there was one action for which – whatever the strictures of Essex partisans, and of the anti-Stuart writers of the following generation – he did not deserve this opprobrium, it was 'the fresh bleeding of that universally beloved Earl of Essex'.[52]

Most historians today consider that Cecil showed remarkable patience towards Essex. There is no evidence that he planned his opponent's downfall.[53] And when Essex turned on him at the trial with the absurd charge (based on a misheard remark, immediately disproved and later withdrawn) that he had maintained the Spanish Infanta's right to succeed Elizabeth, Cecil's grief can be heard through his indignation. It was a felony at that time to discuss matters of succession, and for once his urbane reserve deserted him.

> You would depose the Queen [he cried], you would be King of England and call a Parliament! Ah, my Lord, were it but your case, the loss had been the less; but you have drawn a number of noble

persons and gentlemen of birth and quality into your net of rebellion, and their bloods will cry vengeance against you. For my part, I vow to God, I wish my soul was in heaven and my body at rest, so this had never been.[54]

Not that Cecil hadn't quietly opposed his rival all along. Years later he confessed to Essex's one-time follower Sir Thomas Bodley that the Earl's daily provocations had been 'so bitter and sharp against him' that he had tried to block his friends' advancement (Bacon's, of course, included).[55] And no doubt Cecil was pleased when Essex claimed the command which took him away to Ireland. But the Secretary's 'subtile' methods, alluded to by the Court libellers and made much of by Strachey, boil down to this: he did not work to destroy the favourite, he was content to let him destroy himself – for the good of the country, as he believed.[56] And he was not wrong. If Essex had lived in 1603, James might well not have succeeded to the throne without involving England in civil war. By his foresight and audacity in dealing privately with the future king at that crucial time – which he could not have done with Essex alive and intriguing – Cecil saved England from a threat that has now been forgotten, though fears had been such (Bacon later remarked) that on the proclamation of James the people rejoiced 'as a man that awaketh out of a fearful dream'.[57]

Elizabeth, Cecil and Bacon move as a wicked trio through the pages of Essex's biographers (except those of Lacey, who, under the influence of recent studies, presented a moderate Cecil alongside an odious Elizabeth and evil Bacon). And not least through those of his faithful descendant in the nineteenth century, Walter Bourchier Devereux, who felt the 'deepest contempt' for the 'abominable duplicity' of the haughty, tyrannical, envious, jealous and 'overwhelmingly avaricious' Elizabeth, and for a Cecil with honey flowing from his pen and poisonous malice 'rankling at his heart'. Devereux's Bacon is Macaulay's, basely deserting a generous, trusting friend, and gratuitously endeavouring 'to deepen his offence while living and blacken his memory when dead'. As for Essex, he can do no wrong. Or, if he does, Devereux lovingly excuses him, and where this is not possible, grieves over his weakness. He would, if he could, change history to prove his ancestor honourable – and right. 'Mistaken Essex!' he calls to him across the centuries, over his Irish campaign, 'the true way to have conquered his enemies, and silenced them, was to have applied all his forces, all his energies to the Northern journey, and by one blow have brought the most important rebel of all to the dust.' This is what Essex would have done had he been the disarming and candid Walter Devereux, quite incapable of harbouring treason in his heart against his own sovereign, Queen Victoria.[58]

7

The Servant and the Dreamer

We have gained an idea, although incomplete, of the man whom Bacon served. If we are to evaluate the quality of that service, it is time to look more closely into the relation between Essex and his follower. The subject has not been tackled, except in fiction. Dorothy Sayers, author of scholarly works as well as detective stories, had one of her picturesque female dons in *Gaudy Night* highly approving a book on Essex by one Winterlake, who, she felt sure, had 'got hold of the master-key to the situation between those two men'.[1] It is a pity we cannot read Winterlake. Failing that, I propose to look at the relationship as they themselves saw it, within the framework of their own and their contemporaries' concept of the loyalty owed by follower to patron and patron to follower. How did Bacon understand the nature of his service? Did Essex, like his biographers, look on Bacon as the villain of his piece?

Our first question must be, why did Essex himself never accuse his friend of ingratitude? (On the contrary, even at his trial, he recognized that, in those 'framed letters', Bacon 'did plead for me feelingly'.)[2] Generous restraint or touching dignity, some would have it. 'That noble heart', wrote Macaulay, 'was too great to vent itself in such a reproach.'[3] It did so vent itself, however, towards others – his conspirator friends, in particular, for their 'slackness and coldness' during his months of confinement in the spring of 1600 – when Mountjoy was in Ireland, Southampton in the Netherlands and planning further travel, Danvers and Cuff in the country, and Bacon alone was at hand, doing everything he could to reconcile him with the Queen.[4] 'Essex thought him wanting in zeal as a friend,' said Macaulay, referring to this same period.[5] On the contrary, that summer, after the York House trial and his release, well aware that his friend was not working against him, he had no hesitation in welcoming his assistance – assistance offered once again with the frank proviso that though he loved few persons better than Essex, Bacon loved 'the Queen's service, her quiet and contentment' and 'the good of his country' better; and that his patron should not fly, like Icarus, with waxen wings against the sun. Protesting that he had never flown with other wings than 'desire to merit his sovereign's favour' (though he was at that time urging his friends to gain him that favour by force of arms), Essex had replied with what Bacon looked on as 'a courteous and loving acceptation of my good wishes'. Both by inclination and choice, he wrote, he could not be 'other than kind' to his friend.[6]

What was the charm? Essex can hardly have been the dupe of a false, hypocritical adviser (if anyone was dupe at this stage it was Bacon). The warmth and simplicity of Essex's expressions bear witness to the sincerity of his feelings for both the Bacon brothers, whatever qualms he may have had in the later years about his own lack of good faith towards them. To the ever ailing Anthony he showed a protective gentleness ('I wish I could lend you strength and borrow pain of you'; or, when about to sail for Cadiz, 'I pray you believe, although your mind, which so tenderly weigheth my danger, be very dear unto me, yet for my sake you must be confident'). To Francis he wrote as to an older brother, openly confiding his thoughts, troubles and, in the early stages, his plans – and receiving from him the same trust (as happy to 'rest in the wisdom of a friend') and gratitude for his own 'free and loving advice'. 'And though my love to him be exceedingly great,' he wrote of Francis Bacon, on another expedition, 'yet my judgement is nothing partial; for he that knows him so well as I do, cannot but be so affected.'[7] All Essex's letters show the same appreciation of the brothers' qualities, and confidence in their sincerity towards him.

None the less, patron and follower held diametrically opposite views on the purpose and implications of the system of patronage under which they lived. Essex's were those of his time, if perhaps more extreme, in accordance with his forceful nature. But Bacon had always been wary of the feudal loyalties he saw around him. Already at the age of nineteen he had offered his uncle Burghley the same 'bounden service' he was to promise Essex some fifteen years later, with the same express reservations (so much as was 'lawful to be enclosed of a common', but no more), and subject to the same priorities he was to voice once again in his letter to Mountjoy twenty-four years later – God before King and King before friends:

> I cannot account your Lordship's service distinct from that which I owe God and my Prince [he wrote]. To your Lordship I can but be a bounden servant. So much I may safely promise and purpose to be, seeing public and private bonds vary not, but that my service to God, her Majesty and your Lordship draw in a line.[8]

Happily service to Burghley did draw in a line with the higher principle which royalty stood for in Bacon's eyes, yet it was because his highest ambition found no scope with his uncle that he was to look elsewhere for support; without turning away from Burghley, however, for Bacon deplored faction in all its forms. 'Mean men in their rising must adhere,' he said, voicing the necessity of his time; and the phrase has often been quoted against him. But he thought they should adhere as little as possible; in other words, so moderately as to 'be a man of the one faction which is passablest to the other'.[9] If a man can content every faction, 'the music will be the fuller'. Learned men in particular, among whom he always counted himself, were, he believed, 'desirous to give their account to God, and under God, to the kings and states they served'; and they were not good at 'applying themselves to particular persons', because 'the largeness of their mind' was too much contracted by such exclusive service.[10]

Essex, on the other hand, looked towards an earlier age, when loyalty and treason were a personal matter between a knight and his lord. His service was not given to the state, but to a princess whom he expected to influence on personal grounds, and all his demands, regardless of broader issues, were person-to-person requests. 'If you value me think of my suit,' was a frequent phrase; and it was literally beyond his comprehension that his Queen could appoint Lord Cobham, whom he hated, Warden of the Cinque Ports, rather than young Robert Sidney, the friend he had been so passionately urging on her.[11] Bacon knew Essex, and he knew the implications of the piece of land with which Essex had 'enfeoffed' him (as he put it), at a time when the old oath of fealty was still practised. When expressing his reservations about the gift, Bacon begged the Earl not to turn 'all his estate into obligations', and be left, like the Duke of Guise, with nothing but people bound to his service.[12] But bounden followers were what Essex wanted; he looked on as enemies, it was said, all those who 'did not wear some badge of his favour'. When he found that Lord Grey, one of the knights he had dubbed in order to attach him, had been favourably received at Court in his absence, he ordered him to choose between Cecil and himself. Grey saw no reason to be the enemy of either, and was accordingly told to look to Cecil for his rewards.[13]

In his military friends Essex found the kind of exclusive personal devotion he understood. When the Queen refused to confirm his highhanded appointment of Southampton, on their way to Ireland, as Master of the Horse, he coolly argued against Elizabeth that his gentlemen volunteers would desert her if Southampton left the army. She, on her side, refused to believe that her soldiers fought merely out of affection for their commander.[14] The allegiance which his officers and men gave Essex – unfettered by any higher loyalty to man or principle, since they acknowledged no duty but obedience to their lord – still arouses a moved response, where a more abstract commitment to serve Queen and state fails to do so. Thus Strachey can turn with a sigh of relief from Bacon to one of the most reckless of the potential regicides in Essex's circle, who protested that he would follow his master to any extreme: 'Sir Charles Danvers was not a clever man; but his absolute devotion to his benefactor still smells sweet amid the corruptions of history.'[15]

Essex demanded the same loyalty of the civilian protégés whom he tried so hard to impose on the Queen, and Bacon was by no means the only man to suffer the disadvantages of his overbearing sponsorship. Like Bacon, and like Philip Sidney, who sought to conciliate the two reigning factions, Fulke Greville tried to remain close to both Cecil and Essex.[16] And years later Thomas Bodley left on record Essex's efforts to win him 'by letters and messages and other great tokens of favour', so as to make him solely dependent on himself. He had been much embarassed, he said, by that lord's 'prodigal speeches' putting him forward as an able secretary – 'ever accompanied with words of disgrace against the present Treasurer' (Cecil), whom Essex wished Bodley to supplant. 'Considering the slender hold-fast' his patron had on the favour of the Queen, and 'his perilous and feeble and uncertain advice', after serving Essex for a time Bodley decided to possess his soul in peace, and he withdrew to Oxford. (Where Essex – no unfeeling man – compensated him with a gift of books which was to form the core of the Bodleian Library.)[17]

Not everyone was able to find such an easy way out of the dilemma Essex posed for most of his dependants when by 1599 his own system had broken down. The only escape route open to most of them was to seek employment under Cecil. One man stayed with Essex to the end, and faced ruin as a consequence. This was Bacon's brother Anthony, quite talented enough to have been another Cecil, had he not chosen to attach himself to the Earl of Essex.[18] He is often cited as a model of loyalty, in contrast to Francis. And the parallel is a valid one, for Anthony Bacon stood for that strictly personal form of service which was unacceptable to his brother. Each of them – devoted as they were to each other through-out Anthony's short life – followed his own concept of loyalty. Anthony's was the generally received standard of his time, though few lived up to it as disinterestedly as he did. Unlike Francis, he took an almost childishly partial stand against his uncle Burghley, whom he enjoyed calling names. 'Our Earl, God be thanked,' he wrote triumphantly after the Cadiz expedition, 'hath with the bright beams of his valour scattered the clouds and cleared the mists that malicious envy had stirred against his matchless merit, and hath made the old Fox to crouch and whine . . .' And he expressed the hope that Essex would soon be rewarded with that title of Earl Marshal which his brother, in the long and earnest letter he wrote to him at this time, was begging him not to seek.[19]

Anthony Bacon had no other aim in life but to serve the master 'to whose disposition and commandment', he told Essex, 'I have entirely and inviolably vowed my poor self . . .' He gave his adhesion body and soul, like the Earl's military followers, but without their illusions of personal gain. And sometimes, inevitably, with misgivings, as we can see from a revealing note he addressed to Essex in 1597, when, during one of the latter's offended withdrawals from Court, he was attempting to coax his master back into action. Regretting Essex's indispositions and 'undeserved' discontents, he is bold to send certain business papers

> to your Lordship, of whose deep wisdom, sound judgement and true magnanimity I rest so assured as that my confidence in them checketh and choketh such grievous and stinging apprehensions as may without offence spring from dutiful care and unspeakable devotion of a continual sympathising heart . . .

A heart that, since his first 'entire vow', despising temporal greatness, prized more his master's 'most worthy love' than 'all worldly happiness whatsoever'.[20]

It had need to. Unapproachable – and, as far as we know, unapproached – with proposals for conspiracy, Anthony was turned out of Essex House without a penny when its owner was confined there in March 1600. He died obscurely, three months after his master's execution, and, just as Francis was to die twenty-five years later, badly in debt. The rest is silence. But we may surmise that Anthony's sufferings and doubts, exacerbated by the conflict in his mind from seeing his much-loved brother arraigned against his equally loved patron, must have worn down his resistance. A last blow may well have been his loss of faith in Essex when he learnt that his revered master had inculpated all his closest friends. Anthony, it seems, had written to one of them for an explanation, but the response did not arrive until two weeks after his death. It would not have brought him much comfort. The writer claimed to remove 'any unworthy aspersions of dishonour' from the name of Essex, alleging that he had been persuaded to make his ignoble confession 'solely from fear of eternal damnation'.[21] For the sincerely religious Anthony the tribunal of the next world was not one before which men could lie.

His devotion smells sweeter than that of Danvers. But no more than Francis did he succeed in influencing Essex against the loyal servants who contributed so largely to his disaster. 'Methinks one honest man or other', wrote Secretary Naunton some years later – betraying, with echoes from Bacon's *Apology* that he had one honest man in mind, who had advised Essex only too well – one man, who 'had but the brushing of his clothes, might have whispered in his ear, My lord look to it, this multitude that follows you will either devour you or undo you . . .' There follow the main points of the advice Bacon had so constantly given.[22] But we know that for at least three years before his rebellion, Essex had been unable to respond to his friend's faithful counsel with that other 'fruit of friendship' (as Bacon put it in the essay 'Of Friendship'), the sharing of one's griefs, hopes and fears. And we can imagine what Bacon must have been through in the way of 'stinging apprehensions', similar to Anthony's, as step by step he saw his patron wading into deeper waters.

For Macaulay and the biographers who followed him, it was a simple matter. Bacon had joined Essex's service for his own ends; he left when the ship showed signs of sinking – whenever that may exactly have been. And we are expected to look with similar scepticism on Bacon's affirmation that he had devoted his service to his patron as 'the fittest instrument to do good to the state', disregarding Bacon's lifelong efforts to influence his rulers through others, where he could not act himself.[23] Bacon's vocation as a statesman will be looked into later in this book.[24] Anthony certainly believed in it, and eagerly awaited his appointment to a post of authority in which 'those gifts that God hath bestowed on my brother shall no longer lie fallow'.[25] Essex was equally convinced, and it could well have been because he had some notion of his friend's ampler views that he continued to be drawn to Bacon, even though this follower never gave him the exclusive loyalty he looked for.

Macaulay, a subscriber to the crude notion of patronage, inevitably scoffed. Bacon, he maintained, owed the Queen no loyalty as she had done nothing for him; he was indebted solely to Essex, who, 'not content with attempting to inflict the Attorney-Generalship upon him, had been so cruel as to present him with a landed estate' (in fact a strip of land near the estate Bacon leased at Twickenham). There follow pages of sarcastic reproof to Elizabeth for condemning the ablest young man of her time 'to drudgery, to obscurity, to poverty' – and to lying 'in a sponging-house for a debt of three hundred pounds'. That Bacon could have served her faithfully without any important advantage to himself did not enter Macaulay's head. 'It is barely possible that Bacon's motives' for taking part in the trial of Essex 'may have been gratitude to the Queen for keeping him poor ... There is a possibility that [Justice] Jeffreys may have been an ardent lover of liberty ...' but (after more of the same rhetoric) 'a man who should act on such suppositions would be fit only for St Luke's' – for Bedlam, in other words; and Macaulay did not see why 'suppositions upon which no man would act in ordinary life should be admitted into history'.[26] Here we have the terms of a syllogism repeatedly used in connection with Bacon. Man does not act for idealistic motives. Bacon appears, at least on occasion, to have done so. Therefore he was secretly acting for his own, probably evil aims.

Bacon's approach could not have been more different from Macaulay's. Many years later he was to recall that he had been bound to Queen Elizabeth rather 'for her trust than for her favour'.[27] And, as he wrote in his *Apology*, she never gave him 'ordinary place'. But he had not resented her appointing the experienced Coke as Attorney General (it was Essex's delusive promises and the long deferral of her decision he had suffered from), still less her choice of Fleming as Solicitor General, of whom he had remarked beforehand that if the Queen were to choose so able a man, 'he would by no means alter it'.[28] 'I am as far from being altered in my devotion towards her,' he wrote to Essex on this last occasion, 'as I am from distrust that she will be altered in opinion towards me, when she knoweth me better.'[29] Nor had he cause for resentment. Already in 1594, a few months after Coke's appointment, she had made him Queen's Counsel Extraordinary – an exceptional, unpaid post which afforded him a good deal of private access; and the opportunity to give his advice on state affairs meant more to Bacon than emoluments and rank. The Queen, as he reminded Mountjoy, 'did sometimes divide private favour from office'. He valued her trust, and was content to enjoy her 'private favour'.[30]

The lowest virtues, in Bacon's view, drew praise from the people, but they had 'no sense of perceiving' the highest.[31] In dealing with both patron and Queen he did not seek the popularity Essex thrived on, and he did not expect to be generally understood. When misjudged and threatened by Essex's violent partisans, he told the Queen he accounted the libel against him an honour. 'I take duty too exactly,' he said, 'and not according to the dregs of this age.'[32] The many recommendations on behalf of friends and relatives in his letters, and his keen interest in their affairs, show that Bacon understood the meaning of personal loyalties, but there was for him another reality – a reality one of his twentieth-century biographers was aware of when he noted that Bacon's 'terrific energy was devoted not so much to putting people right as to putting things right'.[33] If we want to understand his motives, we must at least consider the possibility that his was one of those minds he himself described as 'not embarked in partiality, which love the whole better than the part'. There are many references in Bacon's works and letters to the difference between 'private good' and the 'communicative good', which is part of a 'greater body'. Service to the communicative good, he believed, was 'deeply engraven upon man, if he degenerate not'. These may be somewhat abstract sentiments, but when reviewing his dealings with Essex we must bear them in mind. If, like most of us, Bacon sometimes failed to follow his own precepts, the 'greater body' remained for him a very real concern.[34]

Such was the framework within which Bacon tried to serve the Earl of Essex. But was Essex a man who could be served in this way? What was his real nature? Essex's biographers had no doubts about Bacon. They saw him using his patron for his own ends while that patron was successful, and when Essex fell, procuring his death to save his own skin. But their central character remains, as Strachey put it, 'a complicated and obscure question'.[35] Seen through their eyes, his actions, in Ireland and on his return, are inconsistent to the point of incoherence, and they are generally left unexplained, or attributed to 'frenzy' – if that may be called an explanation. Meanwhile a clear-headed Essex is shown in the well-documented histories of the twentieth century, as he was by Spedding in the nineteenth, multiplying his support early on as a part of his political offensive; seeking command after command to sustain his martial renown; discussing his proposed *coup d'état* with Tyrone, and bringing it to a head step by step throughout the year that followed.[36]

So deliberate a traitor, however, leaves a lingering doubt in the mind. Could this unstable young man have been methodically planning treason over the years, while he rushed from 'o'er-leaping' his competitors in the tilt-yard, or exulting over his rivals, to nursing his grievances in solitude and bemoaning the vanity of life? Spedding's straightforward story of the Irish campaign and the rebellion is still, along with the clear account given in the *Declaration of Treasons*, the only coherent explanation of Essex's actions. But no more than the others does this version account for his incapacity to choose until the last minute between gaining glory by an effectual attack on Tyrone, and achieving his own secret ends by an alliance with him. The intention behind many of those knightings, promotings and exorbitant demands was visible to his contemporaries, and it is visible to us, though perhaps it was not always to Essex himself. But if he had planned his seizure of power with so much premeditation, how can we explain the continual wavering – in 'lightning hopes', as one of his followers put it, of some last-minute return to favour – that exasperated his fellow conspirators?[37] Again, some of those letters of passionate self-pity written to the Queen throughout his campaigns and while he was planning her overthrow have so convincing a ring that it is no wonder he has been thought unlucky and ill-used. They do not sound like camouflage for conspiracy, or even cover for indecision.[38]

Thus, while the Essex of the biographies is one mass of contradictions, the Essex presented by some historians is too consistent to be true. Can we discover in this disconcerting character a tap-root from which both reproachful servant and self-seeking traitor drew their life, in alternate spurts of impulsive action and bouts of indecision and melancholy? His nostalgic biographers describe him in the same rosy light in which he saw himself, as the man in whose breast 'a romantic spirit of knight-errantry' infinitely surpassed all other passions (Devereux); in whose heart 'the blood of a hundred barons pulsed', and in whom 'the flame of ancient feudalism' had sprung up, 'radiant with the colours of antique knight-hood . . .' (Strachey).[39] Honour, a quality recognized by the simplest minds, even in an enemy, yet almost impossible to define ('What is honour?' said Falstaff, 'a word, air!') is invariably coupled with Essex's name.[40] And he had indeed inherited it by direct transmission from its living Elizabethan incarnation, Sir Philip Sidney, who on his death-bed had bequeathed to him his best sword – a spiritual legacy neither of them would have mistaken. But he took over from Sidney the outward dignities of feudal knighthood, not the invisible vow, secretly made and kept, to achieve that perfect virtue through which alone glory could be attained. Before setting out to conquer the enemy, the devoted Christian knight, as sung by Edmund Spenser (whose *Shepherd's Calendar* was dedicated to Sidney), had first to conquer himself. He must attain honour, as Essex's own father had striven to attain it in Ireland, 'by virtue and travail'.[41]

Essex, a contemporary noted, desired 'in all things to reap the whole honour', but there was nothing he desired less than to conquer himself.[42] Visible honours were what he wanted, and looked on as his due, and such was his craving for them that he went off in a rage every time another man's performance was rewarded.[43] We have seen how greatly he preferred the gestures and shows of leadership to its responsibilities. In effect he distinguished so little between them that, as was pointed out in our time, 'he mistook the facade of power for power itself'.[44] Like that other short-lived 'child of honour and renown', Henry Hotspur, never tired of challenging the world at large, he would pluck honour from the pale-faced moon, providing he might wear it 'without co-rival'. But there is an overriding difference between the two great rebels, the impatient prince, whose life 'did ride upon a dial's point' – so fast towards his death that he could not stop to read the letters that carried his free pardon[45] – and the commander who from his earliest campaigns had time to write endless epistles of disgruntled self-dramatization. Unlike Hotspur, Essex did not live his quest for honour, he dreamt it out on an inner stage where all its fruits were granted in advance.

It is here we must look for poles on which Essex's being turned, to use an expression of Bacon's – which might be translated today as 'what made him tick'. Essex preferred a day-dream of power to its hard-working reality. Historians all agree that he was spoiled by premature success, but this was nothing to the premature achievements he carried in his mind. Born a cousin of the Queen, a child for whom his father had already dreamt dreams (among them that he should marry into Cecil's family, an alliance that would have changed history), he had been coached by his stepfather, the Earl of Leicester, for the role of favourite. And from the moment he stepped into it, as effortlessly as he put on military command, Essex expected of fate – via the Queen – the unlimited bounty we receive only in dreams.

Reality may come to meet the dreamer for a time, but, except for brief halcyon spells, it cannot match his insatiable fantasy. Though Essex had neither the discipline to follow in Sidney's footsteps, nor the talent to be another Burghley (as Bacon had tried to make him), nor the diplomacy and patience Leicester had needed to keep the position of principal favourite over the years, he wanted to be at the same time glamorous soldier, trusted counsellor and sole titular lover. This last was a role Bacon had also coached him for, with the courtly devices he wrote on his behalf to persuade Elizabeth – and Essex himself – when they were played before her that he was neither soldier nor politician but her devoted *chevalier servant*.[46] Essex wanted all these positions without working for any of them, and when they did not fall into his lap his resentment was unbounded. Until finally he opted for the short-cut.

Day-dreaming has been described by its student in our time as the all-absorbing exercise of imagining life in advance instead of preparing to meet it.[47] As the dreamer becomes increasingly involved in the imaginary procession within, his interest in the world wanes, until what little reality reaches him from outside appears to him in the form of an attack; to which his response is either immediate and violent counterattack, or a defeatist longing for suffering and death. All his capacity for emotion is used up in anticipation, so that the more he protests, the less he feels for anyone but himself. The process was studied in detail by Essex's contemporary, Robert Burton, in his *Anatomy of Melancholy*. It is, he wrote, a malady which even 'the finest and most generous spirits are prone to'. It comes of allowing the 'seed-bed of folly' we have within us to run on '*in infinitum*', by not resisting our 'vain cogitations'. Those who give way to them 'go smiling to themselves, acting an infinite variety of parts' which they 'strongly imagine they represent'; and ready 'to snarl upon any small occasion, if they be not saluted, invited, consulted with'; they will torture themselves 'if their equal, friend, neighbour be preferred, commended, do well . . . Never pleased, never well in body and mind, but weary still . . . suspecting, offended with with every object, wishing themselves gone or dead.'[48]

All the symptoms described by Burton, down to the 'sad look and neglected habit', were present in Essex. When he went to see the Queen, so his secretary, Sir Henry Wotton, recalled, 'he scarce knew what he had on'.[49] His letters throughout both the Rouen and Irish campaigns dwell almost exclusively on the unkind treatment he has received for his 'more than ordinary services', the crosses he suffers 'and shall ever suffer', and his consequent weariness of a world he would forget, and be forgotten by. In Ireland, at the slightest sign of opposition from home, 'amazed silence', he cries, 'will best befit me!' But it was a silence he never kept. 'Why do I talk of victory or success? Is it not known that from England I receive nothing but soul's wounds?' To which the Queen replied that his proceedings begot his difficulties, and told him to give over 'private humours' and confine himself to 'matters of weight'. Essex, meanwhile, before marching off to his ignominious parley with Tyrone, had written her another long tirade, 'from a mind delighting in sorrow; from spirits wasted with travail, care and grief; from a heart torn to pieces with passion', hoping the rebel would give him means to ransom his soul 'out of this hateful prison of my body'.[50]

How different are the letters sent from Ireland, soon afterwards, by a modestly resolute Mountjoy, who – unlike the defiant, insecure Essex of his best-known portrait – watches us attentively, as he gazes straight out of his own.[51] How different also, had been those of Essex's father, the first Earl, years earlier, on the long, hard Irish campaign that was to be his ruin and death; filled none the less with gratitude to the Queen for her bounties, a 'contentation that easeth away all grief', and generous commendation of his officers and men. In our own Earl, back in England and up to his eyes in conspiracy, pitiful appeals to the Queen and increasingly loud protestations, rather than deliberate falsification, betray a growing sense of unreality, while brutal remarks behind her back give the lie to professions of an undying love which he seems only half aware of betraying. 'I, poor I, must suffer and know no change!' he cries; and he will 'tear his heart out of his breast with his own hands' before losing the desire to do her Majesty service.[52] But where is there a lasting relationship in Essex's life? Cecil's observation that his friendship was not to be trusted is amply borne out.[53] He was faithless almost at once to the wife he had inherited from Sidney along with his sword, and his last thought for Penelope – his own sister and Sidney's muse – who had done all she could to save him, was to denounce her, not for her 'rebellious spirit' alone, but for her adulterous attachment to Mountjoy. 'Would your Lordship have thought this weakness and this unnaturalness in this man?' wrote Nottingham to Mountjoy on hearing of it.[54]

Other men died on the block, like Norfolk, with parting words for their children, or like Ralegh, who recalled the poem he had composed for his wife forty years earlier. Essex's own father, as he lay on his death-bed in Ireland, with the welfare of all those around him on his mind (including the last-minute promotion of a friend), had repeatedly sent his love and blessings to his son and daughter.[55] Essex on the scaffold, as was noticed at the time, 'never mentioned nor remembered there wife, children or friend'. He was busy acting out the part of martyr in which he had so often visualized himself. ('It is fitting that my poor quarters, which have done her Majesty service in divers parts of the world, should now at last be sacrificed and disposed of at her Majesty's pleasure.')[56]

Essex's strange repentance is better understood in the light of the view put forward here that he was caught up in a world of his own dreaming. At his trial he had indulged the most flattering dream of all, a vision of himself rising against the Queen, bound in his conscience, as he afterwards told his chaplain, to save the Queen from her enemies, 'to the infinite happiness of this State ... and the saving of many thousand Englishmen's lives'; and he had repeatedly announced that he had 'forgiven all the world'. But the clergyman soon burst this bubble, reminding him that he had yet to face another judgement. The fear of Christian hell-fire was a stark reality to men living in those times, and every sinner felt an urgent need to make peace with God.[57] Now for a brief moment Essex came face to face with himself. He made the full confession we know of, first to his chaplain, and later, in writing, to the leading members of the Council, thanking God that he was to be justly 'spewed out of the land', since the Queen could not be safe while he lived. 'I wonder', said one of the officials present, surprised by this sudden reversal, 'that your Lord-ship, thus guilty to yourself, should be so confident at the bar. It offended many of your good friends.' 'Yes,' replied Essex, 'but I am become a new man.' He was the same man, he had merely swung to the opposite extreme, and even on the block he would admit no co-rival. He bore witness there against himself, loudly and repeatedly, as if he could never have enough of it, denouncing 'this great, this bloody, this crying, this infectious sin'.[58]

The admirers of the 'parfait gentil knight' are baffled, as were his contemporaries, by a repentance which required the incrimination of all his friends. A late nineteenth-century biographer chose to disregard 'the death-bed estimates and self-judgement made under a servile dread of hell and damnation', and a late twentieth-century one explained them away as 'the similar hysteria of the Earl on other occasions'.[59] They were right, however, in noting that repentance and denunciation were one and the same thing in Essex's mind. 'I that must deal clearly with God and the world' – thus did he introduce his unkindest attack on a fellow conspira-tor.[60] Who then was this God he dealt with? It looks as if, impelled by a new image of himself seizing the Kingdom of Heaven – as he had dreamed of seizing the English Court – Essex saw his Lord as a sort of magnified Queen Elizabeth, whose anger must be placated at any cost by the sacrifice of all his friends.

Essex has been compared more than once to that 'most famous melan-cholic of all time', Hamlet, and it has been suggested that Shakespeare had him in mind when he wrote the play.[61] Although the Prince of Denmark is filled with the thoughts of a far greater mind, the two courtier-soldiers – the 'great expectation of the future', as Hayward ad-dressed Essex, and 'the expectancy and rose of the fair state' – did indeed share one principal flaw. Independently of each other, two well-known writers have noticed it in Hamlet: the Italian thinker, Elemire Zolla, who cited him as a perfect example of one addicted to dreaming his life rather than living it; and the Spanish professor and statesman, Salvador de Madariaga, who saw in Hamlet's incapacity to do more than imagine his life the real cause of all his famous procrastinations.[62] Not least among the moods the two heroes share, in the loneliness of their perpetual mono-logues, are those moments of true friendship with a dependant who, not being 'passion's slave', enables them to relax from the constant pressure to fulfil their dream. Hamlet, addressing Horatio – about Horatio – tells him he will wear him 'in his heart's core'. So did Essex wear the Bacon brothers, and so did he write to Anthony – about Anthony – as 'a gentleman whose virtue I reverence, and love his person'.[63]

Hamlet's real tragedy, as the Spanish critic saw it, was 'not his incapacity to avenge his father; not his frustrated ambition; but his incapacity to be Hamlet. He can think Hamlet. He cannot be Hamlet.' This was Essex's tragedy also, and it explains every inconsistency in his life.[64] The compulsive knightings of his untried followers, whose glory had already been achieved in his mind; the triumphant progress through Ireland with an army flushed with success, turning his back on the difficult task of conquest; and, after all his boasts of 'pulling down the pride of the arch-traitor', the disgraceful truce with Tyrone, with whom his meeting at mid-stream was more like a dangerous dream of power come true than a premeditated plan; the disastrous march through the City, confident of the citizens' devotion to so popular a commander – what need to verify a last-minute message from Sheriff Smith that he would assist him with a thousand men? In his desperate letters to Elizabeth, Essex was not (or not merely) assuming the mask of loving despair, as historians have supposed. His was the mask of a tragedian acting on his own inner stage, and so caught up in his role that he could look upon himself, even after his condemnation, as the Queen's saviour; shutting his mind to the real, inevitable prospect of drawing her blood.[65]

To explain a failing of the spirit in Essex as the effect of a (hypothetical) disease of the body, as some have done, is to deny him all dignity and freedom of choice. His contemporaries, who treated human failings as sins of the mind, were in no doubt as to the effect of allowing too much freedom to 'the imaginations' – often, like Hamlet's, 'as foul as Vulcan's stithy'. It was the loss of their freedom of action.[66] Bacon saw Essex as he was, 'a man of an high imagination, and a great promiser to himself as well as to others', whose 'windy conceits' were 'the very preludes to his actions'. Only in 'the secret reaches' of the Earl's heart, he thought, could an explanation be found for his two incompatible ends in Ireland, the one importing prosecution of the war, 'the other treaty'. But the most secret reaches where he kept his hidden aims, while 'wrapping himself in other actions', must often have been hidden to Essex himself while he attempted the impossible: you cannot except in dreams both win a war and lose it. All the evidence points to long-term premeditation – including his boast, early in the campaign, that 'many of the rebels would be advised by him'. Yet until the last moment he clung to his other dream, that of the victorious knight, faithful till death to his royal mistress. The dream of being crowned king prevailed when the astute Tyrone invited him to parley with the promise that he would make him 'the greatest man that ever was in England'.[67] But he went on switching desperately from one dream to the other throughout the next year, until the loss of his income from the sweet wines set him off once more in pursuit of his most irresistible day-dream, that of – bloodlessly – winning the English throne.

Yet Essex must have had some lucid moments, before he was finally overcome with remorse for 'this infectious sin whereby so many, for love of me, have ventured their lives and souls'.[68] Such moments may explain why any reproach to Bacon was out of the question for him. He must have known at heart that while he pursued these different dreams, his old friend and mentor was continually urging him to wake up, and that, when he finally chose the mirage, he had turned his back on his own Horatio. 'Be your own waking censor!' Bacon had begged him before the Irish campaign, do not place 'the fruition of that honour' before 'the perfection of the work in hand'. Then, when that chance was lost: 'recover the Queen and never lose her again.' And, when all was over, he had called on his friend, even at the trial, to wake up: 'Oh my Lord, strive with yourself, and strip off all excuses!'[69]

This analysis has revealed a series of remarkable contradictions. The man who, on his death acknowledged himself 'the most vilest and unthankfullest traitor that was ever born on this land', and of whom Elizabeth said, he that had forgotten God must also forget his benefactors, is not remembered as an ungrateful betrayer. Bacon is. His biographers shrug off Essex's insurrection as the impatience of a madcap nobleman, forgetting that for many months, and probably years, he had been hatching insurrection, off and on, against Queen and state; it is Bacon whom they present poisoning the Queen's mind against her favourite and plotting his downfall. Essex's attempts to overthrow Elizabeth are 'the errors of a gentle spirit', but her Legal Counsel, when performing his necessary public duty, is depicted as venomously assaulting a fallen man. Essex, known to his contemporaries as 'a great resenter', appears as the soul of chivalry, while Bacon, in whom his acquaintance saw 'no trace of vindictiveness', is made out to have been filled with bitterness. To this day he is also described as faithless and cold at heart, while it is often forgotten that Essex was faithful neither to wife, child nor mistress, sister nor friend, and least of all to his idolized Queen – whose memory Bacon cherished long after her death. Finally, Essex was recalled by every chronicler of his day as *ambitious*, in the pejorative sense in which the term was used of Julius Caesar in Shakespeare's play; but it is to Bacon, in whom earlier historians had seen a man neither covetous nor excessively aspiring, that the epithet has stuck.

Essex lived all his life imprisoned in *dormiveglia*, or 'sleep-wake', the condition of the day-dreamer, despite the fact that he had the good fortune to be counselled for some years by one of the most wakeful geniuses of our Western culture. Bacon on the other hand, not being caught up in any internal monologue, was free to enjoy the infinite variety of the human and natural world; and, incidentally, to observe the various 'idols of the mind' which keep man out of touch with reality. No man was so well aware as Bacon of the tricks played on us by that 'arch-flatterer which is a man's self'.[70] The same arch-flatterer which, in Essex, while it destroyed his life, was also the source of his myth, since the image handed down by his overpartial biographers is none other than his own dream image of himself, and many years before he became the martyr of history, Essex had been a martyr in his own eyes. And it is of course the arch-flatterer in ourselves who keeps that myth alive. Day-dreaming, as Burton pointed out, is 'a malady inbred in every one of us', and we share it with Essex. Is it not because of their ever-present hankering after a dream world that Essex's flattering idea of himself was adopted by more humdrum generations, in search of a heroical image on to which they could project their longing for past glories?

Bacon was in the broadest sense of the word what neither Hamlet nor Essex could be, a man of action. He had the power which they had abdicated of pouring his being into the life outside him, and of transforming his 'imaginings' into works, which comes of a capacity to forget oneself and mate with the world. ('It is a poor centre of a man's actions, himself.')[71] He was quite explicit about the standards he lived by. They were those of the *via media* upheld by Elizabeth, and by his own father, whose motto, *mediocria firma* ('moderate things endure'), he had inherited. It was a rich and, to them, satisfying tradition. 'Honour is but the revealing of man's worth,' he said, and he had no patience with its more glamourous aspects – the 'false show' and the 'satanical illusion' of honour, which he denounced in duellers, and which so dazzled Essex. ('A man's life is not to be trifled away. It is to be offered up and sacrificed to honourable service, public merits, good causes and noble adventures.')[72] As the son of a great judge, Bacon could not have subscribed to the false charity which is yet another of the day-dreamers's vices. Justice, he wrote, requires 'wisdom to discover and discern nocent and innocent, fortitude to prosecute and execute, and temperance' to remedy the effects of anger and over-hasty suspicion.[73] It would no more have crossed his mind to shirk his modest part in one of the principal responsibilities of justice – prosecution – than Robert Sidney, Essex's devoted cousin and follower, could have laid down his arms when he was sent to apprehend the rebel earl at Essex House.

Bacon was speaking the plain truth when he told Mountjoy in 1604 that if he looked back on any of his actions with regret, it was certainly not on his dealings with Essex. 'For any action of mine towards him,' he declared, 'there is nothing that passed me in my life-time that cometh to my remembrance with more clearness and less check of conscience.'[74]

PART II

THE CORRUPT CHANCELLOR

8

The Fall of Bacon: A Tragedy in Three Acts

In the spring of 1621, at the height of his intellectual, political and social career, Francis Bacon, Lord High Chancellor of England, was accused of, confessed to and was condemned by his peers for corruption in office. The complex passage of parliamentary and Court intrigue which led to his condemnation has never been fully cleared up, and perhaps never will be. But one thing is certain: nearly all the varied and contradictory censure bestowed on Bacon over three and a half centuries – not excluding the reproach of ingratitude – had its origin in his spectacular downfall. Content for two hundred years with a pious headshake over the frailty of even the greatest among us, in the late nineteenth century the judgement of posterity developed into an indefatigable search for evil deeds and motives that might confirm Bacon's fundamentally corrupt nature, and build up around it the image of a man who had become the epitome of human vice. When this image had been fully established, the corruption – always in doubt among his more scholarly detractors – was no longer necessary to prove Bacon an evil man, and some of them quietly dropped it.[1]

'The duties of life are more than life, and if I die now I shall die before the world is weary of me.' So wrote Bacon to Buckingham, the royal favourite, in 1617, three months after he had been appointed Lord Keeper, rejoicing in his success in clearing the enormous backlog of cases left by his predecessor, Lord Ellesmere.[2] And had he actually died at any time before the end of 1620, as various biographers have speculated, the world would have lost a number of outstanding works, but Bacon would have lived in the histories of others not only as the author of a great instauration, but as a reformer of the highest moral standing.[3] Did he have an inkling of this? A few lines from his *History of Henry VII*, written soon after his impeachment, are suggestive. The King, he noted, was 'at the top of all worldly bliss' when 'an opportune death' came 'to withdraw him from any future blow of fortune', which might well 'have comen upon him' at that juncture.[4]

In the autumn of 1620 Bacon certainly appeared to have reached that 'top of all wordly bliss'. On 12 October he had dedicated his *Instauratio Magna* – consisting mainly of Part II, the *Novum Organum* – to King James. 'The proclamation and prospectus of the new philosophy', as Spedding put it with Baconian enthusiasm, 'was at length safely and happily delivered into the world,' promising 'endless benefits in which all nations and kindreds of people would participate'.[5] James's reply encouraged Bacon to hope that he would respond to his appeal and, like Solomon, promote 'the collecting and perfecting of a Natural and Experimental History . . . such as philosophy may be built upon'.[6] Equally satisfactory was the response of Bacon's cousin and friend, Sir Henry Wotton, then on a mission in Germany, who was so struck by the book that he planned to have it read paragraph by paragraph to his family circle, 'as if it were a work of the ancients'. He proposed to give one of the three copies he had received to the illustrious astronomer Johannes Kepler, whom he had met in Austria, to show him that 'we in England have some of our own that can honour our King, as he had done with his *Harmonica*' (dedicated to King James).[7]

The link with Kepler was a crucial one for Bacon at this time. His political thought was already known to the well-read in France, particularly since the recent publication of his *Essays* in French. But now that James had finally decided to defend his German son-in-law, the Prince Palatine – 'the best support of the healthiest part of Christianity', Bacon had called him – against the invading Imperial forces, James's Chancellor could at last indulge his hopes that England might regain her leadership of Protestant Europe.[8] Bacon's priorities for the present crisis may be gathered from a letter he wrote to Christian of Denmark on 19 November, declaring his great pleasure that a prince of such 'eminent warlike virtue', while professing 'devotion to peace', was still more devoted to 'the protection of true Religion'.[9] Bacon had warmly welcomed a suggestion from Wotton that the cousins should keep up a correspondence 'in both kinds': on the scientific questions of interest to his German counterparts, and above all on ways of promoting the unity of reformed Christian Europe – a goal Bacon shared also with scholars in Holland and Bohemia, and not least in Italy.[10] In March 1621, only a few months after this exchange, while in London Bacon's colleagues in the Privy Council were staging his downfall, Wotton was in Venice, discussing his cousin's ideas for a united Europe with another great scholar, Paolo Sarpi, and with Fulgentio Micanzio – who venerated Bacon and Sarpi equally, as phoenixes, 'rare upon earth' – and who was soon eagerly publishing in Italian as many of the fallen Chancellor's works as he could lay hands on.[11]

At home Bacon could look back over a satisfying year. The *Rules for the Star Chamber* which he had prepared for the approval of the Lords could, he believed, become 'one of the noblest and durablest pillars for the justice of the kingdom'. The Star Chamber was still rightly praised by Coke as 'the most honourable court (our Parliament excepted) that is in the Christian world', and one that doth 'keep all England quiet'. Bacon's *Rules* were aimed at limiting its jurisdiction 'to cases enormous and extraordinary', and had they been enacted, Charles I could not have used this court to quash all opposition against his illegal proclamations and turn it into the infamous instrument of tyranny it was to become, before it was swept away.[12] Bacon could not then have guessed that his *Rules* were soon to disappear – as he was – from the public scene. Of more immediate importance, with the solvency of the Crown never far from his mind he could celebrate a continuing improvement in the royal finances since he had been appointed, three years earlier, to review them. The King's 'resources and his expenses were now equalled for the ordinary', he had been able to report to James after two years, with a healthy balance of £120,000 a year 'for the extraordinaries'.[13] Now more progress could be looked for, since King James had acceded to his Chancellor's urgent request that he should fill the post of Treasurer – vacant since the trial of Suffolk for corruption two years earlier – with a man who could concentrate his energies on this demanding task. As Bacon wrote happily to the favourite Buckingham, early in that coldest of winters, 'a number of counsels for the establishment of his Majesty's estate' which 'had lain dead and buried deeper than this snow, might now spring up and bear fruit'.[14]

Above all his sources of contentment, however, was the news that the King had at last been persuaded to call a Parliament, as Bacon had been urging him to do for the past five years. He had all the King's business *at heart*, Bacon wrote to him when he received instructions to prepare it, but this was *after his own heart*.[15] He set to work at once on a royal proclamation, inviting electors to bring in a 'well-composed House' with 'the gravest, ablest, worthiest members that may be found'; and not to 'disparage' it with 'mean dependants upon great persons' who could command their voices.[16] This, Bacon believed, was the *sine qua non* for a successful Parliament. As long as any 'turbulent spirit', he had warned James earlier, or any ambitious 'valuer of himself' could find 'a harbourer, overt or secret, in the favour of some great person, let his Majesty look for nothing but tempest'.[17] And he urged the King 'to extinguish, or at least compose for a time the divisions in his own house', which otherwise, 'by influence and infusion', would have the same disastrous effect on the new Parliament as a divided Council had had on the last one – called in 1614, and 'addled' within two months. He could not have foreseen that the Parliament he was at work on was to experience in his own impeachment, as a historian observed in our time, a new and more dangerous variant of the intrigues which had brought the previous one down.[18]

At this moment Bacon had but one purpose in view: the calling of a Parliament 'fit to nourish a loving and comfortable meeting' between the King and his people, 'a noble instrument . . . for the settling of so great affairs' as were before it – the greatest of them being a country deep in a trade depression, with its Prince attacked in the Palatine by the Catholic powers, and the Reformed faith in jeopardy. In hopes of forging such an instrument, the Chancellor now gathered a small team to assist him in framing a series of commonwealth bills – 'good matter', as he saw it, 'to set the Parliament to work'. It was Bacon's most strongly held political tenet that the Crown should initiate policy and, with its ear to the ground, offer to meet just grievances. Members would thus be discouraged from hunting after private or petty ones, and allow Parliament to 'go better and faster to the main errand' – in this case to bring in the 'bountiful treasure' needed to prepare for war, if war should prove essential.[19] The paper he drafted for the King, breaking down 'the main of the Parliament business into questions and parts' is lost, along with his 'good commonwealth bills'. But we can tell from the long list of bills he had produced for the previous Parliament – and from other drafts for this one – that his bills would have included measures to improve 'the defence and strength of the realm', particularly the Navy, proposals for the increase of trade and commerce, including urgently needed plans for the promotion of exports, laws concerning depopulation and tillage, plans for 'the better plantation of Ireland', and, most important in Bacon's eyes, for the reform of the law.[20] (He may also have planned to submit a project for the establishment of a Royal Academy of Science – a likely enough project for Bacon, although our contemporary witness to the proposal cannot be relied on.)[21]

The 1621 Parliament – the first and last he was himself to prepare – could have been one of the most successful yet known had it concentrated its energies on Bacon's draft legislation. It is seen today as a Parliament that failed, largely because instead of passing much needed laws to redress fundamental institutional problems, it was distracted by the more exciting activity of impeaching scapegoats.[22] As Chamberlain wrote to Carleton halfway through the first session, the Parliament was busy taking up so many 'particular and personal faults' that, he feared, if these 'fractions' were not soon made up, its 'fair and plausible beginnings would not have so fair an end.'[23] He proved right. Once the 1621 Parliament had eliminated the only man who had developed a real government policy, it was left without leadership from the Crown, and nothing was accomplished. James failed to use Bacon's draft proclamation declaring the royal resolution to defend the Palatinate with 'the utmost of our forces' – which, as Gardiner believed, would have served as a rallying point for the whole nation. Thus Parliament lost sight of its original purpose, to prepare England for war.[24] No solution was found for the economic crisis. As for the legislation Bacon had so eagerly prepared, as another historian put it in 1979, it 'petered out in trivialities'.[25] When, after sitting from February to June, the Commons were faced with the King's decision to adjourn Parliament within seven days, there were loud recriminations of woe over their failure to ripen any of their business. As well there might be if anyone recalled the forty-three bills passed in three months by the 1597 Parliament. 'Bacon's plea for a detailed programme to be set before parliament', wrote another of its historians, 'was never more justified.'[26]

None of this was apparent in the joyful words Bacon wrote for James to pronounce at the long desired inauguration of Parliament on 30 January 1621, dwelling on the 'great expectation in the beginning of this Parliament', and praying God it would not only be 'as good in the conclusion', but 'generative, begetting others hereafter'. And when on 3 February it was his turn to speak, he painted in glowing terms 'the great felicity which we enjoy' under a King who had laid the corner-stone of two mighty kingdoms, brought 'civility' to Ireland, and 'by the plantation of Virginia and the Summer Islands' had sown 'a grain of mustard-seed that would prove a great tree'; who had kept inward and outward peace, and ruled with justice as well as mercy. Going to the 'main errand', he reminded Parliament that whatever they gave to defend the Palatine would, by impressing their enemies, 'be doubled in reputation abroad, as in a crystal glass'. While he still hoped for a peaceful solution of the conflict, 'good policy', he insisted, 'requires that we should be prepared for war'.[27] His optimistic mood was shared, historians now believe, by many of his contemporaries in both Government and opposition, who saw no reason why, given a united Council and a Parliament made up of honest representatives, the problems facing their country should not be solved.[28]

But Bacon had another special source of contentment. His own carefully matured programme for compiling an amendment of the laws of England was ready. A single exception at this Parliament, it was to bear modest fruit. Two weeks after its inauguration, a commission appointed under his auspices to go through the statutes, with a view to abrogating those that were obsolete, reported that it had found six hundred of them 'fit to be repealed as snaring'; and a committee of principal lawyers was immediately appointed to carry out that major survey of all the statutes which Bacon had been pressing for ever since he had first proposed it twenty-eight years earlier to the Parliament of 1593. His bill for the abolition of eighty redundant statutes – a small step forward in what has been qualified as 'one of the most ambitious programmes for the repeal of obsolete laws' ever undertaken – was the only constructive measure to reach a final stage by the end of the session.[29]

For what he called 'his own particular', Bacon might also feel he had reached that height of worldly bliss attained by Henry VII. Verulam, his new mansion in the country, built, as a visitor was to describe it a generation later, 'to harbour his scientific and philosophical contemplations whenever he could retire there', was nearly finished.[30] In town, York House, the home of his childhood, was once again his own. At the birthday celebrations he held there on 21 January, Ben Jonson, his old friend and admirer, hailing with well-turned verses a well-spent sixty years ('Give me a deep-crowned bowl that I may sing, / In praising him the wisdom of the King!') hinted at Bacon's imminent investiture with the title of Viscount St Alban.[31] 'For his assiduity and integrity in the administration of justice', as stated in the patent conferring it, 'his care and prudence in the discharge of his duty as principal Chancellor', and for his management of the royal revenue 'without respect either to private advantage or to the vain breath of popularity'.[32] Bacon wrote thanking James for this new benefit. This was the eighth rise in his career, he said, 'a diapason in music, ever a good number for the close'.[33] And the close was upon him. On 21 March he was charged in the Upper House for taking bribes. On 22 April he abandoned his defence and sent his submission to the Lords, and on 3 May he was deprived of office, fined £40,000, and sent to the Tower.

It was the function of Nemesis, in the guise of Revenge or Retribution, Bacon had written many years earlier, 'to intercept the felicity' of the fortunate, 'however innocent and moderately borne'.[34] He was to become the perfect victim of her action. 'No hero of Attic tragedy', writes the historian of this Parliament in 1971, 'was ever more primed for a fall.'[35] It came about so suddenly that the very political opponents who had contrived it were taken by surprise. For Macaulay this was not a day too soon. In a few weeks, he claimed, letting his imagination and his righteous indignation run riot in equal measure, the value of those objects for which Bacon 'had sullied his integrity' and 'violated' his 'most sacred obligations', had flattered, persecuted, tortured, plundered, 'had wasted on paltry intrigues' all the powers of his 'exquisitely constructed intellect', was to be put to the test; 'a sudden and terrible reverse was at hand.' After the 'most creditable State-Trial in English history', the Chancellor was justly condemned 'because it was impossible to acquit him without offering the grossest outrage to justice and commonsense'; and deservedly ended his long career of worldly wisdom in misery and shame.[36] Twenty-five years later, at the other extreme of opinion, W. Hepworth Dixon questioned the validity of Bacon's trial, and denounced it as a political rather than a judicial act. Basing himself on documents which Macaulay had never set eyes on – Chancery notebooks, and many as yet unpublished state papers – he presented a blameless Chancellor, who rather than sending out 'his jackals' looking for prey, as Macaulay depicted him, sent his almoner to seek out cases of distress. But, carried away by enthusiasm, Hepworth Dixon gave too much credit to conspiracy theories, in particular to a plot hatched over the years by Lady Compton, the favourite's all-powerful mother, for which there is insufficient evidence.

How can we reconcile these widely differing versions? In 1869 the sober story was unravelled by Samuel R. Gardiner in a hundred well-informed pages – a small item in his ten-volume narrative of the reigns of James and Charles, which is still recognized today as the best documented history of the times.[37] As a Whig historian, Gardiner was critical of Bacon's political positions, but having carefully considered all the charges brought against him in Parliament, he did not find Bacon corrupt. It is Spedding who, after incontrovertibly refuting every one of Macaulay's other accusations, is found in 1874 pleading guilty on Bacon's behalf. He admitted

> that Bacon *was* guilty of corruption, that he had not the means of clearing himself; that the sentence pronounced against him, though severe, was not unjust; that his act, moreover, was not only in law indefensible but in morals culpable, and more culpable in him than it would have been in another man; that he had, in short, allowed himself to do that which he knew ought not to be done.[38]

But, Spedding went on to point out, the term 'corruption' includes acts of very different complexions, 'varying from violations of universal morality of the blackest dye to violations only of artificial and conventional regulations, made to defend the outworks of morality'. Bacon's act, he believed, was a political rather than a moral one, 'from which, though rightly forbidden and punished, the conscience would not necessarily recoil'. It was 'one of those acts that are declared and made to be criminal because they may lead to crime'. In Bacon's case they did not. 'I think', he concluded, 'it may be called a sin of inattention; and if we allow a distinction between vice and frailty, may be classed among the frailties.'[39] Having thus accepted his protagonist's relative guilt, Spedding went on to demonstrate that, far from acting as a court of judges sentencing a moral delinquent, the 1621 Parliament had been carried on a wave of popular feeling into a basically popular indictment, and that the sentence they pronounced was of doubtful value.

Late twentieth-century historians of the period have concluded, with Hepworth Dixon, that, whatever the precise degree of his personal guilt, Bacon's conviction must be looked on as a political act. He is seen as the victim of a *putsch* – the first of three attempts to dislodge the favourite, Buckingham, from power.[40] Macaulay's view of a monolithic House of Commons sitting in judgement on a depraved Chancellor, though still invoked in the late 1970s, has fallen by the board, along with many Whig opinions, among serious historians; most of them now consider that the parliamentary process which brought about Bacon's downfall was not so much a confrontation between Crown and Commons as between the different factions of the Court — whose divisions James did not, as his Chancellor begged him to, compose. The impeachment of Bacon is now seen first and foremost as the forging of a tool which one Councillor could use to attack another, in this Parliament, and in those that followed.[41]

In order to verify how far Bacon was actually corrupt, and to gain as exact a picture as possible of the circumstances of his fall, it will be necessary to examine the new views against the old. I propose to bring the thorough – and still valid – research of Spedding and Gardiner up to date, with the help of the most recent studies made of the 1621 Parliament, studies which exceed all others in detailed information about the participants, and in analyses of their motives, vested interests and other allegiances. I will take this aspect of Bacon's reputation in three phases. The next two chapters will set the political stage for the prologue of this play, in which two forces converge on Bacon, the attack on the monopolies, and the attack on Chancery. The following four chapters will be devoted to those attacks, and to the vicissitudes of the Chancellor's impeachment. The last five chapters of Part II, while discussing the justice of that impeachment, will address the most fundamental question of all: was Bacon an essentially corrupt man?

9

Principal Members of the Cast

George Villiers, Marquis of Buckingham, the spoilt, selfish, all-powerful favourite, is of course the central character part in this Jacobean drama staging the fall of a great man. Already in 1618 King James had declared his intention to advance the Villiers family above any other. 'I live to that end,' he had said; and that end involved a ceaseless flow of royal grants into the lap of the teeming Villiers clan, elevated to a rank they had no means of supporting.[1] It was to involve much further damage to the country under both James and Charles. As regards Bacon, when a crisis came that could have brought down the proud favourite, it meant that James would sacrifice his Chancellor to protect his endangered friend. And Buckingham, not content with saving his own skin at Bacon's expense, and breaking the promises he had made to assist him after his fall, would in the end force him to give up his most prized possession, York House, thus helping to justify the gibe of a contemporary that 'my Lord of Buckingham never did undo any of his enemies, but he ruined many of his friends'.[2]

What was Bacon doing as the follower, and for a time close friend, of such a man? Was his role merely one of sycophantic subservience – a subservience he had never used towards Somerset, the previous favourite? He could not have failed to see the dangers of an invasion of Crown and Council by a single family. The key to his attitude may be looked for in his letter to Christian of Denmark (19 November 1620), mentioned above, expressing his satisfaction with the financial and administrative reforms achieved in England over the past two years.[3] During this time Buckingham had placed himself at the head of a programme of reform and could claim to be a champion of the national economy. In the early stages of his rise to power Bacon was not the only person who looked on him as a promising influence, after the stranglehold of the Howards under Somerset – an expectation which the young man's sweetness of manner did little to dispel. But Bacon had special hopes of guiding the inexperienced Villiers and filling his mind with projects of reform. In his 'Letter of Advice to Villiers', written at the favourite's request in 1616, he had set forth the duties and responsibilities of a man 'in so eminent a place and of so much danger' – but also of so much 'power to do good'.[4]

All Bacon's political ideas were expressed in this paper, and in reproducing it later for a wider circulation he must have been conscious of the beneficial influence he had exerted on his pupil. His satisfaction at seeing a few excellent projects well under way – including substantial reductions in the expenditure of the royal Household and in the ordnance, as well as the reorganization of the Navy, which under the retrograde Howards had become a laughing-stock to foreign nations – goes far to explain what has seemed so great an enigma: Bacon's continuing belief in Buckingham, against all odds.[5] By the end of 1620, however, when the abuses committed by his brothers were coming to light, the first flush of Buckingham's reforming period was over. Success had brought promotion to Lord High Admiral, and a rich estate. Solidly established in power, he was too busy attending to buyers of high office to have any time for Bacon's statesmanlike advice. He had just received £20,000 from the sale of the Lord Treasurership to Sir Henry Montagu (now Lord Mandeville), and may have felt some impatience with a counsellor who had himself been promoted on merit and would play no part in this kind of transaction.

Hand-in-glove with Buckingham and almost as powerful, his mother, Lady Compton, recently raised to the peerage to celebrate her son's successes, sat like a spider at the centre of a large network of intrigue. Her influence over most appointments to high place was all-pervading, and, as Chamberlain's letters show, a surprising number of them were coupled by somewhat more than rumour with 'a marriage into the kindred'.[6] Whether or no she played a part in Bacon's downfall, she had, it would seem, tried her hand at bringing down the previous Chancellor, Lord Ellesmere, four years earlier, in favour of her own candidate to the succession, Sir Edward Coke, who was expected to buy back the favour he had lost with a marriage into her family. Angered by Ellesmere's delay in signing a patent involving one of her sons, she had resolved on the old man's ruin, and a contemporary remarked on the many bills about to be preferred in the Star Chamber against him. Ellesmere, however, evaded all attempts at conspiracy by dying before the bills could be brought in.[7]

Bacon was not in Lady Compton's good graces. Soon after he had been made Lord Keeper in place of her candidate – who was also Bacon's long-term rival – he had offended both her and Coke by refusing her a quite unjustified and illegal warrant against Coke's wife, Lady Hatton, who was opposing the match that was to pave Coke's way back to Court. On this occasion, as an eighteenth-century historian put it, Lady Compton 'gave loose to her tongue and railed at him with a bitterness natural to women when they are thwarted in any favourite pursuit of interest or passion'; and it was then that Dudley Carleton described Bacon as 'walking in slippery places, surrounded by men who would sell their souls for money'.[8] In January 1621, just before the opening of Parliament, he was to thwart Lady Compton again in her pursuit of a similar interest (this time with the full approval of the Lords) by imprisoning a newly ennobled candidate for marriage into her family, a man who had publicly asserted his precedence over a lord of ancient stock by striking him and thrusting him violently aside.[9]

Towards the end of 1620 Bacon's most prominent ill-wishers were all busy marrying into the 'tribe of fortune', as a contemporary called the Villiers clan, and receiving the corresponding promotions.[10] Sir James Ley, turning seventy, after failing to buy the post of Attorney General from Buckingham for £10,000, was happy to marry one of Buckingham's nieces – 'and so to be of the kindred', Chamberlain noted, and rise from obscure attorney to Chief Justice of the King's Bench.[11] In this capacity he was to replace the fallen Chancellor in the House of Lords, and pronounce the sentence upon him. Ley was no friend to Bacon, and a few years later, when he had become one of the most incompetent Treasurers the country had yet known, we will find the now powerless Chancellor indignantly reproving him for an act of ill-will towards him. ('Your Lordship may do well to think of your grave as I do of mine, and to beware of hardness of heart; and as for fair words, it is a wind by which neither your Lordship nor any man can sail long.')[12]

Another who figured prominently in the reigning family was Lady Compton's young chaplain, John Williams, who had had his eye on the post of Lord Chancellor for a long time.[13] As soon as Bacon's difficulties in Parliament began, Williams stepped into his shoes as the favourite's mentor – one who was not likely to preach to him against monopolies, or to keep proposing new parliaments. This 'court comet' (as his contemporary biographer and eulogist John Hacket described him), thanks to the pressures exerted by Buckingham and his mother, was to be made Dean of Westminster, Bishop of Lincoln, Privy Councillor and Lord Keeper, all in the space of fifteen months.[14] 'I had thought I should have known my successor,' was all the comment Bacon made when he heard of his last appointment, a promotion which Hacket attributed, no doubt correctly, to the advice Williams had given Buckingham, when the crux came, that he should jettison his friends – principally, of course, Bacon himself.[15] Dean Williams's 'elastic conscience', wrote Menna Prestwich, fitted him to allay the moral pangs of kings.[16] He was to give the same advice on at least two similar occasions: to James, in 1624, over the impeachment of Cranfield (necessity, he said, would excuse the King 'from inconstancy and cruelty'), and to Charles I in 1641 – who took it, to his everlasting remorse – over the impeachment of Strafford.[17] Meanwhile we shall see the new Lord Keeper, later in the year, withholding the King's pardon from Bacon under pretexts which, by their absurdity, betrayed his fears for his own position as well as his hostility towards the man whose post he now filled.[18]

More significantly, the two men who were to be most directly responsible for Bacon's downfall had both recently married into the tribe. Sir Lionel Cranfield had found himself obliged, much against his will, to give up his betrothal to Lady Effingham and engage himself instead to marry a niece with neither dowry nor looks; for which he obtained a place on the Council, along with promises of high office and a peerage. Sir Edward Coke, after haggling three years before over the dowry of £10,000 stipulated by his daughter's prospective bridegroom, Sir John Villiers – and thus, wrote Chamberlain, 'letting slip' a far better plum, the Chancellorship itself – had finally bought his way back on to the Council by giving his reluctant daughter in marriage to this same brother of the favourite, along with three times that sum.[19] These were the two leaders of the opposition (both more than ready to serve the Crown) who, whether or no they actually conspired against the Chancellor, were to work, as Robert Zaller has shown in his history of the 1621 Parliament, 'consciously and directly at bringing Bacon to the greatest possible discomfiture'; and, faced with the chance of securing his political disgrace and removal from office, to seize it 'gratefully and joyously in both hands'.[20]

In the studies published about them – that of Stephen White in 1977, relating Coke's legal views to his political career, family practice, fortune and situation at Court, and that of Menna Prestwich in 1966, on Cranfield's politics and profits – these two men appear very much as Bacon saw them: hard-working servants of the state, convinced of their own rectitude, and unaware of the large subjective component of their mental make-up which could radically change their views and actions according to their personal situation at any given time.[21] Among the limitations Coke and Cranfield had in common was a tendency to attribute general ills and abuses in the Government to the malevolent action of a small number of offenders.[22] In this they were perfectly matched to the mood of Parliament, which – in need of some outlet of activity after one frustrated session, followed by seven years of silence – found it more rewarding to take strong action against people than to tackle difficult questions. Dissatisfied with their respective positions, both Cranfield and Coke were lobbying for parliamentary support in their struggle for power. They saw in the new Parliament an opportunity of gaining influence at Bacon's expense, and were accordingly very careful to placate the Court while they championed the opposition.[23] Although their ends were different, as Zaller noted, 'their separate purposes converged on at least one point': a common and very personal animosity against Francis Bacon. Coke's seasoned antipathy calls for no comment;

'Cranfield's was of more recent date, but it made up in rancour what it lacked in vintage.'[24]

Bacon was not the sole recipient of Coke's particular brand of rancour. He had vented it on many others – among them, when he was Attorney General, Essex and Ralegh, and as late as November 1620, in demanding a life sentence on another Attorney General, Sir Henry Yelverton, for an apparently technical (in fact a purely political) offence.[25] He was to prosecute Cranfield in the same spirit in the next Parliament. 'I do believe', wrote James's Secretary, Sir Edward Conway, 'that if once in seven years he were not to help to ruin a great man, he should die himself.'[26]

Bacon's personal attitude towards this great lawyer and warm-hearted family man – and arrogant, insensitive, self-righteous and quarrelsome colleague, as Coke was generally seen in his own time – will be looked at in a later chapter.[27] On Coke's side, if we are to believe their contemporaries, there was not a little envy, but also the distrust aroused in a narrower mind by one so much lighter and quicker than his own: Bacon must often have thoroughly disconcerted his authoritarian and sententious opponent. Their early rivalries had been exacerbated, and Coke's bitterness increased, as he found himself outstripped by the younger man. When in 1616, after the last of a long series of arbitrarily obstructive acts, he was dismissed from the post of Chief Justice of the King's Bench, against Bacon's express advice, the latter continued to enjoy the King's favour – and not long afterwards received (for free, to Coke's disgust) the Seal that Coke himself had failed to buy.[28] We will hear of him around this time, 'heaving' at Bacon by every possible 'engine', and, for the few weeks in which he held the favourite's ear, blackening his rival so successfully that Buckingham spoke for a time in Coke's phrases and 'menaced in his spirit'.[29]

On Bacon's side the difficulty – shared with many others, including the King – was that of working with a man who identified the public good with his own eminently subjective and changeable opinions; who, said Bacon, 'plowed according to his own tides, not according to the tides of business'.[30] This view of Coke has been confirmed by the historians of our time, for whom the conscious and coherent defender of constitutional reforms against the Crown turns out to have been a Whig illusion. Coke now appears as an opportunistic politician, whose statements reflect his specific objective of the moment, whether in favour of particular parties or to promote his own advancement.[31] Consistency, as Menna Prestwich observed, was never his strong suit, and in the forthcoming Parliament he was to revise his views as and when he found it to his advantage.[32]

Bacon, for whom state affairs ('business') came first, praised his difficult colleague whenever he could, and never gave up trying to work in harmony with him. And for all their incompatibility of temperament, we will find the two greatest jurists in the land collaborating on a number of matters; not least, towards the end of 1620, in preparing the coming Parliament, about which they were in agreement both as to aims and tactics. What happened after 24 November, when his signature appeared under Bacon's in the paper the Chancellor submitted to the King, to exacerbate Coke's hostility? Barely five days later it became known that another high office had passed him by, that of Lord Treasurer, for which already in 1616 Bacon had particularly recommended him to James; and to make matters worse, it had gone (for a high price, as we have seen) to Sir Henry Montagu, the very man who had replaced Coke as Chief Justice in 1616, when James had committed the fatal error of dismissing him.[33] Thus the King, in his short-sighted eagerness for cash to advance his minion, instead of winning over the lawyers, as Bacon had been urging him to do in preparation for the new Parliament, had once again succeeded in alienating the most aggressive – and the most capable – of them all. When Coke realized that his hopes of high office were at an end, rather than choose between undistinguished teamwork in the Council and embittered retirement, he sought a new opening. For the first time in twenty-eight years he had a seat in Parliament. Here, instead of serving one man, he found he could rule four hundred; and if, in the process, he could pull down a detested rival, so much the better.[34]

Bacon was right: the close-fisted Coke, as Menna Prestwich pointed out, with ambition and greed both satisfied, would have made an excellent Treasurer. Had James taken Bacon's advice about him five years earlier, and had he also appointed Cranfield to one of the posts he hankered after, the country's finances could have been turned over, as she put it, to the 'safe, crabbed hands of Coke', Bacon would have been left free to effect his long-desired reform of the law, and Cranfield kept busy on administrative reforms which could have done away with the country's principal trade grievances. With a programme launched in collaboration by Bacon, Coke and Cranfield, providing a foretaste of that united Council which Bacon so strongly advocated, the 1621 Parliament might indeed have come to a good end. Instead it 'was about to see the diverting spectacle of a privy councillor leading the opposition'. It would also see two privy councillors closely allied in the effort to pull down a third, and when that had been achieved, breaking into open hostilities and insulting each other in the House. A breach that was to be further widened when, in September 1621, Cranfield was appointed Lord Treasurer, thereby dashing any lingering hopes Coke might have had of using his nuisance value in the Commons to force the King's hand and gain office.[35]

No contemporary, and no historian, even when praising his gifts as administrator, has had much to say for Lionel Cranfield the man. 'Whereas other men much faulty have yet had some friend speak some good of them,' Sir John Savile remarked, 'he never heard anyone speak of any virtue or goodness in the Treasurer.'[36] Cranfield is noted today for his rasping tongue (Prestwich); his sententious and sanctimonious bullying (Hurstfield); his domineering arrogance (Zaller); his irresponsible effrontery (D.H. Willson); while his contemporary champion, Bishop Goodman, left a defence of him which, as Hepworth Dixon remarked, 'confesses for him to more dubious conduct, and to more safe rascalities than would have blasted the credit of ten ordinary men'.[37] Safe his rascalities were, for Cranfield meticulously covered his tracks throughout a well-plotted career – from London apprentice to Master of the Wards, Lord Treasurer and Lord Middlesex – in which astuteness, industry and sharp practice all played their part. In the City he made quick profits by selling shoddy wares, mixing bad pepper with good, buying up musty wheat. He was a hard money-lender, and as his acquaintance grew, so did the land he acquired by ruining gentlemen. After his training in fraudulent speculation he spent years assiduously propitiating Buckingham, and, while reforming the King's finances as efficiently as he was allowed, he safely reformed a goodly share of them into his own pocket.[38]

None the less, he did reform them, and, as Menna Prestwich suggested, an entirely new turn might have been given to the destiny of the Stuart monarchy 'by a mind as radical as Bacon's collaborating with an executant as able as Cranfield'.[39] Was it Bacon's fault that this did not happen, as his disparagers, turning a blind eye to Cranfield's difficult personality, have not hesitated to affirm? Cranfield saw eye to eye with no man. Ill-tempered with his inferiors, he exasperated his equals with rigidly negative reactions and moody silences. In the 1621 Parliament, where he had the upper hand, he was to quarrel with Member after Member and threaten not a few of them with punishment after it ended. As the Chancellor's subordinate he cannot have been easy to deal with. Yet Bacon was well disposed towards the up-and-coming merchant, fifteen years younger than himself, in whom as early as 1615 he had seen a valuable link between Crown and City. In one of his many letters urging the King to call a Parliament he had particularly praised Cranfield's proposals for the improvement of trade – 'Sir Lionel,' he said, 'being more indeed than I had looked for in a man of his breeding.'[40]

On the strength of this one 'biting remark', as it has been judged, in isolation from the general context, Bacon is frequently depicted as overflowing with contemptuous dislike of his City colleague.[41] His critics failed to realize that Bacon's condescending attitude was that of all James's courtiers towards a City apprentice, though they did not usually express it so mildly, or mean it so kindly. Judge Whitelocke, staunch anti-prerogative man as he was, found it offensive and insulting that the Mastership of Requests should have gone to an 'apprentice boy', and around this time compared Cranfield to the shady financiers who under

Edward III had climbed to high place, and were duly brought down by Parliament. Chamberlain found it 'hard to credit' that 'a merchant of this town' should rise to Lieutenant of Dover Castle; John Pym similarly rejected him – he would not have reform entrusted to 'such men as leap from the shop to the greencloth'; and as for the Earl of Suffolk, he told the King he would resign his staff as Lord Treasurer and all his other honours 'rather than be matched and yoked with a prentice of London'.[42]

Seen in context, Bacon's remark implied no criticism: he was simply expressing his satisfaction at the discovery of a man of so much ability in an unexpected quarter. Early in 1616, we find him paying tribute to Cranfield's perspicacity over the tricky Cockaygne affair, when he referred to a 'lever' they had found against that dangerous speculator – 'a point hitherto not much stirred, though Sir Lionel Cranfield hath ever beaten upon it in his speech with me'.[43] The alleged break between the two Government officials over Bacon's seemingly contemptuous remark, which Cranfield had probably never seen, is a critic's fiction. So little did Bacon object to being yoked with such a partner that the two worked together – in town or at Gorhambury, where Bacon asked him to stay – for over three years afterwards. Nor did he make any secret, either to Cranfield when he called him urgently to his side, or to the King, of his reliance on the City man's collaboration.[44] On the contrary, from 1617 on, when Cranfield was placed at his disposal for the review of the royal finances, we will find Bacon mentioning him to the King with increasing respect; raising here a good point suggested by Sir Lionel, regretting there his sickness, 'because the business of the King's estate goes better when he is handling', and deferring action 'till Sir Lionel be able to execute his part'; or preparing a draft which he could not conclude, he said, until he could speak with Sir Lionel; and when he noted some success, not failing to point out that it had been achieved 'by the help of Sir Lionel Cranfield'.[45]

The trouble was that the touchy *apprenti parvenu*, revelling in his new-found status and conscious of his value as a formulator of financial projects, was not content with the subordinate role of technical executant. He wanted to play lead, and lacking Bacon's political acumen, he saw no difference between his own narrow, anti-foreign views, his long-winded and repetitious memos, replete with statistics, and the Chancellor's concise notes, keyed to a different level of policy, with vistas onto the future, and usually presented with some additional creative twist.[46] He regarded Bacon, as Gardiner put it, 'with that supercilious contempt which a man who has risen in the world by a thorough knowledge of the details of business' tends to feel for a more polished intellect. On one occasion, being himself prone to boosting his own deals, he suspected Bacon – quite unjustly, as it turns out – of desiring the handling of a particular project in order to 'have the honour and thanks from the King'. The project in question was one which Bacon had in fact originated, and although he mentioned to Buckingham that the work had been done 'upon my foundation', Cranfield's biographer did not find in him any wish to parade the scheme as exclusively his own.[47] Absorbed in 'business', however, and put off, perhaps, by his colleague's rough manners, Bacon may have failed to pay sufficient attention to Cranfield's susceptibilities, and there may have been pinpricks, which, in such a man, could feed an increasingly bitter resentment towards his superior officer – a resentment he was to make no effort to conceal when launching his disloyal attacks in Parliament.[48] He was to maintain a hostile attitude to Bacon long after he had shed the pose of popular reformer; and when, as Lord Treasurer he had it in his power to harass the fallen Chancellor, he would take full advantage of it.[49]

So much for the principal character parts in our drama. What of the other players, that handful of opposition Members so ready to 'aggravate' any attack on Bacon? We can no longer see in them, as Macaulay did, the disinterested representatives of indignant constituencies, single-mindedly intent on sweeping away abuses that stood for the Crown prerogative – itself soon to be swept away. Recent studies of the personal lives of some of these Members have shown that while they claimed to speak for the 'great multitude' of their constituents, they were more often than not defending their own concerns – in particular the shares in trading companies which they had acquired after sitting in Parliament – and were using the cry of reform as a stepping-stone in the attempt to transfer their careers on to a more permanent stage. They sought, first and foremost, the protection of that very favourite whom they were indirectly accusing when they condemned Bacon. And sooner or later they gained the high place they were after; whereupon all passion for reform was suddenly spent.[50]

This is eminently true of the well-known opposition man Sir Dudley Digges, one of the 'turbulent valuers of themselves' whom the perspicacious Bacon had described in 1613 as already won over to the Crown – in expectation, as Chamberlain noted again in 1621, 'that somewhat would fall to his lot'.[51] Digges repeatedly changed sides as his hopes of preferment flowed and ebbed. He was to buy the Mastership of the Rolls when it was at its most unpopular, under Archbishop Laud, and accept office with Charles I at the height of the King's struggle against Parliament. Sir Robert Phelips, another passionate fighter for parliamentary liberties, and also a candidate for Government office, was very careful to steer his attack on Bacon so as not to offend Buckingham; he will also be found in the next decade working in close collaboration with Charles I.[52] William Noy, yet another Member active against the Court – and against Bacon, though he had started his career as official law reporter under Bacon's auspices – continued in the opposition until 1631, when to everyone's surprise he cast off the role for that of Attorney General, becoming a notoriously fierce prosecutor – an Attorney General being, he himself remarked, 'one that must serve the King's turn'. Phelips was notorious for, among other reactionary measures, the famous tax known as ship money, and for the infamous soap monopoly – as Clarendon put it, 'the lasting monuments of his fame'.[53]

As for that uncrowned king of the Commons, Sir Edwin Sandys, praised down the centuries as an exemplary gladiator in the fight for freedom of speech, a study of the records of the Virginia Company has shown that he 'combined his role as tribune with a career as unscrupulous company director', and used his patriotic record as camouflage for his private interests; that he was the author of fraudulent prospectuses, a manipulator of parliamentary votes, and an unprincipled seeker after quick profits.[54] Bacon had been somewhat premature in pointing him out to James in 1613 as a man already gained for the Crown. In the 1624 Parliament, however, Sandys was to use the support of the Virginia Company men (including Digges), backed by a recently forged alliance with the favourite, as a pressure group to revenge himself on Cranfield – who, as Lord Treasurer, had annulled his monopoly by allowing the import of Spanish tobacco – and bring about his impeachment. Early in this Parliament Chamberlain noted with disgust that Sir Edwin Sandys had 'made his peace, with promise of all conformity', and he predicted that the Parliament would not be led by its old leaders, since Sandys, Digges and Phelips were now generally seen to be collaborating with Buckingham, and 'had little credit among them'.[55]

Sandys was allied by marriage and by patronage to another member of the Virginia Company, the Earl of Southampton, leader of the opposition in the Lords, where he was to press the attack hardest against Bacon. Since his rebellion under Essex, Southampton had never found a satisfactory centre of power in Court, and his real aim now was to topple Buckingham, recently appointed Lord Admiral over his head, and take his place. It was well known that Southampton was out for the favourite's blood; the two lords would nearly come to blows during the debate on monopolies. It was less well known that, with his determined purpose in mind, he had secretly built up a cohesive group with Sandys and other clients in the Commons – forming precisely that combination of 'mean dependents on great persons' of which Bacon had stressed the dangers – and was thought to have been responsible for raising almost all the grievances brought up in the 1621 Parliament. He could not touch Buckingham, however, and had to content himself with harassing the favourite's protégé at every stage of his trial.[56] Other lords hostile to Bacon at this time were the Earl of Arundel, later a good friend, but just now bitterly offended with him because he had required the lords to give evidence on oath in Chancery instead of on their honours; and that 'monument of fraudulence', the Earl of Suffolk, dismissed from office two years earlier by a commission which had included Bacon, for embezzlement on a large scale, and only recently back in the House of Lords.

These are some of the men who, in attacking Bacon, Macaulay claimed, were 'righteously discharging their duty to their constituents by bringing the misdeeds of the Chancellor to light', and in whom he could detect 'no symptom of personal animosity or factious violence'.[57] As Conrad Russell sees it today, 'only one of the opposition leaders fulfilled the archetypal image of the "country member", standing firmly by his principles throughout his life': Edward Alford, for twenty years Member for Colchester. Alford sought the reform of Chancery, not the fall of the Chancellor.[58] Alone among these men, he was to be vocal in Bacon's defence.

10

The Grievance of Monopolies and the Tumour of Chancery: A Double Scenario

Two attacks – based on two different grievances, but led by the same two men – were inexorably steered towards Bacon early in the new Parliament, and came to a head, whether by good management or good luck, on the same day. In this chapter we shall look into their respective backgrounds.

One of the views still put forward today about Bacon's fall is that Parliament condemned in him not so much the corrupt judge as the sycophantic minister who failed to stop the flow of monopolies into Buckingham's lap.[1] Our first step therefore must be to find out what exactly these monopolies were in James's time, whether Bacon must be held answerable for them, and if so, whether he approved of them because he was convinced of their utility, or out of subservience to King and favourite. Samuel Gardiner is the only historian to have made a thorough study, not only of the few monopolies in which Bacon had a hand, but of all the fifty odd patents taken up by the 1621 Parliament. He noted the prevailing opinion – that James, and with him his Chancellor, 'resorted without scruple to the most illegal and oppressive devices' for the sole purpose of 'enabling Buckingham and Buckingham's relations to outshine the ancient aristocracy of the realm'; and after carefully investigating each of these devices, he concluded that there was not a word of truth in it.[2] Taken as a whole, he found that, far from being 'mere makeshift contrivances for exacting money from the purses of the subjects', these grants were the expression of a well-defined commercial policy – bearing on occasion the impress of Bacon's mind – and that, given a more favourable atmosphere, they could have proved effective and beneficial.[3]

Monopolies, as resorted to by Elizabeth and James, were grants made by the Crown, awarding to an individual or a group of patentees the whole right to sell a particular commodity or to control a particular service on its behalf. As historians now see them, they formed a stage in the growth of the modern state. The commercial patents enabled the government to supervise the economy more closely, while those granted for some service filled a gap in the administration – which, unlike its French counterpart, had no bureaucracy, and left the enforcement of regulations in the inefficient hands of underpaid local justices of peace.[4]

Why, then, did the successive Parliaments object to them so strongly? The trouble was that, while keeping its genuine commercial or state function, the award of patents had developed into one of the many irregular methods – 'bastard revenues', as they have been called in our time – by which princes rewarded their more deserving servants and kept their courtiers happy, in the absence of any regular system of taxation. Sir Walter Ralegh, for example, had held various lucrative patents, and Essex, as we will recall, had founded his fortune on the monopoly of sweet wines; while under James, Cecil made at least £7,000 a year out of the silk monopoly. The country gentlemen, however – who formed the bulk of parliamentary membership – considered the Court patentees no better qualified to enforce these regulations than they were themselves, and they were none too pleased to see the proceeds of fines and sales disappear into the courtiers' pockets. Furthermore, the monopolies were awarded under the royal prerogative and administered by Court officials empowered to seize goods and imprison and impose penalties in the name of the King. Since there was no appeal against their enforcement, in the hands of unscrupulous officials the monopolies were open to every kind of abuse, from widespread extortion to blackmail by patentees acting as *agents provocateurs*.[5]

Typical of this ambivalent situation was the patent to grant licences for taverns and alehouses. Set up with a view to limiting their numbers, since they tended to become the haunts of robbers and bandits (of Falstaff fame), it was originally bestowed by Elizabeth on the much favoured Ralegh. It is doubtful if drunkenness was kept down in Ralegh's time, since his services as government agent were paid for by the substantial fees he received from all the licensed tavern-keepers. But in the next reign the monopoly lapsed, and the taverns, licensed by irresponsible country justices, went on increasing by leaps and bounds, until drunkenness became so widespread that the King himself was alarmed. Finally in 1618 it was decided that he should take the supervision of taverns into his own hands, and two patentees were appointed to watch over offenders and see that they did not evade the over-lenient justices of peace. In the event, however, these officers did little but extort enormous fines from such keepers as were willing to pay for permission to run their disorderly alehouses as they liked, and the remedy proved worse than the disease. Still, as Gardiner pointed out, there was a disease, and the monopoly had been a serious attempt to cure it.[6]

As a result of this conflict between the administrative and commercial needs for patents, and the failure of so many of them to meet those needs, monopolies had been heading the list of grievances in Parliament after Parliament. Elizabeth had agreed with Sir Nicholas Bacon – her Lord Keeper, and Bacon's father – that they were against the principles of English law; but, whether as investments by enterprising subjects, or as one of the most important sources of Crown revenue, monopolies were built into the economy, and however willingly she, and later James, revoked one batch of them, others sprang up. Indeed the very reason why Elizabeth's famous last speech to Parliament in 1601, revoking all the abused monopolies, was called 'golden' is because it was proposed to write it in letters of gold, 'lest it be . . . not so happily effected'.[7] It was not; neither were the proclamations and promises that followed in 1603 and 1610. 'These patents are worse than they ever were!' a Member had cried in 1601, and in 1620 Chamberlain complained that 'the world doth groan under the burden of these perpetual patents, which are become so frequent . . .'[8] A quarter of a century after they had been used as a pretext to topple Bacon, and abrogated by James, monopolies continued to flourish. During the 1630s they brought £100,000 a year to the Crown. They survived the Civil War, and the reforms made by the Rump Parliament left them unchecked.[9]

We must distinguish, however, between useful patents and the monopolies which were felt as grievances. The distinction was clear, despite some confusion in the terminology – and despite the contradictory definitions provided over the years by Edward Coke, who was to lead the attack on monopolies in the 1621 Parliament, and formulate the Act against them in 1624. In his *Institutes*, published in 1644, Coke was to define a 'monopoly' – in the sense of a grievance – as a grant 'for the sole buying, selling, making or using of anything' whereby a person or persons were restrained 'in any freedom they had before, or hindered in their lawful trade',[10] a definition to which Bacon would have subscribed. Forty years earlier, however, when he was Attorney General and a defender of monopolies, Coke had laid down that a patent should be looked on as a 'monopoly' (or grievance) only if the price of the commodity had risen as a result of it, or its quality declined, or if former artisans had lost work from it. Now, in 1621, acting as chief parliamentary prosecutor, he flatly declared that 'the sole buying and selling of anything', under whatever conditions, was 'monopoly' – in others words, a grievance.[11]

Bacon was a convinced opponent of monopolies, as defined by Coke, both in 1603 and in 1644. Like his father, he believed them to be illegal, because they limited freedom of enterprise, and he never failed to support the revoking of abusive patents in Parliament. At Queen Elizabeth's last parliamentary session in 1601 he had taken an active part in the debate on those that were up for repeal. They were, he said, 'hateful to the subject', and must go; and he had contributed to their – temporary – going by pointing out the best procedure for achieving it.[12] But he went further. He strongly supported a motion put forward by the youngest Member of the House that monopolies should be regulated by common law, without any intervention of the royal prerogative. Elizabeth promised to allow this, and James was to do so again in 1606; but they could not fulfil such a promise, for, as both sovereigns soon realized, this would have meant litigating the system to death.[13] When he came to office Bacon stood just as firmly against monopolies, and in 1616, early in the reign of the new favourite, having no doubt observed his tendency to distribute benefits indiscriminately among his kin, he warned the young Villiers against them in no uncertain terms: 'Monopolies are the canker of all trades,' he said; care should be taken that they 'be not admitted under specious colours of public good'. Later, a list of the suits which the King bound himself to refuse, drawn up by Bacon in the summer or autumn of 1620, was headed with the single world, 'monopolies'.[14]

But there were two kinds of patents which most people did not look on as 'monopolies' at all. Firstly, there were those awarded to an inventor, originator or importer of new techniques, 'where any man', as Bacon had described them in 1601, 'out of his own industry or endeavours finds anything beneficial to the Commonwealth'. A late example of these was the patent for glass, which, although administered like the others by 'idle courtiers', whose favour was always in demand to support a new industry, had recently brought in substantial gains.[15] And secondly, there were patents of special importance to the state, such as those established for the defence industries (the patents for saltpetre and ordnance), or the various monopolies for wines, which yielded a good revenue to the Crown, or the Welsh mines, which were to bring in £40,000 for Charles I in the Civil War.[16]

These were the kind of legally acceptable patents which Bacon looked on as a genuine public good, and did his best to promote. But even these were used to reward courtiers, and no more than the King himself could his Attorney General or Chancellor escape from the administrative dilemma they posed. Bacon, in whom the desire for every kind of reform had been implanted by his father, was convinced that not only monopolies, but all the irregular sources of government funds had outlived their usefulness. Yet he knew there was no way of abolishing the system without replacing it by something better; and that only a financially stable government could begin to undertake the much needed reforms. Which is why, throughout his years as Privy Councillor, Commissioner for the Treasury, and Chancellor, he had given the highest priority to work on the retrenchment of Court expenses, the improvement of Crown resources and the encouragement of trade; besides tirelessly advocating frequent Parliaments, 'the ancient royal way of aid and provision for the King with treasure'.[17] Meanwhile, as Attorney General, like his predecessors – and followers – Bacon approved the legality of such patents as he did not look on as 'monopolies'; while as Chancellor he passed similar patents at the Seal, and was responsible for their enforcement.

As a member of the King's Legal Counsel, Bacon was called on to give his view on the 'conveniency', or usefulness to the Commonwealth of a new patent, and on its legality – this last a matter requiring much study and consultation. It is clear from his correspondence that he fulfilled the functions of referee with meticulous conscientiousness. We can watch him at work, for example, on the 'conveniency' of a petition for the licence of 'the sole transportation of tallow, butter, hides, etc., from Ireland', going into every detail, and even where there was no material objection, suggesting provisos, 'all of which, nevertheless, I submit to your Majesty's better judgement'.[18] For of course, under a Stuart monarch, there was no gainsaying the King. Later, as Chancellor, he would be able to 'stay', or temporarily withhold the seal on a patent, but further than that he could not go. On taking his seat in Chancery in 1617, Bacon stated his intention of 'walking in the light' with regard to the passing of the grants, which had created so many problems for his patron and predecessor, Lord Ellesmere. If a patent was unsuitable 'in respect of the King's honour or discontent or murmur of the people', he said, he would consult with members of the Council, and would acquaint the King of their conclusion. If it was against the law, after discussing it with those who had drawn it up, and consulting learned counsel and other judges, he would inform the King accordingly.[19]

To give false counsel, Bacon firmly believed, was equivalent to high treason, and he has been acquitted by all serious historians of advising in favour of a project which involved breaking the law – in other words of promoting 'those odious patents'.[20] But Macaulay is scathing because, having thus pledged himself, Bacon did not stay every patent that came before him.[21] He was perfectly clear about this in his speech. Once he had given his considered opinion, 'if the King shall repeat his order', he would obey. There was actually no way open to a statesman under Stuart rule but obedience. It is as difficult for us as it was for Gardiner to understand the approach of Stuart officials to an almost divine royal authority, although Carteret, nearer to Bacon in time, had no such problem. He found nothing in Bacon's letters to James or Buckingham 'of a supple, cringing or low spirit, but quite the contrary for he often stopped at the seal patents and grants obtained by the interest of the favourite, and gives him his reasons in very free and clear terms . . .'[22] We shall see below how, by quietly returning to the charge again and again, while keeping within the bounds of submission, Bacon managed to defend – and occasionally impose – his views.

If nevertheless he had persisted in staying a grant, the King could override him at any time, and seal his own patent. In fact, before Bacon was appointed Lord Keeper, James had personally sealed a grant which was to prove one of the most abusive, and would be bitterly attacked in Parliament – the patent for inns, from which Ellesmere, practically on his deathbed, had witheld the seal. Although Ellesmere probably held back no more patents than his successor (the King himself mentioned at least four which Bacon had stayed), he has been contrasted to Bacon as an example of the honest Chancellor who could be relied on to block a grant. The contention has no foundation in fact, and in this case the ailing Lord had blocked the patent not for reasons of state, but because he wanted to force the King to accept his resignation.[23]

The patent for inns had been set up in 1616, so its preamble declared, to remedy the 'great disorders' that had sprung up over the past half century, during which new inns had been opened by 'divers and sundry persons' without any lawful authority; and Bacon, then Attorney General, had advised on its legality.[24] The legal position (quite unrelated to its usefulness, or eventual abuses) was a tricky one, because it represented a phase in the general dispute between the central government and the country gentlemen. Bacon asked 'not to do it single', and three other officers of the law were appointed to act with him as referees. What the team finally approved – and the Commons, in 1621, would attack as an encroachment on local rights – was that the authority to license inns should be removed from the incompetent local justices of peace and handed over to the Judges of the Assizes, in other words to the King, whose authority in the matter of licensing inns had never till then been questioned, not even by Coke. Indeed Coke himself, in 1621, was to pronounce the patent for inns 'good in law'.[25]

Unfortunately, once again, the Government's action was defeated by the misconduct of the two commissioners appointed to supervise the licensing of inns on behalf of the busy judges. Bacon had not been involved in the approval of this patent for convenience, but he seems to have given it his blessing. 'I hear nothing from Mr Mompesson', he wrote to Buckingham in November 1616, not long after it had been set up, 'save that some tell me he is knighted, which I am glad of because he may the better fight with the "Bull and Bear" and the "Saracen's Head", and such fearful creatures.'[26] By 1620, however, this same Mompesson, the principal of the two commissioners, and a relation of Buckingham's, had gone the way of other commissioners, and used the patent to enrich himself by licensing the highest bidders – as often as not the very harbourers of criminals whom it had been set up to remove. When, later in the year, these things came to light, Bacon was the first to denounce the patent for inns: it headed the list of monopolies he urged the King to withdraw before the opening of Parliament.[27]

We must now look at one last patent, where Bacon was more closely concerned, the monopoly for the production of gold and silver thread. He was to be violently attacked for the part he had played in its execution – not, as we might expect, by Parliament, where his connection with it was raised in the Lords and, after a brief explanation from the Chancellor, dropped for good, but by Macaulay, some of whose followers made considerable capital out of it. Indeed, it is because of Bacon's participation in the handling of this monopoly, as Gardiner remarked, that we have heard more about it than of any other.[28] On this occasion, Macaulay declared, 'the chief guardian of the laws' assisted the 'rapacious patentees' in setting up a patent 'for the plunder of the public', and assisted them also in guarding it. 'It is needless to say more.'[29]

Bacon did not set up the patent for gold and silver thread. This grant dated from Cecil's time, before Buckingham or any of the rapacious patentees had been heard of, and before Bacon was in a position to be consulted. In 1611 a group of people under the aegis of Lady Bedford proposed to introduce into England the manufacture of gold and silver thread for lace-making, hitherto imported from France and Italy, and they applied successfully for a patent to produce it on a large scale. We will recall that a patent was considered illegal if anyone was restrained by it in a freedom previously enjoyed. In this case a handful of goldsmiths, who had previously tried to work the gold and silver with primitive methods, protested against the new patent and disregarded it (a difficulty which had not arisen over the patent for glass-making); whereupon Sir Henry Montagu, then Recorder of London, imprisoned some of them and took away their tools.[30]

After both sides had been heard by the Council, a fresh patent was drawn up, giving prominence to the entirely new processes introduced. The patentees undertook to import £5,000 of bullion a year, and to compensate the King for the loss of customs duty on the imported thread; and, aware of the value of Crown patronage, they welcomed the participation of Sir Edward Villiers, a half-brother of the recently established, and still well-regarded favourite, who invested £4,000 in the undertaking. Finally on 10 January 1616, after long and careful deliberation, Lord Ellesmere, satisfied that the invention was in fact a new one and that it provided the only chance for England to compete with the Continent in this rewarding industry, passed it at the Seal.[31] It will be noted that all the elements later complained of, rightly or wrongly – the special privileges granted to practitioners of the new techniques, the imposition of penalties on previous artisans, the presence of a brother of Buckingham – were included in the patents of monopoly approved before Bacon appeared on the scene.

The dissident goldsmiths, however, continued to ignore the new patent and impede its work. In April 1617 the matter was again taken up by the Council, who advised that an information should be laid against the offenders before the Court of the Exchequer. But before anything came of this, the King decided to take the patent into his own hands; the profits would accrue to the Crown, and Villiers would be compensated for his investment with a pension of £500 a year. It was not until the autumn of 1617 that Bacon, newly appointed Chancellor, was consulted for the first time, along with Montagu, Chief Justice of the King's Bench, and Attorney General Yelverton; the latter reported to James on behalf of all three of them, approving 'the fitness of the gold and silver business' as 'a means to set many of your poor subjects to work'. A proclamation was accordingly drafted by Yelverton and the Solicitor General, published on 22 March 1618, and a Royal Commission was issued. It included, besides the two active agents involved, all the principal judicial and Council authorities, any two of whom could be empowered to pursue and punish offenders against the patent.

We may glean something of what Bacon had in mind in thus ratifying the strong measures his predecessors had taken from the preamble of a further proclamation issued the following year, the first in which his hand appears unmistakably: 'And whereas we, esteeming it a principal part of our office as a king and sovereign to cherish and encourage the knowledge and invention of good and profitable arts and mysteries . . .'[32] Anyone reading the whole proclamation is likely to conclude, as Gardiner did, that in Bacon's view the grant had been made not to reward patentees but to benefit the nation, and that he was 'contending for a great public policy'. Concerned as Bacon was about the royal finances, he would not have seen much harm in the diversion of extra funds from the purses of a few goldsmiths into the Exchequer, particularly where the poor workman suffered no loss – indeed, gained much needed employment. Without seeing the materials and techniques used it is impossible for us to judge whether the invention was in fact a strictly new one, involving hitherto unknown ways of spinning gold, aside from the 'wiredrawing', which the goldsmiths claimed as 'a branch of their trade', as practised by a few foreigners from the time of Edward IV. Bacon adopted the decision taken by Lord Ellesmere. The men engaged to work it had learned the technique abroad and introduced it on a far larger scale, and at considerable cost in England, and he thought Ellesmere had been right to conclude that it was solely through their efforts that competition with foreign manufacturers had been made possible.

As for the arbitrary powers of imprisonment invested in the Royal Commission, even Gardiner, in full sympathy with the objections of the Commons lawyers to such a procedure, but considering some of the more violent actions of the Commons (of which more below), thought that Bacon may have been justified in believing that supreme powers could not at once be removed from the prerogative and placed in their hands.[33] For Bacon, as for Ellesmere, gold and silver were no ordinary commodities to be frittered away on lace, but the very wealth of the country –

'fitter', as the King proclaimed, 'for our own immediate care' than for that of private persons. If a few unsupervised artisans had used them for this purpose, they had done so illegally and were robbing the Commonwealth. Only under the royal prerogative could gold and silver be suitably protected, and stringent instructions were laid down in the various proclamations for the patent that foreign bullion must be imported to run it.[34] Unfortunately, a new set of 'private persons' – the unscrupulous agents who ran the project in the King's name – managed to by-pass these requirements and melt down the coin of the realm, thus proving the Chancellor wrong, as Gardiner put it, but not dishonest.

So much for the contention that Bacon supported monopolies in order to plunder the people, a point on which no historian has refuted Gardiner's consistent arguments. We must now examine the second part of Macaulay's accusation: the Chancellor's share in enforcing the 'tyrannous edict'. Sometime in 1619 Sir Giles Mompesson, of inn-patent notoriety, but not yet found out, was included among the active commissioners on this patent, and obtained royal approval of a new procedure whereby the errant goldsmiths should 'enter a bond not to meddle or make any gold or silver thread'. On the refusal of some of them to comply, Sir Edward Villiers told Attorney General Yelverton that the business 'lay a-bleeding', and called on him to imprison the tradesmen for contempt of court, which Yelverton did, subject to confirmation by the Lord Chancellor. Bacon summoned the goldsmiths, heard them and sent them back to prison. Whereupon the City petitioned the King on their behalf, and Bacon promptly discharged them.[35]

This is the story, as told by Yelverton when defending himself later in Parliament. Of Bacon's view of the case we have only the few words he spoke in the Lords, which give the impression that, although he could not entirely support his colleague's version, he did not want to let him down. We may assume, however, that when Yelverton declared that he had never conceived this patent to be a 'monopoly', Bacon, author of the preamble cited above, would certainly have agreed with him.[36] He declared in the Lords that he had committed the men 'for their contempt', and there can be no doubt that he was convinced of the legality of his action. Anyone refusing to obey the Royal Proclamation authorizing the exaction of bonds from the tradesmen involved was to be punished, it stated, 'as a contemner of our royal wish and commandment, by imprisonment or otherwise'.[37] Refusal to obey a royal proclamation was looked on in Bacon's time as an act of contempt, much as contempt of the courts of justice is still an offence liable to fine and imprisonment in ours.

So far the legality of Bacon's intervention, but what of its policy? When these events took place, probably in the summer of 1620, he was eagerly pressing for a new Parliament, and the last thing he could have wished was that the Government should give cause for complaint at such a time by enforcing an unpopular monopoly. Had he been aiding and abetting Buckingham's friends in their depradations – destructive of all his own policies – once they had become generally known he would of course have tried to play down the episode.[38] But nothing entitles us to take his complicity for granted; and if, as Gardiner concluded, and Bacon himself declared, he was entirely ignorant of the patentees' abuses, we may imagine the shock when he personally interviewed the prisoners and found that Villiers and Mompesson, men he had trusted as relations of Buckingham, had exceeded their warrant in every direction, breaking into houses, threatening the goldsmiths that 'all the prisons in London should be filled and thousands should rot in prison', and making counterfeit gold lace with debased materials – when not with good English coin.[39] There is much to be said for Spedding's conjecture that, wondering how best to undo what might never have been done had he been more watchful, Bacon preferred to avoid an inquiry into abuses which would have involved the King himself, because of the King's unlimited support to the favourite (whose first efforts at reform Bacon had himself watched over, and of whose good faith he still had hopes). Instead, James could appear in a gracious and popular role, the prisoners be freed, the city gratified and all scandal avoided – as in fact it was.[40] A hypothetical solution, of course, but one that would be typical of Bacon's approach in difficult cases: condemnation followed by grace.

The unpleasant savour of these discoveries must have remained in Bacon's mind when, in the autumn of 1620, he set to work, with the assistance of Coke, Montagu, Hobart and Crewe, on an exhaustive review of the monopolies that had been complained of. In the balanced and sensible document which resulted, Bacon and his colleagues urged James to revoke at once all those patents 'that are most in speech, and do most tend either to the vexation of certain people, or the discontenting of the gentlemen and justices'. They should be called in as contrary to an earlier agreement about monopolies 'or found since to have been abused in the execution'.[41] Less important patents, 'not so much rumoured', could be left to Parliament, so as to allow its Members leeway for indignation and action. The final aim was to eliminate them all.

Since Bacon knew where opposition could be expected, he wrote a private letter to Buckingham, warning him of the trouble that was likely to arise over three of his special friends, and begging him as tactfully as he could to 'put off the envy of these things', and 'rather to take the thanks for ceasing them' than 'the note' for maintaining them.[42] Buckingham's relations had actually made very little out of the monopolies, but he had come to look on them as family perquisites, and he did not like advice that involved curtailing his patronage and power. He chose the notoriety. Bacon strongly defended his proposals before the Council, and he urged them again on Buckingham a month later, excusing himself, with some reason, for his temerity; he gilded the pill, promising to 'go your lordship's way' if Buckingham would not go his – but made it quite clear that he had very much rather not go his lordship's way.

Immediate revocation was what Bacon thought not merely advisable but essential to the success of the forthcoming Parliament if it was not to be distracted from its 'main errand'; and, he added persuasively, 'it will sort to your honour.' It was decided otherwise, and monopolies were left to Parliament to deal with as it pleased. Acting against Bacon's advice, the King, wrote Gardiner, 'was to abdicate the highest functions of government, and to present himself to the Houses without a policy'.[43] More surprisingly, Edward Coke, after assisting the Chancellor in preparing his proposals for the Government to eliminate abusive patents – in order to allow Parliament to concentrate on worthy causes – was to use those same proposals as a weapon to bring down his colleague, thus effectively distracting the Houses from their main errand for as long as the session lasted.

Meanwhile a justified attempt to carry out long overdue reforms in the courts of justice was to be turned into another political offensive aimed at Bacon alone. As a court of prerogative it was natural that Chancery should be singled out for attack by the practitioners in common law who abounded in the House, although the same abuses were rife in all the courts of justice. The feud between Chancery and the common-law courts, represented at this point by Bacon and Coke, was a long-standing one. The common-law courts – principally the King's Bench (for criminal actions), the Common Pleas (for private civil actions), and the Exchequer (for Crown financial actions) – decided cases by resorting to precedent, for which they depended on an unwieldy and inflexible apparatus of statutes and recorded decisions; and since the only safe way through that morass was to stick rigidly to the letter, they not infrequently awarded decrees that were entirely contrary to the spirit of the law. Against these decrees the individual could appeal to Chancery, the court of equity, where the judge, not being bound to observe strict rules, could ensure that the common law was applied according to its original intention.

In his account of English government in 1583, Sir Thomas Smith defined Chancery as 'the court of conscience, because that the Chancellor is not restrained by rigour of forms or of words of law to judge, but *ex aequo* and *bono*, and according to conscience'.[44] In practice, particularly since the time of Cardinal Wolsey a century earlier, the common-law courts had defended the private property of the rich, represented in Parliament by the country Members, whereas Chancery, which held its more flexible procedures for applying the common law under the royal prerogative, had exerted a form of government intervention on behalf of the needy, who of course had no representation and no vote. That they did so exert it is shown by evidence gathered in our time, justifying Elizabeth's Chancellor, Sir Christopher Hatton, who looked on Chancery as 'the holy conscience of the Queen', when he declared that his court took pains to care for the poor. Bacon's predecessor and friend, Lord Ellesmere, felt very strongly about the role of his court. 'As the Chancellor is, at this day,' he wrote in 1608,

> the mouth, the ear, the eye and the very heart of the Prince, so is the Court whereof he hath the most particular administration the oracle of equity, the store-house of the favour of Justice, of the liberalty royal, and of the right pretorial, which openeth a way to right . . . [and] hath jurisdiction to correct the rigour of law by the judgement and discretion of equity and grace. It is the refuge of the poor and afflicted; it is the altar and sanctuary for such as against the might of rich men and the countenance of great men cannot maintain the goodness of their cause and truth of their title.[45]

Bacon, always a champion of the poor, saw Chancery in the same light. The 'court of equity and the conscience of the King', he said, was the power 'for mitigating the rigour of the law, in case of extremity, by the conscience of a good man'; prerogative law being not only a 'kin of blood' to the common law, but also its 'accomplishment and perfection' – and indeed, since the prerogative was held immediately from God, no more than one of its powers.[46] According to many Whig historians, in holding this doctrine Bacon stood for the forces of reaction, while Coke – who had also upheld it while still Attorney General – when he defended the rich landowners and merchants, was defending the liberties of England. But the father of all Whig historians held ampler views. It was, wrote Gardiner,

> the business of Chancery to supply a correction to the highly artificial rules of the Common Law, and until the time came for the growth of a better and more coherent system, it was sufficient that the Chancellor should be possessed of a mind large enough to grasp the general principles of justice, and quick enough to apply those principles to the case before him . . . [He may know] less of the details of business than his subordinates; but he brings to its transaction a mind less trammelled by routine, and therefore more open to the admission of new and enlarged conceptions.[47]

This was precisely the sort of mind with which Coke was least in sympathy. He could see only the dangers of such an approach.

There were dangers, and Gardiner pointed them out. 'In his eagerness to supersede the imperfections of the existing law,' he wrote, 'Bacon sometimes forgot to calculate the risk of pouring contempt upon the law itself.' And it was true that, under the umbrella of prerogative, Chancery had extended its jurisdiction so as to invade the functions of the other courts, thus increasing the general overlapping of areas of competence, and giving rise to what Bacon called 'the tumour of Chancery'.[48] Under Henry VIII, another famous Chancellor, Sir Thomas More, had urged the common-law judges to make the intervention of Chancery unnecessary by themselves using 'their own discretions, as they were in conscience bound', to mitigate the rigour of the law. 'For as much as yourselves', he told them, 'drive me to that necessity for awarding out injunctions to relieve the people's inquiry, you cannot thereafter blame me.'[49] But as under Henry so under James, most common-law judges thought only of defending their own flourishing practices, so that the courts, which should have collaborated to fulfill the law, were often on terms of hostile rivalry.

No one knew the failings of the different courts of justice better than Bacon. Aware since his youth of the need to define the limits of their action more closely, he strongly condemned the 'foolish doctrine that it is the part of a good and active judge to extend the jurisdiction of his court', and thought it 'an intolerable evil' and 'a most pernicious example that courts, whose business it is to keep the subjects at peace, should be at war with one another'.[50] As the son of Queen Elizabeth's Lord Keeper he was specially familiar with his father's court, and when he himself took his seat in Chancery, on 7 May 1617, he devoted his speech to a detailed analysis of its failings – the same which More had had to contend with a hundred years earlier. Above all, he said, there was an urgent need 'to contain the jurisdiction of the court within its true limits', 'to prevent the multiplication, prolongation, uncertainty and expense of suits', and 'to retrench unnecessary delays'. He went on to set forth a detailed schedule of proposals to remedy these ills, as 'a guard and custody to myself and my own doings, that I do not swerve from anything I have professed', and so that all men might know what to expect, and refrain from asking him anything against the rules he had set himself. And he promised 'many further particulars', to be set down in a public table.[51]

He made a start the very next evening with the revival of a custom instituted by More in 1530, but abandoned after the death of Hatton in 1591, that of giving regular dinners to the judges of the various courts. At this first dinner, in hopes of ending 'all former discords and differences between Chancery and other courts', he begged the judges, 'if anything should be brought to them at any time touching the proceedings of the Chancery, which did seem to them exorbitant or inordinate, that they should freely and friendly acquaint him with it, and we should soon agree.' Chamberlain grumbled at the cost of the dinners, but Bacon, going by the 'cheer and comfort on their faces', reported success, and kept up these friendly dealings.[52]

As for the 'further particulars' he had promised, they came early in 1618, when after less than two years in office Bacon embodied his proposed remedies in a hundred and one *Ordinances*, laying down all that was necessary to contain Chancery 'within its true limits, without swelling or excess', and to make it a model court. 'His lordship's rules', as they soon became known, would effect a considerable saving in time, words and 'swelling': suits already judged under common law, it was laid down, could be admitted only 'after solemn and great deliberation'; reports were to keep strictly to the point, bills of 'immoderate length' were to be penalized with a fine; all documents copied out by Chancery clerks were to be 'written orderly and unwastefully', and, since they were paid by the page, in a minimum number of lines. Typical of Bacon is the last ordinance, which promises further additions and changes, as 'time and experience' may show them to be necessary.[53] Rome was not built in a day. But if not all 'his Lordship's rules' had been implemented before the opening of Parliament, it should be noted that the bills moved later by the Grand Committee for the Reform of Chancery did little but restate them, point by point, and indeed the measures then proposed to regulate the entire system – common law, equity and the ecclesiastical courts – though never embarked on, were entirely Baconian in spirit.[54]

Bacon's lifelong efforts for the reform of many different aspects of the law will be looked into below.[55] Most important of all, as he saw it, was to remedy the law's delay. 'Fresh justice is sweetest,' he said, 'the subject's pulse beats swift though the Chancery pace be slow'; and, remembering the previous Chancellor's dilatory ways, he undertook to pronounce his decrees 'speedily, if not instantly' after the hearing. In fulfilment of another promise, he was already quietly and efficiently devoting not only the usual mornings, but afternoons also, and a part of the precious vacations he reserved for philosophy, to settling the 3,658 cases he had inherited from Ellesmere, some of which had been dragging on for up to twenty years. On 8 June 1616, one month after his speech in Chancery and three months after he had received the Seal, he could proudly report: 'I have made even with the business of the kingdom for common justice. Not one cause unheard, not one petition unanswered.' For the first time in living memory Chancery had cleared off all arrears.[56] So had Sir Thomas More sat one morning 'when there was no man or matter to be heard'.[57] And if both Chancellors were again to accumulate petitions, and leave their own modest backlog to their successors, it is because, as we shall see in Bacon's case, many of their suitors refused to accept settlement and came back with new claims again and again. Emptying the Chancellor's desk was still no mean achievement, and we may presume Bacon did so, as he had also promised, without the 'affectation of dispatch' with which one judge boasted of clearing eighty orders a day, but his orders went on 'begetting one another like Penelope's web, doing and undoing'.[58]

On the other hand Bacon had never thought it advisable to reduce

Chancery fees, another question that was to be taken up in Parliament. He wanted the clerical staff to earn fair stipendiary fees, so that they would not need to supplement their incomes by such underhand ways as trafficking in offices. In 1606, before he himself held office, he had successfully opposed a bill laid before the Commons proposing an unprecedented cut in the fees for copies in the Court of Record.[59] If anything, Bacon believed, some fees should be raised, since rents and commodities had risen 'mightily', while fees had continued at the same rate for a hundred years, a situation which occasioned the proliferation of illegal actions. (Cranfield, ignoring these factors, and intent on denouncing Bacon for the fees exacted by his court, was to forge ahead, after Bacon's fall, with a bill allowing no fees higher than those established in Chancery in 1598, disregarding meanwhile the equally excessive fees exacted in his own court, the Wards, which were to form one of the charges against him when he himself was impeached three years later.)[60] As for the fees paid to lawyers for their personal services, while proposing a few rules 'to ease the client', Bacon thought, characteristically, that they should be left to the 'conscience and merit of the lawyer, and the estimation and gratitude of the client'.

There was, however, one area in which he could do little or nothing. If he had trouble in implementing his ordinances, it is because, as in all James's courts, entrenched practices played havoc with his staff. This was the Achilles' heel of Chancery, and it was to prove the Chancellor's ruin. Bacon could change the rules, but he could not change the people who were to carry them out; nor, as a result, could he eliminate the many corrupt practices he found among his subordinates – masters, registrars and clerks. Many of them had bought their offices freehold with their own money, and were expecting to recover the funds expended from fees and gratuities, and all of them held their posts from people over whom Bacon had no control. The masters in Chancery were appointed by the Crown, the Deputy Registrar by the Registrar, the clerks by the Master of the Rolls. Among these were men who had abused Ellesmere and laid him open to criminal prosecution.[61] But even where Bacon could see that his staff were obstructing the implementation of his rules – in particular by multiplying instead of reducing the number of orders that passed through their hands – he was not empowered to dismiss them. The most he could do was to suspend them from active duty.

The same state of affairs prevailed in other courts. In the Court of Requests, for example, presided over by the Lord Privy Seal, where offices were also held for life and fell vacant very infrequently, office-holders received many times their authorized fees for affixing the Privy Seal on documents, and spent half their time competing for positions or securing the reversion of their own posts to relatives. The Earl of Northampton, Lord Privy Seal from 1608 until his death in 1614, never succeeded in establishing control over the patronage of his own office, and his authority over his staff was strictly limited by long established practices of all kinds.[62] Zaller suggests that Chancery had corrupted Bacon – if corrupted he was – rather than the reverse.[63] One may wonder whether Coke himself would have done any better in his place. Or would have tried, for had he attained the desired position of Lord Chancellor there would surely have been no grand championship of reform, and we may surmise that considerably more attention would have been given to decrying the defects of other courts of justice than to curbing the powers of Chancery.

Among the men Bacon was unable to dismiss was a Deputy Registrar named John Churchill, the undeserving ancestor of Winston Churchill. Rightly labelled by Hepworth Dixon a 'flagitious rogue', he was one of those 'bad instruments' Bacon had described as 'the left hands of courts: persons that are full of sinister tricks and shifts, and bring Justice into oblique lines and labyrinths'.[64] In 1613, when Ellesmere lay ill, Churchill had bought the post of Deputy Registrar from the official Registrar, Laurence Washington (a member of the family that was to produce that other illustrious scion, George Washington), who did little work, relying on the deputies whom his inherited patent allowed him to nominate. The Deputy Registrar held a key position: he was required to attend hearings and enter the orders and decrees into the books. The slightest alteration, a mere change of date, could involve the reputations and fortunes of men and the transfer of thousands of pounds.

Bacon had not overlooked the registrars in his *Ordinances*, where they were required, by Rule 41, to write out decrees with particular care, drawing the Chancellor's attention to matters 'of difficulty and weight' for his perusal before signature. But to what avail? Churchill took full advantage of his situation, and his career, traced through state papers, Journals of Parliament and the Order Books of Chancery, proves to have been a long series of dishonest acts. Until Bacon caught him out he had been drawing up forged orders in the names of eminent barristers, cheating clients and pocketing the fees. In addition, in collusion with a shady attorney, one Richard Keeling – a dismissed servant of Bacon's – he had used his free access to the Book of Orders and Decrees, and to the certificates and reports of the masters, on behalf of such suitors as would pay him a sufficiently high price for his forgeries. In June 1620 Bacon came across a deed that was clearly a forged entry and, remembering the facts otherwise, discovered the fraud. He could not dismiss his Deputy Registrar, but he forbade him the Court and threatened prosecution in the King's Bench – meanwhile, unfortunately, leaving Churchill free to hatch his revenge.[65] These gross abuses were to be investigated by the Committee for Courts of Justice, with Bacon's agreement, at the end of February 1621, when a bill was submitted for the pursuit of the frauds carried out by Churchill and his companions, which of course gave them a special motive for purchasing impunity by informing as they pleased against their superiors.[66] The stage was set for the Chancellor's fall.

To bring down a reforming Chancellor, as Menna Prestwich observed, was what Coke sought first and foremost when sponsoring his bill for the limitation of Chancery jurisdiction.[67] But, as she also reminded us, we should not underestimate his other primary aim, which was not so much to reform Chancery as to do away with its essential function, that of a court of equity. Chancery had long been Coke's *bête noire*. Its action went against his beliefs as a common lawyer, and it had frequently crossed his interests as a common-law judge. In the Parliaments of 1610 and 1614, when Ellesmere was Chancellor and Coke was Chief Justice of the Common Pleas – a court that had been losing business to Chancery for the past hundred years, and from which, under his own jurisdiction, a number of appeals had been made against blatant injustice – he had carried on a personal campaign against the prerogative court. Nor did his view of it improve when, in 1616, Bacon used his influence as Attorney General to assist Ellesmere in winning Chancery's freedom of action against Coke's efforts to pull it down, at a time when that indefatigable battler was waging war on every court but his own.[68]

Coke was to show his hand with two new bills, drawn up after Bacon's fall, by which the common-law courts would be given absolute veto over any decision in equity, and the whole intention of equity be thereby repudiated.[69] Such a bill, Gardiner remarked of one of them, 'would have been highly satisfactory to Coke, as it would have given him back, at a blow, all the ground he had lost in his dispute with Ellesmere in 1616'.[70] Fortunately at that point James put his foot down and opposed 'so retrograde a measure'. He promptly warned Parliament 'not to abridge the authority of the courts nor his prerogative'.[71] By that time Bacon had been sacrificed. Chancery was to remain.

But we must return to the opening of the new Parliament. After this brief review of its leaders' motives, the burden of monopolies and the situation in Chancery, we have some idea of the programme. Assisted by the thorough reconstruction of this Parliament which has become available, thanks to the efforts of Conrad Russell, Robert Zaller and Menna Prestwich in particular, we can now start watching the play.

Prologue: Two Attacks are Mounted and Silently Dropped

When Bacon planned the repeal of a large number of monopolies before the opening of Parliament, he suggested appropriate tactics to introduce those that would be left for it to deal with. 'Some grave and discreet gentleman of the country' should 'at fit times' make 'some modest motion', to which after due consultation the King could give way.[1] It was just such a country gentleman, the experienced Member for Colchester, Edward Alford, who, with Sir Edward Sackville, a friend of Bacon's, raised the issue of patents in the second plenary session of the Commons, on 6 February 1621. They were looking for measures to remedy the prevailing trade depression, and the patent for gold and silver thread, in particular, involving as it did a consumption of bullion, could be blamed for the inexplicable scarcity of silver (now believed to have been caused by events beyond the English frontiers, and beyond English control).[2] This same patent led to the hub of their debate: the country gentlemen could not accept a method of law enforcement by private individuals which might in time supplant their own system of local government.

To the surprise of the country gentlemen, however, without a moment's pause the Court party threw themselves into the fray on their side. Coke had already manoeuvred himself into the chair of the Grand Committee for Grievances, a key position for the attack; now Cranfield was demanding the investigation of the courts of justice, for which, on his motion, another Grand Committee was set up two days later. Casting off all notions of party loyalty, and brushing aside the Government's real business – the passing of 'good bills', and of funds to defend the Palatine – the two ministers proceeded to outdo the opposition in naming and pursuing abuses. 'My motion is to strike while the iron is hot,' said Coke, and two days were assigned every week to hearing those grievances which, in his hopeful opening speech, Bacon had urged Members not to hunt after.[3] Stir only those that 'have sprung from the desires of the country', he had said (knowing how many private petitioners would await them in town), and rather seek 'the effectual ease of the people' than to bring 'envy or scandal upon the state'.[4] It is doubtful if the ease of the people was foremost in Coke's or in Cranfield's mind when, as Zaller put it, 'instead of maintaining a common ministerial front', they forged ahead with the patents, giving the Commons 'the most unreserved encouragement to probe for scandal' at the highest levels, and, 'with deliberate indiscretion', playing up the evils of monopoly so as to maximize the embarrassment of the Government.[5]

The country gentlemen, however, noticed only their zeal. 'The privy councillors are as forward as any of us,' exclaimed one opposition man, and Alford was delighted. 'This was the first Parliament', he said, 'that he ever saw Councillors of State have such care of the state.'[6] Unaware that both Cranfield and Coke had defected – one of them for good – from Government ranks, they looked on them as spokesmen of the Crown, and followed them, wrote Zaller, 'in the naive and happy belief that there was a single concord in the state'.[7] The concord, at this point, lay between the two ministers and some of the more aggressive newly elected Members – like their leaders, only too ready to look on the punishment of a few individuals as a national remedy for England's ills. Thus when on 19 February these Members opened fire on the patents for inns and alehouses (the same which had headed Bacon's list for removal by the Crown) we shall not be surprised to find Parliament quickly abandoning its normal procedure of inquiring into the patents, and plunging into violent castigation of the patentees.[8]

The first target of the Commons's anger was Sir Francis Michell, a Justice of the Peace who was commissioner for the enforcement of the patent for alehouses on behalf of the principal patentee, Sir Christopher Villiers, a brother of Buckingham. After four days' debate he was summarily condemned 'for his many misdemeanours' (unspecified), and sentenced (without a hearing) to be 'sent to the Tower through the street on foot':[9] deservedly, since he had been selling licences to the keepers of disorderly houses, extorting large fines and ill-treating anyone who refused to comply; but quite illegally, for the Commons were entitled to punish only those of its Members who had offended against the House. Michell was not a Member of Parliament, had not offended against the House, and, as one Member pointed out, had committed his offences when no House was sitting. Far from being tried and allowed to speak in his defence, he had not even been charged. Never in its worst days, Gardiner remarked, was the Star Chamber guilty of such contempt of the laws made to protect the subject. Some Members would even have aggravated the punishment, but Coke merely insisted that Michell was not to be heard.[10]

With the next patent he was moving onto more dangerous ground. Two of the patentees for inns were brothers of Buckingham, and its principal projector, the master monopolist Sir Giles Mompesson, was connected to him by marriage. With Mompesson in mind – a Member of Parliament, at least, and no less guilty than Michell – Coke announced that he would not 'spare the quality of persons', and Cranfield, following suit, declared that to exempt anyone would be 'to throw over the whole business'. In order to silence critics of their high-handed treatment of Michell, Coke informed the House that by ancient right they could punish this offender at their pleasure; he had no claim to speak for himself since, according to a rule Coke now laid down for the purpose, 'if anyone accused of a grievance do justify it in this House of Parliament, it is an indignity to the House, and for this the House may send anyone to the Tower.' Michell, he said, had incurred the penalty by presenting a petition to defend his actions.[11]

Neither Coke nor the Commons, however, would now be satisfied with merely sending Mompesson to the Tower, and two lawyers were instructed to search the records for precedents that would show 'how far and for what offences the power of this House doth extend to punish delinquents against the state, as well as those who offend against this House'. They reported back the next day, 28 February. The Lower House had no such right, but some two and a half centuries earlier the House of Lords had functioned for a time as a judicial court; the Commons had acted as prosecutor and the Lords as judge and jury. Initiated under Edward III, this procedure, as shown by recent studies, had fallen into disuse less than a century later. It was associated with political crisis from its beginnings, and had been resorted to principally as a weapon in factional rivalry.[12] In the same spirit, Coke at once decided to put it back into use. Overriding the Commons's misgivings, he resolved that they should persuade the Lords to use the power which the Commons lacked, to punish a criminal patentee. With this radical innovation – the revival of an ancient method of impeachment that could be used as 'an instrument of terror' to the King's servants – the ground was laid for the trial of Bacon.[13]

There can be little doubt that when mustering the forces of forgotten precedent against Mompesson, Coke already had Bacon in mind. Neither in Coke nor in Cranfield can we always distinguish the real work of reforming abuses from their efforts to overthrow a colleague, though their frequently acrimonious tone, entirely absent in such keen promoters of reform as Edward Alford, is a clue; and we cannot be certain at what point Coke sensed that he had his old rival in his power. But, though no names had surfaced, there had been hints in the Committee for Grievances about the passing of monopolies, and now in the Grand Committee for Courts of Justice Cranfield openly moved from attacking Chancery to attacking the Lord Chancellor. He was nearly hoist with his own petard when the inquiry he had launched reported concealed irregularities in his own court, the Wards. To divert attention from his manipulations there, which would not come to light until the next Parliament, he quickly turned on Bacon. 'The plague-spot is the Court of Chancery!' he cried, 'why are ye afraid to touch it? The cause you have to try is not whether the Court of Wards has jurisdiction, but whether the Lord Chancellor has done justly!'[14]

Bacon's follower, John Finch (later Lord Keeper under Charles I), sprang to the defence of Chancery, 'a court', he said, 'that did nothing but justly and honourably'.[15] Cranfield meanwhile went on to present his programme for the reduction of Chancery fees, and Coke to denounce further abuses. Coke was no doubt sincerely convinced that the curtailing of Chancery's powers and the removal of the Chancellor were the best things that could befall the country, and that it was his duty to achieve both aims. But most of all he desired the success of the parliamentary judicature he was now reviving, and this too was inseparable from Bacon's downfall. Throughout his life Coke wanted power to be where he was. His whole effort in this Parliament would be to deny Chancery the authority of a court of record – that of arraignment and punishment – and to invest such a right in the court he had newly made his own, the High Court of Parliament.[16] It would require the impeachment of one of the great (Mompesson being too insignificant a victim) to set the seal on the power with which he was now endowing his court elect. Who greater than the Chancellor? And if by his fall Chancery could be brought low, Coke's success would be complete.

Bacon's two opponents were now working in unison and at a quick tempo, backing each other up in their respective committees, Coke conscious of his new strength as leader of the opposition, Cranfield blissfully unaware that the procedure he was helping to establish was soon to be turned upon himself. Equally dissatisfied with the efforts of their fellow Members – Cranfield demanded 'that we should lay aside all other business' until this one was brought before the Lords, while Coke found there was 'never so little care taken in so great a cause' – they overruled all reminders from the House that by common law the accused should be allowed counsel, or at least be allowed to speak in their own defence.[17] They were now aiming beyond the patentees, at the men who had approved the legality and convenience of the patents. Coke, who had previously given the patent for inns as an example of those that were 'good in law but ill in execution', changed his mind and denounced it as 'an exorbitant grievance in itself and in execution'; Cranfield declared the referees at fault, and repeatedly demanded that they be called to account.[18]

Not that either Coke or Cranfield had any clear policy about monopolies, which they had both supported for many years. Coke had been known to attack a monopoly because it interfered with his own freedom to trade, but he had also argued for the patentee in law suits, and had himself drawn up a number of patents. Later in the year he was to be caught out in his new role of Grand Parliamentary Inquisitor, to his lasting discomfiture. Attacking an old monopoly for the engrossing of bills for law suits, he declared that whoever had drawn up this patent deserved to be hanged. It had been drawn up by the then Attorney General, Sir Edward Coke, in person, the patentee replied.[19] Cranfield, for his part, had made good use of monopolies, along with customs farming and money-lending, as one of his financial tactics to get rich quick.[20] 'It was for no enlarged view of political economy that he opposed the patents,' Gardiner remarked; except that they disarranged the course of trade, he would have found it hard to say why they were injudicious.[21] In the event, his ardour against monopolies was to be short-lived. By November 1621, having failed to obtain the Lord Chancellorship on Bacon's dismissal (for which, said a contemporary historian, he had 'one foot in the stir-rup') but succeeded in becoming Lord Treasurer, Cranfield had shed his pose as popular reformer. To please the Crown, which was facing food riots that winter, he would go so far as to declare that the trade depression for which he was now clamorously blaming the monopolies – and Bacon – was not only over; it had never existed.[22]

Meanwhile both men pressed on: Coke, 'the bell-wether of the flock' (Chamberlain) and Cranfield 'the trumpet' in the affair (Bacon), with Phelips hard on their heels.[23] Who had certified the patent for inns? For its 'conveniency', Mompesson declared, the Lord Treasurer Suffolk, Sec-retaries Winwood and Lake, Serjeants Finch and Montagu, and for its legality, the three Justices, Crooke, Nichols and Winch, and Attorney General Bacon, in other words, the best legal minds in office. Chiefly responsible, however, as Coke well knew, were the two active referees, at present the two highest guardians of the law: Bacon, now Chancellor, and Sir Henry Montagu, Viscount Mandeville, now Lord Treasurer. 'If these did certify it,' said Coke, recalling no doubt that James himself had sealed it, 'no King in Christendom but would have granted it.'[24] He was thus, as Menna Prestwich remarked, successfully pinning down Bacon and Mandeville, 'the one his legal rival, the other the occupant of the Treasurership to which, by desert and ability, he had the greater claim'.[25]

Between two fires, the King's counsel were convenient scapegoats for the patentees to shift the blame on to. They would soon be used in the same capacity by the King and his favourite. But when the question of punishing them was broached to the full House, it was received in silence. It was one thing for Members of the Commons to demand the revocation of patents as illegal grievances and to condemn criminal patentees, but could they be judges over this formidable body of legal officials, and, if the officials presumed to justify their actions, send them to the Tower, un-heard? Even Digges hesitated. It might 'draw opposition', he said, 'and a crossing of the proceedings hereafter.' Only one voice was raised, Cranfield's, again urging that the referees be examined in the Lords, 'for his Majesty's honour, who by them hath been abused'.[26]

On 5 March, however, the House took up the patent for gold and silver thread. A new light of publicity was cast on the misdeeds of Michell and Mompesson, and of Sir Edward Villiers, when Yelverton, interviewed in the Tower (where, we will recall, he had lain since his condemnation for disobedience in November), declared that he had imprisoned the goldsmiths in fear of the consequences of resisting a brother of the favourite. He added, needless to say, that 'my Lord of Buckingham never did write, speak or send to him about it', while Cranfield, when he heard Mompesson and Villiers apostrophized as 'bloodsuckers and vipers of the kingdom', was quick to point out that Sir Edward had had no encouragement from Buckingham.[27] But it was clear that Yelverton, and by implication Bacon, had supported measures of a doubtful legality in the view of the Commons lawyers. Champions of the common law, advocates for free trade, defenders (like Bacon himself) of the preservation of precious metals now spoke with one voice. Sir Dudley Digges proposed a bill denouncing all projectors, along with 'all referees that shall hereafter mislead the King, that they may be branded to posterity'; and a committee was finally set up to lay a complaint against the referees before the House of Lords, demanding an inquiry into their conduct.[28] Parts were distributed to the various Members expected to intervene and Sir Edwin Sandys was instructed to follow 'with general aggravation'.

It was to no avail, for when the appointed Members were received in the Lords, on 8 March, their courage again failed them and referees were not mentioned. Information from Mompesson that was merely verbal, they later explained, as to who the referees were – or Yelverton's allusion, without proof, to 'a great person' – did not seem to them 'good ground' for such a complaint. In other words, as Chamberlain put it, they dared not 'touch matters to the quick'.[29] But the Easter recess was approaching, after which the mood of the House might change. Coke, who had reliable information at his finger-tips (having thoroughly studied the patents while he was assisting Bacon to forestall the very attack he was now launching on them in the Commons) soothed and encouraged, and proposed a new appointment with the Lords. The two principal referees were finally mentioned by name. Phelips accused Members of refraining from confronting the Lord Chancellor and the Lord Treasurer out of respect for their great places, and blamed the Speaker for refusing to charge them to their faces with corruption and illegality. 'Enough has been done to condemn Mompesson,' said Coke, 'let us now go deeper,' even if they could not at once 'get at the two men who are in place'. Phelips suggested sending for the Lord Chancellor's papers. 'The referees are the guilty men,' Cranfield once again insisted, 'nothing but their condemnation can now clear the King.'[30]

James did not agree. 'I am the giver of all patents,' he declared, appearing unexpectedly in the Lords on 10 March, this 'great discourse among you . . . cannot but reflect on me.' Decisions on legality and convenience, he pointed out, belonged properly not to Parliament but to the courts of justice.[31] After Bacon was gone, James, determined that his Treasurer should not fall with his Chancellor, would warn Parliament 'not to condemn men for an error in opinion'. And in the next Parliament he was to inform the Commons in no uncertain terms that their 'doctors of law' were no judges in the matter of patents; only if 'inconveniences' occurred in the execution were they entitled to complain.[32]

Now, however, faced with a massive attack that touched his favourite so nearly, he had not the courage of his convictions. It was true that power rested with the King alone, but he had used it to aggrandize Buckingham's family, and as a result of their malpractices an economic device intended (principally) for the good of the nation had proved highly detrimental to it. The nation was now demanding retribution. What could the King do to repair the royal image, already damaged by the weak stand he had taken over the Palatine? A cold logic would have pointed to the only answer: give up the real culprit.[33] Unfortunately, this was what James could not face. As a result, he ended his speech, so decisively begun, by shuffling off the responsibility he had rightly undertaken. He praised Buckingham as an administrator, and welcomed from Coke the proposal he had refused Bacon: to abolish the monopolies. In any case, he said, they brought him nothing but trouble. Complaining that he had been misinformed by his referees, the King announced, though without much conviction, that he would leave his Chancellor and his Treasurer 'to answer and fall as they acquit themselves, for if they cannot justify themselves they are not worthy to hold and enjoy those places they have under me.'

Justify themselves before whom? Bacon might well wonder. They were accountable only to the King. Yet Bacon does not appear to have had any serious misgivings at this stage. No doubt he was confident that he could acquit himself and that in the end James would uphold his right to be the sole judge of offences committed by his servants against their royal master. Not that he was conscious of any offence. 'I thank God my ways are sound and good, and I hope God will bless me in them,' so he now wrote to his friend Toby Matthew, thanking him for his concern over rumours which had reached him in Brussels, from both Houses, of a possible attack on the Chancellor.[34] To Buckingham he wrote around the same time that he was not alarmed by Cranfield, who, though 'formerly the trumpet' in the matter of the referees, was understood to have climbed down. As for Coke, Bacon still believed that 'a word from the King mates him,' and that the King would speak that word.[35]

But what of Buckingham himself, to whom this letter was addressed? On hearing that Mompesson had escaped through his wife's closet and fled abroad – terrified, as a contemporary put it, 'that the arrow of vengeance' aimed at his brother might graze himself – he had rushed off to the Commons to disown all his relations. Relying on the advice of 'the best and most learned', he said, he had thought the patents good things, but now it had turned out otherwise he undertook to be 'the chiefest and forwardest against his friends'.[36] Thus he not only washed his hands of his delinquent family, but, as Chamberlain noted, left 'the aspersion on those on whom the King relied'.[37] Far from seeing these words as a personal betrayal, however, Bacon wrote to Buckingham approving the 'noble proposition' of his pupil in statecraft, as showing 'more regard of the fraternity you have with great counsellors, than of interest in your natural brother'. In this letter, dated 7 March – when the Commons were busily collecting precedents aimed ostensibly at Mompesson, in reality at himself – Bacon's main preoccupation seems to have been that the Parliament should keep to 'fair and moderate courses', so that 'the sweet and united passages thereof may increase the King's reputation with foreigners'. He feared that 'a far other judgement than we mean' might be made abroad 'of a beginning to question great counsellors and officers of the crown, by courts or assemblies of estates'. He would have said more, he added, had he not been personally involved.[38]

What Bacon could not yet know was that he had been succeeded in Buckingham's confidence by a new mentor, Dean John Williams, the same that was soon to be made Lord Keeper in his place. Buckingham had some excuse for panic when faced with what Russell describes as 'the sheer blundering force' of Coke's attacks, even though they were not ostensibly aimed at him.[39] Strong contrary winds, the Venetian Ambassador reported, were blowing at this time against his ship.[40] He could not be certain that the ageing King's protection would avail him against a cabal of his enemies among the old peers, and Prince Charles was still an unknown quantity. When James wisely refused his plea that he should dissolve Parliament, Buckingham turned to Williams, who at once calmed his fears. 'Swim with the tide,' he said, 'and you cannot be drowned'; give up 'those empty fellows' Mompesson and Michell to the public wrath, there being 'no wares that may be better spared', and 'cast all monopolies and patents of griping projections into the Dead Sea after them' (the very advice Bacon had given him before Parliament began, but how differently conceived!); finally, give out that these devices were 'stolen from you by misrepresentation when you were but new-blossomed in Court'.[41] Bacon, as an author of the 'misrepresentation', was clearly one of the wares that could be cast into the Dead Sea. Williams spoke to the convinced, and a much relieved Buckingham, who had done his best to prevent the calling of Parliament (and, once it was called, to have it dissolved) was soon to step, uninvited, into a committee of the Commons and declare himself 'in love with parliaments'.[42]

Meanwhile, on 10 March, after the King had spoken in the Lords, Bacon and Mandeville were allowed a few words to justify themselves, and Bacon gave a brief and straightforward explanation of his actions. He was ready to submit his conduct to his peers, he said, and was not afraid of their judgement. 'May it please your Majesty,' he added, turning on his real accuser, 'for all my Lord Coke hath said, I hope in future ages my acts and honesty shall well appear before his, and my honesty overbalance and weigh his, and be found heavier in the scale.' Coke got his own back the same afternoon, when Bacon, in an attempt to reply to the charges against Mandeville and himself, now finally laid before the Lords, referred to the patent for gold and silver thread. We have his words only in summary form. It had been 'much abused in the execution thereof', he admitted, 'to the intolerable grievance of the subject'. But 'abuses could not be foreseen; they were nothing to the referees; the thing might be lawful though used unlawfully'.[43] Whereupon, seizing the moment with what Zaller describes as a 'hawklike cunning', Coke enquired whether this statement was to be taken as proceeding from the House, according to whose ancient order Members could not speak without permission in their own defence.[44] At the next sitting Bacon and Mandeville, who had also spoken, were made to apologize for their breach of the rule, and when Pembroke referred to them as 'two great lords', he was called to order. In this House, a Southampton partisan remarked, 'they are all peers'.[45]

Zaller saw a symbolic meaning in this brief exchange. Though no charge had yet been made against him, 'Bacon now stood isolated, the target of every shaft, and with every passing hour his role was being more surely shaped: the victim, the sacrifice, the scapegoat.'[46] The scapegoat himself, meanwhile, was still incredulous. If the prerogative were in question, why should he be the sole target? But, having fought so long for a united Council, Bacon must have been shocked to see the process of judicature used by one Privy Councillor to attack another. In his letter to Buckingham he had deprecated 'the questioning of great counsellors' by the Commons, and around this time he concluded a conversation with the King with this prophetical warning: 'Those that will strike at your Chancellor, it is much to be feared, will strike at your crown.'[47] Bacon was all in favour of frequent and increasingly responsible Parliaments, to whom Government ministers, so far accountable only to the King, should explain their policies. But impeachment was, in his view, too potent a tool of faction to be placed in the hands of a still untutored assembly.[48]

The King knew in his heart that Bacon was right. He saw where Coke

135

was heading with his medieval precedents wrenched out of context, and had angrily protested in the Lords that they were not precedents 'of good kings' times', but of usurpers and tyrants, or silly and weak kings, such as Henry VI, with whom he 'scorned to be compared'; 'I think him an enemy to monarchy, and a traitor to me that mentions my actions with such kings.'[49] And he saw only too clearly that once he allowed Parliament to call his Chancellor into question, the full sovereignty on which he based his rule would never be retrieved. But though 'a word from the King' would still have check-mated Coke, James could not speak it. He was to vent his anger on Coke at the end of the session, but at this juncture, with the salvaging of Buckingham as his top priority, he had not the confidence to face up to his stubborn old antagonist, now self-dubbed Grand Inquisitor of Grievances. As a result, he was to miss every opportunity of halting the process.[50] During the Parliament of 1624, when it was too late, James would vainly warn Buckingham – busy, by then, with the impeachment of Cranfield – that he was making the rod with which he would himself be scourged, and that he would 'live to have his bellyful of impeachments'. Others were to warn Charles I, when the following Parliament was duly preparing to impeach the favourite, that this same rod – first forged by Coke for Bacon – would not spare the King himself.[51] Only with the revolution of 1688, which set up a body of independent judges, was it possible to put an end to the long line of political impeachments, disguised as judicial trials, that followed Bacon's.

What kind of a case would now have been made against Bacon we shall never know, for when, on 15 March, the evidence against Mompesson was finally submitted to the Lords, the referees were barely mentioned.[52] They had suddenly become an expendable target – to everyone's relief, for Bacon was after all only the first among many. To proceed against him alone had never been a realistic proposition, while to prosecute all the referees would hardly leave a member of the King's legal counsel in place. Until this date, however, the Commons had been reluctant to drop the charges altogether. Ready by now to see iniquity in anything Coke told them was against some statute, they were full of the patriotic fervour which cannot be satisfied without a victim. They were looking for such a victim, and since Buckingham could not be touched, Bacon was the obvious candidate. But another charge against him was needed – a charge, unrelated to the monopolies, which would implicate him alone.[53]

In the Committee for the Courts of Justice, where, at the hands of the common lawyers, Chancery had similarly been made a scapegoat for other courts, Cranfield had been working hard at just that. We saw him point a finger at the Chancellor, but Bacon, only too glad to have parliamentary support for his efforts to reform that unwieldy body, had already laid Chancery open to inspection. 'Any man', he said, 'might speak freely of anything concerning his Court'; indeed, 'he would thank any man that would propound the means of reforming his Court.'[54] Chancery was duly investigated, but Bacon was not blamed for the misdeeds of his Registrar; and on the reform of the law he could not be faulted. When an opposition Member asked that obsolete penal statutes be sifted out, it was found that thanks to the Lord Chancellor's efforts throughout the summer the task was well under way. However, Bacon was responsible for one unpopular measure, the issuing of injunctions known as 'bills of conformity', whereby in cases of emergency the payment of a debt could be stayed or its amount reduced. The practice had been set up after he had assisted Ellesmere in defeating Coke's attack on Chancery, in an attempt to establish a more humane interpretation of the savage laws of debt; although, having presumably noted some ill effects, Bacon was in fact planning to do away with it in Parliament.[55]

As S. T. White pointed out in his book on Coke's parliamentary activities, it is not known who exactly was hurt by the bills of conformity, but 'whoever they were, they were obviously powerful, and had powerful friends'. The City merchants were angered by them, and Cranfield, himself a professional lender, although his own court had also issued such bills, considered them harmful to trade.[56] He attacked them now, said Gardiner, 'in the true spirit of a London shopkeeper', and denounced them as the real cause of that depression which, he was soon to declare, had never existed.[57] The Commons lawyers, equally indignant, looked on the bills of conformity as an unjustified extension of equity at the expense of common law. 'It should not lie in the breast of one man, be it whosoever,' exclaimed Sir Dudley Digges, 'to use so large a power.'[58]

Whether Coke was acting out of 'jurisdictional jealousy, common-law chauvinism or enmity to Bacon' (White), whether Cranfield spoke from conviction or to embarrass a royal minister (R. C. Johnson), the joint attack in the Committee for Courts was managed by them both in step to the greatest possible effect.[59] On 12 March the transparently honest Chairman, Sir Edward Sackville, Bacon's friend, was pressured to resign on grounds of ill-health, and replaced by Sir Robert Phelips.[60] On 14 March Cranfield regretfully informed the House that one Sir Henry Finch had escaped paying debt on an order from Chancery; whereupon Cranfield's City crony Sir Bernard Hicks sprang up to complain that he himself was the creditor, and that he had lost £200 by that order. A horrified Coke followed: he could not believe 'that there is such proceedings in any court of justice'. After which Cranfield feelingly deplored an injunction which 'robs the subject – and how it robs the subject! And is a cause of the want of money, for who will lend?' The Mompesson affair was 'but a trifle' compared to this![61] Was Cranfield carried away by 'the irresistible pleasure' of giving Bacon the last push, Zaller wondered, 'or did his attack signify that the Government had decided to throw Bacon to the wolves?'[62] Clearly both, for he was emboldened by the knowledge that

James was not protecting his minister. The King, if we are to believe Cranfield, had never authorized these bills; when he heard about them 'he was so angry as I never saw him'; he would not, he told Cranfield, 'endure' officials responsible for such actions about him.

What effect this new attack might have had on Bacon we shall never know, any more than we can know how the attempt to discredit his actions as a referee would have developed, for the Ides of March were upon the Chancellor, and this accusation too was dropped. Coke was now visibly triumphant, with Buckingham so much enamoured of Parliaments that, he told the Lords, anyone who taxed the old lawyer for his precedents of impeachment was 'an ignoramus', while Prince Charles declared himself 'never weary with hearing Coke, he mingled mirth with business to so good purpose'.[63] To the best of purposes, since Coke now had the game in his hands. But his high good humour sprang, as another historian of this Parliament noted, from 'a more private gladness', for the Privy Counsellor turned leader of the opposition had one more card up his sleeve.[64] And the reason for his euphoria became apparent when Cranfield, with perfect timing, announced the next item on his committee's agenda: two petitioners were ready to come forward and accuse the Lord Chancellor of accepting money to favour their suits. A charge had been found that made all others superfluous, one that marked out a single victim, the chosen scapegoat, worthy to be tried by a newly empowered High Court which would soon make the very calling of a Parliament dangerous to Government ministers, and, a generation later, would claim the life of a king.

12

Act I: Bacon is Accused of Corruption in the Commons

It is just possible, as some historians have maintained, that Coke was in luck, and that Christopher Aubrey and Edward Egerton, who had evidently been waiting backstage for their cue, complete with witnesses to testify for them, had chosen exactly the right day and hour to submit their petitions to Parliament. The time was propitious for dissatisfied suitors to complain of an unfavourable decree in hopes of having it quashed. The Chancellor had been aspersed repeatedly in Parliament but no one had been summoned before the Privy Council or sent to the Tower, as they would normally have been, for vilifying the justice of the realm. Even now one angry suitor, condemned three years earlier to lose his ears for such a vilification, and probably unaware that he owed his reprieve to Bacon, was busily hunting out other petitioners against him.[1]

On this fateful 14 March, the signs were unmistakable. The day before, Buckingham, whom we have seen blaming the ills of monopoly on his 'learned friend', had formally promised both Houses the King's and his own support for their investigations, and informally approved Coke's precedents for impeachment; while James, after disowning his legal counsel, had apparently teamed up with Cranfield to damn his Chancellor's bills of conformity. No wonder there were many petitions, as a contemporary noted, 'ready to be put up against my Lord Chancellor', just as there had been against Ellesmere, his predecessor, when he had offended Buckingham's mother, and were to be against Williams, his successor, during the short time he dared to oppose the favourite. Not to speak of the many petitions made to the King against Bacon himself when in 1617 he had briefly fallen out of favour with Buckingham.[2]

None the less it is more than likely that Coke and Cranfield deliberately sponsored Bacon's denouncers, and that the historian who related in 1984 'how a swarm of witnesses appeared from nowhere' to be organized against him was right in assuming that behind them lay the 'powerful mind' of a 'persuasive advocate' with 'compelling reasons to act'.[3] Indeed

Coke as good as said so when, to prove that the witnesses against Bacon were to be trusted, he declared that these men 'came not to accuse, but were interrogated'.[4] Such things were going on all the time. 'The complainants are underhand set on and countenanced by greater persons,' wrote one John Lambe, called soon afterwards before this same session of the Committee for Courts, in a letter of protest to the King.[5] And Cranfield was to make the same complaint to James when he was faced with a similar accusation in the next Parliament: 'Men are persuaded (I will not say promised reward) to accuse me.'[6]

Did he recall his own efforts in Bacon's case? When Aubrey and Egerton lodged their complaints, Cranfield and Coke had already spent three weeks interrogating not only these two petitioners, and others who followed, but also that principal procurer of witnesses, the dishonest Registrar John Churchill, whom Bacon had suspended from his functions, and who had, it seems, been promised protection in return for what he chose to reveal. According to Chamberlain, commenting on 'the tempest' that had so suddenly fallen on the Lord Chancellor, 'One Churchill, a registrar of the Chancery, hath been the chief instrument of his ruin, who being called in question for divers counterfeit orders and extortions, and sequestered from his place with danger of further punishment, professed that he would not sink alone, but draw others after him . . .'[7]

Here too the timing is important. Churchill's delinquencies, whether volunteered with retaliation in mind or obtained with threats, came to light only a few days after Bacon had offered the Committee for Courts free access to Chancery for their investigations, which, since Parliament had no power over the prerogative courts, could not have been carried out without his permission. On 21 February, while the attack on monopolies was proceeding apace and Cranfield was harping in general terms on the guilt of referees, the Registrar had been made liable to prosecution for fraud, personation and forgery – so that to greed and revenge the motive of fear could be added – and Coke had obtained an order to send for informers on Chancery at any time.[8] On 2 March, the day on which, precedents in hand, Coke decided that the Commons should join up with the Lords to punish Mompesson, and the day Cranfield turned his charge against the 'plague spot' of Chancery into a personal accusation of the Chancellor, the Committee for Courts found that John Churchill had abused his position of trust and defrauded the public of fees. A bill was proposed for the immediate punishment of frauds.

Churchill, however, was not punished by this Parliament. Under Bacon's successor he was reinstated in his post, where abuses again multiplied, and it was not until the Parliament of 1624 that he was brought to justice, for forgery and fraud committed in office.[9] In the meantime, we learn from Chamberlain, he provided his examiners with a list of reluctant witnesses, 'driven to say what they know'. The degree and kind of coercion exerted on these witnesses is still an unknown factor, but coercion cannot be excluded.[10] The witnesses thus recruited had to be identified, tested, organized – and by whom, if not by those who examined them before they came on stage, the two most active members of the Committees for Grievances and for Courts of Justice? Bacon had no illusions about the methods used against him. 'Job himself,' he wrote that same day to Buckingham, 'or whoever was the justest judge, by such hunting for matters against him as hath been used against me, may for a time seem foul, specially in a time when greatness is the mark and accusation is the game.'[11] But he had not so far taken the petitions seriously.

They were unusual to say the least. Not only were both complaints some two-and-a-half to three years old, but the substance of each of them was that Bacon, after allegedly accepting money through a member of his own household to favour their cause, had actually decreed against them. Neither petition looked much like an ordinary case of corruption. Christopher Aubrey's already complex suit was further complicated by a crucial discrepancy between his declaration and the Chancery *Book of Orders* over the date of the decree he complained of.[12] Aubrey had quarrelled with his one-time employer, Sir William Brunker, and had won a common-law suit against him; but Brunker had appealed in Chancery, when, in April 1618, the suit came before him for the first time, Bacon decided in Brunker's favour. Whereupon Aubrey bribed witnesses right and left, and finally, at the suggestion of his counsel – Bacon's follower, Sir George Hastings – put £100 in a box and gave it to Hastings, who told him he would carry it to his master, and later returned with a message of thanks from the Chancellor. Aubrey now looked confidently to a favourable decision, but Bacon, maintaining his original view of the case, awarded him 'a very prejudicial and murderous order'. Aubrey then wrote the Chancellor 'divers letters' which remained without a reply until finally his Lordship answered, 'If he importune him, he will lay him by the neck.'[13]

Hastings, who was a Member of Parliament, had also been waiting backstage. Alarmed at the imputation that he had committed the crime of designing to bribe a judge, he denied that he had advised it, and said he had taken the box to his master, not as a bribe, but as a present from himself. Bacon, he went on to declare, had had notice of Aubrey's petition and had questioned him beforehand about it. Commanding everyone else to leave his chamber, he had addressed Hastings as follows: 'George, I hope you love me, and desire not that anything you have done should reflect to my dishonour; I fear there is one Aubrey purposeth to petition and clamour to the Parliament that you gave me from him one hundred pounds. Is it true George?' Hastings replied 'that it was true, he

did deliver one hundred pounds to his Lordship'. His Lordship, said
Hastings, then told him that he should stay the petition while Bacon
looked into his cause again. With so many cases on hand a mistake was
always possible. But evidently Bacon remained convinced of the justice of
his decree, for he proceeded no further, and Aubrey duly brought his suit
to Parliament.

The second petitioner, Edward Egerton, a lifelong addict to litigation,
was greatly dissatisfied with a judgement made by Ellesmere in December
1615. This restored to Sir Rowland Egerton a part of the inheritance which
Sir Rowland's father had capriciously willed away from his son in favour
of the spendthrift Edward Egerton, his nephew. The latter now made
every effort to overthrow the Chancellor's decision against him. On 2
June 1617, three months after he had succeeded Ellesmere, Bacon made
an order transferring the suit to another prerogative court, where the
validity of the will could be determined, and whence it would go to the
King's Bench for a final decision. As far as Bacon was concerned,
the matter was closed, and could be crossed off the old Chancellor's
backlog. Thus when, a week later, Edward Egerton sent him £400 to buy
a suit of hangings for his new home in York House – for which he was
then receiving many presents from his friends – he accepted the gift as it
was offered, in thankful acknowledgement of services he had rendered
Egerton as counsel in the early stages of his suit.

Apparently, however, this present had been made (like Aubrey's) at
the suggestion of Hastings, as well as of one Sir Richard Young, another
member of Bacon's retinue, and when some five months later Egerton
reopened the case, it became clear that it had been intended as a bribe.
The will had been declared valid, but the two parties, unwilling to submit
their suit to a common-law court, had asked the King to refer it to Bacon
for arbitration. Bacon made an unassailable decision (so Gardiner concluded in his detailed study of the case), awarding Edward Egerton as
large a share of other lands still under dispute as the law permitted. It was
at this point that Bacon quite regularly accepted Sir Rowland's fee of £500
for his services as arbitrator. But Egerton, who wanted a complete
reversal of the original verdict – in other words, the whole inheritance for
himself – rejected the private decision, thereby obliging the Chancellor to
arrange for the conversion of his arbitration into a formal suit. On 16 June
1619 Bacon reaffirmed his judgement in the form of a binding decree, thus
unavoidably laying himself open to the suspicion that the fee he had
taken at the end of a suit was a bribe accepted before it. The indefatigable
Egerton now took his case to the King's Bench after all, where, in 1620,
judgement was again delivered against him. He was therefore more than
ready in 1621 to take advantage of the Chancellor's vulnerability, and
bring the case up once again, in the form of a petition to Parliament – the
last resort, as it was soon to become, of all aggrieved suitors.[14]

To make matters worse, Egerton declared that at the time of giving the money he had also come to an agreement with Bacon's chaplain, Dr Theophilus Field, now Bishop of Llandaff, whereby the latter was to persuade Buckingham to influence Bacon in favour of his suit, for which service the Bishop would be paid £6,000 when Egerton received his decree. Dr Field, however (who was afterwards exonerated from this charge), could not, it seems, persuade either Buckingham or the King to intervene, and Bacon in any case decreed against Egerton. Yet although Egerton's project had thus doubly failed – and was to fail again, since the 1621 Parliament took no action on the matter – this indefatigable suitor continued to press his claims on two further Lord Keepers. Bacon's decision was upheld by Williams in 1622 and by Coventry in 1627.[15]

Critics and admirers of Bacon are equally struck, at this point, by his unawareness of the danger he was in.[16] The same attitude, call it an unpardonable ignorance of his own affairs or plain innocence, which is shown by his question to Hastings about the alleged gift of £100 – 'is it true, George?' – is visible in his letter to Buckingham that evening.[17] Shocked as he was, and ill, since in so highly strung a man every strain told on his health, Bacon was so far from seeing himself as a bribe-taker that, as Gardiner remarked, he could only look on the charges brought against him as inventions trumped up by the Commons, baffled in their assault upon him as a referee. And who is to say he was wrong? Yet however little attention he paid to them, the mere existence of such petitions was an attack on his good name. Must the House of Commons, where he had begun his credit – so he would soon ask James – now 'be the place of the sepulture thereof?'[18] This was the purgatory he wrote of to Buckingham, 'I am now in it, but my mind is in a calm, for my fortune is not my felicity. I have clean hands and a clean heart.'

When his young friend, the scholarly Lord Cavendish, brought him the news from the House on the evening of that same 14 March, Bacon at once called Hastings in and rebuked him, presumably for landing him in these difficulties. Hastings replied (he tells us) that 'if pressed, he would throw the blame on his Lordship'. 'If you lay it on me, George,' said Bacon, 'I must deny it on my honour.'[19] There is a note of regretful warning here. Bacon was famous for his affectionate care of his frequently unreliable followers; he felt responsible for them all, and he had gone out of his way to be helpful to this on.[20] He may have suspected that some form of coercion had been used on him, and if it came to his own word against his follower's, Hastings would be the loser. But when, as Chamberlain observed, Bacon's own friends 'were made special instruments against him', what could he do?[21] Later, in his official reply to this charge, all Bacon would say about the £100 was that he left 'the manner of its giving to the witnesses'.[22]

The next day Hastings, angry with his master, he said, for denouncing him in the presence of Lord Cavendish, changed his story and told the Committee for Courts that he had really given the money in Aubrey's name. John Finch, who, when Egerton had first spoken, had at once declared that as counsel for the petitioner in all his suits he had heard nothing of any present or bond, now sprang up again to defend the Chancellor against 'this ungrateful accusation'. 'Sir George Hastings,' he cried, 'you have been my friend, but you can never be my friend again.' He hoped 'so great a man should not fall by the testimony of one who had most reason to excuse himself for so foul a fact as the delivery of a bribe,' and stated his own conviction that Hastings had taken the money and kept it for himself. William Johnson, Member for Liverpool and a fellow officer in Bacon's household, seconded the accusation. Hastings was silent.[23]

But whatever their contradictions, the charges were serious, and it was agreed that they should at once be laid before the whole House. Accordingly on the same day, 15 March, Phelips, paying due tribute to the Lord Chancellor as 'a man excellently imbued with all parts of nature and art', about whom he would not say more because he was not able to say enough, made his first report on them. He must have met with disbelief in the House for, barring an order to the Committee to consider the matter further, no comment was noted. And there was a wave of reaction in Bacon's favour the next day. After Cranfield had started a debate in the Committee with his usual arrogance, a Member who, in an 'unreverent manner had laid injustice to the charge of so great a person as the Lord Chancellor', was forced to retract his words.[24] On 17 March Phelips gave the House a full account of the two charges, expressing the hope that the Lord Chancellor, 'now on stage in this great Senate', might be cleared there. 'It is a cause of great weight,' he urged, 'it concerns every man here; for if the fountains be muddy, what will the streams be?' He concluded with a moving plea for those 'poor gentlemen' who had been 'fettered with much calamity by these courses', and requested that they might 'by petition to his Majesty have their causes revived and revised'. Members were not to know that justice had been amply done to both of them, and, in the case of Egerton, with noteworthy patience over two decades of appeals.[25]

Indignant objections came in from all sides. 'It cannot be pretended', wrote Macaulay, 'that the House were seeking occasion to ruin Bacon.'[26] They were not. Only two or three men sought – and found it. All the other eminent fighters against abuses – Pym, Hampden, Falkland, Sackville, Crewe, Finch, Wentworth and Selden, some of them friends of Bacon and familiar with his mind and intentions – stood up for him, or at most stayed aloof. The first to speak was Sir Edward Sackville. 'The noble Lord stands but yet suspected,' he said. He would 'bite off his tongue and throw it to the dogs' before he would speak for a guilty man. But he did not hold those gentlemen who had testified against the Chancellor to be 'competent witnesses'. They spoke 'to discharge themselves', and if he were guilty, they were those who had tempted him.[27] Sir John Strangeways, Member for Dorset, who did not know Bacon personally, insisted that Hastings and Young had not cleared themselves of the charge of intercepting the fees; their master denied receiving them, and his word must be believed. Sir Thomas Wentworth (the future Earl of Strafford, who was later to lose his life in one of the series of impeachments initiated by Coke) denounced the two petitioners as guilty men.[28]

The next to speak was the Recorder of London, Heneage Finch, Member for Cornwall, and the most learned jurist in Parliament after Coke. He knew Bacon well, having for the past five years assisted him in his efforts to reduce the statute law to some sort of consistency. The House had 'no sufficient grounds to accuse so great a lord', he said. Hastings should set down his testimony in writing, as every time he spoke he told a different tale.

> If the gentleman be allowed to give testimony, before it shall condemn another it must agree with itself. First I heard him say he gave it as a present from himself, yet after he saith he told my Lord Chancellor he had it from Aubrey. Again, Aubrey speaks not of any delivery of money himself to my Lord Chancellor. Then again it is urged that a discontented suitor wrote letters to my Lord, the letters are rejected, not hearkened unto. What does this do but free him?
>
> In the other case: if Egerton, out of a desire to congratulate him at his coming to the seal for his kindness and pains in former businesses, what wrong hath he done, if he hath received a present? And if there were a suit depending, who keeps a register in his heart of all the causes, nay, who can, amongst such a multitude? And as for the £6,000, there is no colour that ever he should have had any part thereof.[29]

Edward Alford agreed with the Member for Cornwall. 'I think the Lord Chancellor took gratuities,' he said, 'and the Lord Chancellor before, and others before him. I have amongst the muniments of my own estate an entry of a payment to a Lord Chancellor for his pains in hearing a cause.'[30] (Lord Say, no friend to Bacon, was to express a similar opinion in the Lords. 'If giving shall make a decree void,' he said, 'many just decrees, nay, most of them will be voided, for money was given commonly for all.')[31] Alford wanted the House to leave the Chancellor alone and get on with the work of reforming Chancery, in particular by controlling the conflicting powers of all the courts and by devising a better system for rewarding judges than that of fees given after an award, two measures Bacon had been actively pursuing.

Members were struck by the weakness of the evidence against Bacon, particularly by the point Sackville had first made: a man should not be accused on the word of a single witness, and a guilty witness at that. They were right: under common law at least two witnesses were required. But Coke hastened to allay their fears with a precedent. 'It is objected that we have but one witness, therefore no sufficient proof. I answer that on the 37 Elizabeth, in a complaint against a soldier-seller [the rich man who paid to avoid his son's conscription] there was no more but *singularis testes* in one matter.' Similar cases, he maintained, although, each with one witness, had been sufficient 'to prove a work of darkness', and 'if an offence be committed in a brothel-house, the testimony of brothels shall be admitted.' On the second count, 'that these men are culpable, and therefore no competent witnesses, I answer, they came not to accuse, but were interrogated' (as if the fact that they had not volunteered made them any more likely to tell the truth). And, Coke added, 'he that accuses himself by accusing another is more than three witnesses' – a statement which was invalidated three days later, when it was ordered that no witness should be examined about what he had himself received.[32] Bribery, he concluded, applying the word to Bacon for the first time, and to great effect, since until then his accusers had mentioned only gifts and gratuities, would go unpunished 'if he that carrieth the bribe shall not be a witness'.[33] By the prejudgment thus involved, Coke had succeeded in evading the principal objection raised by Bacon's defenders, that in terms of normal Jacobean procedure there had been no corruption at all. According to one historian, his timely use of the word may well have tipped the balance of Commons opinion, and persuaded them to accept the Committee's recommendation that all the evidence should now be forwarded to the Lords.[34]

It has been suggested that from this time on Coke played little part in Bacon's fall. 'Even Sir Edward Coke,' wrote Macaulay, 'for the first time in his life behaved like a gentlemen.'[35] He could afford to. 'I speak not because the Chancellor is under a cloud,' he was to say when a month later he took up his attack on Chancery again; and he may have meant it when he added that he would have preferred 'to speak thus in my Lord's greatness, than now when he is suppressed'.[36] (The suppressed lord could still be sneered at, however, and Coke could not resist the opportunity of repeating in Parliament the 'advice to the author' he had scribbled on his complimentary copy of the *Instauratio Magna*: 'You would restore things to their original condition: restore the law and justice first.')[37] Coke was past master in the art of using words to prejudge a case, and when he had spoken of bribes where others spoke of presents he knew exactly what he was doing. The only difference was that now, at the height of his influence in Parliament, he could steer the debates with the flick of a finger.

He had effected one of those light touches on the previous day, when the debate on Bacon had been delayed by a dispute which might have put a spoke in his wheel. The Lords had asked Members of the Commons who had testified against Mompesson to repeat their declarations under oath. The Commons reacted in anger to this 'preposterous' and 'disparaging' request, and Coke was ready to refuse it as inconsistent with the legal basis of their proceedings. He advanced two arguments – the second to be used if the first failed – which completely ruled out the possibility of their giving way to the Lords. But when a Member pointed out that the Commons proceedings against Bacon 'did depend wholly' on the testimony of two Members of the Lower House, Coke quickly reversed his position. Realizing (as White noted) that any legal barrier he erected against meeting their demand 'would almost certainly prevent the Lords from getting the kind of evidence that they would require to convict Bacon', Coke now declared that, although Members could not be compelled to testify on oath, they could do so if they chose, and he invited them to 'offer themselves' to be sworn.[38]

This was on 16 March. On Saturday, 17 March, Coke's justification of single witnesses dispelled the scruples of the House. Heneage Finch's protest that by presenting Bacon's case to the Lords 'we do in a sort accuse him, nay judge him' was set aside, as also Secretary Calvert's proposal that they should appeal to the King – the last thing Bacon's accusers could wish for. Another Member provided the formula: 'if it be gold, we should have no fear to try it,' and it was agreed that the charges should be transmitted to the Lords at their next sitting, on 19 March.[39] But in what form? The manner of presentation, as Coke realized, would determine the Lords' response. If they were sent as a case already proved before the Grand Committee for Courts, the way would be clear for the Lords to take over their judicial functions without delay; if on the other hand they sent in a mere relation of the existence of these charges, the process of inquiry would take much longer, and there might be occasion for the King to intervene.

A debate ensued. Coke and Phelips wanted the charges transmitted 'with a favourable construction' – favourable, that is, to the petitioners' claims. Sackville insisted that if, notwithstanding his objections, it was resolved to send the accusation to the Lords, it should be presented 'without any prejudicial opinion, to be weighed in the balance by their Lordships' judgements'. Even Noy, conscious of the thinness of the evidence, thought the matter should be delivered 'not as a thing certain, as we did in Sir Giles Mompesson's case, but as an information'. It was so agreed, in principle. But when the heads of the accusation were duly drawn up in writing by Phelips, Coke, Noy and Digges, they were presented with so much confidence that it was in effect little short of an instruction to the Lords. 'In their search of abuses of courts, they have found abuses in certain eminent persons, for which they desire a conference, that such a course may be taken for the redress thereof, as shall stand with the order and dignity of a Parliament.' The choice of time and place of the conference, and the number of committee were all they 'humbly' left to the Lords.[40] Coke's victory, as Zaller noted, 'was in that crucial intangible'.[41] Another flick of the finger.

Having thus definitively influenced the submission of the Commons to the Upper House by its presentation, Phelips deliberately defeated by its timing a project the King had prepared over the week-end. It was a project which, by entrusting the investigations to a more competent body of judges than the House of Lords, might have ensured Bacon a fair trial. On the morning of 19 March, James sent a message to the Commons through Secretary Calvert. Unwilling, he said, that such grave accusations 'should lie long on so great a person', in order to expedite examinations of the proofs, he offered to appoint a commission consisting of six Members of the House of Lords and twelve Members of the Commons, to be chosen among themselves, who could examine the Chancellor on oath. If the Commons agreed, he would put the proposal before the Lords, and the inquiry could be carried out during the Easter recess.[42]

James nearly carried his point. One after the other the most respected Members – Wentworth, Alford, Sir James Perrot (a son of the Lord Deputy of Ireland) – 'approved the course' and 'advised for the commissioners'.[43] Coke, as Zaller observed, was appalled. He saw at once that this commission would mean that Parliament, instead of asserting its own right to try Bacon, would be allowed only a temporary power to investigate. The King would give final judgment himself, and a deadly blow would be struck 'at the yet unfledged judicial power of the Lords, without which Coke's grandiose plan for the High Court of Parliament was a broken dream'.[44] A flick of his finger was sufficient. 'We should take heed', said Coke, 'the commission did not hinder the manner of our parliamentary proceedings.' At Coke's suggestion the Commons requested Calvert to thank the King for his gracious message and ask for 'the like message' to be sent to the Lords, that they might have a conference about it.

Coke was well aware that nothing would make the Lords give up the new-found dignity he had bestowed on them with their revived power of jurisdiction. They might, however, have adopted the King's proposal if the Commons had passed it before they received official notice of the case. No doubt with this possibility in mind, Wentworth urged that the House should delay its proceedings against Bacon until the question of the commission had been settled. All we have of Coke's masterly touch this time is the one word: *contra*.[45] And to avoid any further hitch, Phelips promptly went over to the Upper House to deliver the Commons' own message, whereby the Lords would be confirmed in their new status. No more was heard of the commission. The King could have pressed his point, but once again he took the short-term view. Bacon was regretted, but he was expendable, and the precedent of impeachment did not seem so dangerous at that point as the possibility of alienating Parliament, with the wars in Germany looming. His decision to abandon the temporary commission might well have been, thought Zaller, 'the most important single decision ever made by King James'.[46] It was fatal to Bacon.

Coke on the other hand had every reason to be satisfied, for with this last move he had completed his grand design for Parliament. He had achieved this, as White pointed out, with the least possible exertion, in three main steps. By attacking the referees he had first discredited the Chancellor, thus paving the way for further attacks not normally countenanced against so great a personage. By justifying the proceedings against Mompesson he had laid the legal basis for Bacon's trial. And now he had finally persuaded the Commons to ignore James's proposal for a royal parliamentary commission to try the Chancellor. There had been no need for him to play the vociferous part he so much enjoyed – and was soon to enjoy again.[47]

13

Act II: The Lords Join in the Hunt

The Lords undertook the task entrusted to them, as Macaulay put it, 'with laudable alacrity'.[1] They heard Phelips's presentation of the charges against Bacon on the morning of 19 March. By the afternoon they were already setting up committees and swearing in witnesses. Impeachment, as Russell observed, put the Lords at the centre of the stage, which is where at this particular juncture they wanted to be.[2] The older peers had been suffering in their pride from James's practice of granting titles to his personal retainers and favourites, and of late to almost anyone who could afford to pay cash for the title, so that the peerage had nearly doubled since his accession. No better outlet could be found for their anger and frustration at having to give precedence to new-made lords than their heightened status as judges with a mission to purge the Commonwealth of corruption. Hostility to Buckingham, that great dispenser of new titles, could not be expressed directly, but it could find vent in punishing a plausible substitute, and that substitute had now been delivered to them, ready for the kill.

As we have seen, the leaders of the Upper House were in close touch with the Commons, and Southampton, father-in-law of Sir Edwin Sandys and at daggers drawn with the favourite, was not only fully informed about the Commons' attack on Buckingham's most eminent follower; he was in all likelihood one of its chief instigators. In his efforts to bring down his impregnable opponent, he had been doing precisely what Bacon had so strongly warned the new Parliament against: stirring up grievances to serve personal aims.[3] Declaring now that he would 'deal with the Lord Chancellor as with his best friend', Southampton took the lead in investigating the charges and examining the witnesses, and became the most active among the peers castigating the fallen Chancellor. Even his sympathetic biographer A. L. Rowse cannot acquit him of personal animus in these activities.[4]

When the accusations against him emerged from out of the secrecy of the Commons (whose resolutions no man could repeat outside on pain of committal to the Tower) into the daylight of the House of Lords, Bacon, though still in ignorance of their content, was 'much comforted'. So said Buckingham, who despite sundry betrayals had twice visited his sick protégé.[5] Although beginning to realize that appearances were against him, Bacon looked for justice from his peers, and he addressed them with the confidence of a man who has nothing to hide. Begging them to maintain him in their good opinions 'without prejudice, until my cause be heard', he asked firstly for time to consult his counsel (whose part would be small, for he would 'not trick up innocency with cavillations, but plainly and ingenuously declare what I know or remember'); and secondly to be allowed to cross-examine the witnesses against him, to produce his own, for 'discovery of truth', and to answer the charges severally. Finally he expressed the hope that if any more petitions were forthcoming – as clearly they would be, now that every embittered loser of a suit was encouraged to join the fray – the Lords would not allow themselves to be influenced by a few petitions 'against a judge that makes two thousand decrees and orders in a year', not to speak of 'the courses that have been taken for hunting out complaints against me'.[6]

The Lords sent back a courteous but unhelpful answer. They would be very glad if he would clear his honour, and prayed him to provide for his defence. Bacon had every intention of doing so, but what was he to prepare it against? Far from learning whether he might cross-examine the witnesses, he did not even know what they had deposed against him, since copies of the petitions, asked for by his secretary, had been refused.[7] And he had no idea at all what to expect of a judicial proceeding without precedent in his time, or of a body as unpractised in the law and as ill-qualified to conduct a political trial as were the Lords.

In fact the investigation, carried out by three committees during the Easter recess (16 March to 17 April), was loaded against Bacon. The committees were instructed to ask each witness whether he had given, or advised to be given, or known of anyone who had given (or intended or contracted to give) any gratuity to the Lord Chancellor, his friends or his servants, it being specially ordered that 'no witnesses were to be examined what they received themselves, but only what bribes were given to the Lord Chancellor.'[8] In other words, anyone who had ever heard of an attempt to give a gratuity to any servant of the Chancellor's was invited to say so, with a promise of complete amnesty. Mandeville and Montgomery opposed this procedure, but they were overborne. And when one lord pointed out that, if a decree in Chancery could be reversed when a witness had shown that it had been obtained by bribery, some who had obtained a favourable decree might hesitate to speak, it was decided that no deposition against Bacon was to be used in any other cause; which meant that witnesses of all descriptions might come forward to accuse him without fear of any consequence to themselves.[9]

This decision, as Russell concluded, probably sealed Bacon's fate. But it has one advantage for his historians today: under so watertight a system for hunting out accusations there was little chance of any questionable act of the Chancellor's escaping detection. We know the worst of the case against Bacon, and we may be certain that Macaulay was mistaken in assuming that he received 'very much more than was proved at his trial' – a postulation based on Macaulay's ineradicable conviction that Bacon's principal activity as Chancellor was to practise corruption on a large scale, assisted by a team of agents 'looking out in different quarters for prey'.[10]

Following Coke's lead, the Lords had taken for granted that they were investigating bribes. Yet most of them certainly knew that no judge, from the Chancellor down, could maintain the standard of living required of him on his nominal salary, plus the modest fees laid down for particular services, and that judges lived principally on the gratuities willingly offered to them, after justice had been done. In the reign of James there was no civil list. All high officials such as the Lord Treasurer, the Master of the Wards or the Secretary of State were paid official fees which bore no relation to their responsibilities or to their status. In order to fill this gap, it had long been the custom to reward them for their trouble and to retain their goodwill with presents of undefined amounts; indeed some complained unashamedly if a client failed to do so. Crown judges were not paid by the state, and they depended almost entirely on the income they derived from the hearing of private causes.[11] Although Coke, as Chief Justice of the Common Pleas, earned no more than £100 a year, he owed his huge fortune to the clients who brought in their suits and to the sale of offices within his gift. As Attorney General, Bacon received £81 in fees and allowances, but, as he told the King when proposing to leave it, the place was worth £6,000 to him. His emoluments as Lord Chancellor amounted to £918, whereas his annual income from all sources during that period (which will be looked into below) has been estimated at between £9,000 and £10,000, a sum that would not be considered excessive for a Lord Chancellor of the Reign. No wonder that when Ellesmere died, a hopeful candidate offered £30,000 for the Chancellorship.[12]

The judges' practice of receiving gifts from suitors at the New Year, and, originally, even before their causes were heard, was a long-standing one. It had existed as an honorary perquisite ever since kings themselves had stopped taking money for the purchase of writs to sue in their courts.[13] In earlier centuries judges had been paid for delaying judicial proceedings, or to expedite a process, and in some cases the litigants offered a part of what they were to recover to the Crown.[14] For some time past, presents had no longer been considered acceptable until after the suit was closed, but only in rare cases did a judge refuse such gifts, and if he did, he was cited as an exception. Sir Thomas More's first biographer described him as an exemplary judge, 'even to the rejection of gratuities after judgement given'. Bacon himself recalled with admiration the story of the two silver flagons offered to More, who had promptly returned them to his client, filled with the best wine in his cellar.[15] And when, a few days before the Chancellor received his sentence, James announced in Parliament that henceforth no money should 'be given for the hearing of any cause' – a proposal Bacon looked on with so much favour that, he said, he was glad to be 'the anvil on which these good effects are wrought' – the royal behest was seen as an innovation.[16]

Why then was Bacon prosecuted for doing what everyone did? Or more exactly, how could this have been made the ostensible reason for his overthrow? There was just that degree of ambiguity in the system which made it possible for Parliament to use it as a political weapon. However universally indulged in, the practice was not publicly admitted. As with the presents accepted in the Court of Wards, which have been examined in depth by Joel Hurstfield, it was 'a time-honoured custom to deny that any such money was being received'.[17] It took a transparently honest man like Alford to remind the Commons that presents had been entered openly in previous chancellors' accounts. He was right, and they appeared also in those of the boroughs and towns where justices rode circuit.[18] But Alford's reminder to the Commons was not followed up in the Lords. Like the charges against the referees, it would have been dangerous to pursue it too far, since the entire judiciary was involved.

This ambiguous attitude to a practice which prevailed in all the law courts was compounded by the fact that in the second decade of James's reign, with the escalation of Court consumption, the increase in the number of private causes and in the size of gratuities, and above all with the breakdown of the system of royal patronage now that all the strings were concentrated in Buckingham's hands, a need for change had begun to be felt. Bacon was among those who saw this need, and he had himself attempted a number of reforms.[19] Thus Coke was, in effect, turning a general desire for amendments in the system into an accusation against a reforming Chancellor. But he could only do this because, in a system as yet unreformed, the excessive margin between appearances and accepted practice left so much room for entrapment. Rarely was any official so guarded as never to overstep the limits recognized in his day. And who could tell exactly what those limits were? There was no clear frontier beween a compliment or an acceptable payment for services rendered, and an over-lavish present given with the unspoken intention of obtaining a favorable decree. It depended in each case on the generosity of the suitor and the feeling of the judge. We need not be surprised, therefore, that the majority of the Lords, even when aware of the political overtones, should have failed to distinguish between a gratuity and a bribe. How were they to be bothered with the ins and outs of a judge's feeling?

The test used in the Star Chamber, where charges of corruption were tried by jurists more experienced than the Lords, was based on two criteria: whether a gratuity, or the promise of one, had been accepted *pendente lite* (while the cause was still ongoing), and whether it had clearly been employed as an inducement to breach of duty. In order to prove bribery, the accusation must show that there had been a contract between the giver and the receiver. Suffolk was accused in the Star Chamber not of taking money, but of taking it as a condition of despatching a particular transaction, and we saw Heneage Finch insisting that the onus of proving undue influence rested with the prosecution.[20] Chamberlain also, referring a month later to the indictment of a much more corrupt judge than Bacon, remarked that it would be hard to condemn him for gratuities 'if they prove not contracting'.[21]

In the notes he jotted down when preparing for an interview with the King, Bacon denied ever having any part in 'bargain or contract for reward to pervert justice'. Of this 'degree of bribery' he declared himself 'to be as innocent as any babe upon St Innocent's day'. At no stage was he to confess to it, nor was it ever proved against him. For the charge of receiving money when the cause was ended, he 'conceived it to be no fault', though ready to stand corrected, 'for I had rather be a briber than a defender of bribes'. As for that other form of corruption, 'where the Judge conceives the cause to be at an end by the information of the party, or otherwise, and useth not such diligence as he ought to enquire of it', he suspected he was 'in some particulars faulty'. 'At new-years tides and likewise at my first coming in,' he noted, 'I did not so precisely as perhaps I ought examine whether those that presented me had causes before me, yea or no.'[22]

It would have taken a good deal more attention to appearances than Bacon could spare to avoid this particular form of corruption. A Chancellor who depended on gratuities was in a cleft stick, for when was he to receive them if not at the conclusion of a hearing?[23] But many a suit dragged on from Chancellor to Chancellor – Egerton kept four successive Lord Keepers busy – and the officers concerned might all be dead before it ended. When, over the years, suits were unexpectedly reopened over some insignificant point, when a litigant juggled with two or three suits in Chancery, or when payments for past services on conclusion of one suit turned out to have been made for future services on another, as yet unheard of, how could any judge catch up? Heneage Finch had put his finger on the wound with his question: 'Who keeps a register in his heart of all causes, nay, who can, amongst such a multitude?' In order to gain some idea of these difficulties it is worth pausing over the next petition

presented in the Commons, demanding an inquiry into Bacon's acceptance of £300 from one Lady Wharton, even if her story, gleaned by
Gardiner out of the records of her interminable litigation, can only be
sketched out here. One of the thousands of unsettled causes inherited by
Bacon from his predecessor, it was still going on when the 1621 Parliament
opened. It is of particular interest to us because it is probably the case in
which appearances are most clearly against him.[24]

Lady Dorothy Wharton, already remembered by Ellesmere twenty
years earlier for her 'old and vexatious suits', had been married three
times. She had long been at law with the three daughters (by his first
wife) of her second husband, Sir Francis Willoughby, over the considerable property he had left her. The three equally litigious heirs-at-law had
each brought an action against her, and when Bacon took over in March
1617, these actions formed an inextricable tangle of actions and cross-
actions between the various parties. Later that same year he succeeded in
untying the knots and arbitrating between them, but the case was
brought up again when, in the spring of 1618, a discontented servant of
Lady Wharton's, rummaging among her papers, found a deed drawn up
by Willoughby long before he married her, by which he had made over
to his daughters a large part of the land he was later to bequeath to his
wife. As an act of revenge towards his mistress, the servant informed the
daughters, and their husbands now began a suit to compel Lady Wharton
to surrender the deed, while she herself filed a cross-bill to obtain a
judicial declaration of its invalidity.

On 30 October 1619, having found sufficient evidence that after his
second marriage Willoughby no longer considered the deed binding upon
him, Bacon delivered judgement that it should be looked on as having
been revoked. This decree in effect settled the question, and Bacon was
not to change it. There being now no grounds for compelling Lady
Wharton to surrender the deed, it was left in her possession, and by
mutual agreement of the lawyers (though reached with some difficulty)
the bills of both parties were dismissed. Bacon directed the Registrar,
John Churchill, to see that in entering the order in the Chancery books
the reasons against its validity were clearly stated. Churchill, however,
unwilling to part from a client who had subsidized a whole generation of
lawyers, persuaded Lady Wharton to go back on the withdrawal of her
bill and demand a formal condemnation of the deed. Her opponents,
equally keen to reopen the case, had made the same request. Accordingly, on 9 December 1619, powerless to oppose their united demand,
Bacon withdrew the order for dismissal of the suits, allowing the order by
which he had granted Lady Wharton custody of the disputed deed to
stand until the following term, when a final decision could be made.

Some time afterwards, Lady Wharton, unable to let well alone and
fearing some sinister move on the part of her adversaries, decided to ask

for a new decision confirming her custody of the invalid deed. So keen was she to persuade the Chancellor, who was in any case just about to deliver his final decree, that on 26 June, on the advice of her attorney (Richard Keeling, an ex-servant of Bacon's), she put £100 in a purse 'of her own making' and, accompanied by the attorney and his own servant, drove to York House. Bacon apparently welcomed her: 'Who could refuse a purse of so fair a lady's working?' he said, and graciously accepted it, in the presence of both attorney and servant, along with her promise to bring him a further £200 as soon as the decree was passed.[25] Three days later the final arguments were heard; and he awarded judgement exactly as he had intended, formally adhering to the decision he had made nine months before. The decree was entered in the books, and Lady Wharton delivered the £200, which Bacon must have looked on as a well-earned fee, however irregularly he might have received the first instalment.

He was later to confess that he had taken this money *'pendente lite*, but yet, I have a vehement suspicion that there was some shuffling between Mr Shute and the Registrar in entering some orders, which I afterwards did distaste'.[26] He was right to see a connection here, for this shuffling, soon to be disclosed as a major fraud combined by Robert Shute, Lady Wharton's dishonest lawyer, with Bacon's dishonest Registrar, involved a reopening of the case, which necessarily cast an unfavourable light on Bacon's acceptance of the £300. When examining an appeal in Chancery by Lady Wharton to stop her opponents from renewing their suit once again, at common law, Bacon discovered that his principal decision – the decree he had pronounced on 30 October 1619 – had been drawn up in the Order Book 'contrary to the true intent and meaning of the Lord Chancellor'. Accordingly, on 12 March 1621 he decided that the decree had 'not been duly obtained' and that there was nothing to prevent the Willoughbys from reopening their case.

Although we do not know exactly in what way the order entered in the books differed from what Bacon had laid down, it was clear that Lady Wharton, having tried beforehand to bribe the Lord Chancellor to pronounce in accordance with her wishes, had afterwards successfully bribed his registrar to alter his decree in her favour.[27] Silence would have become her at this point. Instead she loudly complained of having spent £300 on the Lord Chancellor in vain. Bacon, by now in the throes of the campaign against monopolies, must have been exasperated by a client who had already wasted too much of Chancery's precious time – the time his *Ordinances* had been drawn up to save. Presumably in hopes of calming her down, he now unwisely reminded her that reopening a hearing did not necessarily imply defeat. After which, a week later, the Willoughbys, who at this point might be forgiven for suspecting that the whole affair was a swindle devised between Lady Wharton and the

Chancellor, hearing of Aubrey's and Egerton's depositions, brought their own request to Parliament for a reversal of the decree against them.[28]

Coke, as Gardiner noticed, was delighted. 'A corrupt judge', he exclaimed, 'was the grievance of grievances.'[29] A committee, led by himself, was appointed to examine the witnesses for Lady Wharton. But when Phelips, reporting in the Commons on the examination of Churchill, 'conducing to the discovery of corruption in the Lord Chancellor', summed up the case, Sir Thomas Meautys protested.[30] He had long been 'an observer of my lord's proceedings' and watched him sow 'a good seed of justice'. It was the envious man who had sown these tares. 'Touching the persons that inform, I would intreat this honourable House to consider that Keeling is a common solicitor, to say no more of him; Churchill a guilty registrar by his own confession. I know that fear of punishment, and hopes of lessening it, may make them say much, yea, more than is the truth.' ('But that a principal member of this house hath undertaken for his honesty,' said Meautys according to another reporter, 'I might decipher him.')[31] Be that as it may, the case, as Phelips presented it to the Lords next day, 22 March, looked black against Bacon. 'For a bribe of £300 his Lordship decreed the cause for her; and then hearing that Wood and the other defendants complained thereof to the Commons, his Lordship sent for them and damned that decree as unduly gotten; and when the Lady Wharton began to complain thereof, his Lordship sent for her also, and promised her redress, saying "that decree is not yet ended".'[32]

This is what some Members, convinced in advance of Bacon's guilt, were now ready to believe on the basis of Churchill's depositions; but the depositions were a tissue of lies. Bent above all on distracting attention from the forgeries he had perpetrated on this and other occasions, Churchill made out that the Chancellor's unexceptionable decisions had been made under the influence of Lady Wharton. In particular, he represented Bacon's agreement to rescind his order for the dismissal of the suits of both parties, given on 9 December 1619, as a special favour to her.[33] But, as Gardiner pointed out, the wording of this new order (one Churchill was not likely to have forged against himself) proves the exact contrary: it was given upon a petition made on behalf of the co-heirs of Willoughby.[34]

The charge 'that Bacon knowingly and corruptly sold or delayed justice falls entirely to the ground' – so Gardiner concluded his thorough and impartial study of Wharton versus Willoughby. Whatever Churchill might say, it was not Bacon's fault that the whole case had not been closed when, in October 1619, he gave what he considered his final decree, satisfying the lawyers on both sides – though not his foolish and quarrelsome client. His fault, which he was to acknowledge as such, was that, knowing it would not influence his judgement either way, he took the embroidered purse offered him a few days before he gave final judgement on 19 June. It did not influence him. He looked on this decree as a pure formality. It did not even expedite Lady Wharton's suit (which would not then have been looked on as corrupt) since already on 1 June, weeks before her visit, he had fixed the date on which he was to give the decree.[35] His real failing as a judge was that in openly accepting money, which he thought his due, before he had decreed, he was giving the worst possible example to the many unscrupulous suitors who thronged around Chancery, as well as exposing himself to the worst possible construction of his motives.[36] As a comment on the value of Bacon's judgement in this case, it is interesting to note that on 13 March 1624, three years after his fall, a bill was brought in 'to avoid a decree procured indirectly and by corruption between the Lord and Lady Wharton and Edward Willoughby, Esq.' If passed, it would have meant the reversal of a decree given by Bacon, on the ground of undue influence, but it was not passed.[37]

After hearing the petitioners in Lady Wharton's cause, the Lords listened to two further complaints against the Chancellor (one of which was disallowed), and to a long list of Bacon's evil doings, drawn up by Churchill, which had been transmitted to them by the Commons.[38] Out of the twenty-two valid cases that were to be brought in against Bacon, four only had been volunteered; the rest were hunted out in the Commons committees, principally on the strength of Churchill's delations. No one could have been better placed to make them than a registrar privy to the entry of all orders, real or invented, and the payment of all fees and fines; no one was better acquainted with whoever had been duped, fooled or exposed, and with whoever might bear a grudge against the Chancellor – and, in particular, with his more vulnerable servants. Others were no doubt at work behind the scenes. Among them we know of one John Wrenham, who three years before had charged Bacon with ruling unfairly against him and had been condemned, in Bacon's absence, for vilifying justice, but reprieved, through Bacon's intervention, and, as Carteret pointed out, was now industriously searching for petitioners against the Chancellor and 'egging them on'.[39]

As the charges came in, Bacon's purgatory closed around him. 'Many indignities are said and done against him,' wrote Chamberlain, better disposed towards the Chancellor in adversity than when he had prospered, 'and divers libels cast abroad to his disgrace not worth the repeating, as savouring too much of malice and scurrility. God send him patience, and that he may make the best use of his affliction.'[40] God was to do so, but in the meantime Bacon wrote to the King to sound 'his Majesty's heart towards me'. Entering into himself, he could not see what he had done to deserve what was clearly a well-orchestrated political attack. 'Whence should this be?' He had been 'no author of immoderate counsel', preferring always gentle ways; no oppressor of the people, not haughty or intolerant or harsh – attitudes which normally provoke retaliation. 'And for the briberies and gifts wherewith I am charged,' he added, 'when the book of hearts shall be opened, I hope I shall not be found to have the troubled fountain of a corrupt heart in a depraved habit of taking rewards to pervert justice; howsoever I may be frail, and partake of the abuses of the times.'[41]

He would answer the charges against him candidly, he told the King, speaking 'the language that my heart speaketh to me', and 'praying God to give me the grace to see to the bottom of my faults'. In this spirit he set to work to defend himself, not against corruption, but against 'the likeness of corruption', resorting (as Coke had done to revalidate the process of impeachment) to precedent.[42] He looked through the records for cases of eminent judges impeached in Parliament during the reigns of Richard II and Edward III, which might bear some resemblance to his own.[43] But before defending himself in the Lords, he must speak with the King. The time had come to ask for an interview.

14

Act III: Surrender and Sentence

What happened between Bacon and the King on 16 April, when that interview was granted, is possibly the most contested episode in Bacon's life story. By 20 April he had decided to abandon the defence he had prepared, and to this day, despite an abundance of surmise, it is not known for certain why he did so. Yet precisely because nothing was proved against him, ever since he took this momentous step he has been looked on as guilty of all the charges brought in against him. In abandoning his defence he was in effect, as Zaller put it, sentencing himself.[1] Two extreme views have been advanced to explain his act. Macaulay, carried away by his own rhetoric into pure fiction, described Bacon working 'on the feeble mind of the King' and employing all his address to persuade him that he should 'dissolve a Parliament which is universally allowed to have been one of the best Parliaments that ever sat'. The King, he said, 'very properly' refused to do so, and it is only when Bacon found that 'all his eloquence and address were employed in vain' that he took his momentous decision. Other historians, with slightly more foundation for their conjectures, have maintained that during this interview the King commanded the Chancellor to give up his defence.[2]

Both versions are wrong. Yet information is not lacking about what was said on this occasion. There are five documents in all: two memoranda by Bacon setting forth what he planned to tell the King; the Lord Treasurer Mandeville's report to the Lords the day after the interview, showing that Bacon spoke as he had intended; and two letters written by Bacon to the King in the next few days, recalling their conversation. In none of this is there any mention of a royal command. As for Bacon's alleged request that James should dissolve Parliament – the last thing he could have wished for a session he looked on as his own brain-child – the report on his interview, in which he begged James to insist that the Lords should give him a fair trial, gives the lie to it, as does his letter of 21 April:

Your Majesty can bear me witness that at my last so comfortable access I did not so much as move your Majesty, by your absolute power of pardon or otherwise, to take my cause into your hands and to interpose between the sentence of the House; and according to mine own desire your Majesty left it to the sentence of the House, and so was reported by my Lord Treasurer.[3]

It was on the previous day, after writing his first grateful letter to the King, that Bacon had changed his mind. In that letter, as during his interview, he had reaffirmed his plans for his defence and once again asked for details of the charges against him, of which, though they had been discussed behind his back for over a month, he had as yet no precise knowledge. But on that same 20 April a friend brought him an unofficial copy of the examinations read in the House of Lords the day before.[4] After this he had only one request to make: that, subject to his 'general submission', the King, 'with the good liking of the House', would save him from any worse sentence than losing the Seal; in order, he said, that he 'be not precipitated altogether'. Its very taking away would be 'as much example for these four hundred years as any further severing'; and precipitation enough, if we recall that the Chancellor presided over the Star Chamber, Chancery and the House of Lords and in the whole country stood second only to the King.

Spedding is probably right in supposing that when Bacon saw the heads of the accusation against him – twenty-eight of them, in twenty-two different suits, with forty-one witnesses arrayed against him – he realized that he could not win. Recognizing no doubt that by his own negligence he had provided a handle to his ill-wishers; seeing also that his most innocent actions had been bent and twisted into crimes; glimpsing the murky source from which these accusations had sprung; and realizing that after all he would have no chance of querying the evidence – collected in committees where he could not appear and passed by the Lords, as Spedding put it, 'undisputed; unexamined, unexplained' – Bacon, who had been very ill over the past few weeks, not surprisingly lost his courage. The tone as well as the content of the charges must have shown him clearly that he was to be tried, not by the highest justice of the realm, but by a tribunal of popular opinion.

This is when he wrote his will, leaving his name 'to the next ages and foreign nations', and the mournful psalm in which Chamberlain saw 'little or nothing of true humiliation'; fairly enough, because here too Bacon was asking his Lord, in the same terms as he had asked his King, what he had done to bring down this clearly political storm on his head, without which his frailties as a judge would have been negligible. As he had reminded James a month earlier of the moderate counsel he had always offered him, so did he now remind the Lord that before all other things he had worked for the unity of his Church; that 'the state and bread of the poor' had been precious in his eyes; that he had 'hated all cruelty of heart' and 'procured the good of all men'. Finally, 'if any had been my enemies, I thought not of them'. And there, in all probability, lay his mistake.[5] Generally indulgent towards any aggressors who (like Wrenham) aimed at him personally, Bacon had paid little attention to the doings of people who might nurse a grievance against him. A clear-sighted counsellor for state affairs, Bacon had none of the qualities of the 'politique', of whose 'corrupt arts' he had written scathingly on more than one occasion.[6] 'The gracious talent of thy gifts and graces,' he now confessed, not for the first time, 'I have misspent it in things for which I was least fit.'[7] Perhaps he was less fit for a statesman's life than for the things he was now turning his mind to again – a history of England and a digest of its laws – but least of all was he a match for political intrigue, whether manipulated by the ablest lawyer in the land or the most insidious registrar; still less when, as now, these two had joined forces. Bacon must have felt the full impact of those forces when he learnt the extent of the claims that had been piled up against him. Yet the shock, while it probably tipped the balance for him, may not have been the principal source of his discouragement.

Had there not been another factor, indignation might have taken over. He could have reacted as Cranfield was to do three years later, when, subjected to a similar political attack – similarly disguised as a charge of corruption and extortion – he fought back with all his aggressive might. Cranfield defended himself, wrote Chamberlain at the time, 'very dili-gently' against the 'many foul matters that came upon him daily', leaving no stone unturned that might serve his turn, devising 'tricks to prolong the business', importuning the Upper House with continual petitions, and 'insolently and impudently outfacing manifest truths'. It was, Chamber-lain remarked, the second example seen in a long time 'of a man of his eminent quality called in question, and yet this differed from the first in that they had then *confitentem* and now *confidentem reum*' – then a peni-tent, now a self-confident man in the dock.[8] Of course Cranfield was harsh by temperament, while Bacon preferred the 'gentle ways'. On 20 April, however, something else had happened to drain his confidence: James had again spoken in Parliament, and something he said must have finally convinced his old servant of what he had known in his heart for some time, that he no longer had the King's support.

Once again James had said that he would not protect 'bribing judges'. On 10 March he had declared that if his Chancellor could not justify himself as a referee, he was not worthy of his place. On the 26th, the day before the Lords celebrated their new role with a savage sentence on Mompesson, he had compared the state to coppices 'inwardly eaten and spoiled' and urged Parliament not to spare the guilty – those who grieved and vexed his people with 'secret corruption, projecture [meaning monopolies], bills of conformity and such like courses' (the monopolies an allusion, the bills a clear pointer to Bacon). Now on 20 April he dwelt 'with delight and confidence' on 'the happiest Parliament that ever was'; and clearly, the happy Parliament which had been Bacon's highest hope was to exclude him, and him alone. 'Punish so corrupt judges that you dishonour not good judges,' said James, 'go on bravely and soundly, and see whether I'll be backward'; the Parliament should not be 'a doomsday so much as a jubilee'.[9] Bacon's doomsday, in other words, would be the King's jubilee. This elated announcement, coming on top of the earlier speeches – and now apparently justified by the list of Bacon's own mostly forgotten actions, which, though committed without corrupt intent, he could not well defend – must surely have been the last drop in his cup. It was a confirmation that he had been cast adrift as the scapegoat, not merely by Parliament and by Coke and his allies, but by the King to whom alone he had so far been answerable, and by the favourite he had tried his best to advise. Nor would it have helped if what Buckingham was now saying about his old mentor, in a new access of virtue, had reached Bacon's ears: he 'regretted not so much his ruin, for that was richly deserved, as his bad conduct'.[10]

It is generally accepted today that Bacon fell because the King allowed it. The revival of old procedures of impeachment in an entirely new context, which aroused serious misgivings in many Members of the Commons, could never have taken place without James's consent. Bacon fell – and Mandeville, the more strongly attacked of the two, survived – because, as Russell concluded, the King so willed.[11] In the last analysis, and whatever their deservings, no Crown servant was ousted unless he had lost the King's favour; which of course, during the reign of Buckingham over James, meant that of the favourite. And if a man's downfall was sought, corruption was invariably found in him, often by means of his own men (as with Suffolk, who had been denounced by a servant caught stealing in his house).[12] When 'from private appetite it is resolved that a creature shall be sacrificed,' wrote Bacon's early editor and biographer, Archbishop Tenison, 'it is easy to pick up sticks enough from any thicket whither it has strayed, to make a fire to offer it with.'[13]

Suffolk fell, not because he had used the Treasury as if it were his own private bank account, and no business could be done there without enormous bribes, but because the political hour of the Howard clan had struck; just as James's previous favourite, the Earl of Somerset, had fallen, not because he was accessory to murder, but because his enemies had found a charming young man to succeed him. Others, probably as guilty but less politically exposed, never came to trial.[14] And who knows what would have happened to Cecil when he lost the King's favour, if he had not died in good time? Only Coke, born to frustrate James, baffled every effort to pull him down. When at the end of the session the King finally sent him to the Tower, his house was searched from top to bottom, but he failed to provide the usual handle, and an old debt of his father-in-law's had to be exhumed to keep him locked up.

Bacon was not so naive as his emotional protestations to his Maker and to his King might lead us to suppose. His real, if unspoken question to James, underlying the others, was 'have I deserved that you should let this happen?' He was never to express his sense of betrayal by the King and Buckingham in so many words, even to himself, except for a few hints that would crop up here and there, between the lines of some unsent draft. But his interview with James cannot have been quite as 'comfortable' as he told the King in his first grateful letter, if he lost his confidence so soon afterwards. We have one other piece of evidence, both good and bad, on this subject, from a contemporary: good, because its author, Thomas Bushell, who is recalling the occasion (overcome with remorse for having, like so many of the Chancellor's protégés, abandoned him on his fall), was a scholar who waited on Bacon and, said Aubrey, was 'much loved' by him; and bad, because Bushell, the eccentric adventurer – as he had become by the time he was over fifty – is describing events which had taken place when he was eighteen, in order to boost his own project for an Academy of Science by fathering the idea on Bacon. We shall hear more of his dealings with his master below.[15]

Bushell's suggestion that the King gave Bacon 'positive advice' – in other words, commanded him to abandon his defence – though it convinced the eighteenth century, has rightly been discredited since then. He has earned the distrust of most historians, but not all the evidence of this picturesque character need be rejected out of hand. His paragraphs on the Chancellor's impeachment follow the facts quite closely, and since he was much under Bacon's influence at the time, it is perhaps not surprising that almost every sentence should have what Spedding once called 'the stamp of Bacon' upon it, as we may now see if we run though Bushell's principal statements.[16] For some days, he related, the complaints against his Lordship 'put the King to this query, whether he should permit the favourite of his affection, or the oracle of his Council to sink in his service'. Today it is generally believed that, faced with this dilemma, the King did, as Bushell put it, jettison his 'oracle'. James strongly advised Bacon, he wrote, 'to submit himself to his House of Peers, and, upon his princely word, he would then restore him again if, in their honours, they should not be sensible of his merits.'

Here again, the Chancellor's young protégé is close to the truth. Bacon had repeatedly received 'loving promises and hopes' from Buckingham – unasked for, as Bacon later reminded him. He was to set them down in full at the end of the year in a note for an interview he was expecting with the favourite:

> Your Lordship knoweth as well as I what promises you made me, and iterated them both by message and from your mouth, consisting of three things, the pardon of the whole sentence, some help for my debts, and an annual pension which your Lordship set at £2,000 as obtained, and £3,000 in hope.[17]

Restoration to favour (not at all improbable in those times), although not mentioned, may have been hinted at, to go by Bacon's own hints to the King in July about Demosthenes, Seneca and others, 'banished for divers corruptions' but 'recalled with honour'.[18] In all likelihood, those promises had been proffered when, in the early stages of the Lords' investigations, Bacon was lying ill, and the inconstant Buckingham had taken to visiting him almost daily – 'which', wrote Chamberlain, 'the world thinks is not without a mystery'.[19] Buckingham, having weathered the storm of monopolies by jettisoning his friend along with his relations (so the French Ambassador noted) was now doing all in his power to assist him, fancying perhaps that this would be for a time the best way to assist himself.[20] The King must have given some token renewal of those promises during Bacon's interview with him, for in another appeal at the end of 1622 Bacon reminded him of his 'gracious and pious promise' when he had admitted him 'in the height of his troubles' (there had been no other meeting since), namely, that he would not 'meddle with' Bacon's estate 'but to mend it'.[21] Aside from anything Bushell may have recalled, the mere fact that an offer was made at this time argues in favour of some kind of pressure, not necessarily explicit, exerted upon Bacon by the King.

To return to Bushell's pages: 'Now though my Lord saw his approaching ruin, and told his Majesty there was little hopes of mercy in a multitude' – a Baconian opinion which he could well have expressed in this crisis – 'such was his obedience to him from whom he had his being that he resolved his Majesty's will should be his only law.'[22] This was an attitude from which Bacon was never to swerve: 'clay in your Majesty's gracious hands', he had signed himself to James while still eagerly planning his defence, yet willing, even then, to give it up. 'Whatsoever the law of nature shall teach me to speak for my own preservation,' Bacon had also noted to tell the King, 'your Majesty will understand it to be in such sort as I do nevertheless depend wholly upon your will and pleasure.'[23] Whereupon, said Bushell, Bacon took his leave of the King, hoping 'that as he was the first, so he might be the last of his sacrifices'; a hope we shall soon find spelled out in his confession to the Lords.[24] The King, Bushell concluded,

> never restored that matchless Lord to his place, which made him then to wish the many years he had spent in state policy and law study had been solely devoted to true philosophy for (said he) the one, at the best, doth but comprehend man's frailty in its greatest

165

splendour, but the other, the mysterious knowledge of all things created in the six days' works.

Clearly, the man who wrote these lines had often heard his master's voice. And was not Bacon just then regretting that he had misspent his talent in things for which he was least fit?

There are other ways of influencing a devoted servant than the spoken command. Since Bushell echoes Bacon in so many respects, we might look again at the 'positive advice' he recalled James giving his master, that he should 'submit himself to the House of Peers'. Did Bushell not mean that same 'general submission' which Bacon soon afterwards told the King he would make in lieu of the defence he had originally planned: to 'put himself upon the mercy of the Lords only on such points as he could not answer clearly'? Who is to say Bacon was not acting on a hint he received from the King, along with those promises – a hint of which he had perhaps felt the full force only a few days later, when, after James had spoken in Parliament, he realized that royal sympathy did not imply support, something Bushell, in his turn, would be quick to gather by a word or gesture from the master who 'much loved him'.[25] Archbishop Tenison, though sceptical of the project he attributed to Bacon, saw no reason to doubt the testimony of this favoured servant, who was soon to bring Bacon the 'heavy news' of his condemnation from the Lords.[26]

If James did in fact discourage his Chancellor from defending himself, what were his reasons? Bacon's eighteenth-century biographer David Mallet, when explaining that the King's passion 'prevailed over his reason, and my Lord St Alban was made the scapegoat of Buckingham', suggested that Bacon was obliged to abandon his defence because, fearing he might make dangerous revelations, James 'would not hazard his appearing before the Lords to plead his own cause'.[27] A century later, with the same thought in mind, Lucy Aikin, a Whig historian usually hostile to Bacon, suggested that, 'had he not been restrained by a knowledge of what must have been the royal wish', the Chancellor could have palliated his offence by accusing others – with good cause; and, as late as 1981, another historian thought that in defending himself Bacon might have involuntarily disclosed skeletons which the King and his favourite preferred to keep out of sight.[28]

Bacon, however, was no Ralegh, whose dazzling self-justification on the scaffold had won his worst haters to side with him, and had frightened James; nor was Bacon likely to defend himself, as Yelverton was soon to do, with rash insinuations aimed at the favourite.[29] Lucy Aikin suggested that the Chancellor might still have found ways 'of extorting from the King some effectual pledge for his own return to power', and she provided her own explanation for his failure to do so. Lacking the boldness which he himself had indicated as 'the first, second and third requisite for public business', he was constitutionally unable to employ 'that "wisdom for a man's self" which, in theory, no man understood so well'.[30] In fact, the thought of what might come to light about the conditions prevailing in the courts of justice, once he began to defend his actions, could well have contributed to Bacon's decision to abstain. Like Chamberlain, he was aware that 'the eyes of Europe are now upon us and our Parliament'.[31] James, for his part, recalling Coke's hints at startling revelations to be expected from the trial of Somerset, might well have nursed private fears, and he would see no difficulty in imposing silence on a minister. Had he not obliged his Scottish Secretary, Lord Balmerino, to take on the authorship of his own ill-advised letter to the Pope, professing himself ready to become a Catholic, in hopes of securing Papal support for his claim to the English throne? After which, terrified 'of proving a knave', he had felt bound to hush up his blunder.[32]

For Macaulay, born in a different age, 'a man who, to please his patron solemnly declares himself guilty of corruption when he knows himself to be innocent' showed 'a degree of meanness and depravity' so loathsome that he acquitted even Bacon of it.[33] Bacon, on the other hand, living when the relations between monarch and subject had many overtones, looked on sacrifice to King and state as natural and honorable, and had actually preached it to the young Buckingham. (If the King 'commit an error and is loath to avow it, but excuses it upon his ministers, of which you are the first', you 'perhaps may be offered as a sacrifice to appease the multitude'.)[34] When Bacon saw himself as a sacrifice, it was not primarily to please a powerful patron, but, as he put it, 'for reformation sake'. He was on the King's side against himself, and would do nothing to spoil that happy union between Crown and Parliament which James had recently celebrated, and which he himself had so long worked for.[35] When Parliament met again after sentencing Bacon and, carried on a wave of success, made an attempt to bring down Buckingham – 'the only author of all grievances and oppressions whatever, for his private ends' – there was no high-placed scapegoat at hand to screen him from scandal (even if short-lived, since it was quickly suppressed).[36] 'As long as great men were in question, as in my case,' Bacon noted later, 'all things went sweetly for the King. But the second meeting, when no such thing was, the rack went higher.'[37]

Bacon's 'submissive letter' to the Lords, as Bushell described the message he himself delivered, soars high above the levels of political intrigue, and too high, some have thought, above those of his judicial guilt. The 'very strange entrance' with which he admitted introducing it, although sneered at by a critic in our time as inept, earned Gardiner's admiration. 'Even in his misery,' he said, 'Bacon's first thoughts were for his country.'[38] And to anyone familiar with Bacon's reforming spirit, his lines have the ring of truth.

For in the midst of a state of as great affliction as I think a mortal can endure (honour being above life) I shall begin by professing gladness in some things.

The first is, that hereafter the greatness of a judge or magistrate shall be no sanctuary or protection of guiltiness; which, in a few words, is the beginning of a golden world.

The next, that after this example, it is like that judges will fly from anything that is in the likeness of corruption (though it were at a great distance), as from a serpent; which tendeth to the purging of the courts of justice, and the reducing of them to their true honour and splendour.

And in these two points God is my witness that, though it be my fortune to be the anvil whereupon these good effects are beaten and wrought, I take no small comfort.[39]

Refraining, therefore, from all that a defence could extenuate 'in respect of the time or manner of the gift', or 'scruples touching the credit of witnesses', leaving these things 'to spring out' of the Lords' 'own noble thoughts and observation of the evidence', he submitted himself wholly to their pity and grace. He would seek of them nothing contrary to their 'honourable and worthy ends to introduce a reformation'. But still he entreated them, as he had James, to accept that his Majesty's taking the Seal from him, 'which is a great downfall', might serve as an expiation for his faults. Finally he hoped that it would be reserved for him alone, who had been first cast into 'the pool of Bethesda', to suffer, and that the matter might 'stay there and go no further'. ('As he was the first,' Bacon had said, 'so he might be the last of the King's sacrifices.')[40] Tenison referred his readers to these words of Bacon's as a pointer to the truth when he remarked that 'the great cause of his suffering is to some a secret'.[41]

The Lords, however, in their new role as judges, were not satisfied with a general confession. 'He is charged by the Commons with corruption,' said Southampton, 'and no word of confession of any corruption in his submission.' The difficulty was a technical one. Since no part of the case had been proved, Bacon's guilt could only be established if he pleaded guilty to all the articles of the charge, the details of which he had still not seen. The Lords could not vote on rumours, and the evidence amounted to little more. If guilty, let him say so, or defend himself at the bar, Suffolk exclaimed – not sorry, Spedding suggested, 'to reply in kind' for his own condemnation for corruption by Bacon two years earlier; although, as Coke said, Suffolk had 'escaped the better by his mean'.[42] Pembroke, however, insisted that they could not call the Great Seal in person to the bar. Yet if reformation was sought, the proceedings should be as public as possible. In the end it was decided to send Bacon a copy of the charges, without 'proofs' – that is, without the names of the witnesses – asking him to reply to them in detail.

In his full confession, handed in to the Lords on 30 April, Bacon replied to the twenty-eight articles of the accusation with a few factual lines on each one. The examinations of the witnesses are no longer available, but as usual it is Gardiner who made the most complete study of the charges, based on these declarations, as corroborated by the records of Chancery. Gardiner had 'learned by experience', he said, 'to place unreserved confidence in Bacon's truthfulness'.[43] Late twentieth-century evaluations by legal experts include one starting from the opposite premise – that Bacon was an inveterate liar – put forward in 1984 by J. T. Noonan, an author who in other respects shows little knowledge about Bacon, as well as an up-to-date study in 1986 by Clifford Hall, whose conclusions, after considerable further probing, differ little from Gardiner's.[44]

Gardiner concurred with Spedding and Dixon on one point: more than half the charges ought never to have been passed by the Lords. At least ten of them could be summarily excluded. They referred to legitimate payments made after the conclusion of the suits as –, for instance, a dozen buttons to the value of £50 after the cause was ended, for which Bacon nevertheless 'confessed and declared' that he had received money, two weeks, or some months, or he could not recall how long after he had given his decree. In four cases he had received payments from companies for suits which had never been before Chancery but had been submitted to his arbitration. They involved no judicial business, but a composition between the two parties, and the money could in no sense be looked on as a bribe. There was one present about which Bacon had himself discovered something irregular, and which he had promptly returned. Another, a 'rich cabinet', he had never accepted, and had repeatedly asked the donor to collect. On three further occasions Bacon had borrowed money from a suitor, incurring straightforward debts, which he had since paid, or attempted to pay.[45]

Thus nineteen out of the twenty-eight articles prove to be no charges at all. Leaving aside until later one last, more general accusation – that he had given way to 'great exactions' by his servants – there remain eight cases that fall into the category of gratuities a judge accepts without taking enough trouble to ascertain whether the giver still has a case pending.[46] We have seen Lady Wharton's suit (the fourth article of the charge), obscured by the actions of dishonest subordinates behind the Chancellor's back. In Aubrey's (article 16), the lies of the Chancellor's servants put the whole case in doubt. The Egerton cousins' cause (articles 1 and 2) looked black for Bacon because in this case he appeared to have taken bribes from both parties. But Egerton had presented his £400 as straightfoward fees for the Chancellor's past services as his counsel; if he had really intended it as a bribe for future services that for five months had existed only in his mind, a busy judge might well fail to penetrate the disguise. Again, after Bacon had succeeded in arbitrating equitably between the cousins – a method he always preferred for family disputes – Sir Rowland, fairly enough, paid him a fee of £500 for his share of this private service. It is only because Egerton refused to comply with the decision that Sir Rowland asked for the award to be confirmed by a decree in court, thus reopening a case that Bacon had looked on as finally settled, and giving the presents he had received on both sides the appearance of a double bribe.[47]

Sir John Trevor's suit (article 6) was ended at common law, but with equity reserved, which meant it might come up again before the Lord Chancellor, who confessed that he had 'neglected to enquire whether the cause was ended or depending' before accepting a New Year gift. In the case of the £500 given by Hansby (article 14), there were two different decrees, though 'all upon one bill'; Bacon confessed that he had received payment 'some good time after the first decree and before the second', that is, *pendente lite*. But he decided on proofs so conclusive that, as Gardiner once again opined, the evidence in favour of his integrity was overwhelming.[48] In Lord Montague's cause (article 17) six or seven hundred pounds were given 'after the cause was decreed, but I cannot say it was ended for there have been many orders since', caused by the defendant's repeated contempts. Finally (article 19) a gift of £200 from Bacon's cousin by marriage, Sir George Reynell, to buy furniture for York House had been made many months before he brought in his suit. On a subsequent New Year's Day, however, among the presents received by the Lord Chancellor from many people who were 'in no way his suitors', there was a valuable ring from his relative, too costly for a New Year's present, Bacon admitted, though 'nothing near the value mentioned in the article' (£600), and obviously given *pendente lite*. Yet there is not even a suspicion that the gift was made with a corrupt agreement, and Bacon's decree on Reynell's cause stood firm after his fall.[49]

These few inconclusive cases, then, are all we are left with out of the twenty-eight accusations, collected after intensive questioning of those best informed about Bacon's actions – some three or four out of an estimated total of, at the very least 8,000 decrees awarded over the four years he was Chancellor – most of these few cases being from the first years, when he was new to the task and overwhelmed with his predecessor's backlog. 'On a scrutiny unparalleled for rigour and vindictiveness into Lord St Alban's official acts,' wrote Dixon at the end of his own analysis of the charges, 'not a single fee or remonstrance traced to the Lord Chancellor himself could by any fair construction be called a bribe. Not one appeared to have been given in secret. Not one appeared to have corrupted justice.'[50] Bacon 'never knowingly sold justice', Gardiner concluded, and while maintaining nevertheless that many of the acts he was charged with were indefensible, he pointed out that wherever the Order Books of Chancery threw any light on his motives, that light was invariably favourable. 'May it not be fairly supposed that this result would hold good in other instances, and that the misdeeds of the great Chancellor were attributable to contempt of forms, to carelessness of haste, and to an overweening confidence in his own integrity?'[51]

After confessing to each of the twenty-eight articles individually, Bacon begged the Lords, 'if there should be any mistaking', to 'impute it to want of memory, and not to any desire of mine to obscure the truth, or palliate anything'. For a 'great deal of corruption and neglect' he was 'heartily and penitently sorry'. He did however remind his judges that he could not be accounted a covetous and avaricious man, since his estate was 'so mean and poor' that his chief care was how to meet his debts; and, more important, that a habit of corruption did 'commonly wax worse and worse', whereas nearly all the actions of which he was accused were over two years old.

On 3 May Bacon was pronounced generally guilty of the offences he had been charged with, and his sentence was discussed by a full House of seventy-two lords, including two archbishops and Prince Charles. They now had their 'excellent opportunity', as Macaulay described it, of exhibiting 'the inflexibility of their justice and their abhorrence of corruption'.[52] A timely reminder from Coke, expatiating on the evils of bribery before them, had come to strengthen this righteous abhorrence: in the past, he reminded the House, three judges had been hanged for bribery – precedents which, as was recently pointed out, would not have been lost on the Lords.[53] Two alternative sentences emerged out of the confusion of the debate: a formal, political censure of the Chancellor, or a personal, moral censure of the man. Had he been accused of selling justice, and confessed to it, Bacon would have deserved degradation from his title of Viscount St Alban. Saye proposed degradation, and Southampton (in whose merciful sentence for his share in Essex's rising Bacon had probably had a hand) seconded it, as did Lord Howard de Walden, to gratify, it seems, a personal animosity of his family; but Arundel, Pembroke and others protested against so excessive a punishment, 'for that he hath made so clear and ingenuous confession, which men of his sort do not'; and the band of moderates, including Prince Charles and all the bishops, voted the motion down.[54]

As Chamberlain promptly wrote to Carleton, Bacon was 'fined £40,000, to be imprisoned in the Tower during the King's pleasure, disabled to bear office in the court of commonwealth, to have no voice in Parliament, not to come within the verge of the court'.[55] Honour was saved, in part at least, 'thanks to his clergy', said Bacon, who had more than once upbraided the bishops – able to smile even now, when his young messenger brought him the news.[56] Buckingham alone, ashamed perhaps of the words he had used of his protégé, and, possibly, as an earnest of the promises made to him, had voted against the sentence.

15

Epilogue: Evaluation of the Trial

Can we now, with Macaulay, 'venture to say that no State trial in our History is more creditable to all who took part in it, either as prosecutors or judges', for decency, gravity, public spirit and justice?[1] Or should we rather echo Gardiner, who considered the House of Lords 'the most unfit body in existence to conduct a political trial'?[2] The Lords, no doubt, had done their best, but what could their justice be, when they heard only the witnesses for the prosecution? 'My lord's cross-answers of Sir George would clear him,' Finch had pointed out in Parliament, referring to the first petition against him.[3] As it turns out, even if Bacon had chosen to defend himself he would not have been granted his request to cross-examine the witnesses. He never so much as learnt their names.

What of the Lords' own interrogation of them? When he sent in his confession, Bacon had left any 'scruples touching the credits of the witnesses' to the Lords' 'noble thoughts'. Such scruples should have been particularly carefully observed in view of the fact that over half the depositions rested on the testimony of a single witness, which was against the law, since Coke's point – that a witness could be trusted when he was incriminating himself – was no longer valid once the witnesses had been guaranteed immunity.[4] Much might have come to light if the Lords had carried out a more critical investigation, as they were to do in other cases. At the trial of the Bishop of Llandaff, for example, they found that a principal witness against the accused, when examined on oath before them, 'did not affirm the same which he had delivered unto the Commons', and they refrained from sentencing the Bishop.[5]

If, as they declared, the Lords intended to make a precedent of Bacon's fall, their first task was to ascertain how many of the facts alleged had been proved true, and the second, whether any of these facts implied real corruption. Bacon had left these things also 'to spring out of your own noble thoughts'. But to no purpose, for the Lords did not verify the facts. And as they did not systematically examine witnesses, they missed many opportunitities of getting at the truth. And they made no attempt to distinguish cases according to the degree of guilt involved. The notion that an accusation might be true in part but have many extenuating circumstances was beyond their legal understanding. They had asked for, and obtained, an itemized confession of the twenty-eight charges, and considering the complexity of the suits, they should have looked into each one separately. They would at least have distinguished those in which Bacon had been legitimately paid as mediator, as well as the loans. (One result of their neglect of this last point was that three claims against Bacon's estate were to be turned down by his executors on the ground that the Lords had declared these debts to be bribes.)[6]

A court from which there was no appeal, as Spedding pointed out, should not have based its decision on what was no more than a feeling that the accused had done wrong. Yet there was nothing else for the Lords to go by. In a cause that was the first of its kind, they had no rules to guide them, no knowledge of what the law was, and no notion of where the line lay that separated the permitted from the forbidden. The judges could have told them what constituted judicial bribery, what law made it penal, and what the penalty was.[7] But not only did the Lords fail to consult any experienced jurist, they never bothered to follow up the points made in the Commons on the general practice of taking gratuities in those unreformed days. As for the most important question of all, whether Bacon's judgement had ever been influenced by gifts, it never came up in any of the charges. And it is the failure of the Lords to pronounce clearly on this vital matter which caused historians to take his guilt for granted, and still today makes all the difference in most people's judgement of Bacon as a man.

Both the accusation and the verdict were faulty – the accusation because, without sifting the evidence or distinguishing cases in their haste to settle the matter quickly, the Lords simply bundled charges and depositions of every kind into one bag. Overdue fees for private services mixed up with gifts accepted *pendente lite*, loans mixed up with New Year presents or with money received by servants and promptly returned – they treated them all equally as bribes, and called on Bacon to confess the lot. The verdict was faulty because, once they had obtained the itemized confession – on which alone, as Southampton had made it clear, they could 'ground their sentence' – instead of examining the remarks Bacon had made on each article (denying some charges, briefly explaining on others), they proceeded to find him globally guilty of all that he had not confessed to, as well as what he had.[8]

A further doubt arises about the validity of Bacon's trial. How far was the procedure used against him in accordance with the constitutional precedents Coke had claimed for it? The point, noticed by Spedding, was elaborated by Colin Tite in 1974, in his book on impeachment in Stuart

England.[9] We have seen Coke steer parliamentary action carefully off the rocks when he defeated the King's proposal for a royal commission to try Bacon, which, by snatching away the high-placed victim needed to establish the Parliament's authority, would have spelled disaster to its proposed judicial function. But another danger arose. Bacon was aware of the relevance of the medieval precedents to his own case, and when preparing his defence, he had made some notes on the trials which might be turned to his advantage.[10] A defence based on the very precedents on which Parliament founded its impeachment of the Chancellor could have blocked the new procedure. This danger to the High Court of Parliament was averted.

While studying the various degrees of political influence exerted on Sir Robert Cotton and John Selden – the 'antiquarian' historians most frequently consulted when either the King or Parliament wanted to search the records – Tite drew attention to one 'considerable mystery' to be found in a treatise Selden was writing throughout the spring of 1621.[11] A committed champion of common law in Parliament, and from this Parliament on a close collaborator with Coke, Selden was employed by the Lords in March 1621 to set forth the precedents on which Coke had based the new parliamentary judicature. The text he produced consisted principally of word-for-word translations of precedents from the Parliamentary Rolls, without any abbreviation or editing. Only in one case was his treatment different. In recording the trial of the ex-Chancellor, Michael de la Pole, in 1386, as Tite remarked, 'wholesale omission and abbreviation take place'; to the extent that, as it stands, the resulting description of the proceedings (fortunately available to us from other sources) makes very little sense.

When looking up Coke's precedents, Bacon had noted the trial of de la Pole as relevant to his defence, a relevance which some of the Lords must have recognized, for when they were considering precedents for Bacon's sentence, de la Pole's was the first name which sprang to their minds.[12] A man of wise and moderate counsel, Richard II's Chancellor, against whom Parliament's only real complaint was his attachment to an unpopular policy, had not a little in common with the Chancellor of James I – including the timely assistance given to his opponents, in his case by a fishmonger, who came forth to accuse de la Pole in Parliament, as Aubrey and Egerton were to accuse Bacon, of having taken a bribe from him through his servants. De la Pole's impeachment, Tite observed, took place, like Bacon's, 'at a time of great assertion of the power of the House of Lords'. He suffered the same fate as Bacon, also 'without dishonour', and received the same treatment afterwards: as soon as Parliament was over, the King released him from prison, remitted his fine, and called on him as a trusted servant for his advice.[13]

In view of the evident link, it is curious, to say the least, that in this case alone, instead of providing the complete text, Selden should have summarized some parts of the defence, omitted others, and failed to mention that three of the charges against de la Pole had been dropped; while at the same time he printed in full the Commons' reply to the defence he had suppressed. The overall effect of these alterations, Tite pointed out, 'was to weaken de la Pole's very successful defence, leaving a picture of a man unable to answer the charges of fraud, and receiving draconian punishment from the Lords'; although, being less able a forger than he was a historian, Tite added, Selden failed to eliminate completely 'hints that de la Pole was not as great a fool as he is made to appear'.

In considering possible reasons for this intentional falsification of the record, Tite concluded that the explanation could only be found in the circumstances of 1621. Selden was at work on the Parliamentary Rolls during the weeks in which Bacon's trial was under way. As committed as Coke was to reviving the judicial powers of the Lords, Selden was also aware that the success of the attack on Bacon was vital to their cause; and he knew that the Lords needed strengthening in their purpose. This, Tite suggested, 'could perhaps be achieved by judicious alteration of the record of what might appear to be the most relevant of all precedents, the impeachment of a previous Chancellor'.[14]

If Tite's is the true explanation of this tampering with the record – a not unlikely one, since Selden was found stretching the record in another case – he may have regretted its effect.[15] Selden was a good friend of Bacon's, and it is interesting to note that when Bacon consulted him a year later about the legality of his sentence, he pronounced it invalid, precisely because it had been inadequately recorded by the Court of Record which the House of Lords had now become. 'Selden the historian', Tite noted, 'had re-emerged.'[16] Bacon was now at work on his *History of Henry VII*, for which he had borrowed various manuscript histories from Selden, but when he asked for a similar permission from Sir Robert Cotton, it was not granted. Cotton had been consulted by various people for precedents related to their trials, and Tite considers it probable that it was through fear of the use Bacon might put it to that he was officially denied access to Cotton's library. Cotton himself however, always generous with his records, must have provided him privately with the material he needed, for Bacon later recalled that Sir Robert had 'poured forth what he had'.[17]

A final factor to be taken into account in this review of Bacon's trial is that it had come before the Lords as a test case when they were most eager to prove themselves in their new role. A month later, when both Houses had had their fill of convictions, and the Lords, as Spedding worded it, had 'established their credit with the Commons as a Court of Judicature by a readiness to condemn without reason whomsoever they accused', they were to deal very differently with offenders such as the

Bishop of Llandaff and Sir John Bennet – the latter acccused of briberies which, according to a contemporary, 'made my Lord Chancellor an honest man.'[18] So much evidence had, it seems, been collected against Bennet that there was no time to deal with it before the end of the session, and when Parliament resumed work both Houses had lost interest, so that judgement was never given. Chamberlain, commenting on the mildness used in these two cases, noted that 'the fine fury or apprehension of things be with length of time or otherwise relented.'[19] With Chamberlain – and Spedding – Tite attributed this decline in tempo to satiety, and to the fact that, since the Lords were now functioning as a judicial court, 'the process was no longer struggling for survival'.[20]

But on 3 May, when Bacon received his sentence, the fine fury was at its height, and at this point, rather than the outcome of a 'grave, temperate, and constitutional inquiry into the personal integrity of the first judge in the kingdom', as Macaulay saw it, the Lords' decision was simply an expression of the passion of the time.[21] The next day they pronounced upon the monopolist Sir Francis Michell that sentence of degradation which some of them had wanted to inflict on Bacon. The spurs were hacked from his heels, the sword broken over his head and heralds marched with him to prison, proclaiming to the hooting crowd that he would henceforth be known as 'Francis Michell, Knave'.[22] Meanwhile on 1 May, two days before Bacon's condemnation, the Commons had vented their vindictive elation in the trial of Edward Floyd, an aged Catholic barrister who had allegedly expressed his satisfaction over the defeat of the Prince and Princess Palatine in Bohemia and argued that Prince Frederick had no more right than he had himself to the Bohemian Crown. Aside from a few words of hearsay, the evidence against Floyd consisted of a crucifix, beads, a handful of 'popish books' and relics, and a libel against Coke – who himself 'knit up' the case against him with another speech on judicial corruption.

Although, crossing himself, Floyd denied, then and throughout the proceedings, ever having spoken the words attributed to him, the most eminent and respectable Members of the House spent their whole morning turning down sentence after sentence as insufficiently harsh. A just God, said Phelips, demanded Floyd's punishment; he should ride with his face to the horse's tail from Westminster to the Tower, and there be lodged in the famous dungeon known as Little Ease, 'with as much pain as he shall be able to endure without loss or danger to his life'. 'If we have no precedent,' said Sir George More, 'let us make one. Let Floyd be whipped to the place from whence he came.' Sir Edward Giles thought he should 'be pilloried at Westminster, and whipped'; 'Twice pilloried and twice whipped,' cried another Member. And so they continued: 'Let a hole be burnt in his tongue'; 'Let his tongue be cut out, or slit at least'; his nose and ears be lopped off; let him be compelled to swallow his beads;

no, he should have as many lashings as beads, and let hot bacon be dripped into the wounds on every sixth stroke.

At one point John Finch, the same who had recently stood up for Bacon, pointed out that the House had no evidence on which to act, and Sandys reminded them that their actions would be watched by the whole world. But they went on regardless, vying with each other in thinking up horrific punishments. Sir Edward Cecil, the grandson of Lord Burghley, suggested branding, but could not decide which letter would be most suitable. Sir George Goring, Buckingham's special agent, proposed 'whipping at twelve stages, swallow a bead at each, an ass's tail for bridle, nose and chops slit and cut, and hanged at the Tower, and there is an end of him'. After this sadistic effusion, moderation prevailed. Floyd was merely (and again, like Michell, quite unconstitutionally) sentenced by the Commons to be pilloried three times, to ride from station to station on a barebacked horse with his face to the tail, to pay a fine of £1,000 and to spend the night in the foulest dungeon in the Fleet.

When the next morning – the day before they pronounced judgement on Bacon – the Lords came to take their places, expecting, wrote Gardiner, 'to feast their eyes on the sufferings of Floyd as they passed through the Palace Yard', the King had sent Fulke Greville to stay the execution of the sentence. What were the precedents, he enquired, for the Commons to act like a House of Record and punish any man – much less one who protested his innocence – without the oath, which only the Lords were entitled to give? 'Let his tongue cleave to his mouth,' Coke exclaimed, 'who says that this House is no House of Record' – thus again reversing the position he had taken two months earlier, when the trial of Bacon by the Lords depended on his accepting that the Commons could not administer the oath, and were therefore no House of Record.[23] Floyd was handed over to the Lords, who, not to be outdone, increased his fine to £3,000, and added branding, flogging, 'disgentilizing' and imprisonment for life in Newgate, having after some discussion turned down the suggestion that he should have his nose nailed to the pillory.

The severe sentence meted out to Bacon appears moderate by comparison. But whatever the difference in treatment between lesser mortals and those who fell from a great height, the two sentences had this in common: far from being the product of a grave and temperate inquiry, they were in fact an expression of emotion, an emotion composed largely of that 'personal animosity' and 'factious violence' of which Macaulay had seen no symptom in either House. The outrageous sentence on Floyd gave vent to strong anti-Catholic feeling, compounded at the time by a widespread sympathy with the cause of the Protestants in Bohemia; the sentence on Bacon was, as Spedding put it, the outcome of a popular clamour, stirred up and steered towards him by his personal and political opponents, after iniquity in high places.[24] In the event, not only was

Bacon's trial found invalid by one of the few experts on precedents of his time, but the sentence on Floyd was later declared (by that 'pillar of justice', as his contemporaries saw him, Selden's friend Sir Matthew Hale) to have been as unconstitutional as the sentence previously passed on him in the Commons.[25]

To conclude this analysis of the parliamentary proceedings against Bacon, we have a Chancellor who was denounced by a dishonest subordinate, and by men who, years earlier, had attempted to bribe him in vain; who was accused, for obviously political reasons, of taking normally acceptable gratuities which, however, irregularly he sometimes took them, never influenced his judgement; who abandoned his defence because he had himself been abandoned by those he served, and because, a reformer at heart, he blamed himself for grave negligence; who was tried, under a purely political procedure that had been in force for a short time two centuries earlier, as a weapon in factional rivalry, and by hue and cry rather than by any law of the land; and, was pronounced guilty – on the sole basis of his confession, though not a single allegation had been proved against him – of much more than he had confessed.

His condemnation by men without knowledge of the law, ably led along, in both Houses, by a small coalition of politicians determined to achieve their own designs and with the requisite legal expertise, which they ruthlessly exploited, is hardly sufficient ground for us to look on Bacon as a corrupt judge, much less a corrupt man. Yet it is the image of a fundamentally corrupt man that Macaulay, taking the Lords' decision at face value, loosed on the world, and many people still hold that image of him at the back of their minds.[26] In the chapters that follow, while evaluating the justice of Bacon's sentence in Parliament – as distinct from the validity of his trial – with the help of his contemporaries, we will situate him among his masters, servants, colleagues and friends, and attempt to find out whether he acted, or reacted, as a corrupt man will in any age.

16

The Contemporary View of Bacon's Fall

'Good my Lord, procure the warrant for my discharge this day.' So wrote Bacon to Buckingham after spending no more than a couple of nights in the Tower.[1] Death was far from unwelcome, but he could not die before receiving his pardon, 'and in this disgraceful place'. He was released the same evening. He would probably never have been sent there but for Southampton's insistence in the Lords that 'the world', if he did not go, would think they had sentenced him in vain.[2] At no stage did the fallen Chancellor's own wide circle of acquaintances treat him as a delinquent, much less, as later biographers would have him, as a convicted rogue. Even the King, Bacon was later to recall after another interview, addressed him 'not as a criminal but as a man overthrown by a tempest'.[3] As for the Parliament which had condemned him, various lords told him privately, 'as it were a way of excusing the severity of the sentence, that they knew they had left him in good hands'.[4] Soon afterwards Bacon could note that they had repented of what they had done, considering it had 'but served the turns of a few'; and when the Parliament had finally broken up, in December 1621, he again heard from a friend that it had 'died penitent' towards him.[5]

In any case, disgraceful as it might have seemed to the fallen Chancellor, a spell in the Tower did not imply the kind of ignominy which a prison sentence held for Bacon's Victorian biographers, in whose experience imprisonment for political dissent, with or without trial, was something that happened only in outlandish places. To be lodged in the Tower in the sixteenth and seventeenth centuries, rather than the punishment of a crime, was regarded as the sign of that greatest of misfortunes, royal disfavour. Everyone in high place was at risk. Many, from Queen Elizabeth downwards (while her sister Mary ruled), had spent some time there, and always, whatever their actual deserts, for basically political reasons.[6] While some paid only token visits, the Earl and Countess of Somerset, for example, lived in the Tower for many years, entertaining like princes; Ralegh had been receiving his friends there since 1603, collaborating with other inmates in scientific experiments, corresponding with Prince Henry and writing his *History of the World*; and Northumberland had become such an *habitué* that on being offered his freedom, his first reaction was to decline it. James's Secretary of State, Sir Robert Naunton, was to point out as a remarkable exception the fact that Fulke Greville, of all Elizabeth's favourites the one to enjoy the 'longest lease and smoothest time without rub . . . was not once imprisoned by the King'.[7]

Bacon, it seems, was in good company. A year earlier Chamberlain, noting that the standing in high place was particularly slippery, had quoted 'some wags' as saying they now held a Council table in the Tower, 'being furnished with a Lord Treasurer, a Lord Chamberlain, a Secretary', besides one or two lesser councillors; and as late as November 1620 he had again remarked on the number of principal officers who had recently been disgraced in this way.[8] If the passage from high office to the Tower was an easy one, however, so was the return to high office. Among its residents, as now listed by Chamberlain, was Attorney General Yelverton, released some months later, and in favour again in 1625, as a Judge of the Common Pleas; Lord Treasurer Suffolk, sentenced in 1618 for embezzlement of Government funds, but back in the Lords in time to sentence Bacon, and not long afterwards appointed High Steward of Exeter; and Secretary Lake, expected to be soon restored to his place. Naunton meanwhile, the other Secretary, confined at the beginning of the 1621 Parliament (for his unauthorized manoeuvres in favour of a French marriage for Prince Charles), was back at work in 1622, and in 1624 became an exemplary Master of the Wards. It is not surprising that a year after Bacon's sentence there should have been rumours of his restoration to the Council.[9]

Not a few of those who had helped to bring Bacon down in Parliament were now to be imprisoned in the Tower, or in less distinguished prisons, for a variety of reasons. At the end of the first session, six weeks after his sentence was passed – and possibly not without some connection with it – Southampton was arrested for practising 'with some of the Lower House to cross the King' (in other words for plotting the overthrow of Buckingham), along with the Commons Member most involved, Sir Edwin Sandys, and Selden (for supporting the right of the Commons to sentence Floyd).[10] They were all set free a month later, as were Lake, Yelverton and the unfortunate Floyd. But on the closure of Parliament at the end of the year, James gave vent to his long-suppressed irritation with Coke and Phelips for their more serious interference with the royal prerogative while it was in session, by sending them both to prison. Coke stayed seven months in the Tower, after which, in his new role of Buckingham's client, he returned in good time to collaborate with him in the impeachment of Cranfield. Phelips, freed at the same time, was to attain high favour under Charles I.

Cranfield made his own brief stay in the Tower in 1624, under a sentence similar to Bacon's, and (if Chamberlain was well informed) bought his way out of it for £6,000.[11] Dean Williams, who had successfully schemed for Bacon's place, trod so carefully as Lord Keeper that he kept out of trouble, but he was later to spend three years in the Tower, before returning to his post as Archbishop of York – in time to promote the death of Strafford. Arundel, a more picturesque figure among the Lords who condemned Bacon, was imprisoned for an arrogant retort in Parliament and went to the Tower on 8 May, three weeks before Bacon himself reached it. He was welcomed there by the Earl of Northumberland, who had been an inmate for fifteen years for his alleged share in the Gunpowder Plot. Both men were released in July, and in August Arundel was raised to the highest honour in the land, the post of Earl Marshal of England, in time to charge Coke with 'attempting to withdraw subjects' hearts from their King'.[12]

Bacon's letter to Prince Charles, written a few days after his release, breathes his gratitude towards the Prince for 'stretching forth his arm' to save him from a sentence, for holding him 'from being plunged deep' when it came, and for having since then 'kept me alive in your gracious memory and mention'; and towards Sir John Vaughan, the Prince's friend and his own, 'the sweet air and loving usage of whose house hath already much revived my languishing spirits'.[13] Prince Charles had a soft spot for Bacon. It was 'at the time of his declension', when the storm was gathering around the Chancellor, that seeing him go by with his 'goodly troup of horses', and admiring his 'undaunted spirits', the Prince had exclaimed, 'do what we can, this man scorns to go out like a snuff!'[14] As for Charles's sister Elizabeth, the Princess Palatine, now the 'Winter Queen' – 'that excellent Lady,' as Bacon called her, 'whose fortune is so distant from her merit and virtue' – she remained his constant friend, as we may see from one of her letters to him, written a year later to thank him for her copy of the book on Henry VII, which he had recently completed – 'the best I ever read of its kind':

> I am very sorry that I cannot show otherwise than by my letters my gratitude for this and other benefits for which I am beholden to you, and though your fortunes are changed (for which I grieve) believe that I shall not change to be what I am, your very affectionate friend, Elizabeth.[15]

For anyone but a queen to befriend a man officially in disgrace was a risky matter under Stuart rule. Only one of Bacon's followers dared – from Paris – to revile the 'dull Britons', who in their 'senseless fury' had destroyed a man as far above them 'as is heaven from hell'.[16] At home

Bacon was no longer surrounded with throngs of courtiers, yet from all sides we hear similar expressions of sympathy and support, and when he returned to London after a year of exile at Gorhambury, his country estate, visitors were not lacking. ('Visitations by all the noblemen about the town,' Bacon privately noted.)[17] Among them James's new Secretary, Sir Edward Conway, to whom Bacon wrote thanking him for his understanding and 'his offers of love and assistance'; and his old friend, Lord Treasurer Mandeville, whose complaint that he was now being kicked upstairs to be President of the Council provoked the fallen Chancellor, an incurable punster, into exclaiming, 'Why, my Lord, they have made me an example and you a *Precedent.*'[18]

The scholars of Cambridge – those who were to celebrate Bacon 'dressed in white, a spotless judge', ready to 'administer justice among the angels' – and courtiers of the highest standing and honesty, such as Pembroke, Falkland, Greville and Digby (himself soon to spend three undeserved years in the Tower), all showed by their unaltered friendship and respect that the sentence imposed on Bacon, though it involved a change in his fortunes, had not damaged his reputation in their eyes, or his virtue, which, as Ben Jonson later testified, adversity could not harm, 'but rather help to make manifest'.[19] Bacon's colleagues must have felt at this time that 'there but for the grace of God go I', and their view of the gratuities Bacon had accepted, if they had one at all, was perhaps best expressed by the historian Thomas Fuller, a young man at the time. The Chancellor, he later wrote, had expended 'on the trials of nature all and more than he got by the trials at the bar', posterity being all the better for them, 'though he the worse'.[20]

'Never was any man more willing to do your Lordship service than myself,' Selden declared when Bacon consulted him, and Sackville, as Bacon's ever-watchful servant Meautys writes, was 'very zealous to do you service in every particular you shall command'.[21] With the affectionate and saintly Bishop Andrewes, Bacon continued their 'ancient and private acquaintance', and with the religious poet George Herbert, their mutually enriching friendship.[22] Not one friend, public or private, was to fail him – with the single exception of Buckingham, the man who owed his political survival to Bacon's fall. But there was one whose absence, 'always uncomfortable to my mind', was at this time, as Bacon told him, 'grief upon grief'. Toby Matthew must have written at once from the Embassy in Spain, where he was impatiently awaiting leave to come home. 'I have long been a debtor to you for a letter,' Bacon wrote back, 'especially for such a letter, the words whereof were delivered by your hand, as if it had been in old gold.' We do not know what those words were, but can guess them from Matthew's effusive praise elsewhere of his friend's 'heart, will and moral virtue', and his unceasing attentions throughout the years that followed.[23]

Bacon's friendly antagonist, Count Gondomar, the Spanish Ambassador, was not to be outdone. Bacon was barely out of the Tower when Gondomar wrote offering his assistance and that of his master, now King Philip IV of Spain, to interpose with James, on whom he exerted a strong personal influence, and obtain Bacon's return to favour. 'Having received so many kindnesses and good wishes from your lordship in your prosperity,' wrote Gondomar, 'I deem it one of my greatest misfortunes my not being able to serve you as duty and gratitude require of me now you are in adversity'; and he concluded his offer declaring himself for ever 'devotedly at the service of your lordship'.[24] Bacon thanked him for his 'warm and sincere' love, but refused: he was planning, he said, to retire 'from the stage of civil actions'.[25] Later, however, Gondomar did him a much valued service in connection, it is assumed, with the partial pardon he so much desired, for at the end of the year we find Bacon thanking him warmly for his generous conduct and his promptness in 'all offices of humanity and honour'. Only divine Providence, he wrote, could have sent him in his solitude, 'as it were from above, such a friend, who, amid such pressure of business and such straights of time has had care of me and effected for me that which my other friends have not ventured to try or have not been able to obtain'.[26] (The 'other friends' being of course the one and only favourite.) These were no mere words of compliment. He was to echo them soon afterwards in a letter to Toby Matthew, praising the magnanimity, cordiality and wit of the Spanish Ambassador, 'a friend reserved for such a time as this'.[27]

It has been remarked that James's leniency towards Bacon, as well as the arrests he made at the end of the session, were 'an indication of what he thought of the fairness of some of Parliaments's decisions'.[28] If, as Bacon now recalled, the King had 'shed tears at the beginning of my trouble', they must have been, at least in part, tears of remorse over the weakness that had caused him to abandon his servant.[29] He now did his best to repair the damage by honouring some part of his promises of pardon and subsistence. Bacon learned early in September that the King would continue the pension of £1,200 a year he had enjoyed for the past two years, and had freed him from the immediate pressure of the private debts that were then his 'chief care' by assigning his £40,000 fine to trustees named by Bacon himself, which would prevent his creditors from coming on him all at once.[30] The partial pardon which Gondomar probably assisted him to obtain was also on the way, and meanwhile he had been granted permission to visit London in order to see his doctors and look into his affairs.

These signs of favour, coupled with the inevitable rumours of Bacon's restoration to office, must have alarmed Lord Keeper Williams who, fearing no doubt for his post, made various attempts to stay Bacon's pardon at the Seal, on the flimsiest of pretexts, while the new Lord

Treasurer, Lionel Cranfield, repeatedly delayed the payment of his pension.[31] Served by these two able but somewhat blinkered counsellors, James must have missed Bacon's more ample vision. 'O had I my old Lord Chancellor Bacon here,' he is reported to have exclaimed on one occasion, 'I would speedily have overcome the affair.'[32]

Remitting fines and granting pardons, sooner or later, was more or less normal procedure in the case of eminent offenders. But few men sentenced and cast into prison by a Parliament can have been called upon by the head of the state, as Bacon was two weeks after his release, for advice about ways of continuing the programme of reform which that same Parliament had begun with his overthrow. James could not wait for the end of the session to consult his one-time counsellor about the reformation of the courts of justice which he was supposed to have polluted, and the relief of the grievances he had been accused of supporting. No time could be better than the present one, Bacon replied, with the authority of the convinced, for the King to stand 'in his highest chair', the Star Chamber, and declare 'his purpose to pursue the reformation which he hath begun'. It was Bacon's fervent credo that 'all great reformations are best brought to perfection between the King and his Parliament'. Here was James's chance. Used to looking at things on the bright side, Bacon did not point out that much of the good work could have been done before the opening of the Parliament – and his Chancellor saved into the bargain – had he been heard. He was glad, he now said, that monopolies had not been dealt with as originally proposed, for 'it might have been thought to have been done to prevent a Parliament,' whereas now the King would be acting 'to pursue a Parliament'.

The opportunity to advise on what he had most at heart must have been tantalizing to Bacon, knowing that he must now be excluded from all further action. ('Your Majesty in your grace and wisdom will consider how unproper and how unwarranted a thing it is for me as I now stand to send for entries of Parliament, or for searches for precedents, whereupon to ground an advice.') He gave his advice, nevertheless, as follows. The Privy Council, with any specialized assistance that might be required, should comb through all the available memorials of those things which had passed in both Houses, and the Learned Counsel should search for precedents on 'matter of reformation' to act on, just as Parliament had based themselves on parliamentary precedents. Thereupon 'the clock could be set', and resolutions taken as to 'what should be holpen by commission, what by act of Council, what by proclamation, what to be prepared for Parliament, what to be left wholly to Parliament'. In this way many grievances would be answered 'by deed and not by word', and the King's care would prove 'better than any standing committee, in this interim between meetings of Parliament'.[33]

Bacon's advice was followed, in essentials, as perhaps it had never been while he was in office. A declaration was made in the Star Chamber (by Mandeville, in James's name) on the date Bacon had proposed, 21 June, and the Privy Council achieved more solid work in the first few weeks after the adjournment of Parliament than it had done in many years. Eighteen monopolies were abolished by proclamation, a further seventeen sent to the courts for study, and a committee was appointed to consider the balance of trade, which was in effect, wrote Menna Prestwich, an application of Bacon's plan for law reform to the economic field.[34] As Robert Zaller remarked, 'the greater part of the parliamentary programme was now being carried out by executive order.'[35] A Parliament, in Bacon's words, had been 'pursued'. This was James's brief hour of rejoicing, when he was, said a contemporary, 'inthronised in his people's hearts' – at Bacon's cost.[36] 'We have made an end of Parliament,' wrote Sir Henry Savile, another friend of Bacon's, 'where nothing passed but eighteen or twenty weeks, and two subsidies, besides some censures upon great persons.' He was sorry for the persons, but 'at least it declareth the good and perfect union between the King and his subjects.' He attached a copy of Parliament's declaration announcing their willingness to venture their fortunes and their lives for the recovery of the Palatinate.[37]

Nothing could have pleased Bacon more than such a 'perfect union' between the King and his people. Had he not urged on James again and again the 'inestimable importance' of his parting with a Parliament 'in love and reverence'?[38] 'I hear yesterday was a day of very great honour to his Majesty,' he wrote to Buckingham, 'which I do congratulate. I hope also his Majesty may reap honour out of my adversity, as he hath done strength out of my prosperity.'[39] These were no empty words. But we should now enquire what Bacon himself thought of the adversity out of which James – who had allowed it – was to reap this honour. Bacon knew what he was doing when, neglecting every opportunity which a more self-regarding person might have used to fight his case, he had taken full responsibility for his own and others' blameworthy actions, and entrusted his defence to the Lords' 'noble thoughts and observations of the evidence'. What was his private view of the outcome of their noble thoughts?

'The crows were forgiven while the doves were censured,' Bacon entered in his notes (in Greek letters, for safety). 'They were not the greatest offenders in Israel upon whom the walls of Shilo fell.' Was he thinking of Sir John Bennet, between whose case and his own, as he reminded the King three years later, 'there was as much difference, I will not say as between black and white, but as between black and grey, or ash-coloured' – and whom Parliament had never bothered to sentence?[40] In this letter he was asking James to give him the same full pardon which had already been granted to Bennet after his condemnation in 1622 in the

Star Chamber. Bennet had pleaded guilty to stopping and reversing wills for money, or if the legatee was too poor to pay him, taking over the inheritance himself, to misappropriating funds entrusted to him for pious uses (in particular £1,000 left by Bodley to the University of Oxford), and in general to administering the property of intestates 'in consonance with the wishes of the highest bidder'. He was also known to have 'shamefully begged' for bribes, and, being himself a great briber (it was he who had offered £30,000 for Ellesmere's post), he had offered to pay any sum required to stop the petitions brought to Parliament against him, including, presumably, those of one irrepressible accuser who had been collecting petitions against him for years and who declared that he was as yet 'only in the suburbs'.[41]

When calling on Buckingham to release him from the Tower, Bacon characteristically summed up two seemingly contradictory views of Parliament's verdict upon him. He was, he said, 'howsoever I acknowledge the sentence just, and for reformation sake fit, the justest Chancellor that hath been in the five changes since Sir Nicholas Bacon's time.'[42] No one had a higher place in Bacon's estimation than his father, both as man and judge. If in his eyes neither Hatton nor Puckering, nor his much respected friend Ellesmere, had equalled Nicholas Bacon – and himself – as Lord Keepers, we must at least assume that his standards were high. As far as Bacon was concerned, he took it for granted that his own awards were made with unimpeachable justice, since, as he said, he 'never had any bribe in his eye or thought when he pronounced a sentence or order'; but also that, 'his thoughts and cares' concerning the good of his country being 'always beyond, and over and above' his place, he had been an exemplary chancellor.[43] In pursuit of the higher aims he shared with his father, he had devised the best possible rules to protect suitors from unnecessary expense – rules which, indeed, have proved of lasting value – and had made his own awards as promptly as suitors would let him, speed being in his view the key to all other reforms of the law.

Bacon knew the immediate cause of his own fall. He compared himself with Cicero, who, though his case had 'no great blot of ignominy', was overthrown by 'a tempest of popularity'. But the blot, if only ash-coloured, was there, and in the same breath as he maintained his integrity, he could state that the Lords' sentence upon him had been a just one, 'for reformation sake'. Elsewhere he noted that 'it was the justest censure in Parliament that was these two hundred years.'[44] He saw no inconsistency in writing (to Buckingham) that he had 'clean hands and a clean heart', and (to James) that no one would ever find in him 'the troubled fountain of a corrupt heart', while soon afterwards confessing to the Lords 'a great deal of corruption and neglect'.[45] It was in the neglect that the real corruption lay, and he faced it then, perhaps for the first time, and was overwhelmed. Confident as he was in his essential integrity,

Bacon was, as he called himself, 'a broken reed'. 'By the King's great favour I received the great seal,' he told Arundel and the lords sent to take it from him, 'by my own great fault I have lost it.' Worldly affairs were 'but mint and cumin' to him now, considering the bitterness of this cup.[46]

'Avoid not only the fault, but the suspicion,' he had written years earlier.[47] Instead, neglecting his own precepts, he had brought on himself not only the loss of his position and means of living, but the loss of his much prized 'power to do good'. With 'an eye to the future as well as to the present', as Spedding noted, all his life Bacon had laboured 'to give the weight of his authority to precedents of reform'. That future was gone, and with it 'the clearest jewel', honour, which he defined as 'the revealing of a man's worth'.[48] If he remained conscious of his worth, now and in time to come, and would on occasion proudly remind those he had served of it ('your Majesty in doing me good may do good to many, both that live now and shall be born hereafter'), he knew that 'the world' would fail to recognize and to use it.[49] He had of course no inkling of the stream of vilification that was to grow and spread until it influenced even the views scholars were to hold of the works he would bequeath to them.

'A little leaven sours the whole lump' . . . 'a small slip in a very good man' greatly diminishes his character and reputation. This biblical warning was present, in many images, to Bacon's mind. He had used it recently in his opening speech in Parliament, of the grievances soon to be debated. ('The best governments, yea, the best men are like precious stones, wherein every flaw or icicle or grain are seen and noted more than in those that are generally foul and corrupted.')[50] He would strive to cleanse himself of this stain throughout his remaining years. Unfortunately only the King, in Bacon's eyes – and in those of his contemporaries – could remove it. After due expiation, a full royal pardon could wipe the slate of honour clean and make him a 'new creature'. It is in this light, rather than as a more superficial desire to regain favour or power, that we should see his repeated appeals to be allowed to serve his royal master, ('else life is but the shadow of death') and his prayer that the King would not blot his name quite out of the royal book.[51]

The only article of the charge against him for which Bacon confessed unqualified guilt was that he had 'given way to great exactions by his servants'.[52] These were 'the young gentlemen of blood and quality' whom Rawley described as happy to enlist themselves in his retinue, because he was the best of masters, rewarding their services with good places as soon as he could, and 'freely' (that is without taking any money from them, as was usual); towards whom he often took on the role of teacher, even if some of them were among those same 'wasteful knaves, proud, profane, costly fellows' who had exasperated Lady Bacon in bygone times.[53] They held everything in common with the Chancellor, wrote Fuller, 'the men never wanting [lacking] what their master had'. Three of them, Aubrey noted, actually 'kept their coaches, and some kept racehorses'.[54] The result of so much indulgence was predictable. Bacon had not 'bound his servants' hands', as he believed all judges should do. Indeed he had allowed them so free a use of his cash – which they took in handfuls from his chests – that they seem to have looked on the litigants' treasure also as their due.[55]

We may gather from the statements which some of these servants made during the investigation that they had been doing a thriving trade behind their master's back. A great deal of money, whether presented as bribes or as gratuities, had found its way, like the gold in his chests, into their own pockets. Aubrey tells of one present intended for the Chancellor, 'a cabinet of jewels which his page, Mr Cockayne received, and deceived his lord'.[56] This practice was already going strong under Cardinal Wolsey, despite all this Chancellor's efforts to improve Chancery in his day. Most members of the Wolseys' household, from the doorkeepers upwards, had taken their secret cuts, and his servants had developed a private fee system of their own for introducing litigants into his office.[57] Fuller had heard an intriguing tale about Bacon that recalls those earlier arrangements:

> The Chancellor had two servants, one in all causes patron to the plaintiff (who his charity presumed always injured), the other to the defendant (pitying him as compelled in law), but taking bribes of both, with this condition, to restore the money received if the case went against them. Their Lord, ignorant thereof, always did impartial justice; whilst his men (making people pay for what was given them) by compact shared the money betwixt them, which cost their master the loss of his office.[58]

'Sit down, my masters,' Bacon is reported to have said on one occasion, when his gentlemen stood up to greet him, 'your rise hath been my fall.'[59] Only on his impeachment, it would seem, when almost all of them scurried away, did he realize that he had taken their gratitude, loyalty and honesty too much for granted. He compared them, said Aubrey, 'to the flying vermin when the house was falling – such summer birds are men'. But if he spoke the words wryly, it may have been with a rueful laugh. Who if not himself was to blame? Few of Bacon's detractors go so far as to present him as a shameless liar, ready to save his skin by laying all the blame he could on his men. It was the other way round, as one of his servants had the grace to confess.[60] And all Bacon's behaviour towards them suggests that he was reluctant, as he had been with George Hastings – who had procured and, most people thought, pocketed the first bribes complained of in Parliament – to throw on them the blame they so richly deserved.

Where Bacon entered the teacher–pupil relationship there was no limit to his goodwill.[61] It was for the career of that same George Hastings that he had spared time and thought on taking his seat in Chancery. At the end of his memorable speech when it was getting late, Chamberlain complained – 'he would needs the Lords stay to hear a motion of the young lawyer', and poorly performed at that, in Chamberlain's view.[62] Bacon was always a promoter of talent, particularly in the young, and we have found him, again with Chamberlain's disapproval, backing for the post of Provost of Oriel College the bright twenty-six-year-old scholar whom he had made his chaplain. When the Archbishop of Canterbury stood for 'others more in years and gravity', Bacon replied that 'he respected not minority of years where there was majority of parts.'[63]

Quite a few of Bacon's servants were tempted (or blackmailed by Cranfield, when he was going through the books in Chancery) into witnessing against their master. Chief among them was one John Hunt, described by Aubrey as 'a notable thrifty man' who 'loved this world'. He loved it to some purpose, it seems, for he was to leave an estate of £1,000 a year. On one occasion Bacon gently remonstrated with him: 'the world was made for man, Hunt, not man for the world.'[64] But Hunt, as the Chancellor's collector of fines well placed for a spot of private collecting, did not get the message. It is known that in at least one case he took money from a suitor without Bacon's knowledge; which Bacon, when he heard of it, ordered him to pay back immediately.[65] Hunt, with 'the world' in mind, refused to be 'bound' for his master. It was otherwise with Thomas Meautys, a faithful servant to the last, and with Ned Sherbourne, a trusted follower, who, though he too was to bear witness against his master, was afterwards 'fain to hide himself, as being engaged for him for more than he was worth'.[66] These were some of the creditors it had become Bacon's chief care, he said, to repay.[67] And if he did not much blame his gentlemen, it is probably because he blamed himself for their delinquencies. ('I confess it was a great fault in me that I looked no better to my servants.')[68]

Bacon's young seal-bearer, Thomas Bushell, is the only one of them whose testimony of remorse is on record; and perhaps, following Coke's principle, we may give him the benefit of any doubt as to his reliability on this point, since he was inculpating himself. He made his *mea culpa* about Bacon in print, forty-eight years after the event. 'Myself and other of his servants', he admitted, 'were the occasion of exhaling his virtue into a dark eclipse.' He deeply regretted 'that so unparalleled a master should be thus brought upon the public stage for the foolish miscarriage of his own servants – whereof (with grief of heart) I confess myself to be one.' Parliament 'had made his master, the Chancellor, make atonement for all their crimes', he went on, and their 'fatal sentence did much perplex my troubled thoughts', particularly since the Chancellor 'in his own nature scorned the least thought of any base or ignoble act', and 'loathed bribery'. Bushell recalled his master's kindness to him, when he had first entered Bacon's service; his

> clearing all my debts three several times, with no smaller sum in the whole than £3,000; his preferring me in marriage to a rich inheritrix, and thereupon not only allowing me £400 per annum, but, to balance the consent of her father in the match, promised upon his honour to make me the heir to his knowledge in mineral philosophy.[69]

Bacon, it seems, fulfilled this promise (though we can see where some of the gratuities went). Transmitting his discoveries to the younger generation was after all one of his principal aims in life. And he made Bushell the heir to a few other inventions which his brilliant pupil was to put to a good use, having learned from the master who 'much loved him', not only 'the art of running into debt', wrote Aubrey, but also how to practise that art in a good cause – 'the carrying on of his ingenious studies' – for 'he imitated his lord as much as he could'. (Aubrey met Bushell when, around seventy, after a life filled with discoveries and adventures, he had settled down and become, in Aubrey's view, 'a handsome, proper gentleman . . . fresh, hawk-nosed, and temperate'.)[70]

Bushell recalled one occasion in his memoirs when he aroused his master's anger:

> So much was his hatred to bribery, corruption or simony, that hearing I had received the profits of first fruits for a benefice – which his pious charity freely gave – he presently sent for me and, being asked of his Lordship, I suddenly confessed, whereupon he fell into so great a passion that, he replied, I was cursed in my conception, and nursed with a tiger for deceiving the Church, threatening I should no longer be his servant.[71]

Forgiveness was asked and obtained, and after Bacon's retirement Bushell returned to serve his 'old master' until the end. Bacon's rare anger need not surprise us. It was to break out again under similar provocation, in a letter he wrote to Buckingham soon after his release from the Tower. 'Some wretched detractor hath told you' (he had heard through Meautys),

> that it were strange I should be in debt, for that I could not but have received an hundred thousand pounds gifts since I had the seal; which is an abominable falsehood. Such tales as these made St. James say that the tongue is a fire, and itself fired from hell, whither when these tongues shall return, they will beg a drop of cold water to cool them. I praise God for it, I never took penny for releasing anything I stopped at the seal, I never took penny for any com-

mission or things of that nature, I never shared with any servant for any second or inferior profit. My offences I have myself recorded . . . As for my debts, I showed them to your Lordship . . .[72]

In his first letter to the King after learning that he stood accused of corruption, Bacon had solemnly declared that 'when the book of hearts' should be opened, 'a depraved habit of taking rewards to pervert justice' would not be found in him; 'howsoever', he added, 'I may be frail and partake of the abuses of the times.'[73] No one could survive under Stuart rule without partaking of the widespread abuses, or *vitia temporis*, as they were commonly referred to, on which James's unpaid bureaucracy was founded. From such men as Sherbourne and Hunt to the King himself, everyone was to some extent caught in the system. We know how Bacon supplemented his inadequate income as Chancellor, and we have seen him pay dearly for doing so. It is necessary now to situate the corruption he confessed to in context, by comparing his actions with those of his principal high-placed contemporaries – not least those who, with virtuous denunciation, brought him down.

17

The Back-Cloth: Abuses of the Times

'If I were to imitate the conduct of your Republic,' James told the Venetian Ambassador, 'and began to punish those who take bribes, I should soon not have a single subject left.'[1] Though few admitted it in public, everyone knew that James's Court was the centre of a flourishing trade. Honours, pensions and landed estates, rich marriageable wards, the enforcement of monopolies, religious penalties and the fines imposed on traitors, as well as the highest positions in the land, everything under royal patronage was for sale. For every service rendered, a long chain of courtiers, from the King himself down to the humblest messenger, received his tip, and no suitor dreamed of approaching a patron without some offering. It was as appropriate for Sir Francis Cottingham to give Buckingham a suite of hangings worth £800 'in the hope of his future favour', as for Lady Arabella to refuse 'to spend her breath' on Lord Cavendish's behalf when he forgot to mention a gratuity.[2] Even pardons were freely bought and sold – a practice Bacon deprecated – and no one saw anything remarkable in Ralegh's acceptance of large sums of money for procuring the pardon of some of Essex's unruly adherents, or in his giving Buckingham £1,500 to intercede with James for his own release from the Tower.[3]

There was an element of grace in the traffic of pardons. But secret bribes were acceptable to the most powerful noblemen from any quarter and for any object, as we may believe when we discover Nottingham, the Lord High Admiral, accepting money from the English pirates who had almost brought trade in the Mediterranean to a standstill, to prevent the Government from taking action against them.[4] 'The ways to enrich are many,' Bacon observed, 'and most of them foul'; and we will find a descending scale in the ways of 'enriching' resorted to by James's officers, from a purse of gold or a length of Venetian velvet given to the Speaker of the House of Commons (and entered in his ledgers) by the aldermen he had favoured, to the most secret practices, discussed in writing only with the postscript, *burn this*. An instruction that was disregarded often enough for us to realize that it must have been frequently obeyed.[5] Some practices were concealed from the general public until they had become matter for scandal, like those of the monopolists, or of the tax farmers, who farmed a large part of the taxes they gathered into their own pockets. But though everyone indulged in one or other of them, and some in all, hardly one was openly referred to until it became convenient to use it as a weapon against a political opponent weak enough to be attacked.[6] As Gardiner remarked, officials who were prosecuted differed from the others only in being found out.

Up to a point the 'foul ways' in use were vices of the whole Stuart system, burdened as it was with an administration which was growing so fast that the revenues from Crown lands could no longer support it, while parliamentary subsidies covered only the extraordinary expenses of war. Joel Hurstfield, in his studies on corruption in the period, defined the situation inherited by James from the first Tudor king as one in which the landed classes 'could not or would not carry the major share of the costs of the national government'.[7] It was in fact, he pointed out, the resistance put up by Coke and his allies to any form of direct or indirect taxation which drove the Government to search for ways of maintaining its services, and in particular of paying its servants' salaries, through those dubious fiscal devices, which were then denounced in Parliament as national grievances. In such a situation the very efforts made by would-be reformers, Cecil and Cranfield among them, had the paradoxical result we have seen in Bacon's case, that they could not help participating in the evils of the system they were trying to change. (Coke's denunciations of the Court of Wards did not prevent him from making an all-out effort to obtain a particularly valuable ward for himself.)[8]

It was first and foremost for the payment of Government officers that the unofficial or 'bastard' revenues were resorted to. Under Elizabeth, as Hurstfield has shown, up to twelve times as much as the Queen's share of all profits made in the Court of Wards had gone into her officers' hands.[9] Maynard Keynes is quoted as saying that corruption, so long as it is moderately practised, is merely another form of taxation, and it is still so practised, no doubt, in many countries today. In England under Stuart rule it was the Government's way of leaving its officials to collect their own fees, and no questions asked. So widely was it used that the scrupulous honesty needed to avoid every twilight practice flourishing in James's time would have been, as Laurence Stone has pointed out, 'not merely eccentric but impossible'.[10] There were, however, degrees. If a servant was worth his hire, as Hurstfield decided, he had a right to take his pay; and for high-level officers, large, though not outrageous, amounts could be a fair price for years of effective work.[11] In looking, therefore, at the means resorted to by Bacon's accusers, his judges and his peers to make their gains, we must bear in mind the relation between the unofficial payments taken and the value of the services rendered.

The first question to be addressed is the respective size of the fortunes made. 'As for my debts,' wrote Bacon in his indignant letter to Buckingham, 'I showed them to your Lordship, when you saw the little house and gallery beside a little wood . . .'[12] This was Verulam, Bacon's one personal extravagance, the summer house he had set up in the grounds of Gorhambury to harbour his scientific experiments, and which was said to have cost him – or rather his creditors – around £9,000. 'Now this illustrious Lord Chancellor had only this manor of Gorhambury,' Aubrey pointed out; unlike most of his acquaintance, such as Fulke Greville, for example, who had estates in thirteen different counties, while Coke died possessed of over sixty manors throughout England.[13] This was not so unusual. Chancellors Hatton and Ellesmere, Chief Justices Hobart and Fleming, among many others, bought up and founded large estates while in office, and (according to Clarendon) Arundel drew more money from his post as Earl Marshal 'than had ever been extorted by all the officers precedent'.[14]

But it was Coke who had made at the Bar a fortune which James regarded as too great for a subject.[15] Coke was well known for his love of money. Born, in 1552, to a modest income, variously reported as £40 and £300 a year, by the turn of the century he was already one of the richest men in England, and he became a good deal richer on the more or less legal perquisites of a Chief Justice of the Common Pleas – once making, said Aubrey, as much as £100,000 in a single year. He left an estate of £11,000 a year to his five sons – who, said Sir John Danvers, when discussing his 'great scraping of wealth', would spend it 'faster than they got it'. To which Coke replied, 'they cannot take more delight in the spending of it than I did in the getting of it.'[16] The fortune built up with 'safe rascalities' by Bacon's other impeacher, Lionel Cranfield, on his road from apprentice to Master of the Wards, was a good deal larger. After being appointed Lord Treasurer in 1621, he trebled his already considerable ill-gotten wealth in land, and by 1624, through the ruthless pursuit of his own interests – not incompatible, it seems, with his struggle to put order in the royal finances – he had acquired an annual income estimated at between £25,000 and £28,000.[17]

As for Bacon's cousin, Sir Robert Cecil, out of the profits of his three great offices he transformed his modest inheritance into one of the greatest estates in the kingdom, which, a Venetian envoy exclaimed in 1607, 'passes the bounds of all belief'. His income towards the end of his life, as Secretary, Treasurer and Master of the Wards, has been estimated at some £33,000 a year. Of the five large houses he built himself, two are still in existence. Hatfield alone cost him £40,000.[18] Cecil was to be outdone, however, by his successor as Lord Treasurer, the Earl of Suffolk, who spent £80,000 building Audley End, and, he told the King, a further £200,000 in furnishing it. It was, said James – whose total revenues out of the Crown lands did not exceed £300,000 a year – 'too big for a King, but fitting for a Lord Treasurer'.[19] Needless to say, no officer could compete with Somerset, whose expenses in his heyday amounted to £90,000 in one year. And least of all with Buckingham, into whose lap – beginning with £80,000 when he was twenty-three, and spreading throughout his insatiable family – tens of thousands of pounds continually flowed in royal gifts and pensions; quite apart from his virtual monopoly over the sale of government offices and honours, the proceeds of which he spent on buying estate upon estate, building lavishly, collecting the best picture gallery of his time, gambling (£1,000 on his servant in a foot-race) and acquiring diamond-studded finery.[20]

We must not forget that for James's courtiers living grandly, ceremonial dress included, was an essential requirement. No great officer could play his part without a large palace in town and a great house in the country capable of accommodating a royal visitor and his train, as well as a personal court of costly servants, some of whom would be employed on state business. When Queen Elizabeth asked Bacon's father, the Lord Keeper, why his country house was so small, he promptly built a much handsomer version to receive her. As Chamberlain put it when deploring Coke's 'thundering' sentence on Suffolk, 'a man must have the means to hold up his degree'; and according to recent calculations, in the early seventeenth century £5,000 barely covered a nobleman's essential expenses.[21] 'Riches are for spending,' wrote Bacon, and when Toby Matthew said of him that he 'lived nobly' and was 'splendid in his expenses', he was bestowing high praise. As was Bacon himself on Elizabeth's 'happy reign', when he wrote that 'there were never like number of fair and stately houses as have been built up from the ground' since it began, nor 'like pleasures of goodly gardens, and orchards, walks, pools and parks'.[22] Bacon, as Aubrey noted, was his own 'chiefest architect'. Wandering among the Roman remains of Verulam, he recalled that 'this magnanimous Lord Chancellor had a great mind to have it made a city again.' 'Fortune denied it him,' but in building Verulam, his 'little house' (unlike Cranfield, who preferred to purchase ready-made, and bought his pictures in bulk), Bacon must have felt he was making his own modest contribution to the beauty of England. ('Not anything twice,' said Aubrey of the 'delicate figures' carved all the way up the staircase of Verulam House.)[23]

As suggested by D. G. James, a perceptive commentator on his writings, Bacon may have needed the stimulus of 'wide vistas and splendid prospects to release the peculiar power of his ample mind'.[24] But Carteret affirmed that he 'never affected riches', and this was the view of his own acquaintance. For the Cambridge scholars who eulogized him on his death he was 'a despiser of wealth', reckoning 'gold less than light air'; his was 'a mind never dazzled by the brightness of heaped up gold'. And he himself made the psychologically interesting observation that 'the personal fruition of man cannot reach to feel great riches'.[25] Bacon's detailed accounts, available to us over a period of three months in the summer of 1618, the time of his highest expenditure, show a total income, gratuities included, of £3,700; this was balanced with his disbursements, which, along with sums set aside for the builders of Verulam and the interest due to his ever-present creditors, included so many gifts, rewards and alms as to justify Fuller's remark that 'vast bounty . . . occasioned his want afterwards'.[26] We can see how, even with an income estimated in his most prosperous years at some £9,000 to £10,000 a year, Bacon was hardly ever flush. Yet, fed on hopes from a young age (his father's illusory legacy, Essex's good intentions), he never lost the habit of living on borrowed funds, so that, taking all his assets into account, he left £14,000 of debts. A fact that was remarked on as exceptional by at least one letter-writer of the day:

> My Lord Chancellor Bacon is lately dead of a languishing weakness; he died poor, that he scarce left money to bury him, which, though he was a great wit, did argue no great wisdom, it being one of the essential properties of a wise man to provide for the main chance. I have read that it hath been the fortune of all poets commonly to die beggars, but for an Orator, a Lawyer and Philosopher, as he was, to die so is rare.[27]

Although comparisons with today's values are of limited usefulness, we should note that, going by the Retail Price Index for 1993, Bacon's income would amount to some £61,000 a month today. This is a goodly sum, yet it is modest when compared for example with the income of the great French prime minister of the period, Sully, whose monthly income came to some £166,000 in our terms.[28] At home, Cranfield's income would be the equivalent of some £240,000 a month, not to speak of Coke's, amounting for a time to £1,500,000.

Such as it was, Bacon had earned his pay, as he put it to the King, 'by the sweat of my labour'. Excepting, that is, the modest pension of £1,200 which we have seen James renew for him after his fall, and which had been bestowed on him in June 1619 out of the Alienation fines, in compensation for a cut of £2,000 from his Chancery profits (which went, said Chamberlain, to provide pensions for 'two hungry Court cormorants').[29] Bacon had applied for this grant somewhat apologetically, knowing that, like others, he would be living off an abuse he would have preferred to reform away. For his other small grant, the farm of Petty Writs, which brought him £600 a year, he felt no need to apologize, since he had improved the public revenue from it by £400 a year.[30] His share of the £5,000 apiece officially allotted to Secretary Naunton and himself as 'windfalls', out of the fines levied on the Dutch merchants in the Star Chamber, had been earned by the sweat of his brow and – until they got him into trouble – he believed that the gratuities, which he accepted just as openly, had been a fair retribution for his labours.

Probably the most widespread among the secret devices for making money was the sale of offices, particularly of those which could be most successfully 'farmed', as shown below, whether for cash or in exchange for matrimonial arrangements like those we have seen concluded under the auspices of Lady Buckingham. Whereas in France this practice had been abolished and replaced with a regular Crown tax, in England almost every position was bought under the counter, either from the Crown, or the favourite who had innumerable offices within his gift – or the previous holder.[31] A position had come to be looked on as the private property of the man who bought it, and he felt bound to recoup himself by exploiting the public he served. Legal posts were sold with the rest. In 1614, for example, £600 apiece was paid to the Bedchamber when nine new serjeants-at-law were appointed.[32] The sale of office, though never looked on as acceptable, had become so universal that an appointment made without payment was remarked on. Thus in 1596, when Sir Thomas Egerton, later Lord Ellesmere, was made Lord Keeper, Anthony Bacon rejoiced in his 'good hap to come to the place freely'; twenty years later his brother was to have the same good hap.[33]

We have seen Coke's successful efforts to buy back his seat on the Council, and those of that amiably indefatigable briber, Lord Mandeville, when he gave up half his estate to become Lord Treasurer – for only a short time, fortunately, since he was not up to the task. A time he must have enjoyed, none the less, since, when asked what the place was worth a year, he replied: 'some thousands of pounds to him who after death would go instantly to heaven; twice as much to him who would go to Purgatory, and nobody knows how much to him who would adventure to a worse place.'[34] Chamberlain, commenting on Nottingham's sale of the Admiralty to Buckingham for 'a good sum of ready money, besides a pension of £3,000 a year, for life, and £1,500 to his family thereafter', thought it somewhat excessive that Lord Sheffield should have offered his post of Lord President of the Council of the North at auction. 'The world', it appears, also censured Lord Wotton for taking part in similar bargains, particularly since Wotton had publicly deplored that 'offices of that nature, and especially councillorships, should pass as it were by bargaining or sale'.[35] Lord Wotton's half-brother, Sir Henry, was later to win the Provostship of Eton – for which the penniless Bacon was also a candidate – by a more delicate form of bribery: he presented Buckingham with a fine collection of pictures.[36]

Still in 1618, we will find Chamberlain remarking on two positions going respectively *au plus offrant* and *au dernier enchérisseur*. For the first of these, the post of Chancellor of the Duchy of Lancaster, Cranfield – though in the course of his financial reforms he had declared the office redundant – proved the most successful bidder. Fearing, he wrote to Buckingham, that his competitors would outdo him, he offered his money in gold ('I pray your lordship to burn this').[37] The highest bidder for the second post, that of Master of the Wards, was Sir Robert Naunton, who had previously obtained that of Secretary of State by promising to make Buckingham's brother, Christopher Villiers, his heir.[38] Sir Henry Yelverton had done better. Having obtained the Attorney Generalship without the assistance of Buckingham, he presented the King with £4,000, as a gratuity after the event. James was so delighted that he took the new Attorney General in his arms, and told him it was just what he needed to buy himself some dishes with.[39]

As shown by his angry reactions, Bacon felt strongly about the buying and selling of office. Position, he said, should be 'by the King's own act', not 'by labours and canvass and money', which produced 'a wilderness and solitude in the King's service'; and along with his friend Sir John Digby, he was one of the few officials under James who refused to bribe his way to office.[40] He owed his promotion as Attorney General (for which one candidate had offered £10,000) and as Lord Keeper (for which another would have given £30,000) to the King's recognition of his merit.[41] The nearest he ever came to giving a bribe was when, on being made Attorney General, he produced a masque in honour of the marriage of Somerset as an act of courtesy towards this favourite, who, though he had not helped him to the post, had indicated that he wished for the recognition.[42] As Chancellor, Bacon had many opportunities of dispensing patronage, both lay and ecclesiastical, but he stuck to his principle: 'rather make able and honest men yours than advance those that are otherwise because they are yours'; and not a murmur has ever connected him with this particular 'foul way' of making money.[43] Unlike Lord Burghley, who saw nothing wrong with accepting a hundred pounds in gold from the Bishop of Durham for 'extraordinary furtherance' in obtaining his bishopric, Bacon followed the practice of his friend Bishop Andrewes, and his own advice to Buckingham. When awarding a living he sought out and promoted 'well-deserving' and able men, though personally unknown to him, going rather 'by care and inquiry' than by 'their own suits and commendatory letters'.[44]

The racket of the Spanish pensions was a unique 'vice of the times'. Gardiner was horrified by what he found in the documents then available, but the full extent of the damage was not known until the 1940s, when Gondomar's dispatches were published in Spain.[45] It was then confirmed that from the moment peace was signed between the two countries in the summer of 1604, Philip III had been paying out large sums to most of the top people at the English Court, and that by 1621 practically all the principal members of James's Council had been on the Spanish payroll for nearly two decades. They are listed year by year, under imaginative pseudonyms, with the amounts paid out to them, the largest of all being awarded to 'Dante', or Lord Treasurer Suffolk, who, with 'Amadis' – Lady Suffolk – received £3,000 a year for supplying inside information on Court, Council and Treasury. (Lady Suffolk, who was always clamouring for more, once garnered a total of £20,000 in one year.) Dorset and Devonshire appear with various sums against their names, Northampton – 'Roldan' – was paid £40,000 for two years' services; and Admiral Sir William Monson – 'Socrates' – well placed to inform on the strength of the Navy, and the movements of Dutch and English ships in the Channel – appears as a privileged pensioner. Sir George Calvert – 'El Cid' – Privy Councillor, and later Secretary of State, was paid £2,500 a year for news of the deliberations in Council, while his fellow Secretary, Lake, and Admiral Nottingham, 'Jupiter,' were in receipt of a mere £1,000 a year apiece.[46]

The worst shock for Gardiner was to find the reliably anti-Spanish Cecil also listed with £1,000 a year – to begin with, for not content with this supplement to his income, already swollen with secret profits from the Court of Wards, Cecil kept asking for a rise, and brazenly demanded large extraordinary gratuities with every piece of information supplied or service rendered. In the spring of 1608, for example, he received £12,500 to ensure English neutrality at the time of the Dutch–Hapsburg treaty – after Lady Suffolk had reminded Philip of all she and Cecil had done for him over those negotiations. The following year he asked for £15,000, and was allowed £11,000, to be shared out between himself and Lady Suffolk.[47]

Although Cecil's policies were not visibly influenced by his Spanish pension, he would not have been awarded these enormous sums if he had not in some form supplied value for money. But considering the ugly implications of the very notion of 'Spanish gold', we must wonder what can have been his hidden thoughts as he sat beside Coke at the trial of Ralegh, putting in a good word for him against the invective of the hectoring Attorney General, probably out of sheer embarrassment and shame, knowing as he did that Ralegh was to be condemned ostensibly – for this was what most impressed the jury – because he had listened (without accepting it) to the Spanish offer of a yearly pension of £1,500. 'I will show you wholly Spanish,' Coke had shouted at him, 'and that you offered yourself a pensioner to Spain for intelligence!' In other words, to 'furnish the peace with Spain' and 'advertise what was intended' by England against Spanish interests – the very terms of the Spanish pension Cecil was at that time negotiating for himself.[48]

The Spanish pensions of James's reign were a well-kept secret. Sir John Digby, the English Ambassador in Madrid, had succeeded in intercepting

Gondomar's lists and begun to decipher the names on them with the same dismay that was to overcome Gardiner in telling what he had learned of the story. And it was not until 1616 and the trial of the Earl and Countess of Somerset for the murder of Overbury – when Coke, unearthing a confidential dispatch among Somerset's papers, scented treason – that Bacon discovered their existence. Digby was called back to inform on Somerset's private dealings with Spain, and Bacon, responsible as Attorney General for inquiring into the murder, found him (as he told Buckingham) 'somewhat reserved'. Bacon was 'in no appetite for secrets', he said, but it was difficult to carry on investigations in the dark, particularly since he believed (rightly, as it now turns out, though Gardiner had been happy to acquit him) that 'no man was liker to be a Spanish pensioner than Somerset, considering his mercenary nature', as well as his pro-Spanish interest.[49] Digby was accordingly commanded to acquaint Ellesmere and Bacon in detail with the secret of the pensions. James, already in the know, had good reason to be philosophical about the corruption of his ministers by the Spanish Government; and by others too, for Cecil also received an allowance from France, and Naunton, his Protestant Secretary, took money from the Dutch, the French and the Venetian Republic – which, said James, when he heard of the threefold pension, would save him from raising his servant's salary.[50]

There is no comment from Bacon on these revelations, and we may presume that Buckingham did not disclose that he was a pensioner himself. But we know that Bacon felt strongly about this kind of practice. He had already denounced it in general terms in 1592, when, praising Elizabeth, he had compared her with the King of Spain: 'hath she given large pensions to corrupt his Council?' And in 1619, when he learned what was going on, he branded *the Spaniard* for corrupting 'so many of our nation . . . to attempt our weak ones and our false ones withal'.[51] Bacon is occasionally mentioned in Gondomar's dispatches, and no doubt this Spaniard and this Englishman, who enjoyed each other's company from their opposite camps, liked to pick each other's brains. But the only list on which Bacon appears – as 'Plato', with Digby or 'Alcides' and 'Trajan' or the Archbishop of Canterbury, and James himself as 'Leandro' – is a key to the pseudonyms used of all the courtiers. No sum of money is anywhere linked to his name.[52] Garrett Mattingley, commenting on the Spanish dispatches in 1955, noted that the intelligence network which Gondomar had developed at the English Court was not at all to that fastidious Spaniard's taste. He thought the business 'a nasty one', and repeatedly advised his Government to apply the money instead to restoring the decayed Spanish fleet.[53] Gondomar's long-standing affection and respect for Bacon may well have originated in a favourable comparison between 'Plato' and most of the other high-ranking courtiers over the 'nasty business' of the pensions.

Bacon was less uncompromising about that other 'foul way', increasingly resorted to by the Crown to reward its servants, the sale of honours. Titles were still occasionally bestowed for outstanding services; Bacon himself was created a Viscount in this way, but Ellesmere had had to pay for his peerage, as did many of less worth who were now filling the House of Lords with *nouveaux nobles*.[54] If a title involved some real public service, Bacon did not object to its sale, to the right people. It had been at his own suggestion – as a part of his plans for the plantation of Ireland with 'men of estate and plenty' – that James had created the title of baronet. In accordance with Bacon's proposal, the order was set up in 1611 for a limited number of gentlemen, who undertook to pay the Exchequer a sum sufficient to maintain thirty foot-soldiers in Ireland for three years, declaring on oath that they had not paid anything else for the honour; and the Treasurer was instructed to keep the fund apart, that it might 'be wholly converted to that use for which it had been given and intended'.[55] This was the kind of honour – or 'dignity', as he preferred to call it – which Bacon approved of. Unfortunately, in the atmosphere of James's Court, dignities inevitably degenerated. The power of making a baronet went to swell the patronage of Cecil, and of Northampton, who had a hand in the making of no fewer than thirty-four baronets in three years.

A few years later Bacon reluctantly recommended the sale of eight peerages, in order to ensure that the King should not present himself as a pauper before the Parliament he wanted James to summon. They were launched by Cecil (with the opposite aim in view: to avoid the necessity for calling a Parliament at all), and the proceeds of the first baronage, £10,000, were divided between the Crown and its underpaid Secretary, Sir Ralph Winwood.[56] Later, when his debts were pressing upon him, and despite his conviction that 'private suits do putrify the public good', Bacon himself asked for 'the making of a baron' (unsuccessfully).[57] This inconsistency was probably not so evident to him as it may seem to us. What he deplored whole-heartedly was the sale of knighthoods on the open market, as when Cecil, needing to call in a loan, gave his business associate, Sir Arthur Ingram (according to Menna Prestwich 'the most unscrupulous tycoon of the age') the selling of six knighthoods, which were (she noted) 'promptly hawked around'.[58] Bacon could claim good service rendered, and would not think he was breaking his own rule, 'not to beg anything which shall not bring gain to to King'. In his eyes there was a wide gap between a hard-working Government servant receiving his due, and a horde of anonymous suitors with no merit beyond their need; and he would not have placed the making of a baron, entrusted to a Lord Chancellor well able to select a worthy candidate, in the same category as an indiscriminate sale of the dignity of knighthood in the City.

Not that he liked any of it. He would never have advised the selling of these titles – 'which I do not in my judgment approve', he told the King

– had it been possible to avert 'a greater evil' by some other means.[59] But such devices at least were almost entirely above board. The trouble with most bastard revenues was the large gap they engendered between a hypocritical condemnation of the practice in public and its private condoning, which made it only too easy for one man to fall by the wayside while others more guilty raised their voices all the louder against him. Hypocrisy and self-deceit over these gains had been carried to a fine art by such men as Bacon's uncle, Lord Burghley, who, in office for half a century, received ten times his official salary under the counter. In his study of the Cecils, father and son, as Masters of the Wards – Burghley for thirty-seven years, Robert Cecil for fourteen – Hurstfield followed the ins and outs of their convoluted thoughts at length in an attempt to determine whether or not they were, as many in their own generation believed, really corrupt.

The Court of Wards was the source of more glaring abuses than any of the other feudal money-making devices resorted to in Tudor times. When a knight who held his title from the Crown died before his children were of age, they became Crown wards. A guardian was appointed by the Master of Wards to administer their estates, of which, on their marriage, a large portion was shared out between guardian and Crown. Much hardship was often suffered by widows who could not afford to buy back their children's wardships, and by the wards themselves – bought, sold, bequeathed and sometimes 'gambled away between a nobleman and a judge in a game of dice'. The inhumanity of their treatment can be gathered from the fact that when the powerful Coke set out to buy a rich ward he looked on any efforts made by a mother, when begging for her child's guardianship at a rate she could pay, as 'sinister courses' against him.[60]

A generation earlier, as Attorney for that Court, Bacon's father had been so horrified by its 'preposterous proceeding' that he had presented Burghley with a drastic plan of reform, in which he urged that the chief thing was not the ward's estate but his mind, of which no care was taken at all.[61] Nothing came of it, and later Bacon, too, prepared a project for the reform of this Court, stressing the need to watch over the good education of Crown wards, and for 'special care to be taken in the choice of persons to whom they were committed' – preferably their near relations ('no greedy persons, no step-mothers nor the like').[62] Nothing came of this either. Both Elizabeth and James tried to dissolve the Wards, but, as with monopolies, the Government could so little do without them as a source of income that when the Parliamentarians gained power in 1640, far from abolishing them, they established a second Court of Wards to finance their side of the war.[63]

Burghley had inherited from his predecessors the gratuities, the secret sales, the systematic destruction of evidence – and the ability to quiet his own sensitive churchman's conscience with appropriate arguments. It was no easy task for Hurstfield, as a modern historian, to find his way through the 'maze of euphemism and ambiguity', the ceremonial game of refusals in which donor and recipient disguised the gifts they exchanged, as shown by such letters as were left undestroyed, despite the usual injunction, 'fit for burning'. But Hurstfield finally acquitted Burghley of corruption, concluding that he had operated the system with moderation and conservatism, leaving it much as he found it, and that he was after all worth his hire to the Queen. 'She had no better servant,' he said, 'and she knew it.' So did the minister's young nephew Francis, when defending against a libel 'her Majesty's ancient and worthy counsellor, the Lord Burghley, whose carefulness and pains her Majesty hath used in the counsels and actions of this realm . . . in all dangerous times and amidst many and mighty practices'.[64]

There was nothing moderate about the secret takings with which Robert Cecil built up his enormous estates. 'Lust for wealth and power', as Hurstfield wrote, 'marked a great part of his career.' As Secretary of State, exerting almost complete control of political power for well over a decade, he brought the pressure of the Privy Council to bear on his rich monopolies of starch and imported silks, fixing highly profitable new leases for them. He used Government funds to back his privateering ventures, and we have seen him quietly pocketing an allowance for many years from Philip II, as well as exacting big bonuses for every additional service. As Lord Treasurer he bought up large areas of Crown land, and sold them back when he found them unprofitable; he traded numerous minor offices in the Treasury and almost certainly made raids on it for his own investments, as Suffolk was to do after him; he obtained thousands of pounds out of jewellers and goldsmiths anxious to recover their debts from the Crown, and borrowed huge sums for his building projects from the customs farmers, while camouflaging his more shady deals in the City 'behind a cloud of trusts and conveyances'.[65]

Finally, he extended the profiteering racket in the Wards far beyond its relatively modest Elizabethan bounds. Even before he inherited the Mastership of this Court from his father, Cecil had been an expert in the secret sale of wardships to his friends and servants, and, by the most complicated and devious machinations, to himself. When, for example, his brother-in-law Lord Cobham had bought the wardship of a rich heiress, only to resell it two days later to Ralegh (for a profit), on condition that Ralegh transferred it back to Cecil himself, Cecil's explanation to a trusted servant who had particularly asked him for the wardship strikes, as Hurstfield put it, 'the purest vein' of his hypocrisy. He had been driven, he said, to take it for himself, and through an important figure like Cobham, as only in this way could it appear that 'some great person' had the grant, which would be more acceptable to the mother, who had begged in vain for the guardianship of her child.[66]

With unremitting watchfulness over his every act and word, Cecil covered his tracks so well that many of his subtly contrived depredations are only now coming to light, whereas the presents Bacon took as they came were laid bare in his lifetime for everyone to see. There could be no greater contrast than that between the two cousins, the inscrutable manipulator of kings and the Chancellor capable of accepting a well-filled purse in the presence of others, with a compliment to the giver on its embroidery. 'Strange to me', said Coke, 'that this money should be thus openly delivered.'[67] The curious vein of innocence which many have found in Bacon has been variously described as hypocrisy, arrogance and an inept naivety, 'a sublime confidence . . . that fatally disposed him to think all men susceptible to skilful management'.[68] In fact, far from managing other people, as one historian noticed, with his mind on 'large endeavours', Bacon did not sufficiently enquire into the attitude of others towards himself.[69] Had he done so, he would have been more wary of his political rivals, on the watch for other people's blunders. Gardiner compared Bacon with Dean Williams, his successor, who was 'never in doubt of that of which Bacon was certain to be ignorant – the precise light in which any action was likely to be regarded by ordinary men', and who, accordingly, 'shunned everything approaching corruption like the plague'. In no sense of the term could Williams be called innocent.[70] No doubt that 'overweening confidence in his own integrity' which Gardiner had seen in Bacon could be irritating to his contemporaries, as it is to some of his critics today. But he really did have his mind on large endeavours. Or would he have been heartened, 'in the midst of a state of as great affliction as I think a mortal can endure', by the vision of 'a golden world' in which, thanks to his fall, those vices of the times he had shared in would be no more?

18

Bacon's Essential Justice

After following Robert Cecil through long years of tortuous hidden tracks, Joel Hurstfield finally exonerated him of real corruption, on the ground that he fulfilled this historian's principal saving criterion: he was worth his hire. First because, alongside the unrelenting pursuit of his fortunes, James's minister was just as unrelentingly active in promoting what he looked on as the best interests of his country, and secondly because in the end he made one desperate effort, against his own interests, to right some of the wrong he had done. It was an effort that could not 'wholly redeem' the dishonesties of a lifetime, but, Hurstfield believed, went far to counterbalance them. If public service was the criterion, he concluded, Cecil, who had given up his career in this unsuccessful attempt, could not be dismissed as corrupt.[1]

Impressed by the tragedy of this final breakdown, Hurstfield underestimated Cecil's essential injustice, his failure to meet the two other basic criteria, as this historian himself had defined them: that profits should be in proportion to service, and that the public good should not suffer. It suffered in numerous ways, as Hurstfield himself has shown, from Cecil's ministrations, not least among them, from his notorious practice of defending his position by keeping able men out of the King's service.[2] But above all it suffered because, if many of his clandestine takings could be seen as part of the system, others could not, since they affected his judgement and actions. Thus Cecil fails to pass the test on both counts: he grossly overpaid himself, and, in the process, he became so deeply entangled in the network of his own sinister deals that the public good was sacrificed time and again.

Cecil's most lenient critics cannot pass over as 'vices of the times' the stranglehold on government finances held by the customs farmers, brought about by his personal dependence on them. When, as in 1611, he was £20,000 in their debt, how could the Lord Treasurer grant a contract to a rival syndicate, or even negotiate a new lease more advantageous to the Crown – much less attempt to cancel the whole system? How could he insist on a reduction of Court pensions which he knew to be indispensable, when he himself was making deep inroads into the public revenue to line the pockets of any courtiers who might influence the King in his favour? This practice was one of the damaging uses of power included by Hurstfield among the signs of real corruption – rightly, for, unable to institute the sensible policy of retrenchment with which Bacon and Cranfield were later to succeed in reducing the Crown debt, Cecil was forced to resort to unpopular stop-gap measures which created more problems than they solved.[3] A similar situation arose when he made his gains from the scandalous alum monopoly through Cranfield's crooked business partner, Ingram, to whom he had sold the six knighthoods mentioned earlier. The Crown suffered heavy losses, and however honest his intentions, the powerful Minister's hands were tied.[4]

But it is for his damage to human lives that Cecil deserved the profound resentment which made 'so many rejoice, and so few even seem to be sorry', as Northampton noted on his death.[5] He deserved it for the stratagems with which he removed every rival to power in his way, 'the fair promises and underhand rubs to hinder their preferment'; for his unashamed admission to the King that he had feigned friendship 'for such a wretch as Ralegh' in order to draw him on, and his corresponding suggestion to the eternally grateful James, that under the pretext of a technical flaw in the conveyance, Ralegh's ancestral home could be presented to the reigning favourite.[6] Among other such unscrupulous practices, he had secured Lord Hunsdon's parklands and extensive commons on his death, behind the back of Hunsdon's kinsman, the rightful claimant, and transformed them into private enclosures for a highly lucrative sheep exploitation, riding roughshod over the rights of the inhabitants, and forcing the pace, in the face of local rioting and bloodshed. And this in complete disregard of the statutes against enclosures which (with Bacon) he had battled for in Parliament only two years earlier, in 1601.[7] As for the villagers living near his home, they had no love for 'Robin the Encloser', who had similarly enclosed Hatfield Wood, robbing them of their common land to plant his mulberry trees, and the thirty thousand grape vines he had ordered from France.[8]

Neglecting his father's precept not to touch the land or goods of anyone attainted for treason, Cecil had also made a fortune out of the fall, secretly promoted by himself, of his brother-in-law Lord Cobham.[9] He had promptly acquired most of the condemned man's estates well below their market price, and carved them up, by a series of piece-meal transactions, in such a way that Cobham's children could never recover them. After which he put the demoralized heir of the other – loyal – branch of the Cobhams so much in his debt that, ignoring the claims of wife and child, this unfortunate relative willed his whole estate away to Cecil. Small wonder if towards the end of his life, while still collecting his well-hidden rake-offs, Cecil was overwhelmed by the enormity of his sins.[10] It was in all likelihood to salve the pangs of his conscience, as well as to find a way out of the financial impasse he had himself helped to bring about, that in 1610 he revived an old project to dissolve the Court of Wards in exchange for a yearly contribution to the Crown.[11]

The project, which became known as the Great Contract, was a complete reversal of Cecil's earlier policy of 'impositions'. These were in effect an abuse of the prerogative, whereas the Contract involved the surrender of a great part of it. At this point a clear statement in Parliament was required, setting forth Cecil's reasons for this act of 'astonishing altruism', as it has been called, on which he was now staking his power and fame. But Cecil, so long used to concealing his intentions behind a smokescreen of camouflage, presented his project with so much ambiguity and inconsistency that it was generally seen as a lure to bring on further contributions, and a rumour went round that £20,000 had been set aside to compensate the Master of Wards for the loss of income he would suffer.[12] A Cecil ready to sacrifice his personal interests for the welfare of the state (as he himself bitterly noted) was scarcely credible, and the Great Contract broke down because of the widespread distrust he had done only too much to deserve. When, in a last effort to salvage the project, he publicly renounced any compensation for himself, it was too late.[13] Thus, whatever the potential value of the Great Contract – about which historians disagree – it was because of the habit of deviousness in which he had long cloaked his worst corruption, and which he could not suddenlty cast off, that this true scion of Machiavelli failed to bring off the one truly redeeming action of his life.[14] None the less, it was Cecil's sincere effort to launch the Contract, added to his ten years' watchful service as 'a keel to the ship of state', which earned him Hurstfield's exoneration from essential corruption. What will be this historian's judgement – and ours – on the corruption of Bacon, seen against that of his kinsman and fellow statesman?

Hurstfield paused in his study of the Cecils to examine Bacon's case, and, as we might expect, he exonerated Cecil's cousin also of any real corruption. The petitioners' complaint against Bacon, he pointed out, 'was that justice – not the injustice they sought – had been done'. In Hurstfield's view, Bacon had been 'greedy, shortsighted and indiscreet', but, when examined in detail, his judgements 'turn out to be those which an honest and independent judge would have given had he been trying the cases on their merits alone'. In other words, he had obeyed Elizabeth's injunction to Burghley, that he be not 'corrupted by any manner of gift'. If he had admitted 'that to trade gifts in the circumstances was an offence and technically corrupt, he showed item by item that money never corrupted the justice he administered. With the surviving evidence before us,' Hurstfield concluded, as Gardiner had done before him, 'we are inclined to take him at his word.'[15]

This was in 1958. By 1973, however, when he again took up the subject of Bacon's corruption, Hurstfield had changed his mind. 'Clearly,' he now wrote, 'since the anticipation of a gift may distort a trial, for a judge to accept a gift before, during or after a lawsuit, from any party involved, is corruption.'[16] What had caused this shift in perspective? He had come across an allegation – almost certainly a mistaken one, as has now been shown – in Edwin Abbott's bitterly critical biography of Bacon (1885), that on one occasion he had distorted justice, not for money, but under the influence of Buckingham.[17] It was, Hurstfield noted, the only case known to him. But Bacon, in showing that it was possible for him to be corrupt had, so to speak, let him down, and Hurstfield was no longer inclined to take him at his word. A new criterion was thus added to the historian's tests for corruption under Stuart rule: the term should now apply in all cases 'where gifts are accepted while holding judicial office'.[18] At this rate only a very rich man could be Chancellor.

Hurstfield was using the term here in the sense of real and essential corruption, but, rather than a properly grounded moral judgement, this was a conventional, arbitrary decision on his part. After finding that Bacon's justice had not been corrupted by money, it is irresponsible to pronounce him corrupt because he might have been. Had Bacon been central to his investigations, Hurstfield would surely have given the screw one more turn and detected the strong prejudice and the false scholarship so much in evidence in the critic who had convinced him of Bacon's dishonesty. Following his resolve to decide each case of what is loosely termed bribery on its real merits, he would have enquired whether, like Burghley and Cecil, Bacon had been worth his hire. From the point of view of this study it is interesting to note the pull of a delusively authoritative detractor on the mind of so objective and balanced a historian as Hurstfield. We have therefore all the more reason to examine the single case of real corruption through undue influence alleged against Bacon.

The accusation is not a new one: Macaulay had already declared, without looking into the matter, that the Chancellor, violating 'the plainest rules of duty', had 'suffered Buckingham to dictate many of his decisions'.[19] 'By no means be you persuaded to interpose yourself by word or letter in any case depending,' Bacon had advised Buckingham not long before he received the Seal, 'and by all means dissuade the King himself from it . . .'[20] But for the young favourite to refrain from bombarding his mentor with letters on behalf of the suitors who bombarded him was too much to expect. There are thirty 'interposing' letters from Buckingham, spread over Bacon's four years in Chancery, and the mere fact that they exist, and that Bacon did not return them unopened, is enough for Macaulay, reading an earlier century in the light of his own, to condemn their recipient out of hand.

'Interposing' in Bacon's day was not looked on as extraordinary or improper, for the simple reason that the judiciary was not yet a completely independent body. For centuries the King himself, assisted by his judges as mere legal advisers, had been the sole judge between claimants. It was still usual for him to discuss important cases with his judges, who – in Bacon's view, if not, by now, in Coke's – continued to be the King's 'conduits', drawing their power from him. The Chancellor was himself no more than the King's representative in Chancery, and however he might have preferred to administer justice as he thought best, Bacon could not have looked on royal interference in the same light as we should see it today.[21] The perspective was different, as it was for Sir Thomas More, who had received many interposing letters from Henry VIII, and for Bacon's father, who had quite a few from Queen Elizabeth, and there are scores of letters from Essex to the Lord Keeper Puckering.[22] The whole University of Oxford once wrote unashamedly to Burghley 'earnestly conjuring' him to influence the Lord Keeper in favour of a suit they had on hand; and we will recall the lady-in-waiting who, when Anthony Bacon offered her £100 to appeal to the Queen over a Chancery case (on behalf of a man he was trying to save from having his ears cut off), refused because she considered the gratuity too small.[23]

Such letters would not have been written had the respective Chancellors or Lord Keepers not responded, as far as 'in justice' they could – and sometimes, perhaps, a little further. And we may assume that among the thousands of causes Bacon handled every year, those to which the favourite had drawn his attention would be attended to with particular care. There was no secret about these letters; we find no 'PS burn this'. Docketed by honest Meautys with such notes as 'the ear of Buckingham to your lordship on behalf of –', a number of them are requests to expedite proceedings; there was nothing anomalous in this, since queue-jumping, and even payment to expedite a suit, originally honoured with the name of a 'fine' and made to the Crown, were not then accounted corrupt practices. And in many cases it looks as if Buckingham had penned off his notes to get rid of an importunate suitor rather than to oversway justice, following Bacon's own recent advice that he should do suitors 'what right in justice you may'.[24]

However the fact that the letters are less numerous after the Chancellor's first two years in office may be an indication that Buckingham had been discouraged, for it is clear that Bacon did not read them without protest.[25] If some are imperiously worded, quite a few of them are written in an apologetic tone, as if to meet some tactful remonstrance, and on a number of occasions Bacon turned down his patron's request point blank, or opposed it with sufficient firmness for Buckingham to desist.[26] Always assuring him of his wish to serve him, Bacon would add some such phrase as: 'but where the matter will not bear it, your Lordship, I know, will think not the worse but the better of me if I signify the true state of things to your Lordship.'[27] Buckingham, for his part, took the failure of his efforts gracefully. ('The cause, I know, hath gone contrary to his expectations, yet he acknowledges himself much bounden to your Lordship for the noble and patient hearing he did then receive.')[28]

Letters requesting judicial favours often contained a message from the King ('I doubt not but his Majesty has been satisfied with the equity of the cause'), or royal instructions on other matters, as we can see from one of Bacon's typical replies, addressed to Buckingham and meant also for James.[29] He reports, in October 1617, on the litigation between the Egerton cousins (one of whom was later to bring his cause before Parliament), that he planned to 'enter into the treaty of accord, according to his Majesty's commandment, which is well tasted abroad in respect of his compassion towards those ancient families'. Taking the matter up again three months later, Bacon writes, doubting whether the suit for the patent of alehouses is advisable; expressing himself unable to help Mr Levison, since the grant he has asked for 'cannot be good in law'; unconvinced that the business for Hawkins is good either in law or conveniency; happy to say that the Egerton parties have agreed to arbitration – he expects 'to make an end of it according to justice and conscience'; in very good hopes of 'effecting your Lordship's desire' for the good of Sir Gilbert Houghton, but that for Moor's former patent of salt he must first acquaint the Council. Buckingham writes back only that he is 'very glad that there is good hope of Sir Gilbert Houghton's business'.[30]

The one case in which the favourite appears to have influenced Bacon against his better judgement, and as a result affected Hurstfield's judgement of him, is that of *Steward v. Steward*. It was discovered in Spedding by the assiduous Abbott when embarking on his *Francis Bacon* – with the declared purpose of showing the Chancellor in a less favourable light than that in which he had hitherto been seen. Delighted with this windfall, he cited it in his introduction as firm evidence that Bacon had deliberately perverted justice, 'not for money – of which no one accuses him – but *out of servility to some great person*'.[31] Gardiner found the evidence inconclusive, but Spedding's co-editor was shaken. Spedding himself, looking further into *Steward v. Steward*, came to the conclusion that, as a result of Buckingham's intervention, Bacon genuinely discovered he had made a mistake, and – as always when he caught himself in error – acted promptly to repair it.[32] But it was not until 1986 that Clifford Hall, the first legal authority to tackle the case in our time, argued convincingly that there is no evidence whatever of malpractice on Bacon's part, and endorsed Spedding's interpretation.[33]

The story runs as follows. On 16 May 1617 the plaintiff, Steward Junior, claimed from his two uncles (his guardians, and the executors of his father's will) the rents and profits due to him on his share of his father's estate, along with his legacy of £800, and insisted that interest on the legacy, amounting to a further £600, was also due to him, although it was not mentioned in the will. He evoked a death-bed statement by his father to that effect. Dr Nicholas Steward, a civil lawyer of good repute, on behalf of the defendants (himself and his brother), denied all knowledge of such a statement, and declared that interest was due neither in law nor in equity. Bacon referred the matter to three Masters in Chancery, who reported that it had been the testator's express intention that interest should accumulate in favour of the plaintiff. However, investigating in our day, Hall found that the Masters had exceeded their warrant, and that when Bacon, appointed Lord Keeper in March that year and still relatively new to his duties, confirmed their decision (4 November 1617), he had acted too hastily, and failed to pronounce clearly on the substantive issue.

Throughout 1618 Dr Steward resisted various efforts to enforce the decision, and, early in December, Buckingham, to whom Dr Steward finally appealed, wrote asking Bacon ('though I know it is unusual in your Lordship to make any alteration when things are so far past'), whether he could not find 'place for mitigation'. Steward, Buckingham warned – and this was the whole extent of his intimidation – was 'a stout man that will not yield to anything wherein he conceiveth any hard course against him', and it would be a pity if he made a complaint against the Chancellor. No doubt it would have been, but Bacon may by now have realized, as Hall was to do, that Dr Steward was in the right and that, threatened with fines and orders for the interest that was not in fact due, his appeal was justified. Since the case had never been heard in court, Bacon may well have felt that he had put too much trust in the Masters. If there had really been 'hard course' against Dr Steward, neither his reply – that he would speak to him and 'what is possible shall be done' – nor the action he now took need be seen as 'a shameful assent' to an 'intimidatory' command (as it was through Abbott's eyes). Bacon promptly obtained an agreement from both parties that the matter should be placed in the hands of arbitrators, a procedure he always preferred, particularly in the case of unseemly disputes between near relations, and which could now provide the quickest and firmest decision in a cause that had dragged on for two years.

Whether the arbitrators decided in favour of the defendants, or the plaintiff chose to settle for immediate payment is not known. On 22 February 1619 it was ordered that the legacy (£800) together with the rent of the lands (£100) should be paid at once to Steward Junior, no mention being made of any interest accrued. There is no evidence here that, as his detractor put it, Bacon was a judge who, for the sake of favour, 'wrests justice to the wrong side'. He had revised his decision, Hall concluded, 'not in order to pander to Buckingham but to satisfy the dictates of his conscience, since, as Ellesmere had enjoined, the Chancellor's task was to judge according to truth and not upon default of the party, as at common law'.[34]

To some extent this question must remain, like that of Bacon's share in enforcing the patents for gold and silver, a matter of opinion. But one fact points conclusively to the justice of his decrees: none of them was ever reversed. Had Bacon awarded unjust decrees, for whatever reason, his impeachment would have been the signal for their reversal in Parliament. With no one to protect him – the King, after his short-lived support, inattentive to his old servant's most basic wants, and Buckingham, forgetful of all his promises, being intent only on turning Bacon out of York House and doing it up for himself – there was nothing to prevent aggrieved suitors from coming forward in hopes of having their decrees reconsidered. Justice upon petition in Parliament had now become general practice (some two hundred petitions for review were to be made in the 1620s); at the same time, any claim against Bacon would have found immediate support, for as soon as Dean Williams was appointed Lord Keeper, all the orders 'corruptly' issued by his predecessor were referred to him for review. Although a number of Williams's own decrees were later to be reversed, the severe scrutiny of this entirely hostile Lord Keeper produced not a single unjust decree of Bacon's.[35] Several bills of complaint were brought in immediately after the Chancellor's fall – among them that mentioned earlier on Lady Wharton's cause[36] – but not one of them reached a third reading. We recall the results of the repeated appeals made by Edward Egerton in Chancery. As Dixon put it, 'neither Williams nor Coventry, after reference to the Judges and Masters in Chancery, could detect a flaw in the judgement; and the decision which was paraded as Bacon's chief offence in 1621 was confirmed on appeal by Williams in 1622, and by Coventry, on a further appeal, in 1627.'[37] Bacon himself could note after the second session of the Parliament that had spent so much of its first session impeaching him: 'not a petition, not a clamour, not a motion of me.'[38] This fact was noted by Rushworth in the seventeenth century and by Carte in the eighteenth. In the nineteenth, Spedding, not content to rest on the word of reliable historians, carried out his own exhaustive search in the records of Chancery, but he found no trace of a reversal, whether by the Lords, or by the King's Commission, the only two procedures open to appeal.[39] As Carte had rightly concluded, 'the discontented suitors, enraged at the loss of their causes, applied for relief against Bacon's decrees, as supposed to be made by corruption; but they found them too just to be reversed.'[40]

In comparing Bacon with his fellow government officials we should look beyond the vices of the times they shared (although unequally, since the others' share was so much larger than his and the incomes they made out of them were three or four times the size of his own). We should consider the more recondite, inner corruption of the men involved. Bacon's open manner of receiving gratuities shows him less tainted than Cecil, and his weakness in accepting embroidered purses is less offensive than Cecil's cool revelations to his intimates of his round-about reasons for pocketing the loot, and than Burghley's efforts to deceive God, if not himself, about his secret gains. We know that Dean Williams, Bacon's successor in Chancery, frightened of the scandal it could bring him, as his contemporary biographer remarked, 'was never sullied with the suspicion that he loved presents'. He had no need of them. He had prepared himself a safe retreat by hanging on to his various sinecures in the Church. To which another was added when he received the Seal: in order to compensate him for the loss of the gratuities that had been fatal to his predecessor, he was made Bishop of Lincoln on the same occasion. Williams succeeded so well in keeping all his preferments that it was said 'he was a perfect diocese in his own person, being at once Dean, Prebendary and parson.'[41] But Clarendon, who knew him well, describes him as 'a man of a very corrupt nature', a view which is confirmed by his whole life – including the selling of state secrets, and the suborning of witnesses and offers of large bribes in exchange for a pardon, when his offences caught up with him.[42]

And how do Bacon's two self-righteous denouncers stand? For his labours as financial adviser to the Court and later as Lord Treasurer, the pitiless usurer and fraudulent speculator Lionel Cranfield – now Lord Middlesex – deserved some part of the hidden gains he made as extortionate Master of the Wards and as a well-disguised taker of bribes in the Treasury. But his gains were out of all proportion to his services, and corruption was inbred in him. On his condemnation by the Lords in 1624, Chamberlain – with the world – 'marvelled they proceeded no farther to degrade him upon so many just reasons'. He attributed their restraint to fear that through the manifold Villiers connection which Cranfield had acquired in the Bedchamber – 'and not gratis' – he might yet 'live to be a pestilent instrument and crush some of them hereafter', as he had already once attempted to do.[43] Even Southampton now spoke with regret of Bacon, whose faults, he said, could not compare with those of this 'wolf to all kingdoms'.[44] 'In future,' wrote another contemporary, 'men will wonder how my Lord St Albans could have fallen, how my Lord of Middlesex could have risen.'[45]

Coke is not known ever to have taken or given bribes, and Judge Whitelocke was probably right in claiming that those who 'had causes before him found him the most just, incorrupt judge that ever sat on the bench'. True, as Chief Justice of the Common Pleas, he had grown rich on the sale of offices, a practice which, though he had denounced it before taking up the post and was to denounce it again later, may still be described as an abuse of the times. But the acceptance of gifts is condemned for one reason only, because it provokes a judge to act unjustly. Without taking gifts, but impelled by prejudice, pride, and what Bacon picturesquely called his 'plerophoria' (an overweening self-confidence), Coke was often as unjust a judge as he had been a public prosecutor.[46] As Attorney General, in the name of the prerogative, he had strained the letter of the law against the spirit, bending procedures to his purpose, or inventing them if necessary, and ruthlessly editing out of the evidence anything favourable to the accused. As Judge, in the name of the common law, he had defended the most unjust decrees against any intervention of prerogative law on behalf of his victims. On the King's Bench he fought tooth and nail against an appeal in Chancery (reviving an obsolete statute for the purpose), to maintain a decree by which a couple of swindlers had obtained many times the price of their wares. In the Common Pleas, Coke's battle against the ecclesiastical courts, as Archbishop Abbot protested, had become so flagrant that 'there existed no crime so great' as not to win his protection.[47]

These were the kind of 'unjust and scandalous' judgements which according to Bacon ought to be avoided at all costs, because (like many of Cecil's machinations) they often involved not merely the acquittal of the guilty – a mere 'streamlet' of pollution – but the condemnation of the innocent and 'the oppression of the poor and hungry man'. This was an outcome which Bacon strove hard to prevent, and his promptness to repair an error should also be seen in this light. He thought bias was far 'more pernicious than bribery', and he looked on bullying the accused as a serious abuse of justice. 'Even reproofs from authority', he maintained, 'ought to be grave, not taunting.'[48] Coke, whether as Attorney General, inveighing bitterly against Essex (and later invoking 'that noble Earl' to insult Ralegh), or in Parliament, attacking Cranfield with particular brutality and refusing to weigh the evidence, was out for blood.[49] Bacon, on the other hand, while claiming strict justice, was merciful and gentle, and made such efforts to be fair to the accused that, as Brian Vickers has shown, they are apparent even in the way he ordered his state prosecutions so as to give the accused 'a better light'; or, as Bacon explained in one case, so that his 'memory or understanding may not be oppressed or overladen with the length of evidence, or with confusion of order'. A procedure which, as Vickers remarked, 'to anyone familiar with some of the unscrupulous tactics of state prosecutors under both Elizabeth and James (including that of deliberately confusing the prisoner), appears quite admirable'.[50]

By Hurstfield's criterion of service to the state, the really corrupt were the idle courtiers, and above all the favourites, who did little but sell favours, acquire land and urge the dissolution of Parliaments. It is by these people that the indirect revenues were distorted and allowed to seep away into 'the thirsty soil of luxury and greed'.[51] By this criterion most corrupt of all were the two men Bacon was obliged to serve if he wished to serve the state at all, the men who were to deplore his 'bad conduct' in Parliament and glibly congratulate themselves on escaping the contagion of his corrupt ways. The worst was James himself, whose infatuations dictated his policies, and who continually encouraged his favourites to take outsize bribes, and, in particular, gave Buckingham his support in the 'vicious system of spoliation and blackmail' (Willson) which he ran with his mother's assistance – if not she with his.[52] And this, by arousing a general resentment which Parliament dared not manifest against Buckingham himself, was indeed the real cause of Bacon's downfall. James too was caught in the system, but it was nothing if not personal self-indulgence which bound him to extend the network of Buckingham's fortunes far and wide at the expense of the Crown finances, and, in the end, to save the favourite and sacrifice the servant.

Bacon was in his own eyes the justest judge who had sat in Chancery for forty years, and not even Coke, ready as he was to pronounce a corrupt judge 'the grievance of grievances', had ever accused him of contracting to sell justice. (It was at the incontestably corrupt John Bennet that Coke was to brandish Magna Carta, exclaiming, 'to no man shall justice be sold!')[53] If, as Hurstfield originally decided, corruption in judges 'is the distortion and delay of justice in return for bribes', Bacon is exempted. If we are to judge him, as Cecil was judged, by his honest efforts to serve the common weal, his contemporaries must speak for him. 'No man was ever so much in love with equity, and none embraced the interests of the public good with so much passion as he did . . . He was as upright a man as he was a just judge.' So wrote his first biographer, five years after his death.[54] He was, as testified by one who had been intimately acquainted with his struggle for over twenty years, 'a most indefatigable servant to the King and a most earnest lover of the public, having all the thoughts of that large heart of his set upon . . . benefiting, as far as possible, the whole human race'.[55]

Many have wondered, since his impeachment, not only how such a man could have fallen, but that he should have accepted with so much humility the condemnation of men far deeper in corruption than himself, and taken so much comfort in being 'the anvil' on which reformation would, he hoped, be 'beaten and wrought'.[56]

19

The Aftermath

And was that reformation 'beaten and wrought'? Were the courts of justice, as Bacon eagerly foresaw, 'purged and reduced to their true honour and splendour'? Parliament 'intended a reformation', the Lords had declared. Was James's injunction followed, when he told them that henceforth 'no bribery nor money be given for the hearing of any cause'?[1] In Chancery for the time being the example of Bacon made the open acceptance of gratuities too dangerous a practice, but none of the other habitual abuses were affected. A reinstated Churchill, in particular, went on busily spreading his network of forgeries for another three years before he was finally unmasked. We know that the prudent Williams accepted no gifts, but, motivated by 'passion and levity', wrote Clarendon, his were the very 'unjust and scandalous' judgements which Bacon condemned above all others, and a number of them were reversed.[2] They were also considerably fewer, for under his direction Chancery no longer attracted the large numbers of suitors that had been drawn to it by Bacon's expeditious decrees. Nevertheless, it was once again blocked up with causes, among the first people to suffer being our friend Chamberlain, who complained that its 'dilatory courses' were 'one of the greatest grievances of our commonwealth'.[3]

After the King had stopped Coke from regulating Chancery out of existence, no further efforts were made to reform it, or to regulate the jurisdiction of the courts. Corruption continued to flourish in all of them, and by the end of the century nothing in the administration of justice had fundamentally changed. 'Our nation has ever been and is guilty of this sin of bribery, even in the reigns of the best of our kings,' wrote an exasperated subject in 1691 – after a Civil War, a Revolution, a Restoration and a still more Glorious Revolution had come and gone. As Bacon had said, 'Like the leprosy it spreads itself in all the courts of equity and justice, even to the meanest office.'[4] So it would continue until the nineteenth century. It looks as if the condemnation of Bacon had indeed 'served but the turns of a few'.[5]

On the impeachment of Cranfield in 1624, the Treasury suffered a fate similar to that of Chancery. It fell into the hands of Sir James Ley, that corrupt 'old dissembler', as Whitelocke called the man who had sat in Bacon's place in the Lords and pronounced the sentence upon him.[6] Appointed principally because in his old age he had married into the clan, Ley proved as inept a Lord Treasurer as Williams was a Lord Keeper. Nor was his successor, Sir Richard Weston, any more efficient: 'a mean and abject spirit', Clarendon remarked, and his immense gains while in office caused him to be looked on, after the death of the favourite in 1628, as a second Buckingham. Accused some years later of extensive malpractice, Weston evaded impeachment by obtaining a dissolution of Parliament. Meanwhile Charles's Secretary of State, Sir John Coke (no relation to Edward), combined industry with covetousness, as his predecessors had done before him; and Buckingham's gains, while he lived, continued to dwarf all others.[7] Whether or not the part played by Bacon in the award of monopolies was the real cause of his downfall, he was, except for the infamous Michell (imprisoned until 1623), the only one to suffer for them. The inquiry into the patent for alehouses was abandoned a few weeks after Bacon's condemnation in Parliament, and the charges against Sir Christopher Villiers were withdrawn. Before Bacon was out of the Tower, Sir Edward Villiers, the principal patentee for the monopoly of gold and silver thread, cleared of all blame in the Lords, had returned from his prudential mission in the Palatinate to take his seat in Parliament. He was granted a lease of the customs and subsidies on gold and silver thread, in exchange for surrendering his Mastership of the Mint – which was restored to him three years later, with further honours to follow.[8] As for Sir Giles Mompesson, who had been sentenced *in absentia* to degradation from his title, a fine of £10,000 and imprisonment for life, he returned from abroad, also in 1623, free to resume his obnoxious activities. Let us hear the world, via Chamberlain, on the subject:

> The business of making gold thread that was so cried down the last parliament as a monopoly exceeding prejudicial to the common-wealth (and for which Sir Giles Mompesson, Sir Frances Michell, and others were called in question, and divers others in danger) is now proclaimed and set up again under colour of a new corporation. We have Sir Giles Mompesson here again and as it seems in *statu quo prius*, for he begins to put his patents (for alehouses and the like) in execution, because they were not then abrogated and damned by act of parliament, when he was driven to so foul a retreat and had such shameful ballads and pictures made of him, but these are the revolutions of the world . . .[9]

Coke finally steered the Monopoly Act through the Commons in 1624. Just as his proposals for the reform of Chancery had been a recapitulation of Bacon's *Ordinances*, the Monopoly Act embodied all the suggestions for the abrogation of monopolies which Bacon had urged on James in November 1620, and Bacon's text served as its preamble.[10] The same sort of thing would happen, Menna Prestwich noted, when in 1625, after toppling Cranfield, Coke 'unblushingly echoed' in Parliament the financial advice of the man whose fall he had brought about.[11] As we might expect by now, Charles I was to have no trouble in evading the terms of the Monopoly Act, and after considerably enriching the Crown, his monopolies were to be the principal grievance brought against him by Pym in 1640. None the less, the Parliament which abolished the House of Lords, the Privy Council, the prerogative and the monarchy itself did nothing further about this particular grievance.

The principal outcome of Bacon's fall was a long series of impeachments. The downfalls that followed his own bore no more relation to the degree of the minister's personal integrity or to the value of his services than such falls had done in the past, and they continued to be determined by a single factor: loss of the King's, or in other words, of his favourite's support. By empowering the House of Lords as the highest court in the land – thus making the greatest property owners in the kingdom its highest judges – instead of strengthening the Commons's hand, Coke had strengthened that of the favourite. A perfect method was now available for Buckingham to get his way against the ever weaker King's wishes. He almost succeeded with Mandeville, who had been spared when Bacon fell. (One victim was enough, and James wanted no more impeachments.) But Mandeville came near to incurring his predecessor's fate later that year, when Cranfield, now married into the tribe, was claiming the Lord Treasurership. One of Buckingham's minions was set to work collecting petitions to accuse him of gross corruption in Parliament, and only by giving up the Treasury in exchange for the nominal honour of Lord President of the Council did Mandeville escape prosecution.[12]

Again, when Buckingham sought the downfall of Williams (who had briefly supported Cranfield against him), we find Phelips, now the favourite's client in the Commons, selecting for action, out of the many petitions brought before Parliament, those which could help his new patron to impeach the Lord Keeper. But Williams was a born intriguer, and he soon managed to make his peace with Buckingham, so that the Treasurer, as a contemporary predicted, did not take his Lord Keeper with him in his fall.[13] Cranfield's time, however, had come. And like so many others, his ruin was not brought about because of his depredations in the Wards and the Treasury, in the end no worse than Cecil's, and still less because of his fundamental corruption. He fell because of the too-effective measures he had taken against the Crown's disbursements on courtiers, rendered yet more unpalatable by his harsh and overbearing way of enforcing them, and also, and above all, because he had dared to introduce 'a darling of his own', his young brother-in-law, as a potential rival to Buckingham.[14]

Cranfield had manipulated faction, and he was toppled by it. 'Remember a Parliament will come!' Bacon had warned him on his accession to the Treasury.[15] When it came, he resisted the attack launched on him by an overwhelming new coalition with all his obstinate might. But with Coke on the war-path, accusing him of 'many great, exorbitant and heinous offences' and inveighing once more against the 'grievance of grievances', and with Buckingham adamant, his well-prepared defence was swept away.[16] He fell, as Clarendon rightly diagnosed, because Buckingham had decided to crush him, 'as he had done others in the same high station'. It was only too easy for the favourite to procure

> some leading men in the House of Commons to cause an impeachment for several corruptions and misdemeanours to be sent up to the House of Peers, against that great minister, whom they had so lately known as their equal in that House, which (besides their natural inclination to those kinds of executions) disposed them with great alacrity to the prosecution.[17]

James regretted a good minister, aware that Cranfield, as one of his impeachers later admitted, 'had merited well of the King and done him that service but few had done'.[18] He warned Buckingham that his turn would come, and Coke was indeed to cry 'grievance of grievances' against Buckingham two years later. James was old and ailing, and could not resist his still unassailable favourite, but he saw the writing on the wall. As Clarendon recalled, he told Prince Charles, who was siding with Buckingham at this juncture, that 'he would have cause to remember how much he had contributed to the weakening of the Crown by this precedent he was now so fond of'. He knew too well

> that it would shake his own authority in the choice of his own ministers, when they should find that their security did not depend solely upon his own protection; which breath upon his kingly power was made so much without a precedent (except one unhappy one made three years before, to gratify likewise a private displeasure) that the like had not been practised in some hundreds of years, and never in such a case as this.[19]

Other historians saw this just as clearly. Henry Elsing, a reporter on the Lords' debates in 1621, described the impeachment of Bacon as 'a false step made by the King and a leading card to others soon after', and Peter Heylin wrote that in giving up Bacon and his successors to the power of the Parliament, the King not only weakened his prerogative, but 'put the

House in such a pin [so much excitement] that they would let no Paliament' pass (for the times to come) without some such sacrifice'.[20]

Against the 'slippery standing' which was the only real result of Bacon's impeachment, rectitude was no protection. In Chancery, wrote Clarendon, the standing was so unsafe that by the time Bacon's good friend Sir Thomas Coventry, a man 'reputed of great integrity' – and incidentally one of the few who had deprecated the Commons' barbarous sentence against Floyd – was appointed Lord Keeper, no one had died in the post 'for near the space of forty years'. Coventry himself 'had need of all his strength and skill (as he was an excellent wrestler) to prevent himself from falling. Nor had his successors for some time after him much better fortune.'[21] By the end of the decade the threat hanging over ministers' heads was so continual that government by Parliament became impossible, and no Parliament was called for eleven years. It was then only one step from impeachment, which still required some attempt to prove technical corruption, to Pym's keener weapon, attainder on trumped-up charges of treason, a process that could not fail, because the Commons gave themselves the right of declaring any actions they pleased to be treasonable. It was also one step from the illegal and violent methods which Coke had used against Michell and Floyd – in his efforts to endow the Lords with the powers of a judicial court – to Pym's equally illegal and violent transformation of the Commons into such a court.[22]

When 'King Pym' obtained his majorities by whipping up the House with fake alarms of 'desperate designs both at home and abroad', and incited the London mobs to hysteria as a background for his unconstitutional attainders and executions, he was following in the footsteps of Coke, who had led the Commons' clamour for the Catholic Floyd to be beaten and hot bacon-fat poured into his wounds. Like Coke and Phelips in this, his head was full of 'cruel and bloody' – though non-existent – Romish plots. And the Commons, quick to catch fire from such incitements, was punishing anyone who dared to express dissent with far more severity than was ever used in the now abolished Star Chamber, ruled by the very methods they had so strongly attacked in Charles. From here it would be but one more step to a Parliament 'purged' of any claim to represent the nation, which, ignoring the Lords, sentenced the King to death. Not to speak of the ensuing rule of Cromwell, who, wrote Clarendon (while admiring his administrative gifts), 'punished dissidents, bullied judges, imposed taxation and imprisoned counsel for the defence far more effectively than Charles had ever been able to do', and thus destroyed the laws and liberty he had set out to preserve.[23]

If Pym and Cromwell were the legacy of Coke, Bacon's spiritual descendant was this same Edward Hyde, Earl of Clarendon, Charles II's Lord Chancellor, and the generally objective historian of the Rebellion, who has often been quoted in these pages. Bred on ideas of tolerance and humanity under the empirically conservative approach which the 'great Tew Circle' he belonged to had inherited directly from Bacon, like his predecessor, Clarendon looked on violent change as inimical to any society. The very notion of civil war appalled both Chancellors, and they were convinced that it could be avoided if, as Clarendon wrote, political interests did not 'fan a small fire (that could easily be extinguished) into a flame', and if men would defend the foundations, while permitting an open-minded discussion of so much that was inessential in Church and lay controversy.[24] Inspired like Bacon with an urge for reform, and convinced that the King should govern with a united Privy Council and frequent, increasingly responsible Parliaments, Clarendon deplored the new turbulence of the Commons. Again like Bacon, he attributed it to the factious attacks on one minister by another, of which the campaign led by Coke and Cranfield against Bacon had been the first. Had the moderate counsel of these two great Chancellors prevailed, some historians now think, constitutional government in England could have been achieved without any need for the disruption and destruction of a civil war.[25]

After he had faithfully served the first Charles and stood by the second throughout his exile – and, under the latter's rule, laboured for years to achieve a constitutional reform – Clarendon was himself made the scapegoat of Charles II's mistaken policies. Unfounded accusations were raked up against him in Parliament by a political cabal of ambitious young courtiers disappointed of advancement, under the leadership of the second Duke of Buckingham – the evil genius of Charles II, as his father had been of James and Charles I. Impeached in his turn, and left to his fate by the King, in almost the same words James had used of Bacon, Clarendon withdrew to exile, conscious that his innocence would not save him, and realizing, as Bacon probably had, that he could not defend himself without showing the Crown in an unsavoury light.[26] Charles, meanwhile, freed from the moderating influence of his minister, could devote himself to the personal (and religiously intolerant) government he had wanted. Just as the impeachment of Bacon had pointed the way to the Civil War, that of Clarendon would lead in the long run to the final failure of the Stuart kings and the Revolution of 1688.[27] 'It pleased God in a short time', wrote Clarendon of himself, to restore him to entire confidence and serenity of mind, so that 'they who conversed most with him could not discover the least murmur or impatience in him, or any unevenness in his conversations'.[28] It had pleased God to do the same thing for Bacon half a century earlier. During 'all the time of his eclipse of fortune', wrote Archbishop Tenison, there was in him 'no abjectness of spirits'. His mind was 'not distracted with anxiety nor depressed with shame, nor slow for want of encouragement, nor broken with discontent'.[29] A year after his fall, Bacon himself confessed, 'I do most times forget my adversity.'[30] Yet it cannot have been easy for a man who had lived as Bacon had, oppressed by his debts and faced with penury through the petty but effective obstruction of Williams in Chancery and Cranfield in the Treasury – the one because he feared Bacon's return to office, the other because of ineradicable ill-will. 'I like my Lord Treasurer's heart to your Lordship so much every day worse than other', Meautys could write to his master, with justice, eighteen months after Bacon's fall, 'as that I cannot imagine he means you any good.'[31]

Already in the autumn of 1621 the King's measures for Bacon's relief had been rendered ineffectual by Cranfield's delaying tactics over his pension, needed as much to repay his debts as for survival, while Williams, ignorant of the law, was splitting hairs to stay his partial pardon at the seal, as 'prejudicial to the service of the King'.[32] Having given up all expectations of the comfortable income originally promised him by Buckingham, along with some help for his debts and a pardon of his whole sentence, all Bacon hoped for now was to 'keep out of want', and live to study, rather than 'study to live'.[33] But the harassment went on, and by the autumn of 1622 he was reduced to sending James an urgent plea. The pension allowed him by the King had been stayed, and the lease for his one other small source of income (the petty farms, which he kept for his wife's maintenance) had been seized without 'a shadow of a legal course'. He was now 'in great extremity, having spread the remnants of his former fortunes in jewels and plate and the like upon his poor creditors . . .'[34]

Throughout those years he was occasionally, partially, tardily relieved, and he obtained the preliminary pardon – not from Buckingham, but probably, as we have seen, through the kind offices of the Spanish Ambassador. He would have suffered none of these troubles had the favourite not finally forsaken his old friend, to whom he now wrote only the coldest ceremonial notes, when he wrote at all. Buckingham had actually been aggravating his troubles and prompting Bacon's tormentors backstage. The King, he told his one-time mentor, had 'showed with great forwardness his gracious favour towards you'; but any favour was too much, now that Bacon had incurred the favourite's deep displeasure by refusing to hand over his much cherished home, York House, which, as noted above, Buckingham wanted to do up for himself. Not content with seizing Wallingford House from the Howards, in exchange for the release of Lady Somerset from the Tower (as he was to take possession of Chelsea House on the fall of Cranfield), Buckingham was furious with Bacon for refusing to hand over his house also, in exchange for which he was offered the much desired freedom to live in London. To be turned out of the house 'where my father died and I first breathed', as Bacon tried to explain, would be to him 'a second sentence'; but needless to say, the favourite got his way. Bacon gave up his home and in the end withdrew to Gray's Inn, 'for quiet and the better to hold out'; while Buckingham, Chamberlain tells us, took 'great delight' in rebuilding that beautiful mansion overlooking the Thames, where he was to feast the whole Court four years later 'with such magnificence and prodigal plenty, both for curious cheer and banquet that the like hath not been seen or known in these parts'.[35]

More tragic for Bacon than that loss, and than Buckingham's unfulfilled 'yea, undesired professions and promises', was the loss of one who, aside from protector and patron, had been for him the friend whose first steps in statesmanship he had lovingly watched over when he still hoped, as Gardiner put it, that Buckingham's presence at Court 'would be conducive to the better government of the country'.[36] It is sad to see Bacon asking the favourite, in the name of 'our former friendship, which began with your beginnings', to 'deal clearly' with him – which Buckingham never would.[37] When, early in 1622, he finally obliged Bacon to give up York House, he used the Treasurer, Cranfield, as his intermediary. Spedding preferred not to believe that Cranfield was selected 'as the man to whom Bacon would least like to part with it'.[38] But, knowing Buckingham, we may wonder, particularly when we find Bacon later in the year – having just heard from Meautys that Williams and Cranfield were using 'such a savage word among them as fleecing' – complaining to his less than sympathetic patron of the Lord Treasurer's many 'certain messages and promises', clearly made with no intent but to vex and 'to do just nothing upon his Majesty's gracious reference'. 'God in heaven bless your lordship', Meautys had exclaimed, 'from such hands and tongues!' And Bacon now appealed to Buckingham: 'Good Lord, deliver me from this servile dependence, for I had rather beg and starve than be fed at that door.'[39]

The good lord did nothing to lighten the cares of his follower – who, none the less, managed to produce some of his major works at this time, his *History of Henry VII*, the *History of the Winds* and the *History of Life and Death* among them; and who continued to watch over Buckingham's errant footsteps, particularly when he was involved in 'rocky business', as Bacon called the disagreement between King and Prince over the Spanish marriage.[40] In some of the excellent advice he noted in memos (possibly never delivered), and in the brief letters he wrote off to Buckingham up to the last months of his life, there is an unmistakable note of personal concern for his one-time pupil in statecraft, for whom he feared 'the blow of assassination'. He did not live to hear Buckingham called 'the enemy of all Christendom' in Parliament, fatal words that were to be found sewn into the hat of his murderer.[41]

For himself Bacon continued to hope that he might 'live out of want and die out of ignominy', but very specially the latter. And in June 1624, having, as he felt, made sufficient atonement, he appealed for that pardon of his whole sentence, including readmittance into the House of Lords, which Buckingham had promised him, and which alone could remove the blot on his good name. The pardon was drawn up but not signed, and we find him still at the New Year of 1626, three months before his death, when another Parliament was about to begin, recalling – in vain – that 'Sir John Bennet hath his pardon; my Lord of Somerset hath his pardon, and, they say, shall sit in Parliament. My Lord of Suffolk cometh to Parliament . . .'[42] Yet, despite a few passionate protests against such injustice (suitably toned down between draft and final version), Bacon had accepted adversity. A curious combination of sincere repentance with a clear conscience and a fully occupied mind enabled him to endure the rudeness of his enemies and the coldness of his friend with equanimity.

'Let us make the right use of our afflictions,' Clarendon was to write, 'improve ourselves and grow better by them,' and 'practise Christian patience'; and in the same key Bacon, who had long known what it was like to 'descend into himself' and 'call himself to account', had noted, soon after his fall, that 'the joys of the penitent be sometimes more than the joys of the innocent.'[43] His Christian patience extended to the least friendly among his acquaintance. He would write quietly for an interview with Cranfield over the lease of York House (than which nothing could have been more unpalatable to him), 'hoping to gather some violets in your garden'; and in his last will he was to entrust the publication of his orations and epistles to Dean Williams, by then – temporarily – in a humbler frame of mind since he himself had fallen from power, and ready to accept the honour 'with all thankfulness'.[44]

'Virtuous men', Bacon quoted a close friend as saying, 'were like some herbs and spices, that give not their sweet smell until they be broken and crushed.' Some of us may be inclined by now to take Bacon at his own valuation. If the sentence was just, the judge was juster. As for the man, we may begin to feel, particularly when looking through the letters and writings of his last years, that he had some affinity with 'those sweet herbs and flowers' he had his table strewn with, because they refreshed 'his spirits and memory'.[45]

Part III

The Servile Self-Seeker

20

Thirsting for Power

The corruption and ingratitude of which, in Macaulay's view, Bacon was a living example, were allegedly founded on the 'boundless ambition' for which he 'stooped to everything and endured everything', and on his unredeemable coldness of heart. The present section will be devoted to the first of these two evil propensities, the supposed craving for precedence and patronage. For which, Macaulay declared, Bacon was willing to abase himself to the dust – so greatly did he fear 'being left behind by others in the career of ambition', his sagacity having 'early enabled him to perceive who was likely to become the most powerful man in the kingdom'.[1] Since this image of Bacon was first launched, his 'unworthy ambition' has come to be looked on as his principal characteristic, the advancement of learning being of far less interest to him than the advancement of Francis Bacon. Indeed wrote one critic in 1894 that 'his consummate policy in the pursuit of his own interests was almost without a precedent'. A children's history book dwelt on it exclusively in 1959. In 1976 one of his most sympathetic biographers took for the title of her story 'the winding stair to great place'; a rickety period staircase is reproduced on the cover.[2]

Before Macaulay no reputable historian had looked on Bacon as a self-seeking politician. We have seen his contemporaries' recollections of him as an indefatigable servant of King and state, who embraced the public good with passion.[3] To John Carteret, his most thorough biographer in the eighteenth century, it was clear that he had neither a 'very aspiring' nor a 'very covetous' disposition', but 'was content to wait the proper seasons and favourable opportunities of rising which are brought forth by time'.[4] But in the twentieth century a curious situation developed. However consistent, pertinent and objective historians may have found Bacon's advice, and however much they might deplore that it was not taken, they felt bound to remind their readers that it had been tendered principally, if not solely, with a view to improving his own position. That his primary aim was self-aggrandizement is now taken for granted. But the historians' own findings are often quite different, and they may be carried away by them for a few sentences of admiring narrative, before they stop to catch up, and declare – with no attempt to substantiate their remarks – that whatever the appearances, Bacon's motives were essentially self-serving.

Thus we will find one writer (in 1927) convinced that his 'careful and discriminating scrutiny' of all the burning questions of his time was 'in harmony with the soberest judgement of the present day' and 'wise far beyond the wisest wisdom of his century' – and, of course, that he had prepared it with his own self-advancement in mind. Another (in 1966), after noting that Bacon felt strongly about the Parliament he was urging King James to summon – in order 'to carry out financial reforms he considered of the highest importance' – adds that he was obviously prompted by his anxiety to be made a Privy Councillor. A third (in 1977), after informing us, with particular reference to his advice to Villiers, that Bacon's motivations 'were infinitely more profound and idealistic than those of his colleagues', goes on to remark – without hiatus or explanation – that his motives in writing it were 'predominantly self-seeking'.[5] In some authors Bacon is hardly ever free of this kind of running commentary. If he spoke for a project that was against his own financial interest, he was 'hoping to impress the Queen with his unselfishness'. If during James's first Parliament he worked with admitted enthusiasm and efficiency on a number of national causes, his every effort is 'primarily a ploy for gaining attention' or 'palpably designed to impress'. When brilliantly summarizing the major issues involved in the union of England and Scotland, he was in reality 'making certain to assure James of his continued devotion to the cause'.[6]

A study of the personal motives behind people's actions – provided the analysis is based on facts, without a prejudging thesis – can be useful to illuminate obscure historical episodes. If research in the records of the Virginia Company shows that Sir Edwin Sandys, when he made his patriotic speech in Parliament urging that only Virginia tobacco should be imported into England, was a fraudulent manipulator of votes who had reduced his company to bankruptcy, we are entitled to look for ulterior motives.[7] But except where motives are the centre of interest, it is not generally thought necessary to remark on a character's personal aims at every turn. In this Bacon is the exception, and the practice is so habitual that it goes unnoticed. Thus a historian reviewing the parts played in Parliament by twenty-four of the King's legal advisers will make no reference to the motives of twenty-three of them. Only over Bacon does he pause to remark that, clearly, he was 'striving to make his activities in the Commons a stepping-stone to advancement'.[8] When, on the other hand, it looks as if Bacon was acting without an ulterior motive in view, a biographer is unable to take this for granted, but feels obliged to defend him against an imaginary sceptical reader or historian – if not against the biographer's own previously expressed censure. We will come across emphatic statements like this one (with reference to Bacon's speeches for the Statute of Tillage): there is 'every reason to believe that he was motivated solely by his own conviction'. And sometimes writers can be seen struggling to overcome the prejudices they share with their readers: 'We may have our suspicions, may be eager to find indications that the motives ascribed to him did not operate; but we can confidently assert that in Bacon's parliamentary career there is nothing to fix a dishonourable stain on his name.'[9] Finally when Bacon is found acting unmistakably against his own interests, his behaviour is put down as 'inexplicable'.[10]

The game of politics has always been played in part for self-advancement, but who is to say exactly where the frontier lies between a desire to fulfil the ego by exerting power, and the consciousness of a power within, which a man or woman may exert for the benefit of others? Most politicians manage to blend personal motives with higher aims, to their own satisfaction. In the forceful Coke, as one historian has seen it, they were so fused as to be indistinguishable.[11] This would not do for Bacon. Imbued from his earliest years with the Protestant doctrine that man is not to be judged by his actions but by his intentions, there have been few people more convinced than he was of the need for continual self-watching, particularly when in 'great place'. As far as conscious motives are concerned, we have more to go on in his case than for most of his contemporaries in public life. His declared aims are available to us in the prefaces to his works, in the explanations of his actions in letters to the King or to his private friends; and we have his writings on the value – and the traps – of power. For oneself, that is. In judging other men's actions he never claimed to have 'windows into men's hearts'. 'The justice of every action consisteth in the merits of the cause,' he maintained. 'As for the inward intention, I leave it to the court of heaven.'[12]

In attempting to ascertain whether Bacon was in practice a selfish power-seeker or a faithful servant of the public good, we should look first at his clearly expressed ideas on the thorny question of ambition. We can then examine the merits of the causes he espoused; compare his life's aims, as he saw them, and his views on the main issues of his time, with his actions in Parliament and in office; and note, in particular, whether he acted against his beliefs in order to gain, or retain power.

Among the three types of ambition distinguished by Bacon, the first – the 'vulgar and degenerate sort' of those 'who with restless striving seek to augment their personal power in their own country', and 'refer all things to themselves' – is now generally attributed to Bacon himself. In his own age the most noteworthy example was the Earl of Essex.[13] For the second, less selfish ambition, 'of those who seek to advance the position of their country in the world', Bacon would have had statesmen like Cecil in mind. 'The third is of those whose endeavour is to restore and exalt the power and dominion of man himself, of the human race over the universe.' This aim – 'the noblest and the holiest a man could set himself' – filled the sails of all Bacon's writings, from his early 'devices' to the posthumously published *New Atlantis*, and was the principal ambition of his life. 'Believing I was born for the service of mankind', he wrote at the age of forty, in a preface that was not published in his lifetime, and wondering what service he was best fitted to render Bacon decided that

> if a man could succeed in kindling a light in nature – a light which could in its very rising touch and illuminate all the border-regions that confine upon the circle of our present knowledge; and so spreading further and further, should presently disclose and bring into sight all that is most hidden and secret in the world – that man, I thought, would be the benefactor indeed of the human race . . .
>
> For myself I found that I was fitted for nothing so well as for a study of truth . . . Nevertheless, because my birth and education had seasoned me in business of state . . . and because I thought that a man's own country had some special claims upon him more than the rest of the world . . . I both applied myself to acquire the arts of civil life, and commended my service, so far as in modesty and honesty I might, to the favour of such friends as had any influence.[14]

In choosing to serve the state 'against the inclination of his genius', Bacon was not only meeting the demands of an age which looked on that service as the first patriotic duty of any man qualified to perform it; he was fulfilling his father's dearest wish.[15] Projects for political reform had been part of the very air he breathed in his father's household, and Bacon was animated throughout his public life with the urge to emulate the richly endowed Sir Nicholas on whom he had modelled his political aspirations – quoting and invoking him in and out of season – and from whom he had drawn his image of the ideal statesman-king, finally embodied in the priest-governors of the *New Atlantis*.[16] His contemporaries were aware of the connection. 'What then his father was, that since is he,' wrote Ben Jon~ e Lord Chancellor's sixtieth birthday; an ographer described him as 'bound to im her, so greatly loved by Queen Eliza- bet ngdom in his hands'.[17]

Y reform, the reform of learning – his Gre art from his father, as was his interest in e al ambition of Bacon's life. Not all students of his writings are aware of his profound emotional involvement with this project to 'illuminate the border regions' of knowledge, conceived before he left Cambridge at the age of fifteen: 'the greatest birth of time', as he described it in his twenties; 'so fixed in my mind', as he wrote at the age of thirty, 'as it cannot be removed'; which when he was forty was his 'only earthly wish'; and beside which, at sixty, when at the height of power, 'all other ambition seemed poor in his eyes'.[18] Although it was so solitary an enterprise that, he warned possible followers, 'it may frighten us a little by its loneliness'.[19] There were, however, the rare joys of being understood, as when he learnt of the 'full approbation' given to the *Instauration* by his friend Toby Matthew 'with much comfort, by how much more my heart is upon it, and by how much less I expected consent and concurrence in a matter so obscure'.[20] The longing to find 'a quiet entry into minds choked and overgrown' comes up repeatedly in his writings. 'I yearn for some secret of initiation which, like the coming of April or spring might avail to thaw and loosen your fixed and frozen minds,' he cried in 1608; and three years before his death we find him still exhorting his fellow men in the same urgent tones:

> Wherefore if there be any humility towards the Creator . . . any zeal to lessen human wants and sufferings; any love of truth and natural things, any hatred of darkness, any desire to purify the understanding, men are to be entreated again and again . . . that they should humbly draw near to the book of Creation [and meditate on it] . . . This men must learn, and resuming their youth, they must become again as little children, and deign to take its alphabet into their hands.[21]

Finding an entry for new ideas into minds often 'beset and blocked' against them was no easy matter. It was not only Coke, and the 'Scholar-King' who were bewildered by the *Novum Organum* (though James promised to read it with attention, even if he must 'steal some time from his sleep').[22] During the first decade of the new reign, Bacon tried out nine different ways of introducing his project, finally publishing only the *Advancement of Learning* and one other treatise. He lived in a continual tension between the desire to give his idea to the world, and the need to hold it back, for fear its unfamiliarity might frighten people not yet ready to receive it. As it did. Even Toby Matthew did not always approve, and Bacon's kinsman and trusted critic, Sir Thomas Bodley, did not approve at all.[23] As Aubrey put it later, ''twas held a strange presumption for a man to attempt an innovation in learning' and 'a sin to make a scrutiny into the ways of nature'.[24] Bacon, however, declared his determination 'not to yield to his or to anyone's impatience, but keep his eyes fixed on the ultimate success of the project'.[25]

Insensitive to his difficulties – or ignorant of them – critics preoccupied with the notion of the philosopher as a 'fortune-hunter' remarked that 'it needed some hope of office to bring him to write the *Advancement of Learning*' (1938); or that after he was made Attorney General there would be no more science, the 'steady climb to office' not requiring such aids (1976).[26] In reality nothing could distract Bacon from his *Great Instauration*, which embodied the same argument, he said, as the *Advancement of Learning*, 'only sunk deeper'; and he was so keen to launch it that the 'delay became unbearable'. 'My time is running out, sons,' he called to future generations, 'and I am tempted by my love of you and of the business in hand to take up one topic after another'; and throughout all his active years 'I number my days!' was his continual cry.[27] Already in 1607, the year he was made Solicitor General, he had felt he was 'immersed beyond his wish in civil business'.[28] The progress reports he had been sending abroad to Toby Matthew 'in the midst of a term and parliament' ('my *Instauration* . . . sleeps not'; 'my great work goeth forward . . . I alter ever when I add') continued, as we learn from Matthew himself; and on taking his seat in Chancery in 1617, while outlining his plans to clear an enormous backlog of pending cases, Bacon made a point of reserving 'the depths of the three long vacations' for those studies to which he was 'by nature most inclined'. (Unlike Shakespeare's lawyer, who slept 'between term and term'.)[29]

Despite much other legal, parliamentary and ministerial business, he fulfilled this promise. His friends went on receiving his 'vacation's fruits', and, when, still in 1617, he wrote to Buckingham that he had left not a petition unanswered, though under a 'flood of business of justice', he could truly add that his mind was 'upon other matters'. Those matters were the thirty odd philosophical treatises he had been intensively at work on from 1613 to 1619, in addition to the *Novum Organum* – the second part of his *Great Instauration* – which he had been 'altering and adding to' since 1590, and which he published, incomplete, in 1620, so 'that in case of his death there might be some outlines and project of that which he had conceived'. The work went on, and in his last months he was still outlining his plans for the whole *Instauration* to a scholar abroad, in hopes that God would favour his scheme 'by reason of its infinite utility'.[30]

This, then, was the 'holiest' ambition to which Bacon's thoughts flew in 'the spaces of other business', to the extent that after nine years of government service he could describe himself as 'not versed in state affairs', having so far led a studious rather than an active life.[31] So deeply was he involved in his studies that more often than not a promotion brought on some psychosomatic trouble (a 'melancholy' or 'distaste', with a sense of 'present peril'), while he remained quite unruffled by any setbacks in his worldly career.[32] Yet if he ever considered escaping from public cares to devote himself to 'leisure and letters' – evoking the biblical line, 'my soul hath been a stranger to her pilgrimage' – it was only when he saw his way blocked to a position of influence, or when he felt his labours in office had been vain. Those contemporaries who, like the historian Peter Heylin, thought he should have been 'abstracted from all affairs of state' and provided with means 'for the going on of his design', could have been right, but this was not Bacon's view.[33] 'To write at leisure what is to be read at leisure', he confided to the French scholar, Isaac Casaubon, 'does not interest me; but to bring about the better ordering of man's life and business, with all its troubles and difficulties . . .'[34]

The distressing conflict conjured up by some of Bacon's biographers between the ambition of the will and that of the understanding – both of which he condemned – was no such thing.[35] Like More and Sidney, like Clarendon and Milton, and like many others involved in the great Renaissance debate on the merits of action and contemplation, Bacon was drawn to the peace of a scholar's life, and when he chose the turmoil of politics he was only too well aware of its 'indignities and perturbations'. No doubt the practical difficulty of leading two lives at once was considerable, particularly for a man who confessed himself, as Bacon did, 'by inward calling to be fitter to hold a book than play a part'.[36] But the so-called conflict was in Bacon – and probably in all of them – no more than a fertile tension of the mind. Bacon saw no opposition between serving the state and serving 'the kingdom of man'. On the contrary, contemplation and action, theory and practice – Saturn and Jupiter – were in his view 'strictly conjoined', and he was convinced that action, the *matter* in which they were founded, could not but enrich all forms of thought. The art of politics flowed from the same fountain as natural philosophy; it was indeed 'a great part thereof'. Speculative studies acquired 'new grace and vigour' when 'transplanted in active life'; and both history and the law were always best written by 'those who had handled the helm of government' and understood 'the grounds of nature, manners and policy'.[37] One commentator in our time has described Bacon as 'the first great statesman of science', another called him 'the supreme Legislator of the modern Republic of Science'; and the condescending remark of his doctor, William Harvey, that he wrote philosophy like a Lord Chancellor, has been seen as his greatest merit: he could think about scientific questions with the experience of a judge in human affairs.[38]

Laying the foundations of his *Instauration* was a task for a king or a pope, requiring 'a thousand hands and as many eyes', and in seeking high office Bacon hoped also for that 'larger command of industry and ability to help him in his work' – the theme of his early letters to Burghley, and of his lifelong efforts with the great and the scholarly, at home and abroad.[39] Burghley thought him too speculative, Essex referred all things to himself, and Bacon's efforts to interest a more likely patron, Prince

Henry, who appreciated him and had made him his personal solicitor, were brought to an end by the Prince's premature death in 1612.[40] His status as Lord Chancellor gave him for a short time that 'commanding ground' from which he could begin to launch 'the greatest birth of time', to influence some of the best minds on the Continent, and to work for 'the stilling of controversy' in Europe, without which there was no hope for that world-wide correspondence between learned men which was to form his Universal College.[41] For it is with this purpose in view that Bacon's whole policy was geared to the aim of averting the civil wars of which he had seen the effects at first hand in France, and which he feared, only too justly, would spread through many countries, portending for literature and the sciences 'a fatal tempest'.[42] For Gardiner in 1869, Bacon's philosophy was the key to his political life. At the turn of the 1990s three scholars discussing his 'grand political strategy' and his inspired *New Instauration*, while each emphasizing a different aspect of them, saw the two programmes as the inseparable components of a single vision.[43]

There is so far little evidence of that craving for power for its own sake denounced in Bacon by Macaulay and his followers. Still less of the extreme view taken by the German and Austrian critics who, following earlier critics at home, have targeted Bacon as the war-minded champion of British imperialism. 'Possessed by the hunger for power, possession, honour and influence,' wrote one of them in 1968, 'he wanted to hold the world in the palm of his hand.' As an editor of the *Essays* had remarked in 1890, 'if it served himself it was enough'. Bacon condemned the very notion of 'world dominion' as 'the evil dream of a prosperous brigand'. But this did not deter an Oxford professor, in 1980, from endorsing the view that his 'drive to power made him the natural advocate' of imperialist oppression.[44] If there was in Bacon any desire for power, it was expressed in his ringing call to all men to make peace among themselves, and with 'united forces' to 'storm and occupy' the 'castles and strongholds' of Nature – and this, not for the oppression of other nations but for the well-being of all mankind.[45]

A craving for political power could be detected in the calculated concentration with which Robert Cecil camouflaged his wide network of corruption over the years, so successfully that it has only recently been uncovered.[46] It is unmistakable in the conspiratorial methods of Cecil's ally, Henry Howard, Earl of Northampton, a secret Catholic, whose own rise to power was the fruit of shameless intrigues carried out with a long-nurtured malice. Of this 'master manipulator', as his biographer describes him, it may truly be said that his scholarly works – written to placate Elizabeth (who saw through him), while serving Mary, and later to charm James – were aimed, one and all, at securing patronage. In the man who earned a decade of influence by teaching Cecil, with diabolical ingenuity, how to destroy their joint rivals, and who sealed his alliance with Somerset by an even more venomous treatment of his own particular rival (Overbury), we may diagnose an insatiable craving for power.[47]

Not in Bacon. If, as an editor of the *Essays* recently noted, 'The Vantage Ground to doe good' was genuinely behind Bacon's efforts to attain high place, this was because the wish to serve his country in office, and his longing to remedy the poverty of man through his works, were inseparably linked in his mind.[48] It was George Herbert, the friend of Bacon's later years, who saw the essential nature of that link. His office 'blesses' his own time, wrote Herbert, and makes it possible for his book 'to bless the future'.[49]

Using his Ideas as Counters in the Power Game

The political climate of Bacon's time, we are told, produced some who sought place for its own sake, some who sought it to forward a programme in which they believed, and many grades in between.[1] If anyone had a programme it was Bacon. He had important points to make about almost every issue that came up in his lifetime, and he made them – in his works and letters, in speeches he wrote for his own or another's delivery in Parliament, in reports and proposals to Queen, King, favourites and ministers, whether commanded or volunteered. His ideas have been variously interpreted by historians in the light of their own beliefs. While some of them see him today as 'the most acute political observer of his time' (Menna Prestwich), or as 'the clearest sighted discerner of the critical problems of the monarchy in the seventeenth century' (Hugh Trevor-Roper), he is still presented by others as a blind, obtuse and doddering Justice Shallow.[2] Most historians, however, have recognized the moderate yet firm tone of his advice and the ample vision and intellectual unity that pervades his political thought – even those who, in the same breath, will denounce his political writings as the work of a presumptuous busybody, or as mere counters to be taken up or put down with the sole aim of gaining royal approval.

Bacon's aspirations for his country can be summed up as follows: a Church at one with itself, laws reduced to a manageable code so that people could know what they were, and a strong and economically stable monarchy, founded on a mutual affection between the sovereign and his subjects. Like many of his contemporaries he saw the King and the people's representatives as the head and limbs of a single body, 'that strengthen and maintain the one the other'.[3] For Bacon it was only in musical terms, point and counterpoint, that their relations could be properly expressed. Never as an opposition between two parties, and still less, as Cecil had tried to effect it in his Great Contract, between two parties to a bargain. However indispensable, the subsidy must be treated as a secondary matter. The Commons should not vote supplies in exchange for the redress of grievances, nor should the King redress grievances in expectation of funds. Parliament should not be 'invited to give' with the offer of 'sprigs of prerogative'. Its true function and purpose, never to be lost sight of, was the enactment of good laws.[4]

In this primary task, to be carried out jointly by the sovereign and his subjects, the King played the solo part. If he sang well, as Bacon never tired of reminding him, the choir would 'fall in sweetly and solemnly' with him.[5] At the opening of every session he must propound 'gracious and plausible laws for the contentment and comfort of the people', devising remedies 'as fast as time breedeth mischiefs', and attend to proposals put forward by the people's representatives.[6] The 'good or evil effect' of a session, Bacon frankly told his royal master, depended entirely on the way he dealt with his Parliament. 'Until your Majesty have tuned your instrument you will have no harmony.'[7] But, as Bacon wrote, 'fitness to govern' was 'a perplexed business', demanding the initiative to create precedents and the 'courage to protect'; these were qualities which were notably absent in this King, who had so little natural talent for the solo part that Bacon once toyed with the notion of playing it for him, if he succeeded Cecil as Secretary, while amusing him 'with pastime and glory'.[8] Some of Bacon's biographers have found fault with him for his supposed failure to realize the King's incapacity for strong leadership.[9] Far from it. If Bacon tirelessly coached his master, encouraging him to learn from his mistakes, it is because, only too well aware of his limitations, he continued to hope that they might be overcome. He also saw those points in the King's favour, a dislike of intolerance, a certain breadth of political vision, patriotic intentions – unfortunately betrayed by his all-absorbing attachments – which historians are now beginning to rediscover.[10] And who could be asked to lead, if not the King?

Bacon supported a vigorous royal prerogative, 'not slackened, nor much strained', and all the stronger for being 'kept within its banks'. In his view, however, prerogative was for times of crisis. He did not adhere to James's personal concept of the divine right of kings – the 'power of a god' to use his subjects like chessmen, as the King described it in Parliament, to 'make or unmake at his pleasure, to give life or send to death, to judge all, to be judged nor accomptable to none'.[11] James, as he once confessed to Gondomar, had no use for Parliaments: 'I wonder that my ancestors should have permitted such an institution as the House of Commons to have come into existence. I am a stranger, and found it here when I arrived, so that I am obliged to put up with what I cannot get rid of.'[12] For Bacon there could be no concert without the people. He never tired of declaring himself 'ever of Parliament', 'the *cardo rerum* and the *summa summarum* [pivot and sum] for all occasions'. It was, he said, 'a great surety for kings'; particular Members might have their private ends, 'yet one man sets another upright.'[13] He wanted Parliaments to be held every third or fourth year, or even yearly. And not only for the promulgation of gracious laws, but because a responsible opposition was essential to restrain the Crown and prevent it from abusing its prerogative. Good laws, he believed, were 'some bridle to bad princes', and if the people's vote proved dangerous to popes, emperors and kings, it was right that it should, to such of them 'as shall transcend their limits and become tyrannical'.[14]

On the other hand Bacon did not wish to see too much power entrusted at once to the House of Commons. He subscribed to the Elizabethan doctrine that premature action was to be expected from the people, in whom 'usurping rebels put their trust'.[15] And he did not think the direction of government policy or the choice of ministers could be safely left in the hands of their representatives, a miscellaneous collection of lawyers, merchants and untutored country gentlemen, many of whom were only too ready to be manipulated in hopes of honour and office, and were responding with increasing violence to the conflicts between their patrons at Court. He advocated – and did his best to promote – a gradual but constant increase of Parliament's share in decision-making. This was to be won, he believed, not by speeches on constitutional privileges or the rights of the people, but by the spread of political knowledge and by the restraint which comes with an increase of responsibility. And with this aim in view he repeatedly urged the King's 'loving subjects' to vote in 'a well-composed House of the ablest men in the kingdom . . . according to the pure and true institution of a Parliament'.[16]

It is curious to find the clear-sighted Bacon dismissed in the 1970s as a reactionary dreamer, hankering after to the good old days of Queen Elizabeth, and so caught up in the delusion of a mythical harmony between Crown and people that he failed to gauge the growth of parliamentary power and influence. A 'strange want of insight', Wallace Notestein remarked in 1971; 'faulty perception', wrote another historian in 1976, surprised that 'so presumably astute a man' should have 'lacked the foresight to evaluate the institutes of his time in the context of a rapidly changing society'.[17] It is of course Bacon's critics who were failing to catch up with the revisions of history, which by then was rapidly casting off the straightjacket of *a priori* Whig theory. The decades before the Civil War could no longer be seen as 'the winning of the initiative by the House of Commons' through milestone after milestone of constitutional conflict; it had become evident that if none of Bacon's contemporaries recognized the growing strength of the Commons – not even Coke, who was supposed to have brought it about – the reason was that the Commons' strength was not growing.[18] Once the Whiggish notion of an 'inexorable constitutional conflict' is defused, as a critic of that false perspective wrote in 1978, the constant invocation of unity, balance and harmony – by the Crown and so-called opposition Members alike – begins to make sense.[19]

We cannot reproach Bacon for underestimating the importance of an anti-Crown party which was never more than a historical projection. If, as remarked by another critic of outdated Whig perspectives, 'the well-known advice given to James I by his most able counsellor, Francis Bacon, has not been studied seriously, it is presumably because Bacon has been thought blind to the inevitability of a constitutional conflict.'[20] He did not see it because it was not there. He did see, more clearly than most, the real problems of his time, though he did not conceive them as leading necessarily to extreme conflict; nor would they have done so, in all probability, if his advice had been followed. Foremost among these problems was one to which he constantly called the King's attention: that breakdown of the process of counsel which is looked on today as leading directly to the Civil War. Under Buckingham's overwhelming influence, James had gradually ceased to hear his appointed councillors, and a balance between factions could not be maintained. The result was a series of crises in the Parliaments of the 1620s, when – beginning with the demolition of Bacon himself by Coke and Cranfield – one Privy Council-lor openly instigated his clients against another, and on one occasion both favourite and Prince together opposed the King himself.[21] 'Kings had need beware how they side themselves . . . as of a faction or party,' Bacon had warned early on, and this was the theme of his many appeals to James 'to extinguish, or at least compose for a time those divisions of his own house' which made effective royal collaboration with Parliament out of the question.[22] The encouragement of disruptive elements in the Commons by Court faction could have been tempered by the presence of a few experienced Government councillors in the Commons who were capable of initiating policy, as there had been under Elizabeth; and Bacon, who was aware of this, begged the King to consider strengthening the Lower House with some councillors of state.[23] James's failure to do so is now seen as one of the main causes of the Civil War.

The joint work accomplished by King and Parliament through the enactment of good laws was reform. Interest in reform has always been a politician's most obvious ploy, and many a high-flown speech has sprung out of less high-flying motives. But in Bacon's case the idea of reform, bred into him by his father, who had inherited it from an earlier generation of reformers, was not only the *leitmotiv* of his political thought, it was the very basis of his philosophy. 'Things constantly alter themselves to the worse' was his perpetual reminder; 'Laws not refreshed with new laws soon wax sour.' The refractory retention of custom was 'as turbulent a thing as an innovation', and 'he that will not apply new remedies must expect new evils.'[24] In every field, from religion to weights and measures, there was a continual need for repair and renewal, and Bacon identified it in each case. 'No abuse escaped his notice,' Gardiner rightly observed, 'no improvement was too extensive to be grasped by his comprehensive genius,'[25] Yet however urgent the need, it was Bacon's conviction that reform could only be effective if carried out slowly, almost invisibly, like the processes of nature and of time itself, 'the greatest innovator'. 'It is the soaking rain and not the tempest that relieveth the ground.' Just as the noblest work of philosophy was the renovation of things corruptible, 'by sweet and gentle measures', so reform in civil matters must be worked out patiently, without premature meddling. Every violent remedy was 'pregnant with new evil'.[26]

How strongly Bacon felt about the improvements he spent so much thought on may be gathered from the tone of his 'Letter of Advice to Villiers', in 1616, when he saw the opportunity of briefing the still open-minded young favourite as a unique chance of getting his ideas across. A sense of the vital importance of each point he had to make keeps coming through the respectful courtesy of his address in passionate denunciations and appeals: you must 'put the King in mind of it!'; 'by all means cry down that unworthy course!'; 'I utterly condemn the practice!' Since his 'Advice' covered the whole spectrum of government, its different heads may serve us as a guideline in recalling the principal issues he was concerned with – and had been for decades, since most of his ideas could already be found in the private diary he had kept, eight years earlier, in 1608, when not in the 'devices' he had written in 1594.[27]

Religion came first in the political scene in Bacon's day. He was in his early twenties when he plunged into a world in which passions ran high between the two enemies of the Church of England, as he described them to Villiers, 'the extremes on either hand'. In the reign of Elizabeth, Catholic injunctions to assassinate her and plots against her life were the order of the day, and James's life, after the alarms of the Gunpowder Plot, was threatened by Puritans, who, as Bacon put it, 'under colourable pretensions of zeal for the reformation of religion' were now 'the nourishers of conspiracy'.[28] Throughout his early 'Letter of Advice to the Queen' and his 'Considerations on the Controversies of the Church', and later his treatise on the 'Pacification and Edification of the Church', dedicated to the newly crowned James, when a breath of change was in the air, we hear the same pressing appeal. While in office he kept in touch with various authorities abroad who thought as he did, and after his fall he continued to urge his views in a number of papers, finally condensing them in the essay 'Of Unity in Religion', which he published in 1625, a year before his death.[29]

Unity in religion, on which depended 'the infinite blessing of peace', was the basis on which all Bacon's work rested. He understood that 'men cannot contend coldly and without affection about things which they hold dear and precious'; but he had more sympathy with the heathen – the fathers of whose church, he said, were the poets – than with churchmen, who, by making 'the cause of religion descend to the execrable actions of murdering of princes, butchery of people, and firing of states', brought down the Holy Ghost 'in the likeness of a vulture'. If Lucretius had known the massacre of St Bartholomew or the gunpowder treason, Bacon claimed, 'he would have been seven times more atheist than he was'.[30] Like Sir Nicholas, who had urged men to refrain from all 'opprobrious words (as heretic, schismatic, papist)', Bacon never gave up trying to calm passions and smooth the way to agreement. 'If we did but know the virtue of silence and slowness to speak,' he insisted, 'our controversies of themselves would close up and grow together'; and he spelled out for both Elizabeth and James, with balanced and sensible suggestions on the liturgy, preaching, finance and the limiting of bishops' powers, the ways in which he thought this could be achieved.[31] This was not, as generally practised, by imposing a rigid conformity on deviants, but by making every possible concession on issues that were 'too small and light to matter' (including the vexed question of the wearing of cap and surplice, on which Bacon suggested that the stronger yield to the weaker, and the non-conformists be free to wear them or not, as they preferred). For the Catholics he wanted the rigour of the oath of allegiance relaxed, and well-trained (and liberally paid) Church of England preachers to attract them; for the Puritans, freedom to do their own preaching. And on neither side, he maintained, should consciences be forced or secret thoughts examined.[32]

For Bacon the key to the pacification of the Churches was reform of the many abuses which, in his view, were the cause of all schism. ('If the sword of the spirit were better edged there would be little need for penal laws against the Papists.') How could the Reformed Church be looked on as reformed forever, and continue unaltered, with all its dilapidations, 'upon the dregs of time'? He did not advocate replanting and rebuilding the spiritual edifice; only that it be 'pruned from corruptions', repaired and restored.[33] But at the Hampton Court Conference, convened soon after Bacon had presented his paper, James was overruled by the Bishops, who did not wish, as Bacon did, to see their inquisitorial powers reduced, and peremptorily rejected his proposals. 'I will have none of that,' he declared. 'I will have one doctrine, one discipline, one religion, in substance and ceremony. Never speak to me more on that point.'[34] Had Bacon's 'sensible and statesmanlike views been adopted', wrote one of his sharpest critics a century ago, the Church of England would have included almost all the nation, and the Civil War could have been averted.[35] Unfortunately James, 'the most wise Christian moderator', as Bacon hopefully addressed him, did not have the courage to achieve that 'golden mediocrity in establishing what is sound and repairing what is corrupt and decayed' which his servant sought in him; and there was nothing Bacon could do about it.[36]

The reform of the law, next on the list of his 'Advice to Villiers', was as close to Bacon's heart as the reform of learning. He greatly admired the laws of England, he told Villiers, 'the equallest in the world between prince and people', and all the richer for being 'mixed and compounded', like the English language, of the customs of so many nations. But England had been rapidly developing from a simple agrarian community into an increasingly complex mercantile society, and the law had not followed suit. There had been for over a century, wrote Bacon, a 'continual heaping of laws without digesting them', and such an accumulation of 'cross and intricate' statutes on the same subject that 'the certainty of the law was lost in the heap'. How could the citizen by made 'more and more happy' – which was 'the end and scope of laws' – when left in so much uncertainty about their application?[37]

Bacon was ten years old when, as he later reminded the Queen, his father had first sowed 'the precious seed of a project for the reform of the law' in her mind – and clearly in his own, for he was to look upon law reform as an essential part of the law.[38] He brought it up first in his early thirties, when he exhorted the mock Prince of Purpoole at the Christmas revels of Gray's Inn – in the same urgent tones he would use to exhort his royal masters – to 'purge out the multiplicity of the laws, clear the uncertainty of them, repeal those that are snaring', and to define the jurisdiction of his courts and eliminate unnecessary suits and causeless delays. And from then on he waged a ceaseless battle for what he called the 'animation of laws' – a fairer, more flexible and dynamic concept of the law, 'mitigated by equity' – so that the judge could be guided, the counsel warranted, the student eased, the contentious suitor disarmed, and the honest suitor relieved.[39] In this radical and original programme he was opposed, as we might expect, by his perennial rival, Edward Coke, who maintained a rigid adherence to the complicated procedures of the common law. 'For bringing of the common laws into a better method,' he said, 'I doubt much the fruit of that labour.'[40]

Coke need not have feared the patient Bacon, as wary as British lawyers still are today of the dangers of a written civil code, fearing it might give rise to more doubts than did the unwritten law. 'Customs are laws written in living tables,' said Bacon. 'I dare not advise to cast the law in a new mould.' As with the Church, he wanted to prune and graft it, not plough it up and plant it again ('for such a remove I should hold indeed for a perilous innovation'). Its 'entire body and substance' would remain, 'only discharged of idle and unprofitable or hurtful matter, and illustrated by order and other helps towards a better understanding', so that it could acquire the consistency and coherence of a code.[41] Two major tasks faced the pruning and grafting reformer: an independent review of the statute laws, including the repeal of 'ensnaring penal laws' which, 'if in bad times they should be awakened', would grind the subject to powder; and a digest of the common case-laws that would simplify them by omitting overruled cases, and would bring out their analogies and relate them to more general principles.[42]

We shall see him taking up both these projects time and again in the successive Parliaments. No words were too strong for him to plead the importance of his proposed Digest of the Laws. It was, he told Elizabeth in 1597, a work 'of highest merit and beneficence towards the subject that ever entered the mind of any king: greater than we can imagine'. In 1607 he entreated James to set up a commission that would carry out this 'heroical work', than which nothing could be 'more politic, more honourable, nor more beneficial to his subjects of all ages'; and which, he declared, 'if I might live to see it, I would not desire to live after'. There could be no task 'more proper for your Majesty as a master nor for me as a workman', he insisted in 1616, when presenting his detailed 'Proposition Touching the Compiling and Amendment of the Laws of England'; and he described the Digest, when on his fall he once again offered to undertake it – if James would supply the necessary assistance – as 'one of the greatest dowries' that could be conferred upon the kingdom.[43]

The work to be done – 'reducing and perfecting' the body of the common laws and purging them of obsolete, repetitive and irrelevant matter, as well as amending misprints and other results of poor reporting – was to be complemented by the compilation of various auxiliary books. Among those would be a highly original thesaurus of related legal terms, in which 'the one may serve to explain the other', and a treatise of Rules and Decisions, or collection of 'grounds dispersed throughout the body of the laws', that would explain 'the naked maxim' by generalization from existing cases, and would reconcile doubts, 'grace argument' and enable both student and professor of the law 'to see more profoundly into the reason of such judgements', so as to procure the greatest possible certainty.[44] Coke's *Reports*, much as Bacon appreciated them for their 'infinite good decisions and rulings over cases', were too idiosyncratic, tendentious and inconsistent to serve this purpose; they lacked the essential properties Bacon had laid down for his rules, 'the one a perspicuous and clear order or method, and the other an universal latitude or comprehension . . . like a model towards a great building'.[45] Bacon himself had tried his hand early on at such a collection. The twenty-five admirable *Maxims of the Law* he presented to Queen Elizabeth in 1597 (which have recently aroused a new interest among Baconian scholars) are all that remain.[46] The rule, he said, like a magnetic needle, 'points at the law', and he saw in these maxims an attempt 'to visit and strengthen the roots and foundations of the science itself'. Thirty years later, in his 'Example of a

Treatise on Universal Justice or the Fountains of Equity' – described in 1927 by William Holdsworth, an outstanding expert in our century, as 'the first critical and jurisprudential estimate of the English law ever made' – he outlined a 'character and idea of justice', a 'law of laws' by which the laws of any country could be tested and amended.[47]

As a legal thinker, according to Holdsworth, Bacon was 'not only among the great of his age, but among the greatest of all time'. That view was echoed in 1992 by another legal expert, Daniel Coquillette, who saw him as a profoundly innovative legal mind, consciously transcending national boundaries, and 'the first truly analytical and critical jurist in the Anglo-American tradition'.[48] For his own time, however, Bacon's chief virtue was that he alone saw that all the evils he had early enumerated – including the law's delay, and that 'tumour of Chancery' which Coke inveighed against – sprang from a single root, the lack of the certainty of the law, without which there could be no justice. Had he been given the necessary support, he could have achieved a major, indeed a unique reform. But James was no Justinian to this Tribonius, and the legal *Instauration* was not to be. The treatise praised by Holdsworth was published in France in 1646, and eventually embodied in the *Code Napoléon*.[49] In England, barring a brief attempt during the Restoration, no new effort would be made to reform the law until in 1826 the Home Secretary, Sir Robert Peel, prefaced his speech in Parliament with the same treatise. 'The lapse of two hundred and fifty years', he said, 'has increased the necessity of the measures which Lord Bacon then proposed, but it has produced no argument in favour of the principle, no objection adverse to it, which he did not anticipate.' The same could be said today.[50]

On Government, or 'the Council Table', Bacon's first recommendation was the most obvious rule for administrators, though, as he rightly said, never practised in his lifetime: Villiers must 'countenance, encourage and advance able and virtuous men', and not allow money and 'cunning canvasses' to go on prevailing. ('Choice of persons active and in their nature stirring,' he had noted in his diary eight years earlier, 'and assure them.') He then made a proposal, new in his time, that Privy Councillors should specialize; there should be a bishop for Church government, a man 'skilled in the laws', and others expert in martial and foreign affairs, with consultants to be called in as required. Four years later he was to propose another 'innovation' which, he was convinced, would 'eternize' the King's name and merit: the establishment of standing commissions to strengthen the administration – the forerunners of latter-day government offices; and he drew up a list of the specific matters to be dealt with. Nothing came of this. Bacon, as one of his biographers commented, was too far ahead of his time.[51] Finally he took the opportunity to interest Villiers in a favourite project, an academy for the training, at home and abroad, of 'young men of whom good hopes were conceived' in foreign affairs, a need to which he had drawn attention some ten years earlier. He urged the young Villiers to 'breed up a nursery of such plants'; and Buckingham did indeed submit a proposal for such an academy to the 1621 Parliament. But we know that this Parliament was too busy impeaching his mentor to deal with its bills, and in 1623 Bacon was once more lamenting the dearth of able men trained in 'business of state'. A similar academy, which he would have come across in France, was to take final shape as the Ecole Nationale d'Administration, set up by Napoleon, and still flourishing; and suggestions for a school of this kind are still being considered in Britain today.[52]

Bacon could not be explicit with Villiers on foreign policy, a strictly royal prerogative. It is therefore to his private diary we should turn for the best summary of his hopes. The 'fairest' prospect, he had noted in 1608, was

> the general persuading of the King and people, and course of infusing everywhere the foundation in this isle of a monarchy in the west, as an apt seat, state and people for it; so civilizing Ireland, further colonizing the wild of Scotland, [and promoting] confederacy and more strait amity with the Low Countries.[53]

But the growth of this happy isle was not to be achieved through 'ambitious predatory wars'. 'In my disposition and profession I am wholly for peace,' Bacon declared to Villiers, not surprisingly, since it was the *sine qua non* for the spread of his life-work; and he strongly opposed any war of invasion 'to enlarge the bounds of our empire'. Only a truly defensive war could be justified, one, that is, where there existed a 'clear foresight of immediate danger'.[54] The strength of a growing state, such as Britain then was – and Bacon wished her to continue – was not, he insisted, primarily a question of territorial extension, which could be a disadvantage, or of riches and fruitfulness, of fortification, but of the unity of this 'entire isle'. It was founded above all on the vigour and free spirit of its men, which the Government should do everything to encourage. 'Provision for war' was in Bacon's view the best way to prevent war, and his parliamentary battles against the enclosure of farm lands were waged for the yeomen of England, the free men from whose ranks alone good soldiers could be drawn.[55] But there was a better way to prevent war. In 1617, a year after writing his 'Advice to Villiers', Bacon instructed the English Ambassador in Madrid to include in his negotiation for a treaty with Spain the erection of a tribunal 'to decide the controversies which may arise amongst the princes and estates of Christendom without effusion of Christian blood'. Nothing came of this idea. As Spedding pointed out, the world was too young for it (though not to think about it, since four years later Sully was to publish the 'great design' conceived by

Henri IV of France for the peaceful coexistence of Catholic and Protestant powers in a united Europe).[56]

How then can we explain that this man of peace was to be found not only proposing, on more than one occasion, a combined crusade led by England and the Netherlands against Spain, and another led by England and Spain against Turkey, but ready and eager for either possibility? We shall understand Bacon's political approach better if we look at these proposals in some detail. In May 1619, when Prince Frederick was trying to engage England in the cause of the Bohemian Protestants, Bacon gave him his whole-hearted support, expressing the hope that King James would contribute to his greatness – which meant war with Spain.[57] This was to be expected, for in the breach that had been developing in the Privy Council between the Protestant party, in favour of support to the Prince Palatine as its champion in Europe, and the pro-Spanish party – which included James himself, unwilling to disturb the *status quo* – Bacon's sympathies lay with the Protestant group.[58] For all his friendly relations with the Spanish Ambassador, he had never trusted 'the Spaniard', who, he maintained, 'had trodden more bloody steps than any state of Christendom', had corrupted the ministers of other princes and had disturbed the nations with his yearly alarms and armadas.[59]

England, at this juncture, with the newly rebuilt Navy which Bacon had encouraged Buckingham to promote, was strong at sea, whereas the Spaniard's root was 'a great deal too narrow for his tops'. Bacon now proposed to James a 'just, preventive war', whereby Spain would be divided from the Indies, and bankrupted with a double blockade.[60] 'A right design and a great one', he maintained; and a timely one, as we know now from the Spanish dispatches, for Spain had never been so entirely unprepared. In a matter of days, wrote Gondomar, 'the sea would swarm with English privateers, and whoever was master at sea would soon be master on land'; the King of England would find himself at the head of a powerful confederacy, 'and it was impossible to say what he might not inflict upon the Catholic Church and the Spanish Monarchy.'[61]

Had James acted on Bacon's proposal, things would have been different a few months later, when Frederick accepted the throne of Bohemia; the Spanish invasion of the Palatine could have been averted and the Protestant cause might well have triumphed. But Philip III – or rather his wily Ambassador – had managed to seduce James with the offer of a wealthy Spanish Infanta as a bride for Prince Charles, and had persuaded him to undertake the flattering but hopeless task of mediator in Europe, without even a guarantee of Spanish neutrality.[62] James continued his policy of appeasement at all costs until September 1620, when, faced with the Spanish invasion of the Palatinate, he was forced to call the Parliament which Bacon had been urging on him for the last five years. Bacon's draft royal proclamation for its opening, a sober but firm declaration to recover and resettle the County Palatine, 'so long in the hands of the Princes of our Religion', sounds much like an exhortation to the King himself to defend his son-in-law. Gardiner was delighted with it. Here was statesmanlike language, he exclaimed. A king who, in the name of England, could put forth such a manifesto as this, on which Catholic and Protestant factions could have joined hands, would speedily have become a power in Europe which neither Spain nor Austria could afford to despise.[63] James, however, was not such a king.

Again in 1624, when negotiations for the Spanish marriage had finally broken down and James at last declared the Spanish treaties at an end, the now fallen Bacon sympathized so heartily with the popular rejoicing that, regardless of his insolvency, he contributed four dozen faggots for their bonfires and twelve gallons of wine.[64] And he prepared a speech for Sackville to deliver in Parliament (where he himself was not allowed to sit), once again recommending that England declare war on Spain and sever the country from its silver mines, thus weakening it in Europe – rather than rush blindly, expensively and vainly, as Buckingham was to do, into the Palatinate. He followed this proposal with a detailed analysis – meeting all the possible objections to 'that mighty work', a war with Spain – which was to be widely appreciated in Protestant circles on the Continent through the next decades. 'Although I had wholly sequestered my thoughts from civil affairs,' he began, 'it is a new case, and concerneth the country infinitely . . .'[65] It did concern the country, among other reasons because the fresh source of supply from the Spanish Indies which England would have gained from blocking the Spanish fleet would have enabled Charles to reorganize his bankrupt administration. With no need to lean on a weakened Spanish Empire, he might have remained committed to the Protestant cause, and the spectre of internal war, dreaded by Bacon for over twenty years, might never have made its appearance.[66]

So much for Bacon's warlike intentions against Spain. But there were two occasions, during these years, when the marriage between Prince Charles and the Spanish Infanta appeared imminent, and Bacon immediately set out to use them also, as he put it, 'for the good and happiness of the Christian world'. 'This conjunction', he wrote in 1617 to the Spanish Ambassador in Madrid (after obtaining the approval of the King, then in Scotland), should be 'the seed . . . of a holy war against the Turk'. The Turk was in Bacon's eyes a greater scourge than 'the Spaniard'. While 'no nations are wholly alien and strangers to one another', the invading Turks, he believed, were not a nation but 'such routs and shoals of people as have utterly degenerated from the laws of nature'; in fighting against these inhuman people he hoped the Spanish and English Kings might 'lay aside and forget their difficulties'.[67] Bacon's efforts fell through on this occasion, because each country mistrusted the other's intentions. None the less, when negotiations for the marriage were resumed, although he was no longer in office, he took up the project again, interrupting his work on Henry VII to write a brilliant dialogue between a 'Protestant Zelant', a 'Catholic Zelant', a military man and a 'politique', presided over by 'a Moderate Divine', aimed at exhausting all the different lights in which the marriage could be seen. ('Here be four of you', cries the Chairman, 'I think were able to make a good world; for you are as differing as the four elements, and yet are friends!')[68] The work was not concluded: the final breach with Spain that followed soon afterwards closed down this brief opportunity.

What was Bacon doing, preaching contradictory crusades, when he had declared himself 'wholly for peace' and explicitly condemned all religious wars? In looking at this double inconsistency, we should first remember that Bacon feared no danger so much as a civil war, 'from which God and his mercy defend us', he wrote to Villiers, for that was 'the most desperate and bloody of all others'. 'Honourable war' on a foreign nation was infinitely preferable, provided it was kept 'moderated and limited', bearing in mind that war is 'the sentence of death upon many'. It was in hopes of a lasting peace in Europe that Bacon's immediate advice was, like that of Shakespeare's dying Henry IV, 'to busy giddy minds with foreign quarrels', and so distract them from the factions that were drawing the country fatally towards that 'most desperate' of all conflicts, 'a war in our own bowels'.[69] To propose war to a war-hating ruler, as Max Patrick remarked in his study of these contradictory projects in 1971, was a risky matter; and arguing against his own, and others', prevalent image of Bacon, Patrick concluded that in doing so he had behaved as a loyal subject and a patriot. In 1985 Bacon's Italian editor was to commend him warmly for his courage in opposing the King's arguments on these delicate questions.[70] The long-cherished hope that a popular war would bring the King closer to his people was not to be. When James failed to promote the only foreign quarrel he could have afforded, he laid the ground for his son's disastrous wars in Germany, and probably strengthened in the still anti-Papist Charles those Catholic sympathies that were to alienate him from the most influential sector of his people.

We have yet to understand how Bacon could extol both war and peace, as it were, in one breath. In 1992 Marku Peltonen argued convincingly that the greatness of Britain – founded on the warlike valour of its men and the commercial and scientific prosperity of its people – did not form for Bacon a single consistent and coherent programme.[71] But let us not forget that both projects were the constant preoccupation of a single mind. Bacon, who tended to see reality through the play of antithesis, was not overdisturbed by the contradictions entailed. So that while he firmly believed (and told Villiers) that 'money . . . is the sinews of war', we will find him reminding Parliament, when the occasion was right (during the debate on the Union of England and Scotland, in 1607, or the Palatine crisis in 1621), that money cannot be the sinews of war, 'where the sinews of men's arms, in base and effeminate people, are failing'. Similarly, while he could look on war as a 'healthful exercise' to promote the greatness of kingdoms, he made it quite clear that the greatness of kingdoms did not include the happiness and well-being of its citizens. Bacon could see, and where necessary emphasize, the different facets of a question in different ways, but, as with the various kinds of ambition recalled above, his own priorities were not in doubt. As a statesman the greatness of Britain was never far from his mind, yet it remained entirely subordinate to the gaol of all his philosophical endeavours, the relief of 'the human family'. That age-old dilemma, the degeneration of states after a prolonged peace, as against the progress and happiness which prosperity affords, is still with us. Bacon could not resolve it – except in the New Atlantis, where distance and isolation enabled the inhabitants to concentrate all their energies on working for the well-being of man.[72]

'For matter of trade,' Bacon told Villiers, 'I confess it is out of my profession,' and he made the same disclaimer on financial questions – with undue modesty, if we are to believe a contemporary critic, who declared that on 'impositions, monopolies etc., the meanest manufactures were an usual argument' and 'he did baffle' the Earl of Middlesex (Cranfield), born and bred in the City.[73] Economic and administrative reform, in particular that of the King's overmanned, unproductive Court bureaucracy, was the corner-stone of Bacon's programme. Already at James's first Parliament in 1604, he had not hesitated to tell the King that his Court was like the root of a stinging-nettle: though not poisonous in itself, all the leaves it bore were 'venomous and stinging to the touch'.[74] If James could be deluded into supporting the disastrous 'monopoly of monopolies' (got up by Alderman Cockayne and supported by Coke, but deplored from the start by Bacon), because he was offered a basin full of gold, if he was caught up in Ralegh's dream of a gold-mine in Guiana, or promoted the Spanish marriage in hopes of a dowry, it was all done to fill his gaping coffers.[75] Only when unhampered by financial pressures, as Bacon never wearied of repeating, would James be free to choose his policies.

The cure Bacon advocated was no stop-gap or panacea, like Cecil's Impositions, devised to avoid antagonizing Court and City, and levied indiscriminately, without concern for trade, on exports and imports alike. 'The work of one morning', Bacon called them, and 'a cause of much mischief following'. Nothing could be achieved, he declared, without the retrenchment of Court expenses, which Cecil had struggled with and found a hopeless tangle. But above all he insisted on the encouragement of every form of trade and industry throughout the country, from the 'meanest manufactures' upwards.[76] 'Money is like muck,' Bacon was fond of saying, 'not good except it be spread,' and he felt as strongly about the engrossing of pasturage as he did about the 'devouring trades' of usury. States whose wealth lay stagnant in the hands of the nobility and gentry could not defray the charges of wars and other public disbursement. It was to the Netherlands, he said, where the nation's wealth was in the hands of 'merchants, burghers, tradesmen, freeholders and farmers', that England should look for an example. And he probably had the Nether-lands also in mind, with its flourishing Jewish culture, when he recom-mended unlimited immigration. ('States that are liberal of naturalization towards strangers are fit for empire.') Jews were honoured in the New Atlantis, and, as Bacon explained, because they were made to feel at home in the island they had 'no secret inbred rancour' against the people they lived among.[77] Bacon did not, like some of his contemporaries, preach equality, but the whole aim of his *Instauration* was to do away with human want. If England husbanded her soil, dried her marshes, culti-vated her wastes, garnered in 'the hidden and rich treasure of fishing', if she distributed her riches among the many and opened herself to over-seas trade (he advocated 'free trade into all parts of both East and West Indies'), if she filled her navigable rivers and increased her population with intake of foreigners, for which there was abundant room – as there was 'sea-room for herself and her neighbours in the sea' – he saw wealth flowing through her 'as in a spring tide'.[78]

'Two great works, amongst the acts of kings have supreme pre-eminence,' Bacon declared to Villiers: 'the union, and the plantation of kingdoms'; and he looked on the 'happy union' of 'these two ancient and mighty realms of England and Scotland' as 'the great and blessed work of Almighty God'. In the memorable parliamentary debate on Anglo-Scottish union in 1606–7 – in which, as has been noted, the ten-sions involved and the tasks to be undertaken to effect it were similar to those which face the European Community today – we will not be surprised to find Bacon arguing with conviction for common citizen-ship.[79] His draft proclamation of the sovereign's new title – 'King of Great Britanny' – bears witness to his celebration of all 'uniting and conjoining', 'compounding and incorporating', 'commixture of bodies and conjunc-tion of states'.[80] While warning James that here too 'unnatural hasting' could 'disturb the work', he took a leading part in the commission that was to pave the way for it, and prepared a detailed analysis of the different items that would have to be dealt with, from names to seals and from stamps to taxes. Above all he rejoiced at the prospect of uniting the Scottish and English laws. Not, as some would have it, by imposing the English law, but by drawing both laws together, since, like the legs of a body, they had 'the same roots and grounds'. The operation would involve reviewing and recompiling the English law, one of Bacon's dearest wishes. And he began to outline a few maxims towards that end. Some 'hostile laws' between the two countries were actually repealed, but the King had gained his new title only in name. Despite all Bacon's efforts to promote it, a United Kingdom, secure in its new strength – 'one of the great monarchies in the world', as he envisaged it – was not to be for another hundred years.[81] The union of their laws has not yet been achieved.

Bacon's 'impassioned interest in colonization', as illustrated by D. G. James in 1967, must of course be seen in the context of a still largely unpeopled New World. It is evident throughout his works, but in none is it so strongly expressed as in the *Declarations* entrusted by the Virginia Council to their eminent member, in 1609 and 1610, after the two expeditions that had met with disaster in the Bermudas. The second, *A True and Sincere Declaration of the Purpose and Ends of the Plantation* – 'a masterly, noble and moving document', as this student of Bacon's thought qualified it – begins with the Baconian resolve to create 'a vast extension to the Kingdom of Man', and concludes with the typical Baconian prayer (which he was to repeat at the opening of the 1621 Parliament) that this grain of seed might be nourished, so 'that it may spread till all the people of the earth admire the greatness and seek the shades and fruit thereof'.[82] In his essay 'Of Plantations' (1625), Bacon made a series of practical and sensible recommendations. It was preferable to select empty lands where 'people are not displanted to the end to plant others' (but 'if you plant where savages are . . . use them justly and graciously'); and, with the lesson of Spain in mind, to situate plantations 'in one continent and near together'. On the planters themselves his views were diametrically opposed to those of nearly all his contemporaries. Ralegh, for example, saw colonization as a way of getting rid of the starving unemployed, and a chance for bankrupt gentlemen to recover their fortunes, in line with James's own policy, which was to drain away unwanted population and stock the plantations 'out of all the jails in England'.[83] Bacon, deploring the 'base and hasty drawing of profit', declared that it was 'a shameful and base thing to take the scum of people, and wicked condemned men to be the people with whom you plant'. Neither were merchants suitable, who 'look ever to present gain', but noblemen and gentlemen, and governors of a quality that might 'lay the foundations of a new kingdom'.[84]

Among the countries 'planted', none was nearer to Bacon's heart than England's closest neighbour, 'that miserable and desolate kingdom' of Ireland, which he wished to see 'like a garden, and a younger sister to Great Britain'.[85] He was almost unique in his sympathy for the Irish, at a time when everyone, from the Queen downwards, looked on them with distaste, if not horror. This was the period when English officials sent out to Ireland – including Sir Henry Sidney, the poet's father, and Edmund Spenser – carried out indiscriminate slaughter of men, women and children; when Ralegh strung up rebels by the dozen, without trial; and when Walter Devereux, the first Earl of Essex, received nothing but praise for inviting the Irish chieftain, Sir Brian MacPhelim, and his wife to his house, entertaining them royally and then seizing them on their way to bed (to execute them later) and slaughtering their two hundred retainers.[86]

In 1598, while Ralegh was advocating the assassination of another Irish chieftain (Tyrone), Bacon, as we will recall, tried to interest Essex in the 'much neglected Irish causes', hoping that he might 'put life into them'. Again in 1602, taking immediate advantage of Mountjoy's victory in Ireland, he entreated Cecil to take those causes 'by the right handle'. Peace should be quickly restored, he urged, the people's hearts recovered, and 'the root and occasion of new troubles' removed by a policy of rewards rather than punishments; which, had it been practised in the past, 'things would never have grown to this extremity'. Contrary to the prevailing practice of segregation between colonizer and colonized, and to the implantation of Protestantism by force, he maintained that religious toleration should be granted, education in the Irish language liberally endowed, knighthoods awarded and the Irish nobility encouraged; that 'men gracious and well-beloved' should be appointed as town governors, and 'an even course' held between English and Irish 'as if they were one nation'.[87]

Instead the King opted for expropriation, and the planting of a new Protestant elite. In vain had Bacon set forth his ideas – in 1597 for Essex, and in 1602 for Cecil – in hopes of interesting them in Irish causes. In 1608, when the statesmanlike proposal of Sir Arthur Chichester, another promoter of conciliation, was turned down, Sir John Davies was sent out to impose the full panoply of the English legal system (complete with English dress) and a plan by which most of the land was allocated to the new settlers.[88] As James's historian put it in 1956, when, in accordance with the views first expressed by Henry Sidney and finally implemented by Oliver Cromwell, the English colony of Ulster was thus inaugurated, James laid the ground 'not only for the Irish rebellion in 1641, but for the whole problem of modern Ulster'.[89] All Bacon could do, when consulted after the event, was to insist that 'planters of estate and plenty' be sent who might at least benefit the country, and that their supervision be entrusted to commissioners who knew Ireland and could feel 'the pulses of the hearts of people'.[90] 'Go slow in sending new people,' he later admonished a newly appointed Lord Chief Justice of Ireland, 'the bane of a plantation is when undertakers or planters make such haste to a little mechanical profit, as disturbeth the whole frame of the work for time to come.' And once again, in opposition to James's policy of enforcing 'one doctrine, one discipline', he urged 'temperance and equality in the matter of religion, lest Ireland civil become more dangerous than Ireland savage'.[91]

Glancing back over this summary review of Bacon's political ideas, we find the same refrain running through them, one and all: the pressing need to reform, but slowly; to prune and graft, but not uproot; to look beyond petty disagreements and work for the durable at the expense of the immediate – bearing in mind the wider harmony of those interrelated issues within the framework of the grand reform he was continually ruminating. Given the recognized validity of each of Bacon's projects, and his keen interest in them, born in adolescence and as vivid as ever in his last years; the fact that most of his projects met with indifference, when not active royal opposition; that his urgent appeals for a digest of the law and for the reform of the Church fell on deaf ears; and that he proposed foreign wars to a frightened pacifist and put the brakes on a ruler impatient for the immediate union with Scotland, which he himself desired – what are historians and biographers about when they assert that he took up legal reform in his youth for no other reason than that 'he knew it was close to the Queen's heart'? How can they claim that in supporting the Union with Scotland, or in urging that 'one just and complete history be compiled of both nations' – a history which no one has yet succeeded in writing – he was merely 'trying harder than ever to prove his value as a royal servant'? That, when he argued for a new Parliament, 'Bacon now saw a splendid opportunity to impress James'? On what grounds do they go on attributing a self-serving motive to every one of his endeavours to advise his royal master?[92]

Bacon's thorough grasp of the political scene of his time is increasingly recognized by scholars. In 1885 Gardiner was surprised to note that in so many people's view Bacon's 'supereminence' as the 'prophet of scientific knowledge' had eclipsed his 'equally great claim as a prophet of political knowledge'.[93] In 1993 his political strategy, based on an extensive study of the 'particulars' of Civil History, was hailed by B. H. G. Wormald as of equal if not greater importance to Bacon than his scientific programme.[94] Beside these findings, the derogatory statements we have looked at verge on the ridiculous. Clearly, if Bacon chose an opportune moment – as anyone would – to present his enlightened, humane, practical and well-timed proposals, it was above all because he wanted to be heard. And if on occasion he also had his career in mind – as anyone might – it was, at least in part, because he hoped promotion would give him a better chance to put them into effect.

22

Hunting for Popularity

There were two platforms from which Bacon could hope to launch his
ideas: Parliament and government office. He did not come to office until
middle age, but, elected to Parliament in his twentieth year, he worked
untiringly through every session from 1581 until 1621. Did the efforts of
forty years' parliamentary activity go to remedying some of the ills
on which he had spent so much thought, or were they aimed principally at attracting royal notice, achieving popularity, or – as so often
with Members of Stuart Parliaments – winning the support of some
high-placed courtier, by adapting his views to a patron's changing
requirements?

That Bacon was appreciated is not in doubt. After a first unremarkable
speech in the Commons in 1584, his name appears on every possible
committee – frequently as reporter, often as chairman – originating bills,
supporting useful measures and supplying precedents. He is seen unfold-
ing his views with good humour, speaking briefly at times to clarify
obscure situations, at other times speaking with energy and vehemence,
but always, where he could, pouring oil on waters that were growing
increasingly troubled. 'My Lord Chancellor,' said Ben Jonson, 'wringeth
his speeches from the strings of his band, and other councillors from the
pickings of their teeth.'[1] Expert orator as he was from the start (one
Member confessed he was almost 'transported' to another opinion,
against his own better judgement, by Bacon's eloquence), he had
early learned that 'long and curious speeches' were about as helpful in
discussion as wearing 'a robe or mantle with a long train' when running
a race.[2]

The succeeding Parliaments must have found something unusual in
this Member, since they repeatedly chose him to present their grievances
to the King, even when he had actually opposed the message he was
entrusted with. During the early sessions of James's reign the 'reconciling
statesman', as Gardiner called him, was at the same time the Crown's

leading, if unofficial, servant in the House, and the Commons' principal spokesman; and by 1612 he could rightly describe himself as 'a peremptory royalist' who, nevertheless, had never been 'one hour out of credit with the lower house'.[3] These words were borne out two years later, when he first attended a session as Attorney General, and after some protest at the presence of a Government official in their midst, the Commons made an exception – which, they insisted, was not to form a precedent – for the man whose services as their delegate to the Lords could not be spared.[4] Indeed the very Parliament that was to impeach him sent him first with a message to the King from both Houses. Bacon thought he had been acceptable to those assemblies principally because of his moderation.[5] But it is clear that they trusted his efficiency and discretion, and above all they must have felt that he was in sympathy with the reforms on hand. We know that wherever reform was wanted, Bacon's name was associated with it, and his fellow Members must have realized that in this staunch defender of parliamentary privileges the reformer took precedence over the politician.

The need to raise the pitch of parliamentary debate above the level that frequently prevailed in his time was in Bacon's mind from the beginning of his career. That the primary purpose of Parliament was the discussion of important measures of reform – with the subsidy 'to come in upon the bye' – was for him no mere question of tactics. 'I mean it not in point of dissimulation, but in point of majesty and honour', he wrote to James in 1613, when, after Cecil's death, he was at last in a position to urge his views, 'that people may have something else to talk of and not wholly of the King's estate.' He spoke in vain, for in his opening speeches James showed little sign that he could think of any business for Parliament to do other than 'supply'. As a result, in passing ever fewer acts, it was fast losing its principal function, that of supreme legislation.[6]

Practising what he preached, Bacon regularly introduced measures of intrinsic value as early in a session as he could. Only a failure to recognize this, his central tenet, could have led such a historian as Neale to attribute his interventions to frivolous personal motives. In 1593, for example, after briefly supporting the Government's motion for the subsidy, Bacon, changing the subject, declared his 'great contentment' that Parliament, which was there not only 'for money but for laws', had taken up the important task of purging the statutes. Neale dismissed his speech as irrelevant and ill-timed, and hinted that he was showing off.[7] A later historian, equally unable to credit Bacon with sincerity, concluded that he was trying 'to convince his colleagues that he was not a Government lackey, and was genuinely concerned with the legislative function of the House'.[8]

In reality Bacon was speaking from a double conviction: that the enactment of 'good laws' should come before any discussion of the subsidy, and that if there was a law worth enacting, it was the repeal of those 'obsolete and snaring statutes', which brought a gangrene on wholesome laws, whereby 'the living lie in the arms of the dead' – a repeal which Bacon, not content with repeatedly urging it on Queen and King, was to pursue throughout his parliamentary career.[9] Five years earlier, at the age of twenty-seven, he had been appointed to a committee of sixteen lawyers from the Inns of Court, all men of years but himself, to review the existing statutes for the Parliament of 1589.[10] In 1597 he seconded a motion 'for abridging and reforming the excessive number of superfluous and burdensome penal laws' – which was not pursued.[11] In 1601, with the same twofold aim in mind, he spoke eloquently for the setting up of a commission to repeal statutes 'both needless and dangerous', and, aware that Members had other priorities, begged each of them to report 'what statutes he thinketh fitting to be repealed'.[12] He went on intervening with the same consistency – and persistence – on this vital subject to the end of his parliamentary career. Prominent among the Bills of Grace he prepared for the 1614 Parliament was a proposal that twenty-four commissioners be appointed to prepare a list of the 'obsolete and snaring laws' which could be replaced with 'laws more mild and fit for the time', for submission to the next Parliament.[13] Having persuaded the King to select these commissioners (including himself), Bacon and his colleagues took such 'good pains' with this list that when it was duly submitted – and before impeaching him, as we will recall – the 1621 Parliament appointed a committee to study it, thus taking the first step towards the 'amendment of the laws of England' for which he had fought so hard.[14]

An effort to raise the level of parliamentary debate will be found in Bacon's speeches on all the important issues he took up, in particular in the 1593 and 1597 Parliaments (of which more below). In 1606–7, battling for the naturalization of Scotsmen in England, in hopes of achieving the Union, against isolationist Members like Sir Edwin Sandys, who were filled with suspicion and racial prejudice, Bacon exhorted them to rise above the shopkeeper's standpoint and take a more statesmanlike view. England, he believed, could only benefit from absorbing and integrating Scotsmen. And in any case, 'by the law of nature all men in the world are naturalized one towards the another, they were made of one lump of earth, one breath of God'. How was it possible for Members of the House to forget 'the considerations of amplitude and greatness, and fall at variance about profit and reckonings – fitter a great deal for private persons than for Parliaments and Kingdoms?'[15] Had Bacon sat at this Parliament with the prestige of a Privy Councillor, a historian concluded in our time, he might have inspired James to launch the kind of joint royal and parliamentary programme which he never ceased to advocate.[16]

By 1610 it was too late. The principal subject discussed by the new

Parliament was the Great Contract, Robert Cecil's project to dissolve the much abused Court of Wards by exchanging it for a yearly contribution to the Crown. Bacon was not happy with a contract the very notion of which implied that 'the King should never after need his people more, nor the people the King'. Like his colleague Sir Julius Caesar, he thought that the time was not ripe for it; retrenchment of royal expenses must come first or the contract would break down. All he could do at this point was, once again, to raise the tone of the debate. He presented the Commons' offer of a regular allowance to the King as a 'loving dowry', and the Wards – 'this tree of tenures planted in the prerogative by the ancient common laws of the land' – as a magnificent gift from the people.[17] Carteret, writing in 1747, believed that he had set the Contract in so clear a light 'as excited that spirit which at length produced the dissolution of the Court of Wards'.[18]

The most unfortunate effect of the embittered debate over the Great Contract, in Bacon's eyes, was that Parliament had now acquired a taste for bargaining. For the next Parliament, called in 1614, he urged James to 'put off the person of merchant and contractor and rest upon the person of a King'; only thus would he be able 'to part with his Parliament in love and reverence'.[19] James, as we might expect, chose the bargaining approach – defended, now Cecil was gone, by Bacon's kinsman, Sir Henry Neville, a diplomat inexperienced in parliamentary ways. Bacon made every effort he could to reverse the negative mood fostered in this Parliament by the Howards, led by Henry Howard, the Earl of Northampton, who, as Bacon put it, had 'set up a flag unto all those that . . . would frustrate its success'. With an inspired speech, he attempted to repair, among other blunders made, that of the new Secretary, Sir Ralph Winwood (another inexperienced diplomat), who had launched into a long tirade on the miseries of the Crown for want of money. He reminded the Commons that they were meeting 'upon an interchange of affection', and invited them to consider the Bills of Grace proposed by the King to do away with their grievances – prominent among them his own bills for depopulation and tillage, the repeal of snaring laws, and the plantation of Ireland.[20] His efforts were wasted, however, for after two months' session the Howard clan provoked the desired dissolution. Yet the Parliament had barely 'addled' when Bacon started out to prepare a new one – nothing being 'a greater spur' to renewed action, he told James, than 'when he knows where he failed', reminding him that his authority would continue to suffer 'as long as money was made the mere object of Parliament'.[21] We have watched his efforts in 1621 to promote a Parliament that would at last unite King and country in a positive policy initiated by the Crown. And we have seen how, once that Parliament had ousted him, the legislation he had promoted failed to get off the ground.[22]

There is one intervention of Bacon's, his speech on the triple subsidy voted by Parliament in 1593, which deserves to be looked at in detail, since it was used by Macaulay to create yet another legend, one that still flourishes today. We can hear Bacon's voice beside Macaulay's in the following page. In the attempt 'to be at once favourite at Court and popular with the multitude', Bacon, wrote Macaulay,

> indulged in a burst of patriotism which cost him a long and bitter remorse . . . The Court asked for large subsidies and for speedy payment. The remains of Bacon's speech breathe all the spirit of the Long Parliament. 'The gentlemen must sell their plate, and the farmers their brass pots, ere this will be paid; and for us we are here to search the wounds of the realm, and not to skim them over. The dangers are these, first we shall breed discontent and endanger her majesty's safety, which must consist more in the love of the people than their wealth. Secondly . . . we shall put an evil precedent on ourselves and our posterity; and in histories it is to be observed, of all nations the English are not to be subject, base or taxable.' The Queen and her Ministers resented this outbreak of public spirit in the highest manner. Indeed, many an honest member of the House of Commons had, for a much smaller matter, been sent to the Tower by the hot-blooded Tudors. The young patriot condescended to make his most abject apologies . . .
>
> As soon as he found that the smallest show of independence in Parliament was offensive to the Queen, he abased himself to the dust before her, and implored her forgiveness in terms better suited to a convicted thief than to a knight of the shire . . . The lesson was not thrown away [Macaulay concluded]. Bacon never offended in the same manner again.[23]

A compelling story. Except that Bacon made no attempt to curry favour with the multitude, indulged in no burst of patriotism, did not oppose the subsidy, and never apologized. He was actually the first to speak in favour of the subsidy, having supported it in previous Parliaments. In this one he alleged 'four causes', the least of which would cost 'more than double what we last gave' (the French King's revolt, the taking of Calais, 'the bleeding ulcer of Ireland', and Spanish 'provocation of sea-matters').[24] And if he now 'breathed all the spirit of the Long Parliament', said Spedding, it could only have been inasmuch as the Long Parliament imposed heavier taxes than any king had ever done, since Bacon was supporting a greater tax than any approved before.

Writing in Calcutta, with no access to parliamentary reports, Macaulay had only the confused view of these events which he gathered from the 'Life' he was reviewing. A closer look shows that what Bacon objected to was, firstly, the Lords' cool announcement from on high that they would accept nothing but a triple subsidy, whereas it was the Commons' privilege to initiate taxation without dictation from the Upper House. He carried this point. His second objection was that, if the threefold tax was made payable in three years instead of the usual six (two years for each tax), the heavy burden 'upon the poorer sort' would breed discontent, and create a harmful precedent; and he may well have been right in suggesting that it should be collected with a freer hand, as and when the need arose. He gained this point also, to the extent that it was agreed to raise the first two subsidies in the usual way, allowing four years, and that the third should be treated as extraordinary, so as not to become a precedent.

Far from courting popularity, Bacon, always as he put it 'involved with few', had spoken against the general feeling of the House, as is clear from the answers of Heneage, Ralegh and Cecil. Why then should a still unfledged Member, with his fortune to make (so Spedding argued), and the hopes of an Attorney Generalship in the wind, go out of his way to oppose the Government party on so popular a cause? There could be only one reason: it was his candid opinion, and he was still young enough to give it boldly – and to underestimate the Queen's displeasure at finding in her young courtier only a qualified allegiance.[25] And when that displeasure broke over his head, at no stage did he retract his speech or acknowledge himself in the wrong. (It is significant that two weeks after these events he began a speech on a bill for the better expedition of justice in the Star Chamber, declaring that 'neither profit nor peril' would move him to speak against his conscience 'in this place'.)[26] To Burghley he upheld his view, pointing out that he had spoken 'simply and only' to satisfy his conscience, and begging him to perform 'the part of an honest friend' in restoring him to royal favour. To Essex he expressed indignant surprise at the Queen's failure to see that he had spoken from 'duty alone'. 'I am not so simple', he exclaimed, 'but I know the common and beaten way to please.'[27]

Nor did he take the 'beaten way' when writing to the Queen herself, a little later, about his application for that 'place of my profession' which his friends were pressing on her. He hoped she would give him back the favour which ('encouraged by your own speeches') he had ever sought. But he would not wrong his 'own good mind' by standing upon that favour, now that his appeal might appear interested. A mind which, he added, 'turned upon other wheels but those of profit'. In conclusion, he begged the Queen's pardon for his 'boldness and plainness' – as well he might.[28] The 'plainness' did little to undo the ill effects of Essex's misguided persistence in demanding the Attorney Generalship for his follower. None the less, when two years later Burghley made another effort to advance him, Bacon still maintained he had been right in proposing a different method of payment, and that his speech should have been 'no great matter, since there is variety allowed in counsel, as a discord in music, to make it more perfect'.[29]

Here, then, are the 'apologies' which Macaulay compared to those of a convicted thief. Soon afterwards an eminent biographer depicted Bacon sobbing while he wrote them.[30] Twentieth-century historians, reading the record more attentively, were to find fault with him for *not* apologizing. 'For so astute a person', wrote Neale, it was 'a strange blunder . . . Perhaps he had merely become intoxicated with popularity, an unaccustomed experience for him.'[31] Following suit twenty years later, another historian described Bacon's protestation of innocence as the foolish attack of 'rectitude and stubbornness' which lost him the office he could have had if he had apologized.[32] And to this day historian after historian, repeating Macaulay's assertion that he 'never offended in the same way again', has maintained that after the Parliament of 1593 Bacon gave up his youthful ideals and, changing sides, became 'pro-Government' and 'anti-reform'; that in subsequent Parliaments he dutifully supported the subsidy – as though he had not supported it in this one – and that he never defended the privileges of the Commons again. 'At that stage of his life,' wrote Notestein in 1971, 'he seems to have valued the historic rights of the Commons and to have been willing to throw his cap over the wall for them'; he had not yet lost 'the zeal of his early thirties' (or as another historian put it in 1992, 'the youthful parliamentarian's fervour').[33]

He never lost it. At the next Parliament, in 1597, he waged a battle royal on behalf of the Commons against the joint efforts of the Lords, including those of his patron Essex.[34] Shocked by the poverty he had seen when examining a band of rebel yeomen in Oxfordshire, Bacon set out to study the conditions that had provoked their anger, and found that because of the recent conversion of thousands of acres of ploughland into deer-parks for 'a few private men', devastating poverty and hunger prevailed in many parts of the country.[35] He opened the session with an impassioned speech on the ills of enclosure, 'that pulled down whole towns' for sheep pasture, and himself brought in two bills against enclosures ('his children', as he called them): one for the increase of tillage and the other for the increase of people.[36] Would Ovid's verse about Troy prove true of England, he exclaimed: 'instead of a whole townful of people, none but green fields, but a shepherd and a dog'? He urged 'a sharp and vigorous law to be made against these viperous natures' who destroy the bread of the poor.[37] The bills, 'well liked' by the Commons, it was reported, were soon passed, but the Lords, assisted by Edward Coke, fought against them tooth and nail. There began a duel of words between the two great rivals, Bacon defending the dispossessed farmers, Coke the park-owning landlords, Coke refusing the Commons a copy of the thirty-one legal objections he had drawn up against their bill, and Bacon refusing a conference with the Lords until they had seen the objections. Bacon won the day, and the Statutes of Tillage and of the Decaying of Towns were passed with only minor amendments.[38]

Bacon's denunciation of the engrossing of tillage sprang from a conviction so strong that enclosures turned up in his images, and even in his jokes. (The Queen once asked him his opinion about a cause which had been referred to a small committee for private trial. 'Oh Madam,' he replied, 'my mind is known; I am against all enclosures, and especially against enclosed justice.')[39] After his fall he was to applaud Henry VII for his exemplary legislation against this abuse.[40] He probably also had those destitute yeomen in mind when in that same 1593 Parliament he actively supported what was later described as 'the first comprehensive measure of legal charity' and 'the great charter of the poor', a statute for the relief of the poor which considerably influenced the destiny of many sufferers, and, as a recent study has shown, remained in effective use for over two centuries.[41] Although when the 1601 Parliament was opened, the production of corn had improved and both these statutes came up for repeal, Bacon again defended the Statute of Tillage – with success. And he fought so passionately against the repeal of the Act for the Relief of the Poor that one Member was amazed at his 'heat'.[42] It would be 'a most uncharitable action' to repeal this statute, he maintained, which had been passed by the previous Parliament in 'a feast of charity'. Excusing himself for speaking so hotly, 'not out of the fervency of my brain' but 'out of the very strings of my heart', he pleaded with his fellow Members. 'We should rather tenderly foster it', he urged, than 'roughly cry away with it'.[43] At this same Parliament, Bacon also supported a petition for the abrogation of a number of abusive monopolies, and spoke in favour of the removal of monopolies from the royal prerogative, so that they should be 'hereafter of more force than they were by common law'. Both of these requests, as we saw earlier, Elizabeth graciously granted, thus providing him with a lifelong model for the dealings between Crown and Parliament.[44]

Must we then look to the Parliament of 1604 to discover when Bacon 'lost his zeal'? Not in the view of the Whig historian Lucy Aikin, who wrote in glowing terms of his honourable stand against the odious right of purveyances, a much abused arrangement whereby the Crown could compel subjects to sell their products at a heavy discount to the royal Household. 'At that time,' she said, 'he had not yet prevailed upon himself to make an entire surrender of the principle of genuine patriotism which resulted from the comprehensiveness and benevolence of his mind.'[45] Bacon was in fact, as a historian of that Parliament put it in 1979, one of the 'leading agitators' in the battle against purveyances, which he had been waging in committee after committee and in every possible debate since 1588.[46] Speaking now as the Commons' messenger to King James, he denounced the 'great misdemeanours' committed in the King's name by commissioners, who worked 'by twilight and in the night-time, a time well chosen for malefactors', who took far more than was needed – even the trees, 'which by law they cannot do; timber-trees, which are the beauty, countenance and shelter of men's houses'. 'There is no grievance in your kingdom', he told James, 'so general, so continual, so sensible and so bitter unto the subject.'[47]

Bacon continued to attack this grievance until in the next Parliament, opened in 1606, purveyance was abolished. At this Parliament he also gained another victory for the Commons' privileges. Thanks to his tactful handling of the controversial admittance of a Member (a disturbance created by the still pro-prerogative Coke, who had unseated an elected Member to install a Crown councillor in his place), their right to decide on the validity of an election to Parliament was never questioned again.[48] In 1610, *pace* Notestein, Bacon was still defending the historic rights of the Commons – in this case their right to discuss the exaction of impositions under the royal prerogative. If, he said, as on earlier occasions under Queen Elizabeth, an inhibition came to restrain them from discussing a question which concerned the interests of the Commonwealth or of any subject, they should inform the King of their ancient liberty to do so, and proceed with the debate.[49]

After 1610 all Bacon's energies – and innumerable pages of exhortation – were needed to persuade the reluctant James to call a Parliament at all, and once it was called, to prevent him from dissolving it; not to speak of framing those 'gracious laws' which could enable the King and his Commons to work together in harmony, laws which he had been putting forward in every parliamentary session for more than two decades. Even so, in 1614, as Attorney General and 'King's man', he was once again sent by the Commons as their messenger to the Lords, this time to explain to them that in levying impositions without their consent, James, no doubt misinformed about his rights, had assumed powers which no former king had ever resorted to.[50] Finally we find Bacon, at his last Parliament, moving so far towards constitutional government as to suggest that the Commons play a part in that exclusive domain of the prerogative, foreign affairs, by 'assisting and strengthening' the King with their views on ways of recovering the Palatinate. James, convinced that the people 'were not capable' of matters of state, vetoed the proposal.[51]

A thorough survey of Bacon's parliamentary interventions would show up lights and shades neglected here. But from what we have seen, whether he was right or mistaken, Bacon would appear to have spoken on most of the important issues of his time from long-held – often passionately held – conviction, born of his awareness of the human suffering involved, and to have done his best to serve his own high idea of the House of Commons as a partner in the dialogue between Parliament and the Crown.

The Parliamentarians of the following generation were in no doubt about his role. Far from seeing themselves as the residuary legatees of the opposition under James – whose most vocal members (Sir Dudley Digges and others) had now become the Royalists of the Civil War – they looked to Bacon as the leading spirit of their revolution, and made serious efforts to put his proposals on trade, the codification of the law and the plantation of Ireland, among others, into effect.[52] On the reform of law, one historian has seen him joining hands 'across the divide of the Civil War' with the Independent gentry, with Cromwell and the Levellers.[53] And it is surely not without significance that a list of the most enthusiastic supporters of Bacon's scientific programme, which Hartlib, Dury and Comenius tried to implement in the 1640s (beginning with John Pym) should turn out to be a list of the principal Members of the Long Parliament.

23

Cravenly Suing for Power and Complacently Savouring its Fruits

Bacon sought office, he tells us, for two reasons: first, because he dearly hoped that 'if I rose to any place of honour in the state I should have a larger command of industry and ability to help me in my work' – that is, in 'kindling a light in nature' which could disclose 'all that is most hidden and secret in the world'; and secondly, because of the special claims his country had upon a man seasoned as he was in 'business of state'.[1] But owing to the premature death of his father, he did not, like his cousin Robert Cecil, inherit the office he had been trained for. Left to fend for himself, he had not even the advantage of the secure estate his father had planned to set up for him. Before we consider how he used his ideas when in high place, therefore, we must look at his method of reaching that place. Is it true, as claimed by Macaulay, that he 'stooped to everything, endured everything', sued 'in the humblest manner', and when repulsed began to sue again?[2] Or, as one critic put it in 1980, that 'he never gave up his lifelong habit of pestering the great for preferment'?[3]

Certainly Bacon sued: there could be no survival at Court without it. The courtiers of Elizabeth and James, that 'illustrious order of mendicants', as Neale described them, sued the monarch, the favourite, and the favourite's favourite – for honours, for land, for justice, for preferment, for pardon, and above all, from the moment a man died and his place fell vacant (or more often before), for office. It was a game everyone at Court had to play, and only a glorious death saved Sir Philip Sidney, who did not want to play it, from ineffectual obscurity. To later ages, however, it has appeared not merely distasteful, but almost incomprehensible. The hyperbolic praises lavished by Tudor and Jacobean personages on their patrons, and their self-abasement before them, have never ceased to astonish their respective biographers. Whether it is Fulke Greville they write of, tirelessly reminding friends at Court of his virtues and of his zeal in the Queen's service, or Ellesmere, begging for rewards and honours to the last, or John Donne, persistently pleading with Somerset ('the instrument of God's providence in this kingdom') for a renewal of the favour he had lost when eloping with that same Ellesmere's daughter, or a multitude of others, their biographers' dismay is the same; if somewhat more justified, perhaps, in the case of such a notorious flatterer as Henry Howard, whose efforts to secure patronage by 'unctuous adulation' of King James passed all bounds.[4]

What surprises about Bacon, when we look at his correspondence, is the modesty of his suing. There are only five surviving letters addressed over fifteen years to the powerful Burghley, gracefully accepting avuncular admonition, thanking him for avuncular support, and referring to his hopes of some position in which he might 'command more wits than of a man's own'. Rather than suits, they read like a sharing of his thoughts with a benevolent relative in a position to help him.[5] A favourable biographer, casting his eye over the twelve years of Somerset's ascendency, when the whole Court was suing him for advancement, found in Bacon's case 'a complete blank in such intercourse' – surprising on any count, he remarked, and 'bewildering, if Bacon was the time-server and opportunist he is often thought and sometimes seems to be'.[6]

It has been observed that the qualities needed to attain power and those required to make the best use of it are not often found in the same person. Spedding thought Bacon ill-qualified to 'tread the quicksands of politics' and work his way up through a Court; and the relief with which, on the accession of James, Bacon exclaimed that 'the canvassing world is gone and the deserving world is come' is in keeping with that view. Bacon himself, as he once told James, felt at a disadvantage because of his comparative 'slowness to sue'.[7] With his mind on so many other things, more often than not he needed the prodding of Essex or some other protector before he could get round to the chore of canvassing for himself. ('Awake your friends,' Greville wrote him in 1594, when the Queen had relented towards him, after his act of independence in Parliament.)[8] When suing became urgent we will usually find him writing off a whole batch of letters in one day, as if to get them over and done with, so that he could get back to what really occupied his thoughts. During the famous rush to Scotland, when every high-placed official at Court flew to meet the new King – 'a spring-time sport', Bacon called it – he himself dispatched a series of hastily penned letters 'commending his love and services' to the various friends who were posting away, though he knew them to be needless, he told Sir John Davies, 'save that I meant to show that I was not asleep'.[9] Bacon's 'uncoordinate' way of dealing with his own affairs was noticed by a historian in our time, and this is a case in point. Seemingly embarrassed by the whole suing business, he would resort to conventional excuses – 'for the comfort of my mother', 'to satisfy my wife's friends' – or when applying to Cecil for the Solicitor-Generalship, that it would have been 'arrogance' in him not to have written.[10]

What more did Bacon do by way of 'pestering the great'? Aside from two straightforward applications to the King for posts for which he was eminently qualified, and to which he was appointed as the obvious candidate – Solicitor General in 1607 and Attorney General in 1613 – he applied for two further appointments. One was that of Secretary, on Cecil's death in 1612, which he failed to obtain, though historians are generally agreed that had James had the courage and foresight to appoint him, the growing estrangement between Crown and Parliament might have been healed, with inestimable consequences for his own reign and that of his son. The other was the post of Lord Keeper, on the death of Ellesmere in 1617, which he obtained.[11] He does not appear servile, mean or irksome in these applications. He thought the promotion was his due, but he did not beg for it or offer to buy it. He asked for it, and gave his reasons, on the whole with remarkable objectivity, speaking rather as adviser than as applicant and coolly comparing his usefulness to the state with that of other potential candidates. In his application for the Lord Keepership, in particular, he correctly stressed his value as moderator in the Council, and the 'inventive part' he could play in the initiation of good laws. His fair assessment of himself on such occasions should be seen beside his dispassionate judgement of himself on his fall, when he saw – and condemned – his frailties with the same impersonal detachment as he had estimated the value of his services to the Government. Carteret, in 1734, closer to the Jacobean scene than we are, admired his ability to explain his fitness for a post, 'with nothing forward or hasty, much less mean or indecent', without 'wrong to others', but with 'honour to himself' and 'duty and benefit to the King his master'.[12]

And when finally in place, did Bacon resort to subservience and flattery in order to stay there – as did Sir Edward Conway, James's Secretary, whose views (said Gardiner) 'changed with every shifting fancy of the great man to whom he owed his office'?[13] We must distinguish here between deliberate sycophancy, on the one hand, and on the other, the flattery then universally practised to oil the machinery of state, which Bacon described as 'a mere form due in civility to Kings and great persons', such praise being in effect 'a submission to the occasion, not the person'.[14] Bacon had no language strong enough to condemn sycophants, 'the bane of all courts', those flies, he told the young Villiers, 'who will not only buzz in every ear, but will blow and corrupt every place where they alight'; and he would have been very much surprised to learn that the future ages, to whom he left his name and works, have counted him among them. Telling his master the truth was, he believed, a counsellor's principal duty. 'If you flatter the King,' he wrote to Villiers, 'you are as dangerous a traitor to his State as he that riseth in arms against him.'[15] In effect, Bacon cannot be shown on a single instance to have misinformed the King, in order to curry favour, by approving what he considered wrong or by failing to express disapproval. It was sometimes safer, he conceded, to keep silent, but it was 'more loving' to speak.[16] And speak he did. He rebuked Essex 'with much freedom', as that Lord admitted, and admonished Buckingham, asking pardon for the freedom of his counsels (among them that the favourite should not give cause for scandal by 'light, vain or oppressive behaviour'), and got into considerable trouble for doing so, as we shall see.[17] But more than that, he repeatedly exhorted James in no uncertain terms to behave more like a prince, and on one occasion, impelled, he said, by 'an infinite desire that your Majesty's affairs may go well', he told the loquacious James to bridle his tongue.[18]

This did not mean that the servant of an absolute monarch could disobey, or even demur, once that monarch had expressed his intentions. Opposition to a sovereign was not merely dangerous and destructive, it was useless – indeed, within the system, impossible.[19] But before the King's will was known, Bacon insisted, a counsellor's duty was to speak his mind. This was established practice, inherited from Burghley, and he thought it best for the commonweal.[20] 'Vote and thoughts are free,' he said, but 'after the King hath resolved, all men ought to cooperate . . . especially when a few, severing from the rest, might hurt the business.'[21] So we find him practising the gentle art of bringing up some neglected point, time and again, in hopes that water would were down the stone, as it sometimes did. Or working indirectly, as when, three years after his fall, on the 'dark business' of the royal match with Spain, over which the King and the favourite were at loggerheads, he urged Buckingham, if in his conscience and judgement he was persuaded (as Bacon was) that the match was 'dangerous and prejudicial to his Majesty's kingdoms', to deliver his soul 'and in the freedom of a faithful counsellor . . . declare yourself accordingly, and show your reasons'. If, however, 'the King in his high judgement, or the Prince in his settled affection, be resolved to have it go on, then you must move in their orb, as far as they shall lay it upon you.'[22]

Following his own precept, Bacon kept his judgement free. Indeed, he sometimes pushed it to the limits of brinkmanship, as happened in the summer of 1617, when, newly appointed Lord Keeper, he was left in charge of the kingdom during James's visit to Scotland. The story reads like a scene out of some Elizabethan drama – as Chamberlain must have realized, when he remarked of one of its characters that 'Burbage could not have acted better'.[23] The case includes Bacon's long-term rival, the disgraced Edward Coke, now trying to buy his way back into favour by offering his daughter, with a rich dowry, to the Buckingham tribe, represented by the favourite's brother, Sir John Villiers; Lady Hatton, Coke's quarrelsome wife, who was expected to provide the dowry, but would have none of the marriage; and the reluctant bride, Frances Coke, who had been carried off by her mother to friends. Coke, until recently Chief Justice of England, pursued her with a band of his armed sons. After ramming down the front door of her refuge, he dragged her out of a cupboard and bullied (some said flogged) her into obedience, and posted her off to the prospective bridegroom's mother, Lady Compton – another character part. Last but not least, enter *deus ex machina*, the intractable Secretary Winwood, who, resenting Bacon's vice-regal authority, had been intriguing against him behind his back and had deliberately concealed the fact that, having originated with Buckingham himself, the project had the King's support.[24]

Bacon heartily disliked all wrangling. Earlier that year he had helped to mediate between Coke and his wife in one of their scandalous quarrels, and he considered this one 'ill on all sides'.[25] His only part in the play so far had been the dangerous one of refusing Lady Compton a warrant for Coke to recover his daughter by force, a warrant which Coke promptly, and illegally, obtained from Winwood. Whereupon Lady Hatton burst in on Bacon during his siesta with an urgent appeal against her husband. The next day she laid it before the Council, and Coke, summoned to answer her complaint, was told with Baconian moderation, that 'that noble gentleman', Sir John Villiers, should be able to seek his (Coke's) daughter 'in a noble and religious fashion, without any forced consent of the maid, and with the consent of both parents'. Charged with 'riot and force', Coke amazed all present by claiming that a father was legally entitled to break into any house in the land in pursuit of a fugitive daughter. An information was filed against him in the Star Chamber, and he was enjoined to deliver his daughter into the Council's care. At this point, like a rabbit out of a hat, Winwood produced a letter from the King approving the marriage. Whereupon Frances was sent back to her temporarily reconciled parents, to be courted by Villiers, and the proceedings against Coke were dropped.

Bacon had behaved throughout with complete consistency. As soon as he learned of the proposal, he had written to Buckingham warning him against his brother's marrying into 'a troubled house', and, more seriously, against a return of Coke to the Council, which, as some other Councillors also maintained, 'would greatly weaken and distract the King's service'.[26] There was no question of acting against King James's wishes, but even now Bacon did not hesitate to write to him once again, 'in plainness and no less humbleness', his opinion of the match – well aware that it might be taken for a personal jealousy ('umbrage') of Coke – as it has been by many historians since. He felt freer, he said, 'than other men in giving your Majesty faithful counsel, and more bound than other men in doing your commandments when your resolution is made known to me' (a tacit, and deserved reproach to the King for keeping him in the dark). Of Buckingham he wrote, 'I had rather go against his mind than his good, but your Majesty I must obey.'[27]

In further, equally dignified letters, Bacon answered the petty scoldings of the infatuated King and the cold notes of the offended favourite, whose anger the triumphant Coke, 'as if he were already upon his wings', was busily stoking up in Scotland (so a colleague wrote to Bacon) with 'misinformation'.[28] Apologizing for his admittedly 'somewhat parent-like' attitude to Buckingham, Bacon gave the King eminently sensible reasons for opposing the match. He had done his best, he said, in ignorance of James's wishes, as 'a true servant to your Majesty', and 'a true friend to my Lord of Buckingham', and he hoped 'all mists and mistakings' would soon be dispersed. To Buckingham he wrote, more personally, 'I rely upon your constancy and nature, and my own deserving, and the firm title we have in the King's service'; adding, with some feeling, 'God keep us from these long journeys and absence, which makes misunderstandings and gives advantages to untruth.'[29]

Both King and favourite were finally satisfied of Bacon's good faith. James publicly defended his own conduct on the grounds that he loved Buckingham 'more than all those who were here present', for 'just as Christ had his John, so he, James, had his George'. And soon afterwards Bacon was appointed Lord Chancellor of the Realm. The mists were dispersed. Or almost, for the seed of resentment had been sown in Buckingham's self-absorbed heart, and we have seen its results. It was Buckingham's single misfortune, Clarendon observed, that 'he never made a noble friendship with a man so near his equal that he would frankly advise him for his honour and true interest against the current, or rather the torrent, of his impetuous passions.'[30]

Bacon did not so easily satisfy his biographers. Macaulay poured scorn on him for allegedly begging the favourite's pardon with the most humiliating self-abasement, while in our time he was sneered at for defending his over-zealous interference with so much obtuseness that it was no wonder James never trusted him again.[31] Why then, we may wonder, did he promptly make him his Chancellor? Bacon was proved right, however, as we can see from the epilogue of the play. Back at Court, after more than doubling his daughter's dowry, Coke 'distracted' not only the Council, but the Parliament that followed; and Frances, as Bacon had warned, brought the troubles of a disunited family into her marriage with Villiers, and eventually eloped with another man.

The reasons Bacon had given James for opposing the match were real and cogent, and there is no need to attribute them to a personal enmity towards Coke, from whom he had nothing to fear at this time, except his nuisance value in the Council. Bacon was well aware that in defending the match, the King had merely been indulging a craving to shower riches on 'his George', at no cost to himself. That Bacon could none the less submit, without revolt or resentment, was put down by nineteenth- and twentieth-century historians to cringing subservience. They forgot that for Bacon and his contemporaries there was a sense in which the monarch – God's representative on earth – could be right against all evidence. It is difficult for us to conceive the quasi-religious emotion aroused in people's minds and hearts by the royal image of Elizabeth as Astraea, the Imperial Moon, the Vestal Virgin, the living symbol of English empire – with all the processions and rituals taken over from its arch-enemy, the Pope; or by that of James, the Scholar-King, surpassing Solomon in his wisdom.[32] That her courtiers could be more than half in love with a bald old woman; that Ralegh meant it when he said she rode like Alexander, hunted like Diana, walked like Venus, 'the gentle wind blowing her fair hair about her pure cheeks'; that the physically repulsive James could be hailed as an incarnation of Phoebus Apollo – 'the most religious learned and judicious King', said Ellesmere, 'that ever this kingdom or any island had'; surmounting, wrote Cecil, 'in his excellent virtues, natural, moral and political . . . all of other kings, living or dead', a very *visio beatifica*, restoring life to his spirits, that were 'ready to expire' in the King's service – all this, if they meant it, passes our comprehension.[33] And they did mean it.

This was the awful god to whom his followers addressed their prayers, in the form of suits, on whose breath 'four lagging winters and four wanton springs', could hang – the worst of all lots being that 'darkness in which a man may not behold his sovereign's face': banishment. So that, if Elizabeth frowned, Burghley trembled in his shoes, and when James clenched his fist at him, Coke fell 'weeping and grovelling on all fours'.[34] Ralegh's Victorian biographer describes the 'strange, sad spectacle' of the condemned adventurer, who 'on the knees of my heart' bombarded the King with letters, begging life, time, compassion for 'a miserable, forsaken man', and when life was granted cried, 'how can so unworthy a creature make payment of so unaccountable a debt? . . . Only my sovereign Lord, who might justly have beaten me and justly have destroyed me, hath vouchsafed to spare me.'[35]

Bacon had imbibed the Tudor myth at his mother's knee, while she was translating the Latin works of Bishop Jewell, its principal exponent, and it is against this background that we should read his praise of Elizabeth's graces, later construed as gross flattery – though Chamberlain saw nothing in it to carp at, barring the writer's poor Latin.[36] His similarly criticized praise of James, which pales by comparison with some of his contemporaries' panegyrics, was not – or not merely – an attempt to win favour. James's failings were only too visible, but his divine kingship was apprehended with a different faculty. When enumerating his virtues, it was the ideal monarch Bacon addressed, the Father in New Atlantis, whose 'large heart, inscrutable for good, was wholly bent to make his kingdom happy'.[37] And it was because the King's voice was 'the voice of God in man, the good spirit of God in the mouth of man', that Bacon could accept what with his reason alone he would have rejected: that the King's judgement was 'higher and deeper' than his own. James believed it too.[38]

We cannot question the sincerity of this irrational conviction that the King, because he was King, knew better, and was better than he appeared to the naked eye.[39] And when disgrace came, we should not read fawning servility into Bacon's despairing lines, 'That which I thirst after as the hart the streams is that I may know . . . your Majesty's heart (which is an abyss of goodness as I am an abyss of misery) towards me.' Nor, though he knew in his own heart that James had deserted him and Buckingham betrayed him, should we mistake for sycophancy the submission to destiny with which he signed this same letter: 'clay in your Majesty's gracious hands'; or the joy with which he later wrote to Gondomar, 'I have been admitted to see and speak to my King.'[40] And if the man who could so imperiously demand his release from the Tower is found in his last years appealing for grace, let us remember that a single need runs through those letters asking for the pardon of his sentence: the King alone, God's representative on earth, could remove the 'blot of ignominy' which, in so far as he had deserved it, Bacon had expiated by his fall, and with a full pardon restore to him the 'precious jewel' of his good name.[41]

Nineteenth- and twentieth-century critics found these attitudes, and this language, unacceptable, even in such personages as Cecil and Ralegh. Still less could they be suffered in a philosopher, venerated by some of them as 'the Founder of a revolution scarcely less important for the sciences . . . than Luther for the world of religion and politics'.[42] Unique in that they voiced their criticism before Macaulay had published his essay, two of the thinkers who have best understood Bacon's writings and were most profoundly influenced by him were so shocked by his – to them – inexplicable subservience to royalty that it created a serious conflict in their minds. Coleridge, who looked on Bacon as a great unifying spirit, and felt a close affinity between Bacon's creative style and his own, is found exclaiming sorrowfully on 'his courtly – alas! – his servile, prostitute and mendicant ambition!' He could not even face 'the general meanness' of a first-rate genius 'submitting to being a Solicitor at all'. And Emerson, in America, was caught in the same dilemma. The works of 'this pivotal Lord Bacon', his 'trusty counsellor', ruled Emerson's attitudes and actions, inspired his favourite images, and so filled his horizon that for many years he thought he would need 'no other book'.[43] But he could not take what he interpreted as an 'Asiatic prostration', the 'nauseous' spirit of compliment he found in Bacon's letters to the King. The suing, as Emerson's biographer noted, had fallen 'with an ugly ring' on his New Englander's ear. As she saw it, his judgement had little to do with Bacon, but much with 'the American democrat in conflict with an English monarchist'. That a man entrusted with the high office 'of opening the doors and palaces of knowledge to many generations', Emerson wrote, should have suffered 'infusions of this alien spirit of courts' was a contradiction with which – unable to see Bacon in the light of his time – he grappled in vain.[44]

Yet, looked at more closely, a good deal of Bacon's so-called fulsome praise of his masters was something quite different. When attributing to Elizabeth or James the ideal qualities of a benevolent monarch, Bacon was reminding those familiar, all too fallible beings to live up to their higher symbolic reality, thus consciously practising a well-known and legitimate form of flattery which he called *laudendo praecipere*, or teaching through praise.[45] It has been noticed that his early praise of Queen Elizabeth – moving from 'the excellencies of her person' to the benefits of her 'politic, clement and gracious government', her rare eloquence, prudent temper and her 'exquisite tact in choosing and finding good servants' – forms the *Urtext* of his ideas of what a prince should be.[46] Similarly, in highlighting the intelligence of the newly crowned James (which involved undervaluing his own), he was in reality doing all he could to quicken the virtue he hoped to find in his master; to enkindle not merely the religiously tolerant prince who would support Henri IV of France against the forces of the Counter-Reformation, but the threefold King-Priest-Philosopher, ready, as Bacon was himself, 'to take flame and blaze from the least occasion or the least spark of another's knowledge delivered'.[47] Teaching through praise, when good counsel proved unpalatable, involved gilding the pill. There is a way, Bacon remarked, of 'conveying and imprinting passages amongst compliments and respects which is of singular use, if a man can hit upon it'.[48] Thus when he wished to 'imprint' upon James the need to curb his parliamentary speechifying, he introduced the suggestion with a reference to the King's 'excellent and incomparable ability' in speaking.[49]

He used a similarly indirect technique in his *History of the Reign of King Henry VII* (1622) – a book seen by his more jaundiced critics today as no more than a last bid to flatter his way back to power, whereas it was in reality part of a lifelong project, and was better understood in his own time as the work of a teacher of kings.[50] Far from gratifying James by praising his cold, suspicious and dangerously secretive ancestor, Bacon, as he told Prince Charles in his dedication, 'took him to the life as well as I could'. But he read into Henry's more enlightened actions a purposeful awareness and breadth of vision than he could have found in that king.

In particular he made much of Henry's commendable custom of resorting frequently to his councillors; of his policy of initiating the relief of abuses and the enacting of good laws (such as his acts against enclosures); of his care to keep his coffers full; and of that excellent practice of consulting his subjects in Parliament on 'all affairs that are of a public nature at home and abroad', a sure way of 'knitting' the people to their king. These are all strategies Bacon had long been preaching to James, as also Henry's policy of making 'offers and fames of war till he had mended the conditions of peace', highly relevant at the time of writing, when James and his son faced a similar situation, with a Spanish enemy instead of a French one.[51]

Attempting to guide a stubborn, all-powerful king, under the sway of a spoilt favourite, was no easier than finding an opening into set minds for the New Instauration. Yet they badly needed guidance, and Bacon, trained to look upon himself as the counsellor of kings, felt he could give it. His detractors today regard all his efforts to advise the favourite privately, after his fall, as part of a determined campaign to regain favour. But a glance at some of his notes for interviews that never took place – which have recently been studied with interest by a historian of the 1624 Parliament – will show also how keenly he continued to follow the issues facing his country, and how much he wished to avert the troubles he saw looming ahead. Issues such as keeping trade with the West Indies open for the Low Countries, the importance of 'the uniting of the states of Europe against the growing ambition of Spain', and 'above all you must look to the safety of Ireland . . . because it is most dangerous for this state.'[52] We have noted the undiminished concern with which Bacon followed the career of his one-time pupil in statecraft in those years, but he was probably at least as preoccupied for the affairs which Buckingham was then mishandling. The following paragraph is from a letter Bacon actually sent to the favourite, then engaged on his famous escapade in Spain with the Prince to negotiate Charles's marriage, which Buckingham was to be principally responsible for wrecking.

> When I look abroad and see times so stirring, and so much dissimulation, falsehood, baseness and envy in the world, and so many idle clocks going in men's heads; then it grieveth me much that I am not sometimes at your Lordship's elbow, that I mought give you some of the fruits of the careful advice, modest liberty and true information of a friend that looketh to your Lordship as I do.[53]

Self-seeking ploy, or zealous watchfulness? Before we can truly estimate his motives, we should take a look at the use Bacon made of such power as he attained. Once in office, did he put his admittedly excellent ideas into practice to the best of his ability, or did he, as one recent biographer asserted, merely sit back and enjoy the fruits of power with 'a self-seeking complacency'?[54]

To begin with, Bacon never wielded the exceptional, and largely secret, power which a Cecil, for example, had built up over fourteen years' tenure, on paternal support, compounded by intensive intrigue. Some degree of discouragement may be allowed for, even in so buoyant a spirit as Bacon's, when he made the inevitable discovery that high office provided less of the 'vantage' to do good than he expected, and little of that 'larger command of industry and ability' he needed for his Instauration. 'Men in great place', he had noted before reaching it, 'have no freedom . . . in their actions.' Yet how narrow was the margin of freedom allowed to the greatest officer in the land surprised even Bacon when, with the agreement of the whole Council, he suspended a proclamation decided on earlier but which, after James had left for Scotland, had become unnecessary and irrelevant. On hearing of this, it is recorded, James 'broke into a great choler, saying that he was contemned and his commandments neglected', and, reminding Bacon that *he was King of England*, instructed him to despatch the proclamation 'without any more excuses'.[55]

Under an absolute king much of an official's work consisted of giving good counsel, and Bacon saw counsel as 'the greatest trust between man and man'. It was a servant's task to offer it, and a king's function to receive it, for which purpose he should draw to himself men by nature 'faithful and sincere, plain and direct', who could 'ripen his own judgement'. Bacon included himself in this category, and as a learned man he thought himself best placed to provide valid counsel – counsel, that is, based on his knowledge of the 'particulars' of civil history, duly 're-freshed' by his own political experience. After his fall we have seen him reminding James that he had never been 'author of any immoderate, unsafe or unfortunate counsel' to his master.[56] Macaulay thought otherwise. 'The years during which Bacon held the Great Seal', he declared, 'were among the darkest and most shameful in English history.' In his view Bacon shared the blame for James's 'wavering and cowardly' foreign policy, and for a whole pageful of other evils; though when those evils are closely examined, it is found that Bacon had drawn attention to and proposed valid remedies for every one of them.[57] Was he at fault for his advice, or because it was not followed? On the first count we have seen historian after historian concluding, each in his own field, that had Bacon's proposals been taken up – his appeals for a united Council, his statesmanlike views on religion, his anything but cowardly foreign policies – there might never have been a Civil War, or even a Thirty Years' War. Not to speak of the ills that would have been averted had his advice on colonization, and on Ireland, been adopted.[58]

Wherever the causes of the Civil War have been pinpointed by his-

torians today, Bacon has been there before them, even to warning against
the dangers of that Scottish rebellion which, in the event, was to pre-
cipitate it.[59] And above all he was fully alert to the danger of the
general administrative breakdown which is now looked on as the
most important cause of the Civil War. Besides advice, he devoted much
time and energy to warding off that breakdown, and we know that
throughout the 'evil years in which he held the Great Seal' he was hard
at work, with the efficient Cranfield to assist him, on a review of the
royal finances. Remembering no doubt the remarkable recovery made by
his brother's friend, Henri IV, with a similar effort in France, Bacon
launched an all-out campaign to reduce public expenditure, by cutting
out redundancy, recovering Crown debts, and improving the yield of
Crown lands; with some success, as we have seen him report.[60] But James
was not as conscious as Henri had been of the link between Crown funds
and Crown power, and the consumption went on, as Bacon wrote to
Buckingham in 1620, praying that God might give his majesty resolution
'to do that which may help it before it be irremediable'.[61] Buckingham
was himself the bottomless drain down which all savings went, and he
did not take the hint. Under his aegis the reform of the Court could not
take place.[62]

'States, as great engines, are moved slowly and not without efforts,'
Bacon had observed – before he tried to move them – and superficial
critics of his efforts have failed to realize that without the cooperation of
those who really control power, a minister's attempts at reform are
doomed to failure.[63] No man besides Bacon, as Trevor-Roper concluded in
1959, had diagnosed the evil of his time 'so completely in all its forms
and ultimate consequences; but he could do nothing to cure it except by
royal permission. This was refused . . .' and both he and Cranfield were
overthrown, despite (and in Cranfield's case because of) their sustained
but unwelcome efforts to make James's Court workable. Comparing
Bacon's proposals for the reform of Church, Court, Crown estates, law,
education and trade to the demands of the radical party in the 1640s,
Trevor-Roper's considered opinion, like Gardiner's before him, was that
Bacon's programme, if carried out, could have made the revolution
unnecessary. Here too the same conclusion is drawn: it is above all
because Bacon's mercantile programme was – like his proposals on
religion and on almost everything else – too far ahead of its time to meet
with support that in England the crisis could only be resolved by violence
and revolution.[64] Yet, if Bacon's various programme's were not carried
out in his lifetime, correct diagnosis, as was recently pointed out, is in
itself a success, and time has fully vindicated him.[65] Some of his projects,
as we have seen, were adopted a century later, others not until the
nineteenth century, others again are still being studied as desirable
improvements today.

Is it Bacon's fault that James did not listen to him? He was censured by late nineteenth-century historians for not exerting a greater influence on his royal master, and in the late twentieth century one biographer explained this failure by supposing that, although useful to the King, he was in all likelihood antipathetic to him.[66] It is true that Bacon was less prized by James than Burghley or his own father had been by Elizabeth. But, as Hurstfield reminded us, 'the difference was at least as much in the monarch as in the servant'.[67] Had the King been less anxious to please his favourite, he would no doubt have paid more attention to his counsellor. He did take Bacon's advice on occasion, and greatly admired his 'true passages of business', as on the Court of Wards, or when Bacon reviewed the situation in Bohemia, in a paper James was so eager to see that he snatched it out of the favourite's hand.[68] And he must have known what he was doing when, regardless of the high bids offered him for the post, he appointed as his Lord Keeper, and later his Chancellor, a man who had offered him nothing at all.

Was James mistaken in his choice? Did Bacon, as soon as he had gained this long-desired position of 'vantage' from which he hoped to launch his double programme, drop everything, as his political biographer Joel J. Epstein has it today, and treat it merely as a prize to be 'cuddled, nurtured and used to every possible advantage'? Was his 'originally clear perception of the abuses of his court', as Robert Zaller alleges, 'gradually blurred by identification'? Had his political perception deteriorated, as Derek Hirst writes, so that he was 'no longer fit for reform'?[69] Bacon's *exposé* of the abuses of Chancery, which he had presented on taking his seat there, was precisely the kind of analysis that most impressed James in his 'wise counsellor'; as he once described it to Buckingham, his 'first setting down the state of the question and then propounding the difficulties, the rest being done in its own time'.[70] 'The rest' was done as soon as possible, in this case with the production of Bacon's revolutionary hundred and one *Ordinances* – 'all the rules necessary', as Zaller noted, 'to make his court a model of efficiency' – which, despite the inevitable time-lag involved in implementing them against the dead weight of traditional malpractice, were to determine Chancery procedure for two centuries.[71] And we will find that, just as Bacon regularly set out to fill the gaps in knowledge he had uncovered in his *Advancement of Learning*, so did he follow up his analysis of Chancery's administrative deficiencies, wherever he could, with practical remedial action.

Where did the Chancellor find the time to cuddle his prize? Not when he was working overtime through those first three months, in the effort to clear his desk of hardly fewer than four thousand decrees left him by his tired predecessor; or when himself pronouncing thousands of new ones, many of which have been found to contain salutory innovations foreshadowing the provisions of modern legislation.[72] Nor when he was drafting his excellent *Rules for the Star Chamber*, then still, like Chancery, a poor man's court, which might have survived had his *Rules* not fallen into oblivion after his impeachment; or when he was enthusiastically preparing for the 1621 Parliament, in a way that, according to Menna Prestwich, compares very favourably with the preparation of the next one in 1624, when he was gone, which failed to put out an agenda of new legislation and discussed only the revival of old bills.[73] Surely not when he was taking such 'good pains' in pursuit of 'snaring laws' that eighty redundant statutes were repealed – by that same 1621 Parliament; or when, as was recently noticed by a student of his law, he 'used his new position to pursue his ideas for accurate, professional court reporting' – so essential to ward off the uncertainty of the law – by securing the appointment of two 'grave and sound lawyers', as he put it, to posts he had proposed years earlier. (First on his list of those who could 'give much life' to law reports was the highly qualified judge, James Whitelocke, though he was personally hostile to Bacon.)[74] With all this going on, we should recall, he was attending to his daily practice in Chancery and running the complex trials of high-level personages then under way in the Star Chamber, as well as carrying out his activities as Commissioner of the Treasure, Councillor, manager, moderator, supervisor of the District Judges, dispenser of minor livings . . . No wonder Bacon neglected his servants! No wonder Chamberlain feared, when he was made Lord Keeper, that 'so tender a constitution of body and mind would hardly be able to undergo the burden of so much business as the place required'.[75]

And we must not forget that this heavy pressure of business represents only one half of Bacon's life. When he published the *Instauratio Magna*, near the end of his career, he apologized to the King for having stolen from his affairs 'the time required for this work'.[76] 'My mind', as he once confessed to Bodley, 'hath often been absent from what I have done.'[77] Had he not been distracted throughout by his plans for 'the total reconstruction of sciences, arts, and all human knowledge' – including the knowledge of man and all his works – we may be sure he would have climbed the political stair with his mind on the job.[78] And would not have fallen off it. But, unlike Cecil and many others, Bacon was quite incapable of what he called 'the sabbathless pursuit of a man's fortune'. He needed his sabbaths too badly. And sabbaths are not like week-days; they favour a receptive frame of mind which is quite different from the active tensions of politics. They gave Bacon his chance to switch from an intensely active involvement with public affairs to 'the survey of the universe, the variety of nature unbounded, deep and noble thoughts concerning the infinite, the stars, the heroic virtues . . .', to a state in which the mind, 'washed clean of opinions', allows the hidden connections of things to rise to the surface. He called it '*wonder*, which is the seed of knowledge'.[79]

Wonder formed a perpetual undercurrent to Bacon's thoughts. We find it in his diaries, in his notes in the margins of old law-books, with the little word '*quaere*' beside them – 'enquire'. ('They have in Turkey a drink called *coffa*, as black as soot, and of a sharp scent, which comforteth the brain and heart . . . *quaere* of mandrake, of saffron . . .'; or, concerning 'beasts royal', lions, elephants, eagles, '*quaere de porpusses*.'[80]) His own books are full of allusions to subjects he planned to follow up, 'If God gives me leave'. And there are five single-space pages of a *Catalogue of Particular Histories*, covering some of the subjects he wished to investigate, drafted in the thick of his activities as Chancellor. Let us skim through one paragaph:

> History of Comets, of Fiery Meteors, Lightning, Thunderbolts, Thunders and Coruscations; of Winds and sudden Blasts and Undulations of the Air; History of Rainbows, of Clouds as they are seen above; History of the Blue Expanse, of Twilight, of Mock-Suns, Mocke-Moons, Haloes . . . of Hail, Snow, Frost, Hoar-frost, Fog, Dew and the like, and of all other things . . . generated in the Upper Region; History of Sounds in the Upper Region (if there be any); History of the Air as a whole, or in the Configuration of the World.

Similar paragraphs are devoted to the greater Motions and Perturbations in Earth and Sea, the History of the Greater Masses, including the History of Flame and of things ignited; the History of perfect Metals; of Quicksilver, Fossils, Gems and Stones; of Fishes and the Parts and Generation of them; of Worms; of Man – his conception, vivification, gestation, and every aspect of his existence; of Sleep and Dreams, of Life and Death, of Vision and Things Visible, of Manufactures and of every kind of Art; ending with a History of the Nature and Powers of Numbers.[81] 'I have such a large field for contemplation . . . to occupy my thoughts,' Bacon wrote to the King, at the height of his preoccupation with the royal budget, 'that nothing could make me active but love and affection.'[82]

Men thus absorbed, he believed, were 'the best servants of kings and commonwealth'. But they were 'not so clever in founding and promoting their own fortune'; they had no time to 'wait occasions, and devise and meditate on plots' to advance it.[83] This was Bacon's case. If, like everyone in public service, he had an eye to his career, he had the eye of a fly with a thousand facets turned on other matters; and he probably devoted to his own affairs a good deal less attention than did any other statesman of his day.

PART IV
THE COLD FISH

24

'With Not a Trace of Pity for Any Human Being'

In the eyes of Macaulay and of the critics who followed him, two grave flaws in Bacon's nature lay at the root of all the evil actions laid at his door. We have seen the first: he would stoop to anything to become 'the most powerful man in the kingdom'. His second fault was this – 'we write it with pain – coldness of heart and meanness of spirit'.[1] The claim against Bacon that he was a heartless man who 'loved and could love no one' survives all others in many people's minds today. 'When all the charges against Bacon have been examined,' Trevor-Roper concluded in 1962, 'one thing only remains: Bacon was not treacherous, not despotic, not corrupt, but he was a cold man.'[2] His contemporaries thought otherwise. They dwelt on his affable disposition, 'his love to relations tender, to friends faithful, to men universal, to his very enemies civil'.[3] Yet Trevelyan could declare in 1904 that love and friendship were 'little more than names to him'; Neale could exclaim in 1961, 'What coldness of heart!', when outlining his anxious briefing of Essex; and Menna Prestwich could conclude in 1966 that all his actions could be explained by 'the coldness that lay at his heart'. In 1985 an editor of his *Essays* was still depicting him as a misanthrope.[4] We have seen something of Bacon as servant and master, colleague and friend. In order to uncover, beneath the accumulation of unexamined opinions, a truer picture of his emotional and affective life, we must now look further into those relationships as they appeared to his own acquaintance, and see him also as a family man. But, first and foremost, he must be cleared of the worst accusation brought against him by Macaulay, that of extreme and cold-blooded cruelty, which, though in his own age this idea never crossed anyone's mind, was still being presented to students in the 1990s as an accepted fact.

Without doubt the greatest injustice done to Bacon by those to whom he bequeathed his name has been the constant reiteration that this 'tender-hearted' prosecutor, as his contemporaries knew him, was not only engaged in deliberately torturing his fellow beings, but was practically the sole convinced torturer of his age. 'He was', Macaulay asserted, 'one of the last of the tools of power' who persisted in this barbarous and illegal practice, a practice repented of by Burghley, forbidden by Elizabeth 'upon any pretence whatever', execrated by the public, and which soon afterwards 'no sycophant in all the Inns of Court' would have the face to defend. A few years later another biographer improved on this story – false on every count, as Spedding demonstrated a century and a half ago – with a description of Bacon as himself directing 'the stretching of the rack, and administering his questions' while 'diabolically delighting' in 'the agonizing shrieks of the fainting victim'.[5] The association of Bacon with such a role was bad enough at a time when torture was thought of as an obsolete institution, long abandoned, at least in Europe. It is worse in our century, which has seen the most refined forms of torture at close range, and continues to witness its routine practice by one nation in three throughout the world, even among countries with a tradition of civil rights. We must therefore look for the reality behind these statements, irresponsibly advanced in 1837, thoroughly refuted in 1848 and again in 1862, yet still offered to us with embellishments throughout the 1980s, and viciously retailed in 1992 and 1995.[6]

The use of torture in criminal investigations was universally condemned and disavowed in Queen Elizabeth's time, as a foreign practice, by the very men who, whether by choice or against their will, continued to apply it. Very much against his will, in the case of Sir Thomas Smith – enlightened philosopher, historian, astronomer and physician, and the most upright of statesmen. In 1566 Sir Thomas denounced this 'servile torment and punishment' as something 'the free nation of England would not abide'. But he applied it himself a few years later, under instructions from the Privy Council, to two servants of the Duke of Norfolk implicated in the Ridolfi plot – not, as he reported back to Burghley, in any hope of obtaining information that might justify such pain or fear, 'but because it is so earnestly commanded to us'. (He was later to try another suspect by the rack.)[7]

Edward Coke applied it less unwillingly. As Attorney General from 1594 on, he often authorized its use, personally conducted examinations under torture, and on occasion expressed his regret that it had not been resorted to. At Essex's trial, for example, he thought that the Queen's 'overmuch clemency' in ordaining that 'no man should be racked, tortured or pressed to speak' had damaged the Crown's cause. And in the proceedings against the gunpowder plotters, in 1606, he cited as an example of King James's admirable lenity and moderation that he would not 'exceed the usual punishment of law nor invent any new torture or torment'.[8] James's lenity may be appreciated in his directions for the interrogation of

Guy Fawkes: if he would not speak, 'the gentler tortures should first be used unto him' (suspending by the thumbs) and gradually extended to the most severe – 'And so God speed your good work!'[9] Although Fawkes was so crippled from his racking that he could not climb to the scaffold, Cecil still managed to complain, at the arraignment of a priest involved in the Plot, that 'we dare not proceed against them by such means as they do in other countries to get out the truth'.[10]

Coke had no such regard for appearances. He was not above publicly bullying prisoners with threats of torture – often as effective as the rack itself – and at the trial of Father Robert Southwell, poet and martyr, in 1595, he lashed out against this priest and all his kind. To explain why his memory was bad, Southwell had pointed out that he had been severely tortured ten times, to which Chief Justice Popham replied that 'such things are done among all nations'; and when the notorious Richard Topcliffe, his torturer, attempted a confused defence, Coke interrupted him. 'Mr Topcliffe has no need to go about to excuse the manner of his torturings,' he cried. 'For think you that you will not be tortured? Yea, we will tear the hearts out of an hundred of your bodies!'[11] Some of those present were shocked, but it is clear that neither Popham nor Coke had any qualms about the Government's use of torture. Coke's first known theoretical statement about it was a remark he made in 1612, that 'the bodies of the nobility are not subject to torture'; but he is not known ever to have protested against its use on the bodies of commoners, and in 1620 he was still acting as commissioner for a racking. It was not until eight years later (two years after Bacon's death) that, in his new role as champion of the people's liberties, he categorically laid down in his famous *Institutes* that all torture of an accused person was contrary to the law of the land.[12] What had he been doing then for the past thirty-four years? Nevertheless, it is in Coke's name and with this often cited declaration in mind that Macaulay, and many others after him, have inveighed against Bacon as a 'renewer' of this allegedly obsolete practice. 'Bacon far behind Sir Edward Coke!' cried Macaulay, 'Bacon clinging to exploded abuses', when the enlightened Coke had declared all torture illegal![13]

As Macaulay knew from David Jardine's book, *A Reading on the Use of Torture in the Criminal Law of England Previously to the Commonwealth*, published shortly before the first appearance of his 'Essay on Bacon' – and cited by him soon afterwards, without comment, in a new edition – extrajudicial torture had been practised in England for at least four centuries before Bacon came on the scene. It had been regularly recorded for some fifty years, and it was still in use fourteen years after Bacon's death. Duly supervised to ensure that the rules were followed, torture was resorted to wherever the realm was threatened with imminent danger. In principle at least, it was not used for punishment, or to obtain further evidence against a suspect, but for cases of high treason when there was 'half-proof' or 'a vehement suspicion of guilt', in order to discover the wider ramifications of a conspiracy.[14] Late twentieth-century works by other experts on the subject, including an article published by Clifford Hall in the *Anglo-American Law Review* (1989), have merely confirmed and amplified what Jardine, and Macaulay after him, had learnt.[15] First known to have been used under Henry II, in 1188, torture was practised against the Templars under Edward II; it was the norm under Richard III, and commonplace under Henry VIII, Thomas Cromwell being a ready advocate.[16] As shown by recent research in the Council Register – where torture warrants were recorded from 1540 – whatever the disclaimers of face-saving or wishful-thinking men, fifty-three cases of extrajudicial torture were recorded in the time of Queen Elizabeth. Under James the record is incomplete, but in any case, since the pressure of foreign invasion was off, there were not so many. Charles resorted to it on various occasions, but though still theoretically in use under George III, it was only rarely practised after 1640.[17]

Although not expressly enjoined by the common law (as was the burning of apostate clerics, for example), executive torture was condoned as an acceptable part of the administration of justice when authorized, in exceptional cases, under the King's 'absolute prerogative'. This was distinct from the 'ordinary prerogative', which was subject to parliamentary approval. In Coke's view, as in Bacon's, the King was empowered to use his absolute prerogative – which they both looked on as an inseparable part of the common law – at discretion for the public good.[18] Torture was thus authorized, not as 'the casual, capricious, or unjust act of particular kings', but, at least from the fifteenth century on, as a uniform practice, directly commanded by the monarch, or by the Privy Council speaking 'with his mouth'. And it was administered by high-ranking common law judges, under warrants shown to the prisoner and recorded, throughout the late Tudor and early Stuart reigns, in Council proceedings, most of which are still extant.[19] Elizabeth issued no general prohibition. True, in 1583 Burghley published a defence of the Government's action towards the Jesuits, claiming that only the guilty were (mildly) racked. But the Queen went on authorizing 'the ordinary torture', which in her reign meant the manacles, or suspension by the arms, more cruelly effective than the rack had been, though its effects were less visible. And throughout the 1590s she had Richard Topcliffe, an expert and addicted torturer, at her disposal.[20]

Conspirators abounded against the life of Elizabeth, and the many torture warrants issued during her reign must be seen in the light of the continual threat of assassination under which she and her ministers lived – particularly after the Pope had declared in 1580 that 'whosoever sends her out of the world' would be doing God a service by 'so glorious a work'.[21] In those years England was a small nation engaged in a struggle for its life against heavy odds. Had any of the successive plots to murder Elizabeth and place her cousin Mary on the throne succeeded, all efforts at resistance would soon have been annihilated by the redoubtable Spanish army, standing ready in the Netherlands on each occasion. The Prince of Orange had been assassinated in 1583, and no one was in any doubt that the death of Elizabeth would mean civil war for England, and very probably the end of the Reformation. Throughout the next two decades, while the Catholic powers planned their military invasions and financed and smuggled in a continual flow of Jesuit priests, prepared for martyrdom and sworn to subvert her regime, the whole effort of the Government was to keep the Queen alive. And no one was more conscious than the young Bacon – as shown in the various letters of advice and papers in defence of the Government's actions which, encouraged by Elizabeth, he drafted during the 1580s – of the danger of those 'wicked and barbarous' attempts against her life. But he was also aware of the need to find ways of 'weakening the discontentment' of loyal Catholics, so as not to drive them to desperation, and to ensure that none be executed, as he said, 'but the very traitors'.[22]

In the mid-1590s, while he continued to think about 'means to stop and divert' these attempts at violence, Bacon was called on to serve in another capacity.[23] With Walsingham dead and his intelligence network dissolved, with Burghley worn out, and with the impatient and intemperate Coke, who had little talent for discovering the truth, in charge of criminal prosecution, Bacon's exceptional ability as investigator came to the fore, and the Queen, though still offended with him for his insubordination in the last Parliament, began to employ him on state interrogations in the Tower. This was not a task that Bacon, conscious as he was of his country's 'special claim upon him', would wish to evade.[24] So between 1594 and 1598 we will find him on a number of occasions, as unofficial Counsel Learned for the Crown, holding private interrogatories of suspects, all connected with some well-attested or freely confessed attempt to assassinate the Queen – most of them carried on without intimidation, this being, in Bacon's view, the best way of elucidating the truth.[25]

During this period his name appears on four warrants for interrogation with torture, should a prisoner refuse to answer. He was summoned in a subordinate capacity, with the Attorney General (Coke) in charge in the two first, and the Solicitor General (Flemming) in the others.[26] We do not know whether torture was actually resorted to in three of these cases, which were all related to conspiracies against the Queen, or whether, if so, Bacon was actually present. He was present in the last of them, with both Coke and Flemming, and with William Wade, then Secretary of the Privy Council, when on 14 April 1597 Father John Gerard was put to the manacles. After three years in prison, Gerard had been caught forwarding papers from abroad to Father Henry Garnet, the English Superior, who had been leading the Jesuits' campaign so successfully from his secret hiding places that he was, not unnaturally, feared as a dangerous enemy of the state. Whether or no Gerard – the reputed author of a *Treatise on Equivocation* – was equivocating when he denied having anything to do with political matters at this time, both he and Garnet were to be compromised in the Gunpowder Plot.[27]

Did Bacon think Gerard guilty? He is always found urging lenity towards those who were 'Papists in conscience, not in faction', but the priests he knew of from earlier confessions had all been involved in faction. Of the part he played in Gerard's examination we know only that, with the other commissioners, he left the torture chamber almost at once, and did not return. Wade carried on the questioning alone, and at the two examinations that followed, Bacon was not present.[28] It is difficult to imagine the man who looked on all offenders 'with the eye of pity and compassion'; who commiserated with weak and hunted creatures – 'the poor deer', 'poor harmless lambs', 'poor maimed soldier', 'the poor Indians', 'racked' by their Spanish conquerors – witnessing the suffering of a fellow human with indifference.[29] But though not bound, as Sir Thomas Smith had been, to supervise the racking, Bacon was caught in the same dilemma as that unhappy servant of the Crown had been – a dilemma which sprang from that of Elizabeth herself, forced as she was by the aggression of the new Catholics to take ever harsher measures against them, when she would greatly have preferred to let them keep their beliefs in peace.

Very different from the Jesuit missionary – forbearing towards his enemies, full of love for his friends, and ready at any moment to die for his cause – was that other offender whose examination under torture Bacon was instructed to attend, as Attorney General, on 18 January 1615, eighteen years later. Edmund Peacham, a Puritan clergyman in his sixties, filled with resentment against the Government 'for taxes and oppressions', had composed, although not delivered, a number of sermons riddled with virulent invective and scandalous defamation. They included threats of popular risings to wreak vengeance on the royal family, and incitements to rebellion, the assassination of King and Prince, and the massacre of all the King's officers.[30] Peacham belonged to the Puritan band whose violence Bacon had denounced in his writings as a young man, and who were now clamouring more and more loudly for the death of noblemen and kings, consigning to hell those who did not share their beliefs. In writing his sermons, Peacham was of course following his own religious leaders, as the Jesuit plotters followed the Pope. Luther had enjoined 'whoso can strike, smite, strangle or stab, secretly or publicly' to do so, since – 'such wonderful times are these' – he

would 'better merit Heaven than another might by prayer'.[31] And Thomas
Cartwright, the leading English Puritan, who demanded the death penalty for blasphemy and for adultery, had announced that backsliders –
those, that is, whom Father Gerard looked on as saved – should be
punished by death without pardon, even if they repented; 'if this be
bloody and extreme', he added, he was 'content to be so counted with the
Holy Ghost'.[32]

Peacham's examination, the subject of Macaulay's strictures, is known
to us principally because of a dispute between Coke and the King as to the
method employed by James to consult his judges before a trial. (Macaulay
was uninformed about this time-honoured practice, which Coke, only
too willing to give his opinion on such occasions, would have been the
last to condemn. Thus he confidently, but quite mistakenly, declared
Bacon 'guilty of attempting to introduce into the courts-of-law an odious
abuse' – royal consultation – 'for which no precedent could be found'.)[33]
The Puritan Minister's first seditious sermon, written in his own hand,
with text and prayer copied out ready for preaching, was discovered in his
house in Somerset when he was brought before the High Commission to
answer for a libel against the Bishop of Bath and Wells. In this long
premeditated paper, Peacham, wrote the outraged James, heaped up 'all
the injuries that the hearts of men could invent' to disable him, leaving
him neither king nor Christian nor man, and 'not worthy of breath here
or salvation hereafter'.[34] Demanding that the King and his son 'be
stricken with death' and 'all the King's officers be put to the sword',
Peacham showed an acquaintance with Government proceedings that
suggested powerful backers.

In the troubled times that followed the breakdown of the 1614 Parliament, the preaching of such a sermon could well have been the signal of
rebellion for the leading landowners of that unruly county. Under Tudor
and Stuart law, incitement to conspiracy was high treason, although
there was a margin of doubt here (was the incitement against the King's
title, or only against his person?). However, the judges concurred in
opining that the case was good in law. Coke alone stood in opposition,
against all his former opinions – and practice – and probably actuated, as
Gardiner suggests, 'as much by temper as by reason'.[35] Peacham was
transferred to the Tower to be examined, in accordance with the instructions of Sir Ralph Winwood, Principal Secretary of State, about his
intentions, his possible accomplices, his reasons for threatening the King
and all those about him. When, being questioned by the Archbishop of
Canterbury, he refused to answer these points, a warrant for his torture
was issued by the Privy Council to the two examiners in charge,
Winwood himself (who was hostile to Bacon) and Sir Julius Caesar,
Master of the Rolls. As Privy Councillors these officers had precedence
over the Attorney General, so that Bacon, although required to attend,

did not act as 'principal examiner', responsible for the execution of torture. Peacham was put to the manacles on 19 January 1615, to no effect. Winwood drew up the official record, and Bacon wrote privately to the King that he wished they had not been driven to make their way 'through questions'.[36] Had Bacon been in charge there might have been no racking, for on learning of this measure he had expressed himself firmly against it. As he later reminded James, 'when others had hope of discovery and thought time well spent that way' (meaning Winwood, presumably, with whose harsh and narrow-minded attitudes Bacon often disagreed), he had warned the King that the accused would merely 'turn himself into divers shapes to save or delay his punishment'.[37]

And so it proved. Bacon then decided to examine the prisoner himself – without torture, needless to say, since his aim was not to extract confessions but to clarify contradictory statements and eliminate any that could be disavowed as extorted in fear of the manacles. Peacham had maintained on one occasion that he had never meant to deliver the sermon, on another that 'he would have taken the bitterness out' before preaching it (which would have been difficult, said one witness, for it was all made up of bitterness). He now retracted even what he had freely confessed at his first interrogation by the Archbishop, as spoken 'wholly out of fear and to avoid torture'. Disowning his own handwriting, he denied writing the sermon, and tried to inculpate his patron and other eminent personages entirely ignorant and innocent of the accusations. Until Bacon, disgusted, exclaimed that he would not detain anyone 'upon this man's impeaching, in whom there is no truth'.[38] Peacham was tried in Somersetshire six months later, by Tanfield and Montagu, judges known for their humanity – his offence, Chamberlain reported, being 'so foul and scandalous that he was condemned for high treason', although not executed, nor likely to be if he 'show some remorse'. He died the following year, as we hear again from Chamberlain, 'in jail at Taunton, where they say he left behind him a most wicked and desperate writing, worse than that he was convicted for'.[39]

Bacon's role as the torturer of Peacham, therefore, amounts to this: he did not (and could not) refuse to appear, as directed and warranted by the Privy Council, at an examination with torture which he was not in charge of, had neither advised nor approved and could in no way have prevented, and which he wished it had been possible to avoid.[40] As to his personal reaction, rather than delighting in the shrieks of the fainting victim, he may have been near fainting himself, being prone to fainting fits.[41] 'Many upon the seeing of others bleed, or strangled, or tortured,' he noted, 'themselves are ready to faint'; and also, 'to delight in blood, one must be either a wild beast or a fury.'[42] On the other hand we cannot expect Bacon to preach the complete abolition of torture, which our own age has not achieved, or be surprised to find him, on one occasion – along with Coke and the rest of the Council – signing a similar warrant to that applied to Peacham.[43] Bacon, we should recall, was not only a humanitarian thinker, but a practising statesman, and he served a Government which lacked a police force to collect trustworthy evidence about the plots that constantly threatened its existence. (Though in some respects it may have faced its unpleasant realities more honestly than we do. What prisoner today can insist on seeing 'the warrant for his racking'?)[44]

A glance at those who signed the warrant for Peacham's racking may help to place Bacon in perspective. Among these high officials, which include the Archbishop of Canterbury, the Treasurer (Suffolk), the Lord Steward and the Lord Privy Seal, and of course the Secretary, we find the Chancellor of the Exchequer, Sir Fulke Greville, the friend of Sir Philip Sidney and the very prototype of the gentle courtier, and Sir Julius Caesar, Bacon's nephew by marriage, who also took part in the interrogation. Caesar was famous for his 'prodigious bounty to all of worth or want', and was said to have been 'kept alive beyond Nature's course by the prayers of those many poor whom he daily relieved'.[45] We may also remember that torture for state purposes was taken for granted by Shakespeare's gentlest dukes, when restoring order at the end of a play – whether for discovery (in England) or for punishment (abroad).[46]

These were rough times, when not only Ralegh, but kindly men like Sir Henry Sidney carried out the most brutal massacres in Ireland; and at home everyone, women and children included, lived under the threat of public whipping, branding or the loss of an ear or a hand for the most trivial offences. Vagabonds were regularly flogged, women were burned to death for treason, or for the murder of a husband, and thieves were hanged alive in chains and left to starve. Far worse than the manacles used to uncover a conspiracy was the 'penance', the *peine forte et dure*, applied under common law to any felon who refused to answer or plead, and under which prisoners had hard stones laid on their prostrate bodies and were gradually crushed to death over a period of days. The 'penance', occasionally imposed as a torture device to discover evidence (as it was by Coke in 1615 on the Under-Keeper of the Tower, when, on trial for the murder of Overbury, he refused to plead), was still in use for another two centuries; and if torture was no longer used for criminal investigations after 1640, the number of witches executed in England under the Commonwealth for actions confessed under torture was greater than in any other period.[47]

Strangely insensitive to these sufferings, the public was more often found expressing horror at the crime than at the barbarous methods used to fight it, methods the mild Chamberlain frequently described as though they were the most natural thing in the world.[48] Times have changed since the Catholic Earl of Arundel would take his five-year old son to see a priest hung, drawn and quartered.[49] 'I did see Mr Christopher Love beheaded on Tower Hill,' wrote Aubrey a generation later, 'in a delicate, clear day'; and maybe he understood what drew men to these spectacles, for he made one of the characters in a play he wrote cry, 'Ah, 'tis the best lechery to see poor wretches whipped at the Court at Bridewell!'[50] Perhaps Aubrey has also given us a clue to the nature of the persistent interest in this theme – an interest which has induced the editors of Bacon for schools to linger over the horrific image of a philosopher causing 'an inoffensive elderly gentleman to be tortured', and, as late as 1984, prompting one of the outstanding judges of our time to describe him, with a wealth of imaginary detail, as the eager and officious organizer of Peacham's torturing.[51] Such is the hold of this notion on people's minds that the temptation to invent new incidents to illustrate it appears irresistible. Thus in a glossy programme offered by the Royal Shakespeare Company for its production of *Richard II* at the Barbican in 1987, the public learned that the contemporary author of another work on Richard 'was imprisoned and tortured on the orders of Francis Bacon, in an attempt to force a confession of treasonable intent'.[52] The man in question is Dr Hayward, who was not tortured, and this quite possibly because of Bacon's quick-witted intervention (described above) on his behalf. Thus are legends born. Bacon? Torture? To the writer of the Shakespeare programme the mere mention of these words, as she read the anecdote, would evoke a vicious link, forged in her mind while she was still at school, and strong enough for her to reverse the facts as she picked them up. As a mere unofficial Counsel Learned in 1599, Bacon could never have given orders for a man's racking – had Hayward been racked. But no matter, the writer had already jumped to her preformed conclusion.

More damaging, because more widespread, is the same false image presented in Peter Levi's attractive and poetic biography of Shakespeare in 1988, where Bacon's only significant appearance, on page 4, comes after a description of the use of the rack in England. In the 1580s, Levi writes, 'Topcliffe and Bacon were determined to succeed in that world, and they did so.'[53] (This way of condemning Bacon by twinning him with a vicious historical character will be met with again.)[54] Levi's source is an unsupported remark by the Jesuit writer Christopher Devlin, in 1963, that the associates of Topcliffe as 'torturer and prober of minds' were Richard Young 'and, a mere stripling, Francis Bacon', who, Devlin added, must have found this 'a most irksome path to preferment'.[55] In the 1580s Bacon was serving the Government principally with his pen, as a defender of Elizabeth's religious policies, although from 1586 onwards his legal talents were also found useful to analyse the depositions of Catholic plotters, and he is known to have interviewed one conspirator – without torture.[56] As for his taking 'so irksome a path', in those years the young Bacon's mind revolved more often on 'things reserved', as he described them, 'which Kings with all their treasure cannot buy', and of which 'their spials and intelligencers can give no news'.[57] And, curiously enough, the only letter from Bacon to Secretary Walsingham that has survived involves a very different kind of preferment. He is appealing for help, not to Elizabeth's grand spy-master, but to 'the great Maecenas of this age', as the Secretary was also known, 'the highest patron of good letters, virtue, learning and chivalry', in connection with that project in which he had been trying to interest the Queen ever since his return from France, and which would have involved him in studies 'of more delight' than the law.[58]

Topcliffe was a pathological sadist. His 'bloody and butcherly mind', in the words of Father Garnet, was the extreme antipodes of Bacon's, and Bacon would certainly have given him as wide a berth as he could. In fact the only time we find his name linked to that of Topcliffe is in a note to his brother, enclosing a copy of Father Robert Southwell's *Supplication* – an appeal to Queen Elizabeth for toleration towards loyal Catholics – which Bacon had obtained from the rabid priest-hunter in May 1592, a month before Southwell was betrayed into his torturer's hands. 'A most traitorous written book', Topcliffe called it. Bacon, as he told his brother, already interested in Robert Southwell's poetry, thought it 'curiously written' (a fine piece of writing), though on the wrong side, and, as the poet's biographer noted, Bacon's tribute is the earliest known reference to this remarkable work.[59]

An incompetent examiner, Topcliffe relied on blackmail, bullying and torture to gain his ends: the persecution of all Catholics, wherever possible, to the advantage of Topcliffe. Before he was finally denounced and disgraced in 1598, he spent his time trapping victims with infamous procedures (not excluding personal rape) in order to take possession of their lands, humiliating prisoners and terrifying them at length with grisly threats, and boasting publicly of his worst successes (in particular, of a machine he had invented for private torturing in his own house, compared with which, he said, common racks were child's play).[60] This is the brute whose name has been carelessly coupled with that of a thinker so concerned with the precarious human condition that all his philosophical works were geared to the relief of misery and the welfare and happiness of humankind. This unnatural coupling is a classical example of how the truth about Bacon has been bedevilled by his denigrators. Far from contemplating man's physical suffering with equanimity (let alone with sadistic gloating), Bacon proposed a search into ways of mitigating pain. He urged doctors 'to acquire the skill and bestow the attention whereby the dying may pass more easily out of life'.[61] And it is surely under the impact of the suffering he had witnessed in the Tower that he included in this search a proposal for ways of increasing 'man's ability to suffer torture', just as his perseverant efforts through two Parliaments on behalf of the ill-treated yeomen were inspired by the misery he had seen with his own eyes, when interrogating a band of starving rebels.[62]

25

The Lukewarm Hater

Bacon, a historian observed in 1971, as others had before him, 'inspired remarkably little affection'.[1] Yet Amboise, in 1631, had described him as 'loved by the people and cherished by the great', and Aubrey evoked him surrounded with 'great friends', 'admiring', 'loving and beloved'.[2] They were right. Improbable as this may seem to the readers of modern biographies, Bacon was an affectionate friend, and, like many Elizabethans, more emotional than people admit to being today. We recall his passionate speeches in Parliament on matters he felt strongly about, and the tears of tenderness which stood in the eyes of the official who welcomed the lost sailors to New Atlantis – as they are said to have filled the eyes of Heraclitus, a philosopher Bacon liked to quote, in his compassion for mankind.[3]

In 1933 Bacon was perceptively described by James's historian David Mathew as 'a somewhat solitary figure in the Jacobean scene', not having the gift for commonplace 'so essential for the reassurance of his equals' – in particular of King James himself, in his heart of hearts a little afraid of his brilliant Chancellor.[4] Bacon knew this. He had early on confessed to being one of those people who are 'by nature bashful' and, lacking 'the plausible familiarity which others have, are often mistaken for proud'.[5] There could of course be little intimacy between one whose mind was so often on 'things reserved', and James, at ease only with handsome courtiers such as Montgomery, with whom he could share his predominant interest in horses and dogs. Yet James liked his old servant well enough, and Bacon recalled that once, when both men were seriously ill ('which was no time to dissemble'), 'I never had so great pledges and certainties of his love and favour.'[6] We know that he enjoyed the disinterested friendship and favour, as well as the admiration, of James's daughter, that 'good sweet, devout princess', whose beauty as a girl had touched him and whose fall he grieved for, as she did for his. He urged Buckingham to do all he could for 'that excellent Lady, whose fortune is so distant from her merit and virtue', and he was still writing to cheer her with good hopes a few months before his death.[7]

Bacon had never been shy with Queen Elizabeth, who treated him with the same familiarity, alternating with irate rebuke, as she did others of her inner circle. The link was established in boyhood, when she had called him her 'young Lord Keeper', and, said Rawley, 'delighted to confer with him and prove him with questions'. This may explain the element of personal pique in her resentment of Bacon's independent stance at the 1593 Parliament, as well as his own overconfidence in taking it for granted that she would understand his motives. Though, as he recalled, she never gave him 'ordinary place', he was proud of the 'extraordinary access' she allowed him and of her 'other demonstrations of confidence and grace' towards him.[8] 'I do yet bear an extreme zeal to the memory of my old mistress Elizabeth,' he wrote after her death (to James, never too pleased with praise of his predecessor), 'to whom I was rather bound for her trust than for her favour'; and other references to his 'good old mistress' bear him out. In 1616 he was still recalling, in his 'Advice to Villiers', her 'in whose time I had the happiness to be born and to live many years'. He confessed that on her subject he could not pass for a disinterested man. This was five years after her death, when, with her memory 'strong and fresh' in his mind, he had written of her in glowing terms in a brilliant *Memorial* – the last of his various defences of Elizabeth – bearing witness to 'her felicity and the marks of God's favour towards her'. It is of all his works the one he was keenest to publish. He sent it at once to the great French historian, Jacques Auguste de Thou, hoping he would 'do right to the truth and to the memory of that Lady' (which de Thou did, including it in his widely acclaimed history of the times). And he left particular instructions for it to appear after his death in England, 'as her tomb'.[9]

Among the important personages at Court, we have seen Bacon attach himself only to those with whom he had a natural sympathy – Essex and Buckingham, principally, while they were still in training for statehood. As pupils they both disappointed their mentor, and Buckingham failed him also as a friend. But we should see Bacon with a better patron, Sir Thomas Egerton (later Lord Ellesmere), who stood towards him as his constant friend and protector. Egerton was one of Elizabeth's most trusted advisers and, according to the historians of his day, the best, if not the most expeditious, of Chancellors. 'I do find in an extraordinary manner', Bacon wrote to Essex when Egerton was made Lord Keeper in 1596, that he 'doth succeed my father in his fatherly care of me and love towards me'.[10] Egerton appreciated Bacon's worth. Two years earlier, while Master of the Rolls, he had drawn up for him special instructions on the duties of a Solicitor General, confident that the post would fall to his protégé. When it did not, Bacon, grateful as ever, wrote thanking him for his 'singular favour so far to comfort and encourage me'. The two men worked in close and friendly collaboration for the next twenty years, and Egerton named Bacon as the fittest man to succeed him. During the old Chancellor's last years of illness Bacon was often at his bedside, from where he wrote progress reports to King James. ('It pleased my Lord Chancellor out of his ancient and great love to me, which many times in sickness appeareth most, to admit me to a great deal of speech with him this afternoon'; or 'He used me with wonderful tokens of kindness. We both wept, which I do not often.')[11]

Bacon's friends at Court – those who were to rally round him in his disgrace, ready to spend long hours in anterooms to serve him – were noted for their integrity. They included the witty Edward Sackville, Earl of Dorset, who had treated Bacon with so much forbearance in Parliament; William, Earl of Pembroke, 'the most universally loved and esteemed of any man in any age', according to Clarendon, devoted to his country, religion and justice, and 'whose friendships were with men of those principles'; Henry Carey, Viscount Falkland, lauded by Ben Jonson for his brave deeds, and whose son was to be a leading light in the Baconian 'Great Tew Circle'; and Fulke Greville, the trusted confidant of Bacon's young days.[12] Another such friend was his respected colleague John Digby, Earl of Bristol, for some time English Ambassador in Madrid, to whom he wrote, when Bristol was undeservedly out of favour, that he had ever estimated him, 'not according to your fortunes, but according to your inward value'.[13] And, of course, there was his constant antagonist, Gondomar, the Spanish Ambassador, who, as we know, came to his rescue in time of need, earning Bacon's admiring gratitude. The two of them enjoyed their official correspondence, sharing jokes, over many years, and we find Bacon happy to bridge his absence with a letter, transmitting some good news 'with more pleasure because of my affection for you', or worried about Gondomar's health, 'endangered with heavy cares'.[14]

Bacon showed the same kindly interest, gratitude and willingness to do service in much of his official correspondence. We find him writing eagerly to a 'very good friend' to assist one person or to request help on behalf of another, responding cordially to someone's advances, sending warm remembrances to mutual acquaintances, and repeatedly declaring himself 'beholden' to one or another for expressions of love or for services rendered. One letter may serve as a sample of Bacon's gratitude. In autumn 1593, when he was lying ill at Twickenham, Lady Paulet who had been kind to him when he served under her husband, Sir Amyas, English Ambassador in Paris, sixteen years earlier – now a widow outside the current of affairs, had evidently written recommending a nephew to him.

Bacon answers by return of post, regretting that he cannot visit her at present; he has never forgotten her 'ancient and especial kindness' towards him, and will certainly do all he can for the nephew, and anything else she may require. He hopes she will accept what he can offer – so much less than she deserves – 'in respect of the unfeigned goodwill from whence it proceedeth', and concludes, after beseeching God 'to bless you with increase of comfort in mind and body, and admit you to his holy protection', with 'your ladyship's assured and ready in all kind affection to do you service'. Many years later he was to save her grandson, John Paulet, from ruin when he was falsely accused by Peacham.[15]

Bacon's feelings were 'kind', Macaulay conceded, 'though not warm'. But, strange to say, even Bacon's known 'civility to enemies' offended his great detractor. 'The temperature of his revenge,' wrote Macaulay, 'like that of his gratitude, was scarcely ever more than lukewarm.'[16] Lord Campbell, echoing him soon afterwards, declared that Bacon 'had not even the merit of being a good hater', and reproached him with feeling no satisfaction at the trial of Essex's old enemy, Ralegh.[17] Bacon was not a lukewarm hater. He was not a hater at all. True, he could flare up if abused, as he did when Coke, standing on his greatness as Attorney General, tried to silence the still unofficial Legal Counsel, in the Court of the Exchequer, apostrophizing him as a nobody. 'The less you think of your own greatness,' Bacon replied, 'the more I will think of it.'[18] No doubt he was nettled, on this and on other occasions, by his overbearing and self-assertive senior, who (as old lawyers of their generation told Aubrey) was always 'envying him and undervaluing his law' – and explaining his jokes; and he was often frustrated by Cecil, whose ostensible cousinly support was underlaid with quite uncousinly counteraction.[19] But we shall never find him pursuing, or even remembering a quarrel. Thorns will prick, he said 'because many can do no other'.[20] But he had to work with these men. He thought their policies disastrous, yet while he criticized them he was also liberal with his approval. We have seen him bestowing praise on Cranfield whenever he could. For the rest, he forgot them. His was the mind he described as 'planted above injuries'. Which is no doubt why he was so vulnerable to the vengeful actions of both Cranfield and Coke.

Bacon was known in his time as 'no heaver of men out of their places'. Yet it is the fashion among present-day historians to show him not merely gloating over Coke's downfall, but deliberately plotting it, and in his eagerness to get his own back on Cecil, viciously slandering his cousin when he was barely in his tomb.[21] Carteret, in the eighteenth century, seeing Bacon's dealings with 'near relation' and with 'old antagonist' in a different light, concluded that he had behaved towards both his rivals in a manner 'that became him'. If, he wrote, these two 'great men' were always crossing him and affecting to slight his professional knowledge, it was because they 'envied his general reputation and feared his abilities as a statesman'. Bacon had 'perceived very early how little service the one, and how much disservice the other' meant him. And no one saw clearer than he did into matters of this nature, Carteret added, perhaps recalling the essay in which Bacon declared that revenge was the worst temptation man is subject to. It was indeed, Bacon believed, 'a weakness and impotency of mind to be unable to forgive'; and he reserved his highest praise for one who, when evil overtook his enemy, was grieved and distressed, and, looking into 'the recesses of his heart', could 'feel no touch of joy'.[22]

Bacon was never quite at ease with his secretive cousin, whom many people looked on as 'readier for revenge than for affection'.[23] But he admired Cecil's qualities, supported him loyally in Parliament, was prompt to serve him, and acknowledged his help, when forthcoming, with gratitude.[24] In order to show him coldly flattering his cousin for his own purposes, Abbott selected a few complimentary passages from his letters to Cecil over ten years, and placed them alongside the judgements he expressed to James after Cecil's death – a comparison under which few of us would look our best.[25] 'No one ought to be judged by such testimonies,' as one of Jane Austen's characters remarked, since 'no private correspondence could bear the eye of others.'[26] But Bacon did not do so badly. In a letter of congratulations for New Year's Day 1608, for example, when the cousins were collaborating satisfactorily, he told Cecil he esteemed the world but trash beside 'the honour and happiness to be near and well-accepted kinsman to so rare and worthy a counsellor, governor and patriot'. Barring the emotional tone, typical of a less inhibited age than ours, Bacon expressed the same view to James in 1612, when applying for Cecil's post: 'Your Majesty hath lost a great subject and a great servant.'[27] And when he went on to say that despite 'fine passages', Cecil's results came 'slowly on', or when he wrote later – how rightly – that Cecil 'had a good method, if his ends had been upright', Bacon was telling James no more than he had once tactfully hinted to Cecil himself. (In 1602, that is, when by way of encouragement he had urged Cecil to undertake action on Irish affairs that would show him 'as good a patriot' as he was thought a politician, and 'make the world perceive' his – so far invisible – 'generous ends'.)[28]

Bacon's other famous remark to the King, that Cecil 'was no fit counsellor to make your affairs grow better, but yet he was fit to have kept them from growing worse', has been looked on as an unkind sally. But Rawley had seen it as proof that Bacon was 'no defamer of a man to his prince', and was, besides, a true Christian, since this was 'the worst he would say of Cecil'.[29] Whether or not Bacon was right is still an open question. Menna Prestwich, like James, thought he erred on the side of charity.[30]

If, as Chamberlain believed, Bacon in his famous essay 'Of Deformity' was recalling his cousin 'to the life', he will have recognized in Cecil the 'perpetual spur' to industry, harboured, as he had observed, by many a deformed man.[31] It was an industry which we know Cecil spent on clandestine exploitation and ruthless duplicity in the amassing of his huge fortune; though also, when the pressure was off and remorse had set in, on a sincere effort to eliminate that very Court of Wards he had so greatly abused. Bacon had been tied for years – 'as a hawk to another's fist' – to his cousin's policy of bargaining with Parliament, which he was convinced had done James 'inestimable prejudice'. On Cecil's death he was at last free to propose economic measures that would enable the King to appear before a new Parliament 'upon terms of majesty, not of necessity'. If he now denounced Cecil's mistakes, it was to show James the vital importance of not making them again.[32] Bacon was not vindictive, as Toby Matthew remarked; if he spoke a word against anyone, 'and that seldom', it was 'to emit an impartial judgement'.[33] In no sense can his judgement of his cousin, however severe, be compared with the systematic denigration of Cecil on his death by nearly all their contemporaries, in particular with the jibes and sneers of Henry Howard, who had been Cecil's closest friend and collaborator.[34] James, who thought much less kindly of his departed minister than Bacon did, believed he had spoken as a 'true man' (a loyal servant of the state) when he criticized Cecil, and as a kinsman when he praised him, but in fact he spoke as a true man also when approving him. 'Give frame . . . to matters before you place the persons,' Bacon now advised the King, and he was himself wholly absorbed in 'the great matter on hand', a new Parliament, when he turned his cool eye on Cecil.[35] This very objectivity has contributed to Bacon's reputation for coldness, since few people place the *res publica* above private considerations. But objectivity is compatible with a warm heart, and we are not entitled to conclude, as Notestein did, that he took little interest in others except as 'useful pawns'.[36] It was of Cecil, not Bacon, that Ben Jonson said 'he never cared for any man longer than he could make use of him'.[37]

Towards his other rival, Edward Coke, Bacon was remarkably forbearing. The two great lawyers of their century were not only at loggerheads on matters of policy – in the case of Bacon a far more consistent one than in that of Coke, whose political views changed with his employment – they were temperamentally incompatible. Coke saw the *Novum Organum* as a foolish book, and he felt towards Bacon the age-old suspicion of the specialist before a man with a quicker mind, wider interests and broader views than his own.[38] Bacon on the other hand must have drawn on his reserves of patience when working with one whom Audrey described as 'so fulsomely pedantic that a school-boy would nauseate it'.[39] Like most people, from the King down, he found the 'perpetual turbulent carriage' of his 'streperous' colleague exhausting, and he thought Coke's over-weening self-confidence subjected things 'to a great deal of chance'.[40]

But did his opposition to the colleague involve ill-feeling, lukewarm or otherwise, towards the man? Their contemporaries did not see envy in Bacon; they remembered it in Coke. It was not until 1976 that Bacon was to be described as 'throbbing with resentment' when he argued his first case and scored a point against the older and more experienced lawyer (newly appointed to the post he had himself applied for), while in 1992 he was again presented as filled with 'personal hatred' for Coke.[41] In reality Bacon's rivalry was of a quite unblushing sort. He was showing off on that occasion, and was to do so again. And he was delighted to deserve Coke's rare approval. ('It pleased my Lord Coke', he wrote to the King after arguing a case for two and a half hours, 'to say it was a famous argument.')[42] Nor was everyone as tolerant of Coke as Bacon was. One of Coke's own political sympathizers denounced him to his face as a vainglorious, bitter, money-grabbing man, in love with his own argu-ments – while unable to listen to those of others – and inclined 'to make the law lean to his own opinion'.[43] Yet, although he could not have disagreed with these statements, Bacon spoke well of his rival to the King whenever he could (as, in 1615, 'I must say, my Lord Coke hath done his part,' or in 1619, 'Sir Edward Coke did his part, I have not heard him do better'). Over the murder of Overbury, he stressed the 'indefatigable pains' Coke had taken, and praised him highly for his 'communion of service' with Chancellor Ellesmere – a communion which Coke did not often indulge in. And it was when disgrace hung over Coke's head that Bacon chose to remind James of his unruly servant's worth, by praising his law.[44]

There is no historical evidence to support the allegation that the removal of Coke from the King's Bench was in any way Bacon's doing; all the evidence points the other way. It is true that he influenced Coke's destiny when, on his advice, the latter was kicked upstairs from the Common Pleas to the King's Bench; 'with as much honour', said Chamberlain, 'as ever went with that place'.[45] From here, instead of raising fewer 'new troubles and questions', Coke turned his energies into attacking almost every court but his own.[46] Until finally in 1616, after one of his more unjust decrees – in favour of a couple of fraudulent jewellers who had obtained many times the price of their wares – had been reversed by Chancellor Ellesmere, he coolly revived an obsolete statute set up to prevent an appeal from an English court to the Pope, in order to block Chancery's action. Whereupon the King lost patience with him, and called in his Attorney General to investigate this and other similar offences.

It may be argued that Bacon, relieved at the prospect of Coke's transfer to some less actively obstructive position, could afford to be generous, but the fact remains that he was so. Indeed he could not have been more generous throughout Coke's months of suspense. Agreeing that his public affront to the dying Chancellor 'could not pass lightly', Bacon nevertheless set forth every possible argument in Coke's favour, and went out of his way to stress the value of his services, particularly with regard to the financial problems then facing the Government. His first effort was to effect a reconciliation. When that failed, he gave his opinion 'plainly' that Coke should not be disgraced, and suggested, with the eminently suitable post of Lord Treasurer in mind, that if his hopes were at an end in one way, they 'should be raised in some other'.[47] The King wanted Coke dismissed out of hand. Bacon, resisting this as best the could, advised that he should not be charged, but if he were, it should be openly, before the whole Council. And when James would have none of it, Bacon insisted that 'he be heard and called to answer', as 'justice requireth', and that details of the charges be put before him in writing, and time granted him to produce his proofs 'tending to excusation and attenuation'.[48] These were advantages that would later be denied to Bacon. The King's reply was to inform the Council of his resolve to remove Coke at once from the Bench.

Even the usually hostile Chamberlain, remarking on the 'coarse usage' and 'uncivil carriage' Coke had received from the principal judges and from others in Chancery, and noticing 'divers speeches' of Bacon's – 'as, that a man of learning and parts is not every day found, nor so soon made as marred' – observed that in the whole affair, Bacon had 'ever used with him more respect than the rest'. Unable to appreciate (in Bacon) generosity to a fallen rival, or (in anyone) recommendations primarily keyed to the needs of government, Chamberlain suspected him of some inexplicably motivated change of sides.[49] Carteret understood Bacon's motives better. In respecting Sir Edward Coke, he wrote, and always presenting him as 'labouring heartily in the King's service' (which, said Carteret, showed him 'far from being of an unforgiving nature'), Bacon's 'whole study' was at this time 'to keep all who were concerned in the King's affairs on good terms with each other'.[50]

This then is the Bacon who inspired little affection, and who had not 'the merit' of being a good hater. Inconsistency is often found among Bacon's denigrators, but it is difficult to believe that the two critics who saw this as a reproach – Macaulay and Campbell – are the same who launched his reputation as a sadist, 'diabolically delighting' in the shrieks of his victims. What these two historians could not understand appeared natural to King James, who (so Rawley noted) bore witness to Bacon's gentleness in all his dealings, as 'the way that was the most according to his heart'.[51] We have seen Bacon appreciated by his patrons and peers, and neither vindictive nor indifferent towards them. We may now turn to his private life, to learn whether among his family and close friends he justifies the generalizations about his coldness which have been bandied about ever since Macaulay first pronounced him 'incapable of feeling strong affection'.[52]

26

'Without Steady Attachments'

Bacon looked on the ordinary 'ties of relationships' as 'sacraments of nature', and he took his responsibilities seriously towards his nephews and cousins, to whom he acted as legal adviser, and, in the case of his widowed aunt, Lady Anne Cooke, and her young children, as family trustee.[1] It is only by accident, however, that we have any of his personal letters to family and servants, since (unlike his brother Anthony) he made no arrangements to keep them. Among the letters which have survived are cordial exchanges with Sir Thomas Lucy of Charlecote (the son of the Lucy of Justice Shallow fame), whose daughter Joyce had married Bacon's cousin, friend and fellow reveller in Gray's Inn, William Cooke. 'I doubt not your daughter mought have married to a better living,' he said, when expressing his approval of the alliance to Sir Thomas, 'but never to a better life, having chosen a gentleman bred to all honesty and virtue and worth.'[2] We hear also that when, in 1615, Sir Julius Caesar married Bacon's niece Anne, he himself gave away the bride. The two lawyers had been companions since their youth, and Bacon is reported to have written some of his works in Caesar's country house. He was to die in his nephew's arms.[3]

We can gain some idea of Bacon's interest in his dependants from accounts that have survived for the three summer months of 1618. We will find here weekly doles to the needy, amounting to some £300 in all; regular payments, such as those 'to Mr Johnson's son at Eton', and numerous specific payments or gifts 'to a poor woman, one knight's wife, one pound two shillings by your lordship's order . . . to a poor man, late a prisoner . . . to a poor pilgrim . . . to a washerwoman, for sending after the crane that flew into the Thames . . .'[4] Again, in his will there are many pages of legacies to friends and servants, and to the children of friends and servants, each one mentioned by name, as well as to all kinds of relations – including no fewer than four godchildren. 'To my very good friend . . . to my ancient friend . . . to my wife's late waiting

woman . . . old John Boyes . . . old Thomas Gotheram, who was bred
with me from a child . . .' As well as £5 each 'to any mean servant that
attends me and is not named'.[5]

Servants, whether dashing or lowly, played an important part in the
family life of Bacon's day. We have seen him with some that were less
than trustworthy. Let us look at him now with his faithful secretary,
Thomas Meautys, whose love for his master clearly reflects Bacon's for
him. 'A gentleman of sweet conditions and strong abilities', according to
Wotton, Meautys was twenty-nine and newly elected Member of Parliament at the time of Bacon's fall. He moves in and out of his master's life
at this time as an attentive, healing presence, speaking for him in the
House, using his own influential friends on Bacon's behalf, and giving up
his savings to tide him over the crisis. We will find him bringing home a
friend he is sure Bacon will be glad to see; giving bad news reluctantly
('yet I hope it will mend too'); brushing off the distrust he received at
Court as Bacon's messenger ('persons apt to be suspicious . . . certainly
trouble themselves most'). In September 1622, he reports as follows on a
proposal made by Bacon for his own future career:

> I come in these to your Lordship with the voice of thanksgiving for
> the continuance of your accepted noble care of me, and my good,
> which overtake me, I find, withersoever I go . . . And now, my good
> Lord, if anything made me diffident, or indeed almost indifferent
> how it succeeds, it is this: that my sole ambition having ever been,
> and still being, to grow up only under your Lordship, it is become
> preposterous ever to my nature and habit to think of prospering,
> receiving any growth either without or besides your Lordship. And
> therefore let me claim of your Lordship to do me this right, as to
> believe that which my heart says, or rather swears to me, namely
> that what addition so ever, by God's good providence, comes at any
> time to my life or fortune, it is in my account, but to enable me the
> more to serve your Lordship in both; at whose feet I shall ever
> humbly lay down all that I have, or am, never to rise thence other
> than your Lordship's in all duty and reverent affection.[6]

It was Meautys who erected the monument to his master in St Michael's
Church at St Albans, inscribing it with these words: 'That the memory
might remain of such a man, Thomas Meautys, living his servant, dead
his admirer, placed this monument.'[7]

If Bacon was more at ease with his followers than with his fellow
courtiers and politicians, it is because he could share, with the brightest
of them at least, some of the thoughts that filled his mind. He could
impart his knowledge of mining to young Bushell, or wander in those
'delicate groves where he did meditate', as pictured by Aubrey, with the
good-natured and 'pleasantly facetious' Thomas Hobbes, the future

philosopher; with whom, said Aubrey, he 'loved to converse', and to whom, 'whenever a notion darted into his head', Bacon could dictate it, without fear of it being garbled.[8] Few people have appreciated the depth of Bacon's desire to transmit his message to these 'sons of the dawn', and his eagerness to promote any talent which might make them readier to receive it. Small wonder, then, if his indulgence of his servants 'opened a gap to infamous reports which left an unsavoury tincture on him'. So wrote Arthur Wilson in 1653, adding that of course they were calumnies.[9] Aubrey had also picked up these reports ('he was a *paiderastes*: his Ganimeds and favourites took bribes'). 'Unnatural vice', however, was the stock-in-trade of political propaganda in James's reign, and we ought not to pay more attention to these 'fames' than did that great rumour-monger Chamberlain himself, who refused to repeat them, as 'savouring too much of scurrility'.[10] Even Macaulay, ready as he was to believe the worst of Bacon, remarked that he 'was never charged, by any accuser entitled to the smallest credit, with licentious habits'.[11]

In the nineteenth century, of course, any such suspicions were hushed up by right-thinking men. Today, when it is almost *de rigueur* to see things *sub specie homosexualitatis*, it is taken for granted that Bacon was 'gay', and little stigma is attached to the charge. Unless, that is, we count the novel, and quite unsubstantiated, remark made in 1974 by Queen Elizabeth's biographer, Paul Johnson, that she gave Bacon 'little preferment, probably because she knew of his pederasty' – which, in that writer's view, explains her 'deep distrust' of his character, and her uncertainty of his 'moral capacity for higher office'.[12] Though we should also consider an equally novel suggestion advanced by Rowse a few years earlier, that Bacon's alleged pederasty 'may have been a powerful factor in his sudden (and otherwise craven) submission' when charged with bribery. Aside from the only two known references by contemporaries (of which more below), Rowse's reason for presuming pederasty was the fact that Bacon spoke warmly – 'so far as such a cold nature could' – only of male friendship.[13] We may wonder if those who so confidently diagnose coldness in others speak from the experience of their own warmth? Rowse has himself been described as 'of a fishiness' or 'coldness of temperament' that 'prevented him from ever achieving the sort of relationship associated with loving and giving'. And Macaulay, the first to inform the world that Bacon 'wanted warmth of affection', was also seen in our time (by Rowse in particular) as a cold man, and was reproached (by Strachey) for his lack of 'the embracing fluidity of love'. In his own time Macaulay was notorious (wrote one contemporary) for his 'total ignorance of the feelings which take their rise in the passion of love'. He talked about love (wrote another) 'with a complete conviction that he knew all about it, but the actual experience was absent'.[14]

Cold or otherwise, was Bacon a practising homosexual? Sir Simonds D'Ewes, Rowse's first authority, is entitled to very little credit. A rabid Puritan, who supported inquisitions against Moors and Jews, he could not mention any member of the Stuart Court without vilification. His 'uncharitable prejudice', wrote his contemporary Thomas Hearne, induced him to believe all kinds of nonsense, and he has been dismissed as a libeller by the best historians of his own and later ages. Expatiating on the 'Fall and Vices of Sir Francis Bacon' in diaries he began to write, at the age of nineteen, in the year of Bacon's fall, D'Ewes dwelt on this particular vice with gusto, as 'a most admirable instance how men are enslaved by wickedness and held captive by the devil'. Having partaken of it with Buckingham, D'Ewes declared, even when humbled by disgrace Bacon would not 'relinquish the practice of his most horrible and secret sin of sodomy'; and some thought 'that he should have been tried at the bar of justice for it, and have satisfied the law most severe against that horrible villainy with the price of his blood'. D'Ewes quoted some low verses left by an unknown hand at York House, carefully explaining, in case his readers should miss the point, that the word 'hog' alluded 'both to the name of Bacon and to that sinister abominable sin'.[15]

Rowse's other authority, one of Lady Bacon's letters, is the imaginary product of misreading and misinterpretation. When berating Bacon for keeping 'that bloody *Per . . .*' (the word is incomplete in the original) 'as a coach companion and bed companion', she was not referring to the effeminate Spanish refugee, Antonio *Pérez*. She was angry with him for allowing himself to be exploited by his servants, first among them that 'proud, profane, costly fellow', Henry *Per*cy – but also one Jones, 'who never loved your brother but for his credit'. The term 'bed companion' was used here without sexual implications, since beds were scarce in those times, and were normally shared with family, servants and friends. What upset Bacon's staunchly Puritan mother was not that her son should share his bed with a servant but the fact that the servant in question was a Papist.[16]

Nevertheless there was undoubtedly around Anthony and Francis Bacon an atmosphere which could give rise to rumour. As we read in Daphne du Maurier's biography of the two brothers, Anthony, while living as intelligencer at Montauban, was once denounced by a servant and arrested for sodomy; he might have been in serious trouble had not his good friend, King Henri of Navarre, come to the rescue. The real trouble, as he confessed when back home, was that he had offended one of Henri's chief councillors by ridiculing his wife's hair-do – and refusing to marry his daughter.[17] Aged twenty-eight at the time, Anthony was crippled with arthritis, and it is clear from a letter he wrote to a physician, twelve years later, that even if he had been seen stroking the curls of a favourite page in Montauban, he had as yet – regrettably, thought the physician – had no sexual intercourse either with man or woman.[18]

Certainly the brothers were more at home with their own sex. They were in the classical situation in that they had an affectionate, intellectual mother who had brought her sons up on strict Calvinist principles, and whom they preferred not to offend. Her letters show her worrying to the point of hysteria over their poor health, their shaky social position between the rash Essex and the double-dealing Cecil, and their still shakier finances – what with their extravagance, their 'riotous' followers, and the service they rendered to Essex, most of the time without remuneration. And above all she feared for their spiritual welfare, much endangered by 'feasting on the sabbath' and staging dramatic shows at Gray's Inn.[19] Francis, full of concern for his mother, may too often have had occasion to write, 'I humbly thank your Ladyship for your good counsel everyway, and I hope by God's assistance to follow the same.'[20] And we find Anthony on one occasion, 'emboldened with warrant of good conscience, and by force of truth', protesting against her high-handed treatment of one of his men, and her 'dangerous humours and uncharitable misconceits', which sprang, he said, 'from a sovereign desire to over-rule your sons in all things'.[21]

We know little of Bacon's youthful revels at Gray's Inn, or of his courtship of the flirtatious Elizabeth Hatton, his uncle Burghley's grand-daughter, when he was thirty-six and she a young widow of twenty. Were his feelings involved? He had written some years earlier in praise of love, that 'happiest state of mind and the noblest affection', which 'doth so fill and possess all the powers of the mind . . . The only passion that openeth the heart . . . A fountain of curiosity, a most sweet ground set with infinite change' and perpetuated in 'the common and natural desire of children . . .'[22] In any case Lady Hatton married Edward Coke, the richer man – and gave him a good deal of trouble. But Bacon stood by her twenty years later, as we have seen, when the couple quarrelled over the marriage of their daughter, and though this was a matter of policy, we cannot exclude an interest in the girl he had courted and was still confident he could influence. With Lady Hatton 'I can prevail', he told the King, 'more than any other man' – and perhaps she prevailed with him: she certainly knew the way to his heart, for we find her a year later sending him seeds from her famous garden.[23] Spedding may have been right in speculating that, with her talent and her beauty, Lady Hatton, who had been happy with her first husband, Sir William Hatton, would have been no bad wife for Bacon: 'He could have kept her temper in order for her, and she would have kept his household and finances for him.'[24]

Bacon spoke warmly in the *New Atlantis* of 'the faithful nuptial union of man and wife', regardless of alliances and portions. His own marriage to 'an handsome girl to my liking' is presented by his detractors as yet another of his cold and calculating actions – 'a mere scheme to make his pot boil' – because, like most marriages in his time, it was arranged with the fortunes of both partners in mind. The disparity in their ages – he was forty-six and she fourteen – was not unusual, and her dowry of £220 a year was appropriate to a man of Bacon's standing, soon to be appointed Solicitor General, with an income of £5,000 a year.[25] However, though, according to Rawley, he treated his wife 'with much conjugal love and respect and with many rich endowments', the marriage does not seem to have been a source of lasting happiness to either partner.[26] In their early years Bacon celebrated 'the joys of a good wife', and he defended Alice with spirit against his quarrelsome mother-in-law; and later he mentioned as one of his greatest griefs that his wife, 'no partaker of my offending', should have had to suffer for his fall.[27] But the portrait of Alice Bacon shows a hard face, and she was said to have a sharp tongue. And though he made generous provision for 'my loving wife' in his will, a few months before his death he revoked this clause, for 'great and just causes', leaving her only her due. He did not wish his much loved Gorhambury to pass into the hands of his gentleman usher, John Underhill, whom Alice married two weeks after his death. If there is anything in Aubrey's gossip, that she made her new husband 'deaf and blind with too much Venus', it could be a pointer to what she had missed in her first marriage.[28]

Whatever his inclinations, however, there is no evidence that Bacon was a practising homosexual, still less a brazen or convinced one. His references to friendship, like Shakespeare's – and unlike Marlowe's – are not sexual, neither are his allusions to friends and servants, or his expressions of affection to them.[29] He excluded 'unnatural lust' from New Atlantis. 'As for masculine love, they have no touch of it, and yet there are not so faithful and inviolate friendships in the world as are there'; and 'there is not under the heavens so chaste a nation as this of Bensalem, nor so free from all pollution and foulness. It is the virgin of the world.'[30] The qualities Bacon most admired are those he attributed to his close friend, Jeremiah Bettenham (of whom more below): *Vir innocens, abstinens et contemplativus.*[31] His friend could well have said the same of him.

This does not mean that there was no passion in Bacon, but that its outlet was not sexual. His was that 'secret inclination towards love of others' he wrote about, 'which if not spent on one or a few doth naturally spread itself towards many'.[32] And his sexuality found expression in his writings. It was to sexual images that he resorted again and again to express the core of his message, that 'true relation between the nature of things and the nature of the mind', which he described as a 'strewing and decoration of the bridal chamber of the Mind and the Universe' – divine goodness assisting as midwife. Bacon saw himself sowing the seed of his invention in young minds, and contemplating the spirits in 'the womb of the elements'. Knowledge was for him 'a spouse, for generation, fruit and comfort'. He wanted his thought, like that of the early Greeks, to be 'firmly rooted in the lap and womb of nature', and the function of his all-important Natural History was 'to supply a suckling philosophy with its first food'.[33] So he announced the *Great Instauration* in 1620. In a preliminary outline, drafted in 1603 in the form of a letter from a master to his pupil, he had written:

> My dear, dear boy, what I propose is to unite you with things in a chaste and holy wedlock, and from this you will secure increase beyond the hopes and prayers of ordinary marriages; to wit, a blessed race of heroes who will overcome the immeasurable helplessness and poverty of the human race. Take heart then, my son, and give yourself to me so that I may restore you to yourself.[34]

We have found Bacon not without feeling in the circle life had placed him in. But a different note is struck here. Undoubtedly the people he felt closest to were the scholars with whom he could share some part of his greatest ambition – to kindle that 'light in nature' which he believed could 'in its very rising touch and illuminate all the border-regions' of knowledge and procure lasting benefits to humankind. As he wrote to the illustrious Isaac Casaubon, librarian to King Henri IV or France, 'Why should I not converse rather with the absent than the present, and make my friendships by choice and election, rather than suffer them, as the manner is, to be settled by accident?'[35] And indeed, wherever his own inquiring mind came in touch with another, Bacon found a friend. As he wrote back to young Father Baranzano, a teacher of mathematics at Annecy who had asked him to elaborate certain points in the *Novum Organum*: 'between lovers of truth ardour begets candour.' He joyfully explained all his plans for the *Great Instauration* to Baranzano, signing himself *tui amantissimus*.[36] Another such kindred spirit was the diplomat and scientist, Sir Kenelm Digby (devoted husband to the fascinating Venetia Stanley), who discovered that plants need 'vital air', and invented a 'sympathetic salve', which he later claimed that Bacon had approved. Digby, Bacon remarked to Toby Matthew, had 'much greatness of mind, a thing almost lost among men'; and to Digby he professed himself 'most glad of his friendship'.[37] Another bond was with the Marquis d'Effiat, whose foremost wish on his appointment as French Ambassador after Bacon's fall (Rawley tells us) was to visit him, 'after which they contracted an intimate acquaintance, and the Marquis did so much revere him that, besides his frequent visits, they wrote letters one to the other under titles of father and son'.[38]

Bacon was particularly attached to friends whom he could rely on to

criticize his writings. Foremost among these was his kinsman, Sir Thomas
Bodley, founder of the Bodleian Library and sixteen years Bacon's senior,
who had followed the younger man's career with interest since his early
days in France. Twenty years later Bacon was reminding Bodley to send
his impatiently awaited comments on the first draft of *Thoughts and
Conclusions*:

> You are, I bear you witness, slothful, and you tell me nothing; so as
> I am half in conceit that you affect not the argument; for myself I
> know well you love and affect. Therefore if I had you but a fortnight
> at Gorhambury, I would make you tell me another tale; or else I
> would add a cogitation against libraries, and be revenged on you that
> way.[39]

Bodley wrote back his gratitude for the 'singular love' that allowed him
'first perusal' of this essay, assuring Bacon of the depth of his affection 'to
your person and spirit, and to your work and words, and to all your
abilities'; but, he said, he valued his cousin's affection for him more than
all.[40] There follow pages of the kind of criticism Bacon appreciated as one
of the best 'fruits of friendship'.

Another much trusted critic – his 'inquisitor', as Bacon called him, and
a companion of his student days – was Bishop Lancelot Andrewes, Queen
Elizabeth's much loved chaplain, whom James also appreciated for his
rare sense of humour.[41] He was general editor of the Authorized Version
of the Bible, and composed prayers still familiar to churchgoers. His
name is 'sweeter than spices', a contemporary exclaimed, admiring him
also for his 'venerable gravity' and 'courageous independence', and
for carrying out all his good works in secret.[42] The Bishop's favourite
recreation, we gather, was to observe the grass, trees, waters, heavens,
and any of the creatures – a natural friend for Bacon, whose writings he
much appreciated. We may assume that Andrewes did not fail his friend
in disgrace, for we find the ex-Chancellor soon afterwards writing him
a long, open-hearted letter, full of his plans of work. In 1622 Bacon
dedicated to him his *Advertisement touching a Holy War*, 'in respect of our
ancient and private acquaintance'.[43]

But it is not only to the erudite that Bacon applied. He would give his
manuscripts to one of the quite unintellectual men with whom he also
formed lasting frienships, such as Sir John Danvers, according to Aubrey
his 'great acquaintance and favourite', in whose 'elegant garden' Bacon
'took much delight'. 'Your Lordship knows I am no scholar,' said Danvers
when Bacon gave him his *History of Henry VII* to read. ''Tis no matter,'
Bacon replied, 'I know what a scholar can say. I would know what you
can say.' And when he had heard Danvers's impressions: 'Why,' said he,
'a scholar would never have told me this.'[44] Another such companion was
Essex's one-time secretary, Sir Thomas Smith, on whose death Bacon

regretted one of the few he 'accounted no stage-friends, but private friends', with whom he could 'freely and safely communicate'.[45] And there was also, last but not least, his fellow reader at Gray's Inn, Jeremiah Bettenham, 'one of his intimate and dearly beloved friends', as Aubrey described him, whose *bons mots* Bacon particularly liked to recall. 'Good cousin,' he wrote to Sir Thomas Hoby on this friend's death, 'no man knoweth what part I bear in the grief for Mr Bettenham's departure. For in good faith I never thought myself at better liberty than when he and I were by ourselves together.'[46] The monument Bacon later erected for his 'innocent, abstinent and contemplative' friend was a fitting memorial for both of them: an octagonal seat under the elms where they had walked and conversed together, covered by a roof and surrounded by a circle of trees.[47]

So far we have found little to justify Campbell in concluding his life of Bacon in 1875 with 'the formidable admission that he was without a steady attachment', or F. C. Montague, editor of the *Essays* in 1907, who could find nothing in Bacon's writings 'to show that he had ever lived in close communion with another person'.[48] What kind of attachment were they thinking of? Friendship means different things to different people, still more to different generations, and in Bacon's time close friendship between two men involved more emotion than any non-homosexual relationship would today. Bacon's critics may not have noticed his description of the solaces of 'friendly love' (1592), which comes 'to perfect what nuptial love has made', and is 'the sweetest contentment'. 'Assuredly no person ever saw at any time the mind of another but in love,' he wrote, or enjoyed so fully 'the delight of concurrence in desire without emulation'. 'What vigour, what alacrity' is inspired by 'friendly love'! Gathering in 'the beams of so many pleasures to inflame the soul', it offers 'the greatest union of mind, the most refreshing repose from action . . .'[49] Yet they would have read in the essay 'Of Friendship' that 'it is a mere, miserable solitude to want true friends'. And they must have seen his pages on the 'fruits of friendship' among them, that an hour tossing one's thoughts with a friend was better than a day's meditation, and 'the liberty of a friend' the best way of showing us our errors and 'extreme absurdities'.

But the best fruit of all was friendship itself. 'It is friendship when a man can say to himself, I love this man without respect of utility. I am open-hearted to him, I single him out from the generality of those with whom I live; I make him a portion of my own wishes.'[50] For Bacon, to say that a friend was 'another himself' was an understatement: 'A friend is far more than himself.' If we now look at the three people he singled out above all others from among his many friends, as Montaigne put it, 'because he is he and because I am I', we shall see that the communion his critics have denied him – the 'faithful and inviolate' friendship to be found in New Atlantis – is precisely what he sought and achieved: for the first forty years of his life, with his brother Anthony until Anthony's early death; for his last few years, until his own death, with the poet George Herbert; and his whole life long with the friend of his masque-playing days, Toby Matthew.

'How firmly thy love stands by those admitted to it!' – so Thomas Campion, doctor, poet and musician, addressed Bacon in 1617; and he had reason to know, for their friendship dated from 1588, when they had acted together in a play presented at Gray's Inn before the Queen.[51] We have seen Bacon as a frequenter of poets: John Davies, Chapman, Beaumont, and especially Ben Jonson, who like Herbert was employed to translate his works into Latin.[52] We hear from Chamberlain that Bacon attended the sermons of John Donne, and from Aubrey that Donne was his admirer and was employed to revise some of his books. Donne himself recalls that it was Bacon who first introduced him to the man who was to become his own 'ardent and faithful friend' and best patron, James Hay, later Earl of Carlisle. The poet was secretary and afterwards unapproved son-in-law to Bacon's patron, Lord Keeper Egerton, as well as the fast friend of Toby Matthew and Bishop Andrewes, and he was in close touch with Bacon's cousin Wotton and his nephew Caesar, near whose mansion in Sussex, where Bacon was a frequent visitor, Donne lived for many years. But if they wrote to each other, no letters have survived.[53]

Of Bacon's relations with George Herbert we know a good deal more, since their mutual influence – particularly Bacon's on Herbert – has been well studied. The poet-parson's seventeenth-century biographer, Izaak Walton, gives us a glimpse of the first meeting between Bacon aged sixty and Herbert aged twenty-seven, when they began 'the desired friendship' – desired, because they had already recognized each other through their writings. As Public Orator at Cambridge, Herbert had thanked 'nature's high priest' on behalf of the University for their copy of his *Great Instauration*. 'We welcome the book,' he wrote, 'not to our bosom alone, but with both arms,' and he celebrated his new friend in various Latin poems. Bacon responded in kind. He 'put such a value on his judgement', said Walton, 'that he usually desired his approbation before he would expose any of his books to be printed'.[54] He dedicated his own *Translation of Certain Psalms* to Herbert, and made him his literary executor; and it is apparently under his aegis that Herbert was able to retire from Cambridge and take up his vocation as a country parson.[55] Alone among Bacon's 'inquisitors', Herbert was himself a creator, which may explain why, as has been abundantly shown, he understood all the different aspects of Bacon's message so exactly. The two friends had one taste in common. Herbert's greatest pleasure, his biographer recalls, was 'blessing people'. He indulged it to the full among his parishioners, and it seems they enjoyed it as much as he did, for they would 'let their ploughs rest' and join him whenever his bell rang for prayer. Bacon did his blessing vicariously in the *New Atlantis*, where the Father of the House of Salomon lost no opportunity of holding up 'his bare hands as he went, blessing the people'.[56] Their letters and the poems Herbert addressed to Bacon bear witness to a mutual understanding which was only too brief, for Bacon died six years later. Herbert's sorrow for the loss of his friend is visible in these lines from his elegy, which we saw earlier in a different translation: 'While you groan beneath the blight of your long slow sickness, and your wasting life halts on uncertain foot, slowly I come to understanding what fate intends . . .'[57] Herbert himself had a good share in preparing the *Manes Verulamiani*, in which his elegy appeared.

Anthony, three years Bacon's senior, his 'dearest brother, unto whom he was most nearly conjoined in affection', was, according to Rawley, 'a gentleman equal to him in height of wit, though inferior in the endowments of learning and knowledge'; Aubrey recalls him as 'much beyond his brother for the politiques'.[58] Had he 'but half as much health as honesty', Elizabeth once protested, 'she knew not throughout her realm where to find a better servant, or one more to her liking'.[59] Except during the thirteen years Anthony spent in France as Walsingham's intelligencer, the brothers were always in close touch – when not actually living together, as they did at their chambers at Gray's Inn during the years of their joint service with Essex. In absence they wrote each other frequent notes and open-hearted letters, which show a constant care of each other. Anthony, in particular, worried over his brother's shaky finances, and Francis was much concerned with Anthony's stone or his gout. In April 1593, when Francis was in trouble with the Queen, we find Anthony beseeching Lady Bacon to believe

> that being so near and dear unto me as he is, it cannot but be a grief unto me to see a mind that hath given so sufficient a proof of itself in having brought forth many good thoughts for the general, to be overburdened and cumbered with a care of clearing his particular estate.[60]

This was the letter Lady Bacon replied to with a scolding to Francis for the costly servants he maintained. But she expressed also her approval of Anthony's good care of him – a recurrent theme in her correspondence – 'God forbid but that ye should always love each other heartily and kindly.'[61]

They did. And they had many good times together, at work and at play. At Bacon's country house in Twickenham, where they received every kind of visitor, from Thomas Phelippes, the brilliant cipher-reader whose services Essex had inherited from Walsingham, to Lancelot Andrewes, the future Bishop. Or in town, where we hear of their gatherings with

Essex and his sister, Lady Rich, of their 'masking and mumming', to Lady Bacon's distress, or being 'twanged asleep' with virginals and lutes. Or making fun of their more tedious acquaintance – in particular of their 'wandering neighbour', Antonio Pérez, the exiled Spanish Secretary, who called himself *el Peregrino* (the Pilgrim), and was drawn to the life as the 'peregrinate' Spaniard in *Love's Labour's Lost*.[62]

As we can see from his letters, Anthony had the most complete faith in his brother's merit, and in his judgement. In 1595, for example, when Francis had suggested that the time was ripe for him to bring his well-deserving activities abroad to the attention of the Queen, Anthony wrote back thanking his brother for his kindness, confessing himself 'incapable of what is best for myself', and committing himself entirely 'to the resolution and direction of my most honourable friend and dearest brother'. And in 1596 we find Anthony writing to Lady Bacon, delighted with the improvement in his brother's prospects:

> Thus your Ladyship sees that though loyalty, patience and diligence may for a time be shadowed and disgraced by malice and envy, yet it pleaseth God, the fountain of all goodness, by his extraordinary power, to make them sometimes shine to the Prince's eyes, through the dark mists of cunning and misreports.[63]

In the following year Francis dedicated his *Essays* to his 'loving and beloved brother . . . such as they are, to our love, in depth whereof I assure you that I sometimes wish your infirmities were translated upon myself'.[64]

There is little evidence of the coolness imagined by Anthony Bacon's biographer, Olive Driver, and by Daphne du Maurier, between the two brothers when they began to diverge in their attitude towards Essex; and none at all of the romantic notion that Francis agreed to play a part in Essex's trial in exchange for his brother's safety, although there may well have been a tacit understanding between them to counterbalance and protect each other from their respective positions.[65] Anthony, who had been ill for some time, died on 17 May 1601, three months after the execution of Essex. An affectionate line to him from Francis, written on 5 May, bears witness to his presence until the end.[66] 'My last Essays I dedicated to my dear brother', wrote Bacon in the second edition, 'who is with God.' In the third edition, published in 1625, he included a new essay on friendship, composed at the request of Toby Matthew – 'proof', Bacon wrote to him, 'of your great friendship towards me'.[67]

Toby Matthew, later Sir Toby, Bacon's principal confidant and critic throughout his life, was a gentle, courageous, erudite and witty man, whose 'sweetness of behaviour' charmed all those he came in contact with.[68] Much given in his youth to 'feasting and debauchery', he became a Catholic convert in 1607 (and, in 1614, a concealed Jesuit priest), apparently persuading many people to return to the 'old religion', and he was particularly feared by the Protestant authorities as a 'dangerous man to our collapsed ladies'.[69] We can gain some idea of what he was like from the qualities he admired in others. Writing home from Madrid about the Spanish Infanta, whose marriage with Prince Charles he was helping to negotiate, he was struck by her 'kingly born' yet unassuming manner, her sensitiveness to unkindness, which she bore silently, 'a great sweetness and goodness' shining 'from her soul through her body', and by one sovereign virtue, 'a resolution she has maintained inviolable from her infancy never to speak ill of any creature'.[70]

Toby Matthew was seventeen years old when, in 1595, he acted the part of squire in one of the 'devices' written by Bacon for the entertainment of the Queen at Gray's Inn, while Bacon ('I wax somewhat ancient') had reached the advanced age of thirty-four.[71] There began the friendship which lasted through many years of absence and through both men's respective rises and falls at different times, until Bacon's death. In 1604, after he had replaced Bacon as Member of Paliament for St Albans and prepared a parliamentary report in his stead (Bacon being at that time 'wholly employed about invention'), Matthew left for Italy and a correspondence began which they kept up through every separation, writing on many subjects of interest to them both, but principally to bridge the gap of absence. Thus Bacon notes, after describing the reforms he hoped the new King would bring about, 'I have written this to you in haste, my end being no more than to write, and thereby make you know that I will ever continue the same, and still be sure to wish you as heartily well as myself . . .'; or, after expatiating on the 'astronomical delusions' of Italian philosophers and the effect of certain planetary positions on the climate, 'you see that though I be full of business, yet I can be glad rather to lay it all aside, than to say nothing to you. But I long much more to be speaking to you, and I hope I shall not long want my wish.'[72]

It was during his stay in Florence that Toby Matthew became a Catholic. He returned to England prepared to face the consequences (though not without 'sore and grievous temptations' to avoid the sacrifices involved), duly refused to take the oath of allegiance, and was sent to prison. Bacon was no fair-weather friend, as Matthew's biographer pointed out. Shocked as he was by Matthew's conversion, Bacon did not forsake his friend. 'Do not think me forgetful or altered towards you,' he wrote, expressing his regret that he was so powerless to help – but still hoping to persuade him:

> I myself am out of doubt that you have been miserably abused. Good Mr Matthew, receive yourself back from these courses of perdition . . . I pray God who understands all better than we under-

stand one another, confine you, as I hope He will, at least within the bounds of loyalty to His Majesty and natural pity towards your country.[73]

This God apparently did, for if he went on helping to 'collapse' ladies into the Catholic faith, Matthew remained a thoroughly loyal subject. But an unfamiliar light is cast on Bacon by Matthew's view of his friend's attempts to reconvert him to the Reformed Church. After explaining to a co-religionist that Sir Francis Bacon, 'my noble and true friend', had been 'so earnest with many of the great ones' that he had at last obtained permission for Matthew to visit him, he added that Bacon had obtained this liberty

> with less difficulty by promising that he would deal earnestly with me about my return to Protestant religion; but for my part I was not of the plot. It is true that now and then he would be speaking some little thing to me of that kind; but he was quickly and very easily answered; for he was in very truth (with being a kind of monster both of wit and knowledge also in other things) such a poor kind of creature in all those which were questionable about religion, that my wonder takes away all my words.[74]

Bacon made one objection that appeared so elementary to Matthew that he raised his eyebrows in surprise, whereupon Bacon told him 'with more feeling than ordinary' that his surprise betrayed his ignorance. 'We seldom met after upon such argument,' Matthew concluded, 'but I passed my time with much gust [pleasure], for there was not such company in the whole world.' Vital as the religious question was to both of them, it is clear that they valued their friendship more.

Bacon's constancy throughout Toby Matthew's inevitable disfavour – a stand which could easily have got him into trouble, though Toby Matthew had kept his ordainment secret – should be seen against the more prudent attitude of the latter's other friends. Thus we find Dudley Carleton, whom Toby had addressed in the old days as 'my very much beloved' and 'my best brother', writing to another acquaintance, when Matthew had been four days a prisoner in the Fleet: 'I wished him better entertainment, but I cannot say he deserved better . . . If he fall alone, I shall grieve the less, and therefore the sooner his friends are rid of him the better.' When after eight years' banishment Matthew came back as the guest of Bacon, now Lord Keeper, Chamberlain deprecated Bacon's generosity. Toby Matthew, he wrote, 'was indeed so exceedingly favoured and respected by that Lord that it is thought *aliquid nimium* [somewhat beneath him] that a man of his high place should give countenance to one so affected. And some stick not to say that former private friendship should give place to public respects.'[75]

Bacon and Matthew, meanwhile, had continued on the same affectionate terms. Throughout Matthew's banishment Bacon shared his plans of work with the friend who knew 'the good end to which it was dedicate', welcomed and discussed Matthew's criticisms, and hoped that his 'discreet and temperate carriage' would restore him to his country and friends. 'Two letters of mine', he wrote in 1609,

> are now already walking towards you; but so that we might meet, it were not matter though our letters should lose their way . . . my knowledge both of your loyalty and honest nature will ever make me show myself your faithful friend without scruple . . . Thus in extreme haste, I have scribbled to you I know not what, which therefore is the less affected, and for that very reason will not be esteemed less by you.

And in 1610, after reporting the progress of his work, 'I have written in the midst of a term and parliament, thinking no time so precious but that I should talk of those matters with so good and dear a friend.'[76]

We catch a glimpse of Toby in 1618, during a brief stay in England (which he owed to Bacon's zeal in mediating for him), before he was again banished. He has forgotten to deliver the messages entrusted to him, because he was overcome with 'the grief I have to leave your Lordship's presence', and hopes he may one day be able to cast 'some small mite into the treasury of his friend's happiness'.[77] In 1619 he wrote to Gondomar, of Bacon, 'There never was a man more bounden to him than I am. He makes me still keep my lodging in his house, with the keys of it, in hope to see me there again ere long, whereof I shall be exceeding glad.'[78] The lines Matthew wrote to Bacon from abroad, on hearing of his disgrace, more than filled his friend's 'treasury', as we can see from Bacon's response:

> I have too long been a debtor to you for a letter, and especially for such a letter, the words whereof were delivered by your hand, as if it had been in old gold. For it was not possible for entire affection to be more generously and effectually expressed. I can but return thanks to you; or rather indeed such an answer as may better be of thoughts than words . . . Your company was ever of contentment to me, and your absence of grief; but now it is grief upon grief. I beseech you therefore make haste hither, where you shall meet with as good a welcome as your own heart can wish.[79]

The positions of the two friends were now reversed. Toby Matthew, aged forty-four, back from a diplomatic mission for which he was eventually knighted (to Chamberlain's disgust), was now a man with prospects and patrons at Court, while Bacon lived in exile in the country. But it was an exile, however, allieviated by Matthew's frequent visits and acts of kindness, for which we find Bacon affectionately thanking his friend, as, in the spring of 1622, 'Your incessant thinking of me, without loss of a moment of time, or a hint of occasion, or a circumstance of endeavour . . . in demonstration of love and affection to me, doth infinitely tie me to you.'[80]

These passages may be enough to show how fully Bacon experienced, over more than thirty years, the 'solaces' of friendship, as described by himself – and still better by St Augustine in his *Confessions*, which Toby Matthew had translated and brought out for the first time in English, in 1620: 'To talk and jest together, to do kind offices by turns; to read together . . . To dissent at times without discontent, as a man might with his own self . . . sometimes to teach and sometimes to learn; to long for the absent with impatience, and welcome the coming with joy . . .'[81] 'He was a friend unalterable to his friends,' wrote Toby of Bacon; and Bacon of him, 'a dear friend of mine, and to me another myself'.[82] Bacon's opinion of Matthew's worth is shown in a note entrusting him with a delicate affair: 'I had rather you dealt between us than anybody else because you are in no way drenched in any man's humour.'[83] This was high praise from Bacon. And we will recall the concluding lines of Matthew's encomium of his friend, published in 1618, with the *Essays* in Italian. 'It is not his greatness I admire, but his virtue: it is not the favours I have received from him (infinite though they be) that have thus enthralled and enchained my heart, but his whole life and character.'[84]

Part V

Vicissitudes of Bacon's Legend

27

The 'Meanest of Mankind'

Bacon was celebrated by philosophers, scientists, poets and historians for two centuries after his death. To be precise, until July 1837. They praised him, as his friend Toby Matthew had done, not for his greatness alone, but for his 'life and character'. In the forthcoming chapters we will trace his reception until the advent of Macaulay, and the very different reception awarded him after that date.

When he died – on Easter Day, 1626 – from the after-effects of an early attempt at refrigeration ('why should not flesh be preserved in snow, as it is in salt?'), few of his contemporaries, and no one outside England looked upon Bacon as anything but the victim of an envious fortune.[1] Abroad there was only one great Chancellor of England, the 'late most wise Chancellor' who had lost his Seal. In France 'that honourable sage', esteemed by one writer 'no less than Pythagoras', was commemorated as the man whose 'truly heroic resolution' in following an unknown path had opened the way to 'a new and perfect philosophy'.[2] Elected 'grand homme de ce siècle' by French officialdom (so one among them noted) he was looked on as the counsellor of princes by such eminent statesmen as Cardinal Richelieu and Sully, to whom the French translations of his works were dedicated. And the only picture in the library of King Louis XIII was Bacon's full-length portrait, brought over by his friend Effiat, the French Ambassador – 'as if', a traveller reported, 'he alone were worthy of that honour who had taught all kings in his *Henry VII*'.[3] All over Europe 'the brightest star in the dawn of a new age', as that other bright star, the Bohemian philosopher Comenius had called him, received no less praise for his integrity and fortitude than for the gifts of his mind.[4]

Pierre Amboise, in the brief 'Life' with which, in 1633, he introduced his French translation of Bacon's *Sylva Sylvarum, or a Natural History* (prepared in London while he was on the staff of the French Embassy), expressed his horror at the Chancellor's 'so rude and strange end'. The 'unparalleled brutality', he wrote, with which Bacon's country had treated a man 'who could reckon the years of his life by the signal services he had rendered to the state', and to whose 'judicious counsel' and 'good conduct of affairs' England owed 'a part of the peace she had so long enjoyed', could have but one explanation. Obviously,

> the sea, that surrounds England on all sides imparts to her inhabitants something of its own fickleness and inconstancy . . . Vanity, greed and ambition, vices so often attached to great dignities, were unknown to him. He was as upright a man as he was a just Judge [and was] loved by high and low. But Monsieur Bacon was too deserving to be happy for long, and though his probity was unquestioned, he was declared guilty of his servants' crimes . . . His rectitude was the sole cause of his poverty. Placing the interests of the state above those of his house, he neglected his own, and took no advantage of his many opportunities for enrichment.[5]

Peter Boener, the translator of Bacon's *Essays* into Dutch, who had been for many years his domestic apothecary and assistant, saw Bacon as 'a phoenix without equal'. Although envied in his own country, wrote Boener, he had acquitted himself of his task as High Chancellor of England so

> that all eyes were fixed on him, and that many foreign kings and potentates and ambassadors honoured him greatly. [He was] by divers authors in Italy, France, Germany, the Netherlands, high esteemed, and often greeted by them in letters, some of which I have seen and read. [But] how runneth a man's fortune! He who seemed to occupy the highest rank is, alas, by envious tongues near King and Parliament deposed from all his offices and Chancellorship, little considering what treasure was being cast in the mud, as afterwards the issue and the result thereof have shown in that country . . .
>
> [Yet] whilst his fortunes were so changed, I never saw him – either in mien, words or acts – changed or disturbed towards whomsoever . . . he was ever the same, both in sorrow and in joy, as becometh a philosopher; always with a benevolent allocation. He was also bountiful, and he would gladly have given more, and also with great pleasure, if he had been able to do more; therefore it would be desirable that a statue or bronzen image were erected in his country to his honour and name, as a noteworthy example and pattern for everyone, of all virtue, gentleness, peacefulness and patience.[6]

At home, where it was not safe to protest against the verdict of Parliament, Bacon's fame, as one of his editors put it, 'grew secretly like a tree'.[7] A sincere sorrow comes through the conventional phrasing of the Latin elegies devoted to him on his death – the *Manes Verulamiani*, privately printed in Cambridge – where the fourth-century martyr, St Alban, is

called on to mourn the saddest event since he himself suffered martyrdom.[8] The scholarly contributors were unanimous in considering Bacon's
death 'a vast catastrophe'. 'You who could immortalize the muses, could
you yourself die, oh Bacon?' 'Now truly robed in white, a spotless judge,
he listens,' and 'reigning in the citadel of gods, shines with a golden
crown'. Strangely different, this acclamation – however much a stereo-
type – from the way Cecil's death had been received twelve years earlier,
and of which Chamberlain wrote that he never knew so great a man so
soon and so generally censured.[9]

The one Englishman who voiced his indignation aloud was safely
across the Channel. This was Dr William Lewis, the young scholar whose
appointment as Provost of Oriel Bacon had supported.[10]

> When you awake, dull Britons, and behold
> What treasure you have thrown into your mould,
> Your ignorance in pruning of a state
> You shall confess, and shall your rashness hate,
> For in your senseless fury you have slain
> A man so far beyond your spongy brain
> Of common knowledge, as is heaven from hell . . .
> O that I could but give his work a name
> That, if not you, your sons might blush from shame!

Lewis concluded his tirade with a favourite Baconian image:

> But as in purest things the smallest spot
> Is sooner found than either stain or blot
> In baser stuff, even so his chance was such
> To have of faults too few, of worth too much.

Ben Jonson's tribute, that of a friend and collaborator, was not published
until 1640, after his own death.

> I have and do reverence him for the greatness that was only proper
> to himself, in that he seemed to me ever by his work one of the
> greatest men and most worthy of admiration that had been in many
> ages. In his adversity I ever prayed that God would give him strength;
> for greatness he could not want. Neither could I condole in a word or
> syllable with him; as knowing no accident could do harm to virtue,
> but rather help to make it manifest.[11]

When Macaulay quoted these lines he left out the last sentence. Greatness he would allow Bacon, but not virtue.

By this time the dull Britons had woken up. Milton saluted one who
needed 'a mighty continent' in which to display the largeness of his spirit,
and the precursors and founders of the Royal Society greeted that 'excellent Chancellor' as the Master Builder who had first conceived their

grand design. He was generally seen as a subject for admiring compassion.[12] 'Bacon, like Moses led us forth at last,' wrote Abraham Cowley, a poet increasingly appreciated today, whose proposals for the Royal Society were based on the *New Atlantis*. This was a sacrificed Moses, 'his life divided twixt excess / Of low affliction and high happiness'.[13] Robert Hooke, Curator of Experiments to the Royal Society, compared his sufferings to those of 'poor Galileo' under the Inquisition.[14] Most of his admirers believed, with the eminent lawyer Charles Mollay, that 'no wisdom could increase or affliction diminish' this great man, whom 'neither pleasure could allure nor riches persuade, nor greatness tempt to the least dishonour'. Envy alone had 'laid his honour and virtues bleeding in the dust'.[15] That this would be generally recognized, they were convinced, was only a matter of time.

> Oh give me leave to pull the curtain by
> That clouds thy worth in such obscurity,
> Good Seneca, stay but awhile thy bleeding . . .[16]

These verses were affixed to a portrait of Bacon in 1630, four years after his death. In 1656, under another portrait, we read:

> Grace, honour, virtue, learning, wit
> Are all within this portrait knit
> And left to time that it may tell
> What worth within this peer did dwell.[17]

Early in the eighteenth century, Joseph Addison illustrated his belief that 'the greatest and wisest men of all ages . . . were renowned for their piety and virtue' with a single example, Francis Bacon. 'To forbear replying to an unjust reproach', he wrote, 'and overlook it with a generous, or (if possible) with an entire neglect of it, is one of the most heroic acts of a great mind.' In illustrating his precept that silence was the best reply to calumny and defamation, he gave two examples of those who had practised it: Jesus Christ, and Bacon. Like Ben Jonson, Addison saw Bacon's fall as an occasion for these qualities to manifest themselves. 'Humbled with affliction, which at that time lay heavy upon him, we see him supported by the sense of his integrity, his zeal, his devotion and his love to mankind, which gives him a much greater figure in the minds of thinking men than that greatness had done from which he had fallen.'[18]

So much for the poets and scholars. The historians could not so easily disregard Bacon's fall, and we find William Camden, his contemporary, commenting ironically: 'The Chancellor, being convicted of bribery, pretends, being weary of honour, he would resign his place, being much loaded with calumnies.' But Thomas Fuller thought Bacon had spent on service to mankind more than he had gained as a judge.[19] And John

Rushworth was sympathetic towards 'this learned peer', who, 'known to be no admirer of money, yet had the unhappiness to be defiled therein. He treasured up nothing for himself or family, but was over-indulgent to his servants, and connived at their takings, and their ways betrayed him into that error . . .' Another contemporary attributed Bacon's 'great failure in prudence' to his 'noble soul, which, disdaining all dross, and terrene considerations, never descended to know the value of money until he wanted [lacked] it.'[20]

A century later, in 1755, the scholarly Thomas Carte, in his *General History of England*, indignant on Bacon's behalf, identified Coke as the principal contriver of his fall:

> A greater man never appeared in any age or in any country; he was an honour to his own; and yet with all the merit of which human nature is capable, with all the modesty attending it that ever graced infant innocence, with all the real disinterestedness and contempt of money that ever was pretended by any Stoic or Cynic philosopher, he was accused of bribery.
>
> Sir Edward Coke hated him for his superiority in every respect, even in his profession of law, and because he enjoyed a dignity which his pride and vanity made him think nobody so capable of filling as himself; and though he was in his own nature the most avaricious mortal upon earth, and in practice grasped at everything, raising an overgrown estate by pleading the most iniquitous causes for his fee, and by other the worst of methods, he yet was not ashamed to accuse Bacon of corruption for what had been done by all his predecessors without reproach . . . He died, the greatest man on earth died . . . poor as the most disinterested of his enemies, for ever to be honoured, admired, loved and lamented.[21]

John Carteret, Earl Granville, the statesman and historian whose long article on Bacon in *Biographia Britannica* (1747) has often been quoted here, had considered the case more coolly. He thought it 'very particular' that because his decrees were just, the Chancellor, although willing to own corruption, 'did not think it amounted, strictly speaking, to taking bribes'. But Bacon's good faith and serenity breathe throughout Carteret's pages. He too pointed out that Bacon had never 'affected riches', was not personally ambitious and took no advantage of the positions of influence in which he found himself; he 'laboured only to arrive at truth and not to acquire a mighty reputation'. Bacon was not a 'supple, cringing, or low spirit, but quite the contrary', he noted. 'There was nothing narrow or selfish in his composition'; he was only too generous, his principal fault being 'the excess of that virtue that covers a multitude of faults'. For this virtue as much as for his knowledge, Carteret concluded, and above all for 'his zeal for mankind', while men have gratitude, 'the name of Bacon, Verulam or St Albans can never be mentioned but with admiration'.[22]

'Spots on the sun', wrote David Mallet in 1740, and this was the general consensus of eighteenth-century opinion on Bacon's failings. Archbishop Tenison, in 1679 – with an image that would have gladdened Bacon's heart – had compared them to excrescences 'which grow on those trees that are fit to build the palaces of kings'.[23] 'Whatsoever his errors were,' Tenison said, 'they are overbalanced by his virtues, and *will die with time.*' As Carteret saw it, they 'hurt only his contemporaries, and they were expiated by his sufferings'.[24] In 1770 David Hume still looked on Bacon's disgrace as a calamity that had befallen 'a man universally admired for the greatness of his genius and beloved for the courteousness and humanity of his behaviour'. He deplored 'the dreadful sentence, dreadful to a man of nice sensibility to honour' under which 'with unbroken spirit his genius continued to shine'.[25]

If the moderate criticism of these historians was all Macaulay had to go on, aside from the remorse of Bushell, the silence of Rawley, Tenison's hint that the cause of Bacon's suffering was to some a secret, and the indignation of all Bacon's admirers, where did he find his base and obsequious schemer, the epitome of greed, ambition, vice, cruelty and 'meanness of spirit'? The answer is not far to seek. Bacon is depicted with every one of these traits – except cruelty, which was invented later – by the anti-Stuart 'libellers', the writers of 'secret histories' vilifying dead or exiled monarchs, who flourished in the middle of the seventeenth century and were looked on as beneath notice by the historians of their own time.[26] Fuller described them picturesquely:

> There is a generation of people who, to enhance the reputation of their knowledge, seem not only, like moths, to have lurked under the carpets of the Council table, but even, like fleas, to have leapt unto the pillows of princes' bedchambers, thence deriving their private knowledge of all things which were not done or thought of.[27]

Both Addison and Swift inveighed against such 'prostitute writers', as Gulliver called them, 'who will repeat the discourse between a prince and his chief minister, where no witness was by'. Tenison had brushed them aside ('Men who mete with their own measures think no man can be great and innocent too'), and Carteret thought any faults attributed to Bacon by the libellers, as they were begotten by malice, could be left in oblivion. But he took the trouble to refute a number of their allegations.[28]

The man particularly alluded to by Fuller – and refuted in detail by Bishop Sanderson – was Sir Anthony Weldon, author of *The Court and Character of King James* (1651). Notorious in his own time as the most 'malicious-minded' of authors, Weldon was rightly labelled in ours 'as scurrilous a chronicler as ever set pen to paper'.[29] A Puritan animated by personal resentment against the English Court, from which he had been expelled for a libel against the Scottish one, he professed to have been an ear- or an eye-witness of every one of the 'secret passages' he presented, or to have had it straight from one of the principal actors, and he promised 'unquestionable, undeniable' truths. His preliminary verses are his best introduction:

> Reader, here view a picture of our times
> Drawn to the life: the foulest secret crimes
> Discovered with their authors . . .

The book fulfils this programme. It moves from the 'venomous and cankered' disposition of Northampton to Lake's 'mean birth and meaner breeding' (his wife beat him, and he won the King's ear with bawdy revelations about all the great men at Court); from Bishop Williams, who, he declared, exceeded even Bacon in bribery, to Buckingham's 'unchaste pleasures'. But Weldon's favourite theme was hatred. He was never so pleased as when he could write that 'the Duke and Bristol hated each other mortally'; 'the King did now hate Buckingham' or, better still, 'Buckingham's extreme hatred to the King was believed the cause of his speedy death'; or that Yelverton told Buckingham to his face, 'the King your master hates you more than any man living.'[30]

We will not be surprised therefore to find Bacon, as a prominent member of the Court Weldon was thus reviling, presented in his pamphlet as 'an arrant knave . . . apt in his prosperity to ruin any that had raised him from adversity', and as so obviously 'the worst among the basest' that baseness is coupled with his name six times in one paragraph. There were 'never so many brave parts and so base and abject a spirit tenanted together in any one earthen cottage as in this one man', Weldon declared, 'nor could any age but a worthless and corrupt in men and manners have thought him worthy such a place of honour.'[31] 'Very hard language', wrote Carteret, 'of a man so eminent and well-known, and this from a person of no character at all, or which is worse, a very bad one.'[32] Weldon had advanced his allegations against Bacon without a shred of evidence and in contradiction to all the known facts, as Carteret proceeded to demonstrate in detail, a century before Macaulay published his essay. Nevertheless they were to inspire a long line of detractors, from Macaulay to this day.

Weldon must at times have been that moth under the carpet, for he picked up, or rather invented, a few very peculiar scraps of gossip. One of them may serve as an example. When Bacon was in disgrace with Buckingham for having advised against his brother's marriage to Coke's daughter, and had written to the King with dignity that he had rather go against Buckingham's mind than against his good, Weldon presents him sitting on an old wooden chest in the favourite's antechamber, among the lackeys ('such as for his baseness were only fit companions'), for two whole days ('myself', said the omnipresent Weldon, 'told a servant of my Lord Buckingham it was a shame'), and when admitted at last, falling flat on his face and kissing Buckingham's feet.[33] The King, Weldon recalls (regardless of the fact that he had by this time already been expelled from Court), read out Secretary Winwood's letter complaining about Bacon to Buckingham and to Weldon himself, 'and we were very merry'. 'Good God!' exclaimed Sanderson in his reply to the pamphlet, 'The King opens his bosom to him at that instant when this man so vilely studied and plotted his Sovereign's and that Kingdom's dishonour?'[34] Carteret thought the facts here presented so improbable that they were not worth refuting. Not so Macaulay. 'Unhappily,' he commented, when retelling it, 'there is little in the character either of the favourite or the Lord Keeper to make the narrative improbable.'[35]

Weldon was the most vicious, but by no means the only libeller of the Stuart Courts, and of Bacon. Arthur Wilson, in his *Annals of King James I* (1653), written at the instigation of Essex's son, the third Earl, described Bacon, with the same glee, as 'the true emblem of human frailty'. After condemning others for similar crimes, he wrote, Bacon came to suffer them himself as a delinquent, they being 'proved and aggravated against him' and 'falling very foully on him'. Wilson, a picaresque character, who lived quite shamelessly, begging, tricking, duelling, repenting, and starting all over again – and bragging of it all in his autobiography – was repudiated by the serious historians of his time.[36] His testimony, wrote Sanderson, was 'so utterly worthless as to be wholly unworthy of credit', and Heylin branded his *Annals* as a 'most infamous pasquil of the reign of the King'.[37]

Sir Simonds D'Ewes, whom we have already seen heaping gross insults on Bacon's head, nursed the same bias against James and his Court as did Weldon and Wilson. In 1729, when his *Autobiography* first appeared, the historian, Thomas Hearne, for many years Librarian at the Bodleian, pronounced its author totally unfit to write a history of England. Sir Simonds D'Ewes, he wrote,

> lived in times when every step was taken to render the kingly power disgusting, and set it in a disagreeable light. He has drawn the character of the King under whom he was born in the strongest terms of abhorrence. While we spurn at the detested Cecil and Carr, we shudder to find the learned Bacon involved in the same censure . . . His account of Bacon is eminently malignant, indeed it ought never to have been written unless it had been substantiated by undeniable evidence.[38]

D'Ewes devoted a whole chapter of his *Autobiography* to the 'Fall and Great Vices of Sir Francis Bacon'. The Chancellor, he wrote, lost his Seal

> for his notorious and base bribery . . . His vices were so stupendous and great that they utterly obscured and outpoised his virtues. For he was immoderately ambitious and excessive proud, to maintain which was he necessitated to injustice and bribery, taking sometimes of both sides.[39]

After speaking elsewhere of the much hated Cecil, whose 'subtle head', he maintained, had contrived the death and destruction of the Earl of Essex, D'Ewes added that Francis Bacon was 'much hated also for his ungrateful treachery to that Earl'.[40] Except for Buckingham's unjust reproach, noted above, this is the only known reference made by a contemporary to Bacon's supposed ingratitude. Carteret was surely right in regretting that Bacon's dealings with Essex had not been set forth 'by men of knowledge and capacity, but left to the pens of such' people as resorted only to memoirs 'enlarged and pieced by their own fancies'.[41]

From these writers, refuted by all serious historians in their own and later times, Macaulay drew not only Bacon's principal vices – ingratitude from D'Ewes, servility from Weldon, ambition and greed from all of them – but the ready-made paradox of Bacon's character. His whole 'Essay on Bacon' swings like a pendulum with their time-worn antitheses. Marching in step with them, he echoed D'Ewes, for whom Bacon's life of brilliant scholarship 'might have been as glorious as by his many vices it proved infamous'; Wilson, in whom Bacon was seen to 'fly so high above reason and yet fall so far below it'; and Weldon, who had exclaimed, 'thus behold him, a memorable example of all that is great and exalted, of all that is little and low.'[42] And he outdid them all with the famous tirade that students in the second half of our century were still being taught to admire, evoking 'the checkered spectacle of so much glory and so much shame'.[43]

Early in the eighteenth century the anti-Stuart libels were perpetuated by the satirists of a new generation, and we find them again denounced, this time by an anonymous 'Lover of Truth', inveighing against that 'low race of men' who 'spend their lives writing libels and lampoons against the best men of their times . . . well knowing the pleasure the generality take in reading the most ill-natured scandalous pieces that can be published'. 'Lover of Truth' was denouncing an article published in the *London Journal* in 1725 in which the 'candid, generous and unresenting Lord Bacon' had been treated as a delinquent.[44] Its author, 'Britannicus', a notorious Government sycophant and known for his savage attacks on his enemies, political and personal, had made Bacon his target, not doubting, exclaims this impassioned critic, that what he has advanced will pass for the truth, and thereby gladden his wicked heart through a belief that he has in part destroyed the character [of one who] stood high in the opinion of mankind; [whose] name and memory is now as universally revered and respected at home as it was, before his death, in foreign parts.[45]

Britannicus had copied his text from Wilson. In 1732 a leading article in this same paper repeated Anthony Weldon's remarks about Bacon almost word for word. 'Though covered *with learning*, so covered that his *sense* could not many times be seen through it', Bacon 'was one of the *meanest* men in the world, vicious in prosperity and an abject coward in adversity'.[46]

Ignorance about Bacon could be expected in an official anti-Tory paper, disposed to be rude to anyone connected with the hated Stuarts. But it is surprising to find an illustrious poet, whose sympathies were entirely on the Tory side, expressing the same harsh paradox two years later, in verses so striking – and so quotable – that they set the stage for Macaulay's Essay:

> If Parts allure thee, think how Bacon shin'd,
> The wisest, brightest, meanest of mankind.[47]

Alexander Pope's couplet appeared in his famous poem, *An Essay on Man*, published in 1734 and followed immediately by numerous editions and translations into most European languages. From that day to this, the couplet has been served up *ad nauseam* in prefaces and articles about Bacon, without reference to the disapproval it aroused in his own time or to the blame Pope has since received for his 'shallow epigram'.[48] It is the more surprising, since Pope thought nothing 'so odious as a libeller', to find him sinking to the level of a Britannicus (who had also maligned his own 'chief intimate', the fallen Atterbury, in closely similar terms), and taking his view of Bacon from a libellous article in the *London Journal*.[49] Carteret dismissed his lines in a few words. 'To the memory of such a man' it could be of no importance if Pope, 'forgetting at once the distance and the resemblance of their characters, suffered his petulant muse to say, *If parts allure thee* . . . His glory cannot be blasted by such envious flashes as these.'[50]

A. B. Grosart, the nineteenth-century editor of poets, was not so sanguine. The wrong which Pope had done with his 'false and perverse' lines 'on the great, but human Chancellor' was the more inexcusable, he wrote, in as much as all his recorded sayings reveal that Pope did not believe it himself; 'only it was too smart and good a thing to be suppressed.'[51] That he did not believe it is amply confirmed by Joseph Spence, a close friend of Pope's, who regularly noted down his confidences throughout their long acquaintance, and whose *Anecdotes* are looked on as a reliable record. Pope was not lavish with his praise, he preferred to 'bite'. But we will find here not one remark about Bacon that does not express unstinting admiration and sympathy for the man who, a hundred years before him, had filled his eyes with the same sights he now looked on, from the riverbanks of his own 'Twickenham retreat' – to use Bacon's expression.[52] It is clear from Spence's pages that Bacon held a very high place in Pope's regard. Nor is there a trace of disapproval or disparagement of Bacon in any of Pope's writings, aside from the fatal couplet whether he is indignantly reproving the dunces:

> 'Tis yours a Bacon or a Locke to blame,
> A Newton's genius, or a Seraph's flame.

or other inferior beings:

> Shades that to Bacon could retreat afford
> Are now the portion of a booby lord!

or resting his mind's eye upon Bacon's face, among those of his fellow thinkers whom their country would soon 'lovingly commemorate in sculptured medals':

> Then future ages with delight shall see
> How Plato's, Bacon's, Newton's looks agree.[53]

How can we reconcile these lines with the contemptuous couplet? Why should a booby lord not enjoy shades that had refreshed a far more despicable Chancellor? And who could look with delight on the meanest of mankind? Still less find in him 'the divine in man', which, Pope explained, was the source 'of Newton's light, of Bacon's sense'?[54]

Pope's couplet becomes even more inexplicable when we consider the extent of Bacon's influence on him. His variations on some concisely expressed Baconian notion, complete with Baconian image, have been remarked on by commentators from his own time to ours, and some of his borrowings have become proverbial ('A little learning is a dangerous thing,' or 'Bear, like the Turk, no danger near the throne').[55] His lines relating beauties which 'no precepts can declare' to the 'nameless graces of music' recall Bacon's on the beauty 'a picture cannot express', if not 'by a kind of felicity, as a musician that maketh an air in music, and not by rule'.[56] Echoes of Bacon are found among Pope's political observations, his projects for learning and his speculation on questions physical and metaphysical. He was reputed to have been 'remarkably fond' of the *Essays* (his annotated copy is in the British Library). But it is on the subject of virtue or 'moral philosophy' that Pope most frequently resorted to 'the meanest of mankind'. The practical suggestions for 'medicining the mind', set down by Bacon in the *Advancement of Learning*, are foundation stones for the system of Ethics that Pope sought to embody in the very *Essay on*

Man in which his famous couplet appears; and where, he announced to his readers, he 'proposed to write some pieces on Human Life and Manners, such as, to use my lord Bacon's expression, *come home to men's businesses and bosoms*'.[57]

The passions, Bacon had written, though 'they behold only the present', 'carry an appetite for good'; in Pope, they see 'immediate good by present sense'.[58] But 'lack of some predominant desire, that should marshall and put in order all the rest, maketh man's heart hard to sound or find.' Knowing their 'predominant desire is the surest key to unlock the minds of men': without it their hearts remain 'inscrutable', and there can be no improvement. We should therefore examine men's natures and ends, 'and find what it is that predominates and directs all the rest'. Once this is achieved, the mind can be gently trained through 'habit and experience', as we harness 'the predominant affections to suppress and bridle the rest'.[59] 'This clue once found', writes Pope, 'unravels all the rest.' We can now take 'Nature's road', treating 'this passion more as friend than foe', and, through 'attention, habit and experience', practise 'the virtue nearest to our vice'.[60] The 'clue' – which, Pope believed, made human nature 'plain' – is the 'ruling passion' every man is born with. Driving off all others, it continues with him until death; and it is in death that it is most strongly felt, as Bacon and Pope agreed.[61] This concept of the ruling passion is seen today by Maynard Mack, Pope's principal editor and biographer, as the central thesis of the *Essay on Man* (indeed of his whole *Opus Magnum*), and as the poem's one claim 'to originality of a sort'.[62] Pope could have found it in other writers (including Montaigne, who described 'a notion of the soul that overrules all others'), but it is Bacon who set it forth most completely. And, as so often, it is with two vivid Baconian images that Pope illustrated the power of 'one master passion' – 'the Mind's disease' – over man.[63]

Could Pope have developed the central principles on which his poem is founded in such close connection with those of a man whose whole life, as he declared in that same poem, belied them? If so, must we suppose, with Grosart, that he had the *meanness* to launch a damaging epigram which he knew to be false, on a man of whom he thought so highly, merely because he could not resist the opportunity of being quoted down the centuries?[64] A plausible case was made by H. Kendra Baker in 1937 for the possibility that he had never intended his couplet as an epigram.[65] The term 'mean' today normally describes a defect which Pope more often described as 'base'. Like many of his contemporaries, he generally used the word 'mean', of himself and others, in the sense of 'modest, unassuming, lowly' (occasionally with the connotation, irrelevant here, of low birth or degree). Thus when invoking the blessing of the great poets on his work, he cried: 'Oh may the spark of your celestial fire / The last, the *meanest* of your sons inspire!'; or wrote, in a prayer, '*Mean* though I am, not wholly so / Since quickened by thy breath.'[66] This acceptance of the term, as Pope would realize, was not improperly applied to Bacon, who, while he claimed to be no more than one 'who rings a bell to call others together' – which 'is the *meanest* office' – was conscious that 'our *meanness* attempteth great things'.[67] Meanness in the sense of 'unassuming' was a quality Pope greatly admired, and another man has since explicitly admired it in Bacon. It is this spirit, wrote Macaulay, for which we 'almost forgive Bacon all the faults of his life . . . this majestic humility, this persuasion that nothing can be too insignificant for the attention of the wisest, which is not too insignificant to give pleasure or pain to the *meanest*.'[68]

Seen in the context of his somewhat involved argument, Pope's use of Bacon as an example makes a good deal more sense this way, for throughout the section of the poem in which he invokes the brightest and meanest of mankind – 'Nature and State of Man with Respect to Happiness' – he is contrasting eminence not with vice, but with felicity:

> More rich, more wise; but who infers from thence
> That such are happier shocks the common sense.[69]

A series of examples (with more Baconian echoes) reviews the cases of people who have enjoyed riches, yet suffered every misfortune, from disappointment to ridicule.[70] After that, under the subheading '*Superior Talents*, with pictures of infelicity in Men possessed of them all', the sufferings of the wise and gifted are described as those of blameless martyrs – a Sidney or a Socrates, content, when they fail in their aims, to 'bleed'.[71]

> In parts superior what advantage lies?
> Tell (for You can) what is it to be wise?
> 'Tis but to know how little can be known;
> To see all others' faults, and feel your own;
> Condemned in bus'ness or in arts to drudge . . .
> All fear, none aid you, and few understand.
> Painful preheminence! yourself to view
> Above life's weakness, and its comforts too . . .
> Think, and if still these things thy envy call,
> Say, would'st thou be the man to whom they fall?

They fell to Bacon, and he is the only example named:

> If parts allure thee, think how Bacon shin'd,
> The wisest, brightest, meanest of mankind.[72]

The 'You' addressed is Pope's revered friend and patron, Lord Bolingbroke, superior in his eyes, he told Spence, 'to anything I have seen in human nature'. And it was with both Bolingbroke and Bacon in mind that, in conversation with Spence, Pope once dwelt on the 'painful preheminence' which is 'one of the misfortunes of extraordinary geniuses'.[73] We should also note that Pope's early critics saw no meanness in Bacon. Joseph Warton, his first editor, who traced Bacon's influence on Pope's life as well as on his works, when illustrating his line on 'unthought frailties' of the wise, alluded to Bacon with an indulgent smile.[74] And the poet John Dennis, replying to a satirical remark of Pope's against himself, recalled the 'cruel treatment' which extraordinary men, Bacon in particular, had received from their country for the past hundred years.[75]

Now if 'meanest' is taken in its usually accepted sense, Pope's line on Bacon would be his first and only departure from his argument in the *Essay on Man*: the contrast between 'preheminence' and happiness. A remarkable, and entirely gratuitous inconsistency. Yet we must not forget that the contrast between 'learning' and 'meanness' had been used about Bacon by the 'libellers', and that Pope indulged in similar paradoxes, and was quite capable of inconsistency.[76] A long line of scholars has taken the pejorative meaning of 'the meanest' for granted, beginning with Warton and ending with Maynard Mack, and this must be accepted as the view of those who know Pope. But among those who know Bacon, Benjamin Farrington, who in the 1950s and 1960s wrote a number of illuminating studies on Bacon's life and works, and published three of his philosophical treatises in English for the first time, believed that Mack was thereby doing Pope an unforgivable injury.[77] If the experts on Pope are right, by disowning a lifetime of affectionate admiration for the man he had made his model, he would be the one person of any repute in his century to deny Bacon the moral worth which the poet's own friends, Cowley and Addison among them, accorded him. And Carteret would be justified in pointing out that Pope had forgotten, not only how close he was to the man he was maligning, but how great was the distance between them – a distance measured by those who know both of them, not so much in 'virtue' or in 'parts', as in amplitude and depth of spirit. Be that as it may, and whatever Pope's real intention, his seemingly paradoxical couplet – so carelessly tossed off, so easy to recall – was to do considerable damage to the reputation of the man he wholeheartedly admired. Though not until Macaulay had taken it up and turned it into a hundred pages of resounding dichotomies.

28

The Two-Souled Monster

Disregarding Pope's epigram, the historians of the early 1800s continued to pass judgement lightly on the fallen Chancellor. Before Macaulay arrived on the scene the general tendency was to look briefly at the single flaw that had brought about Bacon's fall, and pass on. In 1813, 'A New Editor' of the *Essays* (anonymous) confirmed Carteret's verdict: 'Peace be to the failings of this wonderful man! They who alone were affected by them, his contemporaries and himself, have long since passed to their account.'[1] In 1822 Lucy Aikin drew a vivid picture of Francis Bacon, the active, resourceful, efficient reformer, popular in the House of Commons, loving and loved by his learned friends in England and overseas; even though, as a Whig historian, she could not look upon the servant of King James as other than 'the base betrayer of the rights and liberties of his fellow countrymen'.[2] In 1827 Henry Hallam, another Whig historian, still placed Bacon among the greatest men the country had produced for his political writings, and thought that his principles were constitutional, if his practice (allegedly) was not; and he remembered one illegal monopoly on which Bacon had refused to set the seal. 'Yet', he added, with more puzzlement than conviction, 'the general disesteem of his contemporaries speaks forcibly against him, Sir Simonds D'Ewes and Weldon, both indeed bitter men, given him the worst character.'[3] In failing to note that the better historians of Bacon's time had given his two authorities a thoroughly bad name, Hallam showed the damage libels can do. A last fair *Character of Lord Bacon* was published in 1835, two years before Macaulay's essay.[4]

After 1837 the tone changed radically. From bemoaning the frailty of man in piously conventional terms, and occasionally expressing alarm at the general 'infirmity of human nature', the writers of ever longer biographies moved into distress and moral indignation.[5] Macaulay expatiated sorrowfully on Bacon's faults, and others followed suit, until towards the end of the century Dean R. W. Church could begin his book with the sad confession that 'the Life of Francis Bacon is one which it is a pain to write or read'.[6] But in telling his story Macaulay was faced with an obstacle which all his followers would have to deal with: the other Bacon. When he turned from the meanest – not only of his country but of all mankind – to 'the great apostle of experimental philosophy', Macaulay was as extreme in admiration as he had been in scorn, and after sixty pages of detraction there follow forty of extravagant praise.

> In keenness of observation he has been equalled though perhaps never surpassed. But the largeness of his mind was all his own. The glance with which he surveyed the intellectual universe resembled that which the Archangel, from the golden threshold of heaven, darted down into the new creation. [Bacon's wit] possessed him to a morbid degree . . . the feats which he performed were not merely admirable but portentous and almost shocking.[7]

We appear to be dealing with an entirely new person. The man whose desires 'were set on things below' – and who indulged in torturing his fellows – now has for the object of all his speculations 'the multiplying of human enjoyments and the mitigating of human sufferings'. Bacon had cringed abjectly throughout the first half of Macaulay's essay; we now find in him 'a singular union of audacity and sobriety'. He has become, in life, the 'great English teacher'; in death a martyr to experimental philosophy.

It was in an attempt to tie these ends together – or perhaps just to bypass his dilemma by carrying his readers off their feet – that Macaulay delivered the famous page of rhetoric which has been quoted alongside Pope's couplet from that day to this. 'Alas that his civil ends did not continue to be moderate', as he had declared. Had it been so, to cite only a few of the ringing parallels,

> we should not be compelled to regard his character with mingled contempt and admiration, with mingled aversion and grati-tude . . . We should not then regret that there should be so many proofs of the narrowness and selfishness of a heart, the benevolence of which was large enough to take in all races and ages. We should not then have to blush for the disingenuousness of the most devoted worshipper of speculative truth, for the servility of the boldest cham-pion of intellectual freedom . . . We should not then be forced to own . . . that he who first summoned philosophers to the great work of interpreting nature was among the last who sold justice. And we should conclude our survey of a life placidly, honourably, benefi-cently passed . . . with feelings very different from those with which we now turn away from the checkered spectacle of so much glory and so much shame.[8]

The black and white checkerboard was thus launched, a good simile for the perplexing two-headed monster Macaulay had engendered with so much gusto. 'Bacon was all himself' when 'apologizing abjectly' for his opposition to the Queen in Parliament; and some twenty pages later, when 'branded with dishonour', he turned to those noble studies he had never forsaken, 'Bacon was Bacon still.'[9] But which Bacon was he? How often, as a later biographer exclaimed, must he have uttered with Faust the despairing cry, 'Zwei Seelen wohnen ach! in meiner Brust!'[10]

With Lord Campbell's 'Life of Lord Bacon', one of his series of *Lives of the Lord Chancellors* (1845–7), the monster was back in full strength. Damned by professional historians, including Gardiner, as 'among the most censurable publications in our literature', this work was shown up soon after it appeared as 'a compound of unblushing plagiary and unscrupulous misrepresentation'.[11] Yet because of Campbell's eminence as a judge and chancellor, regardless of all scholarly criticism, the 'Lives' were a success in their time, and became a standard work for consultation. Forcibly presented and very readable, they went into edition after edition, and, as the historian J. A. Froude remarked after ten years, 'threatened to take a permanent place in English literature'.[12] Their influence may be appreciated from the title of an American work published a few years later: 'Atrocious Judges, Lives of Judges Infamous as Tools of Tyrants and Instruments of Oppression, Compiled from the Biographies of John, Lord Campbell, Lord Chief Justice of England'.[13] Campbell's 'Lives' were riddled with gross errors of fact (nearly always unfavourable to his subject), which is perhaps not surprising, as he had taken no more than four busy professional years to cover a hundred and fifty chancellors. None the less, in 1984 an eminent judge was still taking his facts about Bacon from Campbell's mis-statement.[14]

Froude, in 1854, denouncing Campbell's many false pronouncements about Sir Christopher Hatton, remarked on Campbell's supreme disregard of any criticism of his mistakes. A typical 'correction' is the one he made when challenged as to his authority for the remark that Hatton was 'idle and volatile'. In the next edition, the line was altered to 'he is said to have been idle and volatile'.[15] Spedding, meanwhile, had published in *The Examiner*, in 1852, a list drawn up in parallel columns, of twenty-eight out of some sixty serious blunders he claimed to have found in Campbell's 'Life of Lord Bacon', with his corrections. When in 1853 a new edition of this 'Life' was published separately in the popular 'Railway' series, Spedding noted that only three errors had been corrected. As he pointed out soon after (in a small volume, signed 'A Railway Reader'), some of the remaining blunders had been made less obvious, but most of the statements he had challenged stood 'uncorrected, undefended, unnoticed'. The number of *The Examiner* where his article had appeared, he surmised, was by then bound into some unwieldy volume, if not in the waste-paper basket, while the *Lives of the Lord Chancellors* continued to be consulted and quoted. As for Campbell's 'Life of Bacon', it 'glows scarlet on every railway-stall, and may be had for half a crown'.[16]

The mistakes in this book are often five or six to as many lines. Typical is the omission of the first part of Bacon's speech in the 1601 Parliament in support of a proposal to abolish monopolies, so that he is made out to have 'taken a most discreditable part' in opposing them, when in fact he supported them. Campbell corrected this mistake, and promptly introduced a new one: Bacon's 'abusive attempt' (his insistence 'that the proper course' for the abolition of the royal prerogative of monopolies 'was humbly to petition the Queen') was, said Campbell, defeated. On the contrary, it was adopted, and if the House was, as Campbell put it, 'thrown into an ecstasy of gratitude', it is precisely because the conciliating approach advocated by Bacon was matched by a conciliating Queen, who gave the grace before it was asked for.[17] Herewith a last example of this author's practice. During the trial of the Earl and Countess of Suffolk, Edward Coke, he wrote, 'pursued his constant course, activity in detecting the offence and moderation in pursuing the offender' – a most unusual course indeed for Coke. Spedding found the explanation: copying word for word from a previous biographer (Montagu), Campbell had simply skipped a line. With the restored line (in italics), the remark reads: *'Bacon commended Coke to the King as having done his part excellently*, but pursued his own constant course: activity in detecting the offence, and moderation in pursuing the offender.'[18] This time the author corrected his mistake.

Campbell's story of Bacon was, as Spedding put it, a coarser version of Macaulay's. Occasionally he lifted a paragraph out of the original almost word for word, but he often improved on his model; and he went to the trouble of unearthing snippets of gossip from the libellers which Macaulay himself had turned down. (Rehashing Weldon's fabrication, for example, about Bacon waiting for Buckingham among the lackeys, he tells as a savoury fact what Macaulay had passed as a probable exaggeration.) 'It is with great pain', Campbell began, 'that I have found myself obliged to take an impartial view of his character and conduct.' The impartiality may be gathered from the headings of almost every page: 'His Atrocious Conduct', 'His Abject Apology', 'His Eagerness for the Great Seal', 'His Pretended Joy' (over the recovery of Lord Ellesmere). Campbell made no secret of his intention in writing this 'Life'. It was to show Bacon up for what he was, 'THE MEANEST OF MANKIND!!!'[19] Over Bacon's dealings with Essex the myth is in full sway. The 'unwise and unfortunate Earl', we learn, had – with 'the sincerest loyalty' – 'most earnestly done his best to serve his country'. It is now Bacon's 'selfish resolve' to meddle no longer that caused 'the fatal catastrophe which soon followed', Essex's rebellion. Had Bacon continued to visit Essex and warn him of the dangers involved, Campbell asserts, 'it would have been utterly impossible for that attempt . . . ever to have been hazarded'.[20]

Feelings of resentment or glee are gratuitously attributed to Bacon throughout these hundred and fifty pages, regardless of chronology. He is shown in 1593, for example, 'intoxicated with the success of his first effort' in Parliament, when in fact it was his fifth Parliament, and he had already spoken in two of them.[21] Appointed Lord Keeper, 'with what rapture must he have written the letters *CS* after his name!' (a rapture perhaps not unknown to his biographer, who was described in his time as a notoriously vain and ambitious man). 'To gain professional advancement, official status and political power,' Macaulay's imitator declares, 'there was no baseness to which he was not ready to submit, and hardly any crime which he would not have been willing to perpetrate. I still readily ackowledge him to be a great man, but can only wish he had been a good man.'[22]

No more than Macaulay did Campbell attempt to make any sense of his double Bacon. No one, he said, had yet written a 'Life' that explained Bacon's motives. Campbell longed to know 'as if we had lived with him' the man who – in a long series of black and white parallels outdoing Macaulay's – 'truckled to a worthless favourite with slavish subserviency' and gave the most admirable advice on legal questions; who, while cold-blooded and calculating, was 'a most delightful companion . . . merry and playful', with 'a smile both intellectual and benevolent'; who, though he was the meanest of mankind, 'had no mean jealousy of others', and while creeping abjectly, preserved his 'venerably pleasing majesty of manner'; and who 'amid his low, grovelling and disgraceful occupations' was 'indefatigably employed upon his immortal work'. On page 141 (as with Macaulay) Bacon was 'perfectly free from malignity', while on page 77 his biographer had never met with 'a greater display of vengeful malignity' than that he had shown in a letter to Coke (which Bacon could not possibly have written, and did not).[23] Yet – and this is a common feature among disparagers – where Campbell was most competent to judge him, Bacon had his critic's unconditional approval. As a statesman, he 'deserved high commendation'; his advice on Ireland was 'beyond all praise'. His wisdom and caution in reforming the statute book would, in what was still to be done, 'be our safest guide'. When a judge himself, he fulfilled the order he had promised with hundreds of statutes, 'wisely conceived and expressed with the greatest precision and perspicacity'.[24] Whatever else may have been wrong with Bacon, the one aspect of his life in which virtue was allowed him was that which, as a Lord Chancellor himself, Campbell knew best.

The historians who took up Bacon's defence against Macaulay and Campbell, however fallible, are not in the same category as his detractors. Even an uncritical, enthusiastic champion like Hepworth Dixon introduced much new documentary material into his two lively biographies (1861 and 1862), and is worth serious attention. As for Spedding, he devoted his whole life to exhaustively examining every scrap of evidence he could find about Bacon, and to setting forth his conclusions with the utmost objectivity. Out of reverence for the truth, as a contemporary pointed out, he stated 'with cautious reserve what a less conscientious writer would affirm as ascertained fact'.[25] From the results he finally published in his seven-volume *Letters and Life* (1861 to 1874), there emerges a man who strove to achieve high aims, and lived through forty years of public life with remarkably few acts of negligence or inconsistency; who was truthful and charitable, and erred, if anything, on the side of diffidence, and whose essential nobility was brought out by his very weaknesses. Spedding was aware that his two antagonists, when confronted with their mistakes, relied on the fact that their readers would probably not consult the sources quoted against them, and he did not hope to convert his own generation. His whole effort was to to make the evidence available to those born after 1850.

But historians of this quality fought a losing battle against Macaulay's vigorous partisan style. We will still find reasonably fair 'Lives' by such students of Bacon's philosophy as John Nichol (1888) and Thomas Fowler (1884). But whether in passing references or in full-scale biographies, most writers now presented Macaulay's two-headed monster, with the same high-minded reprobation, and in the same time-worn phrases. J. R. Green, for example, in his widely read *Short History of the English People* (1874, still in print in the 1960s), concluded, after a few disparaging remarks, that 'the grandeur and originality of Bacon's intellect' parted him from the honest patriots employed by Elizabeth 'quite as much as the bluntness of his moral perceptions'.[26] And B. C. Lovejoy, in a 'critical review' of Bacon's 'life and character' (1888), invoking Macaulay's 'honest and eloquent appeal' on behalf of 'the principles of morality that are eternal and universal', and citing that 'champion of judicial integrity', Lord Campbell, set out to reveal 'the frailty of the man, in order to avoid confusing his intellectual excellence with his moral weakness', an error against which the reader 'must fortify himself'.[27] By this time Macaulay had acquired a follower armed with far more subtle arguments than his own. The Reverend Edwin A. Abbott, a literary critic whom we have already come across as one of Bacon's most systematic detractors, expressed his increasingly sombre view of his character in a 160-page biographical introduction to the *Bacon's Essays* (1876); in *Bacon and Essex* (1877); and in a lengthy biography of Bacon (1885), which, recommended by Sidney Lee in 1898 as the best summary of Bacon's life, was more aptly described by J. M. Robertson in 1907 as a masterpiece of 'industrious injustice'.[28]

Though, like the others, he claimed to write 'with sorrow rather than with pity or unmixed contempt', Abbott was animated from the start by a passionate indignation against the man he was writing about. Among Bacon's 'great and numerous faults', the one flaw for which his contemporaries had sentenced him paled into insignificance: Abbott exonerated him from judicial corruption.[29] But he was so convinced of Bacon's low worth that when he came across a favourable remark about him, he would quote it in italics, with sarcastic intent. Only once did Bacon earn this critic's (almost) unqualified approval. Of his intervention, against the Queen's wishes, in the 1593 Parliament, 'it may almost be said it was the only unselfish and inconsistent action of which Bacon was ever guilty, and therefore it must not be passed over.'[30] (It was not: we have seen the capital made out this 'inconsistent' act by twentieth-century historians.) Abbott maintained that he had not 'knowingly omitted a single good or kind action of any importance' – and perhaps he had not; he simply obliterated them in a thick fog of mistrust.[31] He found in Spedding the facts of Bacon's life, but he twisted them out of all recognition. Proceeding by laborious, microscopic vivisection, he selected isolated expressions and feelings, spoken or written at different times, in a different context, and pieced them together into a superficially convincing mosaic. Any slight discrepancy is thus made to look like a deliberate falsification, any testimony of Bacon's becomes a dishonest elaboration.[32] Abbott's complicated accusations, many of them a tissue of contradictions, will have to be looked at with some care, since his indefatigable pursuit of detail, combined with a false appearance of fairness – sometimes achieved by adding back-handed praise to the blame he never withdrew, or by referring to a refutation he had tacitly set aside – looks so like assiduous research that late in our century students of Bacon have still been taking it for the real thing.

If disposed to embark on the saga of Bacon and Essex, Abbott's reader must renounce any attempt to rely on the principal source from which all historians so far had liberally drawn, Bacon's *Apology*. Basing himself on one lapse of memory over his use of an argument and on a single mistake of fact in the *Apology* – a misdating of no importance – Abbott claimed that, although without any 'definite and conscious falsehood', Bacon's 'chronic inattention' to 'inconvenient facts' led him to 'a complete distortion of history': he remembered, not what he said, but what he 'afterwards thought he should have said'. As a result, Abbott concluded, this record, although interesting from a literary point of view, 'can never be regarded as a contribution to history – unless it be the psychological history of the manifold and labyrinthine self-deception to which great men have been subjected'. Although neither substantiated nor justified, this assertion about a document which has been abundantly confirmed by contemporary evidence was to be echoed by many later detractors.[33] Meanwhile Abbott felt free to replace Bacon's sober story with the wildest speculation about its author's statements and motives.

Taking the latest accusations – Campbell's – one step further, he now described the tragedy of Essex as 'the tragedy of Bacon's degraded soul'. Bacon and Bacon alone, he declared, was responsible for both the rebellion and the execution of Essex. No illustration of his thesis was too absurd for Abbott's freewheeling imagination.[34] An Earl of Essex straight out of *Schoolboy's Own* is shown yielding to his own noble and altruistic impulse on behalf of his rival, Mountjoy, and jostling the Queen into appointing him her Commander in Ireland, solely 'to deliver Mountjoy from the perilous appointment'.[35] Bacon meanwhile, his own long-held and insistently urged views set aside – along with his passionate declaration in the *Apology* that the Irish command would be 'ill for the Queen, ill for him and ill for the State' – simply forgets what Abbott has known all along: that, far from advising against it, he had actually advised in its favour. Contemporary opinion, Abbott concluded, which unanimously condemned Bacon for 'the attempt to injure and destroy his friend', would have been 'ten times more vehement' if it had been known (as Abbott knew) 'how Bacon's advice and promptings led Essex to the very conduct which afterwards issued in his ruin'.[36] Abbott's uncritical follower, Sidney Lee, was soon to take this improvement on the myth one step further. Bacon, he asserted as a known fact, 'plainly told Essex that Ireland was his destiny', and 'steadily pressed his patron to seek the embarrassing post of Governor or Lord Deputy of the distracted country'.[37]

Lee was to embellish another episode on which Abbott had already done his best. Bacon, we will recall, had angered the Queen by staying away from the first arraignment of Essex. Before the York House proceedings, which he had strongly advised against, he asked her as 'one of her highest favours', so he tells us, to spare him from attendance – while accepting 'the entireness of duty' he owed to her.[38] Abbott saw duplicity in every word. 'To some it may appear', he remarked in 1877, that in writing these lines Bacon 'virtually sought the task which he affected to decline'. By 1885 insinuation had solidified into fact. Bacon is now shown requesting 'to have a substantial part assigned to him', and disappointed with a small one.[39] Soon afterwards, we will read in Sidney Lee's 'Life', as another statement of fact, that Bacon, setting to work 'with Machiavellian skill to turn an apparently unpromising situation to his own advantage . . . sought and obtained permission to appear at the inquiry into Essex's conduct.'[40]

From the semi-conscious, self-deceiving Bacon of the *Apology* we move to the deliberate deceiver of the *Declaration of Treasons*, the report on the trial of Essex of which Bacon had prepared the first draft. Here a piece of treasure-trove fell into Abbott's hands. In 1832, in his study of that report, David Jardine had published the original depositions of the prisoners, with notes jotted down by Coke in the margins, and a number of passages marked *om* (omit) in Coke's hand and in Bacon's. He concluded that the passages in question had been struck out by Bacon after the trial, with the intention of strengthening the Government's case against Essex, by presenting his rebellion as a more premeditated act than it was.[41] Campbell had also taken up 'this melancholy discovery', but before Abbott chimed in, Spedding had thoroughly sifted the matter, and proved the charge against Bacon 'absurdly wrong'.[42] Producing a complete text, with all the missing passages and discrepancies clearly marked, Spedding, as usual, placed his readers in a position to judge for themselves. Three things are clear from his analysis. First, that the facts Bacon was accused of suppressing from the depositions, which were attached to the report as appendices, were fully reported in the narrative of the *Declaration* itself. Secondly, that all the actual omissions, whether marked *om* or not, and whether or not Jardine had noticed them (he passed many by), had one obvious explanation: they were made to spare the reputation of people who were implicated in the conspiracy but whom it had been decided to pardon – because of their youth (Southampton, Rutland), or because Essex had accused them on insufficient grounds (Neville, Sussex and others). Thirdly, a number of passages were omitted because they told too strongly against Essex himself.[43]

Undeterred by disproof, Abbott simply repeated the charge of dishonesty, insisting that the confessions had been 'systematically mutilated by suppressions, and occasionally perverted'. The report, he said, 'must be put entirely on one side if we are to do justice to the folly of Essex in his outbreak, and to the unfriendly vigour and cruel unfairness of Bacon in the subsequent prosecution'.[44] Sidney Lee, as usual without bothering to verify his predecessor's conclusions, took up the refrain. Spedding's view, he wrote, 'cannot be upheld when the original authorities are carefully examined. Dr Abbott, in his "Bacon and Essex", has examined the evidence exhaustively, and Spedding's conclusions should be corrected by it.'[45] But both the *Apology* and the *Declaration* were confirmed up to the hilt by Essex himself. Abbott could not deny the authenticity of Essex's own confession, which substantiates all the conspirators' statements about his plans. Nothing daunted, this Dean of the Church declined to attach any importance 'to death-bed estimates and self-judgements made under a servile dread of hell and damnation'. When, 'cringing before the Supreme Being like a slave in prospect of the lash', the Earl 'discovered the whole scene' and accused himself of hypocrisy, Abbott was 'driven by all the evidence to believe that Essex was striving to make his peace with Heaven by taking his chaplain's view of himself'.[46]

Driven by the same kind of evidence, Abbott declared in his next book that Bacon was 'one of the most pernicious counsellors for a man in authority'. As his advice had led Essex to his ruin, so it led Charles I to his death; for Bacon was 'not following but guiding the King on the path that . . . brought his successor to destruction'. How, we may ask, can Bacon be made responsible for the execution of Charles I? By advocating, it appears from Abbott, 'a course which could but ultimately lead to conflict and revolution' – while, of course, it 'had the immediate effect of strongly recommending Bacon himself to the King and facilitating his advancement'.[47] Not that there was anything wrong with Bacon's advice to James. Abbott admitted that he 'honestly and earnestly' desired to see King and Parliament work harmoniously together. But he had 'no political backbone, no power of adhering to his convictions and pressing them on unwilling ears'. In 1614, for example, he proposed that James should levy no more impositions. But because he did not go further and insist that the King sweep away all the existing impositions (which James, needless to say, could not have done), Bacon 'must be regarded as one of the main agents in bringing about the abortive results of the Addled Parliament, and in preparing the way for a Civil War'. It was in Bacon's 'invariable subservient pliancy in the presence of great persons' that Abbott saw the cause of his evil influence. 'As he bowed to Nature . . . so he bowed to Kings.'

Yet when it came to proving his point, this dean's scholarly training got the better of him, and he often adduced more examples for the defence than he could produce for the prosecution. Thus, in any case, we are rightly told, do what he might, Bacon 'could not have persuaded James to change his nature'.[48] Bacon's frankness in criticizing Essex and others, and the 'lofty tone adopted by a young barrister of three and twenty when addressing his sovereign', could be explained: he was not yet 'fully grown in servility'. The very pliancy is sometimes justified. Bacon's 'subtleties of negotiation' with his royal masters were indispensable at Court in his day, and 'far from natural to him'; his 'gross flattery' of Cecil, Villiers and the King 'was probably not all flattery, but a sanguine view of particular persons'.[49] On one occasion Bacon is 'almost redeemed from the accusation of being too courtierlike' by the impression he gave 'that he really did mean a great deal of what he said'. Finally, as a flatterer, he was a failure, 'for he could not succeed in altogether divesting himself of an element of greatness', and James did not attach himself to the great.[50] True, but what is left of Abbott's basic charge of a pliancy so damaging that it brought about the death of a king?

Yet whatever he conceded in favour of the man who seemed to be always slipping between the meshes of his condemnation, Abbott remained firmly convinced that Bacon's motives for political action were necessarily of the worst. He based this conviction on a few pages in the *Advancement of Learning* which Bacon had devoted to a knowledge only too much practised, he said, but not as yet properly studied. He called it the 'Architecture of Fortune', after a favourite adage of his father's much quoted in the Renaissance: *Faber quisque fortunae suae* ('every man is the architect of his own fortune').[51] In these pages, said Abbott, Bacon drew 'too lively a picture to be pleasant of the arts with which he had become acquainted in the process of rising'. The arts in question, which by 1605, when he published this work, Bacon had not used to any great effect, since he had not yet begun to rise, included the art of accommodating oneself to other people, the art of showing off one's abilities to the best advantage, and a few other equally inoffensive social arts, practised, then as now, in all the capitals of Europe by every politician bred to the game. But Abbott, automatically assuming that these 'petty tricks' were the sole guiding principles of Bacon's career, claimed that they had established him in a meanness, 'hollow, false, demoralizing, fatal to all purity and nobility in social life, because it is – truth compels us to say it even of so great a genius – marvellously and portentously contemptible'.[52]

Far from launching a dangerous Machiavellian concept of political man, Bacon was candidly setting down actual practice as he had seen it carried out around him since childhood. His frankness in describing what everyone was doing – and no one was talking about – probably explains the success of his early essays on these subjects, as well as the fame of this particular section of the *Advancement of Learning*.[53] Burghley, wrote one of his biographers, practised what his nephew preached.[54] It was the other way round: Bacon described what Burghley had been practising long before he was born. But he did not preach it. Interested as he was in all human arts, he would allow this one only a modest place in his inquiry into moral and civil knowledge. Learning, he said, neither advises nor esteems it 'otherwise than as an inferior work, because no man's fortune can be an end worthy of his being'.[55] The most 'skilful carpenter of his own fortune', he would later point out, was Julius Caesar, who 'ever pressed forward', in search of 'personal aggrandizement' and power for power's sake, but he 'never once thought of restoring the common-wealth'. In the pages Abbott reproaches him with, Bacon compared 'those who press their own fortune' but 'are weak for government or counsel', to the ant, 'which is a wise creature for itself, but very hurtful for the garden'. And we will find that most of his precepts for the speedy advancing of a man's fortune are thus negatively qualified.[56] 'I did ever hold it for an insolent and unlucky saying, *faber quisque suae fortunae*,' Bacon had also declared, 'except it be uttered only as a hortative or spur to correct sloth.' He would prefer the sentence 'were turned to this, *faber quisque ingenii sui*' (the architect of his own character), 'which could teach men to bend themselves to reform those imperfections in themselves, which now they seek but to cover'. And it was 'as spurs to industry, and not as stirrups to insolency' that he used the phrase when begging Essex, by 'reforming and conforming', to be 'the architect of his own fortune'.[57]

Abbott, if ever he registered any such thoughts as these, qualified them as self-delusions. 'General objects', he was convinced, never induced Bacon 'to forget the particular object of self-aggrandizement'. Bacon's vision of himself as 'the faithful servant of the King but the trusted friend of the Commons' was all part of the delusion. He was 'so manifestly addicted to the constant contemplation of his own interest' that in him public considerations could not be disentangled from private ones – although no doubt, Abbott conceded, when explaining his ideals for the benefit of mankind, 'his self-deceit, if it was self-deceit, was as sincere as most of such convenient self-deceits usually are.'[58] Bacon's 'unsatiable ambition', the principal theme of Abbott's book, has become the constant refrain of historians in our century. Their very vocabulary betrays the origin of the prejudice noticed earlier, whereby few references are made, even in passing, to any useful contribution of Bacon's while in public service without the saving remark that of course he was striving primarily for his own advancement.[59] So convinced was Abbott of his thesis that everything he came across was made to agree with it. Thus when Bacon wrote that the 'envious dispositions' of misanthropes 'are the very errors of human nature', fit only to make 'politiques' of – who practise their corrupt art without caring 'what becomes of the ship of estates' – he was, Abbott concluded, recommending 'tortuosity and deceit' as a positive value in politics.[60] Nowhere did Bacon do so. He recommended that 'hard and severe' thing, 'to be a true politique'.[61]

But Abbott was past-master of slight changes in wording which alter the whole meaning of a sentence. With such equivocations we enter that area in Abbott which he himself so often claimed to find in Bacon, where self-deceit merges into deliberate deception. If, Abbott was prepared to concede, Bacon's rules for the betterment of one's fortunes were subject to the proviso that they should not interfere with the general welfare, they could be justified. 'But this cannot be shown.' His evidence: a few lines in 'Of Truth', where Bacon deplored all 'winding and crooked courses'. 'It will be acknowledged, even by those that practise it not, that clear and round dealing is the honour of man's nature, and that mixture of falsehood is like alloy in coin of gold and silver; which may make the metal work the better, *but* it embaseth it' (my italics). Replacing 'but', however, with 'though', Abbott changed the emphasis of these lines, and subtly altered their meaning. Bacon, he wrote, 'is obliged to admit that "mixture of falsehood is like alloy in coin of gold and silver, which may make the metal work the better," *though* the metal is debased by it'. Bacon, he added, 'considered this alloy not unfrequently necessary'.[62] Lee, as so often, finished Abbott's job for him. He introduced Bacon's thought with a tendentious interpretation of his own, and eliminated the last clause altogether. 'Practise deceit, dissimulation, whenever it can be made to pay,' he wrote in Bacon's name, 'but at the same time secure the reputation of being honest and outspoken.' Bacon is then made to confirm Lee's precept – not his own – with a truncated line: 'mixture of falsehood is like alloy in coin of gold and silver, which may make the metal work the better.'[63] Thus a plea for 'clear and round dealing' had been turned into a recipe for dissimulation and deceit.

In support of his thesis that Bacon's principal aim in life was the architecture of his own fortune (as, according to Aubrey, it was Ralegh's), another piece of treasure-trove fell into Abbott's lap from Spedding's busy editorial pen. This was Bacon's *Commentarius Solutus*, written in the summer of 1608, the only one of his diaries which has survived. In addition to his plans for the greatness of Britain, this covers, as he put it, 'all manner of form, business, study, touching myself, service, others, without any manner of restraint'.[64] Items entered 'for my particular' include his thoughts on the amendment of the law, efforts to 'call wits together' and to find pensions for a college of inventors; 'to apply myself to be inward with Lady Dorset' (the old Treasurer's widow, who might bestow funds for this college); to make use of the Attorney Hobart's weaknesses, of which there were plenty (he was later kicked upstairs to a place for which he was less unfit); and ways of recommending himself at Court – as, by trying to speak without panting. In this somewhat naive collection of suggestions to himself, which those who act constantly on such precepts would never bother to note down, there is nothing (so one of his more hostile biographers remarked) which 'a moderately ambitious politician would be ashamed to recognize in himself'.[65] And as Spedding had observed, if at the age of forty-eight Bacon needed to remind himself of the courtier's art, he cannot have been very good at it.[66] But Abbott, of course, was scathing. Taking Spedding up on this point, he replied out of the depths of his conviction. 'No mistake can be greater than to suppose that Bacon reminded himself in this extraordinary fashion of the duty of advancing himself in life ... The *duty* was *always* present to his mind' (Abbott's italics). In his diary, where he imagined Bacon was showing himself at his worst, Abbott was prepared to take him at his word, something he would not do where 'we find him making himself out much better than we have reason for thinking him to be'.[67]

Men, as Bacon told Villiers, were born 'not to cram in their fortunes but to exercise their virtues'. While making so much of his precepts for the 'Architecture of Fortune', Abbott passed over the series of rules that precede them, and to which Bacon gave a far greater importance. These rules were little written of, he said, and practised by few men, while the others are only too often in use. They are the perfect counterpart to the guidelines for politicians which Abbott inveighed against. 'The good government and composure of the mind I hold to be the chief firmament of human life,' Bacon declared. Moralists enjoined it, but failed to show how it could be achieved. He would like to see an art that could 'work out the knots of the mind, and make the mind sound and without perturbation, beautiful and graced with decency; strong and agile for all the duties of life'.[68] But before starting on this new 'tillage', which, after his favourite poet, Bacon called 'the Georgics of the mind', man must look deeply into 'the roots of good and evil, and the strings of those roots'. This traditional belief was central for him.

> Therefore it behoveth him which aspireth to a goodness not retired or particular to himself, but a fructifying and begetting goodness, which should draw on others, to know those points which be called in the Revelation *the deeps of Satan* . . . neither let any man here fear infection or pollution; for the sun entereth into sinks and is not defiled.[69]

Anyone disposed to doubt that the precepts set down in his 'Georgics' were the guiding principles of Bacon's life can turn to the letters in which he asked his friends to criticize his writings, or to the prayers with which he headed them, or to his lines on the joys of calling oneself to account – 'the pleasure of that *suavissima vita, in dies sentire se fieri meliorem*' (that delightful life in which one feels oneself growing better day by day).[70]

We know that Pope admired Bacon's pages on the tilling of the mind. Another man admired them: Macaulay. He devoted one of the white squares of his checkerboard to their praise. Bacon, he wrote, 'was far too wise a man not to know how much our well-being depends on the regulation of our mind'; he was thoroughly acquainted with man's cravings and his sufferings from 'poverty, disgrace, danger, separation from those to whom they are attached'; and 'it was precisely because he dug deep that he was able to pile high.' Unlike Abbott, Macaulay found in him 'no cant, no illusion', and he entirely approved of Bacon's search for practical methods by which men could cure the diseases of the mind, as he put it, not by 'the resounding nothings of the moralists, but by setting themselves rigorously to work'. How then could Bacon have combined such a keen interest in the cultivation of virtue with all the moral degradation Macaulay had found in him? Macaulay's solution of the puzzle was simple: he cut Bacon in two.

> Those only judge of him correctly who take in at one time Bacon in speculation and Bacon in action . . . In his library all his powers were under the guidance of an honest ambition, of an enlarged philanthropy, of a sincere love of truth. There no temptation drew him away from the right cause. Thomas Aquinas could pay no fees. Duns Scotus could confer no peerages.[71]

Bacon, of course, did not write his books in a Victorian library. He dictated them to young attendants in the leafy avenues or on the roof-tops of Verulam; and he certainly did not look to the 'schoolmen' for his mental companions. But this explanation satisfied Macaulay.

It could not satisfy the painstaking dean, as deeply fascinated as he was horrified by a character who 'the more he is studied, bewitches us into a reluctance to part from him as from an enemy'. Abbott devoted two chapters to 'The Problem' – which, like the schoolmen Bacon objected to, he had spun out of his own substance, with 'no great matter and infinite agitation of wit' – and to 'The Solution'.[72] He found 'something in the nature of a psychological problem in the contradiction between Bacon as he appeared to his friends and Bacon as he appears to us'. To them this man who 'loved and could love no one' seemed 'not only genial, kindly and affectionate, but also a bright example of lofty virtue'. The faults of which Bacon 'seems to stand convicted' appear to be

> Precisely of the kind that would repel inferiors and familiars in private life – [faults arguing] a disposition so lost to all sense of consistency and shame that we can hardly understand how a man guilty of such time-serving can have attracted a single sincere friend; [faults revealing] an absence of healthy moral instinct which – one might have expected – Bacon's immediate dependants and friends would not have been slow to detect.[73]

'The truest character', as Bacon remarked, 'comes from a man's own household.'[74] How then can he have presented to 'such intimate associates as Rawley, Boener and Toby Matthew a character of "ideal virtue"?'

But Abbott's puzzlement did not end there. How could Bacon 'retain so high an opinion of himself that self-respect is too weak a name for it? . . . do bad things and yet believe in his own particular goodness?' And do them deliberately, 'look them in the face before doing them, by setting them down on paper'? How could this man, who stooped to 'despicably mean' conduct, retain such a high self-respect? The answer, wrote Abbott, was a 'complicated' one. It had need to be, since he could not face the only solution to his non-problem – that Bacon's friends living near him in his own time knew him better, and knew him to be better – and so did Bacon himself – than Abbott 'thought he had reason for thinking him to be'.[75] Through ten long and convoluted pages of answer, Abbott fought his way towards a solution, without managing to explain away the virtue Bacon's friends saw in him. Finally, with a new twist to Macaulay's crude answer – the devoted truth-seeker tempted out of his library by the lure of fees – he reached the following conclusion. Bacon's 'inherent deficiencies' account for a part of his 'moral derelictions'. Because he 'could "strive for truth unto death" in Science but not in politics', he was increasingly drawn by his self-deceiving and self-indulgent nature to the excitements of a political life for which he was 'morally unfit'. But since he fatally subordinated every emotion and moral instinct to the pleasures of the intellect, it is to Bacon's 'enthusiasm for science' that we must look for the principal source of those moral derelictions. His 'crowning deliquency' was this. He was not 'a taker of bribes'. Neither riches, honour nor reputation were of any importance to him for their own sake, but he could not resist them

> when they presented themselves under the mask of friends and servants of Truth. It was Satan, tempting as the Angel of Light. And surely no story of unhappy wretches bartering away their immortal souls to the Evil One for a hollow pretence of present happiness, and afterwards beating themselves idly against the narrowing net that presses them towards the inevitable pit, is much sadder than the record of the retribution, artistic if ever retribution was, that befell this Traitor to Truth.[76]

Following this apocalyptic solution to the imaginary problem of Bacon's character, another critic would soon declare that Bacon opened men's eyes to the world around them but closed their minds to the world which lies within, and that he was a friend to no man; 'only the Truth, whose faithful servant he seems unswervingly to have been, could claim him for her own.'[77] Where but in a country as mistrustful of intellect as England so often is, could such a statement have been seriously advanced? But perhaps we should hear Bacon himself: 'Moral baseness cannot be allied with love of truth. Truth of being and truth of knowing are one.' And 'Certain it is that truth and goodness differ but as the seal and the print, for truth prints goodness.'[78]

Goodness being, as Bacon defined it, care for 'the weale of men'. For he subscribed to the view – immortalized by John Donne – that a good man's heart 'is no island, cut off from other lands, but a continent that joins them'. And he saw man's heart as a 'noble tree, that is wounded itself, when it gives the balm'.[79]

29

The 'Creeping Snake'

Abbott did not have to wait for a following. Among the historians of his own generation who immediately adopted his views was another dean, R. D. Church, whose *Bacon* (1884) was still recommended to students in 1980 as 'the best short account of his life'. Church admired Bacon so much that he could not pile on enough hyperbole:

> in temper, in honesty, in labour, in humility, in reverence, he was the most perfect example the world has yet seen of the student of nature . . . with whom the whole purpose of living and of every day's work was to . . . enlighten and elevate his race . . . [and whose] first and never sleeping passion was the search for knowledge at the service of man . . . No one ever had a greater idea of what he was made for, or was fired with a greater desire to devote himself to it.[1]

And so on. Yet, impressed against his will by Dean Abbott's relentless brief, Church found himself 'most reluctantly obliged to differ' from the admittedly 'high intelligence and honesty' of Spedding's work. 'It is vain', he cried, 'to fight against the facts' of Bacon's 'poor', 'vicious' and 'unhappy' life. And clearly Church had fought.

> With all his greatness . . . with all the charm that made him loved by good and worthy friends, amiable, courteous, patient, delightful as a companion, ready to take any trouble – there was in Bacon's 'self' a deep and fatal flaw . . . He chose to please man, not to follow what his soul must have told him was the better way.

Thus he was willing to 'hunt to death a friend like Essex', and with all his political wisdom and statesmanlike vision, though 'he had the courage of his opinions', Bacon did not have the public spirit to enforce them. His 'many deplorable shortcomings' came to this: he believed that men, like nature, 'must be won by yielding to them . . . and the ruin of a great life was the consequence'.[2] Macaulay and Campbell are present, but this is Abbott speaking.

A more important, and equally reluctant, casualty appears to have been the great eminence, Gardiner himself. There is a remarkable contrast (noticed in particular by B. H. G. Wormald in 1993) between the conclusions Gardiner reached about Bacon in his *History of England* (1869), and the views he expressed in his article on Bacon in the *Dictionary of National Biography* (1885).[3] Gardiner had no occasion to read Abbott until he set out to write this article, but he did so then, and while he expressly rejected some of Abbott's censure – and did not propose him for further reading, as he did Church – only the overwhelming effect of Abbott's persuasive denigration could explain the change of mood we find here. In 1869 Gardiner had written scathingly of that 'most brilliant of historians', Macaulay, when, following 'satirists who knew nothing of his life', he had 'painted the great statesman and the great philosopher in colours as odious as they are untrue to nature', because Bacon's principles did not square with those of a Whig politician. From his thorough study of the events Bacon was concerned in, Gardiner himself had learned to trust his truthfulness. Even his mistakes, as seen by the greatest of all the Whig historians, were no more than 'the errors of a generous spirit'. Bacon was not, Gardiner emphatically stated, 'that strange congeries of discordant qualities . . . never found united in any human being. He was not one man as a thinker, and another man as a politician. In every part of his career he was indefatigable in the pursuit of truth and justice.'[4]

In the *DNB*, however, sixteen years later, the discordant qualities, along with the 'lower part of Bacon's nature', are with us again. For the first time in Gardiner we hear of Bacon's boundless hopes of advancement, his misplaced optimism, his 'thorough hatred' of Cecil. Bacon's 'poverty of moral feeling cannot be denied', though his 'hypocrisy was for the most part unconscious', and 'he was not himself conscious of wrong.' In his letter of advice to Essex after Cadiz (against which Abbott had inveighed) 'Bacon unintentionally displays the worst side of his character as fully as he did afterwards in the *Commentarius Solutus*.' Finally, his alleged failure to recognize that it was impossible to bring James and the House of Commons together was rooted in his own 'moral and intellectual nature', and it 'led to the great catastrophe of his misused life'.[5]

If Abbott's bias could deflect such a clear mind as Gardiner's (as it appears to have swayed Joel Hurstfield's, many years later) it will not surprise us to find that he left a deep mark on the first few decades of our century.[6] His opinions were swallowed whole by the literary critics Sidney Leé (1904) and George Saintsbury (1920–22), who felt that all the necessary research had now been done for them, and while Bacon found defenders (such as J. M. Robertson in 1907, cited earlier), few historians were uninfluenced.[7] G. M. Trevelyan, in particular, whose *England under the Stuarts* (1904) was immediately successful and was still circulating in the 1960s, attributed Bacon's 'characteristic pettiness' and his ignorance of the very meaning of love, friendship and virtue to 'the absence of any lofty ideal of personal conduct', adding (again after Abbott) that 'the advancer of human learning could not read the book of human life'.[8] In 1926 the tercentenary of Bacon's death was fittingly celebrated by C. D. Broad with a lecture in Cambridge on the philosophy of Bacon.[9] But at the Rice Institute in Houston, where eminent members of academe also commemorated Bacon's works, they vied with each other to cry down his life. A professor of philosophy from Cornell University, invoking Pope and Macaulay, repeated all the hoary calumnies and added one from his private knowledge: Queen Elizabeth, it seems, 'never forgave the man who had been directly instrumental in causing [Essex's] ruin'. After which a professor of jurisprudence – reminding his hearers that Bacon 'had a record as an office-seeker that is likely to stand for all time', and pointing out that as a Chancellor 'he seemed intoxicated by his own greatness' – proceeded with his personal contribution to the legend: on Bacon's impeachment 'the righteous indignation of all England was centered on him' and 'the wrath of a people outraged by general misrule came upon him.' A professor of English history compared Bacon with Coleridge and Shelley – in whom, whatever their failings, 'something remained intact' – and discerned in Bacon the 'shrivelling' of a 'damaged soul'.[10] Meanwhile in England a literary critic could find

> nothing in the man that appeals to the universal heart; nothing to stir enthusiasm, nothing to win admiration. His literary partisans struggle desperately for his good name; but the utmost that their efforts, if successful, could gain for us is that we should refrain from condemning.[11]

In 1928 the complicated image of Bacon evolved by Abbott out of Macaulay's plain black-and-white one took a great leap ahead with the publication of Lytton Strachey's *Elizabeth and Essex* (discussed above in connection with the myth of Essex). Immediately translated into various languages, this highly readable book made publishing history in the United States, and was last printed in paperback in 1981. Strachey took Abbott's industrious injustice for serious research. His was a talent for turning straw into gold, and he transmuted the piecemeal collages into quick and fatal images, broadcasting Abbott's dim view of Bacon to a far wider public than the Victorian dean had addressed. Strachey's historical characters are known to have been largely fictitious, but, as Neale put it, 'they lived'.[12] In these pages a sincere, misunderstood Essex and a lethal Bacon, the villain of Strachey's piece, have lived on as he painted them. Here Abbott's self-deceiving deceiver is 'in his element' when in a position to poison the Queen's mind against his benefactor, and repeatedly experiences 'a peculiar satisfaction' at the thought of some new advancement. When Essex suggests making him Attorney General, Bacon quickly skips thirty years into the future. 'Ah, he smiled, judgeships! high offices of state, a peerage! Verulam, St Albans, Gorhambury – what resounding title should he take?' When his brother dies, thinking, of course, only of what he may inherit, Bacon contemplates his prospects of sensual and intellectual satisfaction against the background of a 'strange cackle' (Lady Bacon's mind gave way in old age, a subject Abbott had also exploited). As for Bacon's allegedly insidious omissions in the *Declaration of Treasons* (on which Strachey liberally embroidered), 'so small and subtle were the means by which Bacon's end was reached', said Strachey, that he may not have been conscious of what he was doing. 'Yet such a beautiful economy. Could it have risen unbeknownst? Who can tell? The serpent glides off with his secret.'[13]

It was Lytton Strachey who launched the image of a Bacon whose 'qualities blending, twisting, flashing together, gave to his secret spirit the subtle and glittering superficies of a serpent'. In this guise Bacon winds in and out of Essex's tragic story, hypnotizing its author. When Bacon wrote his by now notorious letter of advice to his patron: 'inspired with the ingenuous grandeur of the serpent, he must deploy to the full the long luxury of his coils'. When he spoke at the trial, 'the double tongue had struck, and struck again'. 'A serpent indeed', Strachey thought, 'might well have been his chosen emblem – the wise, sinuous, dangerous creature, offspring of mystery and the beautiful earth'. He wished 'to turn away from the unconscious traitor, the lofty-minded sycophant, the exquisite intelligence, entrapped and strangled in the web of its own weaving'.[14] But the weaving was Strachey's, and with his vivid image all the grovelling vices and unattractive, earthy virtues attributed to Bacon by previous detractors were given visible shape.

The metaphor is straight out of the *Advancement of Learning*. Bacon frequently resorted to the biblical contrast between the grovelling snake and the winged creature – angel or dove – to illustrate the essential unity of man's being, little dreaming that it would be seized on to depict him as the 'heart double and cloven' which he most despised.[15] 'Nowhere in the universal nature of things', wrote Bacon, 'is there so intimate a sympathy as between truth and goodness. The more should learned men be ashamed if in knowledge they be as winged angels, but in their desires as crawling serpents.' When he deprecated 'the Architecture of Fortune', the image came naturally to his mind: 'What advantage is it to have a face erected towards heaven, with a spirit perpetually grovelling upon earth, eating dust like the serpent?' And it was present when he urged the truth-seeker to face the 'deeps of Satan' in his own heart: 'It is not possible to join serpentine wisdom with columbine innocency, except men know exactly all the conditions of the serpent: his baseness and going upon his belly, his volubility and lubricity, his envy and his sting, and the rest; that is, all forms and natures of evil.'[16]

Discarding the unmistakable intention of these lines – which were Christ's injunction to his disciples – Macaulay turned them scornfully against their author:

> It did not require Bacon's admirable sagacity and extensive converse with mankind to make this discovery. Indeed, he had only to look within. The difference between the soaring angel and the creeping snake was but a type of the difference between Bacon the philosopher and Bacon the Attorney General, Bacon seeking for truth and Bacon speaking for the Seals.[17]

Abbott followed suit. How could a man 'creep like a snake in public and pose as an angel in private?'[18] And, after Strachey, few are the biographers who have failed to apply this metaphor to Bacon's life, some of them in passages of lyrical prose that rival his own. 'The sinuous mind could indeed twist and turn, loop and reloop, slide, untie and recover,' writes one of them in 1963, 'the agile mind could coil and curvet before it struck.'[19] Meanwhile another image used of Bacon in his lifetime came to reinforce it, a comparison probably made in all innocence, but now regularly recalled with a pejorative meaning which its author surely never intended. 'He had a delicate, lively hazel eye,' wrote Aubrey; 'Dr Harvey told me it was like the eye of a viper.' Aubrey was reminded of the eyes of Bacon's pupil Thomas Hobbes, like Bacon's 'of a hazel colour', and 'full of life and spirit'.[20] For a naturalist like Dr Harvey, the discoverer of the circulation of the blood and Bacon's personal physician – who, as again noticed by Aubrey, made many 'curious observations on frogs, toads and a number of other animals' – the viper's eye would not in itself have an unpleasant connotation. He may simply have meant to suggest a quicksilver liveliness in the human eye. But those who, after Strachey, turned the snake image against Bacon have been fascinated, one and all, by the 'cold viper gaze'; from which it is but a flash to the darting double tongue.

Strachey's much quoted summing up of Bacon's character is undiluted Abbott. 'Profound in everything but psychology', he declared, Bacon failed to know himself. In lines that echo the Victorian Dean's doom-laden denunciations, we learn that he 'could not see into the heart of things', that 'among the rest, his own heart was hidden from him,' and that 'his psychological acuteness, fatally external, never revealed to him the nature of his own desires.'[21] This 'fatally external' insight, though a blatant contradiction in terms, was to be attributed throughout the twentieth century to the man who conceived his essays as 'the inwards of things', until it was finally discovered that there are no 'inwards' to look into.[22] A failure 'to read the book of human life' is a strange diagnosis of one who was regarded in his time as 'a soul equally skilled in men and nature'; who, wrote Hume in the eighteenth century, 'had begun to put the science of man on a new footing'; who was looked on by Hallam, in the nineteenth century, as a greater philosopher of human nature than of the physical world; and whose influence on modern psychology, from Hobbes to our day, is increasingly appreciated.[23]

Once Bacon's degradation was established, the game was to hunt out new misdemeanours, preferably signs of meanness, however imaginary. Any trifle served as an excuse for a little extra blackening. Already in 1913, in a lecture delivered at the British Academy, Bacon had been stigmatized for failing to acknowledge an entirely hypothetical debt to Bernard Palissy, the great French potter and naturalist whose lectures he *might* have attended as a young man in Paris (though there is no proof that he was influenced, if he did attend them). Conceding that in any case in Bacon's time no one quoted his sources, the author of this lecture had in mind a philosopher 'unlikely to pay a generous tribute to any forerunner', who was now adding 'yet another to his meannesses by stealthily stealing the credit of the French working man'.[24] A new and even more improbable form of meanness was attributed to Bacon in an article on the essay 'Of Beauty' published in 1945, and recommended to students in 1985. In speaking of the awkwardness of youth compared with the graceful motion of the mature, Bacon, it appears, was 'consoling himself' for entering his fifties. Overlooking his many pages of praise for the magnanimous excesses of youth, into whose minds 'imaginations stream' better and 'more divinely', this critic adduced as a confirmation of Bacon's 'meanness' that he could thus 'belittle youth as a prop to middle-aged vanity'.[25]

As noted earlier, the trouble with smears so thoughtlessly distributed is that while it may take no more than a few lines to impress a lasting black mark on the reader's mind, as many pages are needed to present the actions in question in a more objective light. The following smirch is perhaps a more glaring example than usual. In a book entitled *The Charities of London* (1960), a Harvard professor, W. K. Jordan, remarked in passing that Sir Francis Bacon, 'ever-ready to bend a great mind to ignoble deeds', wrote an 'infamous brief' to King James in an 'outrageous attempt' to break the will of Thomas Sutton, endowing what was to become the famous charitable institution of Charterhouse.[26] The story is, briefly, as follows. Known as 'the richest commoner in England' (immortalized, some think, during his lifetime by Ben Jonson as *Volpone*, the Fox), Sutton had made his fortune buying up lands rich in coal, and had greatly increased it by marrying the widow of a wealthy old brewer and by lending out funds on a large scale to the landed gentry. He was courted by many, said Aubrey, 'hoping to have been his heir'; but on his death, in December 1611, it turned out that he had left all his money to charities, including the large sum of £8,000 for the maintenance of an alms-house and a boys' school in the old estate of Charterhouse, which he had recently bought from the Earl of Suffolk.[27]

A nephew of Sutton's, one of the 'poor kindred' Chamberlain mentioned as having been left out in the cold, disputed the will, and Bacon, then Solicitor General, as well as Legal Counsel for the nephew, was among those appointed by the Privy Council to report on the case. If the nephew were to win it, the Government would have more freedom to determine the exact terms of the bequest, and this interested Bacon, who had long-held convictions about the right use of charitable trusts.[28] The will of the testator, he wrote to the King, should not be interfered with so long as the bequest held good in law, or could be made good in equity. But if it turned out that a birthright had been 'planted in the heir', and the bequest came within the King's 'power and grace', Bacon, thinking in terms of a welfare state rather than private charity, expressed the wish that 'this rude mass and chaos of a good deed were directed rather to solid merit and durable charity, than to a blaze of glory' that would 'crackle' a while and 'quickly extinguish'.[29]

The bequest as it stood, wrote Bacon, with its far too high endowment of a single institution, would soon degenerate into 'a preferment to some great person to be master and to take all the sweet, and the poor to be stinted and take but the crumbs'. Bacon wanted, instead of 'one hospital of exorbitant greatness' (which could too easily become 'a corporation of declared beggars' or 'a cell of loiterers' and drunkards), a series of houses all over the country, so organized that they might 'take off poor of every sort' where they were most needed, and put them to such work as they could manage, with a view to eliminating beggary altogether. As for the school, he said, more scholars were bred by the grammar schools than the state could employ, 'unfit for other vocations, and unprofitable for that in which they are brought up'. Instead he wished 'Mr Sutton's intention were exalted a degree, that that which he meant for teachers of children, your Majesty should make teachers of men', by increasing the niggardly salaries of readers in the arts and professions at the universities. He concluded his proposal, hoping (with one of his favourite images) that thereby 'that mass of wealth that was in the owner little better than a stack or heap of muck, may be spread over your kingdom to many fruitful purposes'.

When the legal question was tried in 1613, before all the Judges of the Exchequer, judgement was given in favour of the will as it stood, and we hear no more of Bacon's proposal.[30] It was natural for the faithful alumni of Charterhouse, coming across his letter, to protest against arguments that assailed the principles of their foundation. But Bacon was expressing beliefs he had set forth in many of his writings. Whether or no he was right is not the point. In his own time Chamberlain thought 'Master Solicitor' had spoken 'wittily and ingeniously' against Sutton's will, while

Thomas Fuller disagreed on the schools, believing there could not be too many, since good would always flow out of them.[31] Carteret opined in 1747 that he had 'opposed this charitable institution from no other principle than that of an extensive charity'. In 1927 a usually denigrating writer concluded that with these proposals Bacon had shown himself 'wise beyond his century'.[32] And Trevor-Roper, in 1959, saw Bacon's efforts in favour of institutes for skilled training, rather than the grammar schools that turned out unemployable bureaucrats, as part of the enlightened mercantile policy which, in the countries that adopted it, was to avert revolution.[33] Our only conclusion here must be that with three lines of abuse Professor Jordan was able to give another twist to Bacon's reputation as a creeping snake, whereas it has taken as many pages – and could have done with quite a few more – to show how greatly he mistook Bacon's intentions in writing that 'infamous brief'.

It had become customary by now for historians and biographers to use Bacon as a foil for some other character closer to the author's sympathies. Not only had he been for a long time black knight to Essex's white one, and dry-as-dust pen-scratcher to the carousing author of Falstaff; he was also made out, in accordance with Whig tradition, a Tory traitor to Coke's defender of the people. Thus in an overseas broadcast on 'great figures of the bar' in 1947, a kindly and virtuous Coke was contrasted to Francis Bacon, 'a corrupt judge, servile and mean of soul'.[34] The comparison came down from Macaulay, via Abbott, who saw Bacon 'holding up to posterity for ever the contrast between his courtier-like servility and Coke's manly independence'.[35] Even Conyers Read described Coke in 1960 as a loyal and devoted public servant, where Bacon was exclusively 'for Bacon'.[36]

In 1952, in *The Murder of Sir Thomas Overbury*, by William McElwee, a villainous Bacon confronted a less than heroic hero. As Attorney General at the trial in 1616 of James's ex-favourite, the Earl of Somerset, and his wife, Lady Somerset, for the murder of his friend and mentor, Sir Thomas Overbury, Bacon was presented as implacably hostile to the accused, because of his commitment to George Villiers, the new favourite. The whole case, we are told, was a put-up job, in which Bacon played his part with the usual 'sycophancy of his all-absorbing ambition', 'threading his way' through the political labyrinth 'with contemptible skill', 'bullying and cheating his way through the accusation' – while making 'a great show of treating the accused with exaggerated fairness', and acting throughout with 'flagrant dishonesty', to 'his eternal shame'.[37] New biographers were soon to elaborate the theme. One, in 1960, gave Bacon the part of stage villain, ready to have a cloak thrown over Somerset's head should he say too much (while he fixed his 'viper eye' unswervingly on the prisoner). Another, in 1970, depicted him as an even greater scoundrel than the murderess, Lady Somerset (the subject of this author's book), as he moves with 'one glittering eye on the Lord Chancellorship', purrs when contented, weeps crocodile's tears, and foresees with that same 'beady eye' the downfall of the favourite.[38] None of this should surprise us when we consider that already in 1846 Bacon had been branded, in an extravagantly unhistoric narrative of the poisoning, as 'one of the most wicked men in recorded history'.[39]

These authors of fictitious history were apparently unaware that a century earlier Campbell had just as indignantly accused Bacon of being in collusion with the King 'to spare the two great offenders' and secure their pardon.[40] Still less did they seem to know that Carteret had praised the 'wisdom and caution' with which he had conducted himself in that affair, and Montagu the 'impartial and merciful treatment of a man whom in his prosperity he had shunned and despised'.[41] In real life Bacon had nothing to do with the reprieve of Somerset, in 1622, a year after his own fall, or with his pardon three years later – except to wonder why Somerset had been pardoned and he had not. Nor had he any obligations whatever to Somerset, during whose time of favour he managed to carry on his dealings directly with the King. He obtained the post of Attorney General without the favourite's help, and when, after the event, as Bacon later remarked, Somerset 'thrust himself into the business for a fee', he managed to pay off the obligations he had not incurred with an elegant gesture: resorting to his friends, the students of the Inns of Court, he produced a masque in honour of the favourite's marriage, entirely at his own expense.[42]

Bacon conducted the trial of Lady Somerset – who had confessed and repented – with compassion, and that of Somerset with such scrupulous fairness that critics determined to blame him, one way or another, have had to interpret it either as collusion or as camouflage. Indeed it was on this occasion that he attempted to introduce into the system a form of *viva voce* testimony, then rarely allowed, by which prisoners could cross-examine witnesses for the accusation.[43] It would take many pages – and a more thorough understanding of the background of high intrigue to this story of love potions and poisoned tarts than Bacon's various disparagers have shown – to tell it in full. Various legal eminences were involved, and Bacon was not called in until after Coke, then Chief Justice, with proofs – and red herrings – furnished, as Gardiner observed, by his own vivid imagination, had thoroughly prejudiced the case. Anyone reading Bacon's thoughtful presentation to the King of the alternatives before him, and his speeches at the different trials, will appreciate his efforts to secure justice for a man he had never liked, while sparing the King's feelings for the disgraced, yet regretted, favourite; steering clear of Coke's baseless hints at further conspiracies; restricting the evidence to what had a direct bearing on the case; and preventing Somerset, if possible, from giving away irrelevant but embarrassing secrets of state.[44]

Bacon certainly thought him guilty. Two months before he was apprehended, Somerset had endeavoured to obtain a general pardon (for himself alone), covering – against all precedent – murder by poison; and with only two days to spare he had secured and burned thirty letters which were part of the evidence, and forged others.[45] Information brought to light by Garrett Mattingley in 1955 suggests that although he was an accessory after the fact, he may not have been personally guilty of the cold-blooded murder of his friend. But Gardiner had seen no reason to doubt that Bacon's conclusions were drawn in perfect good faith, and Mattingley does not involve him.[46] As it turned out, the evidence against Somerset was insufficient to prove guilt. In such cases the seventeenth-century practice was to maintain the credit of the Government by pronouncing the accused guilty, but to right the situation with a pardon. Bacon's own view, which he was to hold for himself when faced with impeachment, was that downfall and confession were a sufficient punishment for the great, and he wrote in those terms to the King:

> There may be evidence so balanced as it may have sufficient matter for the conscience of the peers to convict him, and yet leave sufficient matter in the conscience of a King upon the same evidence to pardon his life; because the peers are astringed by necessity to acquit or condemn; but grace is free.[47]

Bacon had hoped all along for some 'clear confession' from Somerset. Failing this, however, he did his best to charge him so as not to 'make him odious beyond the extent of mercy'. Somerset was found guilty by the Lords 'without the difference of one voice'. Bacon's role in the affair has been fully elucidated, but we still find him presented to students in 1985 as 'fitting up' the royal favourite in a 'fixed' trial.[48]

Bacon had also been serving as foil for a much more interesting hero, Sir Walter Ralegh, whose own legend, celebrated in the nineteenth century and in a number of mid twentieth-century biographies, was born out of the same mixture of self-proclaimed martyrdom, popular misunderstanding and Whig interpretation as that of his admirer, the Earl of Essex. The execution of Ralegh for a deliberate act of piracy against a country with which England had been at peace for twelve years was looked on in Macaulay's time as an outrageous injustice. Hankering after Elizabeth and Drake, Ralegh's admirers felt (and many still feel) that deliberately burning down and pillaging a Spanish town, complete with churches and convents, and destroying some hundreds of civilians – an act which Ralegh brushed aside as not worth complaining about – could not be considered strictly criminal.[49] They continued to refer to Spain as 'the enemy', and this emotional attitude has obscured the truth about Ralegh. Indignation against the irregularity of his final sentence has blinded historians to the justice of his punishment, and to the fact that the first death sentence, in 1603, for his undoubted involvement in the plot to dethrone James in favour of Arabella Stuart, was not as undeserved as it has seemed, after he so successfully turned the tables on Coke at his trial.

Macaulay predictably implicated Bacon in Ralegh's 'dastardly murder', and to this day he is still denounced as the judicial murderer of a war-minded Ralegh for being 'in conflict with the peace-seeking James'. But Bacon played too marginal a role in this saga to make it worth devoting much space to the laying of 'Ralegh's Ghost'. The many 'ghosts' that were later circulated by the Puritans to make Ralegh out a victim of Spanish intrigue were investigated with exemplary impartiality in 1853 by Macvey Napier, who, French and Spanish sources in hand, felt bound to face the 'unwelcome truth'; and later by Gardiner in 1869 and Spedding in 1872. A summary of Napier's principal conclusions, which have not been seriously contested, can be referred to as a background to the following brief outline (see Appendix). His view of Ralegh was recently confirmed in a brilliant study of the first voyage to Guiana by Charles Nicholl (1995).[50]

Loved by Queen Elizabeth, befriended by Prince Henry, and described by Aubrey as 'a wonderful waking spirit' although 'damnable proud', Ralegh quoted 'that excellent gentleman', Francis Bacon, with approval in his *History of the World*.[51] Bacon mentions a prolonged tête-à-tête between himself and Ralegh, whom he had long wanted to interest in his scientific experiments, just before the latter set off for Guiana in March 1617, ostensibly in search of a gold-mine. This was not, as has mistakenly been assumed (because of a misreading of 'Lord Chamberlain' as 'Lord Chancellor'), the famous dialogue which Ralegh actually held with the Chamberlain, Lord Pembroke, one of the principal patrons of his expedition.[52] To Pembroke (and not to Bacon) Ralegh would naturally confide his plan of attacking the Spanish fleet, trusting that James would be only too ready with his pardon. 'Why you will be a pirate!' Pembroke exclaimed. 'Tush, my Lord,' said Ralegh, 'did you ever hear of any that was accounted a pirate for taking millions? They who aim at small things are pirates.' It was in this spirit that Ralegh, the survivor of a generation in which the Queen herself had abetted her pirates against the Spanish enemy, set forth on this new adventure, his bid for freedom after thirteen years in the Tower, and also a gamble for his country's greatness – if not for that of France, since before leaving he secretly offered to transfer his services and eventual gains to the French King.[53]

Ralegh had formally pledged himself to King James to abstain from hostile inroads into any Spanish settlement, on pain of the execution of his suspended death sentence – which was James's pledge to Philip III, the prospective father-in-law of Prince Charles, not at all happy about this allegedly peaceful, but exceptionally well-armed exploration of his *Lebensraum*. No serious student of Ralegh's own words, however, or of the evidence of his captains can doubt that his real intention all along was not to seek a mine but to conquer the land of El Dorado, which he had been dreaming of since he first set foot in Guiana twenty years earlier. He hoped, as he wrote to his wife, to be 'a king among them'; or failing that, to seize the Spanish fleet. Nor can it be doubted that his son's famous cry, when attacking Santo Tomé – 'come my hearts, there is the mine we must expect, they that look for any other mine are fools!' – sprang out of his own brain.[54] Disastrously, of course, for Ralegh lost his son and, when his captains left him, all hope of the success of his great aims. The King's folly in authorizing an adventure rightly labelled 'the veriest hallucination that ever crossed a madman's brain', in expectation of gold to fill his coffers, is only too patent. But when Ralegh broke his formal pledge, he had no choice, he could not become an accessory after the fact to his unfortunate – but also faithless – servant's crime.[55] The victim, he felt, of a huge hoax performed on him by his rogue subject, the King was further infuriated when Ralegh attempted to escape to France, and his long-term secret dealings there leaked out. Having experienced the effects of Ralegh's eloquence at his earlier trial James regrettably turned down the advice of both Bacon and Coke – that he should be charged before the Council and Judges in full array, and their joint decision made public in a formal record – and demanded a private hearing.

A Commission of Inquiry was set up, including the Archbishop of Canterbury, Caesar, Worcester, Bacon and Coke, with Secretary Naunton (a friend of Ralegh's) in charge, before which Ralegh contradicted himself so brazenly that they ended up believing there was not a word of truth in his assertions, and convinced of his guilt. Lord Chancellor Bacon announced their unanimous decision, that Ralegh had abused the King's confidence, and Chief Justice Montagu awarded execution, as called for by Attorney General Yelverton, in the only way it could be done – since a man attainted of high treason could not lawfully be tried for any crime he committed afterwards – by putting his earlier sentence into effect. It was a potential sanction which Ralegh had accepted before he started on his venture, but because of James's insistence on a private hearing people did not know what he had been charged with, or why the anomalous procedure had been used.[56] They heard only his speech on the scaffold, a masterpiece of audacity and skilful evasion, in which this consummate actor, refuting at length various irrelevant and minor charges, presented himself as a misunderstood but forgiving hero, and entirely by-passed the issue of his real offence.

With this speech, his 'last mirth in this world', he said, on this second 'happiest day of his life' – the first being that of his brilliant defence in 1603 – and with his exemplary death, Ralegh cast himself for the role of martyr to a Stuart monarch. From that day on, this man most hated in his lifetime became the idol of all patriotic Englishmen, and the revolutionaries of the next generation were to look on him, quite mistakenly, as their precursor.[57] Bacon thoroughly disapproved of piracy, and of 'plant-ing' in a land already planted 'by another Christian prince'. But he had not known of James's unworthy undertaking to the Spanish Ambassador that if Ralegh broke his word he would be handed over to be executed in Spain; indeed he had voiced the strong opposition felt by all but Buckingham at the Council when they heard of such power being offered to a foreigner.[58] Yet because of his share in pronouncing a fundamentally just sentence, he was contrasted unfavourably by Macaulay with this new legendary victim, the great Elizabethan adventurer, expert in effrontery and double-dealing, as his best-disposed biographers have shown. And to this day Ralegh, the dreamer-cum-confidence trickster, still carried on the wave of his own fictions, is seen by less scholarly historians as the white sheep, while Bacon, playing his straightforward part as Chancellor of the Realm, probably with sorrow, is cast as the black one.[59]

One of Ralegh's more picturesque biographers was Margaret Irwin, author of *The Great Lucifer* in 1960. This writer succeeded in dyeing Bacon's supposed mistreatment of Ralegh a deeper shade of black by joining two conversations, allegedly held by them before his voyage, neither of which is authentic. In the first (which actually took place between Ralegh and Pembroke, as noted above), Bacon is made out to have condoned Ralegh's intention of attacking the Spanish fleet. In the second (known to be apocryphal), Bacon allegedly assured Ralegh that his Admiral's com-mission would automatically secure his pardon.[60] After this, on Ralegh's return from his disastrous voyage, we are told, Bacon ate the words he had never spoken, and promptly brought up his earlier conviction against him.

Having misattributed two documents, Margaret Irwin proceeded to split up a third, the paper drafted by Coke on 10 October 1618 on behalf of the Commissioners (Bacon included) who had heard the charges against Ralegh, and signed by all of them, advising the King on ways of proceed-ing against the accused. The first part of the Commissioners' advice, that Ralegh should be given a public hearing, is presented as by Coke alone, in so-called opposition to Bacon, who had certainly supported, if not orig-inated it. The King's misguided reply that he would have none of his counsellors' suggestion, and that Ralegh must be heard and sentenced privately, is attributed to Bacon on no ground at all. The second part of the advice in which, with Coke as their draftsman, the Commissioners jointly proposed that Ralegh should be sentenced on his earlier convic-tion, is given out as Bacon's alone. James is described as snatching 'at this perfect solution, put forward so smoothly by his supreme head of the law', fortunately 'quite simple, and moreover legal'. After this, we learn that Coke, 'whose life-long pride had been to embody the law' (his efforts to strain it to the limit at Ralegh's first trial, and his brutal bullying of the accused, conveniently forgotten) was to be spurned from on high for failing to degrade the law, as Bacon had done, into 'a trick to serve the King'. Meanwhile Bacon had seized his chance to give Ralegh 'the death-sting'. Why had not James, who had called Cecil 'my little beagle', thought of calling Bacon 'my little viper'? (In fact it is Cecil, not his cousin, who was called a viper in his time.)[61]

A. L. Rowse, in *Ralegh and the Throgmortons* (1962), deplored the literary biographies that go on perpetuating old mistakes, and he was too good a historian to maintain these untenable charges against Bacon.[62] But he shared one indulgence with Margaret Irwin: that of confronting a freedom-loving Ralegh with a pompous bureaucratic-minded Bacon in the debate on the enclosures of common lands, held in the 1601 Parliament which they both attended. Bacon, as we know, was a convinced denouncer of enclosures – which meant the conversion of tillage into grass, and consequent depopulation – while Ralegh spoke for the individual's freedom to cultivate his own land as he wished. In the seventeenth century the free trade approach prevailed whenever an improvement in the supplies of grain made it possible, and at such times (as in 1592) Bacon rejoiced.[63] But it was the four years' scarcity and famine that followed, to which he was an eye-witness, that had provoked him to launch his two bills for tillage and against enclosures. In 1601 corn was cheap, and some Members proposed the repeal of the Statute of Tillage. Bacon defended it hotly, insisting that the wealth of the kingdom should not 'be engrossed in a few pasturers' hands'. 'I think the best course is to set corn at liberty,' Ralegh replied, expressing a sincerely held view, no doubt. But we must bear in mind that Ralegh's lands were particularly suited to pasture, and among the many monopolies he held was that of the prosperous wool trade. He also enjoyed the monopoly of the Cornish tin-mines, one of the principal commodities of the kingdom, and if he approved of free corn, he expressed himself in no uncertain terms at the same Parliament against free tin. Clearly this public exchange of views between two great minds of their age on a problem that is still with us today – one speaking for the commonweal, the other for private profit, and both in the name of the free yeomen of England – would have been worth looking at with a more objective eye.[64]

Writing on the same subject, in her haste to show Bacon in a poor light, Margaret Irwin confused, not letters this time, but speeches in different Parliaments four years apart, and mixed up two entirely unrelated statutes. Reproving Bacon for supporting, with 'heavily embroidered eloquence', Cecil's 'paternalist' policies against sheep-grazing, she has Ralegh in 1601 making short work of his speeches, with the House so carried away by Ralegh's (presumably unembroidered) eloquence that they shouted 'Away with the Bill!' and persistently rejected it, until Bacon was forced to 'pronounce its obloquy'. Those allegedly ill-received speeches, however, are taken from Bacon's first intervention, in 1597, in favour of the bill – which was passed by that Parliament, and ratified in 1601, whereas the bill that was so eloquently shouted down was a proposal on the compulsory sowing of hemp for cables and cordage, with which Bacon had nothing to do.[65] So with one more misreading of history it was possible to attribute to Ralegh, in the name of the free English farmers, a political victory over Bacon, whose life-long concern for those same English farmers is derided in this story as the empty rhetoric of a 'stunted heart'.

The same emotional tone, if not the extravagant history, is found in the description of another exchange between Bacon and Ralegh, at the same Parliament, this time by J. E. Neale, in 1957. Had Bacon been a central character in Neale's Elizabethan story, this thoughtful historian would certainly have discovered how greatly Elizabeth's Counsel Learned differed from the prevailing image. Sadly, it is Macaulay's cold-hearted and thoroughly worldly politician who moves through his pages, 'ever drawing the veil of noble motive over his activities'; a 'young prig', 'untouched by the fires of youth, immune from infection by his audience'; an officious, blundering busybody, who, when he submitted his favourite project for the reform of the law in the 1593 Parliament, could only have been 'showing off'. In 1601 Bacon had spoken in favour of a particular tax which was to be shared by rich and poor alike, 'bearing the same yoke'. Said Ralegh, 'Call you this an equal yoke when the poor man pays as much as the rich?' The poor man's estate, Ralegh insisted, was no better than he was assessed at, whereas the rich were assessed at not one-hundredth of their wealth – as this well-endowed favourite of Elizabeth had good cause to know. Bacon's reasons for supporting what looks like a poll tax have not been identified. Neale, however, oblivious of the battles Bacon had fought and won in Parliament to improve the poor man's condition – and of Ralegh's adamant opposition to the abolition of rural servitude, or of the ballads then circulating about him ('He polls the poor to the skin') – was happy to see Bacon's 'false and priggish sentiment' scorned by his free-minded opponent. 'As a verbal miniature of two supremely famous men,' he remarked, 'how revealing this incident is.'[66]

Bacon was to go on playing the villain in Ralegh's 'Lifes'. In George Garrett's popular biography *Death of the Fox* (1972), a hotch-potch of absurdities (which may none the less be some people's first encounter with Bacon), we find a double-dealing politician, 'a grinning knave' with a 'hungry soul', whose life was spent in constant efforts for 'the advancement of Francis Bacon', and whose 'viper-eye' would never meet Ralegh's.[67] And we come across him again in *The Voyage of Destiny* by Robert Nye (1982), where Ralegh, forgetting, it seems, how much he appreciated 'that excellent gentleman', avers that Bacon 'would welcome the chance to put the knife in my back, as he had put it so often into others'. Knowing that Ralegh knows he knows this, Bacon dare not meet his glance, but ever 'shuts his viper eyes'.[68]

30

The Venomous Atheist, the Traitor and the Coward

Before we follow Bacon's image into the last decades of our century, it will be worth our while to cross the Channel and find out what the foreign nations to whom he entrusted his name had been doing with it. On the Continent, throughout the seventeenth century and most of the eighteenth, little interest was shown in Bacon's life, beyond the horrified indignation of Amboise, in 1631, at the treatment he had received from his compatriots, or Voltaire's remark a century later: 'He was so great a man that I have forgotten his faults.'[1] People were more interested in his books. The acclaim with which these were hailed 'from so many parts beyond the seas' – and which, for so abstruse a work as the *Novum Organum*, had surprised Bacon himself – had continued unabated.[2] For two centuries he was translated, read and quoted by the cultivated public of many European countries, as far afield as Hungary, and studied by such men as Leibniz in Germany and Vico in Italy. 'As the Greek Plato had no Tacitus,' wrote Vico, 'so both Rome and Greece lacked a Bacon.'[3] Over-flowing with praise, Bacon's admirers had only one reservation, but it was a vital one at the time: his deplorable religion. With Father Mersenne, they felt that Bacon was 'a great loss to the Catholic world' – so great a loss that while in the 1620s the Christian reformers around Paolo Sarpi in Venice and the Catholics of Florence vied with each other for the honour of translating his *Essays* into Italian, among the latter this honour involved suppressing, or mutilating, such of the essays as steered too close to heresy.[4] Writing in Spain in 1773 the Benedictine encyclo-pedist Father Benito Feyjoó, a warm admirer of Bacon as one who 'did not regard his own glory and thought only of the truth', still deeply regretted his religion. 'Oh misfortune,' he cried, 'that heresy should keep these bright lights buried in the gloom of its shadows!'[5]

In France philosophers of the Enlightenment, Voltaire, d'Alembert and specially Diderot, claimed to have first taught the world to read and understand the great Chancellor, newly emerged out of 'the black night of an ignorant age'. They looked to Bacon as their founding father, and the revolutionaries followed suit. 'Neglected by his own country', cried one of them, Bacon 'bequeathed his name and writings to foreign nations. It is up to us, the men of liberty, to save the legacy of the martyrs of philosophy.'⁶ But no longer the adviser of princes, theirs was a denuded Bacon, shorn of many of the facets of his rich being; and they now proceeded to remove the last of them, the religious foundation stone of his thought – incompatible with the rational scientific outlook of enlightened philosophers – and to proclaim him an atheist. Nothing Bacon wrote on religion should be taken seriously, wrote J. A. Naigeon. The famous remark, he said, that 'a little philosophy inclineth man's mind to atheism, but depth in philosophy bringeth men's minds about to religion' had clearly been written in a fit of mental aberration. Nevertheless, Naigeon conceded, profound and subtle thoughts were to be found in Bacon's works – inspired during his lucid moments. Readers, he warned, should take care to follow the scientist, but not the believer.⁷

On the 25th Brumaire, year III of the French Republic – of which Bacon was hailed as a precursor – Antoine Lasalle, a disciple of Diderot, was appointed by the Convention to translate Bacon's complete works into French. By this time science had become synonymous with atheism, and from the fifteen volumes he produced between 1799 and 1803 Lasalle rigorously excluded all Bacon's writings on religious subjects, and any lines suspected of a religious intent – the *oremus*, as he called them ('let us pray's'). Where he could not easily cut, he added notes to protect the unwary reader, or sarcastic comments. His preface included a long 'monologue' in which Lasalle's Bacon confided to the reader the plans his translator had invented for him, in the following terms:

> Addressing a bigoted theologian-King in the presence of tyrannical and suspicious priests, I cannot express my opinions clearly . . . Bound as I am to wrap my thoughts in vague and general terms and obscure expressions, I may not at once be understood . . . I will not openly describe the rights of man [so violently and perfidiously suppressed]; I will not directly attack the Throne or the Altar, because, resting as they do on each other, and on a threefold foundation of ignorance, terror and custom, they are at present unshakable. But, while paying lip-service to them, I shall undermine them both with my principles . . . For the best way to destroy the Priesthood and the Monarchy in one blow, and to make kings and priests forever useless, is to work for the enlightenment of men . . . Sooner or later my explanations, or a part of them, will reach the people, and they will lose their stupid faith . . . of no use to anyone but the priests.⁸

The reaction which now set in against the enlightened philosophers was forcefully represented by the ultramontane Piedmontese diplomat, Count Joseph de Maistre, for many years Ambassador at the Court of St Petersburg. This paladin of the counter-revolution, as he saw himself, abominated the materialistic philosophy on which the 'Satanic' French Revolution was founded. And although his diatribes were really aimed at Voltaire, Diderot and company, for the first time on the Continent a note of personal invective against Bacon came into play; for Maistre (who, before he realized that the encyclopedists had made the English philosopher their figurehead, had greatly admired him) saw the enlightened philosophy as a river of mud 'swollen with the venom of Bacon', indeed, literally issuing out of Bacon as he 'raged against every precept of the spirit'. In 1803 he devoted two volumes to denouncing the works of this 'enemy of science'. Bacon's philosophy, he wrote, was 'a continual aberration'. His *De Augmentis*, 'a totally worthless and despicable book', bore the manifest signs of 'a sick imagination and a disordered mind'. His *Novum Organum* was worthy of Bedlam, 'so ridiculous that we must hoot with laughter at every page'. Finally, 'there is nothing more to be said about Bacon. Only the blind can be taken in. He is wrong when he affirms, wrong when he denies, wrong when he doubts, wrong, in a word, wherever it is possible to be wrong.'[9] In seven hundred pages of condemnation aimed at the thinker, the man could not escape calumny, and Maistre expatiated on the 'innumerable evil traits' he had gleaned from the notes of Bacon's translator – annoyed with his subject for so frequently deviating from the straight and atheist path. But if the man was vicious, Maistre concluded, it was because the thinker was. Bacon was vile because he transmitted a vile philosophy; a hypocrite because (as Lasalle had also averred) he wore the mask of a Christian to impose on James I; he was a gross flatterer, because, to please James, he spoke well of Henry VII. And in any case, 'if the encyclopedists praised Bacon, he could not but be evil'.[10]

In 1800, three years before Maistre had embarked on this crusade, Lasalle had already been denounced for the traitor translator he was by J. A. de Luc, who in *Bacon tel qu'il est* defended him as a religious philosopher against the atheists of the *Encyclopédie*.[11] The same year had seen the publication of *Le Christianisme de François Bacon*, a monumental study relating Bacon to Leibniz and highlighting in both philosophers religious aspects that had previously been disregarded.[12] Its author, J. A. Emery, devoted a hundred pages to a life of Bacon which has had no equal in France for thoroughness combined with a broad overall view. Drawing on contemporary testimony, including that of the libellers, and citing the opinions of later writers such as Addison and Carteret, all of which he critically analysed, Emery set out to fill the gap left by such a 'partial and superficial' 'Life' as that of David Mallet. (Mallet's 'Life' had been circulating in French since 1755 as the preface to a quite unreliable *encyclopédiste*'s account of Bacon's philosophy.)[13]

The Bacon we meet in these thoughtful and scholarly pages looks very like the man who was to emerge from Spedding's discussion in *Evenings with a Reviewer* half a century later.

> We may truthfully say [Emery declared] that Bacon's heart was no less excellent than his mind. It is impossible to read his works and not to like him. One would look in vain for any hostile personal remarks or criticism. There is no malice in them, no bitterness. Both before and after the disaster that befell him, everything in him breathes a candid zeal for truth and a most tender charity towards men.

And on his ingratitude:

> Read his Apology, he is justified by the straightforward narration of the facts . . . He is admirable for the way in which he manages to excuse his own actions without ever aggravating the Earl's guilt.

On his servility, with reference to James and Buckingham:

> Bacon has been called a vile flatterer, but he never praised in the one or the other what was not truly praiseworthy . . . Nor could he himself be reproached for incapacity or lack of zeal.

Emery denounced D'Ewes and Wilson for their libels, citing in particular Wilson's remark that a rumour he had just noted about Bacon's sexual *mores* was almost certainly false – 'then why mention it?' Emery asked. Like Addison, he saw Bacon's fall as an opportunity for his religious piety to shine forth. If Bacon was justly condemned, he wrote, there was nothing more noble or more generous than his confession. Indeed, said Emery, 'the Parliament that owed its convocation to him had more to be forgiven for than had Bacon himself'.

> He proceeded in this affair with so much simplicity and candour that when we see the advantage his enemies took of him we cannot help feeling it is almost a pity that Bacon refrained from using his brilliant gifts to turn on his accusers . . . His century, similar to ours in this, was too corrupt to realize his worth . . . But he felt himself to some extent to blame; he felt it, and his naturally upright and generous soul preferred to expose itself rather than go against the testimony of his conscience.[14]

In a second volume Emery published an anthology of all Bacon's religious works, which now appeared for the first time in France. Maistre could have found enough matter here to calm his anti-Republican ire. Instead, having made up his mind that Bacon was irredeemably evil, he set off in search of venom, and landed with particular force on a paper discussing Christian paradoxes, mistakenly attributed to Bacon, which he described as 'infinitely suspect', while typical of the man ('All of Bacon is in it').[15] So much misdirected vituperation, as De Mas pointed out in 1985 in his study of these trends, completely by-passed the moral and intellectual personality of the Chancellor of England, as indeed did the whole ridiculous controversy, so that there was little left of Bacon but his name.[16]

The vituperation was soon to take a new turn. By one of the coincidences which tend to justify the notion of ideas germinating in the air, while Macaulay was writing his essay in India in 1836, a crop of denigrating biographical introductions appeared in France, where Bacon's works were by now included, with those of Descartes, in the dissertations set for school-leaving examinations. Their source of inspiration was not far to seek. The years of the Revolution had seen the translation of a *History of England*, in eight volumes, by the famous ultra-Whig, Catherine Macaulay, who had been acclaimed in revolutionary Paris.[17] A distant relation of T. B. Macaulay's, her anti-Stuart Philippics, along with her black-and-white concept of history, similar to his own, probably influenced him; she may even have introduced him to Weldon, on whom she drew copiously. Her passionate bias, combined with a brash ignorance, was such that it occasionally led her (so the historian D'Israeli claimed, on the testimony of the Librarian of the British Museum) to tear out of the manuscripts she consulted any page she came across which was 'unfavourable to her party, or in favour of the Stuarts'.[18] Mrs Macaulay could find no words scathing enough for the vices of James and his Court, in contrast to the candour, integrity and masculine virtue that prevailed in the rest of England (the females being characterized by chastity, modesty and industry). And we can identify in her diatribes against Bacon the origin of every disparaging remark made by the new French biographers, from the absurd episodes she retailed out of Weldon, to her overall estimate of Bacon, as summed up in the following lines:

> Blind and insensible to the superiority of true dignity, he eagerly pursued in the most disgraceful manner that deceitful image of it which attracts the vulgar . . . Despicable in all the active part of his life and only glorious in the contemplative, him the rays of Science served to embellish, not to enlighten, and philosophy herself was degraded by a conjunction with his mean soul.[19]

These French professors had little regard for historical facts beyond their frontiers, as we may see from J. A. Buchon's preface to Bacon's philosophical works (1836). Buchon has Bacon giving up a timid attempt at parliamentary opposition (1593), and when this 'apostasy' failed of its effect, dedicating a ridiculous discourse of praises to the Queen (1580), whereupon he demanded – and obtained – the death penalty for Essex (1601), and so on for page after page of wild mis-statement, until his final conclusion: that if Bacon's own age absolved him of his misdeeds, the more enlightened morality of later times could not follow suit.[20] J. B. de Vauzelles (1833) and A. F. Ozanam (1836) were no more trustworthy.[21] Vauzelles, like Macaulay, cited Weldon at first with some hesitation ('his truthfulness has often been rightly doubted'), but, again like Macaulay, he was soon found reporting Weldon's anecdotes as accepted fact, without reference to their conclusive refutation in *Biographia Britannica*, in 1747, though this appears in his list of works consulted.[22] And, like other denigrators, once he had made up his mind about Bacon's servile ambition and general ill-repute, Vauzelles set off to hunt for confirmation in Bacon's own writings. His account of one of his discoveries, followed by Ozanam's presentation of the same subject, may serve as an illustration of these two authors' notions of historical accuracy. An apophthegm of Bacon's reads as follows:

> When any great officer, ecclesiastical or civil, was to be made, the Queen would enquire after the piety, integrity, learning of the man. And when she was satisfied in these qualifications, she would consider of his personage. And upon such an occasion, she was pleased once to say to me, *Bacon, how can a magistrate maintain his authority when the man is despised?*[23]

Bacon evidently admired the Queen's way of proceeding, and was proud of her confidence in him. Here is Vauzelles:

> The Queen, it appears, did not think very highly of Bacon's character: she said to him one day, 'how can the magistrate maintain his authority when the man is despised?' This from a Queen who had persistently refused him the Solicitor-Generalship looks very much like a derogatory personal remark. Thus humiliated, Bacon was reduced to speech as servile as his behaviour.[24]

Three years later Ozanam produced his own improved version. He placed the conversation after the death of Essex, a time when Elizabeth was expressing her regret that Essex had not taken the advice of his wiser friends (Bacon prominent among them) and confessed his guilt, thereby possibly saving his life: 'It was even said that one day, on Bacon's importuning the Queen more than ever after Essex's death, she replied to him, "How can the magistrate maintain his authority, when the man is despised?" '[25] No more than Vauzelles, of course, could Ozanam appreciate Queen Elizabeth's esteem for Bacon, or his devotion to her. The angle was too different, as we may realize when we read that Bacon's memoir on Queen Elizabeth is described in this biography as cynical praise – he called her a *'merciful* Queen'![26] Ozanam will often be found jumping to unhistorical conclusions. Here is the ignominious Bacon, for example, standing before a romantic and chivalrous Essex,

> with whom he must have exchanged promises of eternal friendship
> – hardly daring to raise his eyes to the man whose knees he must
> more than once have embraced. [And this] when he had before him
> the example of Yelverton, who had preferred to incur the displeasure
> of Edward VI, rather than plead against the Earl of Somerset, his
> protector.[27]

Ozanam meant James I, not the child King Edward, who had died seventy years before these events, and the alleged exemplary conduct held up to Bacon occurred some twelve years after Essex's death. But these are no more than improvements on an original misunderstanding, from another story of Weldon's, itself a tissue of blunders.[28]

This writer was faced with the same dilemma as Macaulay, though more poignantly. Accepting without hesitation (from Weldon via Mrs Macaulay) an image of Bacon as a base flatterer from his childhood – who had contrived, 'with hateful perseverance', the disgrace of Coke, was responsible for the death of Ralegh, and generally 'dragged himself in the muddy roads of power . . . stopping at neither crime nor ignominy' – Ozanam admired Bacon with all his heart, both as a scientist and a poet. He saw him as 'the priest initiator', for whom all things 'were harmony, splendour and ravishing vision, intoxication of the soul', and he maintained that 'this magnificent genius was profoundly religious' (however regrettably Protestant). Was it Bacon's fault, he argued, if first Hobbes and Locke, and later Voltaire and d'Alembert had 'sat him down at their Sophists' banquet and overwhelmed him with the infamy of their praise?' Compelled, like his English counterparts, to split Bacon into two halves – a sort of schizophrenia that invaded subject and author together – he wept for

> the debasement of a great soul, a sublime creature to whom God had
> given a glorious mission, but who sank into degradation. You were
> sent, O Bacon . . . for vast discoveries . . . but your example could
> make men curse science and doubt virtue . . . You are great but you
> were wicked . . . No good man, whatever the glory of your name,
> looking at you across the ages with a holy jealousy will cry: 'How I
> wish I were he!'[29]

Ozanam would have been happy indeed could he have bypassed the deluded Vauzelles and the lying Weldon and heard about Bacon directly from Toby Matthew – a Catholic after his own heart.

In the next generation Macaulay's influence came to reinforce this combination of religious censure with radical anger. A careful study of Bacon's philosophy, life and influence by Charles de Rémusat (1857) had one defect which vitiated it from the start: Macaulay was Rémusat's authority on the facts of Bacon's life, and naturally enough Rémusat adopted the English historian's interpretations (and sometimes his very words), enriched, on occasion, by Campbell's. Thus when describing Bacon the Privy Councillor, Rémusat was inevitably reminded of his remark about men who are 'winged angels for their knowledge and creeping serpents for their passions'. 'We can no longer imitate the indulgence of writers in the last century,' he concluded, 'today we do not have the excuse of not knowing history'; after all, England's 'best writers have not hidden the truth from her'. Now that he believed he had learned the truth about Bacon, the same thing happened to Rémusat as to Macaulay and Campbell: on page 71 of his book, we read that 'not a day went by without his returning to his great, cherished idea', and on page 87 that not one of his days was honoured by 'a noble counsel, a dignified resistance, a generous initiative'. This biographer could not bring his double Bacon into focus, because, unlike Emery – who distinguished between more or less reliable recollections and tales distorted or invented out of spite – he could not 'harmonize' the statements of Aubrey with those of Weldon. Macaulay, whose historical scholarship he took for granted, weighed too heavily on the wrong side of the balance. Rémusat noted the announcement of Spedding's *Letters and Life* with interest. Had they come out a few years earlier, he would no doubt have written a different book.[30]

In *La vérité sur la condamnation du Chancelier Bacon* (1886) Camoin de Vence saw Bacon once more as a man who was the victim of his servants, and whose good faith and justice would be 'proclaimed with admiration and respect down the centuries', despite such violent attacks as Macaulay's.[31] But for most of our century, in France as in England, the darker version prevailed. In 1922 a new presentation of Bacon's philosophy by Gaston Sortais was introduced, under the shadow of Abbott, with pain over that 'singular alloy', Bacon's life,

> in which the highest qualities of intelligence are found mingled with a fundamental weakness of the will. This violent contrast brings to mind in its awe-inspiring appropriateness a passage from *De Augmentis* which one might think had been addressed to Bacon himself by another man: 'the more should men be ashamed if in knowledge they be as the winged angels, but in their desires as crawling serpents.'[32]

In 1938 Bacon was misunderstood and sneered at by the philosopher Gaston Bachelard, and ten years later, in a brief biography strewn with errors of fact, André Cresson ('Membre de l'Institut') once again expatiated on that 'rare phenomenon', a divided and delinquent genius.[33] Meanwhile Romantic biography also had its day in France. Souky de

Cotte, in *La Reine Vierge* (1938), later staged as a play, presented the same vicious Bacon who had now appeared in Strachey's widely translated story of Elizabeth. Walls covered with graffiti denounce him as a traitor to his friend, while he ceaselessly stirs the Queen's hatred against the long-suffering and dignified Earl of Essex. 'Qu'on lui donne le coup de grâce, Bacon s'en charge' (Finish him off, Bacon will take care of that). Bacon does, and Essex expires, without for an instant breaking his faith to his God and his Queen.[34] Not until 1991, with Michèle Le Doeuff's illuminating study of the *Advancement of Learning* – published two centuries after Emery's book on the philosopher and the man, when there had been a revival of interest in his works – would the French public be able to read an outline of Bacon's life sensitive to the realities of his mind and time.[35]

In Germany, 'that most wise philosopher, Francis Bacon of Verulam, Chancellor of England' was recognized in his lifetime by such scholars as Tobias Adam. Interest was revived in the late eighteenth century by Immanuel Kant, and half-way through the nineteenth by the great naturalist Alexander von Humboldt, whose mind, like Bacon's, ranged across every discipline, and whose vast vision of the *Kosmos* (1845) emerged in Baconian fashion out of the innumerable minute observations he made throughout his travels. Humboldt looked on Bacon as a pioneer, greatly admiring his works on the winds and on the movement of light.[36] But in the years that followed, which saw Campbell's 'Life of Bacon' in England, and Rémusat's *Bacon* in France, two distinguished writers were to devote a different kind of attention to Bacon's life and character. In 1856, in *Francis Bacon of Verulam*, Kuno Fischer, author of a ten-volume History of Modern Philosophy, saw Bacon as a man of considerable charity and nobility of mind, but (with Macaulay's help) he discovered 'blemishes' in him which were 'not mere human errors but debased sentiments and political crimes'. Fischer made an elaborate attempt to bridge the gulf beween the philosopher and the politician, and finally came up with a new solution. 'Neither was the one . . . a "soaring angel", nor the other a "creeping snake".' The key to the mystery lay in a quality of 'elasticity' which somehow, as Fischer saw it, held the two separate personalities together. Bacon was ruled, in thought as in life, he said, by an 'elastic morality'. Facility was his strength, a 'natural elasticity'. 'We know of no philosopher more *elastic* than Bacon.'[37] Thus, by dwelling on a key-word – that short-cut to thinking which Bacon had deprecated – the 'problem' of a double Bacon was eluded.

For the distinguished German biochemist Baron Justus von Liebig, as for Joseph de Maistre, whose detestation of the Enlightenment philosophers he shared, there never had been a problem: he too opted for a Bacon who was evil through and through. The whole purpose of his book on the *Novum Organum*, he announced, was to dethrone Bacon and tear down 'the pompous edifice' of his thought, until then mistakenly considered 'one of the most solid monuments of human greatness'. All Bacon's works, Liebig declared, and in particular his inductive method, were the trumpery goods of a charlatan, and Bacon himself 'a Dr Marvellous', standing at the door of his shop to boost his panaceas and depreciate all competitors.[38] In a page that out-Macaulays Macaulay, he made short work of the two-souled Bacon:

> Mr Macaulay thinks it is not impossible to separate character, which determines man's actions in private life, from the tendencies out of which his scientific action spring. We are to see in a man like Bacon a respectable ambition, a vast philanthropy and a sincere love of truth, while at the same time Macaulay presents him elsewhere as vain, selfish, untrustworthy, boasting, greedy, and without honour, unable to recognize merit in others, or to mention any name without dragging it in the mud, and speaking always of his own deeds and of the rewards owed him by humanity.[39]

Liebig was filled with disgust by the efforts of Bacon's admirers 'to veil the hideous deformities of his character', deformities 'revealed irrefutably by his own confession', and by their 'poverty-stricken arguments' to make him out a true scientific investigator. And he could let no opportunity pass to label Bacon a plagiarist, an ignoble hypocrite, an impostor. This irritable critic (in whose pages, needless to say, Weldon figures prominently) had a positive gift for reading his sources upside down, and for reviling Bacon where he was most to be praised. Thus the philosopher who set up his own laboratory and continually encouraged others to make experiments ('a workshop is wonderfully like a library'), who thought it was only by imitating the ways of mechanics and artisans that man could begin to fathom nature's mysteries, and who, said Rawley, had his knowledge, not from books, but 'from some grounds and notions within himself' is berated, in Rawley's name, for obtaining all his information from books and for 'proudly and disdainfully' looking down on scientists and explorers as 'nobodies'.[40] Liebig (where was he looking?) could find no trace anywhere in Bacon's works

> of the joys and intimate affections aroused in great explorers of nature by their investigations and discoveries, nor of the feeling of humility they were filled with whenever the accomplishment of a great work allowed them to appreciate better what still remained to be achieved.

'In dealing with Bacon,' he concluded, 'we may assume without hesitation that all his actions were animated by particularly bad intentions.' It is entirely to his wickedness as a man that Bacon's alleged failure as a scientist must be attributed:

Nature, that had richly endowed him with brilliant gifts, had refused him truthfulness and good faith; because he approached her with a heart full of lies, she refused to obey him, and would reveal nothing to him . . . Just as he was in the other actions of his life, so he showed himself in science . . .[41]

Liebig's book was widely read not only in Germany, but also in France, where it appeared three years later. Its French translator, thoroughly convinced by the author's views, added his weight to them in a series of asides. 'Moralists can only applaud Bacon's fall,' he commented. 'It is a satisfaction to their noble cause that there should be one man the less of those who, by a shocking, and unhappily too frequent discordance, unite in their person the most seductive intellectual beauty [a beauty Liebig himself had failed to discern] with the most hideous moral deformity!'[42] After Liebig, a low view of both the life and works of Bacon prevailed in his country for many decades. It was in 1926 that Oskar Kraus launched the idea of Bacon as the advocate of military imperialism, noted earlier, while in 1936 J. Schick thought it worth devoting a whole essay to Bacon's abysmal inferiority to Shakespeare, Galileo and Kepler.[43]

So much for Germany. We know that Macaulay had made his way to St Petersburg, for we find E. F. Litvinova's Bacon, in 1891, attaining great heights and sinking to great depths for lack of firm moral principles. 'How to conciliate such intellectual greatness with so much moral baseness? Plato would never have conceived of a philosopher in whom mind and heart were so divorced. As Macaulay wrote, "while the great minds soar, men crawl on the ground like snakes." '[44]

Macaulay had also found his way to Madrid, where the great Spanish novelist Benito Pérez Galdós, a whole-hearted admirer of all things English, was a reader of his essays. We shall not be surprised, therefore, to find a character in one of Galdós's novels (1894) 'praising Bacon to skies for his intelligence and wiping the floor with him for his conscience'.[45] In the Spanish encyclopedia, *Espasa Calpe*, some years afterwards, we will see Bacon summarily dismissed as a man dominated by ambition, in love with intrigue, and distinguished neither for probity nor for gratitude. However, since in Spanish eyes Queen Elizabeth was even more wicked than he was, he earned a new, if undeserved distinction here – that of losing her favour because of his moderate attitude towards the Catholics.[46] A more recent casualty to Macaulay's persuasive eloquence was the Spanish historian Antonio Ballesteros, the editor of *Documentos inéditos* (1936–45), five erudite tomes of Spanish dispatches. When he came across a remark by the Spanish Ambassador, Gondomar, to the effect that Bacon was *un hombre de muy buen natural* – 'a man of a very fine character', or 'naturally good' – Ballesteros paused for a long and puzzled note. Gondomar's 'high estimate of the Chancellor', he wrote, 'is indeed curious, for he is speaking of the famous Francis Bacon' in whom there was 'a complete divorce between his brilliant intelligence, and his behaviour, that of an ambitious man who did not scruple to remove every obstacle in the way of his career, who . . .' (there follows a page of the usual denigration). It did not cross this historian's mind (which is 'indeed curious') that Bacon's friend Gondomar might have known Bacon better than he – or Macaulay – could have done.[47]

Around this time Bacon appeared before a wider Spanish-speaking public as the alleged companion and lover of one of the worst scoundrels in Spanish history, the great renegade, Antonio Pérez, one-time Secretary to Philip II, and for some years a refugee at the English Court. This man, as presented by Dr Gregorio Marañón in his well-researched *Antonio Pérez*, is the bird to whose feather Bacon is made to belong. A proven double-dealer, who while in power diverted enormous sums into his pocket and bled place-seekers implacably, Pérez was also a cold-blooded murderer. With forged documents he induced King Philip to doubt the loyalty of his half-brother, John of Austria – wrongly, as the King found out too late. And when one of Philip's high officials was about to denounce his machinations, Pérez persuaded the King that he deserved to die. He then arranged for the official's assassination, and by again tampering with letters, made it appear to have been carried out on the King's instructions. This was his most cynical lie, according to Marañón, who concluded that Pérez thoroughly deserved his fall.[48]

Little was known about this exotic and dandified foreigner when, in 1594, he appeared at the English Court. Queen Elizabeth was amused for a while by 'her Spanish traitor', as she called him, but Essex and the Bacon brothers, who bore the brunt of his pretentious manners and of his unremitting tales of woe, ended up fleeing his presence. The *canard* now launched by Marañón – that Pérez had found in Bacon 'muddy backwaters in which his radical immorality . . . could swim at ease' – springs from the doubly mistaken reading of a letter of Lady Bacon's, mentioned earlier. As noted above, she was expressing her anger with Francis not for sharing his bed, which everyone did at the time, but for sharing it with 'that bloody Per . . .' – clearly meaning his Catholic follower, Henry Percy, of whom the Puritan Lady Bacon disapproved. Birch, in the eighteenth century, misread 'Per' for Antonio Pérez', but Spedding cleared up the mistake.[49] Marañón, finding Pérez in Birch and Percy in Spedding, imagined that Lady Bacon had written two angry letters, on two different occasions, complaining of her son's friendship, in one case with the Spanish courtier and in the other with a 'good-looking and evil-living page' (Marañón's epithets). 'Once more she augured that divine wrath would fall on his head. And she was right.' We are given to understand that Bacon's homosexuality, thus doubly proved, was the cause of his downfall.

The injustice done to Bacon in 1948 by this distinguished Spanish doctor was compounded in 1956 by a Swiss hispanist, Gustav Ungerer, who, in a brilliant study of Antonio Pérez as Armado in *Love's Labour's Lost*, took Marañón's conclusions for granted and pronounced Pérez and Bacon 'as like as two peas'. In both men 'splendour of intellect' – a splendour, in Pérez's case, strictly limited to the gift of the gab – was 'paired with a vicious propensity for the lower savours of temporal existence', and both 'became traitors and lofty-minded flatterers entangled in the web of their own intelligence'.[50] Philip II had declared with some justice that Antonio Pérez's misdeeds were such as no vassal had ever been guilty of towards his King and master. Macaulay himself might well have been shocked to find Bacon, whose worst treason in his eyes was to have assisted in the prosecution of a traitor, coupled with such a man.[51] Denigration continued regardless, and in Spanish students are still being taught in a preface to the *Essays* that Francis Bacon obtained his high government positions through his immense ambition, his capacity for intrigue and his disloyalty to his friends, and that he ended his life surrounded with enemies, a typical case of 'the moralist who fails to follow his own counsels'.[52]

And how did Bacon fare in Italy, to whose thinkers he was so much indebted? And they to him – Galileo, in particular, who developed his theory of the tides partly in response to Bacon's.[53] The Italians gave him a warm welcome from the beginning. In Rome they would have voted him into the Accademia dei Lincei, founded in 1603 for 'the study of the great book of nature', but that their statutes excluded Protestants; in Florence the Grand Duke Cosimo II was the first to publish his *Essays* outside England, and in Venice the scholars clamoured for his *History of the Reign of King Henry VII* 'and whatever else he shall compose', exercising 'the talent of his divine understanding'.[54] Italy is the country that most appreciated Bacon's *Wisdom of the Ancients*. Thanks to Vico, a century later, the vital role Bacon assigned to poetry, and to the interpretation of fables, in his general scheme of things, was never lost sight of in that country, and did not have to be rediscovered, as it finally was in Britain.[55] In the *Enciclopedia Italiana*, published in 1930, Bacon was treated with a fairness and sympathy not shown to him by those of his own country, and he was honoured for renouncing a defence which might have endangered the monarchy (a motive for his submission which Macaulay had scornfully rejected as even more loathsome than judicial corruption).[56]

This favourable attitude cannot be attributed to the illusions of ignorance, for it is doubtful if any country has shown a greater interest in Bacon, as we may see from the numerous editions of his books in our century. Between 1920 and 1960, for example, aside from excellent editions of the *Essays*, and of *Henry VII*, fifteen editions of the *Novum Organum* were brought out in Italian, compared with one in English; and the 1970s saw the publication, by Enrico De Mas, of the reorganized, annotated works, political, juridical and historical, prefaced by the kind of objective and appreciative biographical note which in England students will look for in vain.[57] The Philosophical Works, edited by Paolo Rossi in 1975, were reprinted in 1986, and throughout the second half of our century scholarly studies of Bacon's works have abounded, including, in 1957, Rossi's crucial reassessment of Bacon as a scientist in modern times, De Mas's brief and illuminating *Francis Bacon* (1978), and many other valuable contributions.[58] Interest in Bacon is often met with in Italy. Unlike my grandson in England, presented at school with a 'dangerous' and a 'shifty' Bacon, my granddaughter Serenella, at school in Tuscany, could read only praises of a Renaissance pioneer in the mine of truth, in her *World History from the Fall of Rome to Waterloo*. Nor do we hear, when Bacon's name comes up, such epithets as 'a crook if there was one!' Instead it is (from a foot surgeon in the capital or a mechanic's daughter in a small hill-town) 'Ah, Bacone, a great man if there ever was one!' – with gestures to match.

Did Macaulay never reach Italy? He did, but the Italian outlook on human failings is not generally one of denunciation, and De Mas, for one, welcomed the arrival on the scene of critical presentations of Bacon, whereby 'the image of the philosopher acquired a more human physiognomy which was far more interesting to posterity'.[59] This scholar had little interest in disparagement. The *Commentarius Solutus*, for example, was for him a source of such fascinating insights into the workings of Bacon's mind that he had not time to linger over those jottings 'for my particular' which Abbott had found so offensive.[60] In the brief biography which precedes De Mas's *Francis Bacon*, we see a philosopher influenced by and influencing his friends all over Europe; looking always for able men to work with him; renouncing his defence because he was probably aware of the political motives behind his impeachment; remaining after his fall deeply interested in national affairs, and still offering valid counsel. Bacon's death of pneumonia as a result of his attempt to freeze a chicken, De Mas concluded, 'set the seal to an existence entirely devoted to the two greatest resources of humanity, scientific effort and political wisdom'.

This has been the usual approach in Italy. Only one writer, under the influence of a newly imported bias, took a different line. When Mario Manlio Rossi wrote his well received essay on Bacon in 1934, Strachey's *Elizabeth and Essex* had recently been translated into Italian, and this set the tone for Rossi's research. Like Abbott, he now devoted a chapter to 'il problema Bacon', and he was very pleased to discover a new key-word to explain the double, 'snake-like' soul. Kuno Fischer's had been 'elasticity'. For Rossi, the notion of Bacon's 'legalistic mind' was the solution. The problem, however, remained. Should he harken to Aubrey, or to Weldon – who, Fuller had said, related 'things which were not done or thought of'? Rossi could not choose between them. But it was Weldon he passed on, with large chunks of Macaulay and Strachey thrown in. There was also, however, 'that unknown Italian' (in fact, Toby Matthew) who, in a preface to the first Italian version of the *Essays*, had spoken of Bacon's moral virtue. '*Moral virtue?*' Rossi echoed. Unfortunately we cannot see the gesture which must have accompanied these words.[61]

There was also Spedding, in *Evenings with a Reviewer*. But no, Macaulay's 'classical opusculum' was not essentially destroyed by this work, Rossi decided – without proffering any argument in support of his decision. And he proceeded to follow Spedding, fact by fact, on the 'sad story' of the torture of Peacham, so as to expose the 'unforgivable guilt' of Bacon, but without once mentioning Spedding's demonstration that it was non-existent. And, 'I ask you', will anyone believe that Bacon acted against Essex out of faithfulness to the Queen, rather than spurred on by some despicable personal motive unknown to us? Perhaps a particular – 'to us incomprehensible' – form of cowardice? As for Bacon's fall, the Chancellor was so obsessed by ambition, and by the urge to surround himself with courtly adulators, that when the blow came he was stupefied. 'We can hear him clearly, asking himself: "How could I have done this? Was I really so vile?"'[62]

31

'England's One Scoundrel'

We left Bacon's reputation in the English-speaking world as it stood halfway through the present century, when he served as a foil for an idealized Ralegh. Meanwhile Bacon had long been similarly contrasted with the greatest of his contemporaries, the gentle and easy-going poet – few of Shakespeare's biographers being able to resist a passing thrust at their hero's 'serpentine adviser'.[1] Before we follow Bacon into the last decades of our century, therefore, I would like to look at the extraneous influence which, while creating an entirely different and equally false image of him, added another turn of the screw to the image we know. It is when his reputation was at its lowest ebb, in the late nineteenth century and early twentieth, that a considerable minority of cultivated opinion in Britain and all over the world began to look on Francis Bacon as the secret author of Shakespeare's plays. And as late as 1970, Rowse found, after lecturing to hundreds of audiences in Britain and America, 'that the great heart of the English-speaking public isn't sure whether Shakespeare wrote his own works'.[2]

First mooted in 1781, the Baconian theory was officially launched in 1856, with the support of Ralph Waldo Emerson, Bacon's keenest admirer from overseas, and of Nathaniel Hawthorne. Around this time such varied personalities as Coleridge, Disraeli, Bismark, Freud, Mark Twain and Henry James felt, with Emerson, that they could not 'marry' the 'ignorant rustic' to his poetry.[3] So many links had been found by different scholars between the two great Elizabethan minds that in 1853 one critic, impressed with the Baconian spirit of Shakespeare's plays, could write:

> It is as if into a mind poetic in form there had been poured all the matter that existed in the mind of his contemporary, Bacon. The only difference between him and Bacon is that Bacon sometimes writes an Essay and calls it his own, whilst Shakespeare writes a similar Essay and puts it in the mouth of an Ulysses or a Polonius.[4]

In 1888, three years after the publication of Abbott's *Francis Bacon*, an indignant opponent of the Baconians had no trouble in explaining these coincidences. He depicted a rascally lawyer sitting in the stalls, feverishly taking notes on the plays. There was, he maintained, 'something conscious, not to say sinister, in the silence of Bacon respecting Shakespeare, whom he must have known' and 'whose work he pillaged in the printed plays, but whose name he never even whispered to posterity!'

> We now *know* [he continued] that Bacon recognized Shakespeare's genius, and that he was enormously indebted to his plays for felicitous expressions and words, old sayings, profound reflections, antitheta, and the ripe results of wisdom; indeed, that he derived *so much mental sustenance* from them, beginning as a listener to them on the stage, that much of the wisdom attributed to him is really originally the property of Shakespeare.[5]

Enthusiastic adepts, meanwhile, found an increasing number of Baconian parallels in Shakespeare. Nor were they discouraged when similar parallels began to appear in all the Elizabethan playwrights. While orthodox scholarship was busily 'disintegrating' Shakespeare and sharing his works out among his contemporaries (as too erudite – or not poetic enough – for the rustic bard), Baconians reversed the process and began attributing all the best Elizabethan drama and poetry to a single author, Francis Bacon, or to a team of authors under his direction. The theory attracted every sort of amateur and crank. Frustrated mathematicians who might otherwise have tried to square the circle, free-ranging cryptographers, dreamers on Atlantis and pursuers of the occult joined in the chase, and a mythical Bacon emerged, a literary superman and magus, author of most of the works written in England and quite a few abroad, founder of a Grand Lodge of Freemasons, and, last but not least, the son of Queen Elizabeth by a secret marriage with the Earl of Leicester, and the legitimate heir to the throne. ('Either Bacon was the Prince of Wales,' exclaimed one zealous defender of the 'royal birth' theory arguing against unbelieving Baconians, 'or he was not Shakespeare.')[6]

For a much wider public than the philosopher had so far enjoyed, this was the real Bacon, and most of the books published about him in English during the first half of our century dealt not with his own works, but with the controversy over his authorship of the plays.[7] Even today the word 'Baconian' generally indicates, not a student of Bacon's works, but someone who believes he wrote Shakespeare's. (Indeed, according to Longman's *Dictionary of the English Language and Culture* (1995), Bacon 'is known especially because of the suggestion that he may have written some or all of Shakespeare's plays'.) While a handful of doctors and lawyers with time to spare exchanged lengthy tomes of polite sarcasm, thousands of 'staunch' and 'ardent' Baconians lived 'to further the name and fame of Francis Bacon' in the pages of *Baconiana* and other reviews devoted to the subject in Europe and America. We hear of 'whole-hearted members of the Baconian fold' gathering frequently (as one of them put it) 'to express something of the ardour of our souls for Francis, Viscount St Albans, his thought, his work, his deeds'; and even, on occasion, carrying 'their ungrudging labours and propagandist activity' so far as to permeate 'the confines of His Majesty's prisons, to give change and enlightenment to the abandoned convicts there on our great subject'.[8]

Some very strange Bacons were brought to light by the faithful, out of a growing collection of ciphers, of which twenty-two varieties had already been noted by 1910.[9] An epic tale of his life was unfolded by the Irish American Senator, Ignatius Donnelly, in 1888, in a mammoth two-volume book *The Great Cryptogram*. Unfortunately, after 900 pages his publishers compelled him to condense his story, at a crucial moment – Bacon had just been warned of the Queen's intention to seize 'Shaksper' (as the Baconians called the false Bard of Stratford) and force him to divulge the name of the real author of his plays. Horrified to think that it 'would humble his father's proud and most honourable name in the dust' to learn that his son had shared in the profits of the plays with such a low creature (Sir Nicholas had been dead by now for fifteen years), and fearing that he himself would be 'hanged like a dog' for the politically risky play of *Richard II*, Bacon attempted suicide by taking ratsbane, and fainted in an orchard in Gorhambury. The Bishop of Worcester advised that Shaksper – the 'gross fat rogue' whom Bacon had ridiculed as Falstaff – should 'have his limbs put to the question' (*sic*), but 'the rascally knave' escaped abroad, in time to save the real author of the plays – and just before his publishers closed down on Donnelly.[10]

In 1900 a tragic Bacon was revealed to the world by the famous Mrs Elizabeth Wells Gallup, who had painstakingly deciphered his harrowing life-story, allegedly encoded by Bacon in numerous Elizabethan and later works (including of course his own), by means of the 'bi-literal cipher', a cipher which Bacon had actually invented. Mrs Gallup's explanations – and her text – were so convincing that as late as 1938 the Head of the Cryptological Service at the French War office was inspired to publish Bacon's supposed confession in French. That, without any knowledge of Greek or Latin, she also managed to 'decipher' a literal translation of some parts of the *Iliad*, allegedly composed by Bacon himself in quite readable Elizabethan blank verse, adds to the mystery of her own life.[11] 'Though constantly hedged about, threatened, kept under surveillance', Mrs Gallup's Bacon began: 'I have written this story in full, in cipher, being persuaded in my own mind and heart that not only jesting Pilate, but the world asks "What is truth?"' The cipher, he went on to explain (with a real Baconian image), 'doth hold as in imperishable amber the story'.[12] And he proceeded to pour out in passionate and poetic prose his early romance with Princess Marguerite of France ('love's little sunny hour'), his frustration as the unrecognized heir to the English throne, his grief over the death of his younger brother, Essex, like him a legitimate son of Queen Elizabeth, and his remorse for having aided his detested mother against this noble brother. Finally he revealed the secret of his writings, 'guarded chiefly by such as are known names', that is by Greene, Peele, Shakespeare and Marlowe. Of Elizabeth, he wrote: 'She was my mother, yet more than any other I have cause to curse her . . . It burneth as an injury no lapse of time can cure.' And strange as it may seem, quite a few people still look on this travesty of Bacon's patient friendship for Essex – and of his faithful affection for Elizabeth – as the product of his pen.[13]

In vain did two cryptographers of high repute, in 1957, demonstrate beyond all doubt that none of the systems proposed by these, or by other decipherers, could have been used in Elizabethan printed texts.[14] Once seized by decoding fever, its practitioners are proof against all disproof, and they require ever increasing doses of their drug. Not least surprising, however, among all the new and often contradictory personalities allocated to Bacon, is that of the encoder himself. The phenomenal amount of work that would have been involved for a busy Lord Chancellor, with his mind on the *Great Instauration*, in inserting long and prolix explanations in numerous different and conflicting ciphers, each more complicated than the last, into practically all the literature printed in his time did not disconcert the decipherers, who themselves seemed to have endless time at their disposal. In Donnelly's cipher a thousand pages of small print yielded no more than eight double-space pages of deciphered text. He explains the process. Bacon first wrote his secret story, then devised the subjects of the play Shakespeare would sign, so as to fit the cipher's needs. If, for example, he had to refer to his servant Henry Percy, he could resort to the battle of Shrewsbury, where Prince Henry Percy was slain. As an admirer of his efforts exclaimed, not only had Bacon 'to construct his cipher, but he had also to compose the exterior writing which contained it, in sufficiently attractive, occult, enigmatic words, as in a cleverer age to invite, and eventually obtain solution'.[15] Thus did Bacon conceive and set forth the whole of his *Great Instauration* – not to speak of all Shakespeare's plays – as a vehicle for his personal disclosures.

Other exploits were laid at his door. For a hundred years many Baconians have been convinced that he was also the author of the essays of Montaigne, principal grounds for this belief being Anthony Bacon's friendship with the French philosopher, and the fact that a critic had called Montaigne *our Pharos of illumination*, 'in other words, our *Beacon*, pronounced, in Elizabeth's day, *Bacon*'.[16] Meanwhile another school contended that Bacon was the real author of *Don Quixote*, of which the 'alleged translation' was obviously the original, while the Spanish text was 'a more or less stilted effort', and a bad translation at that, by the pretended author, Cervantes.[17] Few supporters of this theory knew any Spanish, which is perhaps why one of them announced that it was much easier to prove Bacon the author of *Don Quixote* than to show that he wrote Shakespeare's plays. Examples of parallels that betray Bacon's hand are the comparison of sleep to death, common references to Helen of Troy, and the suprising interest Cervantes showed in the English story of the Knights of the Round Table. It was 'a joke of someone' (we are not told whose) to make Shakespeare and Cervantes, both masks of Bacon, die on the same day.[18] Bacon, however, was not content with this achievement, for we learn that he also composed all of the two hundred odd plays till now thought to have been written by the Spanish dramatist Lope de Vega, as well as many other works which, 'when divested of their Latin, French, German, Italian or Spanish mantles', also appear to have been translations of his originals.[19]

But there was more work in store for him. It had already been noted in the 1880s that the Rosicrucian aims corresponded under many heads to 'the mighty schemes of Verulam'; in Baconian eyes, therefore, 'they could have been conceived by no lesser mind'.[20] Thus, with the blessing of the Theosophical Society, we witness the birth of yet another persona for Francis Bacon, who, as Fra Rosie Crosse, or Head Shelezer, had founded the fraternity of the Rosie Crosse in England, his secret League for the Advancement of Learning, which emerged in 1726 as the Grand Lodge. The pursuit of this Bacon involved a pleasurable hunt for the typo-graphical irregularities and paper-marks in which he had left his 'secret signatures'. At the same time some of his devotees were in direct commu-nication with him, 'thanks to a link forged during a previous life on earth', as one of them explains, surprised but happy that so great a mind and soul should stoop to a person as insignificant as herself, and commu-nicate 'his simpler thoughts' to her.[21]

The activities of the Great Magus, who, we learn, also knew Hebrew and Chaldean, were not confined to his own time. Himself a reincar-nation of Roger Bacon – which explains his apparent borrowings from his medieval namesake – he continued his watch over philosophy and letters. At first, as some Baconians still believe, by living on secretly, after his official death, until he was over a hundred; and later by means of successive reincarnations, or in the person of the mysterious Comte de Saint Germain, who himself did not die, as is supposed, in 1784, but, when his Baconian identity was revealed in 1928, was still living in seclusion.[22] In the course of so long a life we will not be surprised to discover that Bacon turns out to have fathered every literary work of importance, from *The Canterbury Tales* to *Robinson Crusoe*, not forgetting *The Ancient Mariner* and FitzGerald's *Omar Khayyám*. In particular, he was the real author of

Pope's *Essay on Man*, including, presumably, the couplet about himself.[23] Around this time a learned German critic supported Bacon's claim to have been an incarnation or reincarnation of, among others, Shakespeare, Jehovah, the Devil, Jesus Christ, and his own mother.[24] 'With these vast and bottomless follies men have been entertained' – thus wrote Bacon of some of the tenets of the esoteric society he is held to have founded.[25]

Despite the good work done by the more sober Baconians in unearthing interesting details of Bacon's life, and in defending him against some of the defamations studied in the present book,[26] the Baconian follies could not but have an adverse effect on his already damaged fame. Indignant with the 'wretched group of dilettanti' who were 'bold enough to deny William Shakespeare the right to his own life-work' and to 'bespatter him and his invulnerable name with insane abuse', the 'Stratfordians' gave back as good as they got, and protests rained in.[27] 'The idea of robbing the world of Shakespeare for such a stiff, legal-headed old jackass as Bacon!' (1874); of transferring allegiance (1882) to 'Elisabeth's shifty Lord Keeper', who had composed his ciphers, if at all, 'to steal an immortal reputation from the dead'! In 1903 the famous Marie Corelli chimed in, denouncing 'the scandalous business of robbing the world's greatest genius of his name and reputation' in favour of a conceited pedant, Lord Bacon, 'the *traitor to his country*'.[28] Since the Baconians were merely attempting to oust a usurper, they could not see the logic of these counter-attacks, and the usurper himself loomed ever darker in their minds. 'Shaksper' became a 'drunken and illiterate clown', 'the sordid money-lender of Stratford'. Whereupon the orthodox retaliated against a doubly imaginary Bacon, the heretics' magus and martyr, and Macaulay's servile betrayer, ready-made for their abuse.[29] 'The true character of Bacon is black enough,' said the Chairman of the National Memorial to Shakespeare, in 1909, 'why rise to intensify it?' And he apostrophized as 'a bundle of villainies . . . England's one scoundrel, Lord Chancellor, Lord Verulam, Viscount St Alban'.[30]

In 1912 G.K. Chesterton joined the fray: 'why should the Baconians boil with abhorrence of poor Will from Warwickshire?' he exclaimed, and in a two-page tirade worthy of Macaulay's best, he set out to show that that historian had not done justice to the evil in Bacon. 'The brilliant effect of Macaulay's breathless essay depends on depicting Bacon as a monster of inconsistency, a misadmixture like a merman; above, in thought, he is as pure and graceful as a god; below, in action, as cold and fugitive as a fish.' Not so, Chesterton asserted: 'vulgar and shallow in philosophy', Bacon was consistent throughout. 'I do not see the two men of Macaulay – I think the man who fawned on Villiers was exactly the same as the man who despised Plato. And I am not at all surprised that the same individual who set himself higher than St Thomas also set himself lower than King

James.' Chesterton saw 'all the tangled tree' of the mad and mystical 'Baconian' extravagance, 'dormant and implicit in the seed of Lord Verulam's philosophy'. Like so many others, projecting the problems of his own time onto Bacon, he concluded that

> all those who trust science more than art, or experiment more than intuition . . . whitewash the wrinkled wickedness of the Tudor statesman and courtier, just as they whitewash the yet meaner wickedness of our own statesmen and men of power today. The mad duel between Bacon and Shakespeare . . . is really significant and menacing as a part of contemporary history.[31]

In 1926 a more impartial partaker in the controversy deplored

> the absurd and indiscriminate abuse which is now showered on the memory of Francis Bacon by certain Shakespeariolaters . . . venting their spleen on poor Lord St Alban, with entire disregard of historical justice, as though he were himself to blame for a wicked conspiracy to appropriate to himself the glory of Shakespearian authorship.[32]

Once again, Bacon was 'the least part of his own matter'.[33] But the abuse continued, and he soon aroused the anger of yet another group: those who had discovered new authors for Shakespeare's plays, and who looked on Bacon as a threatening rival candidate. A Russian champion of the Earl of Rutland, for example, informs us in 1940 that after Rutland's death the succeeding Earl handed his unpublished manuscripts to Bacon, who, since he was a crook, betrayed his dead friend and claimed the works (in cipher) for himself. 'We can only say with a sigh that the greed for even a distant fame must have hardened the Philosopher's mind and poisoned his conscience.'[34]

The demarcation line between Bacon's two fames occasionally crossed, so that we will find J.M. Robertson, one of the fairest vindicators of Bacon's character, fiercely attacking the 'Baconian heresy' in 1913, and E. G. Harman – convinced that Bacon wrote not only Shakespeare's poetry, but Spenser's also – describing him in 1914 as a self-deceiving time-server.[35] We should also hear W. G. Thorpe, a Baconian lawyer steeped in Abbott, on the real author of Shakespeare's plays. There are two men in Bacon, he wrote in 1897,

> as distinct as the two sides of a medal . . . On the obverse are the noble head, the eloquent features, the speaking eyes. On the reverse not a redeeming feature: drunkenness, debauchery of the vilest kind, according to current reports, gambling, extravagance, forgery, fraud, ingratitude, treachery, and finally the judicial murder of Essex, his patron, for the sake of the plunder it might happen to bring. Not a trace of either love or pity for any human being! For his mother

inspired only fear . . . Not one act of charity records itself in Bacon's life. [All in all he was] an aggravated paradox of humanity, inwardly concentrated all in self; outwardly the revealer to Humanity of a new philosophical universe . . .

And a good thing too, Thorpe concluded, for 'of all the mighty host which has no other hope save the mercy of God, none could stand more in need of [such a philosophy] than he'.[36]

These variously disreputable Baconian Bacons continued to thrive in the late twentieth century. In 1973 Joan Ham, who was also a follower of that other heresy, the belief that Richard III had nothing to do with the death of the Princes in the Tower, denounced Bacon (or rather the Shakespeare in him) as a dishonest historian. When writing the play of *Richard III*, she claimed, with Richard cast as murderer, he was well aware that this king was not responsible for the Princes' death, but he did not make up for his villainy until he published the *History of Henry VII* twenty years later. In fact Bacon maintained, as Bacon, the view he had supposedly illustrated as Shakespeare; Joan Ham read in *Henry VII* his fair assessment of Richard III as a well-intentioned king, but she overlooked another page in which he expressed the conviction that Richard had murdered his nephews.[37]

In 1979 Pierre Henrion again reminded us that Bacon was the real author of *Don Quijote de la Mancha* (*Mancha* meaning Channel – clearly of the English Channel). He presented elaborate and, in his view, irrefutable proof that Bacon had 'fathered' an early version of *Don Quixote* which had been circulating *sub rosa* since 1575. There was one difficulty: in 1575 'this young prodigy' was fourteen years old. We now learn, however, that he was in fact nearer twenty, since all the known references to Bacon's age (Henrion overlooked his certificate of baptism) were misleading, being 'parts of an astutely engineered plan to mask the truth', that he was really the Queen's son. In asking him how old he was, Henrion explained, and thus provoking the well-known reply that he was two years younger than her happy reign, the Queen had deliberately intended 'to fool the public and all future historians'.[38] Throughout the 1980s 'our gallant band of cipher analysts' continued to fill the pages of *Baconiana*, while another twist was given to Mrs Gallup's story, with the suggestion that her bi-literal cipher 'may have been a blind to conceal an inner system, the secret of which was known to her but not revealed'.[39]

Still in the 1980s a glossy reprint of *Francis Bacon's Personal Life-Story*, by Alfred Dodd, first published in 1949, explained the mystery of Bacon's (royal) birth, his (sham) death, and the real reason why he deliberately allowed himself to be ruined.[40] In an equally glossy biography, Jean Overton Fuller, recapitulating the same themes, found them clearly illustrated in the plays, where Bacon was obviously Hamlet (Gertrude being

Essex's mother, 'or more probably the Queen'), but also Titania's 'changeling boy' ('who is "the little changeling boy" if not Francis?').[41] And, despite the efforts of the Freemasons best acquainted with the history of their society to disclaim Bacon as a Mason, we find that the myth of the Grand Master is now kept alive in a new Trust, which holds frequent celebrations and conferences on his 'secret fraternity of poets and scholars', and on his 'initiatory training in preparation for attaining the supreme degree of Fra C.R.C.' – an illumination Bacon himself attained at the age of fifteen.[42]

Finally, in December 1992, after learning in an article in *Baconiana*, of the 'Athenian Order' apparently founded by Francis and Anthony Bacon in 1580 – with Fulke Greville as Grand Master, and every third member a Rosicrucian – we are introduced, in another article to a more deliberately evil Bacon than any yet invented. The son of Elizabeth by a wicked Leicester, under the influence of a 'sinister' Roger Bacon and in league with the 'black magician' John Dee, Bacon, we discover, was 'a Satanist'. His whole aim, as the author of all Shakespeare's works and those of many other writers, and as the founder of Freemasonry and of the Rosicrucian Society, was to overthrow Christian belief and replace it with a 'shell' of religion, emptied of its meaning; to substitute for the true philosophy of Socrates, Plato and St Thomas Aquinas his own 'perverted philosophy', and to reconstruct the whole world – including the North America he had himself founded – on Masonic lines.[43] As A. E. Waite, historian of the Rosy Cross, had already observed a hundred years ago, 'There never was such a mad world as that which has been formulated around the central figure of Viscount St Albans.'[44]

Meanwhile Shakespeare's orthodox biographers were struggling to keep up at all costs their image of a cold, unimaginative and humourless Bacon; a man, that is, who could never have written the plays. Bacon was pronounced, by Edward Dowden in 1875, as being incapable of friendship and 'without a spark of genial humour'; by Churton Collins in 1904, as being without trace of 'any light play of wit and fancy, of any profound passion, of any aesthetic enthusiasm'; by Edgar Fripp in 1938, as being without humour or courage, unloved, and 'unenthusiastic, save for knowledge'; while Dover Wilson, addressing a birthday lunch at Stratford-on-Avon in 1948, strongly suspected that he 'had no heart at all'.[45] Nor did he fare any better in the biographies produced in 1964 to celebrate the fourth centenary of Shakespeare's birth. But the most unkindest cut of all was surely his treatment in 1988, in Peter Levi's delightful array of contemporaries of Shakespeare.[46] Here Bacon could fittingly have taken his place, not without panache, beside the greatest of poets; in their young days, perhaps, on that evening of Gray's Inn revels, when first his own 'devices' and later the *Comedy of Errors* were shown; or when collaborating with Francis Beaumont, in the spirit of the *Winter's Tale*, to produce

his *Masque of the Thames and the Rhine* for the wedding of Princess Elizabeth; or pleasing Thomas Campion and George Herbert with his own
poetic efforts.[47] Instead we find only a careerist, 'eager' to turn against
Essex, 'frantic to rise high' in the pursuit of criminals, and bracketed in
this frenzy, as we have seen, with the sadistic Topcliffe.[48]

32

The 'False Persona'

In the mid-twentieth century there was a noticeable shift of attitude in various lives of Bacon, written by scholars such as Benjamin Farrington in Britain and Fulton Anderson in the United States, laying more stress than others had done on what he was attempting to achieve, and showing his unity of purpose.[1] They were received with scepticism. One reviewer declared himself unconvinced by Anderson's contention that Bacon was a 'moral statesman', trying to put his theories into practice in public life. Bacon, he still believed, 'was basically a self-seeking politician'. Or 'perhaps he was both; a crass politician as well as a philosophically oriented statesman?'[2] Nor did the new approach keep other scholarly writers from the usual sneers. Max Patrick could still celebrate the four hundredth anniversary of Bacon's birth in 1961 by stressing that his vigorous prosecution of Essex 'was death to the popular Earl, and the blackening of his own reputation by charges that he was a son of Judas'; and in 1962 G. P. V. Akrigg could go out of his way to observe that feeling 'was never Bacon's long suit' ('not for nothing did Aubrey later report that he had the eye of a viper').[3] There was, however, a tendency to tone down the invective. Familiar disparaging remarks were sometimes quali-fied with expressions such as 'let's be fair to Bacon'. and a sort of two-way trend developed: after automatically repeating the negative opinions which everyone took for granted, a writer might grudgingly note others, discovered on the way, which ran counter to the general bias.

This approach is particularly evident in the study of Lionel Cranfield by Menna Prestwich (1966), often cited here. The Bacon presented by this historian is a grasping materialist with a 'devastating' capacity for double-think, whose 'gnawing ambition' had corroded 'the most cynical mind of his age' – which explains why a man who could 'soar to horizons far beyond those of his contemporaries, could also stoop so low'. And yet . . . time and again the author's perspicacity, objectivity and sense of justice get the better of the inherited image in her own mind. Bacon was sycophantic, 'but he had his moments of truth', 'cynical, but perhaps he was right'; his advice that Coke should be kicked upstairs, where he would be less obstructive, does not after all 'seem so odd', while his reluctance to strike Coke down 'tells in his favour'. 'Possibly his views should be ignored, because of his notorious cynicism,' but 'there is flesh on the bones' of his notes, and however unscrupulous his suggestions for dealing with opposition leaders, 'it is legitimate to enquire whether his ideas of political management should be rejected out of hand'.[4] Strange that a historian of this quality, well into the second half of our century, should still feel a kind of surprised reluctance to find herself speaking at all favourably about Bacon.

In the long run, however, the revival of interest in Bacon, which has since produced many scientific, historical and literary studies in learned volumes and journals, had little effect on Bacon's reputation as a man. The growth of the highly specialized study, as has been noticed, tends to remove Bacon himself out of the province of general readers.[5] They are thus left at the mercy of biographers who pass on the vivid image tossed off by Macaulay – and etched into their brains by Abbott – without ever pausing to look at it; and, of course, of those academics who do not seem to have read the new studies, and are happy with denigration. In the United States, for example, while in 1962 Anderson's book embraced the thinker and the man in a rounded evaluation, we saw Bacon in the study by W. K. Jordan (Harvard) ready, as ever, 'to bend a great mind to ignoble deeds'.[6] In 1966 Anthony Esler (Duke University) endorsed Macaulay's 'slashing condemnation' of the 'despicable' conniving politician', self-serving courtier and corrupt judge, who 'deluged his powerful relatives and patrons with petitions for high office'. Esler's own conribution was to depict Bacon as 'the Tamburlaine of the mind', whose 'egotistic self-confidence was as towering as that of any of Marlowe's heroes', and whose 'surging sense of unlimited power', seeking an outlet in 'both political and philosophical triumphs', found it in 'a single splendid image – the image of himself as the Great Lord Bacon'. ('How glorious a statue of himself Bacon must have expected posterity to raise . . . !')[7] In 1968 the *Encyclopedia Americana* once again presented a 'servile, ruthless, unfaithful Bacon, still torn between ambition for office and the craving to achieve his immense program', still 'fascinating and disconcerting historians' and still betraying his perfidy towards Essex by skilfully suppressing parts of his story.

Writers on other personages to whom Bacon served as a foil were in no two minds about him. In Robert Lacey's biography of a demythologized Essex (1971), without a hint at the known refutations, every calumny so far circulated was heaped upon a quite unrevised Bacon's head. Having 'painfully' established himself as a member of Gray's Inn, bought a seat in Parliament with 'judicious bribes and flattery', and in other ways 'abjectly pursued' his career, Bacon accepts the gift of Twickenham Park and Garden (*sic*) from Essex – the condition he made, that 'I can be no more yours than I was', being sneered at as 'a likely story!' He then promptly 'plays Judas' to his friend, intervening with 'vicious irrelevance' at the first trial; assists Essex with letters, 'more to hedge his bets than to make amends for his treachery'; 'craftily insinuates malice and not hysteria' at the final trial; is treated as a pariah by all and sundry, and fails to profit by his treachery. End of Bacon.[8]

But what are we to think when in a study illustrating his brilliant achievements in the field of scientific thought, *Francis Bacon, The First Statesman of Science* by J. G. Crowther (1960) – Bacon's whole life is presented as 'a dialectical struggle between the active and the contemplative, the personal and the social, the noble and the ignoble'? The key to the 'problem' of this double Bacon is Abbott's, with another turn in the lock. In a chapter entitled 'Criminal or Mental Invalid?' the author suggests that Bacon was suffering from a disorder 'which was the price he paid, socially and mentally, for probing the utmost end of knowledge'. The psychological abnormality of a man 'who kept the two different activities of his mind in separate compartments' would help to explain the attitude of Elizabeth and Burghley towards him, and may have contributed 'to the distrust in which he was held'. Such cases, Crowther pointed out, could sometimes be cured by electroshock treatment – indeed, he thought, the shock Bacon received on his fall from power may actually have 'brought into communication areas of his mind which had lost contact with each other'.[9] Of all the 'charitable speeches' with which men have honoured Bacon's bequest of his name to a later age, this is surely the one that would have astonished him the most.

Bacon's popular biographers, meanwhile, were doing their best, but they were defeated by the two-headed monster. C. D. Bowen, in 1963, suffered from the 'darkness' in Bacon's life, and found him 'a great trial to his biographers'. She was as fascinated as Strachey had been with the man she described as 'clever, restless, crafty', with his 'liquorish viper eyes', 'who took bribes yet cannot be called dishonest, who betrayed Essex but was not mean or base'; and as puzzled as ever Abbott was by the fact that 'his prime champions' were found not only among the worldly but among the virtuous – scholars, clergymen whose lives were blameless and devoted. 'Is this part of the riddle,' she wondered, 'or was Macaulay right in his verdict that Bacon's champions, dazzled by the effulgence of his brilliant mind, forgot the standards of ordinary decency and morality?'[10] Daphne du Maurier, in her biography of Bacon, *The Winding Stair*, published in 1976, after her attractive first volume on those two 'golden lads', Anthony and Francis, was just as puzzled. He had a mind 'with so many facets that he must have bewildered his contemporaries', yet he was so greatly admired by those who knew him best; she wondered what a twentieth-century psychoanalist 'might have unravelled from a recumbent Francis on a couch'. Francis Bacon, she decided, was an enigma, in his time as in ours.[11] He had been no enigma to his contemporaries. 'There cannot be one colour of the mind, another of the wit,' as Ben Jonson was prompted to remark, after praising Bacon's character and his works, 'for the greatness that was only proper to himself.'[12] We, however – so A. Johnston put it in 1965 – 'must accustom ourselves to the intermingling of two figures', to this 'strangeness in the man'. Why should we? Why follow writers who are trying so hard to solve a non-existent problem that they never think of looking directly at the man himself, as, according to Carlyle, Spedding had left him, 'washed down to the natural skin'?[13]

We have seen a scientist's view of the scientist. Let us now look at a historian's view of the statesman: Joel J. Epstein's brief outline, *Francis Bacon, a Political Biography* (1977), recommended in 1981, despite many mistakes of fact, as 'the best account of Bacon's political career', and in 1992 as 'a thorough and insightful study'. Epstein tried 'to be fair' to his subject, but again the inherited burden was too much for him.[14] His Bacon is riddled with 'self-seeking aims' and frustrations, struggles desperately through a 'furious period', and is 'driven by the desire for power' and the 'agonizing' search for fulfilment. Occasionally, despite the 'self-seeking motive', there might be something to be said for one of his actions, but in the end his story is that of a gifted individual who, after striving a long time for great place, 'behaved in it without distinction'. He had 'successfully compartmentalized his political and intellectual sides', said Epstein, looking at Bacon with the same double vision as Crowther had done. But in leaving out the scientific thinker, Epstein left out the political thinker also. It is no wonder that when he came across the ampler view put forward by H. B. White (1968), who looked on Bacon as a profound political philosopher, he found it 'a bit unsettling'.[15]

Jonathan L. Marwil, in *The Trials of Counsel* (1976), had faced no such problem when he brought out his own improved version of Abbott's dim view (1885), covering Bacon's thought as well as his life – although his qualifications for judging Bacon's science, and even his history, have been justly queried.[16] Bacon, he claims, is seen here in his true colours: a self-deceiver, a Judas and a 'villain-maker', 'slipping the coils of deadly analogy around the Earl', as he falsely charged an Essex innocent of all plotting; but above all as a man racked with the desire for political power.[17] Bacon, wrote Lee at the beginning of our century, had decided to serve the Crown, 'with the single unpraiseworthy aim of benefiting his own pocket', and after his fall had offered to codify the law solely because of his 'wild hopes of regaining the King's favour'. Marwil now extended this view to Bacon's whole life work. We discover not only that his apparently earnest interventions in Parliament were prompted, one and all, by an overweening desire to convince his royal masters of his worth, but that the 'vast contemplative ends' he had confided to his uncle as a young man were no more than a method of self-advertisement, and his plans for the reform of learning a 'self-justifying formula', frequently resorted to by his biographers to give meaning to 'a soiled life'. And finally we hear that all his works – legal, scientific, historical, religious and literary – inspired both as to content and timing by calculated self-interest, were taken up or put down as they might serve his plans for self-advancement.[18] (It is 'odd', Marwil remarked, that the *Advancement of Learning* should still be read as though it were 'untainted'.)[19]

This historian adopted not only Abbott's judgements but his all too effective methods, including his way of influencing the reader by pre-judging an issue, and the devious practice of making the author he is quoting say the opposite of what he meant. Thus, in support of his conviction (after Abbott) that the *Apology* was an unreliable piece of self-deception, he stated that Spedding himself 'had some doubts about the work'. Spedding, with no doubts whatsoever, was commenting on a statement made in the *Apology*, and, as always, conceding every possible advantage to his imaginary opponent. He pointed out (and Marwil cites him) that Bacon's account should 'be taken with caution, being his own story in his own defence when nobody could contradict him'; but, he added (and Marwil does not cite him), the statement was made 'under the most solemn asseveration that a man can tell of its truth', an asseveration that entirely convinced Spedding. We have seen Macaulay and will see others making their point simply by suppressing the second half of a sentence.[20]

We will look in vain in Marwil's book for reasoned argument or demonstration. Contemporary witnesses favourable to Bacon are rejected out of hand. Rawley is disqualified: he was 'devoted'. And all we hear of Toby Matthew's encomium is that he admired Bacon 'to a fault'.[21] We are warned not listen to Ben Jonson on his friend's gifts (his praises, not retailed here, might be 'misleading'); nor must we let our confidence in Jonson's remarks 'persuade us that Bacon generally won the minds of his listeners'; 'his speeches might well have annoyed those who knew themselves less talented or believed themselves more serious.' They might – but did they? Nor must we assume that because Bacon became chief spokesman in Parliament the King prized him as a Counsellor; as for the Members, they might have been merely 'taking advantage of his talents' – as why should they not?[22] Habitually attributing his own views to those among whom Bacon lived, Marwil suggests that Bacon 'may well have sounded like Justice Shallow to his contemporaries'. But did he? They spoke of the Judge's piercing eye, and recalled that men 'durst not conceal the most intrinsic part of their mysteries from him'.[23]

Marwil's thesis is based on the premise that everything in Bacon is false. Not a word he spoke is to be trusted, even his jokes 'should be treated with skepticism', and every action requires 'translation' or 'construing' to detect its hidden purpose.[24] If Bacon liked living at Gray's Inn, it is because there alone he found people 'submissive to his will'. His pleasure in building, which he inherited from his father and shared with many of his contemporaries, and even his love of gardens, sprang from an obsession with putting things in order.[25] It is difficult to write fairly about someone you dislike, and when this critic is not scornfully condescending, he is exasperated by unpleasant traits 'typical' of Bacon, or by his 'predictably' unworthy actions. In success, Bacon is sanctimonious, whimsical, preening, strutting; he 'exceeds the limits of puffery' and 'exudes' a misplaced confidence which 'oozes' from his letters; in defeat he is tawdry yet pathetic, and seethes with resentment. 'For Bacon to persuade himself that he was meant for contemplation required minimal self-deception.' His works, 'disturbingly obtuse', betray sloth and ineptitude; his conversation is a show of learning, and he expresses himself with a 'largesse of words' and a 'windy ignorance' which would greatly have surprised Ben Jonson, who wrote that he 'could not but love' him for his diligence, and for whom 'no man ever spoke more neatly, more precisely, or suffered less emptiness, less idleness in what he uttered.'[26]

And yet . . . While reducing Bacon's 'planned' production of learned works to 'platforms' from which he could 'air his hopes and frustrations', Marwil was faced, once again, with a Bacon who did not fit, and he had to resort to the usual qualifying formulas. Self-promotion cannot *by itself* explain the *Maxims of the Law*; the 'Discourse on the Union of Kingdoms' is not *'purely* a matter of flattery'; *The Advancement of Learning* is not *exclusively* an exercise in 'self-advertisement'; and we might do Bacon an injustice 'to see calculation as the *sole* motive for his attachment' to Essex (my italics).[27] The contradictions Abbott floundered in are much in evidence in Marwil's Bacon, who is drawn on the jacket of his book, staring down at his black negative image, upside down, and who is continually achieving the most improbable feats. He gives James advice often conceded to be unimpeachable, merely to impress him. In Parliament he is found pushing himself forward and 'posturing' as he presents the bills with which he was attempting to deal with the savage depression by which, Marwil admits, Bacon had been deeply shocked, when 'he had seen its consequences at first-hand'. He broaches his great project to Elizabeth as a young man, and later to James in every way he can think of; makes one more effort in his last years to gain Eton as a launching ground for it, and gives it forceful posthumous expression in the *New Atlantis*: all this with the single aim of forging a 'false persona' with which he could 'rationalize a sense of failure'.[28]

Bacon's whole life, Marwil concluded, was a failure – as it had need to be if his aims were what Marwil thought them. He failed, not because he was impeached for corruption (like Abbott, Marwil exonerated him from this charge), but because he could never fulfil his 'racking desire to have the world recognize and reward his genius'.[29] He did not win the trust of those he served, and if he won that of posterity it was on false pretences, however much the 'seemingly wisdom-filled sentences . . . still beguile us'.[30] Or did, until 1976. Now, after a century and a half surviving disparagement, exit Francis Bacon for good. He has deceived us all. Through his 'disreputable' arts of rhetoric, he managed to impose his own 'convenient assessment of himself' on his friends while he lived, and on generations of followers. Macaulay – in his pages of high praise – was deceived, along with the others. And none so much as Bacon himself, who thought he had been born to serve mankind.

We are still in the United States, eight years later – or rather with readers of *Time* magazine the world over. Many people will never have heard of Bacon except as he is presented here, with Presidents Garfield and Nixon, as one of three typical examples of takers of bribes in history.[31] They will learn that in 1617 one John Wrenham had charged Bacon with ruling unfairly against him; that, being unable to prove bribery, he had both his ears cut off and paid a heavy fine; and that he was justified, too late, when in 1621 Bacon 'confessed to a whole array of bribes', and, adding insult to injury, 'got off easily'. What they will not learn is that Wrenham was sentenced in the Star Chamber by Coke, seconded by the other fifteen judges – the irreproachable Bishop Andrewes among them, but not Bacon – for 'vilifying justice', which was then looked on as a 'foul crime', implicating not only the Chancellor, but the whole Bar, and even the King. And that, although condemned to the savage punishment Coke demanded for him – life imprisonment, a thousand-pound fine and loss of his ears – he neither lost his ears nor paid a fine, and was released after a few months in prison, because Bacon would not hear of his slanderer being disfigured or punished (the seat of justice being vindicated by his trial), and pleaded with the King to set his condemnation aside.[32] They will not hear Wrenham's Legal Counsel, Yelverton, testify at the trial that nothing had come 'between God and [the Chancellor's] conscience but the merits of the case', or Serjeant Crewe, Counsel for his opponent, declare that, having 'always despised riches and set honour and justice before his eyes', Bacon had judged 'out of his noble conscience and the integrity of his heart' and that 'no magistrate hears with more attention' and 'attends with more understanding and patience'.[33] Nor will they learn, of course, that in later years Wrenham, forgiving the Chancellor neither his decree nor his leniency, used his regained liberty to hunt out petitioners against him, and, as Carteret put it, 'proved his ruin'.[34]

When presenting this image of Bacon to the world, *Time* was reviewing an eight-hundred page book entitled *Bribes* (1984). Its author, John T. Noonan Jr, a legal scholar of repute at the University of California, had used his authority and expertise to revive once again the Macaulay/Campbell version of a corrupt Chancellor presiding over 'a ring' of shady barristers. Prompted by Buckingham, 'abetted in his game' by the Keelings and Lady Whartons, assisted by such Chancery personnel as Churchill, and 'with the judicious employment of bagmen', Bacon is shown running Chancery as 'a money-making machine'. Noonan underpinned his evaluation with an impressively thorough analysis of the parliamentary proceedings against Bacon, and of his detailed confession. Unfortunately, starting from the premise that the Chancellor was a crook animated by the lowest of motives, he took every dubious bit of gossip assiduously collected against Bacon – including Churchill's denunciations – at face value. He disregarded Gardiner's equally thorough but more impartial study of every cause relevant to the confession, and dismissed all Bacon's explanations as the plausible excuses of a man at bay, 'craftily' professing ignorance of his suitors' gifts and shamelessly laying the blame on the servants he had himself corrupted. The biased testimony of enemies goes unquestioned, but everything said by others – not excepting the unimpeachable Sackville – in Bacon's defence is discounted as the biased testimony of servant or friend. And that exemplary priest and scholar, Toby Matthew, of whom the French Ambassador reported that he worked 'for honour's sake alone, and from zeal', appears as one of Bacon's accomplices, 'busily negotiating for payments from litigants and doing Bacon the double service of screening him from contact and of letting him accomplish more business than he could have handled by himself'.[35]

Bacon is the only taker of bribes to earn a whole chapter in Noonan's book; indeed, two, since an extra one was required to present him as an impersonation of that other unjust judge, Angelo, the merciless and icy justicer, adulterer and 'virgin-violator' (*sic*) who is the villain of Shakespeare's *Measure for Measure*. This play was enacted, it now appears, 'not on an English stage but at the center of the English system of justice'. In the chapter entitled 'Angelo, the Shaken Icicle', Bacon is placed on a par with this frigid, lecherous and cruel Shakespearian character. Like Angelo, Bacon was 'so imprisoned in his confidence and self-sufficiency, that he was the ready victim of great temptations'. Noonan supports his novel thesis by reading overtones of sexual corruption into an image Bacon had noted down for use in his promised interview with the King: he would deal ingenuously with his Majesty, 'without seeking fig-leaves or subterfuges'. Meaning, said Noonan, that he 'would show how his genitalia worked'. Bacon, he went on to explain, reverting to the ancient role of the corrupt official as whore, posed as 'the King's virgin' (which 'no doubt tickled James'), while he 'conceded sin'.[36]

But the connection of judicial with sexual corruption which Shakespeare was illustrating in *Measure for Measure* is not present in Bacon. 'Without fig-leaves' is a figure of speech, which he also used in his confession to the Lords. And he was not hinting at virginity, doubtful or otherwise, but claiming truthfulness. This Noonan would have realized had he recalled that Truth is traditionally represented naked, as it is in Bacon's essay 'Of Truth', where it is described as 'a naked daylight', and in his Plan of Work for the *Great Instauration*, where he designed 'to set everything forth . . . plainly and perspicuously (for nakedness of the mind is still, as nakedness of the body once was, the companion of innocence and simplicity)'.[37] 'What drove Bacon to it?' Noonan wondered. Among the various psychological explanations he offers (repression by his mother, rivalry of his father, the spectre of past poverty, or excessive pride), he suggests that Bacon's 'great betrayal' in 'prosecuting his patron Essex for treason and sending him to have his head cut off' may have haunted him 'so the memory could be obliterated only in magnificence and opulence'. The chapter concludes with the humiliated philosopher in one of Dante's hells as the living incarnation of the 'unjust man' – taken from Bacon's translation of Psalm 1: 'so shall he not lift up his head in the assembly of the just.' A role Bacon has now recognized as his own.[38]

That is how a reputed American legal scholar has seen the Chancellor who looked on himself as the justest judge in fifty years, and whose proposals for the reform of the law were to have considerable influence on American legal theory. We might expect a more complete understanding – or at least a greater familiarity with Bacon's life and background – if we turn to one of his own countrymen, like Bacon a reforming judge, and with all the authority of a distinguished career in the profession behind him. Bacon almost entirely fills one of the thirteen sketches presented by that 'judicial colossus', as he has been called, Lord Chief Justice Alfred Denning, in *Landmarks in the Law* (1984).[39] It is entitled 'Torture and Bribery', and the author's express purpose is to tell us about Bacon's 'wicked doings'. This Jekyll who 'would do no good', we learn, coupled with an evil Hyde, has been 'accused of torture' and 'found guilty'. He was also false and perfidious, an unjust judge, and a hypocrite besides, who denounced these vices in others.

Judge Denning had little regard for facts, as we may note when we read, for example, that Bacon married 'an alderman's elderly and ugly daughter for money'. (When Bacon married the 'handsome maiden' he had found 'to his liking', and settled double her dowry upon her, she was fourteen years old.)[40] We will find Denning's other statements on a par with this one. His account of Bacon's arraignment in Parliament is a travesty, and every statement presenting him as a torturer is false. Bacon was not consulted by the King as to whether Peacham could be put to the rack; he did not tell the King that it was his prerogative to apply torture; he did not 'get the Privy Council to allow it'(in fact he advised against it); and he did not write a letter to James 'full of venom' against a 'poor old man' who had been 'appalled by the wickedness of the King and his favourites'. Finally, he did not propose to the King 'that he and his fellows should go to the Tower and threaten Peacham with torture by burning', an absurd misreading of Bacon's suggestion, with an apt metaphor, that 'it were not amiss to make a false fire'; in other words, that if Peacham were told that his trial was imminent, he might confess. Denning's blunder is the more surprising when we recall that in present-day inter-rogation the expression 'to light a false fire' with this connotation is standard terminology.[41]

Were it not for the ever prevailing bias, it would be difficult to conceive of a respected Chief Justice – who, we may presume, had summed up the evidence on countless occasions with impeccable impartiality – setting out to poison the jury's mind against this prisoner at the bar, quoting only *ex parte* witnesses against him, without hearing a single word in his defence, and completely misunderstanding what the accused has said. In *Landmarks in the Law* Denning showed no interest in Bacon's writings, except to cite Coke's 'cutting criticism' of the *Novum Organum* as 'fit to be freighted in the *Ship of Fools*'. He passed over in silence the admirable works of judicial criticism written by other distinguished experts in the law, where he would have found a very different view of the essential probity shown by 'the greatest legal thinker of all time'.[42]

Bacon fared no better at Oxford, where in 1980 Professor Anthony Quinton devoted seven depressing pages (as unlike as could be to De Mas's lively sketch, in a similar preface two years earlier) to reminding the students of Bacon's philosophy that 'England's most important Re-naissance thinker' was a mean, servile, cruel and corrupt man. In this preface the usual episodes are rehearsed in the same poor light. Pope's 'remarkably concise' couplet is cited, and Macaulay's 'rollickingly injudi-cious essay' is recalled with obvious enjoyment. Bacon's rich and varied experience is reduced to a series of deserved misfortunes: he was disliked by Queen Elizabeth, 'not much admired' by anyone, and finally frus-trated, despite his lifelong habit of 'pestering the great'. As we would expect, he manifested the 'somewhat reptilian qualities' of his character, and he was also 'a fairly cold fish'; which, Quinton concludes, may help to explain his achievement of 'so much glory and so much shame'.[43]

One more sample of the shadow Bacon which many scholars still carry in their minds came from Edinburgh in 1992, where, in a study principally devoted to his legal attainments, Daniel Coquillette praised this 'creative, profound and innovative man' as 'one of the paramount thinkers of his age'. There was, however, Bacon's 'darker side', and the life of this 'flawed man' is vitiated here by the same old themes of disparagement. On his 'role in the execution of his first supporter', we learn yet again that Bacon 'was instrumental in securing the Earl's conviction'. We hear that a thoroughly frustrated Bacon spent his youth 'seeking to advance his fortunes' with 'begging letter' after begging letter, entreating his uncle Burghley in vain. And no wonder, since Queen Elizabeth 'thoroughly distrusted him', probably rightly, for 'she was a shrewd judge of character'. Bacon is recalled, needless to say, as 'one of the last English jurists to use torture', and finally, because he was 'immensely proud of his establishment', we meet him as the self-confessed receiver of huge bribes. With reference to the 'passionate disputes between Macaulay and Spedding on this issue' (posthumous disputes, we should note, as far as Macaulay was concerned), Coquillette has only one comment: 'careful modern research has confirmed Bacon's own confession.' When looked up, the modern research turns out to be a 'scholarly and thorough account' of Bacon's corruption given by John T. Noonan in *Bribes*.[44]

Finally in 1995 the old ground was gone over once again in an article by Adrian Berry in the *Sunday Telegraph*, recapitulating what he had written about Bacon in 1982, with embellishments.[45] Enter the 'wicked benefactor', a 'towering genius who hid the coldest of hearts'. In Macaulay's ringing sentences, we read once again that 'when Essex attempted a childish *coup d'état* Bacon, wishing to curry favour with the Queen' prosecuted him 'to death' and then 'blackened' his memory. After which he proceeded to 'pervert the laws of England to the vilest purposes of tyranny' by having an aged clergyman 'tortured until he confessed to non-existent crimes'. (It should be pointed out for the record that, when advising against torture, Bacon had told the King that Peacham would merely go on inventing a variety of lies, as he had done till then, and as he was to do again – though not on the day he was put to the manacles, when he did not open his mouth.) Finally, Bacon was 'no ordinary accepter of bribes', as indeed becomes clear when we discover that on his appointment as Chancellor he 'let it be known that justice would go to the highest bidder'. To complete the picture, we are offered another new fact. When Bacon stuffed a dead chicken with snow – an experiment in refrigeration which, we will recall, brought about his death from pneumonia – 'he had stolen the chicken'! (The author must have forgotten that Hobbes, from whom we have the story, was quite explicit. He told Aubrey that alighting from his coach with Dr Witherborne, the King's physician, Bacon 'went into a poor woman's house at the bottom of Highgate hill, and bought a hen', and the woman eviscerated it for him.)[46]

Berry concluded his article remarking that the crimes of 'great but wicked benefactors' are soon forgotten. But he has not forgotten Bacon's supposed crimes. And, suprising as it may seem on the threshold of the twenty-first century, all his allegations (except about the stolen chicken) are still taken almost verbatim from Macaulay, whom he mentions as 'one of the first to perceive both sides of Bacon's character' and to identify him as a 'creeping snake'. The ball rolls on.

33

The Sterile Philosopher

It was inevitable that the habit of finding fault with Bacon should pass from his biographers to the commentators on his writings. While many of his defamers managed to combine a high estimate of Bacon's thought with a low view of his character, we know that others opted for a philosopher who was evil through and through. Among these, we have seen an eminent German scientist claim that the venality of Bacon's life had invaded his work, and a famous English author conclude that the man who could fawn on Villiers was necessarily a vulgar and shallow philosopher.[1] 'Can we conceive', wrote Bacon's one Italian detractor, that 'such a serpentine soul would not have its effect on the thinker?'[2] Scholars seriously engaged in the study of Bacon's real purposes remain unaffected by such opinions. If they notice them, they may express their dissent, or merely laugh. But among the less dedicated many have been influenced in their judgement of Bacon's mental quality by the prevailing climate of moral condemnation. Jonathan Marwil was perhaps an extreme case when he claimed to show – to the satisfaction of the historian reviewing him – that Bacon's alleged 'failure as statesman and lawyer, his weakness as historian, philosopher and prosewriter' and his 'narrowness of moral and political vision' could all be attributed to his 'flawed personality'.[3]

The vicissitudes of Bacon's reputation as a thinker are outside the scope of this book, but we are concerned with the shadow cast by Bacon the man on Bacon the philosopher. More than one student of his works has noticed the exceptional treatment meted out to Bacon alone among the thinkers of his time. Paolo Rossi, speaking at an international symposium on Bacon in 1984, was surprised to note how often his thoughts are taken out of historical context and 'perverted to discredit him'.[4] 'I know of no other Renaissance writer', Brian Vickers remarked in 1989, 'who is so regularly vilified'.[5] It is not just because philosophical viewpoints have changed that 'the sage of Verulam', whose 'fearless genius', in 1626, challenged 'the deepest recesses of our nature', could be dismissed in 1948 as 'a new manager descending upon the old firm . . . with the familiar bric-à-brac cleaned up and offered as a new line'; in 1954 as 'a solemn pretentious ass'; in 1975 as a failed philosopher, a mere entertainer, a 'dabbler in natural studies'; in 1976 as a writer who had 'failed to master scientific lore', and in 1986 as a 'sham thinker', whose 'revolutionary stance' has long since been 'debunked' and whose claims to originality are mere 'bluff'.[6]

There can be little doubt as to the animus behind such appraisals. Scorn for the philosopher and scorn for the man are often overtly linked, as they were in the well-known scientist J. W. Draper, who in 1862 wrote: 'It is time that the sacred name of philosophy should be severed from its long connexion with that of one who was a pretender in science, a time-serving politician, an insidious lawyer, a corrupt judge, a treacherous friend, a bad man.'[7] The same animus is found a century later, in such diverse critics as Lynn Thorndike (Columbia University), who concluded in 1958 that Bacon 'could not think straight', that he 'was a crooked chancellor in a moral sense and a crooked naturalist in an intellectual and scientific sense'; Edmund Cahn (Boston), who, in a chapter entitled 'The Lawyer as Scientist and Scoundrel', in 1966 described Bacon as 'a sort of chanticleer whose crowing had nothing to do with the rising of the sun'; and Friedrich Heer (Vienna), who decided in 1968 that Bacon's hunger for power had driven him to formulate his Induction as 'England's answer to Spain'.[8] Where the indignation aroused in scholars by a delinquent Bacon is not as explicit as this, it is apparent in gross misjudgements whereby he is castigated for holding ideas diametrically opposite to those he unmistakably stood for, in sweeping statements ascribing to him a deleterious influence over a whole age, or in the marked gap to be found between a commentator's normally appreciative attitude to a subject and the hostile tone reserved for a despicable Bacon.

Nowhere else in the writings of George Saintsbury, for example, one of the most influential literary pundits of the 1920s, do we meet with the scathing disdain that came naturally to his pen when he touched on Bacon's opinions. Why did he so impatiently brush aside, as not worth considering, everything Bacon wrote? The answer will be found in a biographical note obviously inspired by Abbott, stressing the evil actions in the life of 'this much debated' and 'strangely blended' character, in whom, Saintsbury informs us, passion and enthusiasm were entirely lacking. How otherwise could the man under whose aegis Kant published his great critique, whose every sentence filled Emerson's horizon and whose achievement and breadth of experience Nietzsche did not feel qualified to evaluate, be summed up as a pusillanimous, insensitive and superficial thinker, of whom 'little but glowing rhetorical generalisation' was to be expected, and whose ideas it was hardly necessary to take 'with any seriousness at all'?[9]

That was in the early 1920s. In 1985, John Pitcher, Fellow of St John's College, Oxford, introduced a Penguin edition of Bacon's *Essays* aimed, it would seem, at discouraging students from ever reading them. They will learn here that Bacon's prose is clumsy and cluttered, and also spineless, wobbly and flatulent, and his sentences are 'dead limbs', ornamental and leaden; that his writing, deliberately 'mindless', goes on 'looping unattractively round its subject' with a 'phoney gravity', and that he 'displays his reading' in 'a literary mortuary'. Bacon's language, once seen by the young Shelley to 'burst the circumference of the reader's mind and pour itself together with it into the universal element', is now forced, 'sweating', through a series of analogies from the kennel, or the butcher's table, 'in among the bones, flesh and viscous humours'. The heart is 'a bag of blood' which Bacon is doing his best not to eat; understanding is 'grabbing', working on a subject seen as 'worrying at it'. And if the philosopher who sought in all things 'their inward virtues and powers' entitles his own essays *The inwards of things*, it is because he despaired of reaching what he really wanted to see: the arteries, the alimentary canal, the urinary ducts, et al. Finding him 'shut out from these, for want of a microscope', his critic wonders 'what kind of insides can he be thinking of for the *Essays*, what interiors are there to masques, customs, envy, death or love?'[10]

In this reading there are few inner resources to Bacon the man, for, not surprisingly, we are back with the 'reptilian nature' and the 'viper's eyes'. Pitcher's Bacon was a born hater of mankind, interested only in 'heaps of money' and 'smart gardens'. He was 'as base as he was talented', see Pope's couplet. And read Abbott's biography: 'a well-documented study' by a 'not unfair critic'. Vickers, on the other hand, is reproved for his failure to mention, in a small pamphlet on Bacon, 'the important essays which have attacked Bacon's writings and morals'. Many 'have told Bacon's life', Pitcher concludes, but his reputation today is somewhat too 'glossy'; 'he still awaits his biographer.'[11] Pitcher's view of Bacon's life is Abbott's, as is his practice of manipulating quotations. By *addition*, as when he cites Ben Jonson, who (differing notably from this critic) recalled that Bacon's language, 'where he could spare or pass by a jest, was nobly censorious', and relays it to his students as: 'as Ben Jonson pointed out, Bacon couldn't resist a joke, *especially at the expense of an enemy.*'[12] By *subtraction*, as when, dwelling only on the left-hand column – *pro* – in a series of typically Baconian antitheses, and disregarding *contra*, he depicts Bacon busily noting down 'reels of advice on cruelty to be memorized strip by strip, ready for the occasion', ready, that is, for anyone to use, including a Lord Chancellor, 'or someone who was simply tempted to kick a dog'.[13] We may remember that Bacon once quarrelled with a prime minister for hitting a dog, and this minor misjudgement is a pointer to the ignorance about Bacon's life, work and time which these critics share with the predecessors whom they echo and endorse.

On this point Vickers did not give due attention to Bacon's denigrators. He showed that the unargued and unsupported attempts of Marwil, Pitcher and other recent writers to discredit and trivialize Bacon's philosophy are based on a profound ignorance of his science and a complete disregard of his repeatedly declared aims. Their failure to study his major texts, as well as the historical background against which his science can be understood, has led them, Vickers concluded, to 'spectacularly wrong' readings of crucial questions and grotesque inversions of the truth, and in the end to a 'total distortion of Bacon's significance as a natural philosopher'.[14] Three years after Pitcher's introduction to the *Essays*, Antonio Pérez-Ramos made what Vickers describes as 'a devastating exposure of the hollowness' of those judgements. In a fresh examination of Bacon's thought, based on a reconstruction of its conceptual and scientific background, he demonstrated that it lies 'at the root of one of the main trends of our philosophical legacy', and his thoroughly argued book has finally rehabilitated Bacon as one of the principal founders of modern science.[15]

Denigrators, however, do not usually read their demolishers, and the Bacon they have fashioned may be with us for some time yet. This is a philosopher bereft of all spirituality, a crude utilitarian, the source of all our ecological misfortunes, and a pedestrian logician, in whom, as Liebig had exclaimed, no trace is to be found 'of the joys and intimate affections aroused in the great explorers by their research'. It is also – in the eyes of scholars and popular biographers alike – a blinkered careerist, whose world 'excluded not only faith but poetry as well', and whose end was miserable, because the true explanation of his 'worldly and spiritual ruin' is that 'it is probably always disastrous not to be a poet'.[16] Finally, wherever he looked, Macaulay's double Bacon cast a dividing eye. He severed poetry from science, art from technology, imagination from reason, the divine from the natural world.[17] In this chapter we will look at the image of Bacon's thought which has prevailed for over a century, and at its connection with the equally prevailing view of his degraded character.

The most widespread misattribution is that of the false prophet who led humanity, not to the promised land, but to the wilderness of rank materialism and crass utilitarianism. All the ills of industrialization, from soil erosion and the fumes of car exhausts to the loss of human values in an alienated consumer society, have been laid at Bacon's door, and he was denounced by Heidegger and Marcuse as the evil animus of science, a very symbol of its 'nefarious identification' with technology.[18] At a time when people had begun to feel the damaging effects of industrial development, who better fitted than the author of the *New Atlantis* for the role of scapegoat so often awarded him? The deposed father of experimental science became its wicked stepfather. A pointer to the influence of disparaging biographers here is the fact, noted by Paolo Rossi when refuting this thesis in 1984, that Bacon's philosophy is rejected for diametrically opposite reasons. Those who have exalted scientific knowledge declare that science owed nothing to his writings; those who look upon it as thoroughly evil see in Bacon 'the very essence of science'.[19] Convinced in advance, neither group has felt any need to confirm their negative view by a closer study of his texts, or to look into the cultural background of ideas with which they were connected. Had they done so, they would have discovered that the philosopher who advocated the marriage of the mind with things was also the first to unite scientific knowledge with traditional ethical and religious ideals; and that he had in mind not only material comforts, but an entirely new concept of 'fraternity in learning and illumination' among scientists the world over, to extend knowledge and procure 'the weal of man'.[20]

The denigrators of Bacon's motives as a scientist resort to the same dubious methods as did the disparagers of his personal and political aims, and in particular to the arguments *ad extremas* (taking an opponent's idea to absurd extremes, where it may be condemned out of hand), which Macaulay was so fond of. Thus did Anthony Burgess, in an article on terrorism in our time (1978), attribute one of its most fearful forms to 'a Baconian faith in the virtue of destroying the past so that a better future may automatically be established'.[21] Nothing could be less Baconian, since alone among the thinkers of his time Bacon had entreated men not to forget, 'in the euphoria of novelty', that in order to move forward science must preserve 'the anticipations of the past'.[22] Another damaging procedure, also used in the biographies, was to suppress the second and most important part of the concept a critic was attacking. Bacon's responsibility for our present plight was argued on two counts, both by means of this unscholarly manoeuvring. First, it was alleged, he aimed only at what he called fruit, or 'payment', and he placed his faith in machinery and wealth as precious ends in themselves.[23] 'Fruit', as Bacon meant it, was not the payment of a few; it was the raising of mankind out of the poverty he had seen at close range. Yet urgent as might be 'the relief of man's estate', we rarely find a mention of fruit in Bacon's writings without its counterpart, 'light', which is the discovery and contemplation of knowledge, on which fruit depends. Truth and utility – theory and practice – were for him the two faces of a medal, for 'what in operation is most useful, that in knowledge is most true.' But the only valid search was that which imitated 'the divine procedure, which in its first day's work created light only'; and Bacon never ceased to warn those who would run ahead, like Atalanta, 'after profit and commodity' that they did so 'to the infinite loss of mankind'.[24] His critics left out the first day's work.

For the other charge, they cancelled the second and most important half of a crucial sentence. It is, they contended, the 'Faustian urge', or 'diabolical aim', of exerting power over nature as an end in itself which has given to science its 'demonic character', with all the consequences that ensue. Casting off his 'filial bond' with nature, Bacon offered mankind 'as its main ideal the limitless expansion of human power'.[25] There is no such notion in Bacon. The arrogant claim of unlimited power for man is precisely what he deplored in 'the magicians', as he deplored the pride and greed of all those who attempt to 'domineer over nature'. In the 'chaste and holy' wedlock between the universe and the mind of man that his scientific reforms were designed to achieve, there is no place for the rape of nature which we have since perpetrated. It is true that Bacon sought 'to extend the bounds of human empire', but let us read on: 'as far as God Almighty in his goodness may permit'. This is the all-important clause which Bacon's defamers left out of account, though it is everywhere present. In the *New Atlantis*, where the expansion of human power is illustrated, Bacon solemnly disavowed 'both power and knowledge not dedicated to goodness and love', failing which, all knowledge turned 'malign and serpentine'.[26]

'Malign and serpentine' – are these not the attributes most frequently used to describe Bacon himself? Yet, alone among the forerunners of modern science, Bacon had foreseen the potential dangers of man's dominion over nature. In each case it is possible to identify the point at which we transgressed the natural laws he had respected, and in our attempt to dominate nature, failed to obey her.[27] In his pages on the myth of 'Daedalus, or the Mechanic', famous for his 'pernicious genius', 'unlawful inventions' and 'depraved applications', Bacon warned against the dangerous 'fruits of mechanic invention' – 'and well we know how far in cruelty and destruction they exceed the Minotaur himself.'[28] Bacon hoped, as many have after him, that the mechanical arts might 'serve as well for the cure as the hurt'.[29] In the meantime, in New Atlantis, the brotherhood of Salomon took an oath of secrecy to conceal all dangerous inventions, and since, for Bacon, the only reliable safeguard was prayer, they held daily services 'for the blessing and illumination of our labours, and turning of them to good and holy uses'.[30] The religious solution will not do for today's scientists (although the ecological ideals which many people fight for may be a kind of substitute). Still less will it do for those students of his works who question his sincerity. For Abbott, Bacon at prayer did not succeed in 'imposing upon others more than he imposed upon himself'. But for Bacon the efficacy of prayer was not in doubt. He placed similar prayers before many of his writings, begging 'God the Father, God the Word, God the Spirit' to 'guide this work, both in its ascent to His glory, and its descent to the good of man'.[31]

'Knowledge', Bacon affirmed, 'is a plant of God's own planting,' and the central place of Christian doctrine in his programme (not surprising in this scientist in whose works quotations from the Bible have been estimated at one per page) has been well studied.[32] Basing the advent of his *New Instauration* on a biblical prophecy, he conceived it as a restoration of the dominion over nature with which God had endowed Adam and which Adam had doubly forfeited: first when he sought 'to depend no more upon God's will', and in recent times, when his posterity moved away from God's creation and gave up looking for 'the seal of God on things' – a predicament Bacon's *Instauration* was intended to remedy.[33] Bacon was a regular churchgoer, according to Rawley, 'conversant with God' and with the sacraments. He wrote an inspired Credo, and in many places, including the *New Atlantis* – a religious fable, where the shipwrecked sailors find God 'everywhere manifest' – he lingered with evident enjoyment over the doings of Christ and the angels. He liked to describe 'the true temper of a man who has religion deeply seated in his heart', and he spoke with what looks almost like envy of 'the elected saints', who have wished themselves 'razed out of the book of life, in an ecstasy of charity and infinite feeling of communion'.[34] No wonder Addison, when illustrating his conviction that the greatest and wisest men of all ages were renowned for their piety, and rejecting 'many shining examples from among the clergy', chose one instance only, Sir Francis Bacon.[35]

Bacon's twentieth-century students, however, who had in mind a treacherous friend, a dishonest judge and a power-hungry politician, knew better. When they did not contemptuously dismiss his professions of faith, they ignored them and substituted their own views. He was declared a concealed atheist (1799); 'an unenthusiastic Christian' who looked on the Church of England as 'a branch of the Civil Service' (1926, endorsed 1980); and an agnostic, whatever his own statements to the contrary (1938). In the 1970s his religious approach was brushed off as 'infantile' by one author, while another pronounced him incapable of understanding 'how men give themselves to God'; and finally in 1985 he was shown using the Christian theology of redemption to 'edge out' of his writings and 'evade the here and now' of his own senses, leaving behind 'a surrogate flesh and blood', which was Christ's body but not his own.[36] Whatever this many mean.

As so often, Bacon was used as a foil for others. Thus Harold Fisch contrasted his 'grave defects' in religious understanding with 'the truer visions of other thinkers'. Fisch found in Paracelsus an 'excitement and awe' before nature, and in Robert Boyle 'a note of humility' and a sense of 'the mystery of things' altogether 'absent from the writings of Bacon'.[37] According to this writer (1952), Boyle saw what Bacon failed to see: that nature is 'God's epistle to man'; that the sun shines 'to declare the glory of God'; that the Divine plan may be revealed in the feathers of a peacock's train; and that the world is a temple, and the natural philosopher its priest. But these were all well-established notions, which Boyle, who was looked on in his time as 'a second Bacon', executing 'what Verulam designed', had naturally inherited from his predecessor; as he did the contagious excitement with which Bacon looked on the natural world, seeing everywhere 'the Creator's own stamp upon creation impressed and defined in matter by true and exquisite lines', and rejoicing in the 'infinite flight' of birds and the 'glorious colours' of their feathers. And we know that before Boyle it was Bacon – 'the high priest of the universe and the souls of men', as George Herbert saw him – who sought to lay the 'foundations in the mind of man of a holy temple, whereof the exemplar is the universe'.[38] Fisch, however, was convinced that Bacon had 'excluded religious faith from his life', so that when the sun rose, he averred, Bacon could see nothing but a ball of fire, where Blake was to behold 'an innumerable company of the heavenly host crying, Holy, holy, holy is the Lord God Almighty!' – the very words which, in Bacon, 'those who, abasing themselves, refer all things to the glory of God' cried out when they discovered the three 'true stages of knowledge', and found each of them 'Holy, Holy, Holy'.[39] Were it not for the prevailing image of Bacon the man, sanctioned in those years by historians such as Neale and Rowse, could a scholar have strayed so far from the reality?

Fisch's final charge against Bacon (who had recently been branded as a 'dissociator' in another context) was the familiar one that he made 'a clean cut', severing divinity completely from 'the rest of our experience'; after which it was to be abolished by others.[40] Whatever others may have done with his teachings, Bacon himself made no cut between nature and what he called the 'perennial philosophy'. True, he preferred not to 'confound the two forms of learning', which he saw as 'liquors poured through different funnels into the same vessel'. And rather than 'adapt the heavenly mysteries' to our changing rational knowledge, he thought we could attain the 'heavenly truth' by 'direct apprehension of the mysteries of God'.[41] But he believed that 'the two clear eyes of religion and natural philosophy' were coupled by 'an indissoluble bond', and that natural philosophy was, 'after the Word of God . . . the most approved nourishment for faith'. 'So far are physical causes from withdrawing men from God and Providence', he maintained, 'that contrariwise, those philosophers who have been occupied in searching them out can find no issue but by resorting to God and Providence at last.' In his own cosmogony, the 'supreme divine Providence' educed from blind atoms – 'by a fatal and necessary law – all the order and beauty of the universe'. (In no different spirit did Schroedinger declare in our time that each individual part of a living organism was 'the finest masterpiece ever achieved along the lines of God's quantum mechanics'.)[42]

If it is difficult for twentieth-century critics to see religious vision, awe and humility in 'the meanest of mankind', few of them have found any value in him as a natural philosopher. Bacon's more scholarly students have been puzzled to find his subtle, precise, complex thought reduced to little more than slogans handed down from one historian of philosophy to another, just as his many-sided life was reduced to a handful of misdemeanours.[43] Where no explicit reference is made to Bacon's life and character we may not assume that the hostile biographies have affected a particular commentator's views. Yet it cannot be by coincidence that throughout the five or six decades in which his personal reputation was at its worst, he was sneered at as a retrograde philosopher, 'the herald of the new Science', who, 'wishing to produce a scientific revolution, produced nothing of lasting scientific value' (1938). The 'grand Verulamian design' for the reconstruction of the sciences was set aside and all attention centred on a single volume, Book II of the *Novum Organum* or 'New Instrument', now seen as a huge and useless 'logical machine', a blind enumeration of data, unguided by any hypothesis, which could 'only be taken seriously by the most provincial and illiterate' (1968).[44] In 1987 Peter Urbach found this generally received view of Bacon as a plodding 'fact-collector' an inexplicable mystery.[45] There are quite a few such mysteries in Bacon's variable reputation as a philosopher which the ordinary controversies of academe cannot entirely explain.

To begin with, we should ask how an allegedly deluded thinker, whose method was dismissed as a fraud, could have been looked to by the founders of the Royal Society, the Académie des Sciences, the French *Encyclopédie*, as the inventor of modern science? Why a French correspondent of Hobbes, comparing Bacon to the practising scientists Galileo, Gilbert and Harvey, and to Descartes and Gassendi (both admirers of Bacon), declared that England had won the palm, because he alone had 'carried it over all others'? What made Leibniz, when Bacon's works first came into his hands, feel himself 'transplanted into another world', and believe that it was *De Augmentis* that had set his feet on the path of philosophy? Why did Coleridge pronounce the *Novum Organum* 'one of the three great works since the introduction of Christianity', or Darwin, setting out on the *Origin of Species*, vow that he would proceed 'on true Baconian principles'?[46] And how could an incompetent philosopher have persuaded so many people to undertake the inquiries he proposed, or urged 'as a very great favour to myself', and have influenced generations of thinkers to develop their new experimental science in his name,[47] bearing in mind that the gift of inspiring others is not a purely mental one, but stems from the heart as much as from the head, and that it presupposes precisely that affective interest and enthusiasm which his more biased critics failed to see in their cold-hearted Bacon?

Benjamin Farrington's essay in 1953, 'On Misunderstanding the Philosophy of Francis Bacon', prompted a new line of scholars to question the worm's eye view of Bacon's method – and in some cases that of his life at the same time.[48] But only in the late 1980s was it finally recognized that Bacon explicitly rejected the indiscriminate accumulation of experience attributed to his Induction. While he warned against premature conclusions, drawn 'on the authority of too few cases', he deprecated the purely empirical approach as 'a mere groping as of men in the dark'.

> The true method of experience on the contrary first lights the candle, and then by means of the candle shows the way; commencing as it does with experience duly ordered and digested, not bungling or erratic, and from it educing axioms and from established axioms again new experiments, even as it was not without order and method that the divine word operated on the created mass.[49]

In 1988 Pérez-Ramos demonstrated that Bacon's logic, which he called 'the interpretation of nature' or 'a voyage of discovery' was, exactly as he had announced it, an entirely new 'art'. A logic of content, not form, and immensely different, said Bacon, from the ordinary logic, for it extracted knowledge not merely 'out of the depths of the mind but out of the very bowels of nature'. 'My logic', he could claim, 'embraces everything!'[50] Beginning in observations and ending in arts, it proceeded in a two-way movement, from a large and various inventory of observed 'particulars', through the intuitive analogical leaps of conjecture which formed Bacon's hypotheses, and by means of a series of deductive steps – repeatedly checked against 'fresh particulars' – towards 'living axioms'; whence it was only one more step to the useful inventions that were 'the business of the human race'.[51] An essentially correct description of the method of science, as Urbach had pointed out.[52]

Late in our century new light was also cast on Bacon's 'other philosophy', present in many of his works but generally overlooked. Over the past two decades, with the help of a newly discovered text, Graham Rees had been studying the theory of the universe which Bacon planned to include in Part V of the *Great Instauration*.[53] In his early works Bacon had inclined to the materialist universe of Democritus, a universe composed of eternally unchangeable atoms moving in an infinite void; but from 1612 on he categorically denied the void, conjuring up instead a 'starry heaven compounded of ethereal and sidereal nature', all 'fluctuation, waves and reciprocation', and an earth in which 'all things emit rays'.[54] He perceived the dynamic processes of nature, organic and inorganic, as a simultaneous flow and ebb of weightless – though subtly material – 'vital' and 'inanimate' spirits, the vital spirits struggling against the inanimate to preserve youth and beauty, and to develop higher organic forms.[55] With this 'explanatory framework', said Rees, 'he sought to interpret all natural phenomena – from plant to planet, from spirit to star': a vision 'unique to himself', whatever he may have borrowed from Paracelsian and other sources.[56] But it was a vision at first sight incompatible with the quantitative science which his method was to promote. Already in the 1920s Bacon had been admired, among others by the distinguished mathematician and philosopher Alan Whitehead, for harmonizing a dynamic concept of nature with the mechanical aspects of his experimental science.[57] Rees now saw this act of synthesis as a 'highly original feat', by which Bacon 'contrived to unite modes of thought then regarded as quite disparate'.

A union of disparates – which is, according to T. S. Eliot, the basic poet's work – may be easier to grasp outside the framework of classical physics.[58] For Einstein, we will remember, 'mathematics bordered on poetry'; and the atomic physicist Werner Heisenberg compared the scientific concepts dealing with 'the more remote parts of reality' with artistic styles.[59] 'Exact science passed him by,' remarked a condescending critic of Bacon's philosophy in 1938, finding in this 'an element of tragicomedy'.[60] Too soon, perhaps, for only a few years later another atomic physicist, Wolfgang Pauli, was to celebrate the dethronement of a 'deified measurement' by quantum physics; and it may turn out that it was Bacon who did the passing by.[61] Already in 1713 Giambattista Vico, Bacon's most eminent Italian follower, had congratulated 'il gran Verulamio' on having wisely 'avoided the rocks of Cartesian mechanistic thought'; and he has been seen in our time also as one who stopped short of 'the pitfall of classical mechanism'.[62] Heisenberg, writing in 1956, stressed the dangers of a Cartesian partition of nature into mind and matter. It was a partition no longer compatible with physics, but which, he said, had 'penetrated so deeply into the whole structure of our minds and our society' that we were unable to accept the two pictures which had established themselves, the particle and the wave, as 'two complementary descriptions of the same reality'.[63] William James may have been right in suggesting that Bacon would have been 'satisfied with a wave or corpuscular theory of light, but not with mere geometrical optics'. Indeed he might have had less trouble than we have in accepting a reality which James likened to 'an alternative of flight and perching' in the life of a bird.[64]

Bacon was entirely at home with complementarity. In all spheres of life we have found him joining apparently incompatible opposites: arbitrating between litigants, mediating between King and Parliament, promoting the 'commixture of bodies and conjuncture of states', or balancing the military greatness of kingdoms against the lasting peace that was essential to his search for such principles 'as lie at the very heart and marrow of things'.[65] For this maker of marriages, who noted so many pregnant antitheses as the way to a moral truth, who believed that action and contemplation, statesmanship and study were 'strictly conjoined', who saw light and fruit as complementary aspects of the same reality, and life itself as a precarious equilibrium between contending spirits – what difficulty could there be for him in linking a dynamic theory of the universe to a flexible, open-ended method of discovery, which, as he described it, was itself a 'closer and purer league' between the experimental and the rational faculties, such as had 'never yet been made'?[66] Following the pre-Socratic philosopher, Heraclitus, whom he liked to quote ('the hidden harmony is better than the obvious', said Heraclitus), Bacon declared that 'whoever can accept discord, and penetrates the roots of things, where strength resides . . . embraces the unity of nature in substances most unlike'.[67] Provided they are 'grounded in nature', the 'conjugations between things' (like those borderlines between the senses, where 'light playing on the water' meets 'the quavering of a stop in music') are 'the same footsteps of Nature treading or printing upon several subjects'. It is by closely observing these meeting places that 'the latent processes' and 'the hidden properties of things' can be discovered. 'For these it is that detect the unity of nature' and reveal 'the fabric of the parts of the universe'.[68] And these are the analogies on which Bacon's imaginative hypotheses were founded, the 'leaps between the observable and the inobservable', as Pérez-Ramos called them, which his critics have so long refused to see in his method, despite his unmistakable statement that 'there is no proceeding in invention of knowledge but by similitude'.[69]

Shelley, invoking 'the same footsteps of nature' in his *Defence of Poetry* in 1820, concluded that Lord Bacon was 'necessarily' a poet: as a leading inventor, the author of a 'revolution in opinion', and because his words 'unveil the permanent analogies of things by images which participate in the life of truth'.[70] And William Hazlitt, also in 1820, found in Bacon 'one of the strongest instances of those men who, by the rare privilege of their nature, are at once poets and philosophers, and see equally into both worlds'. Bacon, Hazlitt believed, 'united the powers of imagination and understanding in a greater degree than almost any other writer'; he seized upon his results 'rather by intuition than by inference . . . abstraction or analysis', and reason in him 'worked like an instinct'. He belonged to an age when 'facts and feelings went hand in hand . . . The understanding was invigorated and nourished with its natural and proper food, the knowledge of things,' and ideas 'seemed to lie like substances on the brain'. But in the first half of the seventeenth century an important change, said Hazlitt – he called it a 'dissociation of sensibility' – had taken place 'in the minds and characters of Englishmen', after which the mind became detached from things and entered a 'vacuum of abstract reasoning and sentimental refinement', and poetry ended either in a passionless abstraction or in the 'vague rhapsodies' of a purely subjective lyricism. He chose Bacon to illustrate the nature of the 'unified sensibility' which had prevailed until that time.[71]

Hazlitt published these views in 1836, a year before Macaulay's essay changed the scene. They were to be radically reversed in our time, as far as Bacon was concerned. Already in 1922 Saintsbury had announced that Bacon the thinker, having allegedly decided that the literary arts were 'unfit for serious study', was responsible for 'that partisan opposition between literature and science' which had developed since his time.[72] In 1934 Hazlitt's ideas on a dissociation of sensibility in the English mind were taken up again by T. S. Eliot, in an essay celebrating the 'direct sensuous apprehension of thought' in Donne and Herbert, and deploring its loss in Tennyson and Browning.[73] Then in 1943, L. C. Knights, with an essay entitled 'Bacon and the Seventeenth Century Dissociation of Sensibility', echoing Eliot but making no mention of Hazlitt, set off a remarkable crystallization of the Baconian legend. Like Hazlitt, he chose Bacon for his example, but in reverse. With a 'characteristic separateness of thinking and feeling', he averred, Bacon – who was in any case responsible for all the 'spiritual impoverishment' brought on us by progress – had sanctioned a 'divorce between imagination and reason, emotion and intelligence' that was to have a disastrous effect on English poetry. Strange words, uttered little more than a century after Coleridge had recalled 'that illustrious man by whom SCIENCE was married to POETRY, and in whose writings she always appears in the company of the Graces. Need I mention Lord Bacon.'[74]

Knights, however, was quite unaware of the essential role played by images in Bacon's act of discovery, and does not seem to have noticed his rare gift of embodying highly complex ideas in the powerful metaphors that were to be grasped in a flash by his followers. In this critic's view Bacon excluded any interest in natural phenomena, and ignored 'the creative and vital forces of the mind'. His images, unlike those of his contemporaries, had no 'vivid feeling for both sides of the analogy', no life of their own. Lacking the validity 'that comes from the perception of similarity', and above all the sensitive exploration by which meaning can be deepened, they were coldly '*imposed*' on his preformed arguments as a mere 'rhetorical trick'.[75] The contentions of Knights were successfully challenged by a number of scholars throughout the 1950s. Bacon's tentative, many-sided metaphors, feeling their way as his thought developed, were studied and analysed, and in 1968 Brian Vickers devoted several chapters of his book *Francis Bacon and Renaissance Prose* to tracing their development. He showed conclusively that not only do Bacon's images have a life of their own, but they positively run away with their author, most of them being rooted either in nature itself (like the pruning of the law or the manuring of young minds) or in 'the simple but lasting experiences of man – light, water, food, a dwelling; going on a journey' so that it is possible to follow the onward movement of his thoughts from one work to another, as they branch out in ever fresh analogies.[76]

These studies left Knights's thesis in shreds, but they might as well never have been written for all the attention paid them by the purveyors of Macaulay's Bacon, for whom his charges came in handy to round off their story. Recapitulating them in 1980, Anthony Quinton argued, as Knights had done, that the imagery of Bacon's prose was 'externally applied ornament, deliberately put on for illustrative purposes and not part of the actual fabric of his thought'; and Whitney, restating the same opinions in 1986, found in Bacon an extreme case of control and manipulation of 'the common coin' of similitude, and declared that he had imposed 'an ascetic, sterile orderliness upon the tremendous creative energies of the greatest age of literature in England'.[77]

In the same year John Pitcher upheld Knights's view of a mentally sterile thinker, 'the chief culprit in the break-up of the imaginative life of seventeenth century Englishmen'. Ignoring Hazlitt and brushing Vickers aside, Pitcher endorsed the idea, now forty years old, of a dissociator, all 'thought without feeling', who cut 'the instincts away from the intellect – a lobotomy which ended for good all the integrity of mind and matter'.[78] No mean feat! Neither Quinton nor Whitney offered any substantiation of their judgements, but Pitcher once again deployed an Abbott-like expertise. 'The case against Bacon's writing is made by several literary heavyweights,' he pointed out (in fact by two, C. S. Lewis and Douglas Bush), which, as they published their views in the *Oxford History of Literature*, 'amounts to a kind of blackballing'. Vickers had taken issue with Knights's 'devastating' idea, he said, 'but with no great success', and he cites John Carey's 'highly charged pages'.[79] If the student, so forewarned, bothers to look up these pages – actually two – he will find the first devoted principally to an argument that is far from conclusive against Vickers's book, while in the second Carey virtually confirms his opponent by pointing to an as yet unnoticed form of image, frequently present in Bacon's writings, and comparable, he concludes, for its 'agility and suppleness', to some of the best Elizabethan imagery.[80] A persevering student will also discover that Bush provided little fuel for the strictures of Knights, and none for Pitcher's own contention that the *Essays* lack 'generative powers', or that they hold no 'secret joys' and offer nothing 'from within'. On the other hand he will find that Bush listed a number of critics who, he thought, had justly queried Knights's thesis.[81] What kind of a blackballing is this?

Had C. S. Lewis, Pitcher's other authority, never known Macaulay's disreputable Bacon, would he have experienced the *Essays* as 'a metallic-looking cactus raised on the edge of a desert . . . sterile, inedible, cold and hard to the touch'?[82] Perhaps he might have heard Leibniz, advising philosophers to 'think highly of Verulam, for his hard sayings have in them deep meaning'; or Bacon himself, explaining that they are hard because 'they are *seeds* only, not *flowers*'.[83] There are many such seeds germinating in Bacon's writings, and it is one of the mysteries of his reputation as a philosopher that Bacon of all people could be seen to impose a 'sterile orderliness' on the creative energies around him – Bacon for whom knowledge was 'a spouse for generation, fruit and comfort'; who reproached the Schoolmen for preferring their 'laborious webs of learning' to 'a fruitful womb for the use and benefit of man's life', and whose own method of inquiry began in an abundance of live, earthy experience, drawn from the 'bowels of nature', and ended in the creation of a 'race of inventions' for mankind. Where is the sterile order in the Baconian cosmology, which teems with 'spirits', continually 'leaping and frisking in endless variety and constant motion', as they emerge out of the 'rich and fruitful supply of active power subsisting in the underworld'? Bacon's very lists of items to be studied – his *History of Generations and Pretergenerations*, of which we saw something earlier – are cascades of 'motions and perturbations', 'coruscations', 'vivifications', 'gestations' and limitless 'potentialities'. All these lead to order, certainly, though hardly a sterile one; for, he tells us, it is 'the generative and vivifying power in things' – bearing within it, 'like a second chaos', the air 'in which the seeds of so many things act, wander, endeavour and experiment' – which leads us to principles.[84]

But the controversy over Bacon's images is only one aspect of the crowning mystery of his reputation as a thinker: the allegation that, unlike most writers of his time, Bacon was a 'denigrator of poetry', and that the lack of a poetic element in his mental make-up is the real explanation of his 'worldly and spiritual ruin'. This myth originated, like many others, with Macaulay – even though Macaulay himself had appreciated a 'poetic faculty' in Bacon (while Abbott diagnosed 'a dangerous excess' of it, 'which led him into error').[85] But poetry was not felt to be compatible with the mean and cold-hearted self-seeker his Ur-detractor had launched into the world. 'The great poet's faculty of imagination, which is mainly the fruit of emotion, was denied Bacon,' wrote Lee, summing up the general view in 1904. For Knights, in 1943, there was 'never any indication that Bacon has been *moved* by poetry or that he attaches any value to its power of deepening and refining the emotions'; and, despite Vickers's hopeful remark, in 1971, that the view of Bacon as 'the Antichrist of the imagination' had almost been destroyed, it was still thriving in the 1980s.[86] On the Continent the poet in Bacon had never been lost sight of, but at home the testimony of earlier writers was forgotten.[87] That of Archbishop Tenison, for example, who thought that

Bacon had 'a very good judgement of poesy' and 'some talent that way' himself. And that of Addison, who had again selected Bacon for his example – this time to illustrate his conviction that 'the great end of all arts', and very specially of poetry, was to raise our nature, 'throwing into the shades' its 'mean and narrow parts'. The *Advancement of Learning*, he said, 'gives a truer and better account of this art than all the volumes that were ever written upon it'. And, he concluded, 'no writer who defends poetry but is himself a poet.'[88]

Many of his contemporaries, when complimenting Bacon or lamenting his death, had spoken of him as a poet in his own right. We have seen him hailed by Campion as 'one whom the sweet muse calls'. The dramatist Thomas Randolph addressed him as 'thyself a singer', and 'E.F.' mourned him as 'a poet from Ithaca'.[89] In the next generation, Edmund Waller, another poet who knew Bacon well through a mutual friend, recalled two distinguished men for whom poetry was 'the diversion of their youth' – Sir Philip Sidney and Sir Francis Bacon – as 'nightingales who sang only in the spring'.[90] And the chronicler, John Stow, included Bacon among 'present excellent poets who worthily flourish in their own works' (assigning him the eighth place, with Shakespeare in the thirteenth).[91] Bacon himself, while resorting to the disclaimers that were *de rigueur* for men in public life ('though I profess not to be a poet'), spoke of himself in private as 'a concealed poet', and Aubrey was to describe him as 'a good poet, but concealed'.[92] Who can tell what was lost? The few verses that survive ('The world's a bubble and the life of man / Less than a span . . .') do not resound with all the harmonics we perceive in great poetry, yet they evoke some very pleasant ones.[93]

The 'vein of poetic passion' which Spedding discerned in Bacon is more strongly present in his prose – in those 'harmonious and rhythmical' periods which, said Shelley, 'contain in themselves the elements of verse'.[94] But it is also manifest in many other ways. In his love of poetry, to begin with (in the New Atlantis there was 'excellent poesy'); in the numerous quotations from the poets we find everywhere in his writings and speeches, particularly from *the poet*, Virgil, for Bacon an inexhaustible source of ideas; in the lively interest he took in the drama of his day, as is evident not only from his thoughtful pages on the subject, but from the abundance of expert theatrical metaphors which have been found throughout his writings, and from the active part he played as 'chief contriver', when not as actor, in the production of Court masques.[95] It is present in his concept of poetry as 'a dream of learning', in which 'the divine grace uses the motions of the imagination as an instrument of illumination', the mind being open to 'similitudes, types, parables, visions, dreams', and to the ancient fables by which, 'as it were through a veil', God had spoken to man. And it is surely present also in his own highly idiosyncratic interpretation of these fables, some of which, in his eyes, 'were big to bursting with the secrets and mysteries of nature', as aspects of his own Instauration. His interpretations enchanted many people in the seventeenth and eighteenth centuries, beginning with the poet, George Sandys, who said that he had received 'the greatest light' from the Viscount of St Alban in preparing his translation of Ovid's poem (begun on the eve of Bacon's impeachment). All this did not prevent a commentator in our time from accusing Bacon of using the methods of the fabulists 'strictly in order to undermine them, to thwart their power by draining them of meaning'.[96]

Bacon did not drain away meaning, he multiplied it, and his poetical urge was most powerfully expressed in the abundance of mythological symbols (exceeding, it seems, even those of Spenser in *The Faerie Queene*) with which he embodied his most abstract scientific conclusions. Who but the author of *Wisdom of the Ancients* could have offered us a preview of the Second Law of Thermodynamics in terms of a battle between Cupid and Eros?[97] One reluctant admirer, Joseph de Maistre, was not amused. 'There goes the poet when we look for the scientist,' he exclaimed, 'always an image instead of a reason!'[98] But Bacon's images *are* his reasons, as Shelley could have told his French contemporary. The poets at any rate made no mistake about this philosopher who liked to expound his Great Instauration in dramatic dialogues, or discover it in Greek myths, and who gave it final shape in a new fable of his own. From his time to Macaulay's – and outside England, to this day, if we recall echoes in Baudelaire, Rimbaud and Borges – poets have celebrated in Bacon that feeling for poetry which his later English critics denied him. Campion, who had acted with Bacon in a play in their young days, was delighted with his mythology; George Herbert borrowed metaphors from him, and responded with his own to many facets of Bacon's message; the author of *Paradise Regained* echoed and admired the author of the *Instauratio*, or *renewal*; as did Cowley, Addison and Pope in their different ways.[99] In Coleridge, Bacon's writings – 'that mine of enkindling truths and pregnant expressions' – evoked a high degree of response, and he thought his own style closely resembled Bacon's; and Shelley, on whom Bacon's influence has been well studied, saw in him the only writer who could be compared with Plato for 'the rare union of close and subtle logic with the Pythian enthusiasm of poetry'.[100]

So much for the failure to be a poet which brought about Bacon's 'miserable end'. But we have one more mystery to look at: that end itself, and indeed a whole life which, without *joie de vivre*, as some biographers and students of his writings would have it, was one long series of discomfitures, culminating in 'well-deserved misery'.[101] The image spans our century. In 1904 Lee saw Bacon as 'a pitiable failure', and for Strachey in 1928 'the miserable end . . . was implicit in the beginning – a necessary consequence of qualities that were innate . . . One wishes to turn away one's gaze' from 'his bitterly ironical tragedy'. But one doesn't; and Strachey dwells contemptuously on 'an old man, disgraced, shattered, alone on Highgate hill, stuffing a dead fowl with snow'.[102] In 1958 Paul Kocher described Bacon as the 'prisoner of his own personality', miserable because he knew he was 'the least friended public figure of his generation'. In this author's view, 'the whole wretched complex' of Bacon's distrust, dissimulation and management rolls to 'a final, almost inevitable *débâcle*', with 'five years of misery'.[103] His entire career, Marwil declared in 1976, must be viewed as a failure, his life story 'ends as it began, in frustration'; and in 1980 Quinton described it as a long series of disasters, between which he managed to get himself appointed Solicitor General and Chancellor, and to enjoy only one real pleasure, 'the welcome death of the hated Salisbury'. He was frustrated and hated throughout his youth, wrote this critic, and disliked by both his royal patrons, his fall being merely 'the greatest of his misfortunes' – although that, apparently, was capped by a 'special misfortune' reserved for him: to have been the subject of Macaulay's 'worst constructions'. Might we not add another: to have had Lord Macaulay's worst constructions endorsed with evident satisfaction by Lord Quinton?[104]

It is natural for those who believe that Bacon's principal aim in life was his own advancement to conjure up all that frustration and gloom, but the reality was different. Six months after his fall, when he wrote asking the Lords for leave to see his creditors in London, Bacon did indeed picture himself as 'old, weak, ruined, in want and a very subject of pity'; and we know what he suffered from the blot which 'by my own great fault' had fallen on his name.[105] But we know also that adversity 'neither spent nor pent' his spirits, and that even in those first weeks after his imprisonment he often forgot his troubles altogether. He had discovered 'the joys of the penitent', and that other joy he was soon to describe as a 'truer, surer and more agreeable to nature' than the satisfying of personal desires, a joy which is imparted by 'the consciousness of good intentions, howsoever failing in success'.[106] To Strachey's image of Bacon's sad and lonely end we must oppose the death, in the arms of his lifelong associate and kinsman by marriage, Sir Julius Caesar, of a seeker so intent on his experiment in refrigeration that he forgot to feel the cold; aware that the fate of Caius Plinius – 'who lost his life by trying an experiment about the burning of Vesuvius' – might soon be his own, but pleased that his experiment had succeeded so well. This was surely that best of deaths which he had himself described: 'He that dies in an earnest pursuit . . . scarce feels the hurt'; and 'when a man hath obtained worthy ends and expectations . . . the sweetest canticle is *nunc dimittis*' – 'now lettest thou thy servant depart in peace'.[107]

Throughout those last five years Bacon had pursued the 'worthy ends' he had always been most drawn to, and, absorbed in what he called 'the living life', had been producing some of his best work. Archbishop Tenison records that 'during all the time of his eclipse of fortune' his mind was 'not distracted with anxiety, nor depressed with shame, nor slow for want of encouragement, nor broken with discontent'.[108] As for the image, dear to his denigrators, of a lifelong frustration and misery, his ever renewed enthusiasm and optimism and his openness to new experience give the lie to it. Aubrey recalls him driving out when it rained 'to receive the universal spirit of the world'. Bacon was indeed a great receiver, and what surprises in him is the degree to which he appears to have enjoyed pleasures, both of the senses and of the mind – well aware that those who 'take more pleasure in enjoying pleasures than some other are less troubled with the loss or leaving of them'. 'Pleasure', 'happiness', 'joy', 'comforting to the spirits', these are expressions that came easily to his pen, and few people can have made more frequent use of the word 'delight' for all kinds of experience.[109] See the variety of 'great pleasures' to be glimpsed in masques, for example, or the delights of the mind to be found in the 'direct communities' between ear, eye and thought – indeed, in any transition from one thing to another. (There is 'great pleasure' in 'well-cast stair-cases, entries, doors, windows', and in the 'conveyances and passages' in speech.)[110] In Bacon, 'the eye is never satisfied with seeing, nor the ear with hearing,' while the mind is 'joyful to receive light', and 'not only delighted in beholding the variety of things', but raised thereby to discern their inner laws.[111]

If 'the enjoyment of happiness' was 'a great good', the power of imparting it to others was 'a still greater'. In one of Bacon's works, a man whose face was 'habituated to the expression of pity' describes as 'the happiest experience of my life' an occasion on which he found 'peaceful lodging in able and congenial minds' for 'an Instauration of Philosophy'.[112] This was a pleasure God himself indulged in when he 'took delight to hide his works', so that the 'experiment' of discovering them could be for Abel (and Bacon) a 'matter of delight'. Best of all was the joy of contemplating the 'highest powers and virtues' of men's minds, of watching 'the spirit of man' as it 'dances to the tune of the thoughts'.[113] In an essay he published a year before his death, Bacon saw the inquirer after Truth engaged on that 'love-making or wooing of it' which was for him 'the sovereign good of human nature'. 'Certainly,' he added, 'it is heaven upon earth to have a man's mind move in charity, rest in Providence, and turn upon the poles of Truth.'

With such happy thoughts we may now leave this 'deservedly miserable' man. Enough has perhaps been said of Baconian criticism in our time to show that, even where it cannot exactly be measured, the strong bias against his life and character soon and thoroughly invaded the study of his works. The habit of treating Bacon with contempt proved irresistible; that of uncritically repeating an uncritical predecessor did the rest.

There are no extremes to which writers would not go to indulge their sense of moral superiority over a despised philosopher, as may be seen from Justus von Liebig's considered opinion of the *History of Life and Death*, in which Bacon dealt with a valued project for the 'prolonging and renewing of the life of man'. This book, on which Alexander von Humboldt thought his future as a scientist would rest secure, and which is again arousing the interest of scholars today, was written, Liebig asserted, 'for the express purpose of justifying the propensities of certain Court personages to orgies of the table, and to other excesses'.[114] Liebig's views on Bacon, published in 1863, were common currency for many decades, so we will not be surprised to note that it was by dint of quotations from his book that, as late as 1938, the distinguished French philosopher Gaston Bachelard, in a study of the psychic forces which stand in the way of knowledge – a study which, though he does not notice it, reads like a modern version of Bacon's 'Idols of the Mind' – laid the ground for a fierce attack on Bacon's 'blindly credulous' and 'backward-looking' science.[115]

We cannot know what view the twentieth century would have taken of Bacon's philosophy had he died in 1620, when his reputation stood at its highest, and left no handle for defamation. But we may be sure that the philosophers and other critics of our day would not have produced such gross travesties of his thought, or expressed their dissent with so much unphilosophical violence.

CONCLUSIONS ABOUT THE LEGEND-SPINNERS

34

The Secret of their Success

Before taking up the methods and motives of his critics, what can we briefly conclude about Bacon himself after living with him for so many pages – at his most inspired, at his weakest and frailest? Only those who have eaten and drunk with their subject or have talked to his friends, said Johnson, can write his story. This remark is particularly true of Bacon, who, though an intrepid thinker, was shy in his dealings with the world, so that, in England, only a handful of his intimates fully grasped his life's purposes.[1] We have seen him in many apparently inconsistent roles: as the judge who could read a culprit's thoughts like an open book, and as the all too naive public servant who laid himself open to vicious political ambush; as the Chancellor who indulged in court ceremonial, to the dismay of his young Dutch visitor, but who soon renounced his 'proud pomposity' and fled to his private friends (or played truant to watch a masque put up by the students of Gray's Inn); as the keen financial reformer who was deplorably lax over his own accounts and disastrously negligent of appearances, believing that 'the excessive care for discretion of behaviour is a great thief to meditation'.[2]

Yet we have also learned, as Gardiner did after carefully reviewing Bacon's every judicial action, 'to place unreserved confidence in his truthfulness', bearing in mind that even those who still censure him today as a corrupt judge do so merely on the strength of his own confession to the Lords, while they take no account of his trustworthy, and justified, explanations.[3] And we may now affirm that the 'wooer of Truth', as he saw himself, can be taken at his word when describing his own actions. If Bacon spoke the truth when, more concerned for the common good than for his own, he made that unnervingly dispassionate judgement of himself before the Lords, he spoke the truth also when he solemnly told Essex's closest friend that he could remember no action of his towards any man 'with less check of conscience'; when, during the worst crisis of his life, he reminded his all-seeing Creator that he had cherished the oppressed, and 'hated all cruelty and hardness of heart'; and again when he privately noted, while accepting the justice of his sentence, that he had been the justest judge in England for the past fifty years.[4] On this point we can safely leave the last word to Gardiner: 'The judgement thus recorded by himself may be accepted by history as final.'[5]

Those of us who have 'talked to his friends' will remember another quality they found in him. Bacon believed that 'the inclination to goodness is imprinted deeply in the nature of man', and it was not only his near acquaintance who saw this quality in him. We will recall the distinguished enemy who wrote home in his despatches that Bacon was a man 'of a very great goodness of nature'.[6] If such was the testimony of those who had eaten and drunk with Bacon, how came he to be described as 'the most wicked man in recorded history' (1846) – there being 'no baseness to which he was not ready to submit' to gain advancement, 'and hardly any crime which he would not have been willing to perpetrate' (also 1846)? How could he be depicted as a man whose 'seductive intellectual beauty' was combined with 'the most hideous moral deformity' (1864); who was of a meanness, 'hollow, false, demoralizing, fatal to all purity and nobility in social life'; and who was – not surprisingly, since he had sold his soul to the Devil – 'marvellously and portentously contemptible' (1885)? How was it possible for a biographer in 1897 to see in his life nothing but 'drunkenness, debauchery, extravagance, forgery, fraud, ingratitude, treachery', with 'not a redeeming feature' besides, and 'not a trace of either love or pity for any human being'? And for an editor of his works in 1903 to inform students that 'the only branch of knowledge for which Bacon really did anything is the barren knowledge of how to trade upon the folly, the vanity and the selfishness of mankind'? Such were the opinions that were summed up in 1909 by a Shakespearian authority who called Bacon 'England's one scoundrel'.[7] And can we understand any better why he is still habitually awarded the role of villain when 'Lives' are written of Essex, Ralegh and Shakespeare, and why he winds in and out of our century in the form of a grovelling snake? Why he was depicted in the 1970s as a tawdry, posturing, insensitive and bitter man, his entire creative output no more than a 'self-justifying formula', spawned to give meaning to 'a soiled existence'? Why, throughout the 1980s, he was still reviled, sneered at, debased: in one author creeping, lifeless, joyless, unredeemed, 'with that contemptuous question' – *what is truth?* – 'banging inside his head'; in another, tossed, eternally unredeemable, in the winds of hell, a miscreant whose moral twin is the icy blackmailer, Lord Angelo of the stage – as forty years earlier it had been the Spanish traitor and murderer of history?[8] And why he is held up to us in 1992, hardly less absurdly, as a Satanist, in league with black magicians to pervert humankind?

For the biographers who write of him in these terms, there is no question of taking Bacon at his word. He was by definition a deceiver, and it is the deceiver and the cold-blooded double-dealer who has been circulating for over a century in popular editions, and who is newly circulating in paperback prefaces and introductions.[9] For the readers of these works, the murky stories handed down about him are the reality, while the dedicated seeker who makes nonsense of them – though familiar to all serious students of his thought – remains an abstraction, with little bearing on his life. We have seen the gap between the two visions of Bacon growing ever wider with the increasing specialization of the scholars who write about the different facets of his mind in learned journals, or meet to discuss them at international seminars.[10] They make no mistake about him. The few people actively engaged in Baconian scholarship, as one of them put it informally, know perfectly well that nearly all the charges brought against the man and his work 'are misconceived, wrong or plain loopy'. Yet many of these specialists tend to shrug their shoulders. Bacon the man is irrelevant to the particular aspect of Bacon the thinker they are concerned with. That the vast majority of *Time*'s readers should know Bacon only as a grim-looking official who, like Nixon, 'enjoyed taking bribes' will not bother them – if they notice it.[11] And if a busy colleague in academe adds a bit towards the false image with some potted biographical preface, recapitulating the long-refuted nonsense, what of it?[12]

Historians are still contending with other legends besides Bacon's. There is a saintly Thomas More and a devilish one (unknown to Erasmus), and between them they have crowded out the real man, one of 'the very few who have enlarged the horizon of the human spirit', as a more objective biographer recently reminded us.[13] Two images of Richard III, one wicked, one blameless, have similarly eclipsed the real Richard – no monster, though he could not have usurped a throne in the fifteenth century without eliminating its rightful claimants. (As Machiavelli put it, 'there is generally but a short interval between the prison and the graves of princes'.)[14] Amid the emotional clamour for a king innocent of murder, the trustworthy historians of a human Richard, who had high aspirations and fine qualities – including very probably a capacity to feel remorse – remain unheard. Not least among these is Bacon himself, who, after recording Richard's crimes, concluded that 'although desire of rule did bind him, yet his other action, like a true Plantagenet, was noble, and he loved the honour of the realm and the contentment of his nobles and people.'[15]

Where Bacon is concerned, the final question before us now is why, despite Spedding's entirely satisfactory endeavour over a hundred years ago to establish the truth about this complex, but uncomplicated man, all the untruths he refuted continue to flourish in the minds of many biographers and historians, and in those of the majority of British readers. Could they have failed to note the unscholarly methods by which the critics of both Bacon's life and works, following each other, as Churchill put it, 'like sheep through the gates of error', pass on the inherited censure without examining it – often with additional titbits of their own confection? Rare is the biographer who, like P. M. Handover on Robert Cecil, confesses that in an earlier work she had 'accepted too readily the verdicts passed upon him by others'.[16] A dispassionate look at some of the improbable statements made by Bacon's disparagers should be enough to put off any alert reader. But reading life stories involves a somewhat passive, uncritical stance. A biographer's disapproval often gets across before a particular statement is questioned. So when Abbott declares with conviction that Bacon had 'no liking or care for birds or beasts, wild or tame', it seems natural to believe him – if one has not already noticed that Bacon spoke feelingly of animals, and particularly loved birds.[17]

The legend-spinners get away with the most flagrant exaggerations. We have seen them piling up ever stronger superlatives, as though a simple statement had lost the power to convince. Bacon is not wicked, he is the most wicked man in history; not mean, but the meanest of mankind; and Campbell had to write these words in capitals, with three exclamation marks, before they came near to expressing his feelings.[18] Mounting superlatives of praise are required to counterbalance the blame, in order to keep a two-souled Bacon on his tight-rope. Bacon 'had an amplitude of comprehension such as had never been vouchsafed to any human being', wrote Macaulay, 'the feats he performed with it were not merely admirable but portentous.'[19] And Abbott heaped his praises on the 'gigantic', 'stupendous', 'grandiose' and 'sublime' philosopher who was a 'portentously evil' man.[20] We have seen biographers vying with each other in the attempt to go one better than a predecessor. In 1837, Bacon 'bore a principal part in shedding Essex's blood'; in 1846, his decision to meddle no longer was the real cause of Essex's insurrection; by 1885 it was Bacon who put the whole idea that drove Essex to treason into his head.[21] One biographer felt the need improve on his own image between one volume to the next, and we saw that, without a shred of new evidence, Bacon's request to be excused from appearing against Essex at the York House trial was turned into a shameless demand 'to have a substantial part assigned to him' (whereupon another biographer coolly declared that Bacon had 'sought and obtained permission to appear at the Inquiry').[22] A similar urge drives the purveyors of legend to think up increasingly evil motives for their subject, until finally it can be assumed 'without hesitation' that all his actions 'were animated by particularly bad intentions'. Which of course involves judging Bacon by blatantly different criteria from those used on his contemporaries. So we find both Strachey and Lacey, for example, approving Mountjoy's timely disengagement from so close a friend as Essex as an act of maturity, while they decry the same disengagement in Bacon as a betrayal.[23]

When his critics run short of accusations, they leaf through Bacon's writings, pinpoint one of the ills he diagnosed in humankind, and claim to discover it in him. If, wondering how man could 'win the imagination' away from evil passions, Bacon remembers Ovid on their powerful influence – 'I see better things but follow the worse' – it is he himself who is following 'the worser way', and one biographer after another will quote the line at him in reproof. When in unmistakable terms he deprecates the 'architecture of a man's fortune' as a way of life, they denounce him as if he were recommending it, so as to practise it himself with impunity.[24] As a result, instead of faulting him where he was weak, the denigrators of Bacon's life, like those of his works, attack him where he was impregnable, and take the very metaphors with which he expressed his most central thoughts out of his mouth to twist them against him. Above all things Bacon condemned the 'creeping snake', and the heart 'double and cloven', and we know the creeping, cloven-hearted monster they made of him.[25]

If only for their chronic disregard for facts, from Weldon down, the pedlars of legend deserve no credit. The worst culprit was Macaulay himself, whose habitual inaccuracy was equalled only by his refusal to correct his mistakes when they were pointed out to him, confident as he was that his readers would not bother to check them.[26] Refutation was powerless before Campbell's enormities, backed as they were by all the authority of a Victorian Lord Chancellor. They are now breeding new enormities in writers such as Noonan and Denning.[27] Most of Bacon's detractors succeed in bypassing Spedding's accurate analyses without pausing to argue with him. His 'monumental work' was acclaimed in 1884 as a 'titanic achievement', and still is today, but, since Bacon was really undeserving, 'made in vain'.[28] In 1904 one critic approved Abbott for 'correcting the partial view of James Spedding'; in 1985 another was still advising his students to read Spedding for his 'erudition, industry and fair-mindedness', while he himself tacitly rejected everything Spedding had said.[29] Not surprisingly, the mistakes made by Bacon's critics nearly always tell against him. It was not merely carelessness in reading his sources that led Campbell to denounce Bacon's 'most discreditable part in supporting monopolies' when he was actually attacking them, or Epstein to misread his legacy to his kinswoman, Lady Cooke, as a legacy to Lady Hatton (Sir Edward Coke's wife) – deliberately included in his last will, said this historian, in order to 'spite Coke'.[30]

Readers may be forgiven for succumbing to the deceptions practised upon them by the trained minds who have placed their scholarship at the service of a preconceived image. The best historians have been taken in by the scholarly apparatus with which Abbott and his followers support the deft manipulations whereby Bacon is made to advocate what he deplored and Spedding to express mistrust where he was affirming his belief in Bacon's truthfulness. These unscholarly scholars cite but fail to evaluate the reliability of their sources. They will place a journal writer like D'Ewes, who reviled Bacon without knowing him – just as he sneered at Selden, faulted Camden and saw evil in the best of the Jacobeans – on a par with the sympathetic and admiring Aubrey, who, while usually refraining from judgement, collected from Bacon's intimates all the particulars on which an evaluation could be based.[31] When they do invoke authority, they are not to be trusted. What will anyone familiar with Aubrey make of the statement that he 'dismissed Bacon as an unworthy individual'?[32] Little wonder, then, if the reader is confused when less known witnesses, summoned for the prosecution in a critic's 'case against Bacon', turn out to be witnesses for the defence.[33]

The thoroughly disconcerting Bacon who emerges from methods such as these is continually frustrating his authors. All but the happy few whose condemnation of him is total keep haring back and forth, emphatically affirming what they have just categorically denied. In one page, and sometimes in one sentence, readers learn that Bacon's heart 'was large enough to take in all races and ages', and that there are many proofs of 'the narrowness and selfishness' of his heart; that he 'was all himself' when at his most allegedly abject, and, when he turns to the noble studies he had never abandoned, 'Bacon is Bacon still.' We have heard one critic, having never seen 'a greater display of vengeful malignity' than Bacon had allegedly shown, pronounce him soon afterwards 'perfectly free of malignity'.[34] Today, as a result, after being for so long a puzzle, to which every biographer, dissatisfied with a predecessor's solution, has felt bound to propose a new 'key', Bacon has become a 'false persona', something 'dark and dangerous', whose whole life could be labelled – once again by bending his own words against him – 'a dark saying'.[35]

Some readers will have turned with relief to the more coherent image presented by the 'wiser sort of historians', as Bacon called them, those who bring in 'the entire body of history' as often as the person they are describing 'enters the stage'.[36] Wiser historians also studied the man and his work, and where they criticized, took his whole personality into account and set it in the framework of his age. In this they were following Spedding, who, using Bacon's own scientific method, based on the patient collection of innumerable 'particulars', had spent a large part of his life collating sixteenth- and seventeenth-century documents. In exhaustively examining every divergent view and conjecture, he had, as he tells us, a single purpose in mind: to understand at each step why Bacon chose as he did, in order to find out 'what kind of a man he was'; and to present his readers with all the information they needed to form an accurate and independent judgement.[37] Why did so few people avail

434

themselves of this opportunity? The answer is simple. Few people will take the trouble to read a thousand pages of well-balanced evaluation when they can learn all about Bacon's 'lamentable career' in Macaulay's 160 pages – or glean its essentials from the five pages Strachey devoted to him in his bestselling tale. The public, reading for recreation, prefers a swift and captivating story, delivered with the assurance of conviction, to a careful presentation of the evidence. And practitioners of legend have a special advantage here: they know the truth beforehand. They know it because a century and a half ago one master spinner of tales implanted a concept of the man so firmly in their minds that nothing can dislodge it.

Did they not notice the grave flaws in their principal authority? As was touched on earlier, volumes of criticism have been written about Macaulay.[38] Already in his own time he was convicted of fishing false-hoods out of the 'cesspools and quagmires', and retailing them 'mixed up with facts, as if they were facts'.[39] In the view of many of his fellow historians, then and now, he lacked almost all the qualities essential to their craft, chief among them that of verifying the evidence and allowing it to tell its own story. They deprecated his simplistic approach to the historian's task as that of a judge awarding sentence in retrospect – when not of a zealous public prosecutor; and they were amazed at the 'superb indifference' with which he separated the goats of history from the sheep.[40] 'I wish I could be as cocksure about anything as Macaulay is about everything,' Melbourne is reported to have said.[41]

Bacon's biographers, if they had any historical awareness, could not have helped hearing the chorus of voices that have condemned Macaulay's 'grossly unfair' essay on their subject and his defamatory allegations about many great men besides Bacon – Samuel Johnson, in particular, who was still being 'rescued' from Macaulay's caricature in 1994,[42] and above all that other two-souled monster, the Duke of Marlborough, Winston Churchill's ancestor, whom Macaulay took over from two libellous 'Lives' – *Life of James II* and *Court of Charles II* – which he knew to be the product of a private spite; just as he took over his Bacon from Weldon's *Court and Character of King James*.[43] But if Macaulay's readers heard these voices at all, they heard them too late, for, as was already noted in his lifetime, the pictures he had drawn 'rightly or wrongly stamped themselves ineffaceably upon the popular mind'.[44]

They stamped themselves with equal strength on the informed, critical mind. Historians were not convinced, but they were conquered. One after another, those who used their reason to censure Macaulay for defects unpardonable in a historian were swept off their feet by an irrational wave of surrender to his powerful narrative. Thus Harriet Martineau, Macaulay's exact contemporary, after thoroughly condemning his *History*, admitted that those who were best aware of Macaulay's faults –

including herself – were carried away by 'the delight of reading him'. Gardiner, who reproached 'the most brilliant of historians' for painting his picture of Bacon 'in colours as odious as they are untrue', admired him for writing it 'in a language which will be read as long as the English tongue endures'. Acton, who saw in Macaulay 'a key to half the prejudices of our age', thought him 'the greatest of all writers and masters'. Churchill, exposing the arguments of Marlborough's maligner as a 'tissue of fraud and lies', was resigned to the outcome. 'It is beyond our hopes to overtake Macaulay,' he wrote. 'The grandeur and sweep of his storytelling style carries him swiftly along, and with every generation he enters new fields.' 'Whatever we may think of it as history,' said Rowse in 1994, 'there is no doubt that it makes good reading.'[45] And today the 'Essay on Bacon' is still seen with a smile as 'deplorably convincing' or 'rollickingly injudicious', and its misstatements are given a new lease of life by its admirers.[46] This was the power and vividness which enabled Macaulay, wrong as he often was, to impress 'his own version upon the English mind more firmly than the truth'.[47]

It was a power he developed intentionally. His one self-confessed ambition in writing was popularity. He wanted to reach a wider circle of readers than any historian had done before him. When starting his famous *History of England*, his declared aim was to produce 'something which shall in a few days supersede the last fashionable novel on the table of young ladies'; his 'Essay on Bacon', he hoped, would be 'popular with many, whatever the few who knew something about the matter might think'.[48] His success was complete in both, to his immense glee. His *Essays* proved the best seller of the century, while for his *History* neither Hume nor Gibbon, he could boast, were in the running. And he has continued to enjoy a popularity without precedent among historians.[49] Success came easily to his 'unperplexed mind' (as his biographer, Cotter Morison, described it in 1882), so geared to addressing a crowd that he instinctively omitted anything it would not immediately grasp.[50] He had all the parliamentary orator's tricks of innuendo at his finger-tips. We have seen the fake parallels with which he thundered against his victims, and have watched him insinuating false statements into the reader's mind, disguised as possible exaggerations.[51] Instead of argument, he frequently resorted to sarcasm – the 'pungent rhetoric and elaborate scorn' deplored by Churchill, or the 'contemptuous chuckle' which, as Spedding observed, can have such lasting effects. 'Every reader who is not on his guard', Spedding pointed out, 'will naturally fall into such a sympathy for his writers, as to receive impressions almost unconsciously from direct and impalpable insinuations of this kind. They take him unawares, and bespeak his judgement without his own consent.'[52]

Some found the 'literary pyrotechnics', the forced paradoxes, the 'rocking-horse rythms' and that 'perpetual semblance of hitting the nail on the head without the reality' merely exhausting.[53] But Macaulay's false-hoods, dealt out with genuine conviction in the long repetitive peror-ations which so many historians were to echo, inevitably worked their way into the public mind, fed as it was from childhood, throughout the nineteenth century and half our own, on his *Lays of Ancient Rome* and his *Essays*, awarded as school prizes – fed, that is, on his personal heroes and bugbears, which went back to his own school days, and which he never changed.[54] Macaulay confessed to his sister that he read principally 'for the love of day-dreaming and castle-building'. And that is perhaps why his history is so full of spotless heroes slaying hideous dragons, and, in particular, of glorious revolutionaries who, by bringing down the House of Stuart in the seventeenth century, made nineteenth-century England lawful, secure and happy, as his biographer put it, 'in a world racked with evil passions and streaming with blood'.[55] Bacon had diagnosed the day-dreamer in Essex. Could he ever have expected to be cast as villain in a dream of English history?

The only way for a historian to avoid projecting the present on to past centuries, as one of them has pointed out, is for him to become conscious of his situation.[56] It would be difficult to find anybody less conscious of his situation than Macaulay.[57] He was so blithely unaware of his own inad-equacy as a historian that, while declaring himself a follower of the methods he had 'learned from Lord Bacon' and castigating others for not following them, he denounced in them the practices he himself was most prone to, without realizing that he was describing his own: in particular that very habit of presenting characters in sharp antithesis which we have seen him indulging in with such gusto.[58] Macaulay, said Carlyle, looked on things of the spirit 'with spectacles instead of eyes' (and he must have worn them on his assignment in India, when he dismissed all that country's culture as 'not worth half a shelf of European books').[59] It is hardly surprising that in jumping to discreditable conclusions about Bacon, he should have failed to take into account the complexities of Bacon's character and situation. He never saw them. Before they could reach his eyes, he had turned those spectacles upon them and forced all their lights and shadows into the famous black-and-white checkerboard which was fed to generations of schoolboys. Bacon had himself described the 'distribution of everything into two members' as 'a kind of cloud that overshadowed knowledge'. People who practise it, he wrote, 'when a thing does not aptly fall into those dichotomies, either pass it by or force it out of its natural shape'.[60] How could a man whose 'vast genius' no one had ever been found 'competent to embrace' – and has not yet – be squeezed into Macaulay's narrow categories?[61]

When Spedding tackled Macaulay – then at the height of his triumph – he expected not popularity but indifference, or even hostility, from the majority of his readers. He made no attempt to flatter their prejudices or

stir their emotions. Like Bacon, he addressed his remarks to later generations.[62] And his sole effort was that of the true historian (as laid down by
a critic of historians today): to illuminate 'the secret recesses of the
personality where a man's first responsibility lies'. Thus in his quiet way
Spedding was able to give us many exciting glimpses of the real human
being that was Francis Bacon. For Bacon is exciting. Scholars, when
setting out to explore his works, have often used this epithet to describe
his effect on them.[63] And it is because Spedding had so closely espoused
the subtleties of his mind that he could perceive better than most how
strictly Bacon obeyed his own injunction: 'cleave to the very marrow of
things.'[64] Spedding saw the inner unity of the man who had observed that
'variety is as the rainbow to the sun'.[65] A century later scholars such as
Benjamin Farrington and Brian Vickers recognized in Bacon the single-
hearted lover of humankind, intent on touching in his fellow man, as he
put it, 'that portion of his understanding, however preoccupied and beset,
which welcomes truth'; and whose search for a truth that could help
mankind is visible even in his style.[66]

This is the real key to Bacon's character. It explains his innocence – or
culpable naivety – in believing that no evil could spring from the actions
of one who had dedicated his life to this purpose. It is compatible with
faults of weakness and negligence; with giving way to King James over
matters of policy, when he could not persuade him, or accepting Lady
Wharton's purse and forgetting that her cause was still open. It is not
compatible with insincerity and meanness of spirit. For the simplistic
mind, however, unable to grasp that internal unity without which
nothing complex could survive, complexity spells insincerity – the one
fault on which all Bacon's misconstruers are agreed. And between the
complex reality and the complicated image, biographers made their
choice when they entrusted his reputation to the 'great Philistine', as
Matthew Arnold described Macaulay; 'the sublime of commonplace', as
Carlyle saw him; the 'intellectual dwarf' who, wrote Stuart Mill, was
without a germ of 'further growth in his whole being', and who said
thousands of brilliant things but so few true ones; the man who, according to Gladstone, was 'incapable of fetching from the depths or soaring to
the heights'.[67] It was choice which determined the view of Bacon still held
by a large number of his compatriots.

Today Macaulay is no longer read in schools, and he has lost a good
deal of his magic. But that magic has done its work. 'It is not the lie that
passeth through the mind,' wrote Bacon, 'but the lie that sinketh in and
settleth in it that doth the hurt.'[68] The psychological power of what he
called a 'false notion, or idol' is all the greater when that idol is concealed.
Thus the 'false notion' we now have of Bacon – a few vivid lines of
denigration which reduce the rest of his life to a shadow – is all the more

strongly established because none of those who take it for granted are conscious of its source. Macaulay's image, still intact after a hundred and fifty years of repetition, carries an undiminished emotional charge – a charge so strong that it breaks out in wild invective and spills over, as we have seen, into the virulent language which commentators on his thought reserve for Bacon alone among Renaissance writers.[69] Some powerful emotion must have been at work to keep this animus alive for so long, against all rational expectation. Political bias, which can carry a heavy load of emotion, comes to mind, but in fact, except for the jumping-off ground supplied by the anti-Stuart libellers to Macaulay's historical fantasy, anti-Tory opinion played little part in the blackening process. If Lucy Aikin was sometimes unjust and Caroline Macaulay savage, there are Whigs such as Rushworth in the seventeenth century, Addison in the eighteenth and Gardiner in the nineteenth, who wrote about Bacon with equanimity. This virulence is something more personal, and lies closer to the bone. Where does it spring from?

Bacon described the birth of a prejudice as an opinion 'agreeable' to the predisposed mind, which 'simultaneously and suddenly' fills the imagination, and which afterwards continues to 'infect it', so that it will resist all opposition.[70] In his own case the 'agreeable' opinion had its source in the wounded Chancellor whom his critics found ready to hand, and we all know how satisfying it is to human as well as shark nature to see blood drawn. When Macaulay 'simultaneously and suddenly' filled the imagination of generations with his portrait of a badly flawed man, the hunt – first set going by Cranfield and Coke among the disreputable hangers-on of Chancery – was on. A hunt is a highly pleasurable experience, and the crowning pleasure of this one fell to Bacon's disparagers: an unlimited licence to condemn.[71] We have seen Macaulay indulging in what his biographer called 'the luxury and pleasing sensuousness of moral condemnation', and his followers writing more in sorrow than in anger – but more in pleasure than in either.[72] Few of them, as they 'blushed' for Bacon – or 'very much feared', or 'regretted to say' – managed to tell the 'painful story' of his 'misspent life' without betraying emotions that range from a not very convincing distress to undisguised gloating over his 'well-deserved' misfortunes.[73] Not only did they consign him to a variety of hells; they dwelt at length on the most insignificant punishments meted out to him by fate, and when possible added imaginary misfortunes to the real ones. Thus, in 1976, Marwil savoured the 'intriguing irony' of Bacon's admiration for a Queen whose favour he allegedly failed to gain, adding that 'he tried to get de Thou' to use his *Memorial* on Elizabeth in his *Histoire Universelle*, presumably in vain. (In reality, de Thou acknowledged Bacon's article at once, 'being esteemed', wrote Carteret, 'a most exquisite performance of its kind, and as such it was made use of in his invaluable History.' It was published there in full.) Bacon's imaginary devastation over an alleged 'shattering loss of face' is lingered over with the usual complacency as late as 1995.[74]

Some of Bacon's defamers, no doubt, were moved by disappointed love. A great philosopher is expected to be near perfect, since perfection 'exalts and ennobles mankind', and gives us a better opinion of ourselves.[75] So when Bacon failed to meet their standards, praise turned to invective, the more immoderate for the admiration they continued to harbour for him against their will. And harbour it they did. Of the many critics who have confessed themselves 'beguiled' or 'dazzled' by Bacon, it is those who treated him worst, and who dwelt with most satisfaction on his sufferings, who were the most 'bewitched' (Abbott), or 'fascinated' by his 'glittering allurement' (Strachey).[76] The majority, however, simply enjoyed putting down the great. 'We now approach the highest but one of the peaks of intellectual greatness' – so Sidney Lee embarked on an article of pure denigration.[77] When the hunt is on, the greatness is lost sight of, but it is still agreeably present at the back of the critic's mind – not least when he is content to shake head and let Bacon off with a condescending reproof.[78]

Negative biography, written in a bitter and contemptuous tone, is very much in vogue today, and as we watch its authors at work, the question inevitably arises, are they writing about their subject or about themselves? People often reveal their own secrets when affronting others, as Churchill observed, and he remarked on Macaulay's tendency to accuse those he wrote about of greed for filthy lucre – a vice Macaulay himself was not exempt from.[79] We have seen a biographer criticized for his coldness reproaching Bacon with coldness.[80] Similarly, the notion of a philosopher bent above all things on his own advancement was born in the minds of men themselves thoroughly impressed with the glamour of political and social acclaim. Whether or not Bacon actually envied the courtier who 'could obtain a more cordial salute from Buckingham', we know with what satisfaction Macaulay, who made this statement about him, boasted of dining with people who were 'all Lords except myself', or of being thanked 'by a King in all his glory'. And where did the 'rapture' with which Bacon first signed himself Lord Chancellor – as alleged by another notoriously ambitious Chancellor – originate?[81] A taste for pulling down the powerful from their high place was recently identified in the biographer who fifty years ago drew the most vivid picture of Bacon craving for advancement: Strachey's concern with power, said his own biographer, 'took the form of an assault on ambitious men and women already dead'.[82]

The relief to be gained from projecting onto another something that displeases us in ourselves, and condemning it in him, may go far to explain an appetite for depreciation that can only be assuaged by abusing a man long dead. Macaulay's nineteenth-century biographer remarked on the absurdity of being angry 'with people who lived so long ago, and never did us harm'.[83] Without indulging in fashionable Freudian interpretations, we may assume that a critic's anger against Bacon today is more likely to concern that critic, at the time of writing, than Bacon, who could truly say – as when he was caught up in Queen Elizabeth's anger against Essex – 'I am the least part of my own matter.'[84] Shelley, with Bacon among other 'poets' in mind, was to upbraid critics who, uniting in their own persons the 'incompatible characters of accuser, witness, judge and executioner', decide, without trial or testimony, 'that certain motives of those who are "there sitting where we dare not soar" are reprehensible'. 'Look to your own motives,' he admonished them.[85] Another man was to voice the same indignation. Only once did the imperturbably mild Spedding allow his sense of outrage to break forth, and that only in a private letter. What kind of people are these, he asked, 'who so complacently take it for granted that they are nobler beings than Bacon . . .? Why are these people permitted to go on strutting and moralizing and making the angels weep, when a sudden gift of insight into themselves would make them go and hide out of the way?'

'I have yet to learn', Spedding declared in *Evenings with a Reviewer*, 'that his character was ever ill-spoken of by a man of great spirit who had opportunities of knowing him.'[86] And when we look down the ranks of those who have penetrated Bacon's motives, appreciated his efforts and his humanity, and spoken with understanding of his frailties and failures, we find that they could be described as men 'of great spirit', or better (with a phrase of Bacon's which Hazlitt liked to quote) as people who 'look abroad into universality'.[87] Some had held public office, and could make allowance for the stresses and limitations they were familiar with, and they all shared the amplitude of mind, the unassuming generosity, tolerance and good humour which his contemporaries found in Bacon. These are qualities also noted in Bacon's close friends – George Herbert, Toby Matthew, Bishop Andrewes, Jeremiah Bettenham – as well as in the courtiers with whom he was most in sympathy – Pembroke, Falkland and Sackville, among others. They were eminently present in Spedding himself, described by one of his numerous friends as gentle, wise and luminous, and remembered for his ready smile and his winning, humorous remarks. Among those of his inner circle, Alfred Tennyson dedicated an admiring poem to him, and Edward Fitzgerald called him 'the wisest man I know'. His dying words, not long after he had been run over in the street by a cab, are in keeping with the rest of his life. While still conscious, we are told, his one concern was to assure those around him that the cab-driver was not to blame.[88]

These same qualities are often found in the historians who, before Spedding, saw Bacon with insight and in the round: Montagu, Hepworth

Dixon, Gardiner; Hazlitt – described by Charles Lamb as 'one of the finest and wisest spirits breathing' ('no one who knew him', said Lucy Aikin, 'could help loving him'); and Addison, the poet-statesman, who charmed Pope and was praised by Johnson for his sense of humour as much as for his love of truth. And let us not forget Archbishop Tenison, of whom Evelyn wrote that he 'never knew a man of more universal and generous spirit'; and that best of historians, Thomas Fuller, much loved by Coleridge, with his infectious good humour and exuberant wit, whose favourite virtue was moderation.[89] We will not look for breadth of vision, or for the kind of good humour that comes from our acceptance of our own share of human foibles, among those who have been putting Bacon down from his time to ours. Detraction supposes a strong ego and a generally irritable frame of mind, keener on seeing the worst in others than on discovering the truth about them. The first two who saw Bacon in a poor light – Cranfield and Coke – are sufficiently known to us. Whatever the virtues of the latter (the former had, it seems, very few), we know that harshness, rancour, envy and narrowness of mind ranked high in the list of their defects. Nor shall we expect mellowness of judgement from the libellers of James's Court.

Bacon's detractors down the centuries fall roughly into two categories, each of them exerting a powerful influence on their own kind. On the one hand there is the happy-go-lucky band of clever (sometimes brilliant) but angry story-tellers, galloping off on their various hobby-horses, blind to the real man whose value they so heedlessly depreciate – though some of them are quite pleased to show off their own. Theirs is the style Quinton felicitously labelled 'rollicking'. First indulged in by the picaresque libeller, Arthur Wilson, it was practised among others, by Macaulay, Campbell, Strachey and Denning. On the other hand we have the obsessive burrowers and the zealous crusaders against evil, balancing their far-fetched theses on a scaffolding of minutiae which could be variously combined to distort the truth. First among them, no doubt, was the industrious D'Ewes, 'a mere copyist and collector', as he has been described, without any constructive ability, although a gold-mine for historians with wider perspectives.[90] But most representative of this category, with his self-acknowledged followers today, was Dean Abbott, a headmaster, as we learn from an admirer, full of zeal, energy and virtue, who had a 'deep reprobation' for the vices he disapproved of.[91]

We may draw the obvious conclusion, that a well-disposed, good-humoured critic is more likely to be fair to his subject than an acrimonious one, and that a relaxed frame of mind is more conducive to objectivity. And Aubrey's well-known remark about Bacon – 'all that were *good and great* loved and honoured him' – may be valid not only for their contemporaries, but for many of those who have since frequented Bacon; if, that is, by the 'great' we mean people whose field of vision is large, and by the 'good' those who are at ease with their own souls, ready to look with unclouded eyes on the world about them. Bacon's life, John Pitcher informs us, while recommending Abbott's, 'is not yet expounded'. He 'still awaits his biographer'.[92] He may have to wait a long time, because the qualifications required of such a biographer – involving some degree of professional acquaintance with the aims, methods and language of science, jurisprudence, economics, history, and indeed with almost every branch of human endeavour cultivated in the Renaissance – have not yet been found together in one person. Less than ever today is an exclusively academic writer 'competent to embrace the vast extent of his genius' – without which the man cannot be understood – not only because the history of such a man as Bacon is best written by 'those who have handled the realm of government' (as he thought all history should be written), but also because the task now before a biographer seeking to evaluate Bacon in his own terms as well as in those of our time, is to join the divided Bacons of the popular 'Lives'. And in doing so, to bridge the gap between these 'Lives' and the unified vision – which, as increasingly shown by recent scholarship, animates Bacon's 'grand political strategy', his theory of the universe and his newly studied 'maker's science', so relevant to our time.[93]

Will the twenty-first century bring forth some wide-awake polymath, an updated version, perhaps, of the illustrious diplomat and statesman John Carteret, Earl Granville, whose long article on Bacon we are familiar with here? Carteret was as happy out of the places of power he occupied as in them. 'Void of gall', as he is described in a poem by Horace Walpole, the son of his great political rival, and as much liked for his good humour as for his 'versatile intellect', he was an accomplished scientist, a brilliant linguist, a distinguished scholar and a patron 'of learned men and learned undertakings'. And he was remembered by the best men of his time as 'one of the great'.[94] We know at any rate what Bacon's biographer should not be: a day-dreamer, like Macaulay, making villains to set off his glorious heroes, or like Lytton Strachey, whose 'Life' by Michael Holroyd has shown that his whole effort in writing about Essex was to lose himself (though it 'exacerbated his pain') in a romanticized version of the love affair he was then involved in with Roger Senhouse. In describing Essex playing at cards with Elizabeth late into the night, Strachey was passionately reliving his own sexually charged card-games with his *inamorato*. Craving ever more make-believe, his great wish, he confessed to Senhouse, was to 'pulverize the material and remould it in the shape of his own particular absurdity'. He succeeded. In a book which should have been entitled *Strachey and Strachey*, the supporting cast is entirely made up of loyal friends and vicious enemies; among whom, writes Holroyd, we meet with Bacon 'the serpent', a 'blacker villain than Enobarbus'.[95]

There are other forms of day-dreaming, and while we may wish to see the author of this new 'Life' gifted with the vivid style of the popular writer, we may hope that he will not be caught up in the kind of make-believe practised today by the more extreme literary theorists, who indiscriminately foist onto their subject – with hardly a glance at the subject himself, still less at his or her times – all the discontinuity, ambivalence and equivocation which their theories are compounded of. To see in Bacon, as one postmodern critic predictably does, 'a tragedy of meaning rather than of events' does little to embrace his genius. Promising not to represent him as 'dissolved beyond redemption', Charles Whitney explains that 'the catastrophe of Bacon's modern text is the engulfment of a vision of presence in the web of the text' (and so on, for this kind of commentary can be spun out indefinitely, like those other webs of scholastic learning which Bacon deplored). Of this fatal engulfment, writes Whitney, 'though Bacon could not', the reader can, within limits, achieve a 'tragic recognition'. Whether or no such remarks cast any light on Bacon the thinker, they sometimes turn out to be mere camouflage for a fashionable condemnation of Bacon the man.[96] Perhaps the author of a new 'Life' will realize, with Benedetto Croce, that condemnation is superfluous. Those who 'have already appeared before the tribunal of their day', said Croce, cannot be condemned twice; 'they can suffer no other judgement than that which penetrates and understands the spirit of their work.'[97] At this point our hypothetical author may conclude, as did one historian of the Chancellor's impeachment, that 'all censure is impertinence'.[98] Or, while still using his personal criteria to evaluate Bacon's life and character, may see him in terms of the goals which that zealous well-wisher of mankind had set himself and the ideals to which he aspired.

There is a quality we should look for above all others in Bacon's biographer. In her essay, 'Biography, True and False', Iris Origo, herself a near flawless practitioner, tells us the one thing a writer must do when taking on what she considers almost impossible: to understand a fellow creature in his going forth, and to 'decipher the whole heart of his mystery' across 'a long stretch of generations'. He must, at least for a time, give up self, and cast his own opinions aside.[99] This is not easy. But if a few trustworthy historians have succeeded so far in giving us a glimpse of the rich reality that was Bacon, it is because, as she enjoins, they did not drown his voice in their own.

May Bacon meet with the biographer he deserves. Until then let us be content to take him at his own valuation, agreeing with Fuller that 'none can character him to the life save himself'.[100]

Appendix

Ralegh's involvement in the 1603 conspiracy and his real aim when setting forth to Guiana in 1617, as analysed by Macvey Napier in his essay on Sir Walter Ralegh (1853).

Napier was the editor of the *Edinburgh Review* where the essay on Bacon by his valued contributor, Macaulay, appeared sixteen years before he brought out his own very readable study. He has no criticism of Bacon, but, though ready to defend Ralegh against the charges of his more mistrustful contemporaries, and those of later historians (e.g. David Hume's claim that his report of his voyage to Guiana was 'full of the grossest and most palpable lies', p. 132), he was mortified to find that even when Ralegh's actions were viewed in the best possible light, his veracity and integrity could not be relied on (p. 257). He regretfully endorsed Ben Jonson's remark that Ralegh 'esteemed fame more than conscience' (p. 162).

Ralegh was certainly involved to some extent with his follower, Lord Cobham, in the conspiracy in 1603 to depose the King and place Arabella Stuart on the throne, with Spanish aid. However eloquently he defended himself, his behaviour was not that of an innocent man. He first denied any knowledge of the plot, then he confessed that he had been offered Spanish funds to take part in it, then he sent a secret note of instructions to Cobham in case he were interrogated. Cobham himself twice denounced him and twice retracted his testimony. However, despite more damning evidence from the French Ambassador Beaumont's dispatches, pointing strongly to his direct participation, it is highly improbable that Ralegh could ever have accepted money from Spain (p. 198). Napier concluded that, aware of Cobham's treason, he 'indulged his own discontent and encouraged the schemes of the other' with some secret scheme of his own in view. His real intention was probably (as reported by an intimate friend of Southampton to Aubrey, who had close links the Ralegh family) 'to inveigle Cobham to Jersey [where Ralegh was Governor], and then, having got both him and his Spanish treasure in his power, to make terms with the King' (pp. 199–203). He could not plead this in his defence, and was thus implicated in the plot he had meant to denounce. (See also Rowse, *Ralegh and the Throgmortons*, pp. 235–7.) This would explain both his strong sense of his innocence, and Cobham's anger against him. It is also in character, as Napier pointed out (pp. 203–4): 'It was said of Ralegh by one who knew him well "that he desired to seem to be able to sway all men's fancies – all men's courses"; and perhaps it was this notion of his power to sway others that entangled him in a net of his own spreading . . .' But although Napier considered the sentence unjust, Ralegh was not innocent. Dictating terms to one's sovereign from a position of power – as Essex had also planned to do – was still treason.

Ralegh emerges from Napier's analysis as an intrepid but reckless and unscrupulous adventurer fired with a great idea, the conquest of El Dorado, which, though shared by many (but not by Queen Elizabeth), was nevertheless a delusion. We see him impelled all his life long by an overwhelming ambition, to be the one to 'put an effectual curb' on the power of Spain, thereby promoting English colonization and commerce. He combined a sincere belief in the wonders of the New World (including his dream of an alliance with the imaginary potentate of El Dorado) with extravagant fictions deliberately thought up to promote his plans, and lying promises aimed at hoodwinking the Spanish colonizers, the Indian chiefs, and his own Government at home (pp. 123, 137, 140, 261). Though he had not, as many thought, acted in bad faith when proclaiming the existence of a gold-mine, 'his pacific professions' before he set out on his second voyage to Guiana in 1617 'were intended merely as blinds' (p. 260). His real aim from the beginning was not to work a mine in the desert parts of Guiana, according to his solemn promise, but to conquer territory he knew to be Spanish; for which purpose, as he later admitted, he deliberately concealed the existence of a town near the mine. His own words, and those of his captains, leave no doubt that the capture of Santo Tomé was resolved on before his voyage began, and that Ralegh's men disembarked 'for that express purpose' (pp. 236–7, 258, 265).

Had the expedition succeeded, he might conceivably have gained the immunity he counted on. 'Good success', as he would write in the *Apology for his last Voyage to Guiana*, 'admits of no examination.' When it failed he attempted to carry out the plan he had confided to Pembroke before setting out (and later denied, but confessed to in the end): an attack on the Mexican fleet. But, deserted by his captains, he was forced to abandon it and return home (p. 253). There followed further deceitful behaviour, to Napier's embarrassment. Before his departure for Guiana, while heaping extravagant praise on James and vowing it was his dearest wish 'to be torn to pieces in his service', Ralegh, despite his later denials, had held repeated conversations with the French Ambassador, Count Desmarests (who wrote of him in his dispatches as 'in the highest degree discontented' at his treatment by James), and resolved to abandon his country and make the King of France an offer of his services and acquisitions. Whether or not he was as insincere towards the French King as towards his own, Ralegh clearly meant to secure a refuge abroad in case of failure in Guiana; and when, back in Plymouth, he received an offer of French assistance he made two efforts to escape to France, but was betrayed. The iniquity of the Government agents set to spy on Ralegh is beneath Napier's contempt, but he is again obliged to face the devious and degrading expedients resorted to by the hero of Cadiz, now wallowing in the depths of self-pity, to gain time for another escape (p. 262).

The Commission investigated the charges against him with particular care, and Ralegh was allowed to answer them point by point, a privilege of which he availed himself by telling falsehood after falsehood, and – when he finally confessed that he had formed a plot to seize the fleet – by laying the blame on Winwood, who could not answer him because he was dead. But his best and most effective lies were those of his 'last mirth'. 'It seems that he knew better how to die than to live,' was Dudley Carleton's comment, 'and his happiest hours were those of his arraignment and execution' (14 Nov. 1618, *Dudley Carleton to John Chamberlain*). No rational statement could prevail against the myth he gave life to with his dying speech, when he acted out his vision of himself as the forgiving hero and willing martyr. The Government's official report – of which Chamberlain rightly remarked (19 Nov. 1618) that as the work of Bacon, Yelverton and Naunton, 'in all probability it must be as true as well written' – came out a month too late. By this time the epitaph recalled by Aubrey was already a reality: 'He living was belov'd of none, Yet on his death all did him moan.'

And the irony is that, as Napier pointed out, it is to the behaviour of the 'mean and pusillanimous' James that he owed his 'halo of literary and martyr-like glory' (pp. 272–3). 'Such was the precious result of James's cunning and kingcraft; for had Ralegh been pardoned when he was liberated, he might have been brought to trial in some competent form, and the law would have vindicated itself by maintaining both the reality and the appearance of justice' (p. 266). Indeed had the King made use of the exceptional gifts and energies of this subject – whose high aspirations and 'most lofty, insolent and passionate' poetic vein (so Puttenham) had fascinated Elizabeth – instead of blocking his way from the first, Ralegh would have led a better life, and might have been a different man. James, wrote a contemporary, could have 'had at his command as useful a man as served any prince in Christendom' (p. 267). Ralegh suffered, as did Bacon, from serving a poor-spirited king. But leaving aside the regret of historians, and Ralegh's own dream image of himself, Napier's survey makes one thing clear: no more than Essex was he the guiltless, loyal servant of a monarch who sacrificed him to political expediency; nor could his 'dastardly murder' be laid, along with other fancied misdeeds, at Bacon's door.

Charles Nicholl, in *The Creature in the Map: A Journey to El Dorado* (London, 1995) brings a 'cache' of recently discovered documents to bear on the voyage. While casting a variety of new lights on the 'strange mingling of primitivist nostalgia and anticipated rape' that was Ralegh's dream, Nicholl fully validates the view of this elusive character expounded by Napier a hundred and forty-two years ago.

Abbreviations

Volume numbers in bold refer to the *Works of Francis Bacon*, collected and edited by James Spedding, Robert L. Ellis and Douglas D. Heath, vols i–vii (1857–61), together with *The Letters and Life of Francis Bacon, Including all his Occasional Works*, edited with commentary by James Spedding, vols viii–xiv (1861–74).

For abbreviated titles of Bacon's works, see above, p. xii, Principal Writings of Bacon Referred to Here.

B.	Francis Bacon
AB	Anthony Bacon
Lady B.	Lady Anne Bacon, their mother
Bm	George Villiers, Duke of Buckingham
TM	Toby Matthew
Aikin	Lucy Aikin, *Memoirs of the Court of King James the First*, 2 vols, 1822
Aubrey	John Aubrey, *Aubrey's Brief Lives*, ed. Oliver Lawson Dick (Penguin edn), 1972
BB	*Biographia Britannica, or the Lives of the Most Eminent Persons who Have Flourished in Great Britain and Ireland*, ed. A. Kippis, 6 vols, 1747–66
Birch	Thomas Birch, *Memoirs of the Reign of Queen Elizabeth, from the year 1581 till her Death*, 2 vols, 1754
Bowen, *Coke*	Catherine D. Bowen, *The Lion and the Throne: The Life and Times of Edward Coke*, 1957
Campbell	John Campbell, 'Life of Lord Bacon', *Lives of the Lord Chancellors* (1845–7, ed. 1848 in 10 vols), iii, 1–146
Chamberlain	*The Letters of John Chamberlain*, 2 vols, ed. N. E. McClure, Westport, Conn., 1919
Clarendon	Edward Hyde, Earl of Clarendon, *The History of the Rebellion and Civil Wars in England* (1641, ed.), Oxford, 1888
Clive	John Clive, *Thomas Babington Macaulay, The Shaping of a Historian*, 1973
CD	*Commons Debates 1621*, ed. Wallace Notestein, Frances Relf, Hartley Simpson, New Haven, 1935
CJ	*Journals of the House of Commons*, vol. I
CR	*Contemporary Review*, 1876
CSPD	*Calendar of State Papers, Domestic Series*, ed. M. A. E. Green, 1858
Devereux	Walter B. Devereux, *Lives and Letters of the Devereux, Earls of Essex, in the Reigns of Elizabeth, James I and Charles I*, 2 vols, 1853
DNB	*Dictionary of National Biography*
Dixon	W. Hepworth Dixon, *The Story of Lord Bacon's Life*, 1862
EHR	*English Historical Review*
ER	James Spedding, *Evenings with a Reviewer*, 2 vols, 1881
F. *Phil.*	Benjamin Farrington, *The Philosophy of Francis Bacon, An Essay on its Development from 1603 to 1609 with New Translations of Fundamental Texts*, Liverpool, 1964

Abbreviations

Gardiner	Samuel R. Gardiner, *History of England from the Accession of James I to the Outbreak of the Civil War, 1603–1642,* 1863–9
Jardine	David Jardine, *Use of Torture: A Reading on the Use of Torture in the Criminal Law of England Previously to the Commonwealth,* 1837
JP	*Journal of Proceedings against Lord Bacon* in 'A Collection of Proceedings' etc., repr. Montagu, *Life of Francis Bacon* (1825–34), Note GGG
Journals, coll. D'Ewes	*The Journals of all the Parliaments of Queen Elizabeth, both of the House of Lords and House of Commons,* collected by Sir Simonds D'Ewes, ed. Rev. Paul Bowes, 1682
Lacey	Robert Lacey, *Robert, Earl of Essex, An Elizabethan Icarus,* 1971
Legacy	*The Legacy of Francis Bacon,* ed. W. A. Sessions, *Studies in the Literary Imagination,* iv 1, Atlanta, Georgia, April 1971
LD	*Lords Debates in 1621,* Elsing, ed. Gardiner, 1870
LJ	*Journals of the House of Lords*
Mac.	Thomas Babington Macaulay, 'Francis Bacon', in *Critical and Historical Essays,* 1837; this edn, Everyman, 1961, ii, 280–398
Manes	*Manes Verulamiani,* In Memory of the Greatly Honoured Lord Bacon, Baron Verulam, Viscount St Alban, 1616, ed. W. G. C. Gundry, 1949
Marwil	Jonathan L. Marwil, *The Trials of Counsel, Francis Bacon in 1621,* Detroit, 1976
Northumberand MS	*Facsimile of an Elizabethan Manuscript preserved at Alnwick Castle, Northumberland,* ed. F. J. Burgoyne, 1904
PD	*Proceedings and Debates of the House of Commons in 1620 and 1621,* 1766
Pitcher	John Pitcher, *Francis Bacon, The Essays,* 1985
Prestwich	Menna Prestwich, *Cranfield, Politics and Profits under the Early Stuarts, The Career of Lionel Cranfield, Earl of Middlesex,* 1966
Rawley	William Rawley, *Life of the Honourable Author,* introducing *Resuscitatio,* his edition of Bacon's works, 1657
Russell	Conrad Russell, *Parliaments and English Politics 1621–1629,* Oxford, 1990
Strachey	Lytton Strachey, *Elizabeth and Essex,* 1928
Tenison	Archbishop Thomas Tenison, *Certain Remains of Sir Francis Bacon, Baron of Verulam and Viscount of St Alban,* 1679
Terminologia e fortuna	*Francis Bacon, Terminologia e fortuna nel XVII secolo,* Seminario internazionale, Roma, 11–13 marzo 1984, in Lessico intelletuale europeo, Rome, 1984
Tite	Colin G. C. Tite, *Impeachment and Parliamentary Judicature in Early Stuart England,* 1974
TLS	*The Times Literary Supplement*
Weldon	Anthony Weldon, *The Court and Character of King James,* 1651
Zaller	Robert Zaller, *The Parliament of 1621, A Study in Constitutional Conflict,* Berkeley, 1971

Notes

For full details of works cited see Abbreviations, Principal Writings of Bacon Referred to Here and Bibliography

The Works of Francis Bacon, ed. Spedding, Ellis and Heath (1857–61), 7 vols, and *The Letters and Life*, ed. Spedding (1861–74), 7 vols, reprinted together as vols i–xiv, are cited by volume (in bold) and page number only.

Chapter 1 *'The Peremptory Tides of Reputation'*

The chapter title is from *AL*, **iii**, 469.

1 **v**, 215; *De Aug.*, **v**, 119; *NO*, **iv**, 104; Epistle Dedicatory, *IM*, **iv**, 11.
2 The last will of Francis Bacon, 1626, **xiv**, 539.
3 B. to TM, 1609, **xi**, 132, 135; B. to Bishop Lancelot Andrewes, summer 1622, **xiv**, 374.
4 *De Aug.*, **i**, 714 (**v**, 4).
5 *AL*, **iii**, 476 and 329; *De Aug.*, **v**, 119; *AL*, **iii**, 318.
6 Elizabeth Sewell, *The Orphic Voice* (1960), 60.
7 G. W. Leibniz, *Opera Omnia* (1768), **vi**, 303.
8 G. P. Gooch, *Political Thought in England from Bacon to Halifax* (1914), 22; J. W. Gough, *Fundamental Laws in English Constitutional History* (1955), 56; Hugh Dick, *Selected Writings of Bacon* (1955), p. xv.
9 Gilbert Wats, Preface to *The Advancement of Learning and Proficience* (1640), his translation of *De Aug.*
10 Copy of the *Novum Organum* presented by Bacon to Coke, Holkham Hall; John Chamberlain, *The Letters of John Chamberlain*, ed. N. E. McClure (1939); 3 Feb. 1621, ii, 338.
11 Ben Jonson (1647), *Works* (1925–52), **viii**, 592.
12 I. Vincent, and E. F. in *Manes Verulamiani* (1626), 40 and 43; David Mallet, *The Life of Bacon, Lord Chancellor of England* (1740); Samuel Johnson (1779) on Mallet's *Life*, cited Brian Vickers, *Francis Bacon and Renaissance Prose* (1968), 246, n4.
13 Brian Vickers, ed., *Essential Articles for the Study of Francis Bacon* (1968). p. xxviii.
14 Charles Williams, *Bacon* (1933).
15 Joel Hurstfield, Review of *Francis Bacon* by Fulton Anderson, in *English Historical Review* 29 (July 1964), 603; Julian Martin, *Francis Bacon, The State and the Reform of Natural Philosophy* (1992), 2.
16 *Gemma valde nitida*, *De Aug.*, **i**, 56, translated as 'the clearest diamond', v, 42; *Othello*, III. iii. 160.
17 B. to King James, July 1624, **xiv**, 518.
18 Earlier draft of Bacon's last will, attached to Tenison.
19 Enrico De Mas, *Scritti politici, giuridici e storici di Francesco Bacone* (1971), i, 57.
20 Catherine D. Bowen, *Francis Bacon, The Temper of a Man* (1963), 4.
21 Sheila Wingfield, Viscountess Powerscourt (1983), who has since

given the present work her constant support.

22 *NA*, **iii**, 134; *NO*, **iv**, 167; F. C. Heath, 'Origins of the Binary Code', *The Scientific American*, 227, 2 (Aug. 1972).

23 *History of King Henry VII*, **vi**, 242; as used by John le Carré, of agents under deep cover.

24 Alexander Solzhenitsyn, *Cancer Ward* (Engl. transl., 1969), 435, 550 and 555; *Proceedings of the Session of the Union of Soviet Writers*, cited Soltzhenitsyn, *A Documentary Record* (1970), 141 and 147.

Chapter 2   'That Angel from Paradise'

For chapter title, see note 37 below.

1 From eight contributors to *Manes*, mostly anon., 40–43.

2 See Graham Parry, *The Golden Age Restored* (1981), 198.

3 Jonson, *Works*, viii, 592.

4 Rawley, in Spedding, **i**, 8.

5 David Lloyd, *State Worthies* (1665).

6 Spedding, **i**, pp. xvi–xxi; for portrait by Simon Pass, see jacket of this book.

7 William Camden, *The History of Elizabeth, the Late Queen of England, Annales* (1617, ed. T. Hearne, 1635), iv, 593; Aubrey, 174 (I have also used the more scholarly edition of Aubrey's *Brief Lives* (1694), ed. A. Clark (1898)); John Evelyn, *Numismata* (1697), 370. Evelyn was born six years after Bacon's death.

8 *NA*, **iii**, 154, and *Redargutio Philosophiarum* (1608), in F. *Phil.*, 104, the speaker whose 'face had become habituated to the expression of pity'; M. McCanles, 'Myth and Method' in the Scientific Philosophy of Francis Bacon', *Dialectical Criticism and Renaissance Literature* (1975), 14–51, see p. 51.

9 Francis Osborne, *Advice to a Son* (1656, ed. 1677), i, 151; Jonson,

Works, viii, 591; Bacon, 19 June, in *Commentarius Solutus*, a diary he kept in summer 1608, **xi**, 92.

10 Thomas Campion, Epigram 190, *Works*, ed. P. Vivian (1967), 263; Toby Matthew, *Autobiographical Letter to Dame Mary Gage* (1611), ed. E. Dowden (1904).

11 *Promus* (written 1594–7, ed. E. Durning-Lawrence, 1910); *Apophthegmes New and Old* (1625), **vii**, 123–65.

12 **iv**, 487.

13 Bacon, Apophthegm 58, **vii**, 133, and *Apology Concerning the Earl of Essex* (1604), **x**, 149–50.

14 Aubrey, 171; Jonson, *Works*, viii, 591; Osborne, *Advice to a Son*, i, 151; Rawley, **i**, 12.

15 Rawley; Peter Boener, 'Life of Bacon', prefixed to Dutch edn of the *Essays* (1647); Aubrey, 172, 175; Lady B. to AB, 24 May 1580, **viii**, 114; *SS*, **ii**, 423.

16 **x**, 38 and n2.

17 Rawley, **i**, 17.

18 Tenison, 19; Thomas Birch later recalled 'that wholesome pleasant lodge and finely designed garden', ii, 51–2; on Gray's Inn, see Dugdale, *Baronage of England* (1675), ii, 437, and W. Holden, 'Bacon's Association with Gray's Inn', *Baconiana* 141 (Autumn 1951), 205.

19 Aubrey, 174.

20 Campion, Epigram 90, *Works*, 263; Davies, *Scourge of Folly* (1610), 23; Thomas Randolph in *Manes*, 46; George Chapman, *Georgics of Hesiod* (1618); for Donne see Aubrey, *Brief Lives*, ed. Clark, 68.

21 *Manes*, 38.

22 Rawley, i, 6.

23 Fuller, *Church History of Great Britain*, (1655), iii, 325.

24 See chapter 27 below.

25 Notestein, *Four Worthies* (1956), 78.

26 Chamberlain, 28 Oct. 1620, ii, 324; Goodman, *The Court of King James the First* (c. 1650), i, 283. Chamberlain was also noticed as a prejudiced and malicious critic of Sir

Henry Wotton by L. Pearsall Smith, *The Life and Letters of Sir Henry Wotton* (1907), i, 69 and 131 n4.

27 Smith, *Sir Henry Wotton*, 10 May 1617, ii, 73; 22 June 1616, ii, 9; 7 Feb. 1618, ii, 135; 23 June 1621, ii, 385.

28 Constantijn Huygens's autobiography (Latin 1629–31), Dutch trans. 1946, 114–17; Huygens's letter to Daniel Heinsius at Leyden, 6 June 1621, cited Jacob Smit, *Constantin Huygens* (The Hague, 1980), 88. I thank Gabriela von Humboldt and Wieger Hellema for information and translations.

29 B. to Bm, 8 May 1617, **xiii**, 194.

30 Chamberlain, 10 May 1617, ii, 72.

31 Bishop William Sanderson, *Aulus Coquinariae* (1650), cited Spedding, **xiv**, 227; Chamberlain, 11 Oct. 1617, ii, 102.

32 Bacon, *Essays* in Italian (1618), dedicatory letter to the Grand Duke of Tuscany, translation into English by the author, see 'Address to the Reader' in John Donne, *A Collection of Letters made by Sir Tobias Mathews Kt . . .* (1660), and see **xiv**, 286.

33 Rawley, **i**, 15.

34 Boener, cited Spedding, **xiv**, 576.

35 Tenison, 15. Sir Henry Wotton was appointed, see below, chapter 17, n36.

36 Rawley, i, 13; Aubrey, 'brief life' of Coke, 226.

37 'Quell' angelo del Paradiso', Micanzio to Cavendish, cited De Mas, *Scritti politici, giuridici e storici*, i, 105; George Herbert, 'In Honour of the Illustrious Baron Verulam', in *The Latin Poems of George Herbert* (ed. 1965), 170; Aubrey, 171, italics Aubrey's, see Clark edn, 70.

Chapter 3   The 'Horrible Old Rascal'

1 Adrian Berry in *Sunday Telegraph*, 19 Feb. 1995; Haycock in *Blackwood's Magazine*, Dec. 1930; G. M. Thomson in *Daily Express*, 4 Oct. 1933; Colonel Ingersol in *The World* (New York), 4 Sept. 1887, cited in *Proceedings of the Bacon Society* i (1887): 65; remark recalled by William White in *A Criticism of Macaulay's Essay* (1900), 1.

2 Quotations from R. W. Gentry, 'Garbled History', *Baconiana* 125 (1947): 193–201.

3 Sidney Lee, 'Francis Bacon', in *Great Englishmen of the Sixteenth Century* (1904, ed. 1925), 224, 242.

4 See Benjamin Farrington, 'On Misunderstanding the Philosophy of Francis Bacon', in E. Ashworth, ed., *Science, Medicine and History* (1953); Fulton Anderson, *Francis Bacon: His Career and Thought* (1962); Vickers, *Essential Articles*. Biographers: Bowen, *Francis Bacon*, and Du Maurier, *The Winding Stair* (1976).

5 Slaughter, 'Francis Bacon and the Ideal Commonwealth', 56, and Axson, 'Francis Bacon as Man of Letters', 112, in *Rice Institute Pamphlet* 13, University Extension Lectures on Bacon (1926).

6 Genevieve Foster, *The World of Captain John Smith* (1959), 162–5. The same unpleasing political climber is found in the *Children's Britannica* (1969).

7 Adrian Berry in *Daily Telegraph*, 3 May 1982; John Gohorry, 'Acts of Merit', *Encounter*, Sept.–Oct. 1984, 3–4; Otto Friedrich, 'They Do Not Know It Is Wrong', *Time*, 15 Feb. 1985.

8 Marwil; Epstein, *Francis Bacon: A Political Biography* (1977); Anthony Quinton, *Francis Bacon* (1980); Pitcher; Coquillette, *Francis Bacon* (1992).

9 Aubrey, 170; Pitcher.

10 See in particular part V, chapters 29 and 32.

11 C. J. Dixon, *A Preface to Bacon*; (1963) see also Matheson and Matheson, *Francis Bacon: Selections* (1964), 7.

12 Strachey; A. L. Rowse, *William Shakespeare, A Biography* (1963), 345.
13 Thomas B. Macaulay, 'Francis Bacon', *Edinburgh Review* (July 1837), reprinted in *Critical and Historical Essays*, hereafter Mac. (see list of abbreviations for full details).
14 J. M. Robertson, 'Bacon', in *Pioneer Humanists* (1907), 44.
15 Harriet Martineau, *Biographical Sketches* (1869), 425; Lord Acton, letter of 1 Sept. 1883, in *Letters of Lord Acton to Mary, Daughter of the Right Hon. W. E. Gladstone* (1904), 173; Seeley, *History of England, 1603–1642* (1911), cited Kenyon, *The History Men*, 74, 217. Seeley told G. M. Trevelyan that his great uncle Macaulay was a charlatan (Kenyon, 226). For recent views (Clive, Kenyon et al.), see chapter 34 below.
16 Winston Churchill, *Marlborough, His Life and Times* (1933–4), vol. i, 54, 131–2, 144–6, 426–36.
17 Charles Firth, *A Commentary on Macaulay's History of England* (1938), 2.
18 See below, chapter 34.
19 A. L. Rowse, *The English Spirit* (1944), 102 and 231.
20 See chapter 34 below.
21 C. S. Venables, Preface to Spedding, *Evenings with a Reviewer*, p. xxvi.
22 Paolo Rossi, 'Per una bibliografia degli scritti su Francesco Bacone, 1800–1956' (1957).
23 *ER*, i, 182.
24 Robertson, *Pioneer Humanists*, 51.
25 Basil Montagu, *Life of Francis Bacon*, appended to *The Works of Francis Bacon, Chancellor of England*, 16 vols (1825–34).
26 Mac., 293 and 317.
27 *AL*, **iii**, 430.

Chapter 4   Who Abandoned his Patron

1 John Nichol, *Francis Bacon, his Life and Philosophy* (1901), i, 46.
2 Mac., 321.
3 *ER*, i, 111 and 153.
4 *Of the Colours of Good and Evil* (1597).
5 *Apology*, **x**, 144.
6 For the consistency and reliability of the *Apology*, barring two minor errors of dating, see Spedding, **x**, 127–33, 161–2 and 180–1.
7 *Observations on a Libel* (1592), **viii**, 143–208; Bacon's pleading, **viii**, 267.
8 See *ER*, i, 90–91, and, among others, Bacon to Lord Keeper Puckering, Apr. 1594, **viii**, 292, on his uncle's 'kind course', and to Burghley, thanking him for his assistance over his failed candidature, and his continuing favour 'in regard of my private estate', 21 Mar. 1595, **viii**, 357; also, to same, 31 Mar. 1597, **ix**, 51–2. Bacon was raised to the Bench at twenty-five, compare Coke at thirty-eight and Egerton at forty.
9 B. to Burghley, Jan. 1592, **viii**, 109, and, to same, 16 Sept. 1580, **viii**, 12–13.
10 W. T. Smedley, 'The Mystery of Francis Bacon', *Baconiana* 33 (Jan. 1911): 5–34; see Frances Yates, *The French Academies of the Sixteenth Century* (1947), 4 and 14–30.
11 See **viii**, 31; B. to Bm, on Burghley, 23 July 1620, **xiv**, 110; speech of the Second Counsellor to the Prince of Purpoole (i.e. indirectly to the Queen), at the Gray's Inn revels, Christmas 1594 (**viii**, 335).
12 B. to Walsingham, 25 Aug. 1585, recalling Hatton's encouragement; Anjou's visit, Nov. 1581 to Feb. 1582; re Bacon as inter-

preter, see Burghley's household accounts cited Conyers Read, *Lord Burghley and Queen Elizabeth* (1960), 258.

13 Yates, *French Academies*, 134, see **viii**, 330.

14 Re Sidney, see Julian Martin, *Francis Bacon, The State and Reform of Natural Philosophy* (1992), 27–34; and see La Jessée's poems addressed to the Bacon brothers in 1597, Lambeth Palace Library, ff. *661*, 263–4, and *653*, 281.

15 Edmund Waller, Dedication of his *Poems* (1645) to Queen Henrietta Maria.

16 *Apology*, **x**, 143, and B. to Essex, 10 May 1596, **ix**, 31; B. to Essex, 10 May 1516, **ix**, 31.

17 Anthony Standen to Bacon, 5 Nov. 1594, Birch, i, 154; Essex to Sir Thomas and Lady Cecil, June 1597, ibid., ii, 347–8.

18 Bacon's gratitude in *Apology*, **x**, 142, see **ix**, 36; Essex to Lord Keeper Egerton, 17 May 1596, **x**, 34–5; Essex as reported by AB to Lady Bacon, 5 Feb. 1594, **viii**, 269.

19 Essex to Puckering, Mar. 1595, **viii**, 354; B. to AB, 25 Jan. 1595, **viii**, 348.

20 B. to AB, 25 Jan. 1595, **viii**, 348 (in the *Apology*, **x**, 144, he recalled that Essex had spoken these words to him); 'Nothing cut the throat more of your access,' wrote Cecil to Bacon, 'than the Earl's being somewhat troubled at this time', May 1594, **viii**, 296; Essex to B., 28 Mar. 1595, **viii**, 289.

21 Fulke Greville to B., 27 May and 7 June 1594, **viii**, 298 and 302.

22 Elizabeth's famous remark (as reported by Essex to B., 18 May 1594, **viii**, 297) was made soon after he had scored some points against Coke, when pleading his first case. Bacon himself believed that he had lost the Solicitorship 'the rather' by Coke's influence (B. to Coke, 30 Apr. 1601, **x**, 4).

23 In January 1595, Bacon confided

to Essex his plan to give up these efforts and travel abroad, particularly requesting him not to mention his wishes to the Queen, 'till her Majesty had made a Solicitor'. Essex did so, and stirred up no end of trouble (B. to Cecil, **viii**, 350). For a crucial let-down, see Standen to AB, Apr. 1594, cited W. Hepworth Dixon, *The Story of Lord Bacon's Life* (1862), 88.

24 Cecil, as reported by Lady B. to AB, 23 Jan. 1595, **viii**, 347; Lady B. to AB, 30 June 1595, **viii**, 364 n1.

25 Yielding was the *leitmotiv* of Bacon's letters to Essex, see his letter of advice to Essex, 4 Oct. 1596, **ix**, 42 and 45. *Apology*, **x**, 144–5; Lloyd, *State Worthies*, 603; among those urged on the Queen by Essex were Thomas Bodley as Secretary, and the young Robert Sidney, whom he begged her to appoint as Warden of the Cinque Ports; Neale, *Queen Elizabeth* (1934), 336.

26 17 May 1596, **ix**, 34.

27 *Apology*, **x**, 144.

28 B. to Essex, autumn 1595, **viii**, 373; *Apology*, **x**, 144. 'Proem' to 'Of the Interpretation of Nature', written *circa* 1604 but not published, **x**, 84. *Apology*, **x**, 145.

29 B. to Essex, 4 Oct. 1595, **ix**, 40–45.

30 Mac., 312.

31 **x**, 143; spring 1597, **viii**, 55; *Apology*, **x**, 145.

32 Blount, see 'Sir Christopher Blount', in Christopher Devlin, *Hamlet's Divinity and Other Essays* (1963), 111–27; Wright, in Dixon, 134–5.

33 **ix**, 40; B. to Essex, Oct. 1597, **ix**, 104; A. H. de Maisse, *Journal* (1597), 116.

34 B. to Essex, Feb. 1598, **ix**, 94 and 98. He was to use the same argument with Cecil in 1602. See below, chapter 21; **ix**, 94–6.

35 *Apology*, **x**, 146, see **ix**, 125–7.

36 B. to Essex, Mar. 1599, **ix**, 129–33.

37 Sir Robert Markham to John

Harington, in Harington, *Nugae Antiquae* (1769), i, 240. Simon Forman, picking up the general feeling in the horoscope he cast for Essex on 19 March, a week before his departure, noted at the time that he would 'not do much to bring [the enterprise] to good effect'. He saw in the end of the voyage 'negligence, treason, hunger, sickness and death' (Rowse, *Simon Forman* (1974), p. 220).

38 Strachey, 200. 'The land of mist and bogs', wrote Robert Lacey, 'had ruined his father, and now it ruined him', see Lacey, 238.

39 Essex to Harington, *Nugae Antiquae*, i, 246; see Queen to Essex, 'before your departure, no man was held sound, which persuaded not presently the main prosecution in Ulster, all was nothing without that and nothing was too much for that', 14 Sept. 1599, Devereux, ii, 63. See also Essex on that 'arch traitor', 21 Aug. 1599, ibid., ii, 54.

40 See **ix**, 139.

41 Queen to Essex, 14 and 17 Sept. 1599, Devereux, ii, 63 and 73–5.

42 *Apology*, **x**, 149 and 155.

43 Ibid., 146–7. The white staff was borne by officers of the Queen's Household.

44 Strachey, 206, where Bacon 'had blown upon her smouldering suspicions' until they were red hot, and Abbott, *Bacon and Essex* (1877), 148–9.

45 **ix**, 150; the letter confirms Bacon's remarks in the *Apology* (**x**, 147–8).

46 See in Blount's confession, **ix**, 316, and in Southampton's declaration after his arraignment, 315–16, Essex's first intimation, in 1598, of his 'dangerous discontent'. He made a full confession after his trial, first to his personal chaplain, Rev. Ashton, then, at the latter's persuasion, to Cecil and other Councillors (**ix**,

234–6). The first is reported in an unsigned letter from a follower to AB, 30 May 1601, printed Camden, *History of Elizabeth*, iii, 960, and in part in Devereux, ii, 167–70, and Spedding **ix**, 234; for the second, see Cecil to Winwood, Mar. 1601, Ralph Winwood, *Memorials of the Affairs of State in the Reigns of Queen Elizabeth and King James I (1653)*, 1725 edn, i, 301; also Nottingham to Mountjoy, 31 May 1601, **ix**, 236 n5. The confession, written by Essex in his own hand, was communicated at once to the Council, and attested by Egerton, Buckhurst, Nottingham and Cecil.

47 Rowland White to Sir Robert Sidney, 3 Oct. 1599, *Sidney Papers, Letters and Memorials of State* (1746), ed. A. Collins, 1911, **ii**, 128 and 131.

48 Spedding, **ix**, 157; *A Declaration touching the Treasons of the Late Earl of Essex and his Accomplices* (1601), **ix**, 255; the confessions, **ix**, 292–3; see Cuffe on his 'lightnings of hope that her Majesty intended graciously to call him again to the Court', **ix**, 332.

49 **x**, 154–9, see further in chapter 5 below.

50 *Apology*, **x**, 157; declaration of Danvers, **ix**, 334, see Spedding, **ix**, 156–69, and 169 n9. Danvers' confession, **ix**, 336–7; Danvers, **ix**, 339; see Spedding, **ix**, 170–72.

51 **ix**, 157; **x**, 153–4.

52 **x**, 154; B. to Essex, 20 July 1600, **ix**, 190; *Apology*, **x**, 155.

53 Devereux, ii, 175 and **ix**, 198. 'If he cannot win it back in such measure as before,' Mountjoy added, 'he must be content with less.'

54 'He fell again upon the drawing over of an army,' to which Danvers was convinced Mountjoy would not agree (declaration of Henry Cuffe, **ix**, 340).

55 Sept. and Oct. 1600, Devereux, ii, 120 and 127; Essex's remark was reported by Ralegh in *The Pre-*

rogative of Parliaments in England (1628), 43.

56 Harington, *Nugae Antiquae*, i, 179. Because of his knowledge of the conspiracy, Neville (earmarked by Essex as his Secretary of State) was kept in the Tower until the end of the reign, see various declarations, **ix**, 207, 260–61, 344, 351.

57 Neale, *Queen Elizabeth*, 370.

58 *Apology*, **x**, 156–8.

Chapter 5   And Betrayed Him

1 Account of Essex's trial in the letters of Vincent Hussey, in *CSPD*, *1598–1601*, 19 Feb. 1601.

2 Mac., 313.

3 Joel Hurstfield, 'The Succession Struggle in Late Elizabethan England', *Elizabethan Government and Society, Essays Presented to Sir John Neale*, ed. Bindoff et al. (1961), 370.

4 When contemplating such a retreat under Queen Mary, Burghley confessed to the Spanish Ambassador that if he carried out his intention he could expect to be cast into the Tower (Neale, *Queen Elizabeth*, 86).

5 Olive Driver, *The Bacon Shakespeare Mystery* (1960), 81.

6 *Apology*, **x**, 141–2.

7 See confessions annexed to the *Declaration of Treasons*, **ix**, 286–321.

8 'O tempora o mores!' wrote Coke on the margin of one of the confessions, see Bowen's biography of Coke, *The Lion and the Throne, The Life and Times of Edward Coke* (1957) 118; Egerton, see Hussey, in *CSPD*, *1598–1601*, 556.

9 'History of Squire's Conspiracy', 23 Dec. 1598, **ix**, 116.

10 *Sir Thomas More*, II. iv.

11 **ix**, 225.

12 Article on Bacon by John Carteret, Earl Granville in *BB*.

13 Such as John Nichol, *Francis Bacon, His Life and Philosophy* (1888–9), 52.

14 MS report by Lionel Tollemache, cited **ix**, 218; also David Jardine, *Criminal Trials* (1832); Cobbett, *State Trials*; Camden, *Elizabeth*; Winwood, *Memorials*, etc.

15 Camden, *Elizabeth*, iv, 635; *ER*, i, 129. A year later, with tears in her eyes, Elizabeth warned another French Ambasador, Count Harlay de Beaumont, when news had come that Biron himself had plotted with the King of Spain against Henri IV: 'in such cases we must lay aside clemency and adopt extreme measures' (Devereux, ii, 203–4). Biron was excuted on 19 July 1602. Winwood's reply to Cecil's letter of 7 March 1601 about the trial of Essex: Winwood, *Memorials*, i, 229–301 and 316.

16 See his speech for the prosecution of Lady Somerset for murder, **xii**, 297 ('to confess fully and freely' is 'the nobleness of an offender').

17 **ix**, 221.

18 See *Declaration of Treasons*, **ix**, 215.

19 Confession of Blount, **ix**, 366, and Birch, ii, 478.

20 Confession of Essex, see above, chapter 4, n46. Blount suggested to Gorges that he should 'kill, or at least apprehend Sir Walter Ralegh' (first confession of Gorges, and Blount's confession, **ix**, 267, 295 and 317); report of Blount's speech, 18 Mar., **ix**, 316–17.

21 **ix**, 226–7; *Apology*, **x**, 157. The 'framed letters' were drafted by Bacon, in accordance with a Court practice of the time (one as from AB to Essex, the other as Essex's reply) to 'picture forth unto her Majesty my Lord's mind to be such as I know her Majesty would fainest have had it' (**ix**, 196–201). See Howard's similar letter as from Essex to the Treasurer, with similar intent, 4

22 'I know but one friend and one enemy my Lord hath; and that one friend is the Queen, and that one enemy is himself': Bacon is quoting with approval 'a great officer at Court', *Apophthegms*, **vii**, 167.

23 Bacon's words as reported Jardine, *Criminal Trials*, 352; Mac., 314.

24 Camden, *Elizabeth*, cited Spedding, **ix**, 231.

25 *BB*, 375, note H.

26 Chamberlain, 24 Feb. 1601, i, 120.

27 Confession noted by Nottingham (see chapter 4, n46, above), **ix**, 236 n5.

28 Essex was referring to Tyrone, see *Declaration of Treasons*, **ix**, 251.

29 Confession of Essex, as reported to Anthony Bacon, 30 May 1601, from Camden, *Elizabeth*, iii, 960.

30 Devereux, i, 141–3.

31 Blount, **ix**, 318; Rutland, **ix**, 301. See examinations of Gilly Meyrick and of the actor Augustine Phillips, 17 and 18 Feb. 1601 (E. K. Chambers, *William Shakespeare, A Study of Facts and Problems*, 1930, ii, 324–6). Whether or not the deposition scene was omitted from early productions and text, the show presented to Essex's men is unequivocally described as 'the *deposing and killing* of Richard II'.

32 See among other allusions from 1578 on, the vicious attack on the Queen in 1595 by the Jesuit priest, R. Doleman (= Robert Parsons, Cardinal Allen), *A Conference about the Next Succession to the Throne*, 163, accusing her of being led astray by her favourites, Burghley, Leicester and Hatton, as Richard II was by those 'caterpillars of the Commonwealth', Bushy, Bagot and Green, and declaring that kings may be lawfully deposed;

at top: Oct. 1599 (Linda Peck, *Northampton, Patronage and Policy at the Court of James I* (1982), 16–17).

and Edward Gilpin, 'Skialotheia', a satire circulated in September 1598, describing Essex in verses that echo Shakespeare's on Bolingbroke (*Richard II*, I. iv. 25, Shakespeare Association Facsimile (1931, cited Lacey, 209). The same parallels with Bolingbroke are found three years after the execution of Essex, in a satire on Ralegh (*Poetical Miscellany of the Time of James I*, ed. J. O. Halliwell, 1845).

33 G. B. Harrison, *The Life and Death of Robert Devereux, Earl of Essex* (1937), 266–7, 280. Hayward admitted to tampering with the facts in his history, in particular to slanting the Archbishop's oration in favour of the deposers of kings. He was released soon after Essex's death, and James appointed him Royal Historiographer.

34 See chapter 2 above, and *Apology*, **ix**, 154.

35 Jardine, *Criminal Trials*, i, 337, see Chambers, *William Shakespeare* (1930), ii, 325.

36 William Lambarde, Keeper of the Records in the Tower, 'Note of his conversation with her Majesty on 4 Aug. 1601', in John Nichols, *The Progresses and Public Procession of Queen Elizabeth*, ii, 552, see Chambers, *William Shakespeare*, i, 354 and ii, 326.

37 *Richard II*, II. ii. 144; report of the trial of Essex, cited Lacey, 272. Also, Essex was, like Bolingbroke, determined to 'be his own carver and cut out his way', and his followers cried, 'seize the Queen and be our own carvers!' – although the expression is a common one, it is still a likely echo.

38 Declaration of Essex at his trial, **ix**, 221.

39 *Richard II*, II. i. 241, 165–6 and 75.

40 G. E. Aylmer, *The King's Servants* (1961), 464. For later parallels, see Charge against Oliver St John

(Apr. 1615, **xii**, 141 and 145).

41 P. M. Handover, *The Second Cecil, The Rise to Power 1563–1604 of Sir Robert Cecil* (1959), 224.

42 Chambers, *William Shakespeare*, ii, 353.

43 Probably in October 1597, when Essex spent some time at his home in Wanstead. Blount's declaration, 18 Mar. 1601, **ix**, 316.

44 Declarations of Hetherington, Knowd and Davies, **ix**, 293–4 and 300; Dixon, 134 and 141–3; Faolain, *The Great O'Neill* (1942), 219. The imprisoned Jesuit priest, Thomas Wright, claimed that 'if the Earl of Essex were King it would be a glorious kingdom', for 'he would free us all,' Hussey, in *CSPD 1598–1601*, 549–56.

45 'Now in God's last judgement,' Coke exclaimed, 'he of his earldom shall be Robert the Last that of the kingdom thought to be Robert the First!', Jardine, *Criminal Trials*, i, 321; 'My lord of Essex', said Cecil, 'is a competitor of the throne of England,' ibid., 356.

46 Thomas Fitzherbert to Sterrell from Madrid, 1 Mar. 1594, Birch, ii, 470; Aikin, i, 56–7; Declaration of Danvers, **ix**, 355–6.

47 *Apology*, **x**, 158; see below, end of chapter 7.

48 Lord Burghley, from York, on the impression made there by Elizabeth's clemency, cited Neale, *Queen Elizabeth*, 377. See in Dixon, 182–3, Bacon's care in exonerating Sir Thomas Smith, the Sheriff of London, whom Essex had inculpated (**ix**, 236).

49 Mac., 321–2.

50 Rowland White, 28 June 1600, *Sidney Papers*, ii, 204. These knighthoods (seventy-five) were not annulled; they are all listed in W. A. Shaw, *The Knights of England* (1906), the last being the notorious Bainham, knighted on 14 Sept. 1599, just in time for the fatal meeting with Tyrone.

51 **x**, 148; B. to Cecil, **ix**, 162.

52 B. to Sr Henry Howard, Dec. 1599, **ix**, 161–2.

53 *Apology*, **x**, 141.

54 Bacon at this time 'stood high in the estimation of his contemporaries', wrote Gardiner, i, 164. Only a hint of criticism of his *Apology* has been found (by a hostile biographer, Marwil, 117 n31): a remark made by 'King, the fool', relayed to Bacon's friend Sir John Davies, the lawyer-poet in Ireland to the effect that it was 'the philosopher of his wit' ('the philosopher's saving grace' or 'effort to save his face'); but it is doubtful if, as this critic suggests, the lawyer sending the book 'for an hour's recreation', i.e. leisure, meant 'sport', i.e. 'mockery'.

55 Yelverton to B., 3 Sept. 1617, **xiii**, 246–9.

56 John Hacket, *Scrinia Reserata, a Memorial Offered to the Great Deservings of John Williams* (1693), i, 39–40. Buckingham, wrote Hacket, was 'too ready to cast a cloud suddenly upon his creature, and with much inconstancy to root up that which he had planted'.

57 Mac., 315.

58 *Apology*, **x**, 159.

59 Mac., 313, see 319–21.

60 As also the official sermon preached on Essex at St Paul's, see **ix**, 242. The young Clarendon, author of the remark, later changed his views.

61 **x**, 244; see below chapter 28.

62 Dixon, 186. Thanks to the discreet handling of the charges against him, it was possible to reverse his attainder in 1603, so that his son could become the third Earl of Essex. Ralegh, less fortunate, lost his estate; Mac., 315.

63 **x**, 159.

64 'The Proceedings of the Earl of Essex', June 1600, **ix**, 175–89.

65 *ER*, i, 156. 'The very style bears witness to it – faltering, hurrying, breaking – as a man's voice breaks when it speaks out of too full a heart' (i, 182).

66 *ER*, i, 181–2. 'I must reserve much which makes for me', wrote Bacon, 'upon my respects of duty.'

67 Essay, 'Of Youth and Age'; B, to Essex, 20 July 1600, **ix**, 190–91, and *Apology*, **x**, 145; *De Sapientia Veterum* (1609), **vi**, 754.

68 Robertson, *Pioneer Humanists*, 56.

69 *ER*, i, 182; *Apology*, **x**, 143.

70 Confession of Essex, as reported Nottingham to Mountjoy, 31 May 1601, **ix**, 236 n5. And, added Nottingham, he 'spared not to say something of her affection to you'. Penelope had played an active role in the rebellion; Father Garnett reports her as inciting the mob to kill Chief Justice Popham, when shut up in Essex House (cited Sylvia Freedman, *Poor Penelope* (1983), 140 and n28).

71 Carleton to Dudley, cited Devereux, ii, 158–9. Essex threw the blame also on Lord Sandys, but his wife blamed him: her husband, she wrote to Cecil, had been 'led on by that wild earl's craft, who hath been unlucky to many but never good to any. I wish he had never been born' (cited Handover, *The Second Cecil*, 228).

72 Thomas Fuller, *Worthies of England* (1652), 380–81.

Chapter 6 Essex, Hero and Martyr

1 Jane Austen, *Pride and Prejudice* (1813), chapter 40.

2 See in particular the essays in *Elizabethan Government and Society*, ed. Bindoff et al. (1961).

3 Essex's friend Henri IV of France, a good judge of character, would not believe that he had asked for a private execution, 'nay rather clean the contrary, for he desired nothing more than to die in public' (reported Winwood, *Memorials*, i, 309). In fact the repentant Essex had made his request, ostensibly at least, 'lest the acclamation of the people might be a temptation to him' ('Proceedings after the Arraignments', **ix**, 285).

4 B. to Essex, 4 Oct., 1596, **ix**, 44. 'Only if in Parliament your Lordship be forward for treasure in respect of wars, it becometh your person well. And if her Majesty object popularity to you any time, I would say to her, a Parliament will show that.'

5 Robert Naunton, *Fragmenta Regalia* (1630), 51 (Naunton followed Winwood as Secretary in 1617); John Stowe, *Annales* (1580), 805. In 1594 Saviolo dedicated his manual of swordsmanship to Essex as 'the English Achilles'; in 1598 Chapman dedicated his translation of *The Iliad* to that 'most true Achilles' and 'most honoured now living instance of the Achilleian Virtues, eternized by divine Homer, the Earl of Essex', hoping that politics will not 'stir your divine temper' from the pursuit of eternity. Thus, as Harrison remarked, proving a truer prophet than he knew, for this modern Achilles was now 'sulking in his tents' (G. B. Harrison, *Shakespeare at Work*, 1933, 219. Message sent by Essex. to AB via E. Reynolds, 13 Aug. 1597, Birch, ii, 357. *An Apologia*, defending his military views in May 1596, publicly circulated in May 1600 when he was in disgrace, in 300 copies, promptly withdrawn but finally published in 1603 (*Salisbury Papers* (1892), viii, 545).

6 Chamberlain, 23 Aug. 1599, i, 84. Essex's knights, he said, brought

the order into contempt. Scornfully labelling them 'Rouen' and 'Irish knights', Thomas Wilson excluded them from his count of English knights in 1601, as 'many of them hardly good gentlemen' ('The State of England', in *Camden Miscellany*, xvi, 1936, 23). See further above, chapter, 5, n50.

7   Neale, *Queen Elizabeth*, 323.
8   Clarendon, 'The Difference and Disparity between the Estates and Conditions of Buckingham and Essex', *Reliquiae Wottonianae* (1672), 190. *Memoires de Sully*, cited Devereux, i, 273.
9   Neale, *Queen Elizabeth*, 323; H. A. Lloyd, *The Rouen Campaign* (1973), 116; 8 Sept. 1591, Lacey, 71, 90 and 194.
10   B. to Essex, Mar. 1599, **ix**, 132.
11   His 'points of popularity which every man took notice of', as 'affable gestures, open doors, making his table and bed so popularly places of audience to suitors', were noted in *Declaration of Treasons* (**ix**, 248). For parallels with Shakespeare's Bolingbroke, see chapter 5 above.
12   See Leslie Hotson, 'Roaring Boys of the Mermaid', in *Shakespeare's Sonnets Dated* (1905). 'A most lascivious man, and a contemner of magistrates', Camden remarked of him (*History of Elizabeth*, iv, 549). Three weeks before the rebellion, the Lord Treasurer Buckhurst sent his son to tell Essex that he could have arranged an interview for him with the Queen had the Earl not allowed 'base captains and rascals . . . as Captain Baynham' free access to him (Foley, *Records of the Society of Jesus*, i, 7). Clarendon also mentions Bainham as having previously been 'in prison for suspicion of treason' ('Difference and Disparity', 190).
13   B. to James (**xii**, 250–51), reporting

on an interrogation of Bainham (by Attorney General Yelverton) – this time not drunk, 'or not otherwise than so as mought make him less wary of keeping secrets'.
14   *Hamlet*, IV. iii. 6.
15   Winwood, *Memorials*, i, 316 and 326; full text of letter, 296–9.
16   'Rerum Vulgatorum Nota', diary of Richard Smith, cited Harrison, *The Elizabethan Journals* (1591–1603), 1933, iii, 174.
17   Neale, *Queen Elizabeth*, 377–98.
18   *History of the Most Renowned Queen Elizabeth, and her Favourite, the Earl of Essex . . . A Romance* (1650), see also Devereux, ii, 177–83. Taken up by Francis Osborne in his *Historical Memoires on the Reigns of Queen Elizabeth and King James* (1658), the story was circulated abroad by Aubéry du Maurier (an ancestor of Gerald and of Daphne), who had it from Prince Maurice of Nassau, who had it from Sir Dudley Carleton, English Ambassador in Holland (Aubéry du Maurier, *History of Holland*, Paris, 1680). Clarendon was 'nothing satisfied with that loose report of the ring or jewel' ('Difference and Disparity', 190). *The Unhappy Favourite*, a dramatic version conceived in complete ignorance of the facts, circulated in 1682, remained in vogue throughout the eighteenth century, and a number of rings were claimed as Elizabeth's authentic gift.
19   Published 1624, with the subtitle: 'A Warning against the Spanish Marriage and Peaceful Relations with Spain' (ed. 1885), p. 92.
20   **ix**, 167. It was under the influence of such stories as 'Essex's Ghost' that the young Clarendon (aged fifteen when it appeared) pronounced the official narrative of the treasons of Essex 'pestilent libels'. ('Difference and Disparity', 192–3), see above, chapter 5.
21   Thus Osborne, *Historical Memoires*,

Weldon and D'Ewes, see below, chapter 37.

22 *BB*, 374; Mallet, *Life of Bacon*, 33.

23 *The Private Lives of Elizabeth and Essex*, based on the play by Maxwell Anderson (Warner Bros, 1939), circulating in video (United Artists Television Inc.).

24 Neale, *Queen Elizabeth*, 378.

25 J. B. Black, *The Story of the Reign of Elizabeth, 1558–1603* (1936).

26 Essex. to Harington, *Nugae Antiquae*, i, 246. Contemporary accounts agree with Robert Naunton's (*Fragmenta Regalia*, 53): 'The Queen was fully bent to send my Lord Mountjoy, which my Lord of Essex utterly misliked, and opposed with many reasons and arguments of contempt towards Mountjoy, his then professed familiar, so predominate was his desire to reap the whole honour of closing up that war, and all other.' In fact, he 'jock-eyed himself' into the position (Handover, *The Second Cecil*, 184), and he walked into a trap made by himself (Hurstfield, 'The Succession Struggle', 376).

27 Hurstfield, 'The Succession Struggle', 375–6.

28 Hilaire Belloc, *A History of England in Seven Volumes* (1931), iv, 424ff.

29 Lacey, 236–7, 263, 267, 300. This book is recommended by Paul Johnson (*Elizabeth*, 1974) as one of the two best biographies of Essex, the other being Devereux's.

30 G. B. Harrison, *The Life and Death of Robert Devereux, Earl of Essex* (1937).

31 Black, *Reign of Elizabeth*, 440–41; Strachey, 205, 218–19.

32 Lacey, 236–7, 263, 267, 300.

33 Abbott, *Bacon and Essex* and *Francis Bacon, An Account of his Life and Works* (1885), 73–4. The confessions aroused no doubts in contemporaries, shocked as they were by them. See George

Carleton (cited chapter 5 above) to his brother Dudley, after the execution, on 'these noble and resolute men, assured of one another by their undoubted valour, and combined together by firm oaths' who 'set in the end before their deaths to such plain confession and accusations of one another, that they seemed to strive which should draw one another in deepest . . .' Devereux, ii, 158–9.

34 Abbott, *Bacon and Essex*, 136–47 and 241. The Queen however rested her charges against Essex (as she wrote to Fenton, Nov. 1599) not on 'the disgraceful nature of Tyrone's propositions, but upon his disobedience' (cited ibid., 142). See further, Abbott on the 'garbled confessions', chapter 28 below.

35 Nichol, *Francis Bacon*, 54–5.

36 Abbott, *Bacon and Essex*, 134–47.

37 Queen to Edward Fenton, 5 Nov. 1599, cited ibid., 142. 'If the list were genuine,' said Abbott (60 n1), 'Essex's treason would be unquestionable.' This one clause confirms that it was (Spedding, **ix**, 258).

38 Black, *Reign of Elizabeth*, 2–4; Strachey, 16 and 257; Lacey, 44, 56, 262.

39 Catherine Macaulay, *The History of England from the Accession of James I to that of the Brunswick Line* (1763–83). On Mrs Macaulay's reliability, see further below, chapter 30, n19.

40 Abbott, *Francis Bacon*, 7, 10, 196.

41 C. H. Williams, 'In Search of the Queen', in *Elizabethan Government* (1961), 1–20.

42 John Kenyon, *The History Men* (1983), 207–8; Spedding, **ix**, 77. Elton thought Neale placed Elizabeth on too high a pinnacle, as a reaction against Froude: Elton, *Tudor and Stuart Politics*

(1983), iii, 411–12. But Spedding's impressive Elizabeth is still found in 'Queen Elizabeth I', a collection of articles by leading Tudor historians in *History Today*, no. 6 (1986). This confirms for our century Bacon's conclusion that 'the only commender of this lady is time, which so long a course as it has run has produced nothing in this sex like her, for administration of civil affairs' (p. 318).

43 *Apology*, 154; Neale, *Queen Elizabeth*, 364, 370, 376, 380; Birch, ii, 505. On her conversation with Beaumont, see above, chapter 5, n15.

44 Joel Hurstfield, *The Queen's Wards* (1958), 294–5.

45 Hurstfield, 'Explaining James I', letter to *TLS*, 23 May 1975, 567.

46 *In Felicem Memoriam Elizabethae* (1609), **vi**, 284 and 317. See also in Bacon's earlier 'Discourse in Praise of the Queen' (1592, **viii**, 139) her ability to discover 'every man's ends and drifts, her wonderful art of keeping her servants in satisfaction, and yet in appetite'.

47 Strachey, 267.

48 Spedding, **ix**, 152–3; Handover, *The Second Cecil*, 199; Hurstfield, 'The Succession Struggle', 390.

49 Stopes, *Third Earl of Southampton* (1922), 212; Hurstfield, 'The Succession Struggle', 374–5.

50 Osborne, *Historical Memoires*, 31–5 and 87 (he wonders how Essex's enemies could have brought him to 'an act of such imprudence'). The story was repeated by Mallet in 1740 (*Life of Bacon*, 31), and by Mrs Stopes (*Third Earl of Southampton*, 214) in her build-up of the Essex myth.

51 Strachey, 161.

52 For Cecil, see below chapter 18; for the anti-Stuart writer, Anthony Welden, see chapter 27.

53 Hurstfield, 'The Succession Struggle', 390.

54 Jardine, *Criminal Trials*, 356, and Spedding, **ix**, 234.

55 Thomas Bodley, *Autobiography* (1609, published posthumously 1647).

56 Osborne, *Historical Memoires*, 31–5. Note Cecil's typical remark to Bacon on an unfounded rumour circulating about him (*Apology*, **x**, 148): 'For myself I am merely passive in this action . . .'

57 Strachey, 107–8 and 235–6; Handover, *The Second Cecil*, 317–18 and 282; Bacon, *The History of Great Britain* (fragment), **vi**, 277. See also B. to Kempe on the death of Elizabeth, exclaiming 'with what wonderful still and calm this wheel is turned round', Apr. 1603, **x**, 74.

58 Devereux, i, 183, 375, 380, 389, 393; on Cecil, i, 442; on Bacon, i, 288, and ii, 50, 169, 192 and 140–41.

Chapter 7   The Servant and the Dreamer

1 Dorothy Sayers, *Gaudy Night* (1935), 20.

2 Abbott, *Bacon and Essex*, 226 (Spedding's slightly different version, **ix**, 226).

3 Mac., 313; see Abbott, *Bacon and Essex*, 182–3, and Strachey, 229. 'Because of his deep love of the man', suggests Mario Rossi, in *Saggio su Francesco Bacon* (1934, see further chapter 30 below), following Strachey, without wondering how the odious man he had presented could have inspired such love.

4 Statement of Danvers, **ix**, 338.

5 Mac., 313

6 B. to Essex, 20 July 1600 and

Essex's reply, soon after, **ix**, 190–92, see *Apology*, **x**, 155.

7 Essex to AB, 2 June 1596, Birch, **ii**, 20; Essex to B., May 1596, **ix**, 35–6, see *Apology*, **x**, 143; Essex to Sir Thomas Cecil, 24 June 1597, Birch, ii, 347–8.

8 B. to Burghley, 16 Sept. 1580, **viii**, 13.

9 Essay, 'Of Faction'. As Carteret saw it in 1747 (*BB*, 373), 'too much merit' made Bacon suspect to his Court patrons, and the fact that he was favoured by patrons of both bands, Cecil's and Essex's, while bringing him much credit, 'contributed more than anything to spoil his fortune'.

10 Essay, 'Of Honour and Reputation'; *AL*, **iii**, 279.

11 'I had just cause to hate the Lord Cobham,' wrote Essex (March 1597). 'If therefore her Majesty would grace him with honour, I may have right cause to think myself little regarded by her.' *Sidney Papers*, ii, 27. Another favoured formula was 'If your Majesty valued me as you would do any man that had done you half the service . . .' (Harrison, *Essex*, 209).

12 B. to Essex, Nov. 1595, **viii**, 373 (see chapter 5 above), and *Apology*, **x**, 143–4.

13 Osborne, *Historical Memoires*, 30. According to Clarendon, 'he looked from above, and with a displeasure that had a mixture of scorn more than anger upon such as courted not his protection' ('Difference and Disparity', 191); Neale, *Queen Elizabeth*, 347.

14 Ibid., 359.

15 Strachey, 25.

16 The Queen, who was fond of him, sent him out of town when Essex's trials began. He was a timid man, and did not, like Bacon, use his influence on Essex's behalf (see A. Rebholz, *The Life of Fulke Greville, First Lord Brooke*, 1971).

17 Bodley, *Autobiography*.

18 So Handover, *The Second Cecil*, 262. He was 'a very great statesman' wrote Aubrey (174), see further below, chapter 26.

19 B. to Hawkins in Venice, Oct. 1596, Devereux, i, 392, see B. to Essex, 4 Oct. 1596, discussed above, chapter 4.

20 AB to Essex, 8 Feb. 1597, Birch, ii, 275–6; AB to Essex, 19 Feb. 1597, Birch, ii, 281–2. On the relations between the two brothers, see chapter 26 below.

21 Anonymous letter to AB, 30 May 1601, **ix**, 234 (mistakenly cited by Devereux, ii, 201, as written by AB to defend the reputation of Essex).

22 Naunton, *Fragmenta Regalia*, 54. 'Do not strive to overrule all, for it will cost hot water,' he went on, with an image which becomes clear when we recall Bacon warning Essex that his violent courses, 'like hot water, help at a pang', but 'lose their operation in the end' (*Apology*, **x**, 144, see chapter 4 above). Wotton wrote later that in his contestations with the Queen, Essex forgot the counsel of 'a prophetic friend', who told him that such courses 'were like hot waters that help at a pang . . .' (Henry Wotton, 'A Parallel between Robert, late Earl of Essex and George Villiers, late Duke of Buckingham', *c*.1634, in *Reliquiae Wottonianae* (1621), 161ff.).

23 Mac., 316.

24 See chapters 20–23.

25 AB to Lady B., 11 Sept. 1593, Birch, i, 121–2.

26 Mac. 315–17, see *ER*, i, 152–6. The Queen did not leave Bacon entirely unrewarded: two weeks after signing his bills against enclosures, she granted him an estate in Cheltenham (see further, Dixon, *Personal History*, 92).

27 B. to James, 1 Jan. 1609, **ix**, 114–15.

28 B. to Lord Keeper Egerton, 28 July 1595, **viii**, 365; see Carteret, 'although Bacon received but slender marks of honour' compared with his deserts, 'this was so far from warping him, either in duty or affection, that so long as the Queen lived he served her with both zeal and fidelity . . .' (*BB*, 77–8).

29 B. to Essex, Oct. 1595, **viii**, 372.

30 *Apology*, **x**, 142.

31 Essay, 'Of Praise'.

32 B. to Queen, after the Star Chamber proceedings against Essex, 19 Nov. 1599, **ix**, 160.

33 Charles Williams, *Bacon*, 176.

34 'On the Controversies of the Church' (1589), **viii**, 95; Essay, 'Of Goodness'.

35 Strachey, 248. He saw Essex as 'a devoted servant and an angry rebel – all at once', entertaining treasonable projects 'with intervals of romantic fidelity and noble remorse'. See also Abbott, *Bacon and Essex*, 32.

36 S. T. Bindoff, *Tudor England* (1950, 1965 edn), 300–304.

37 See Cuffe's declaration, **ix**, 333.

38 Essex to the Queen, 9 Sept. 1600, Devereux, ii, 120. The angry self-pity of a much injured man who ignored sound advice, failed to report in time, and blamed all his difficulties on his fellow officers – when not on his employers for failing to encourage him – were all present in his campaigns in France, seven years before the Irish expedition.

39 Devereux, i, 194; Strachey, 231 and 248.

40 *I Henry IV*, V. i. 37.

41 So wrote Elizabeth to her faithful cousin, Essex's father in Ireland, Devereux, i, 74.

42 *I Henry IV*, I. iii. 193 and 204; V. ii. 90 and 82. In his time Essex was described as desiring 'in all things to reap the whole honour' (Naunton, *Fragmenta Regalia*, 52); see above, chapter 6, n26.

43 On the famous occasion when Essex threatened to draw his sword on the Queen, such was his tone of offended innocence that his admiring descendant would have liked to think, 'had any single authority supported it', that it was not Essex who, by an act of disrespect, had first given offence to the Queen (Devereux i, 498–502).

44 Joel Hurstfield, 'The Essex Rebellion', in *History of the English Speaking Peoples* (1970), 1536–8.

45 *I Henry IV*, V. ii. 250. The King had written offering him a free pardon.

46 In particular the discourses presented to the Queen in 1592 (**ix**, 120). See Handover, *The Second Cecil* (130–33) on the contemporary identification of the various parts in the 'devices' written by Bacon for Essex.

47 Elemire Zolla, *Storia del Fantasticare* (1964).

48 Robert Burton, *The Anatomy of Melancholy* (1621), esp. 11, 172–6, 244–6, 265 and 361. Burton is describing the unregenerate humour of melancholy, the day-dreamer's fantasy, under the influence of Saturn, not that which, fired by the rays of Jupiter, leads to the 'heroic frenzy' of genius, or to revelation, as studied in Dürer and Agrippa by Raymond Klibansky et al. in *Saturn and Melancholy* (1964).

49 Wotton, 'A Parallel', in *Reliquiae Wottonianae*, 171.

50 Autumn 1591, Devereux, i, 209–18 and 241. Cursing his birthday and longing for the grave – he was twenty-three – Essex conjures up a pathetic image of himself writing 'till my dim eyes and weak hand do fail me'. Summer and autumn 1599, ibid., ii, 21, 41, 56, 61–2, and 68.

51 As noticed by Freedman, *Poor Penelope*, 151–2; see portrait, ibid., 84.
52 Spring and summer 1574, Devereux, i, 50ff; Oct. 1600, ibid., ii, 127.
53 Cecil's remark, 25 Oct. 1599, *Sidney Papers*, cited Abbott, *Bacon and Essex*, 24.
54 Essex's confession, reported Nottingham to Mountjoy, 31 May 1601, **ix**, 236 n5
55 Elizabeth Jenkins, *Elizabeth and Leicester* (1972), 213, and for Sir Walter Devereux, i, 39 and 143.
56 Report on proceedings after the arraignments, **ix**, 285, see Devereux, i, 143 and 163. See Essex's numerous references to his martyrdom, ibid., ii, 21, 41, 56, 59, 99, and the poem he addressed to the Queen in June 1600, 'I, poor I, must suffer and know no change', 111. Some of his associates shared the day-dreaming, e.g. imagining, as late as February 1600, said Chamberlain, that 'we should see him a cockhorse again'. It was, he adds, 'but a kind of dream, a false paradise that his friends had feigned to themselves . . .' (i, 86).
57 In the first part of his confession to the Rev. Ashton, the minister of his choice (Devereux, ii, 167), before he broke down and told the truth. He was 'bound in conscience', he maintained, to save the Queen from atheists, papists, and other 'mortal enemies of the kingdom', thus tending 'to the infinite happiness of this state . . . and the saving of many thousand Englishmen's lives'. Later he confessed to Dr Barlow, another divine, that sometimes when in danger, in the field, 'the weight of his sins lying heavy upon his conscience, being not reconciled to God quelled his spirits . . .' (cited Abbott, *Bacon and Essex*, 231–2).
58 Essex, confession to Ashton, as reported to AB, Camden, *History of Elizabeth*, iii, 960, see **ix**, 285.
59 Abbott, *Bacon and Essex*, 233–4; Lacey, 312–13.
60 Confession of Essex as reported to AB, cited Devereux, ii, 169.
61 Frances Yates, *The Occult Philosophy in the Elizabethan Age* (1979), 153; see Harrison, *Essex*, 319; and see J. Dover Wilson's edition of *Hamlet* (1934), pp. lxv–lxvi, with a portrait of Essex as frontispiece, recalling the many who have seen him as the model for the character of Hamlet.
62 Zolla, *Storia del Fantasticare*, 52; Salvador de Madariaga, *On Hamlet* (1948).
63 *Hamlet*, III. ii. 71–4; Essex to AB, autumn 1593, Devereux, i, 289. 'Something too much of this', says Hamlet, as did Essex frequently, when complaining to the Queen: 'but no more, neither now or hereafter, of this argument' (ibid., ii, 56). Both saw the world as a prison, and their death scenes, beseeching the world to have a charitable opinion of them, are the same (Harrison, *Essex*, 324; *Hamlet*, V. ii. 365).
64 de Madariaga, *On Hamlet*, 95.
65 This view answers Neale's implied question: how could Essex, knowing the Queen far too well to imagine that she would meekly submit to his commands, put out of his mind the horrible prospect of drawing the Queen's blood? (*Queen Elizabeth*, 371).
66 *Hamlet*, III. ii. 89.
67 *Declaration of Treasons*, **x**, 249 and 251; confession of Blount, **ix**, 250, 253, see Harrison, *Essex*, 324.
68 Confession of Essex, reported Nottingham, **ix**, 236 n5.
69 B. to Essex, Mar. 1599, **ix**, 129–33.
70 Essay, 'Of Friendship'.
71 Essay, 'Of Wisdom for a Man's Self'.
72 Essay, 'Of Honour and Reputation', and 'Charge Touching

Duels', 26 Jan. 1614, **xi**, 399–409. Some of Essex's challenges, such as that to Nottingham, for receiving a title above his own, came within the category of 'satanical illusions'; others, like those to his enemies in the field, were permissible, in Bacon's view, provided they had been approved by the highest authority (**xi**, 405), which of course in Essex's case they never had been.

73 Accusation of Sir John Wentworth, 10 Nov. 1615, **xii**, 213.
74 *Apology*, **x**, 142.

Chapter 8 *The Fall of Bacon: A Tragedy in Three Acts*

1 e.g. Abbott, *Bacon*, p. xix, 291: 'For however great and numerous Bacon's faults may have been, he was not in the ordinary sense a taker of bribes'; and 'if Bacon perverted justice, not for money – of which no one accuses him . . .'
2 B. to Bm, June 1617, **xiii**, 208. 'The lawyers', he added, 'were drawn dry of all the motions they were to make.'
3 Dixon, 376. Spedding (**xiv**, 83) thought 'his example and authority upon all questions of business, politics, administration, legislation and morals would have stood as high and been as much studied and quoted, as it has been upon questions purely intellectual.'
4 *History of Henry VII*, **vi**, 237.
5 *ER*, ii, 395.
6 B. to King, 20 Oct. 1620, **xiv**, 130–31, and Dedication of the *Great Instauration*, **iv**, 12.
7 Wotton to B., 19 Dec. 1620, in *Reliquiae Wottonianae*, 298–300. Wotton, who had earlier described to Bacon his visit to Kepler, was now on a (doomed) peace mission from James to the German princes, on his way to Venice.

8 B. to the Count Palatine, Feb. 1619, **xiv**, 21–2.
9 B. to King Christian of Denmark, 19 Nov. 1620, **xiv**, 142, see comments of Gardiner, 'On Four Letters from Lord Bacon to Christian IV', (1867), 219–20.
10 B. to Wotton, 20 Oct. 1620, **xiv**, 131. A unified reformed Europe was the aim Wotton had constantly pursued throughout his three embassies to Venice.
11 De Mas, *Francis Bacon*, 28 and 34.
12 Edward Coke, *Institutes of the Laws of England* (1628), iv, 5. On the abolition of this 'excellent expedient' to preserve 'the peace and security of the kingdom', as long as it was 'gravely and moderately governed', Clarendon, iii, 401.
13 B. to Bm, 9 June 1620, **xiv**, 96, see below, chapter 31.
14 21 May 1619, **xiv**, 32–3; B. to King, autumn 1620, **xiv**, 85–90; B. to Bm, 29 Nov. 1620, **xiv**, 149.
15 B. to King, 2 Oct. 1620, **xiv**, 114.
16 B. to Bm enclosing his Draft Proclamation for a Parliament (not used), 18 Oct. 1620. **xiv**, 123.
17 B. to King advising him to call a Parliament, autumn 1615, **xii**, 175–91, see 177, 182 and 188.
18 Zaller, 26. Bacon, wrote Menna Prestwich, 'had issued a clear warning against the treacheries to which he fell a victim' (Prestwich, 288).
19 B. to Bm, 23 Dec. 1620, **xiv**, 116, and Draft Proclamation, n16 above; 'Worthy Causes', **xii**, 186.
20 Bacon's proposals for the 1614 Parliament, **xii**, 14–18, and for a new Parliament in 1615, n17 above. He listed a number of pertinent suggestions 'to mend the case of the realm in point of trade', including a proposal for budgets to be allocated to particular programmes.
21 Thomas Bushell, see below chaper 14, notes 15 and 16. Mean-

while on 5 March Buckingham put forward a scheme Bacon, following in his father's footsteps, had urged on him four years earlier, for the training of young sons of good family in foreign affairs (see below, chapter 21).

22 Russell, 114–17.
23 Chamberlain, 18 April and 5 May, ii, 263 and 375.
24 Gardiner, iii, 379 and 398.
25 Russell, 114 and 116; Gardiner, iii, 378–9.
26 Prestwich, 318.
27 Reply to Speaker's oration on the opening of Parliament, 3 Feb. 1621, **xiv**, 173–5, and Draft Proclamation, **xiv**, 126.
28 Kevin Sharpe, 'Introduction: Parliamentary History 1603–1629, In or Out of Perspective', in *Faction and Parliament, Essays on Early Stuart History*, ed. Sharpe (1978), p. 11; Russell, 47–9.
29 **xiv**, 181; see *CD*, iii, fn to entry for 13 Feb. 1621.
30 Aubrey, 175.
31 Jonson, 'Conversations with Drummond', in *Works*, i, 141.
32 Thomas Rymer, *Foedera* (1704), vol. xvii, cited Montagu, *Life of Francis Bacon*, p. ccciv.
33 Probably on 17 Jan., the day of his investiture, **xiv**, 168.
34 'Nemesis, or the Vicissitudes of Things', *De Sap.*, **vi**, 738.
35 Zaller, 26.
36 Mac., 340 and 351.
37 Gardiner, iv, 1–103, see Sharpe, 'Parliamentary History', in *Faction and Parliament*, 2–3. So complete is Gardiner's narrative, he writes, that whatever his bias, 'it is the evidence of the seventeenth century which emerges more than the values of the Victorian age'. He concludes that 'Bacon did corrupt things without being himself corrupt' (Gardiner, 'Four Letters', 225), as did Spedding (**xiv**, 182–270, and *ER*, 295–40).
38 *ER*, ii, 289.

39 **xiv**, 251; *ER*, ii, 289–90.
40 Zaller, 123; see Epstein, *Francis Bacon*, 133.
41 Russsell, 16–17.

Chapter 9   Principal Members of the Cast

1 At a feast given by Buckingham in his honour (Roger Lockyer, *Buckingham, The Life and Political Career of George, First Duke of Buckingham, 1592–1628* (1981), 34).
2 Remark, probably by Cranfield, recalled by Hacket, *Scrinia Reserata*, i, 189.
3 B. to King Christian of Denmark, 19 Nov. 1620, **xiv**, 142.
4 **xiii**, 13–56.
5 Gardiner, 'Four Letters', 219–23.
6 Chamberlain, 3 Jan. 1618 and 9 June 1621, ii, 124 and 381; see Lockyer, *Buckingham*, 68.
7 Sir William Lovelace to Sir Dudley Carleton, 11 Mar. 1617, cited Dixon, 310–13.
8 Letter cited Mallet, *Life of Bacon*, 88. The King reproached Bacon angrily for 'your slight carriage to Buckingham's mother when she repaired to you upon so reasonable an errand', Aug. 1617, **xiii**, 245; Dr George Carleton to his brother, Sir Dudley, 22 Oct. 1617, *CSPD, 1611–18*, 489. See further below, chapter 23.
9 Lord Norris, recently created Earl of Berkshire, so that his rich daughter could marry into the clan. Rather than marry Kit Villiers, she eloped with Edward Wray, a Groom of the Bedchamer, and a protégé of Bacon's (Lockyer, *Buckingham*, 11). Norris was not freed until he had apologized.
10 James Howell to his father, 22 Mar. 1623, of the appointment of Cranfield ('a notable stirring man') as Chief Judge in the

Exchequer Chamber, obtained (Howell hinted) through his marriage into 'the Tribe of Fortune', *Familiar Letters* (1650), i, 41–2.

11 Chamberlain, 3 Feb. and 9 June 1621, ii, 338 and 381.

12 B. to Lord Treasure Ley, 20 June 1625, **xiv**, 528, see further below, chapter 26.

13 So Goodman, *Court of King James the First*, **i**, 286.

14 Hacket, *Scrinia Reserata*, i, 51. 'Out of this bud the Dean's advancement very shortly spread into a blown flower.'

15 July 1621, recalled by Bacon, Apophthegm 31, **vii**, 184.

16 Prestwich, 434.

17 Clarendon, 130.

18 **xiv**, 306–12, see Williams to Bm, 27 Oct. 1621, beseeching him 'to meddle with no pardon for the Lord St Alban'.

19 Chamberlain, 15 Mar. 1617, ii, 64. 'If he had had the grace to have taken hold of the match offered by Sir John Villiers,' wrote Chamberlain, 'it is assuredly thought that before this day he had been Lord Chancellor.' In addition to the £10,000 already promised, he was now forced to redeem by a payment of £20,000 the estates settled upon her at his death, Gardiner, iii, 99.

20 Zaller, 55.

21 Stephen D, White, *Sir Edward Coke and the Grievances of the Commonwealth* (1977), 14–15; Prestwich.

22 White, *Sir Edward Coke*, 43–4; Prestwich, throughout.

23 See Russell, 23, and Prestwich, 328. She saw the lawyer in Coke, which secured him his place in history, at loggerheads with the politician: in the 1621 Parliament the politician was uppermost.

24 Zaller, 54. On personal animosity as the motive for Bacon's impeachment, see also Jonathan Watts, 'Lionel Cranfield, Earl of Middlesex', *Statesmen and Poli-*

ticians of the Stuart Age, ed. Timothy Eustace (1985), 34.

25 When in Nov. 1620 Yelverton was tried for exceeding his authority in the preparation of a new charter for the City of London in favour of the City men, Coke demanded life imprisonment for him, and a high fine. He was to prosecute Cranfield in the same spirit in the 1624 Parliament (Prestwich, 317). See Bacon's own regretful speech, as Judge, and his reduction of the sentence from £100,000 to £40,000. Gardiner, iv, 23; Spedding, **xiv**, 136–40; Prestwich, 317; Zaller, 30.

26 Sir Edward Conway to Carleton, 18 Apr. 1624, cited Prestwich, 436.

27 Chapter 25 below.

28 See chapter 23 below, and Spedding, **xii**, 243.

29 Attorney General Yelverton to B., 3 Sept., 1617, **xiii**, 248.

30 B. to King, 25 Feb. 1615, **xii**, 257.

31 White, *Sir Edward Coke*, 15 and 148. For example, in 1592, and as Chief Justice of the King's Bench in 1616, Coke maintained that the Privy Council was not bound to disclose its reasons for convicting a prisoner – a view he was to oppose forcefully in Parliament, as soon as he was out of office. See also Prestwich, 143.

32 Ibid., 303. 'With unblushing effrontery', she points out, after consistent support of the disastrous Cockayne monopoly, he turned about and castigated it as 'a desperate device to alter an established counsel'.

33 See above. In Feb. 1616, when Coke was in well-merited disgrace (see below, chapter 25), Bacon reminded the King not to 'blunt his industries in the matter of your finances, which seemeth to aim him at another place'; he stressed Coke's value, 'touching your finances and matter of repair of your estate'; if, he said, Coke's

469

hopes were at an end in one respect, he 'could wish they were raised in some other' (12 and 21 Feb., **xii**, 242 and 252).

34 It was said that when someone advised James, early in the session, 'to take down the Lower House a little', he replied that 'he was but one King, they were 400, and everyone a King' (Locke to Carleton, 12 Mar. 1621, cited Spedding, **xiv**, 194).

35 Prestwich, 193, 198, 288–9.

36 Cited Robert E. Ruigh, *The Parliament of 1624, Politics and Foreign Policy* (1971), 325, n16.

37 Prestwich, *Cranfield*, 196; Joel Hurstfield, *Freedom, Corruption and Government* (1973), 190; Zaller, 54; D. H. Willson, *Privy Councillors in the House of Commons 1604–1629* (1940), 151; Dixon, *Personal History*, 261.

38 Prestwich, 49, 157 and 456.

39 Ibid., 198.

40 B. to King advising him to call a Parliament, **xii**, 187.

41 See in particular Robert C. Johnson ('Francis Bacon and Lionel Cranfield', *Huntington Literary Quarterly*, xxiii, 4 (August 1960), 301–20) who asserts without evidence that Bacon's principal defect was 'the arrogant manner he frequently displayed towards his social and intellectual inferiors'.

42 Whitelocke and Chamberlain, cited Prestwich, 194; Pym, in ibid., 465; Suffolk, Chamberlain, 23 Nov. 1616, ii, 39.

43 B. to King, 25 Jan. 1616, **xii**, 257, see Prestwich, 175.

44 See B. to Cranfield, 15 Aug. 1613 (cited Johnson, 'Francis Bacon and Lionel Cranfield', 303), recommending an old servant and asking 'to speak with you if this evening it be not too much trouble'; or letter inviting him to Gorhambury, cited Prestwich, 205.

45 See 3 and 25 Feb. 1616, **xii**, 237 and 258; Bacon's correspondence with Buckingham, **xiii**, 269–73 and 275ff., and B. to Bm, 29 Nov. 1616 (**xiii**, 116) enthusiastically reporting that 'by the help of Sir Lionel Cranfield' he had increased the value of Sherborne Manor from £26,000 to £32,000.

46 Prestwich, 179–80; on Cranfield's piecemeal view of reform, Watts, 'Lionel Cranfield, Earl of Middlesex', in *Statesmen and Politicians of the Stuart Age* (1985), 36, and Prestwich, 198 and 287.

47 Cranfield to Bm, 31 Jan. 1620, **xiv**, 76; B. to Bm, 17 Feb. 1619, **xiv**, 81; Gardiner, iv, 46; Prestwich, 271.

48 Cranfield did not conceal his personal resentment when, in February 1621, he launched his 'rancorous attacks' (David Willson, *The Privy Counsellors in the House of Commons, 1604–29 (1931)*, 151), 'like landmines planted under Bacon's reputation' (Zaller, 54).

49 Meautys to B., summer 1621, **xiv**, 397.

50 Russell, 32–40.

51 Bacon in 'Advice touching the calling of a Parliament', 1613, **xi**, 370; Chamberlain, 21 Dec. 1622, ii, 468, see Russell, 35.

52 Buckingham took no offence at the attack on his friend (Russell, 112, 424–5), and in 1624 Phelips, vying with Coke and Sandys to handle the attack on Cranfield, was acting openly for Buckingham (Ruigh, *Parliament of 1624*, 320–21).

53 Digby in Prestwich, 142 and *DNB*. This monopoly, established in 1630, produced soap that blistered the hands of washerwomen, at double the usual price.

54 Prestwich, 145, 305–15, 436–8.

55 Chamberlain, 21 Jan. and 20 Mar. 1624. In the following Parliament Sandys was rejected by the county of Kent as 'a client of

Buckingham and a tool of the Court' (Prestwich, 145).

56 Russell, 106–7; A. L. Rowse, *Shakespeare's Southampton* (1965), 270–73; see Christopher Hill, *The Century of Revolution, 1603–1714* (1980), 54; **ii**, 543 and 549.

57 Mac., 351.

58 Russell, 34.

Chapter 10   The Grievance of Monopolies and the Tumour of Chancery

1 Clayton Roberts, *The Growth of Responsible Government in Stuart England* (1966), 27. It was also the view of Coleridge, see *Coleridge on the Seventeenth Century*, ed. R.F. Brinkley (1955), 57.

2 Mac., 334 and 341. For the present chapter see Gardiner, 'Four Letters' and *History of England*, iv; Spedding, *ER*, **ii**, 250ff. and **xiv**, 204–8.

3 Mac., 333–4; Gardiner, 'Four Letters', 225–6. Neither were 'benevolences' (a voluntary tax) extracted by force. One only had been requested, solely of the nobility, for the war in the Palatinate, and all Buckingham had to do with it was to contribute £1,000

4 Hill, *Century of Revolution*, 23.

5 Gardiner, iv, 7; Hill, *Century of Revolution*, 26. The notorious Mompesson, for example, patentee for inns, sent a man pretending to be a lost traveller, late at night, to beg an alehouse keeper for shelter, and rewarded him for his kindness by prosecuting him for keeping an unlicensed inn.

6 Gardiner, iv, 4–5 and 42, and 'Four Letters', 237.

7 *Journals*, coll. D'Ewes, cited Russell, 422; Hurstfield, *The Queen's Wards*, 253.

8 Sir Robert Wroth, see J. E. Neale,

Elizabeth and her Parliaments (1957), ii, 380–84; Chamberlain, 8 July 1620, ii, 311.

9 Barry Coward, *The Stuart Age* (1980), 196 and 214.

10 Edward Coke, *Institutes* (1628), p. lxxxv, 181. See Elizabeth R. Foster, 'The Procedure of the House of Commons against Patents and Monopolies 1621–24', in *Conflict in Stuart England* (ed. Aiken et al., 1960), 73.

11 Zaller, 127.

12 **x**, 27–9 and Zaller, 128. James avoided the difficulty by keeping the jurisdiction of monoplies in his own hands and appointing privy councillors and Crown lawyers as referees (Bacon among them) to certify the legality of all new patents before they passed the seal.

13 So Zaller, 24.

14 'Letter of Advice to Villiers', **xiii**, 49; B. to King on the state of his Treasury, summer or autumn 1620, **xiv**, 85–90, and to Bm, 7 Oct., **xiv**, 115–17. Monopolies headed the list of suits which the King bound himself to refuse, see Gardiner, 'Four Letters', 246.

15 The glass patent was to be exempted from those abolished in 1624, see Gardiner, iv, 10, and Hill, *Century of Revolution*, 24. Inventors, usually of the artisan class, could not obtain a patent except through some enterprising courtier, who retained control over it.

16 Coward, *The Stuart Age*, 196 and 241.

17 'Reasons for calling a new Parliament', summer 1615, **xii**, 176.

18 B. to King, June 1616, **xii**, 355–6. See his certificate of the patent for slitting iron bars, 27 Jan. 1617, **xiii**, 135.

19 Speech on taking his seat in Chancery, 7 May 1617, **xiii**, 188–9.

20 Anyone who concealed the truth from the King was 'as dangerous

a traitor to his State as he that riseth in arms against him', 'Advice to Villiers', **xiii**, 15.

21 Mac., 334.

22 *BB*, 395.

23 Gardiner, 'Four Letters', 228–9 and 241; Chamberlain, 8 March 1617, ii, 59. Among the patents Bacon stayed are four which Yelverton had approved (King's speech to the Lords, 1 Mar. 1621, cited Zaller, 117 and n5). See also Bacon's letter to his cousin Barnham on a patent for the survey of coals (14 Mar. 1623, **xiv**, 514).

24 Gardiner, iii, 77 and iv, 3.

25 'No person is for to erect an inn without licence from the King,' an eminent Judge had laid down in 1611 (Gardiner, 'Four Letters', 236).

26 B. to Bm, 21 Nov. 1616, **xiii**, 103.

27 See later in this chapter.

28 Gardiner, 'Four Letters', 237.

29 Mac., 335.

30 Gardiner, iv, 11–20.

31 Gardiner, 'Four Letters', 241. As for the patent of inns (see in next chapter), Ellesmere had personal reasons for delaying his signature.

32 10 Oct. 1619, ibid., 260.

33 See below, chapter 21.

34 By an act of Henry VII, goldsmiths were forbidden to melt gold and silver, except to make a few objects, among which gold and silver thread were not included (Gardiner, iv, 15 and 17, and 'Four Letters', 266). Bacon's strong feelings on this question had led him to take an active part in the prosecution of the Dutch merchants, in 1619, for the exportation of gold.

35 The exact date is not known. See Spedding, **xiv**, 204–8. Gardiner, 'Four Letters', 260; *ER*, ii, 252.

36 'The testimony of a discontented person is but poor,' said Bacon (hinting at the fact that Yelverton was at that time being used as a pawn in a move to attack Buckingham). Outlining the history of the patent, he pointed out that 'the authority of the King was much abused by the execution thereof, to the intolerable grievance of the subject,' and 'that much imposture was used in the trade'. *ER*, ii, 251; Cobbett, *Parliamentary History, 18 James I, 1620*, 12 Mar. p. 1202; Zaller, 72. Yelverton's defence in Parliament, 30 April, cited Gardiner, iv, 14. 'If he used the word monopoly, it was to follow their phrase to him. He never thought of it as a monopoly': Yelverton, reported 30 Apr. 1621, afternoon, LD, 43.

37 Gardiner, ix, 206. The Proclamation, issued 28 Oct. 1619, is printed in Gardiner, 'Four Letters', 200.

38 'Whether he considered the King's interest or Buckingham's, the country's or his own', wrote Spedding, how could he possibly have committed such a blunder? (**xiv**, 207, and *ER*, 254); see Gardiner, iv, 20.

39 Ibid., 17.

40 **xiv**, 208.

41 Ibid., 145–8; Zaller, 22.

42 B. to Bm, 29 Nov. 1621, **xiv**, 148–9.

43 Gardiner, iv, 21; **xiv**, 151.

44 Thomas Smith, *De Republica Anglorum* (1583), 71.

45 Hatton, cited B. L. Joseph, *Shakespeare's Eden, The Commonwealth of England, 1558–1629* (1971), 140; Ellesmere, cited in ibid., 139.

46 Bacon, noted Chamberlain, 14 Oct. 1620, ii, 321 (Chamberlain, as often, was suspicious, see discussion by Spedding, **xiv**, 118); Bacon, *History of Henry VII*, **vi**, 85.

47 Gardiner, iv, 58. On Bacon and the role of Chancery in controlling 'the excessive power of oppressive gentlemen' towards the poor, see his notes for a speech in Chancery, addressed to Whitelocke on the latter's taking

his place as a Serjeant, 29 June 1620, **xiv**, 102.

48 **xiii**, 184.

49 From More's biography by his son-in-law, W. Roper (pp. 44–5), cited J. A. Guy, *The Public Career of Sir Thomas More* (1980), 84. More believed that 'the authority to interpret legal rules equitably was already inherent in their offices'.

50 Aphorism 96, *De Aug.*, **v**, 109.

51 Speech on taking his seat in Chancery, **xiii**, 182–94. See Guy, *Sir Thomas More*, 90, for More's struggle with the same problems. Already in 1595, Bacon's 'Councillor', in a Christmas device played before Elizabeth, had urged his 'Prince' to undertake this task (**vii**, 339).

52 Account of Council business and other matters, 17 May 1617, **xiii**, 198–9; 'at which speech of mine,' Bacon went on, 'besides a great deal of thanks and acknowledgement, I did see cheer and comfort in their faces, as if it were a new world.'

53 Zaller, 95; full text, **vii**, 754–74. Chamberlain noticed their publication (30 Jan. 1619, ii, 206). See excellent analysis of the *Ordinances* by Coquillette, *Francis Bacon* (1992), showing the stress laid by Bacon on fairness and expedition.

54 Zaller, 95.

55 Chapter 21.

56 B. to Bm, 8 June 1617, **xiii**, 208, and Spedding in **xiv**, 302. W. Hepworth Dixon, himself a lawyer, combed through the *Book of Orders and Decrees in Chancery* and the *Reports of the Masters* for Bacon's first two terms (Dixon, 318–19 and 422), and found that he had despatched 3,658 suits – a good deal more than his average later, which as Bacon told the Lords was 2,000 a year (19 Mar. 1621, **xiv**, 216). Dixon gave the

breakdown for his first four terms as: Easter, 1,829; Trinity, 1,829; Michaelmas, 2,968; Hilary, 2,178 (involving some 35,000 suitors) (ibid., 336). This high figure was confirmed for me by Jeanne Stoddard, who examined the *Decree Book* (1618, C33). John Ritchie, *Reports of Cases Decided by Francis Bacon in the High Court of Chancery (1617–1621)* (1932), pp. xviii–xix, noted the remarkable increase in size of the volumes of Chancery Orders for those years, and their 'no less remarkable' sudden decrease in the years following Bacon's deposition.

57 More, who, like Bacon, had set aside his afternoons to hear causes (he had dealt with 912 in one year). Both chancellors made an all out effort to award 'fresh justice'.

58 **xii**, 190–91.

59 Arguments against the Bill of Sheets, Jan. 1606, **x**, 285–7.

60 The bill, which was to have been (unjustly) retroactive, had originated in a spirit of private revenge rather than reform, and came to nothing. 'Was there no one to remind Cranfield, who out of all those present should have known, that prices and costs had risen somewhat since Elizabeth's accession?' G. E. Aylmer, *The King's Servants, The Civil Service of Charles I* (1961), 368–9. Moral justice was done, Aylmer added, when Cranfield himself was charged with excessive fees at his impeachment. (See Bacon in 1612 on the scandalous 'multiplication of fees in that court', **xi**, 288, and Dixon, 368–9.)

61 See Dixon, 338ff for a detailed study of the position in Chancery, with life histories of some of the members of Bacon's staff.

62 Peck, *Northampton*, 48–51.

63 Zaller, 90.

64 Essay, 'Of Judicature' (1612);

Dixon, 340–41; Rowse, *Shakespeare's Southampton*, 271 and n9. A prosperous practising lawyer, Churchill 'solidly improved the fortunes of his family, married into the aristocratic Winstons, and acquired considerable property, partly by enclosing commons to improve his land at public expense' (Churchill, *Marlborough*, i, 30–31).

65 It is not known exactly when Bacon took action against Churchill (clearly before 28 Feb., when the parliamentary journals refer to the Registrar as having been sequestered from office 'with danger of further punishment'). The most probable date is that given here, on the occasion of Bacon's 'vehement suspicion' of 'some shuffling' (**xiv**, 205 and 253; Gardiner, iv, 74–5 and 57, n1).

66 As Gardiner pointed out, iv, 56–7.

67 Prestwich, 299.

68 See B. to King, June 1616, **xii**, 350, and chapter 32 below. Coke, wrote Gardiner (iii, 6) wanted to bring every court in England under the control of that over which he himself presided.

69 The second bill, as Gardiner pointed out, provided 'that the final decision in a court, the main value of which consisted in its readiness to afford redress against the injustice committed by the common-law judges, should be entrusted to a body in which those very judges composed the majority' (Gardiner, iv, 19). Although there was plenty of food for scandal in the other courts, Zaller concludes today: 'Chancery was to be the scapegoat among the courts, as Bacon had been among the referees. The choice of the first victim, indeed, had virtually determined the choice of the second. And as Bacon's case had admirably served both public necessity and private revenge, so Chancery's served the private interest of the common lawyers' (Zaller, 96–7).

70 Gardiner, iv, 109.

71 *CD*, ii, 303–6.

Chapter 11   *Prologue: Two Attacks are Mounted and Silently Dropped*

1 29 Nov. 1620, **xiv**, 146.

2 Russell, 86 (see also 90–99), citing a demonstration that 'the main cause of the depression lay in devaluation in the Baltic, which meant that silver fetched a higher price than it did in England'; Prestwich, 301.

3 Zaller, 51 and 57. Coke brushed aside all thoughts of the crisis and of funds for the war. 'His Majesty's cause', he said, 'was neither deplorable nor desperate.'

4 Bacon's reply to the Speaker's oration, 3 Feb. 1921, **xiv**, 178.

5 Zaller, 51. It was an issue on which ambitious men at Court could hope to discredit one another (Russell, 87–8).

6 8 Feb., see Digges to Carleton, 15 Feb., cited Zaller, 50; Alford, 19 Feb., see *PD*, i, 78; Dixon, 390.

7 Zaller, 52.

8 White, *Sir Edward Coke*, 43; Russell, 104–5. The patent had been impatiently sealed by the King himself.

9 Among other profits, Michell had received an income of £40 a year from Newgate Prison, on condition he made use of it for his prisoners (**xiv**, 185–6, Gardiner, iv, 42–3).

10 Gardiner, iv, 43; **xiv**, 217–19.

11 27 Feb., *CD*, ii, 122–3, and vi, 262–3, 285–6; **xiv**, 186.

12 Tite, 1 and 48. First used for the trial of William Latimer in 1376, the procedure lapsed under Henry IV.

13 So Clayton Roberts, *The Growth of Responsible Government in Stuart England* (1966).
14 2 Mar., *CJ*, 533–9; Dixon, 392–4; Zaller, 62; Prestwich, 293–4.
15 *CJ*, 533–9.
16 Coke's remarks on 17 Apr. 1621, *CD*, ii, 98; Gardiner, iii, 6.
17 Cranfield 6 Mar., Coke 8 Mar., *CD*, ii, 172; reminders came in particular from Sir Humphrey May, Recorder Finch, and Glanville (Dixon, 195).
18 Cranfield had been hammering at the referees since 15 Feb. Coke's definitions, 19 and 21 Feb., *PD*, i, 65 and 77, see **xiv**, 184.
19 See Coke on *Darcy* v. *Allen*, Zaller, 127; his discomfiture over the monopoly for engrossing bills for law suits was still recalled in 1628 (Russell, 128). On these inconsistencies, see further below, chapter 21, n75.
20 Prestwich, 46.
21 Gardiner, iv, 46.
22 Zaller, 145 and 163.
23 Chamberlain, 17 Feb., ii, 345; B. to Bm, 7 Mar., **xiv**, 192.
24 Coke's remark, 20 Feb., *CD*, ii, 108.
25 Prestwich, 295.
26 Spedding, **xiv**, 188–9.
27 Gardiner, iv, 47; Zaller, 64.
28 Digges warned the Commons against being 'too particular in challenging too large a power', 6 Mar., *PD*, 136.
29 **xiv**, 196; Chamberlain, 10 Mar. 1621, ii, 351.
30 9 Mar., *CJ*, i, 541–7; *PD*, i, 134–40.
31 Gardiner, iv, 48; Zaller, 67–70.
32 24 Apr., *CD*, iv, 252–3.
33 On possible policy aspects of this decision, Zaller, 68.
34 Early March 1621, **xiv**, 201.
35 **xiv**, 192.
36 Hacket, *Scrinia Reserata*, i, 49; *CD*, ii, 161; *CJ*, 537. Buckingham's most compromised relative, Sir Edward Villiers, had already fled abroad.
37 Chamberlain, 10 March, ii, 351.
38 **xiv**, 192.
39 Russell, 123.
40 The Venetian Ambassador, cited Gardiner, iv, 51, n2.
41 Hacket, *Scrinia Reserata*, i, 49–50.
42 On 13 March, stepping blithely into a Committee of which he was not a member (Gardiner, iv, 53).
43 10 March, **xiv**, 198; Zaller, 72.
44 Ibid., 73.
45 Gardiner, iv, 50–51.
46 Zaller, 73.
47 Spedding, **xiv**, 199.
48 See Gardiner, iv, 69 and 106–7. On Bacon's views see further below, chapter 21.
49 Coke was so 'puffed up' on precedents, Chamberlain noted, that he brought them forth 'misapplied or perverted to a wrong sense' (18 Mar. 1621, ii, 358).
50 John T. Noonan, in *Bribes* (1984) (343 and n42), underestimating the weakness of James's position, added to Coke's other motivation against Bacon a fear of royal reprisals for his bad precedents. 'I hope you will punish him,' James told the Lords. They did not, and James was to lose skirmish after skirmish until the Lords voted with only one voice *contra*, that of the ashamed favourite (Tite, 141).
51 Clarendon, i, 43.
52 Russell, 111. The Lords, as Zaller remarked (77), when soon afterwards they organized committees to investigate the monopolies (under the leadership of Southampton), conspicuously omitted any mention of the referees.
53 Zaller, 85.
54 Bacon's message to the Commons, reported to the Committee by John Finch on 14 Feb. and by Sackville on the 17th to the whole House (*CJ*, 525).
55 Bacon – a borrower by temperament, as Cranfield was a moneylender – had strong convictions on the remedies that the courts of

equity should be able to apply 'as to conscience appertains' when usurers called in their money too suddenly. He set them forth after his fall in a draft Act against Usury, which he sent to Secretary Conway in April 1623 (**xiv**, 419).

56 White, *Sir Edward Coke*, 61; Cranfield's haste, wrote Locke to Carleton (3 Mar. 1621, cited Zaller, 204 n126) stemmed partly from the fact that his own court had also issued them.

57 Gardiner, iv, 57.

58 Ibid., 58.

59 White, *Sir Edward Coke*, 60; Johnson, 'Francis Bacon and Lionel Cranfield', 311–13.

60 Phelips, 12 Mar., *CJ*, 549. When offered the chair again on his return, 13 March, he said: 'hath an ague; is not well, not fit for it' (*CJ*, 555), but according to a contemporary chronicler, the reason for his removal 'was his refusal to report complaints received against Bacon' (*CD*, v, 258 and n14). Historians have diverged widely in their view of Sackville's attitude towards Bacon on his impeachment. Prestwich (293) describes him as 'the unrelenting enemy of Bacon', but this charming womanizer and gentle courtier should be seen in the context of his constant friendship and assistance to Bacon, before and after his fall (see chapter 25 below). It was for Sackville to speak it in the House that Bacon wrote his speech 'concerning a war with Spain' in March 1624, and he was to write affectionately recommending a young friend to Sackville a few months before his death (xiv, 460 and 529). Zaller is probably right (65, 74, 80) in suggesting that when Sackville launched the attack on monopolies – in the spirit of Bacon's own proposal of 19 Nov. – he had no idea that his insistence that the referees be

questioned would involve Bacon; and he summarized the proceedings 'without in the least grasping their import'. He was the first to speak for Bacon when the charges were brought before the whole House.

61 14 Mar., *CD*, ii, 221–4; *PD*, i, 157–9; Prestwich, 299–300.

62 Zaller, 75.

63 On 17 March, when the final charges were brought in against Mompesson (ibid., 4); see Aubrey, 227, on the fun poked at Coke in the play *Ignoramus*, acted 'with great applause before King James', in which they 'dressed Sir Ignoramus like Chief Justice Coke, and cut his beard like him, and feigned his voice'.

64 Marwil, 42.

Chapter 12   Act I: Bacon is Accused of Corruption in the Commons

1 John Wrenham, see further chapter 32.

2 Dr Mead to Martin Stuteville, 25 Feb. 1621, Birch, ii, 232. For Ellesmere, see above, chapter 9; for Williams, see Lockyer, *Buckingham*, 193. Yelverton to B., 3 Sept. 1617, **xiii**, 248.

3 Noonan, *Bribes*, 344. Noonan thought that historians have underemphasized the part played by Coke and others in toppling the Chancellor.

4 17 Mar., *CD*, ii, 241–2, see further below. Foster ('The Procedure of the House of Commons against Patents and Monopolies', *Conflict in Stuart England* (1960), 66) concluded that there was more behind the petitions and complaints against the patents than met the eye. For Zaller (204 n130) it is clear that the petitioners were well sponsored.

5 Cited Foster, 'Procedure against Patents and Monopolies', 66.
6 Cranfield to King, 29 Apr. 1624, cited Prestwich, 446.
7 Chamberlain, 24 Mar. 1621, ii, 355.
8 'It is ordered that the Sub-Committee for Complaints against Courts of Justice shall have Power to send for any to inform them such as they shall think fit' (21 Feb. 1621, *PD*, i, 78; Dixon, 390).
9 1624, *CJ*, 670–766.
10 Chamberlain, 24 Mar. 1621, ii, 355.
11 14 Mar. 1621, **xiv**, 213.
12 The story of both petitions is in Gardiner, iv, 59ff., Spedding, **xiv**, 212–15 and Zaller, 75 ff. Gardiner (iv, 59 n3) noted an error of transcription in the dates of both gratuity and decree, mentioned in *PD* as 1 and 13 July 1618 – in fact probably 1 and 13 June, since the decree appears in *Chancery Affidavits* as 13 June. In the *Book of Orders and Decrees*, however, the decree condemning Aubrey to refund a large sum is dated 2 July, although the entry was not made until the 4th. Churchill, who was continually cooking the records, may have caused the confusion.
13 Gardiner, iv, 59–60. Bacon refused to pronounce until the accounts between the litigants had been thoroughly examined, but Aubrey could give no satisfactory explanation of his claims. After the 'killing order' (13 June) he finally produced accounts, and in November Bacon announced his award, acknowledging the justice of many of Egerton's claims, but still leaving him dissatisfied. For Aubrey's story, see Gardiner, iv, 58ff. and Dixon, 400ff, and for George Hastings, as reported by Phelips to the House next day, 17 Mar., *PD*, i, 195.
14 *CD*, ii, 224–6; **iv**, 155–61 and **vii**, 578–9. See Russell, 37. For the account of Egerton's petition, see

Gardiner, iv, 60–64, and see further below.
15 Dixon, 426; Gardiner, iv, 64. 'Seldom has any judgement been subjected to such an ordeal', Gardiner concluded, 'with such triumphant success.' See references to the case in Bacon's correspondence with Buckingham, **xiii**, 262–3 and 295. The litigation of these cousins has been made to look black for Bacon because he appeared to have accepted a gratuity from both sides. That this was not the case will be seen in chapter 14 below.
16 If anybody had told him the day before,' wrote Spedding (**xiv**, 212) 'that he stood in danger of a charge of taking bribes, he would have received the suggestion with unaffected incredulity.'
17 B. to Bm, 14 Mar. 1621, **xiv**, 213.
18 B. to King, 25 Mar., **xiv**, 226.
19 Continuation of conversation reported by Phelips in the House on 17 March, cited n13 above, as entered more fully in *Journal of Proceedings against Lord Bacon*, 4. See Gardiner, iv, 65. Meautys, defending Bacon in the Commons, said 'that my Lord Chancellor's speech to Sir George Hastings was that if he did think to frighten a judge with such an accusation, he must deny it upon his honour, and charge him with it' (*CD*, vi, 67). Bacon was to bequeath his 'casting-bowl' to Cavendish (**xiv**, 542).
20 As when, after his inaugural speech in Chancery, he made the Lords wait to hear that same young Hastings present a motion; see also Serjeant Crewe's remark, later: 'Sir Richard Young confesseth he had the money, and now to discharge himself, accuseth the other' (17 Mar.), *CJ*, 561.
21 Chamberlain, 24 Mar. 1621, ii, 354. See in Dixon's examination

(Dixon, 373) of one of these cases from the Privy Council Registers, the story behind the accusation that a diamond ring presented to Bacon by his relative, Sir George Reynell, as a New Year's gift, was intended as a bribe (sequel below, chapter 14).

22 **xiv**, 212.

23 *PD*, i, 171–4; *CD*, iv, 160–61, v, 44–5 and 301–2 and vi, 66–8, cited Zaller, 78; Dixon, 403.

24 *CJ*, 558; Gardiner, iv, 65.

25 *CJ*, 560; *CD*, ii, 239. In the following Parliament, as Russell noted, Phelips would take action only on petitions which assisted Buckingham in his efforts to impeach Dean Williams, Bacon's successor in Chancery.

26 Mac., 351.

27 Zaller, 80.

28 17 Mar., *CJ*, 560–61; Dixon, 404.

29 17 Mar., *CD*, ii, 241. These words are attributed by most reporters to the Recorder, Heneage Finch ('X', in ibid.); *Journal of Proceedings*; William Cobbett, *State Trials* (1806–26); Cobbett, *Parliamentary History 18 James 1620* (1776), ii, 1094. However they could have been spoken by Mr John Finch, who had defended Bacon two days before in the Committee (*CD*, ii, 240 n19). *CJ* merely mentions 'Mr Finch'.

30 See his list of proposals for reform 26 Mar., *CD*, iv, 193–5, see also Spedding **xii**, 14–18, and chapter 29 below.

31 23 Mar. 1621, *LJ*, iii, 39.

32 *CD*, ii, 242 and iv, 168, see Zaller, 81 and Epstein, *Francis Bacon*, 146. The fact, Macaulay argued, that satisfied bribers, with every motive for holding their tongue, came forth to accuse Bacon, was the best proof that 'an extensive system of corruption' existed (Mac., 353). He failed to take this order into account.

33 *CD*, ii, 242. When John Finch had used the word in the Committee, he spoke of the false witnesses, not of Bacon.

34 For Coke's 'unwarranted use of this word' see Tite, 112 n1.

35 White, *Sir Edward Coke*, 153; Mac., 352.

36 April 1621, *CJ*, 574.

37 Ibid., 578.

38 Zaller, 78; White, *Sir Edward Coke*, 151–2.

39 Gardiner, iv, 66.

40 *CJ*, 561; *CD*, ii, 242. See Tite, 117, and Russell, 112.

41 Zaller, 81.

42 Ibid., 82.

43 *CJ*, 563.

44 Zaller, 82–3.

45 Sackville, expressing the wish 'to have no divorce between the Lords and us', apparently supported Coke, but he probably did not see what Coke was heading for. See above, chapter 11, n60.

46 Zaller, 84.

47 White, *Sir Edward Coke*, 153. Below, Coke will be seen egging the Commons on to punish a new and 'dangerous' offender, with a 'popish heart' (chapter 17).

Chapter 13   Act II: The Lords Join the Hunt

1 Mac., 343. Not solely from virtuous indignation, however, but because, as Clarendon saw it, they were 'naturally inclined to those kinds of executions'; Clarendon, i, 43.

2 Russell, 15. 'I see men do with great alacrity and spirit proceed when they have obtained a course they long wished for and were refrained from' (Bacon, speech on the Subsidy Bill, Nov. 1597, **ix**, 88).

3 On Southampton, see chapter 9

above; for Bacon on not hunting after grievances, see chapter 8.

4   *LJ*, 10 Mar. Rowse, *Shakespeare's Southampton*, 271–1; on p. 171 he finds no reason to think Southampton's conduct towards Bacon was 'personally motivated', but on p. 272 he fears he 'cannot after all acquit [him] of personal animus against Bacon'.

5   **xiv**, 216.

6   B. to the Lords, 19 Mar. 1621, **xiv**, 215.

7   16 Mar., *PD*, i, 157–64; Dixon, 407; re Meautys's request: *CJ*, 17 Mar.

8   23 Mar. 1621, see **xiv**, 224.

9   *LJ*, iii, 58; Russell, 113.

10 Mac., 336 and 354, see Spedding, **xiv**, 224.

11 Gardiner, iv, 79; Spedding, **xiv**, 266; Dixon, 367–8; see more fully below, chapter 17.

12 B. to Bm, 30 Jan. 1622, **xiv**, 328; see Noonan, *Bribes*, 360. On the equivalent of Bacon's income today, see further below, chapter 17 and n28.

13 Thomas Carte, *A General History of England* (1747–55), iv, 73.

14 Daines Barrington, *Observations on the more Ancient Statutes, from Magna Carta to the Twenty-First of James* (1766), 22.

15 Apophthegm 23, **vii**, 128, probably from Roper, More's biographer in 1556.

16 21 Apr. 1621, *LJ*, iii, 81; Bacon's first confession, **xiv**, 242.

17 Hurstfield, *The Queen's Wards*, 347–8.

18 See the end of chapter 9 above.

19 See below, chapter 21, on Bacon's proposals for reform. Linda Peck made a penetrating anlysis of the reasons why longstanding corruption, still tolerated and well managed under Elizabeth, became a crucial issue between 1615 and 1621: Peck, 'Corruption at the Court of James I: The Undermining of Legitimacy', in *After the Reformation, Essays in Honour of J. H. Hexter* (1980), pp. 75–93.

20 Suffolk, **xiv**, 561; Heneage, chapter 18 above.

21 For Sir John Bennet, Chamberlain, 18 Apr. 1621, ii, 364; see further, chapter 16.

22 **xiv**, 235–6.

23 Gardiner, iv, 79.

24 See ibid., 72–81; Dixon, 342–7. The longevity of suits, as Guy remarked of Sir Thomas More (pp. 50, 83, 92), was caused not 'by the dilatoriness of the bench, but by the intractability of the parties' (see Guy, *Sir Thomas More*, 50, 83, 92).

25 No more was heard of the extraordinary allegation (reported in *CD*, ii, 247–8) that 'because she had not £200 ready in money, one Shute dealt with her to pass over the land to my Lord Chancellor and his heirs', and 'sets upon Keeling to do it'.

26 **xiv**, 253; Gardiner, iv, 76.

27 Lady Wharton's counsel, Robert Shute, the son of a reputable judge, described by Dixon as 'a more brilliant and sagacious rogue' than even Churchill. In 1618 Bacon had backed this young talent for the Recordership of London, despite the objections of the London Aldermen to his 'want of years and gravity' (Chamberlain, ii, 180), and had sponsored his election in December 1620 as MP for St Albans. But the 'shuffling' over Lady Wharton's case, and another transaction about which Bacon would later state he had known nothing, must have opened his eyes to this protégé's gross abuse of his patron's confidence (**xiv**, 256). Shute was appointed Recorder in January 1621, but died two weeks later (see further, Dixon, 343).

28 Ibid., 77 n2.

29 A favourite expression of Coke's, noted by Chamberlain on this occasion (see Gardiner, iv, 78 n1), 24 Mar. 1621, ii, 356. He was to brandish it against Cranfield in 1624.

30 *CD*, ii, 247; Gardiner, iv, 78.

31 21 Mar. 1621, *CD*, v, 59; also ibid., ii, 252.

32 *LJ*, 22 Mar.

33 *CJ*, 565, see also *CD*, ii, 248: 'Lady Wharton so wrought that he was willed not to enter the last order, so that my Lady was left at liberty to prosecute it in Chancery, brought it to a hearing and at length got a decree.'

34 Gardiner, iv, 75 n1.

35 Ibid., 80 and n1, and 81.

36 Ibid., 78.

37 **xiv**, 558.

38 Gardiner, iv, 81.

39 For Wrenham, see below chapter 32.

40 Chamberlain, 24 Mar. 1621, ii, 356.

41 B. to King, 25 Mar. 1621, **xiv**, 225–6.

42 Ibid., and first confession to the Lords, 22 Apr., **xiv**, 225 and 242.

43 Some of these had successfully defended themselves. He noticed in particular that in the case of Justice Thorpe, under Edward III, the prosecution had stressed the importance of the oath of office, when condemning him for taking bribes. It was laid down that this judgement should not form a precedent, 'specially against any who have not taken the oath' – an oath established for judges, not long before, by which they undertook to accept no reward while they had a process pending. A Chancellor did not take this oath (he merely swore to 'well and truly serve the King'), and was therefore not foresworn – a distinction (noticed also by Coke, *Institutes*, iii, chapter 68) which was not a quibble, since such high-placed men were looked on

as above being corrupted by presents. Bacon so considered himself (viz. his notes, **xiv**, 232–4). See discussion of the legally acceptable gratuities in Spedding, **xiv**, 217–21, Tite, 115, n1, and below chapters 15 and 18; also Noonan on Coke's views of Thorpe's case, see *Bribes*, 753 n55.

Chapter 14 Act III: Surrender and Sentence

1 Zaller, 89.

2 Mac., 343. 'The King', wrote Mallet (*Life of Bacon*, 105), 'absolutely commanded him not to be present at his trial, promising on his royal word to screen him in the last determination; or if that could not be, to reward him afterwards with ample retribution of protection and favour. He obeyed, and was undone.' As rightly pointed out by Gardiner, 'Buckingham's insane demand for a dissolution had never been supported by Bacon,' whose every letter showed his readiness to see the charges against him 'sifted to the uttermost' (iv, 87).

3 **xiv**, 235–42; B. to King, 21 Mar. 1621, **xiv**, 240–42.

4 On the various and somewhat erratic procedures used in Parliament to present charges and to announce punishment, see Tite, 141–2.

5 **xiv**, 228–31.

6 As in 'The Reply of the Squire', in his Device for Christmas 1595 (**viii**, 383–41).

7 'A Prayer or Psalm', Apr. 1621, **xiv**, 230; on this recurrent reflection (from the Vulgate Bible, Psalm 120, line 6), see below chapter 20, and Spedding, **xiv**, 569–70.

8 Chamberlain, 13 May 1624, ii, 559.

9 See above, chapter 11, for King's speech on 10 March; on 26 March, *CD*, iv, 240; on 20 April, ibid., v, 86.

10 Bm's words to Tillières, French Ambassador, cited Gardiner, iv, 85–6.

11 Sharpe, *Faction and Parliament*, 28; Russell, 104.

12 On Suffolk's fall, Gardiner, iii, 187 and 195.

13 Tenison, 69.

14 On Somerset, see Hurstfield, *Freedom, Corruption and Government*, 169. See Sharpe, 'The Earl of Arundel, his Circle and the Opposition to the Duke of Buckingham, 1618–28', in *Faction and Parliament*, 211.

15 Chapter 16, see **xiv**, 199–200 and 235, and J. W. Gough, *The Superlative Prodigal, a Life of Thomas Bushell* (1932).

16 Appendix to Bushell's *Abridgement of the Lord Chancellor Bacon's Philosophical Theory in Mineral Prosecutions* (1659). The language of Bushell's project is not Bacon's, but there are many Baconian echoes to confirm his not unlikely statement that it was Bacon who first aroused his interest in mining, and introduced him to Agricola's *De Re Metallica*, from which he learned its techniques (F. *Phil.*, 33–4). For Bacon's interest in the reclaiming of drowned lands and mines, see, among others, his 'Letter of Advice to Villiers', 1616, **xiii**, 48 and Charles Webster, *The Great Instauration, Science, Medicine and Reform, 1626–1700* (1975), 346; and for his plan to set up a commission for their recovery, Jan. 1620, **xiv**, 71. Bushell may have been familiar with his master's lifelong interest in the scientific and poetic academies he had first seen in France. For Bushell's intimacy with Bacon, see Aubrey, 178 and 202–5, and see Bushell's own remarks in the *Abridgement*, chapter 16 below.

17 Memorial of a conference with Buckingham, Oct. 1621, **xiv**, 313. The meeting never took place. Instead Bacon sent a brief note to Buckingham in which he mentioned 'your undeserved favours' and 'undesired promises' (**xiv**, 315). See also B. to King, 24 Jan. 1624, **xiv**, 452.

18 B. to King, 16 July 1621, **xiv**, 297. On 19 March Buckingham reported to the Lords that he had found the Lord Chancellor 'very sick and heavy', but now he was 'much comforted' with hopes of finding 'honourable justice' in that House. Bacon may well have received other comfort from the man he would write to on the 25th as 'my anchor in these floods' (**xiv**, 216 and 225).

19 Chamberlain, 24 Mar. 1621, ii, 356.

20 Tillières, Venetian Ambassador, and Salvetti, Tuscan Resident at the English Court, cited Gardiner, iv, 85–6.

21 B. to King, summer 1621, **xiv**, 388.

22 Compare: 'Pity in the common people, if it run in a strong stream, doth ever cast up scandal and envy' (*History of Henry VII*, **vi**, 203).

23 Memo for an interview with the King on 16 Apr. 1621, **xiv**, 237.

24 See later in this chapter.

25 Did the King's advice to Bacon, as reported by Mandeville in the Upper House (see n3 above) – that he should put himself at the mercy of the Lords – imply defence or submission?

26 Tenison, 99.

27 Mallet, *Life of Bacon*, 104–5.

28 Aikin, i, 218; Lockyer, *Buckingham*, 99.

29 Ralegh, see below, chapter 29; Yelverton, see Gardiner, iv, 113–15.

30 Aikin, i, 218.

31 Chamberlain, 10 Feb. 1621, ii, 340.

32 Willson, *Privy Councillors*, 234–5. Balmerino confessed to the letter he hadn't written, and was sentenced to death, but reprieved in time to die naturally.

33 Mac., 346.

34 'Letter of Advice to Villiers', **xiii**, 14.

35 B. to Bm from the Tower, 31 May 1621, **xiv**, 280.

36 Led by Yelverton, see Gardiner, iv, 113–15, Zaller, 116ff., and Tite, 119–20.

37 Notes for a conference with Buckingham, 2 Jan. 1623, **xiv**, 444.

38 Marwil, 56; Gardiner, iv, 92.

39 22 Apr., **xiv**, 242–5.

40 As the biblical pool of Bethesda healed only the first to enter it, so the beginning of reformations 'hath commonly strength to hurt him only that is first cast in'. 'There is an honour likewise,' Bacon had written, 'which may be ranked among the greatest, which happeneth rarely, that is, of such as sacrifice themselves to death or danger for the good of their country . . .' ('Of Honour and Reputation').

41 Tenison, 16.

42 *LD*, 14; **xiv**, 248; Gardiner, iv, 92; Dixon, 420. Coke, cited Aikin, ii, 110. At Suffolk's trial Bacon remarked 'with a smile' (Gardiner, ii, 208ff.) that New Year's gifts were 'not to be given all the year round', but it was he who brought down Coke's demand of a £100,000 fine to £30,000. Carteret noted that Bacon had also urged the King to 'tenderness and mercy' (*BB*, 297). Suffolk was freed after ten days in the Tower.

43 **xiv**, 252–62; Gardiner, iv, 94, see also 95–9; Dixon, 422–30. Bacon promised 'a particular confession on every point', but craved liberty 'that where the charge is more full than he finds the truth of the fact, he may make declaration of the truth in such particulars' (**xiv**, 250).

44 Noonan, *Bribes*, 354–63, see further chapter 32 below; Clifford Hall (Senior Lecturer in Law at Buckingham University), 'Francis Bacon a "Landmark in the Law"?', *Baconiana* 186 (1986), 45.

45 These were accepted as genuine loans, see below chapter 15.

46 See chapter 16 below.

47 Gardiner, iv, 64; Dixon, 424–6.

48 It was obvious from the correspondence, Hall noted, that the Masters in Chancery, to whom Bacon had referred the case, would decree in Hansby's favour, and he pressed for expedition – a common practice, not then considered corrupt. 'Nor is it clear that Hansby received the expedition he may have thought he had paid for.' Hall, 'Francis Bacon, a "Landmark in the Law"', 45.

49 In the will Bacon wrote at the time of his fall (10 Apr. 1621, **xiv**, 228–9), he bequeathed his rings to his wife, 'save the great diamond I would have restored to Sir George Reynell'.

50 On the number of decrees awarded by Bacon, see above, chapter 10, n56; Dixon, 429–30.

51 Gardiner, iv, 99.

52 Mac., 345.

53 24 Apr. 1621, Commons in Conference with the Lords, *CD*, iii, 75–6.

54 *LD*, 60–61, cited Spedding, **xiv**, 267–70.

55 Chamberlain, 5 May 1621, ii, 371.

56 As noted by Bushell (*Abridgement*). To appreciate the joke, we must recall Bacon's strong criticism of the bishops from as far back as 1589 ('Controversies of the Church', **viii**, 74–95), and his efforts to curtail their excessive powers (see below, chapter 21).

Chapter 15   Evaluation of the Trial

1 Mac., 351–2. 'No criminal ever had more temperate prosecutors than Bacon. No criminal ever had more temperate judges.'
2 Gardiner, iv, 69. See also Gough, *Fundamental Law*, 56–7.
3 *CJ*, 17 Mar. 1621, i, 561, see Spedding, **xiv**, 245. On 19 March he asked the Lords for permission to cross-examine the witnesses.
4 See above, chapter 12.
5 **xiv**, 246–7. According to Spedding, the Bishop of Llandaff's case (chapter 12 above, see Tite, 111 and 136), closely resembling Bacon's, seemed 'as precise, as circumstantial, as conclusive' as the evidence against Bacon himself. The Bishop was released with a public admonition from the Archbishop of Canterbury, of which, wrote Gardiner (iv, 125), he took little heed, since his first act was to implore Buckingham to promote him to a better bishopric. He was back in the Lords in May, soon after Bacon's condemnation – and even before he had received his admonition. On the case of Sir Thomas Perient, see Gardiner, 'Four Letters', 224.
6 Report to the Chancellor on the state of Bacon's debts after his death, cited Campbell, iii, 146n.
7 **xiv**, 251 and 263.
8 *LD*, 61–2, notes for 24 Apr. 1621.
9 Spedding, **xiv**, 330–34; Tite, 117 and 171.
10 Bacon consulted Selden over some 'passages of Parliament's', probably to find out how far they agreed with constitutional precedents (**xiv**, 330).
11 Tite, 26–8 and 31–5.
12 Wentworth: 'If Poole his case concerns this, to be read in the House' (debate in the Lords on

Bacon's punishment). La Pole's case was referred to by Pembroke, Hunsdon and Spencer, *LD*, 62, notes for 3 May 1621, see Spedding, **xiv**, 268.
13 Tite, 35 (citing B. Wilkinson, writing in 1952 on constitutional history in the fourteenth century), and Bacon's notes on Chancellor de la Pole, **xiv**, 232. J. S. Roskell, in *The Impeachment of Michael de la Pole, Earl of Suffolk, in 1386* (1984), rejects the general view that he was a scapegoat for Richard II's early failures, and presents him as a somewhat inept man who did his best in a difficult age.
14 Tite, 33.
15 He was Bacon's friend, as is clear from the warmth of his expressions in the letters described in chapter 25 below; Bacon was later to entrust him with the editing of his legal manuscripts (**xiv**, 540).
16 Selden to B., 14 Feb. 1622, **xiv**, 332–3. The Lords' judgements were made verbally, he said, and were noted only by the clerks in the Journal, 'which, as I think is no record of itself, neither was it ever used as one.' A judgement not entered into the rolls and sent to Chancery, as they had been in former times, meant that the decision was not final, and could not stand as a precedent. When Cranfield was impeached in 1624, as Tite pointed out, the Commons were careful to set down the charges (on which all the records were based) lest there should be, 'as in the case of the Lord Chancellor Bacon, no memorials remaining' (*CJ*, 11 May 1624, cited Tite, 168).
17 B. to TM, Sept. 1623, **xiv**, 429; see Woolf, 'John Selden, John Borough and Francis Bacon's *History of Henry VII*, 1621'.
18 On the Bishop of Llandaff, see n5

above; on Bennet, Locke to Carleton, 23 Apr. 1621, cited White, *Sir Edward Coke*, 154, see further below, chapter 16; Gardiner, iv, 108; Russell, 113, Tite, 133ff.

19 Chamberlain, 2 June 1621, ii, 377. He was sentenced a year later by the Star Chamber, where he pleaded guilty.

20 **xiv**, 248; Tite, 138–9.

21 Mac., 344, see Spedding, **xiv**, 271–2.

22 Gardiner, iv, 132. For the description of Floyd's trial that follows, ibid., iv, 119–22, and Zaller, 105.

23 When for purely pragmatical reasons Coke had agreed that the Commons could not administer an oath, i.e., were no Court of Record (chapter 12 above). As Gardiner pointed out (iv, 122), in dealing with Mompesson, over whom they finally had jurisdiction, the Commons had 'expressly renounced the right which they had now intemperately assumed'. See White (*Sir Edward Coke*, 155–9) on the ins and outs of Coke's battle with James on this occasion.

24 **xiv**, 277.

25 Hale and Hargrave, cited Gardiner, iv, 123–4. The Lords could only exercise criminal jurisdiction upon presentment of the case by the Commons, which in Floyd's case the Commons had felt it beneath their dignity to do.

26 Mac., 357.

Chapter 16 The Contemporary View of Bacon's Fall

1 B. to Bm, 31 May 1621, **xiv**, 280.

2 The alleged disapproval of Parliament was afterwards used on various occasions by Bacon's ill-wishers as an excuse to make difficulties for him, e.g. by Lord Keeper Williams, when he insisted on maintaining the clause

excluding Bacon from the Verge of the Court (**xiv**, 291).

3 B. to the Spanish Ambassador, Gondomar, 23 Mar. 1623, **xiv**, 412.

4 B. to King, summer 1622, **xiv**, 385; notes for an interview with Buckingham, autumn 1621, **xiv**, 314.

5 Notes for an interviw with the King, Mar. 1622, **xiv**, 351.

6 And risked the scaffold. It was one of the merits of Henry VII, Bacon was soon to note, that 'in twenty-four years reign he never put down counsellor or near servant' (*History of Henry VII*, **vi**, 243).

7 Naunton, *Fragmenta Regalia*, 32.

8 Chamberlain, 20 Nov. 1619 and 4 Nov. 1620, ii, 274–5 and 325.

9 Ibid., 20 Jan. 1621; Locke to Carleton, 22 Feb. 1622, cited Spedding, **xiv**, 330. See also Cotton, sent to the Tower in 1616 for burning incriminating documents and changing some data, in an attempt to prove the innocence of his patron, Somerset, accused of the murder of Overbury. He was pardoned after eight months, and by the end of 1621 was at work for the King looking up evidence against Coke.

10 *CD*, iii, 339; iv, 189–201, 390; vii, 616, and Chamberlain, 4 Aug. 1621, ii, 396.

11 Chamberlain, 5 June 1624, ii, 562; on Williams, chapter 14 above.

12 Chamberlain, 19 May 1621, ii, 375.

13 B. to the Prince, **xiv**, 287–8. Charles always insisted on mercy and consideration towards the Chancellor, and 'the respect to be had of his person', and he voted against Bacon's degradation (*LD*, 16, 41 and 63). Vaughan, later Chief Justice of the Common Pleas, was a close friend of Selden's.

14 Sanderson, *Aulus Coquinariae*, cited Spedding, **xiv**, 227.

15 Elizabeth's letter, 2 June 1622, **xiv**, 366.

16 Dr William Lewis, see below, chapters 23 and 37.

17 B. to TM, Sept. 1623, **xiv**, 429.

18 Conway, Jan. and Mar. 1623, **xiv**, 402 and 407–8; Mandeville, see Aubrey, 174, and Bacon, Apophthegm 9, **vii**, 181.

19 T. P., and Henry Ockley in *Manes* 41 and 46. See Bacon's supportive letter to Digby when he, too, was sent to the Tower to silence his opposition against Buckingham, chapter 25.

20 Fuller, *Church History*, iii, 325, and *Worthies*, 380.

21 Letter to Bacon, 14 Feb. 1622, in answer to an inquiry on the legality of his trial (**xiv**, 332), see on Selden's attitude to Bacon, chapter 15 above; Meautys to B., Dec. 1621, **xiv**, 323.

22 See chapter 26 below.

23 Full text in chapter 2 above. Matthew returned to London on 29 Dec. 1622. On his care of B., chapter 26 below, n76.

24 Letter referred to by Spedding, **xiv**, 284, text in Montagu, *Life of Francis Bacon*, p. ccccxxiii.

25 Bacon's reply to Gondomar, 6 June 1621, **xiv**, 285.

26 Dec. 1621, **xiv**, 235–6.

27 B. to TM, Feb. 1622, **xiv**, 335–6. On Gondomar's relations with Bacon, see below, chapters 17 and 25.

28 Tite, 140.

29 B. to King, 4 June 1621, **xiv**, 281.

30 B. to King, Aug. 1622, **xiv**, 387. On Bacon's pension, awarded June 1619, and the farm of petty writs (bringing in £600 a year) see further below, chapter 17. He assigned this 'farm' to his wife's relations in trust for her maintenance.

31 On Williams, **xiv**, 308–10; on Cranfield, **xiv**, 381 and 395–7.

32 Boener, 'Life of Bacon', see Spedding, **xiv**, 288.

33 Bacon's reply to King, around 21 June 1621, **xiv**, 289–91. On Bacon's efforts in favour of the commissions set up to continue the work of Parliaments under many heads (including depopulation, the plantation of Ireland, and the 'drowned mines' that were to interest his follower, Bushell), see B. to King, urging him to support and publicize these commissions, Dec. 1619, **iv**, 70–72. See further chapter 21 below.

34 Prestwich, 327. On Mandeville's declaration, see Spedding, **xiv**, 291.

35 A year later, when setting up a commission to deal with petitions and complaints, the King was to assure his people that 'his royal care was not confined unto times and meetings in Parliament, but at all seasons and upon all occasions watcheth over the public weal of his kingdom', Zaller, 138–9.

36 Ibid., 87.

37 Saville to Carleton, 7 June 1621, cited **xiv**, 282. That harmony between himself and his people over Bacon's impeachment, which James was later to recall as never 'paralleled by any former time', would not outlast his Chancellor's fall (Prestwich, 289).

38 Advice touching the calling of a Parliament, Dec. 1613, **xi**, 371.

39 Meautys to B., 25 Nov. 1622, **xiv**, 397; B. to Bm, 5 June 1621, **xiv**, 282.

40 Notes for an interview with the King, Mar. 1622, **xiv**, 351; B. to King, July 1624, **xiv**, 519.

41 Contemporary cited Linda Levy Peck, 'Corruption at the Court of James I: The Undermining of Legitimacy', in *After the Reformation, Essays in Honor of J. H. Hexter*, ed. Malament (1980), 85. Bennet was rich enough to obtain bail for £60,000. He had one other advantage over Bacon: he could beg for mercy in the name of ten children

and forty grandchildren.

42 B. to Bm, 31 May 1621, **xiv**, 280.

43 Notes for an interview with the King, April 1621, **xiv**, 238; B. to Bishop Andrewes, summer 1622, **xiv**, 372.

44 B. to Bm, 31 May 1621, **xiv**, 280; private note preserved in cipher by Rawley, see **xiv**, 559.

45 B. to Bm, 4 Mar. 1621, **xiv**, 213; to King, 26 Mar. **xiv**, 226, to Lords, 24 Apr., **xiv**, 261.

46 B. to King, 20 Apr. 1621, **xiv**, 240; B. to Bm, 5 June 1621, **xiv**, 282. Mint and cumin were the herbs paid as tithes by the Pharisees, Matthew 23:23.

47 Essay, 'Of Great Place'.

48 **xiv**, 283–4; Essay, 'Of Honour and Reputation'.

49 B. to King, 5 Sept. 1621, **xiv**, 299.

50 **xiv**, 178. See his discourse on this theme in *De Aug.*, published two years later, **v**, 42. The same thought – with a different image, also a favourite of Bacon's – was applied to him by his follower, Lewis, when denouncing the Chancellor's impeachers, see chapter 27 below.

51 B. to King, 4 June 1621, **xiv**, 281; draft appeal, not sent, summer 1622. The same applies to his reminders to Buckingham of past promises (chapter 20 above), see B. to King, 24 July 1624, **xiv**, 518–19. On his attitude to the King, see chapter 23 below.

52 See article 28 of his confession, 24 Apr. 1621, cited above, chapter 14.

53 Rawley, **i**, 14, and chapter 2 above; Lady B. to AB, 17 Apr. 1593, **viii**, 244 (see further chapter 26 below).

54 Fuller, *Church History*, iii, 325; Aubrey, 172.

55 The plausible anecdote about the visitor who, while waiting for Bacon, twice saw one of his gentlemen come in and fill his pockets with money from the Chancellor's drawers was over-

heard from the visitor himself by M. Pitt as a boy in 1655 (Preface to Pitt, *Cries of the Oppressed* (1691), cited **xiv**, 563–4).

56 Aubrey, 172.

57 J. A. Guy, *Sir Thomas More*, 81. When Lord Keeper Williams succeeded Bacon, presents of value were regularly offered to his secretaries, a procedure that would not have continued after the clamour of Bacon's downfall had it not been long in use (Hacket, *Scrinia Reserata*, **i**, 52).

58 Fuller, *Worthies*, 381.

59 Pitt, see n55 above.

60 Noonan, *Bribes*, see below, chapter 32; Bushell, see below.

61 Aubrey, 173. For his smear that Bacon's pupils were his 'Ganymeds', see below, chapter 26.

62 Chamberlain, 10 May 1617, ii, 78.

63 William Lewis obtained the post in 1617, and was active in restoring the college buildings, but he resigned on Bacon's fall (June 1621) and took up a diplomatic post in Paris. He was afterwards chaplain to Buckingham, and to Charles I, was exiled during the Commonwealth and reinstated on the Restoration. For his indignant diatribe against Parliament for their impeachment of Bacon, see below chapter 27.

64 Aubrey, 172.

65 Southwich versus Wich, **xiv**, 259; see reports for 21 Mar. 1621, *CD*, v, 58 and 315 Gardiner, iv, 81. Strange, Hall noted, that 'if Bacon was corrupt, he did not order the money to be paid over to himself' ('Francis Bacon, a "Landmark in the Law"', 46).

66 Aubrey, 172; Chamberlain, 2 June 1621, ii, 377, and earlier ref., 11 Oct. 1617, ibid., 80. Sherbourne, formerly one of Cecil's secretaries, had also been Sir Dudley Carleton's agent in 1616, before taking service with Bacon. An-

other such servant was Randall Davenport, who when under oath before the Lords denied the evidence he had given in the Commons against the Bishop of Landaff (**xiv**, 247 and chapter 15, n5 above); he was denounced in the Commons as a 'false accuser of honest men' (*CD*, ii, 429). Lady Wharton's lawyer, Robert Shute (chapter 13, n27 above) was also a false intermediary – or accomplice, as Macaulay and Noonan would have them.

67 Confession to the Lords, 24 Apr. 1621, **xiv**, 261; B. to Cranfield, Mar. 1622, **xiv**, 347.

68 Confession to the Lords, 24 Apr. 1621, **xiv**, 261.

69 Bushell, see above, chapter 14, nn 15 and 16. On the death of Bacon he withdrew to the Isle of Man and became an illustrious hermit, in obedience, he said, to his 'dead Lord's philosophical advice', experimenting with a diet of herbs, oil and honey, 'like to our fathers before the flood, as was conceived by this lord'. See A. de la Pryme, *Memoirs of Thomas Bushell*, ed. W. Harrison (1878).

70 Aubrey, 202–4; Bushell, *Abridgement*, see Gough, *Superlative Prodigal*, 7.

71 De la Pryme, *Memoirs of Thomas Bushell*.

72 B. to Bm, July 1621, **xiv**, 296.

73 B. to King, 25 Mar. 1621, **xiv**, 226. 'Attribute these things to the corruption of the times,' said Buckingham to the Lords in the debate over Bacon's first confession, 24 Apr. 1621 (*LD*, 15).

Chapter 17 The Back-Cloth: Abuses of the Times

1 The Venetian Ambassador, 2 Aug. 1618, cited Gardiner, iii, 74–5. Bacon objected to the sale of par-

dons, see *ER*, ii, 181 and **xii**, 187.

2 Clarendon, i, 41.

3 Napier, *Lord Bacon and Sir Walter Raleigh*, 151–2. Among the unruly adherents was the notorious Sir Edward Bainham (chapter 5 above). Littleton, a fellow conspirator, gave Ralegh a bribe of £10,000, and Bainham a similarly large sum.

4 Hill, *Century of Revolution*, 30.

5 Essay, 'Of Riches'; Bowen, *Coke*, 6.

6 Hurstfield, *The Queen's Wards*, 336.

7 Hurstfield, *Freedom, Corruption and Government*, 308.

8 Hurstfield, *The Queen's Wards*, 71.

9 Hurstfield, *Freedom, Corruption and Government*, 154.

10 Laurence Stone, 'The Fruits of Office, The Case of Robert Cecil, First Earl of Salisbury, 1596–1612', in *The Economic and Social History of Tudor and Stuart England, Essays in Honour of R. H. Tawney*, ed. F. J. Fisher (1961), 115.

11 Hurstfield, *The Queen's Wards*, chapter 10: 'Corruption', and *Freedom, Corruption and Government*, chapter 5: 'Political Corruption in Modern England: the Historian's Problem'.

12 Letter to Bm, **xiv**, 296, cited chapter 23 above.

13 Conversion from Retail Price Index, July 1993; Aubrey, 179; Bowen, *Coke*, 454–5.

14 Clarendon, i, 119.

15 C. W. Johnson, *Life of Sir Edward Coke* (1837), i, 25.

16 Aubrey, 226.

17 Prestwich, 419–20.

18 Stone, 'Fruits of Office', 24 and 33.

19 Ibid., 280; Prestwich, 159–60.

20 For Somerset, see Willson, *King James VI and I*, 344. For Buckingham, see Chamberlain, 12 Oct. 1616, ii, 15, and see Lockyer, *Buckingham*, 48–70 and 236–9.

21 Chamberlain, 20 Nov. 1619 (ii, 274), citing a remark of Hobart, Chief Justice of the Common

Pleas, who considerably reduced this fine; Laurence Stone, *The Crisis of Aristocracy*, 547.

22 Essay, 'Of Expense'; TM, see above, chapter 2, n32; Bacon, 'Observations on a Libel' (1592), **viii**, 158. See also, earlier the same year, 'Discourse in Praise of the Queen', **viii**, 131–2.

23 Aubrey, 176–7; Prestwich, 90.

24 D. G. James, *The Dream of Learning* (1951), 25, 'His spacious spirit not thus bounded', as Wats wrote of him in his Preface to *The Advancement and Proficience of Learning* (1640).

25 Carteret, *BB*, 383; Thomas Campion, Epigram 90; *Manes*, 41; Essay, 'Of Riches'.

26 Bacon's accounts: **xiii**, 326–31; Fuller, *Worthies*, 381.

27 Howell, *Familiar Letters*, section 4, for 1558–9.

28 See François Bayrou, *Henri IV, le roi libre*, 329. Bacon's £60,000 a month remains well below the earnings of chief executives in many firms today, privatized and unprivatized, e.g. by the Chief of British Gas, amounting in 1994, with the year's bonus, to £85,000 a month, or by the Director of the Royal Bank of Scotland, estimated at £1.5 million a month for 1963, which only Coke could equal (figures from *Weekly Guardian*, Jan.–Mar. 1995).

29 Chamberlain, 5 June 1619, ii, 213, see Prestwich, 269. The Master of Alienations, said Aubrey, was Bacon's 'right hand' in building Verulam.

30 B. to Bm, 9 Oct. 1618, **xiii**, 342; to King, 5 Sept. 1621, **xiv**, 298.

31 As Gardiner pointed out (iii, 211) an attempt was usually made to select the fittest man for the job, and some large bribes were rejected, but even then Buckingham expected something for his trouble as a necessary intermediary.

32 Prestwich, 161 n5.

33 AB to Hawkins, May 1596, Birch, i, 481.

34 Cited Bowen, *Coke*, 370.

35 Chamberlain, 24 Oct. 1618, ii, 173.

36 Ibid., 3 Jan. 1618, ii, 125. Chamberlain's correspondent, Dudley Carleton, had also applied. The post fell to Wotton partly because the Government owed him large sums of pay as Ambassador in Venice, but above all because he surrendered his reversion of the Mastership of the Rolls to Buckingham, who had been offered £5,000 for it (Logan Smith, *The Life and Letters of Sir Henry Wotton*, 1907, i, 200).

37 Chamberlain, 7 Mar. 1618, ii, 148. Prestwich found some piquancy in this executant of financial reform bribing his way into a department he had declared redundant (257–8).

38 Chamberlain, 3 July 1624, ii, 586; Gardiner, iii, 101.

39 Ibid., 80. From Judge Whitelocke's diary, *Liber Familicus*, 5 Apr. 1617, cited Campbell, iii, 95 note 'n'; also Chamberlain, 15 Mar., on the £10,000 'block' laid against Yelverton – Sir James Lea's offer for the post (ii, 62).

40 e.g. with reference to the making of Serjeants-at-law, Bacon urged Buckingham: 'by all means cry down that unworthy course of late times, that they should pay monies for it' ('Letter of Advice to Villiers', Aug. 1616, **xiii**, 35).

41 For the post of Attorney General, see below chapter 29; for that of Lord Chancellor, John Bennet had offered £30,000 for the Seal, before it was awarded to Bacon for nothing.

42 At a cost of £2,000.

43 B. to Bm, 12 Aug. 1616, **xiii**, 6.

44 B. to a one-time fellow of Bacon's college, Trinity, Cambridge, 23 Apr. 1617, **xiii**, 173. Bishop

Andrewes (Aubrey, 169) 'made it his enquiry to seek out and promote "ingenious persons" in poor livings', and it was Bacon's particular advice to Bm (**xiii**, 31) never to prefer men to Church places 'for any byrespect', but only such as were 'eminent for their learning, piety and discretion'.

45 Gardiner, i, 214, and ii, 224; Laurence Stone, *Family and Fortune, Studies in Aristocratic Finance in the Sixteenth and Seventeenth Centuries* (1973), 16–18. The following pages are based on the dispatches of the Spanish Ambassador, Diego Sarmiento de Acuña, Conde de Gondomar, to King Philip III and (after his death on 21 March 1621) to Philip IV, see Antonio Ballesteros y Beretta (ed.), *Documentos inéditos de la historia de España* (1936–45).

46 See dispatches for 6 Sept. 1613, Ballesteros, *Documentos inéditos*, iii, 86, 12 Feb. 1614, iii, 271, and 5 Nov. 1617, i, 124.

47 Stone, *Family and Fortune*, 277; Gardiner, ii, 216–17. There is no suggestion that Cecil followed the example of Sir Edward Strafford, Elizabeth's ambassador in Paris, who acted as a double agent and gave all the misinformation he could for Spanish gold (Neale, *Essays in Elizabethan History* (1958), p. 58).

48 Jardine, *Criminal Trials*, 444.

49 Gardiner, ii, 347; B. to Bm, 9 Apr. 1616, **xii**, 264–5. On the Spanish pensions, he told Buckingham, there were 'things his Majesty knew, and things which by some former commandment of his Majesty he was restrained to keep in silence', but he thought they had no bearing on Somerset. Somerset (or Apollo) had not yet been found out, and Gardiner was happy to believe him innocent; but it is now known that he col-

lected his £3,000 a year personally from the Spanish Ambassador in gold, and that Buckingham received the same allowance. Disgraced pensioners like Lady Suffolk and Monson continued on the Spanish payroll, though Somerset had the grace to refuse his pension while in prison.

50 Gardiner, i, 216; Gondomar to Philip, cited R. E. Schreiber, *The Political Career of Sir Robert Naunton, 1589–1635* (1981), 91.

51 'Discourse in Praise of the Queen', **viii**, 131. 'Short View of Great Britain and Spain', **xiv**, 27. For Bacon on Spain, see further chapter 28.

52 Ballesteros, *Documentos inéditos*, ii, 189. Garrett Mattingley, in *Renaissance Diplomacy* (1955), 261, suggested that the King, Queen and Prince, who figure at the top of a key list of pseudonyms sent to Spain on 1 July 1619 as 'Leandro', 'Homero' and 'Petrarca' (Ballesteros, *Documentos inéditos*, ii, 182–9), were themselves in receipt of Spanish pensions, but the pseudonyms were used in all sorts of correspondence, and no financial accounts include these names. The list has no link with the regular account of expenses on 30 June which includes forty-two items, among them relatively modest sums allocated to 'Pyramus' (Lady Suffolk), to 'Socrates' (Admiral Monson), and to others who 'helped Leandro' (the King). Digby himself appears in the list of names as 'Alcides', the Archbishop of Canterbury as 'Trajan', and, last on the list, Bacon as 'Plato'. There is no trace of the 'modest stipend' which Mattingley supposed Bacon could have earned with gossip which Gondomar 'knew how to turn to account'.

53 Mattingley, *Renaissance Diplomacy*, 259–60. Gondomar must have dis-

liked it all the more when he found that his dispatches had been regularly intercepted and sent to King James ever since 1613, when Sir John Digby went to Madrid as English Ambassador. Gardiner tells the tale with the same horror that Digby must have felt as he gradually deciphered 'the names of men whose loyalty had never been suspected' – Cecil the first among them (iii, 216–17).

54 Chamberlain said he had paid £20,000 for the honour (29 Mar. 1617, ii, 65).

55 'Discourse on the Plantation of Ireland', Dec. 1608, **xi**, 120–21.

56 Peck, *Northampton*, 53–5; Prestwich, 115–16; Gardiner, ii, 393.

57 Bm to B., Jan. 1621, **xiv**, 158.

58 Prestwich, 24. 'A contract to procure knighthood for money', Bacon ruled, 'ought not to be enforced.' See Ritchie, *Cases Decided by Bacon*, 11, p. xviii and n33. Bacon appears to have forestalled a decision finally made in 1925. The sale of honours is still in vogue, as it was in 1922, when Lord Northcliffe gave £200,000 for his peerage, of which half went to Mrs Keppel, and half to King Edward VII (McEwan, *The Riddell Diaries, 1908–1923,* 1986).

59 B. to King, advising him to call a Parliament, summer 1615, **xii**, 186.

60 Hurstfield, *The Queen's Wards*, 331 and n1, and 71.

61 Hurstfield, *Freedom, Corruption and Government*, 177–8.

62 Draft Declaration for the new Master of the Wards, June 1612, **xi**, 284–9 – a paper which James admired as one of his 'true passages of business' (B. to King recalling his words, 18 Sept. 1612, **xi**, 311). Bacon was then being considered for Master of the Wards after Cecil's death (compare his approach as candidate with that of Essex, earlier, who saw the Wards merely as a source

of income from which to extend his influence). Ten years later Bacon was still dwelling on projects for 'the disposing of wards and generally education of youth' (**xiv**, 351).

63 Hurstfield, *The Queen's Wards*, 329–30. In 1640 the Government were making four times as much out of them (£95,000) as they had in 1610, when Cecil tried to abolish them with the 'Great Contract', and their exploitation, according to Clarendon, was one of the principal causes of opposition to Charles I. The Long Parliament abolished them in theory in 1641, but in effect they continued until the Restoration. In 1660, a month after his coronation, Charles II exchanged this revenue – which weighed solely on the landowners – for duties on beer, tea, etc., obtained from the whole community. See Hugh R. Trevor-Roper, 'The General Crisis of the Seventeenth Century', *Past and Present*, 16 (November 1959), 58–9, and Alan G. R. Smith, 'Crown, Parliament and Finance: The Great Contract of 1610', in *The English Commonwealth 1547–1640, Essays in Politics and Society, Presented to Joel Hurstfield*, ed. Clark et al. (1974).

64 Hurstfield, *The Queen's Wards*, 266, 278, 281–4; Bacon, 'Observations on a Libel' (1592), **viii**, 149–50. Bacon's praise of his uncle is not uncritical; he notes 'the coldness of his nature'.

65 See Cecil in Stone, *Family and Fortune*, chapter 1: 'Acquisition, 1590–1612', and chapter 2: 'The Building of Hatfield House'; Prestwich, and Hurstfield, *The Queen's Wards*, 302–5.

66 Hurstfield, *The Queen's Wards*, 109–12.

67 *CJ*, 20 Mar., 565. The purse containing £200 was delivered in the presence of 'one Gardener', a

servant of Keeling's. Coke was referring also to a New Year's present of £100 from Sir John Trevor, along with the alleged gift of a cabinet.

68 Marwil, 50 and 56.

69 David Mathew, *James I* (1933), 176–7.

70 Gardiner on Bacon, and on the corrupt nature of Williams, iv, 91 and 136. For an opinion in our time on Williams's 'inner irresponsibility . . . mixed with cunning, remorselessness, love of power', see John Maynard Keynes, *Essays in Biography* (1933), 36. Clarendon, i, 130–31.

Chapter 18   Bacon's Essential Justice

1 Hurstfield, *Freedom, Corruption and Government*, 188 and *The Queen's Wards*, 316. On Cecil's faithful service, see Gardiner, i, 144; on his efforts to restrain an extravagant King and to improve Crown revenues, Hurstfield, *Freedom, Corruption and Government*, 147.

2 Ibid., 152, and *The Queen's Wards*, 302–4. See Spedding, **xi**, 223.

3 See Stone, *Family and Fortune*, 115; Prestwich, 25.

4 Ibid., 24 and 113, see chapter 17 above.

5 Northampton to Rochester, 22 May 1612, cited John Gerard, *What Was the Gunpowder Plot?* (1897), 23.

6 Gerard, citing Walter Cope and Cecil to the King on Ralegh, ibid., 27 and 198. See also Father Blount on Cecil's 'pretended letter', to be 'found by chance', in connection with a second Gunpowder Plot, ibid., 224–5.

7 Stone, *Family and Fortune*, 109–10. These operations took place in 1603, two years after Bacon, with Cecil's support, had successfully defended the Acts against enclosures he had put through the pre-

vious Parliament, which provided that no more land could be enclosed without special licence – a licence which Cecil would have no difficulty in granting himself.

8 Bowen, *Coke*, 286. See Osborne's remark that Cecil was neither Robin Goodfellow nor Robin Hood but 'Robin the Encloser', and that he 'had such a dust raised' by 'his inclosure of Hatfield Chase (after he had to his great advantage exchanged it for his Manor of Theobalds) that the black cloud of detraction fell upon all he said or did', *Historical Memoires*, ii, 88.

9 Bernard Beckinsale, *Burghley, Tudor Statesman, 1520–1598* (1967), 214 n65.

10 Stone, *Family and Fortune*, 108–9. Although Cecil continued his secret profits until the end, already in 1606, faced with a paper denouncing his gains and threatening rebellion if the Wards were not reformed, he noted in the margin, 'this is in part my fault' (Prestwich, 35).

11 Hurstfield, *The Queen's Wards*, 310. He could at least prevent others from exploiting the wards to the extent that he had done.

12 For tactical reasons Cecil had begun by offering only reforms, not abolition, and his final offer was so worded that the Commons did not know whether they were being given the opportunity to request abolition or not (Smith, 'The Great Contract', 120–23; see also **xiv**, 159 and 167–8).

13 See Hurstfield, *The Queen's Wards*, 311.

14 For Bacon the Great Contract was a great illusion, like Cecil's 'impositions'. It was merely another way of 'finding the readiest payment', in order to avoid facing the real task of a Treasurer: to cut down Court expenditure and introduce business management.

15 Hurstfield, *The Queen's Wards*, 182–4.

16 'I have here modified the view I expressed in *The Queen's Wards* (1958), p. 184,' wrote Hurstfield (*Freedom, Corruption and Government*, 147 and n2), after citing his authority, E. A. Abbott, *Francis Bacon*, 1885.

17 For the untrustworthiness of Abbott, see above, chapter 5, and below chapter 28. Hurstfield was not alone in suffering this influence; even Gardiner wrote less favourably about Bacon in the *DNB* (1885) that in his *History of England* (iv, 1869) after reading Abbott, whom he cites. See below, chapter 29.

18 Hurstfield, *Freedom, Corruption and Government*, 162.

19 Mac., 335–6.

20 'Advice to Villiers', **xiii**, 33.

21 For Bacon's views on the judiciary as 'lions under the throne', see **xii**, 99–104, and chapter 24, n33 below.

22 In fact, letters of this sort were not considered improper (Monro, *Acta Cancellaria*, cited Clifford Hall, 'Heath on Bacon in Steward's Case', *Baconiana*, 184 (1984), 67).

23 Dec. 1595: AB could not raise the sum demanded by the only too willing Lady Edmundes (Birch, i, 354); see Neale, *Essays in Elizabethan History*, 65. Bacon himself, in 1611, 'finding the honesty of the man and the equity of his cause to deserve favour', recommended a suit to the Court of Requests, and in the last year of his life begged his friend Edward Sackville, now Earl of Dorset, to intervene in the Earl Marshal's Court, in what looks like a real hardship case (**xi**, 261 and **xiv**, 529).

24 'Advice to Villiers', 1616, **xiii**, 28. Buckingham, as Hacket put it, was 'far more apt to believe them that asked him a favour than those that would persuade him it

was not to be granted' (*Scrinia Reserata*, i, 107).

25 Abbott (*Francis Bacon*, 263) found fewer such references as the years went on – a clear sign, in his view, of increasing corruption (i.e. of increasing dissimulation) in Bacon. The argument, whichever way it is read, is unfounded, since Bacon's protests appear more often in later years (**xiii**, 259).

26 As evidenced in the causes of Leigh, Dyer and Monk, 15 Nov. 1617 and 4 Feb. 1618 (**xiii**, 273 and 298–9).

27 29 Oct. 1617, **xiii**, 269.

28 Bm's request on behalf of Sir Rowland Cotton, 20 Apr. 1618, **xiii**, 311; Bacon's reply, 15 June 1618, **xiii**, 313.

29 Bm to B., 15 June 1618, **xiii**, 313.

30 B. to Bm, 11 Oct. 1617, **xiii**, 263; B. to Bm, 25 Jan. 1618; Bm's reply, 28 Jan., **xiii**, 297.

31 Abbott, *Francis Bacon*, p. xix.

32 Spedding's co-editor, D. D. Heath on the Steward case, **xiv**, appendix 1, 579ff. Bacon's readiness to repair a mistake is shown also in his reply to a recommendation of Buckingham's in favour of Sir John Cotton, who had been removed by Bacon from his office as Custos Rotulorum. 'I know no cause in the world why I should have displaced him, but that it was certified unto me that it was his own desire to resign; wherein, if I was abused, I will restore him.' He wished to be certain this was so, for if Cotton had merely changed his mind, Bacon would not 'disgrace the other that is comen in', Jan. 1618, **xiii**, 290–93.

33 Hall, 'Heath on Bacon in Steward's Case', 66 and 73. He found that Heath's account, from which Abbott took his cue, could not be relied on, his legal history being 'somewhat thin and firmly rooted in that methodological fallacy of reading the past with

34 Spedding, **xiii**, 445.

35 Hacket, *Scrinia Reserata*, i, 53; Carte, *General History*, iv, 77. See Fuller, an admirer of Williams (*Church History*, iii, 326): 'never Lord Keeper made so many orders which were afterwards reversed'; for Williams, and for his successor, Coventry, see also Campbell, iii, 184 and 212. One of these decrees was used by Hale as an example of the procedure of reversal (**xiv**, 557).

36 See above, chapter 13.

37 Dixon, 40.

38 The second session of the 1621 Parliament, 14 Nov. to 18 Dec. (Notes for a conversation with Lady Buckingham, Oct. 1622, **xiv**, 392.)

39 John Rushworth, *Historical Collections* (1659), i, 31; *ER*, ii, 343, and xiv, 555–9. The procedure for the reversal of decrees was by petition, either to the King (who would set up a commission) or to Parliament.

40 Carte, *General History*, iv, 77. Bacon's detractors have argued, firstly, that 'the hundreds who have got what they paid for remain quiet' (Mac., 354) – forgetting that for every man contented there would be one aggrieved (*ER*, ii, 340); and secondly that Bacon owed his immunity to the protection of Buckingham (Abbott, *Francis Bacon*, p. xx).

41 Hacket, *Scrinia Reserata*, i, 65. Williams was also criticized for further supplementing his income with 'a vast many orders privately on petitions, for the sake of fees' (Campbell, iii, 184).

42 Clarendon, i, 465.

43 Chamberlain, 13 May 1624, ii, 560.

44 Southampton, in *LD*, for May 1624, cited Prestwich, 454.

45 Words recalled by Locke, writing to Carleton, 13 May 1624, cited Dixon, 473, and by Bacon himself, Apophthegm 3, **vii**, 180.

46 Bowen, *Coke*, 336, see below, chapter 25.

47 Ibid., 182–5, 230, 252, 280, 312–13.

48 *De Aug.* (1623), **v**, 50: 'for it is not everyone that offers a bribe, but there is scarcely a case wherein something may not be found to bias the mind of a judge, if he be a respecter of persons.' Whether for reasons pleasant or unpleasant (as 'shrewd tongues') 'there will be unequal measures everywhere . . . and judgement will be perverted.' See also the Essay 'Of Judicature'.

49 Jardine, *Criminal Trials*, 444; Prestwich, 436. At his pleadings, wrote Coke's anonymous denouncer in 1616, he was 'wont to insult on the misery and to inveigh bitterly at the persons' (cited Campbell, iii, 76). See Spedding, **xiii**, 121ff.

50 Vickers, *Francis Bacon and Renaissance Prose*, 43–5, citing Bacon's charge against Somerset. Bacon's intellectual honesty comes out, Vickers noted, in such comments as that 'he would add nothing of his own, but the order only'.

51 Hurstfield, *Freedom, Corruption and Government*, 193 and 319.

52 Willson, *James VI and I*, 332 and 387, and on the bribes taken by Somerset with royal approval, 338.

53 Coke, 24 Apr. 1621, *CJ*, i, 578.

54 Pierre Amboise, *Histoire Naturelle de Maître François Bacon* (1631), Preface.

55 Toby Matthew, Dedicatory Letter to Bacon's *Essays*, see chapter 2 above.

56 Bacon's first confession to the Lords, 22 Apr. 1621, **xiv**, 242.

Chapter 19   The Aftermath

1 First confession 22 Apr. 1621, **xiv**, 243–4. Wallingford commended

Bacon's person in the Lords but wished him to come to the Bar: 'we intending a reformation, the opener it is the better' (*LD*, 17); James's speech to the Lords, 21 Apr. *LJ*, iii, 81.

2 Clarendon, 465.

3 Chamberlain, 19 June 1612, ii, 564. Williams spent more time on remunerative private orders (chapter 18, n41 above). On the volume of Chancery orders under Bacon, see Ritchie, *Cases Decided by Bacon*, p.xviii.

4 Pitt, *Cries of the Oppressed*, Preface; Bacon in *AL*, **iii**, 423.

5 Notes for an interview with Bm, autumn 1621, **xiv**, 314.

6 Whitelocke, cited *DNB* entry on Williams.

7 Clarendon on Weston and Coke, i, 63–4 and 119, and ii, 81.

8 Gardiner, iv, 116; Zaller, 124. Villiers was made Master of the Mint in 1624 and Lord President of the Council of Munster in 1626.

9 Chamberlain, 26 June and 12 July 1623, ii, 505–6.

10 See above, chapter 10. The Bill was enacted on 19 Dec., just before the end of the session.

11 Prestwich, 464–5.

12 On the petitions amassed against Mandeville, in particular by Coke, see Gardiner, iv, 140 and Dixon, 451–2.

13 'My Lord Treasurer cannot go without his Keeper,' Sir Francis Nethersole to Sir Dudley Carleton, 25 Apr. 1624, cited Ruigh, *Parliament of 1624*, 142 n79.

14 Chamberlain, 10 Apr. 1624, ii, 553. He thought it was Cranfield's 'harsh and insolent behaviour to all' which did him the worst damage.

15 Bacon's warning: Petyt's *Miscellanea Parliamentaria*, cited Johnson, *Life of Sir Edward Coke*, ii, 139.

16 Coke on the war-path: Prestwich, 455–6; Tite, 158. Coke was to brandish this phrase against Buckingham in 1628 (Lockyer, *Buckingham*, 439), as he had done against Bacon.

17 Clarendon, i, 43.

18 Sir John Eliot, the parliamentarian who had advocated Cranfield's impeachment, admitted, when it was done, that whatever his ill-gotten gains the Treasurer had 'merited well . . .' (Prestwich, 460–61).

19 Clarendon, i, 43. For the 'unhappy precedent' other factors were involved, but Buckingham's subsequent behaviour towards Bacon could certainly have given Clarendon the impression of a 'private displeasure'.

20 Henry Elsing, 'Discourse on Parliaments', cited Carteret, *BB*, 406; 'such a pin', Heylin, cited Montagu, p. cccxliii.

21 Clarendon, i, 98. Bacon described Coventry to the King as a 'well learned and honest man', even if too 'well-seasoned' in Coke's ways. See Coventry's modest and courteous lines to Bacon in Oct. 1625, **xiv**, 535.

22 See chapter 15 above. On Pym's obsessive zeal in rooting out that incarnation of evil, the Popish religion, and hunting down its delinquent followers, see Conrad Russell, 'The Parliamentary Career of John Pym, 1621–29', in Clark et al., *The English Commonwealth*, 147 and 160, and Russell, 427. Impeachment, which by the eighteenth century had become a device for legislative control over executive and judicial officers, crossed the Atlantic on the *Mayflower*, and was finally embodied in Article I of the Federal Constitution (attainder being expressly forbidden), with the proviso that punishment be limited to loss of office, and that the House could not exercise judicial powers, or transform impeach-

ment into an instrument of oppression (as Pym did with attainder) by defining impeachment
offences as it pleased. See P. H.
Hoffer with N. E. H. Hull, *Impeachment in America 1635–1805* (1984).
23 Clarendon, i, 4 and xv, 150.
24 R. W. Harris, *Clarendon and the
English Revolution* (1983), 418.
Great Tew was the estate of
Lucius Cary, son of Bacon's
friend, Viscount Falkland – 'the
noblest man of his age', as that
age saw him (ibid., 11–12). For
Bacon's influence on the circle,
ibid., 16–17. See Clarendon, *A Brief
View and Survey of the Dangerous
and Pernicious Errors to Church
and State in Mr. Hobbe's Book
entitled Leviathan* (1673), 207,
cited ibid., 405. Clarendon, as
Harris showed (p.16), was urging
the same need 'to separate
essentials from inessentials' as
Bacon had.
25 This was Gardiner's opinion, as
far as Bacon was concerned. It
was endorsed in our time by
Trevor-Roper in 'The General Crisis of the Seventeenth Century',
n28.
26 Harris, *Clarendon*, 307, 368–70, 386
and 378. The outcome was similar:
a new generation in the Commons had been taught by a new
Buckingham to use the weapon
of impeachment, and they would
use it against the second Buckingham seven years later, as their
predecessors had used it against
the first, and get the upper hand
of the second Charles (ibid., 386
and 391).
27 Coward, *The Stuart Age*, 258.
28 Clarendon, *Continuation of his History* (printed 1759), p.1242, cited
Harris, *Clarendon*, 393.
29 Tenison, 255.
30 B. to Bm, Mar. 1622, **xiv**, 341.
31 Meautys to B., late 1622, **xiv**, 397.
32 Williams to B., 18 Oct. 1621, **xiv**,
308.

33 Petition to the King, autumn 1622,
xiv, 388.
34 Ibid., 387–8.
35 Bm to B., 12 Oct. 1621, **xiv**, 305; B.
to the Duke of Lennox, replying
to his offer for York House, condi-
tional on Buckingham's refusal,
30 Jan. 1622, **xiv**, 327 (the lease
had been assigned to trustees,
who allowed Bacon the use of the
property); memorial for a conference with Buckingham, and draft
letter to him, Oct. 1621; B. to Secretary Cottington, 22 Mar. 1622,
xiv, 405; Chamberlain, 19 June
1624 and 15 June 1625, ii, 565 and
625.
36 Gardiner, iii, 96.
37 B. to Bm, Oct.–Dec. 1621, **xiv**, 316–
17. Sad also, the various emotional
drafts (321ff.) which precede his
final, dignified appeal.
38 **xiv**, 334.
39 B. to Bm, Aug. 1622, **xiv**, 397.
40 B. to Bm, 29 Aug. 1623, **xiv**, 432.
For some of the excellent advice
he gave Buckingham during
those last years, see below, chapter 30.
41 Anti-Jesuit measures might, he
feared, 'draw the blow of an
assassination against Buckingham' (notes for advice to Buckingham, 2 Jan. 1624, **xiv**, 447).
42 B. to Sir Humphrey May, Dec.
1625 or Jan. 1626, **xiv**, 548–9.
43 *De Aug.*, **v**, 7; Harris, *Clarendon*,
402; B. to Bm, July 1621, **xiv**, 296.
There are echoes, major and minor, in the lives of the two chancellors, equally keen on speeding
up the work of Chancery, and on
mitigating the rigours of the law
(Harris, *Clarendon*, 359), from
their youth (when both liked or-
ganizing masques, ibid., 39), to
the end of their lives (when both
devoted commentaries to the
Psalms, ibid., 402). Like Bacon
(chapter 22 below), Clarendon
tried to raise the level of the political debate, and, aware of his

monarch's shortcomings, urged him to live up to his role (253). Both were able to appreciate the qualities of their worst opponents.

44 B. to Cranfield, spring 1622, **xiv**, 346; his will, **xiv**, 347. On Bacon's death Williams paid tribute (*Manes*, 40) to his 'earnestness, loyalty, toil and watchfulness', adding, 'Why do I vainly pour forth profitless words?' Why indeed! A comparison between Williams's flowery speech on taking his seat in Chancery and Bacon's substantial one on the same occasion justifies Clarendon's view of him as vain and frivolous (iv, 130 ff.).

45 One of his friend Bettenham's sayings, recalled Apophthegm 253, **vii**, 160; Aubrey, 172.

Chapter 20   Thirsting for Power

1 Mac., 320, 350.

2 Edmund Lodge, *Portraits of Illustrious Personages of Great Britain* (1894), iii, 191; Foster, *The World of Captain John Smith*; Daphne du Maurier, *The Winding Stair, Francis Bacon, His Rise and Fall* (1976).

3 Toby Matthew, cited chapter 2 above; Amboise, *Histoire Naturelle*. Aside from the 'libellers', discussed in chapter 27 below, only Bishop Goodman (*The Court of King James the First*, 284) opined that Bacon 'continued ambitious after his fall, and did practise much to rise again'. Tenison found (81) that reading the letters written by the fallen Chancellor 'rather cleareth his fame than throws more dirt upon it'.

4 BB, 383. See also Mallet (*Life of Bacon*, 22) He approved Bacon's 'generous ambition', involving the great captains, statesmen and writers who had kindled it.

5 James Rowley, 'Francis Bacon, his Public Career and Personal Character' (1927), *Wordsworth and Other Essays* (1927), 148–52; Prestwich, 179; Epstein, *Francis Bacon*, 49 and 126. Similarly, having perceptively remarked that Bacon would have had a better opportunity to put his political ideas into practice under 'a politically astute and financially stable monarch' like Henry VII than under James, whom he tried in vain to influence, Epstein promptly reverted to the pre-established axiom that he 'pursued power basically as an end in itself' (ibid., 163).

6 Epstein, *Francis Bacon*, 41, 76 and 81. (Like Bacon's other critics, Epstein also remarks on his 'profound insight into the problem' in question, ibid., 68.) See Bacon's vehement speech against a Bill which would have brought him the much needed occupancy of the post of Clerk of the Star Chamber, worth £2,000 a year (**viii**, 102 and **xi**, 21).

7 Prestwich, 308–9.

8 Willson in 1940, *Privy Councillors*, 106.

9 Epstein, *Francis Bacon*, 56; Rowley, 'Francis Bacon', 133.

10 Ibid., 39.

11 Zaller, 31; Gardiner, 30.

12 'Advertisement touching a holy war', **vii**, 28. For 'windows into men's hearts', B. to Archbishop Whitgift on proceedings in ecclesiastical causes, spring 1592, **viii**, 98.

13 AL, **iii**, 279. In Bacon's view the most typical of this ambition was Julius Caesar, 'Character of Julius Caesar', **vi**, 341–5.

14 Proem to 'Of the Interpretation of Nature' (*c.* 1601), **x**, 84–7.

15 De Aug., **v**, 79; see Tittler, *Nicholas Bacon, the Making of a Tudor Statesman* (1976). Bacon, sent to Paris at the age of fifteen to train in 'business of state', was destined

by Sir Nicholas to follow in his father's footsteps.

16 Paul Kocher, 'Francis Bacon and his Father' *Huntington Library Quarterly* 21, 1958, 133, 146, 149–50 and 152–5, presents Bacon as driven by the 'loving but implacable shade of his father', whom he invested with a quasi-religious aura as the symbol of the ideal statesman, trained like himself in law, history and letters, and whom he felt it his pious duty to follow. Francis inherited from his father, among many incentives, his staunch defence of the royal prerogative, and his project for the reform of learning (F. *Phil.*, 12–13). (For a parallel in our time, see Winston Churchill, seemingly possessed with the 'daemonic spirit' of his father, in Roy Foster, 'Winston's *Lord Randolph*', *TLS*, 23 July 1981, p. 87.)

17 Ben Jonson in Aubrey, *Brief Lives*, ed. Clark, 68; Amboise, *Histoire Naturelle*, 5 and 9.

18 'Proem', **x**, 86; see Bacon's letter to Fulgentio in his last year (autumn 1625), filled with undiminished enthusiasm for his life work, recalling 'The Greatest Birth of Time', written forty years earlier (**xiv**, 531–3); B. to Burghley, spring 1592, **viii**, 108; *Temporis Partus Masculus* ('The Masculine Birth of Time', written 1603, transl. in F. *Phil.*, 62) drew attention to the pent-up emotion in these works; Proemium to the *The Great Instauration*, **iv**, 8.

19 'Cogitata et Visa' ('Thoughts and Conclusions', written 1607, in F. *Phil.*, 98).

20 B. to *TM* (who as a Catholic had expressed some criticism of *On the Fortunate Memory of Elizabeth*), 10 Oct. 1609, **xi**, 135–6. In 1620 he still felt how solitary his enterprise was, but resolved 'not to abandon either it or himself' (**iv**, 8).

21 *RP*, F. *Phil.*, 107 and 128; *The History of the Winds* (1623), cited F. *Phil.*, 54.

22 King to B., 16 Oct. 1620, **xiv**, 122.

23 Bodley to Bacon about 'Thoughts and Conclusions', *Reliquiae Bodleianae* (1648), p. ccxxxiii. See also Toby Matthew's strictures on 'The Refutation of Philosophies', 10 Oct. 1619, **xi**, 137. As a result of his friends' advice, Bacon withheld these pieces, which were not published until long after his death.

24 Introduction, Aubrey, 50–51. 'Many', wrote Osborne, 'would have cashiered Bacon's *Advancement of Learning* as an heretical, impertinent piece, but for an invincible strength of contrary judgements that came to his rescue from beyond the seas' (*Advice to a Son*, i, 151).

25 Bacon, *CV*, F. *Phil.*, 101. Bishop Andrewes followed the development of Bacon's work for thirty years, see B. to King, 12 Oct. 1620, **xiv**, 120.

26 Geoffrey Bullough, 'Bacon and the Defence of Learning' in *Seventeenth Century Studies Presented to Sir Herbert Grierson* (1938), in *Essential Articles*, 93; Marwil, 141.

27 B. to King, 12 Oct. 1620, **xiv**, 120; Bacon, *CV*, F. *Phil.*, 100. Only on those rare occasions when nations are free from wars could 'the wheel of knowledge turn' (*CV*, F. *Phil.*, 95); *RP*, F. *Phil.*, 128; B. to King, 12 Oct. 1620, **xiv**, 120.

28 *CV*, F. *Phil.*, 100.

29 B. to TM, 1609, **xi**, 134; TM to B. in *The Life of Sir Tobie Matthew, Bacon's Alter Ego*, by his kinsman, Arnold H. Mathew and Annette Calthrop (1907); speech on taking his seat in Chancery, 7 May 1617, **xiii**, 190; *As You Like It*, III. ii. 325.

30 B. to Andrewes, Sept. 1909, **xi**, 141 (he was planning, if God gave him leave, he said, to write 'a just and perfect volume of philosophy, which I go on with, though

slowly); B. to Bm, June 1617, **xiii**, 208–9; 'Proemium and Epistle Dedicatory', *IM*, **iv**, 8, 11 and 12; B. to Fulgentio, autumn 1625, **xiv**, 532–3.

31 Essay, 'Of Nature in Men' (1612); B. to Bm, Aug. 1616, **xiii**, 27; *CV*, F. *Phil.*, 100.

32 Bacon usually suffered from indigestion and vertigo, e.g., when he was made Solicitor General (as he noted, *CS*, **xi**, 79), and when he finally inherited the clerkship of the Star Chamber. 'He hath not greatly enjoyed his new honour,' Chamberlain remarked when he was appointed Attorney General, 'being overtaken with a painful fit of the stone' (11 Nov. 1613, i, 486); and he was again complaining of Bacon's indisposition (a fit of the gout) soon after he was made Lord Keeper (ibid., ii, 75).

33 Peter Heylin, *Cyprianus Anglicus*, a life of Archbishop Laud (1661).

34 B. to Casaubon, after he was made Solicitor General, 25 June 1607.

35 *NO*, **iv**, 66. For instance, in Bowen, *Francis Bacon*, the titles of chapters 1, 4 and 5 (part 2). Bacon deprecated the illusory 'ambition of the understanding', which, he believed, led to an 'apotheosis of error', as much as he did the ordinary ambition, or 'amplification of a man's power' (*Valerius Terminus*, 1603, **iii**, 223).

36 B. to Bodley sending him a copy of the newly published *AL*, April 1605, **x**, 253.

37 B. to Burghley, spring 1592, **viii**, 108; dedication of *De Sap.*, to Cecil, **vi**, 689, and address to the University of Cambridge, **vi**, 691; *In Felicem Memoriam*, **vi**, 305. Bacon was to dedicate his *Essays* to Prince Henry as 'the fruit of both' his lives, active and contemplative.

38 J. G. Crowther, 'Nature to be Commanded must be Obeyed',

New Scientist (1977), 734–6; Loren Eiseley, who also described Bacon as 'the statesman and strategist of science', *The Man who Saw Through Time* (1973), 36, 48, 81; Aubrey on Harvey, 288. In 1985, Enrico De Mas argued convincingly that his whole inductive method may be a reflection of the judicial processes of inquiry (*Francis Bacon*, 101), and in 1987 the legal expert Clifford Hall stressed the influence of Bacon's professional training on his treatment of all branches of knowledge ('Then and Now, Francis Bacon and the Law Reform' *Baconiana*, 187 (1987)). In 1988 a first-rate Baconian scholar, Antonio Pérez-Ramos, saw the *inductio* as an interrogation, and Bacon as the cross-examiner of nature (*Francis Bacon's Idea of Science and the Maker's Knowledge Tradition* (1988), 240–41), while in 1992 Julian Martin saw in Bacon's proposals for legal reform the blueprint for his reformed natural philosophy (*Francis Bacon, The State and the Reform of Natural Philosophy*, 1992). However, in maintaining that both these reforms were conceived merely to strengthen the prerogative, Martin underestimated his interest in the role of Parliament, and missed the supreme place of the reform of learning in his programme (see the review of his book by Brian Vickers in the *Renaissance Quarterly* (1994), showing that he largely ignores the substance of Bacon's scientific reform).

39 *AL*, **iii**, 229 and 328 and Tenison, 20; see B. to Fulgentio, autumn 1625, **xiv**, 532 on the magnitude of the task; and his efforts e.g. in *CS*, **xi**, 63.

40 B. to Robert Cecil, Mar. 1595, **viii**, 356; relations with Prince Henry and Sir Thomas Challoner, his chamberlain, **x**, 63 and *CS*, **xi**,

63–4; see Strong, *Henry, Prince of Wales, and England's Lost Renaissance* (1986), esp. 334.

41 B. to TM, 1609, **xi**, 137–8.
42 'Proem', **x**, 86.
43 Gardiner, iii, 396. Pérez-Ramos and Martin, see n38 above, and B. H. G. Wormald, *Francis Bacon, History, Politics and Science, 1561–1626* (1993), for whom Bacon's political strategy and the 'grand strategy' of his science were organically connected by an inseparable link.
44 Friedrich Heer, *The Intellectual History of Europe* (1968), ii, 150, cited with approval by Anthony Quinton, *Francis Bacon*, 17; S. H. Reynolds, *The Essays* (1890), 215. See also Oskar Kraus, *Der Machtgedanke und die Friedensidee in der Philosophie der Engländer: Bacon und Bentham* (1926).
45 *De Aug.*, **iv**, 373.
46 Hurstfield, see above, chapter 18.
47 Peck, *Northampton*, 88–94.
48 Kiernan, *Sir Francis Bacon, The Essayes, or Counsels Civill and Morall* (1985), 256, notes 65–6 (to 'Of Ambition'). Kiernan was replying to a sneer from another editor, S. H. Reynolds, about Bacon's remark: 'He that hath the best intentions, when he aspireth, is an honest man.'
49 George Herbert, *Works*, ed. F. E. Hutchinson (1945), 435.

Chapter 21 *Using his Ideas as Counters in the Power Game*

1 Schreiber, *Sir Robert Naunton*, 1. Bacon himself illustrated the ways in which politicians disguise their personal interest, in his analysis of the political scene in 1615 (note 4 below), see Prestwich, 138–9.
2 Prestwich, 137; Hugh Trevor-Roper, *Religion, Reformation and Social Change* (1967), cited Quin-ton, *Francis Bacon*, 73–4 (Bacon diagnosed the evil, said Trevor-Roper, 'no man perhaps so completely'); Marwil, 146.
3 Essay, 'Of Seditions and Troubles'; speech to the Commons, May 1610, **xi**, 177.
4 See Bacon's analysis of the mistakes made in the 1610 Parliament, letter to James advising him to call a Parliament, summer 1615, **xii**, 176ff., specially 179–82. Compare Cecil, who thought no time should be spent in devising and enacting new laws, of which there were only too many (Handover, *The Second Cecil*, 93).
5 B. to King, June 1621, **xiv**, 290.
6 'Incidents of a Parliament', spring 1613, **xi**, 366.
7 'Touching the Calling of a Parliament', spring 1613, **xi**, 371–2.
8 'Touching a Holy War' (1622), **vii**, 29; B. to King, advising him to call a Parliament, analysing the mistakes made in 1610 (summer 1615, **xii**, 179–82); CS, **xi**, 73–4.
9 Gardiner thought that Bacon 'shut his eyes to the defects' in James's character (iii, 379); 'a lack of vision', writes Epstein today, which 'shows a deficiency in him as a political man' (*Francis Bacon*, 106).
10 See Russell, 420, Sharpe, *Faction and Parliament*, 36, and R. C. Munden, 'James and "the growth of mutual mistrust"', in ibid., 43–72. These historians rejoin Spedding, see ER, i, 207.
11 *AL*, **iii**, 307; speech in support of a motion for supply, 1614, **xii**, 37; James I, *The Trew Law of Free Monarchies* (1598), cited Willson, *King James VI and I* (1956), 312. James declared in Parliament that Kings were 'justly called Gods', having all their attributes – 'to create or destroy, make or unmake at his pleasure', while being 'accountable to none' (ibid., 269).
12 Gondomar, despatches to Spain,

cited R. W. Church, *Bacon* (1884), 123.

13 B. to King, 25 July 1617, **xiii**, 233; speech to the 1621 Parliament, **xiv**, 172.

14 Gardiner compared Bacon's theory of Government, attributing large powers to the Crown, which could be kept from abuse by frequent Parliaments, with the constitutional relation which prevailed in France until the second Empire (iv, 43). B. to King on a digest of the laws, Mar. 1621, **xiv**, 359; *Considerations Touching a War with Spain* (1624), **xiv**, 471.

15 Bacon on the 'malignant disposition of the common people': **vi**, 703 and 718, **iii**, 345, **xi**, 202, **xiv**, 127, 145 and 152, and Essay, 'Of Seditions'.

16 Gardiner, iv, 107. On Bacon's efforts to encourage a good choice of Members, without 'packing' a Parliament (**xi**, 367–8), see draft proclamation for the Parliament of 1621, **xiv**, 127. See Gough, *Fundamental Law*, 28–9, on his respect for Magna Carta, and his fear that 'if force prevail above lawful regiment' it would be too easy for Parliament 'to sweep away all these perpetuities' (vii, 633).

17 Wallace Notestein, *The House of Commons 1604–1610* (1935); Marwil, 136–7.

18 Sharpe, Introduction, *Faction and Parliament*, 1–2. Coke now appears as Bacon had seen him, a pragmatic and opportunistic politician, ready to compromise with Buckingham to oust an old ally, in a House of Commons whose Members tended rather to pursue individual grievances than undertake the responsibility of reform.

19 Derek Hirst, 'Court, Country and Politics before 1629', *Faction and Parliament*, 124. Contrary to the Whig thesis, as Sharpe pointed out (ibid., 4, 16 and 38–9) Parliament was now more unwieldy, and less able to put good laws into effect.

20 Sharpe, *Faction and Parliament*, 11.

21 Managed by Buckingham to defeat his rivals, wrote Sharpe, the House 'proffered the programme of a faction, not the counsel of the realm', and under Charles 'the Privy Council was virtually eclipsed' (*Faction and Parliament*, 41); see Russell, 202–3.

22 Essay, 'Of Faction' (1597); B. to King advising him to call a Parliament, 1615, **xii**, 189, 368.

23 B. to King, summer 1613, **xi**, 368.

24 *De Aug.*, **iv**, 489; 'Controversies of the Church', **viii**, 88; Essay, 'Of Innovation', and 'Antitheta' on innovation, *De Aug.*, **iv**, 480.

25 Gardiner, ii, 193.

26 **iv**, 489 (or 'Let a living stream constantly flow into the stagnant water'); 'Touching the Calling of Parliament', spring 1613, **xi**, 372; Discourse 'On the Union of Kingdoms' (1603), **x**, 90–92; 'Orpheus', *De Sap.*, **vi**, 721; 'Antitheta' on violent counsel, *De Aug.*, **iv**, 490. 'Some people would have no change,' he told James, at the start of his reign, 'no, not reformation. Some would have much change, even with perturbation.' He hoped God would direct Elizabeth's successor 'to hold a mean' (B. to King, Apr. 1603, **x**, 73).

27 1616, second version printed 1618, **xiii**, 13–55. See his similar eagerness in other letters to Buckingham (**xiii**, 117–18, 152, 163, 252, and **xiv**, 37, 317, 430, 432). *CS*, **xi**, 40–95, see esp. 73–4.

28 'Certain Considerations Touching the Better Pacification and Edification of the Church of England' (1603), **x**, 103–21, esp. 106.

29 **viii**, 74–95; 'Pacification of the Church', **x**, 103–21, esp. 106.

30 'Controversies of the Church', **viii**, 76; Essay, 'Of Religion' (1612).

31 Neale, *Elizabeth and her Parliaments*, i, 42; 'Controversies of the Church', **viii**, 75.
32 'Pacification of the Church', **x**, 108 and 117–18. He was not heeded.
33 'Controversies of the Church', **viii**, 80; 'Pacification of the Church', **x**, 105 and 109; see Spedding, **x**, 126–7. He wanted the Bishops to exercise their authority in council, with the Dean and Chapter, as in the past; to stop them ruling by deputy, and to limit their inquisitorial powers.
34 See Spedding on Bacon and the Hampton Court Conference, Jan. 1604, **x**, 128.
35 Abbott, *Francis Bacon*, 110.
36 'Pacification of the Church', **x**, 104.
37 'Advice to Villiers', **xiii**, 18; 'A Proposition Touching the Compiling and Amendment of the Laws of England' (1616), **xiii**, 63–5; speech in Parliament on the union of the laws, 28 Mar. 1607, **x**, 336; Aphorism 5, *De Aug.*, **v**, 89; *History of Henry VII*, **vi**, 91, see Spedding, **xii**, 57–61.
38 Epistle Dedicatory, *Maxims of the Law* (1597), **vii**, 316; see Tittler, *Nicholas Bacon*, 78–80, and his article, 'Sir Nicholas Bacon and the Reform of the Tudor Chancery', *University of Toronto Law Journal*, 23 (1973), 384; Kocher, 'Francis Bacon on the Science of Jurisprudence', *Journal of the History of Ideas*, 18 (1957), 2–26.
39 **viii**, 339; *AL*, **iii**, 475–6; *Maxims of the Law*, **vii**, 316. On the 'snaring laws', whereby the living 'lie in the arms of the dead', see below, chapter 22.
40 Coke, Preface to *Reports*, iv, cited Kocher, 'Francis Bacon on the Science of Jurisprudence'.
41 'Touching the Compiling and Amendment of the Laws', **xiii**, 67. The same dilemma is faced today by the Law Commission for codi-

fication, see Hall, 'Then and Now, Francis Bacon and Law Reform'.
42 'Touching the Compiling and Amendment of the Laws', **xiii**, 65.
43 *Maxims of the Law*, **vii**, 316; speech on the union of laws, **x**, 336 and n2 (Bacon suppressed the last sentence from his draft, probably as too personal a reaction); 'Touching the Compiling and Amendment of the Laws', **xiii**, 69–71, see *Maxims*, **vii**, 319. The complementary books were to include among others an abridgement of the whole law, for ready reference only, and a Book of Institutes, or a concise student text, such as we have it today.
44 'Touching the Compiling and Amendment of the Laws', **xiii**, 68–9; 'Example of a Treatise on Universal Justice', *De Aug.*, **v**, 85–110, Aphorisms 80–83; *Maxims of the Law*, **vii**, 319.
45 B. on Coke, 1616, **xiii**, 65. As remarked by John Blackbourne (*Works of Lord Bacon*, 1730, i, 178), 'lord Bacon was the architect and lord Coke the artificer. One saw at once the rights of all mankind, and how they square with and are the ground of laws in particular states.' The other was content to produce a single work that would 'do the office of a dictionary.'
46 *Maxims of the Law*, **vii**, 319; Aphorism 85, *De Aug.*, **v**, 106. See on the *Maxims*, Coquillette, *Francis Bacon*, 46.
47 William S. Holdsworth, 'The Elizabethan Age in English Legal History', *Iowa Law Review* (1927), 329. In his last years Bacon was still hoping 'to have composed a frame of Laws' for the New Atlantis. See on the 'law of Laws', Aphorism 6, *De Aug*, **v**, 109, and *AL*, **iii**, 475–6: The fountains of justice are all one stream, though they 'take tinctures and tastes

from the soil through which they run'.

48 Holdsworth, *History of the English Law* (1909), v, 254. He considered Bacon 'a more complete lawyer than any of his contemporaries', and he remarked of Bacon's lectures at Gray's Inn (*Reading on the Statute of Uses*, **vii**, 391–445) that they had earned him a place 'besides those few great teachers who have appeared at infrequent intervals in the history of English law'. See also Coquillette, *Francis Bacon*, esp. 3 and 295–6.

49 Translated into French by J. Baudoin. The Code Napoléon was in force from 1810 until 1994.

50 Peel, cited Spedding, **xiii**, 61.

51 'Advice to Villiers', **xiii**, 42–4; *CS*, **xi**, 73–6; B. to King, Jan. 1620, **xiv**, 71–2, including a list of the different heads of specialization proposed; Du Maurier, *The Winding Stair*, 160.

52 'Advice to Villiers', **xiii**, 20; *De Aug.*, **iv**, 286.

53 *CS*, **xi**, 74.

54 'Advice to Villiers', **xiii**, 21; *Considerations Touching a War with Spain*, **xiv**, 470. See above, chapter 20, n44 on the German critics who saw Bacon as a warmonger. In Britain, Robertson, vocal in Bacon's defence against every other charge (chapter 3 above), saw in his alleged warlike policies the only 'valid indictment' against him (*Pioneer Humanists*, 111).

55 Bacon against enclosures, chapter 22 below. Any action to discourage them, he wrote in *History of Henry VII* (**vi**, 94–5), 'did wonderfully concern the might and mannerhood of the kingdom', since this favoured a prosperous yeomanry, which provided the principal strength of the army.

56 Letter of instructions to Digby, the English Ambassador in Madrid, 23 Mar. 1617, **xiii**, 157–9. Bayrou, *Henri IV*, 423–34.

57 B. to the Count Palatine, 13 May, **xiv**, 22, see Spedding, **xiv**, 21.

58 S. L. Adams, 'Foreign Policy and the Parliaments of 1621 and 1624', in *Faction and Parliament*, 142. Though he did not share Winwood's narrow Puritan approach, Bacon's vision was closer to the Protestant 'apocalyptical' ideas centred around the Prince Palatine. If Gondomar was Bacon's friend, so were Lord Cavendish, the Danvers brothers and Pembroke, all in the other camp, and, as Prestwich remarked (283), 'Bacon denounced Spain as vigorously in 1619 as Cromwell was to do in 1656.'

59 'A Short View to be Taken of Great Britain and Spain' (1619), **xiv**, 26. He is recalling the Spanish pensions (chapter 17 above).

60 Ibid. In 1585, in 'A Letter of Advice to Queen Elizabeth' (**viii**, 43–6), Bacon had proposed an international league to attack the Indies, in hopes of using Spanish silver to finance land operations against Spain. The idea was taken up again by Digby in Nov. 1621, and by Sir John Eliot in Mar. 1624.

61 From Gondomar's Memoir, Jan. 1619, Gardiner, iii, 283.

62 Had James used 'a more manly tone', Gardiner maintained, and embarked on some of the military preparations which Bacon continually advocated, Spain would not have invaded the Palatine (iii, 281).

63 Draft 'Proclamation for a Parliament', 18 Oct. 1620, **xiv**, 124–8 (see above, chapter 8); Gardiner, iii, 379 and 398.

64 **xiv**, 465–6.

65 'Notes for a Speech . . .', Feb. 1624, **xiv**, 460–65; *Considerations Touching a War with Spain*, **xiv**, 460 and 469.

66 Russell, 452.

67 'Touching a Holy War', **vii**, 36; instructions to Digby, 23 Mar. 1617, **xiii**, 15–19, see Gardiner, iii, 62, 322 and 324.

68 'Touching a Holy War', **vii**, 17–36, debate held by a Catholic zealot, a Protestant zealot, a soldier, a statesman and a courtier, see **xiv**, 369–71.

69 Bacon allowed 'wars defensive for religion', but not offensive, *Touching a War with Spain*, **xiv**, 47; *2 Henry IV*, IV. v. 213–14; 'Advice to Villiers', **xiii**, 21 and 46.

70 Max Patrick, 'Hawk versus Dove, Francis Bacon's advocacy of a Holy War by James against the Turks', *The Legacy of Francis Bacon*, ed. Sessions (1971), 161, 167. The 'self-interested goal of regaining royal favour' is none the less seen as Bacon's principal motive (Patrick on Bacon above, chapter 3). De Mas, *Francis Bacon*, 33.

71 Marku Peltonen, 'Politics and Science: Francis Bacon and the True Greatness of States', *The Historical Journal*, 35, 2 (1992), 279–305. (I thank Brian Vickers for drawing my attention to this article, and to many others.)

72 'Advice to Villiers', 1616, **xiii**, 46; Essay 'Of the True Greatness of Kingdoms'; *Of the True Greatness of the Kingdom of Britain*, **vii**, 49.

73 'Advice to Villiers', **xiii**, 22; Osborne, *Advice to a Son*, i, 151. We catch an unfamiliar glimpse (**xii**, 187–8) of the Solicitor General, praised for his industry 'in digesting masses of evidence relating to the customs'.

74 'Petition to the King on behalf of the Commons, touching Purveyors', 27 Apr. 1604, **x**, 183.

75 For Bacon's view of the gigantic speculation, launched in 1614 by that fraudulent conman Alderman Cockayne – who managed to hoodwink the King, Somerset, Suffolk and even Coke – see Prestwich, 164–70, 168, 178 and 188.

By supporting the project, she remarked, Coke 'was merely substituting one monopoly ring for another'. Bacon had at first 'affected' the scheme, though with misgivings, and has been criticized for inconsistencies in its charter, which, as Attorney General, he drafted (Astrid Friis, *Alderman Cockayne's Project* (1927), 279–80). But he soon saw through it, and strongly warned the King against it.

76 'Reasons for Appointing a Lord Treasurer', early 1620, **xiv**, 76–7. Cecil had laid customs on 700 articles not taxed before.

77 Essay, 'Of Seditions and Troubles', also Apophthegm 252, **vii**, 160; *Of the True Greatness of the Kingdom of Britain* (1607), **vii**, 60–61. *NA*, **iii**, 151. There is no trace of antisemitism in Bacon's 'True Report of Dr Lopez and his Treason' (**viii**, 274–7), even though Jew-baiting was rampant in 1594 around the trial and execution of this Portuguese doctor – accused of attempting to poison Queen Elizabeth – and Marlowe's virulently antisemitic *Jew of Malta* was showing to full houses; even Cecil called Lopez a 'vile Jew' (Handover, *The Second Cecil*, chapter 13), but Bacon, though indignant as always with any conspirator against the Queen's life, and with Spain for sponsoring him, has not a word against Lopez *qua* Jew. Strongly in favour of immigration, Bacon was likely to have been among those who thought that England, having expelled her Jews in 1290, should readmit them, as she was to do under Cromwell.

78 'Advice to Villiers', **xiii**, 24 and 49; Essay, 'Of Seditions'; 'Speech for General Naturalization', **x**, 313.

79 Conrad Russell noticed a similarity between Britain after the Union of the Crowns and the

present pattern of the European Union, including the discussion of many similar themes (a common external tariff and exchange rate), and other parallel occurences during the debate of the bill for Anglo-Scottish Union in 1606–7 ('John Bull's Other Nation', *TLS*, 12 Mar. 1993, pp. 3–4).

80 'Touching the Happy Union of the Kingdoms of England and Scotland' (1603), **x**, 90–99.

81 'The Equalizing of the Laws of the 2 Kingdoms'; 'The Recompiling of the Laws of England', *CS*, July 1608, **xi**, 94; 'Speech for General Naturalization', **x**, 323.

82 D. G. James, *The Dream of Prospero* (1967), 94–8; see lines quoted from Bacon's speech for the opening of the 1621 Parliament, chapter 17, and *De Aug.*, on empires, **v**, 80–81.

83 Hill, *Century of Revolution*, 31. King James, following the practices of Justice Popham, who first 'set afoot the plantations' (Aubrey, 409) and stocked them out of all the jails of England. James advocated plantations in the belief that they would drain away unwanted population, 'idle rogues and sturdy beggars, reprieved criminals and vagrant children' (Willson, *King James VI and I*, 329).

84 See also 'Advice to Villiers', **xiii**, 49–52. In 1592 Bacon had written deploring 'the fate of the poor Indies', 'brought from freemen to be slaves, and slaves of most miserable condition' ('In praise of the Queen', **viii**, 137).

85 B. to Sir William Jones, on his appointment as Lord Chief Justice of Ireland, May 1617, **xiii**, 205–7; 'Certain Considerations Touching the Plantation of Ireland', Jan. 1609, **x**, 47.

86 Shakespeare's Richard II voiced the general attitude (II. i. 156): 'We must supplant these rough,

rug-headed kernes / Which live like venom where no venom else / But only they have privilege to live!'; for Sir Brian MacPhelim's treacherous invitation, 1574, see article on McPhelim in *DNB*.

87 'Advice to Essex, Mar. 1597, **ix**, 95, see above chapter 5; B. to Cecil, Aug. 1602 (**x**, 45), enclosing 'Considerations Touching the Queen's Service in Ireland'.

88 See Hans Pawlisch, *Sir John Davies and the Conquest of Ireland, A Study in Legal Imperialism* (1985).

89 Willson, *King James VI and I*, 324–6. Sir Arthur Chichester, Lord Deputy of Ireland, had proposed that the bulk of the land forfeited by the Irish chieftains should go to the native inhabitants, but they ended up with less than one-tenth of it.

90 'Certain Considerations Touching the Plantation of Ireland', **xi**, 116–26.

91 B. to Sir William Jones, May 1617, **xiii**, 207. See also letter to Villiers, 5 July 1616, on ways of dealing with the recusants of Ireland 'without using the temporal sword', namely, using 'the most natural means', education (**xii**, 379).

92 Epstein, *Francis Bacon*, 76 and 100, and Marwil, 94 and 133 (see further below, chapter 32); also ibid., 112–13 on the 'common misconceptions' of Bacon's role 'from the failure to appreciate how much he desired to convince the King of his worthiness', and ibid., 151 on his alleged attempts to volunteer his services as historian, the dates and titles of which 'suggest calculated self-interest as their inspiration'. Many historians, with Marwil (144) have repeated the crude argument that when Bacon advised Villiers rather to 'make honest men yours than advance those that are otherwise because

they are yours', he was merely asking him to advance Francis Bacon. (See B. to Egerton, Apr. 1605, **x**, 250, where Bacon lamented 'the unworthiness of the history of England and the partiality and obliquity of that of Scotland'.)

93 Gardiner, in *DNB*. For an unsurpassed evaluation of Bacon's political vision, see Church, *Bacon*, 153–4.

94 Wormald, *Francis Bacon*, 17. 'Bacon's provisions for the British state were proposed in terms no less scientific in his intentions than what he offered with respect to the universe of nature.'

Chapter 22 Hunting for Popularity

1 Ben Jonson, 'Conversations with Drummond' (1618–19), in *Works*, i, 142. Some reacted negatively, viz. the parliamentary reporter who introduced Bacon ironically as 'the heir apparent of eloquence' (*CJ*, 10 May 1614). See Karl R. Wallace, 'Discussion in Parliament and Francis Bacon', *Quarterly Journal of Speech* 43 (1957): 12–21, reprinted in Vickers, *Essential Articles*.

2 For the impressed Member, Bowyer, *The Parliamentary Diary of Robert Bowyer, 1606–7*, ed. David H. Willson (1931), 120.

3 B. to King, May 1612, after eleven Parliaments, **xi**, 280. For instance, see Church, *Bacon*, 88–9.

4 There are as many interpretations of this incident as there are opinions of Bacon. For Carteret in 1747, the 'unique honour' showed the 'high esteem' in which he was widely held, and was granted 'purely out of respect to his person' and the services he had

rendered the House (*BB*, 383–4). Spedding, in 1848, found this conclusion of the 'long and eager debate' remarkable for 'the absence of all trace or hint of any personal distrust of Bacon in any quarter' (*ER*, ii, 16–18); Christopher Hill saw it as proof that Bacon was right to consider himself 'a good House of Commons man' cf. his *The English Revolution* (1965) (*Intellectual Origins*, 98–9); in 1976, however, Marwil (136) saw it as a symbol of general suspicion in the House, which Bacon soon afterwards justified by his fall, and Epstein, in 1977 (*Francis Bacon*, 104), looked on it as 'a defeat for both the Crown and Bacon', alleging (without proof) that 'his standing in the House had been shaken'.

5 Petitionary letter to the King, Aug. 1622 (not sent), **xiv**, 385.

6 'Touching the Calling of Parliament', 1613, **xi**, 372; see Russell, 45–6; and Sharpe, *Faction and Parliament*, 23. The Parliament of 1606 remained for Bacon an ideal model, because, as he later recalled, 'the ancient majesty of the Kings of this realm was then preserved'; subsidies were not demanded by the King – 'much less made the business or errand of Parliament', but were moved later in the session, in plain words, by 'an honest gentleman' and adopted on the same day (**x**, 273).

7 Neale, *Elizabeth and her Parliaments*, 299, see further chapter 29 below.

8 Epstein, *Francis Bacon*, 54. Spedding would have turned in his tomb had he known that this was put forward as what he himself had implied when discussing this speech.

9 'Amendment of the Laws', **xiii**, 65.

10 In 1588, as noticed Marwil, 65.

11 **ix**, 79.

12 **x**, 17–19. 'Better it is', he said, as if to anticipate Neale's criticism, 'to venture a man's credit by speaking than to stretch a man's conscience by silence.'

13 Bills presented by the King in response to known grievances. Bacon thought 'such Bills of grace and relief' had not so far been matched (**xii**, 15, 27, 41).

14 See chapter 8 above. It was more important, he said at the beginning of that Parliament (**xiv**, 178), to 'revive good laws' than to make new ones.

15 'Speech for General Naturalization', **x**, 313; 'Case of the Post Nati of Scotland' (1608), **vii**, 664. For a good analysis of Bacon's 'closely argued' speech (Feb. 1607) see Wormald, *Francis Bacon*, 155.

16 Epstein, *Francis Bacon*, 74. Bacon, Gardiner had written (i, 197), was 'the one man who could have guided James through those quicksands'.

17 Speech to the Lords moving a petition to the King for leave to treat of a composition with him for Wards and Tenures, 8 Mar. 1610, **xi**, 164 On the Contract, see above, chapter 18.

18 *BB*, 381.

19 Reasons for calling a Parliament, 1613, **xi**, 371.

20 Speech in the 1614 Parliament, **xii**, 38. Even if, as recent research would indicate (Peck, *Northampton*, 207–10), Northampton did not play the principal role in the intrigues that brought down the 1614 Parliament (despite statements of Wotton and others to the contrary), he was certainly involved, along with other members of the Howard faction, including his nephew, Suffolk, and the reigning favourite, Somerset (to whom Suffolk wrote that he was 'well contented to play the knave in such dissembling').

Chamberlain saw Northampton as the ringleader in what was evidently a plot to provoke the King into dissolving Parliament, and described him celebrating its dissolution by driving through London 'as it were in triumph' (9 and 30 June, i, 537–8).

21 B. to King, advising him to call a Parliament, 1615, **xii**, 177.

22 Chapter 8 above.

23 Mac., 306–7 and 320, see Spedding **viii**, 214–19. Dixon saw these things from a different angle: 'Even Edward Coke with all his authority could not repress the young Member for Middlesex' (Dixon, 64).

24 Spedding, 'Lord Macaulay's Essay on Bacon Examined', *Contemporary Review* xxviii (June–Nov. 1876), 169–89; *ER*, 50–65; **viii**, 214–25, and for Bacon's two speeches, 26 Feb. and 7 Mar., **viii**, 212–13 and 223–4. 'Mr Bacon assented to the three subsidies but not to the payments under six years . . . which would breed discontentment and endanger her majesty's safety and precedent' (*Journals*, coll. D'Ewes, 493). See today Clifford Hall, 'From Little Acorns, How Francis Bacon Lost "Friends" but Influenced People in 1593', *Baconiana*, 189 (1990), 76–87.

25 The vacancy which could have led to Bacon's appointment as Attorney General occurred early in February; the debate on the subsidy began on the 19th.

26 20 Mar. 593, **viii**, 226.

27 B. to Burghley, Mar. 1593, **viii**, 233–4; B. to Essex, soon after, **viii**, 240.

28 B. to the Queen, **viii**, 240.

29 B. to Burghley, June 1595, when he was applying for the post of Solicitor General, **viii**, 360.

30 Campbell; see further, chapter 28 below.

31 Neale, *Elizabeth and her Parliaments*, ii, 309.

32 Marwil, 75. Abbott, writing in the same spirit a century earlier, called his intervention 'the only unselfish and inconsistent action he was ever guilty of' (*Bacon and Essex*, 38).

33 See Notestein, *The House of Commons 1604–1610*, 558 n7, referring to Bacon's defence of the Commons' right to deliberate without dictation from the Upper House. 'Never again', writes Marwil (p. 95) 'will he take a position that might seem to cross the royal interests.' See also Coquillette, *Francis Bacon*, 6.

34 Essex, who had been sulking in the country, rushed to town to join the Lords in opposing Bacon's motion.

35 Dixon, 108–10. See Marwil, 94 and n61. Attorney General Coke and Solicitor General Fleming, called in to advise, found their offence treason, but only Bacon appears to have been impressed by its cause. 'A few private men', as the Bishop of Durham later complained, by enclosing thousands of acres of common land 'had dispeopled whole villages' (cited Maurice Beresford in his study of enclosures, 'Habitation versus Improvement', *Essays in the Economic and Social History of Tudor and Stuart England, in Honour of R. H. Tawney*, ed. F. J. Fisher (1961), 48.)

36 **ix**, 79–82, and for a good outline, Dixon, *Personal History*, 90–93.

37 Speech against enclosures, Nov. 1597, **ix**, 82–3.

38 *Elizabeth 1 and 2*, 23 Jan. (Tillage) and 8 Feb. (Decaying of Towns), **ix**, 79.

39 Apophthegm 40, **vii**, 169.

40 *History of Henry VII*, **vi**, 93–5.

41 An Act to prevent the misapplication of funds devoted to charitable trusts, see A. L. Beier, *The Problem of the Poor in Tudor and Early Stuart England* (1983).

42 **x**, 39.

43 **x**, 38.

44 See chapter 10 above.

45 Aikin, i, 191–2; on the petition presented to the King, 'Touching Purveyors', 27 Apr. 1604, **x**, 185.

46 Smith, 'The Great Contract', 114–15. 'That Elizabethan immortal', he wrote of Bacon, already prominent in the debates and committees working to curb the purveyors in 1589, was to figure as one of the 'leading agitators' in 1604.

47 For the part played by Bacon in this Parliament, *ER*, ii, 1–50.

48 Speech to the Commons on Sir Francis Goodwin's case, 29 Mar. 1604, **x**, 166. 'Let us deal plainly and freely with the Lords . . . It is fit great men maintain their Prerogative, so is it fit that we maintain our privileges.'

49 **xii**, 183.

50 *ER*, ii, 35.

51 Ibid., 292; Adams, 'Foreign Policy and the parliaments of 1621 and 1624', 162–4. In 1624, however, the tired King was to allow the debate on foreign affairs 'by default' (Russell, 126 and Ruigh, *Parliament of 1624*, 383).

52 Prestwich, 149.

53 Webster, *The Great Instauration*, 25, see also 514–19. Bacon he suggests, may be seen as 'the official Philosopher of the Revolution'. See Hill, *Intellectual Origins*, 96–100. In 1992, Martin, focusing on the 'peremptory royalist' and bypassing the 'Parliament man', imagined that Bacon would have been appalled by the Parliamentarians' claim to be carrying out his ideas (*Francis Bacon*, 174). But Trevor-Roper, enumerating the aims of the Parliamentarians, found every one of them high on Bacon's list, from military aggression abroad in defence of the Protestant cause, to the reform of the universities

(*From Counter-Reformation to Glorious Revolution*).

Chapter 23 *Cravenly Suing for Power and Complacently Savouring its Fruits*

1 'Proem' to the 'Interpretation of Nature', **x**, 85.
2 Mac., 320.
3 Quinton, *Francis Bacon*, 6.
4 Rebholz, *Life of Fulke Greville*, 144; W. J. Jones, *Ellesmere and Politics, 1603–1617*, (1967), 19, 20 and 61; on Donne, see J. B. Leishman, *The Monarch of Wit* (1951), 35–8, and on Northampton, Willson, *King James VI and I*, 156. See Neale, *Queen Elizabeth*, 286, and J. H. Barcroft, 'Carleton and Buckingham: The Quest for Office', *Early Stuart Studies, Essays in Honour of D. H. Willson*, ed. Reinmuth (1970), 122.
5 E.g., B. to Burghley, 16 Sept. 1580 and Jan. 1592, **viii**, 13 and 109, or 21 Mar. 1595, **viii**, 357.
6 Williams, *Bacon*, 163–4, and Mac., 340. There are no letters to Bacon from Somerset, and despite the tacit rule that every suit must go through the favourite, only one from Bacon (on his candidature for the Mastership of the Wards, in 1612, **xi**, 342). For Bacon's dealings with Somerset see chapter 29 below.
7 B. to a friend, **x**, 73–4; B. to King, autumn 1611, **xi**, 241.
8 B. to Greville, May 1595, **viii**, 359; Greville to B., 27 May 1594, **viii**, 298, warmly supporting his young kinsman.
9 B. to Cecil, 25–28 Mar. 1603, **x**, 58–70. The letters offering his services to James were all written off on 25 and 28 March.
10 B. to Cecil, 10 Mar. 1606, **x**, 289; B. to Ellesmere, summer 1606, **x**, 284; See chapter 25 for the views

of David Mathew, in *James I*, 176.
11 Gardiner, ii, 145 and iv, 107, and Willson, *Privy Counsellors*, 135, and see Bacon's application for the post of Secretary of State in 1612 (**xi**, 280), and for that of Lord Chancellor in 1616 (**xii**, 243); note 6 above for his candidature to the Mastership of the Wards. See his advice to James in 1620 (**xiv**, 86) on the appointment of a Treasurer: 'let not the regard of persons be the principal, but the nature of your affairs and the times', and Gardiner (iii, 29 and 80) on Bacon's motives in applying for the Chancellorship, 'the desire of benefiting his country' was no doubt mixed up with that of 'a sphere in which to exercise his talents'. But in applying to the King, whose policy he wanted to strengthen and broaden, it is enough 'that he believed with justice that he was eminently fitted for the place'.
12 Carteret, in *BB*, 390.
13 Gardiner, iv, 410, the great man being Buckingham.
14 Essay, 'Of Praise'.
15 'Advice to Villiers', **xiii**, 15 and 28.
16 'Concerning the Undertakers', **xii**, 48.
17 For Essex, Spedding, **ix**, 42 and 132, and chapters 2 and 5 above; for Buckingham: 'Letter of Advice to Villiers' in 1616, **xiii**, 13ff. (chapter 22 above), which Carteret admired (*BB*, 387) for its 'spirit of freedom'; letter of Jan. 1624 (**xiv**, 451).
18 Advice to James, 'Reasons for Calling a Parliament' (1613), **xi**, 369, and advice to call Parliament (1615), **xii**, 190. After the King had made his opening speech in a Parliament, Bacon thought it would be 'right if he spoke no more', and in 1614 he told him he should undertake 'not to entertain his people with curious tales and vain

hopes, but to prevent words with deeds' (Memorial for the King's Speech to Both Houses, **xii**, 27). Compare with Ralegh expressing to the French Ambassador his disgust at his treatment by James, and his resolution, if successful in Guiana, to offer his services to the King of France, while at the same time declaring to James that it was 'his dearest wish' to die for him (French dispatches cited Napier, *Lord Bacon and Sir Walter Ralegh*, 241–4, see Appendix).

19 The young Bacon, as we saw above, for merely wishing to tone down the effects of a Government motion was considered worthy of banishment, if not the Tower (Queen, cited Essex to B., 24 Aug. 1593, **viii**, 254). Buckingham demanded 'undiscoursed obedience' (Hacket, *Scrinia Reserata*, i, 39–40), and James took it for granted. When Archbishop Abbot presumed to disagree with him over the divorce of Lady Essex, James told him that, as his 'creature', he should 'reverence and follow' his judgement, and have implicit faith in it (Willson, *King James VI and I*, 341).

20 'I will not change my opinion,' Burghley told his son, 'but I will obey her Majesty's commandment, and in no wise contrary the same' (Peck, ed., *Desiderata Curiosa* (1732), i, 64–6).

21 B. to Bm, 17 May 1617 (**xiii**, 199) with reference to the divergence of views over the Spanish marriage. He had reminded James a month earlier (**xiii**, 171) of the 'bitter fruits' of a divided Council, as experienced in the 1614 Parliament; much damage might be done, he warned, in proceeding with a treaty with Spain if the Council did not 'draw all one way'.

22 B. to Bm, 24 June 1624, **xiv**, 449, still on the Spanish match.

23 *De Aug.*, **iv**, 484; Chamberlain, 24 May 1617, ii, 77, on Lady Hatton declaiming against Coke.

24 There was no love lost between Bacon and Secretary Winwood. Their disagreement when Bacon reproached Winwood for hitting a dog (chapter 2 above), betrayed a deeper irritation.

25 B. to Bm, 12 July 1617, **xiii**, 22.

26 Ibid., 223–5.

27 B. to King, 25 July 1617, **xiii**, 232–4. Bacon fancied ('though I do not wager with women's minds') 'that I can prevail more with the mother than any other man'.

28 Yelverton to B., 3 Sept. 1617, **xiii**, 247–9.

29 B. to King, 31 Aug. 1617, and to Bm 23 Aug., **xiii**, 245–6 and 242–3.

30 James in the Council, 28 Sept., Gardiner, iii, 96 and 98; Clarendon, i, 68.

31 Mac., 338; Marwil, 147.

32 Frances Yates, *Astraea* (1975). In James's reign the myth flowered again around his daughter Elizabeth, the 'Winter Queen'.

33 Ralegh to Cecil, when in the Tower because of his clandestine marriage, July 1592, Edward Edwards, *The Life of Walter Ralegh Together with his Letters* (1848), ii, 51; contemporaries, cited Willson, *King James VI and I*, 170; Ellesmere, speech on the Post-Nati, cited, ix, 152.

34 *Richard II*, I. iii. 214; on Coke, Bosworth to Milbourne, Feb. 1610, cited Gardiner, ii, 42 n.

35 Stebbing, *Sir Walter Ralegh*, 232, and Edwards, *Life of Walter Ralegh*, ii, 278–83, 268–91 and 296–7.

36 Lady Bacon's English version of Jewell's *Apologia Ecclesiae Anglicanae*, where Elizabeth appears as 'the nursing-mother of England', appeared in 1564, when Bacon was three; 'Discourse in Praise of Elizabeth', 1592, **viii**, 126–43; Chamberlain, 16 Dec. 1608, i, 276.

37 *NA*, **iii**, 144.

38 B. to Bm, on James's reasons for turning down his draft proclamation for the 1621 Parliament (chapter 8 above), approving 'his Majesty's judgment and foresight above mine own'.

39 B to Bm, 8 May 1617, **xiii**, 195.

40 B. to King, 25 Mar. 1621, **xiv**, 226. The letter Bacon wrote to Buckingham (16 Dec. 1620, see chapter 10 above) urging him, despite a first refusal, that the worst monopolies be abrogated by act of Council before the 1621 Parliament, is cited as characteristic of his servility (Abbott, *Francis Bacon*, 259) because of his apparently timid approach: 'I opined (but somewhat like Ovid's mistress, that strove, but yet as one that would be overcome...).' In fact he was trying to get his unpalatable measure through without antagonizing Buckingham – the best way to failure. After his disclaimer, *de rigueur* when dealing with such a man, he set forth the reasons for his opinion with conviction, and ended with a last effort to tempt the favourite (one he had used before with Essex and Cecil): 'it will sort to your honour.'

41 B. to Bm, 31 May 1621, **xiv**, 280; B. to Bm, Nov. 1622, **xiv**, 397; Spedding, **xiv**, 512, see among other such letters, B. to Southampton, 32 Jan. 1623, welcoming the calling of the 1624 Parliament, and hoping he might serve in it, 'that since the root of my dignity is saved to me it might also bear fruit, and that I may not die in dishonour'.

42 Coleridge ('The Friend', Essay 8, in *Essays*, ii, 1818). A fervent admirer of the 'immortal Verulam', Coleridge thought Bacon neither ungrateful nor corrupt, and looked on his fall as a punishment 'for trifles'. But failing to see in historical perspective the fallen Chancellor's appeals to James (aimed above all at a restoration of honour which only a King could grant), Coleridge found in him a 'servile compliance' which ran counter to his whole concept of Bacon's unity of spirit. So compelling was the conflict in his mind that he wondered, against all his beliefs, 'whether Lord Bacon does really form the only known exception to Baseness in union with a first rate genius?' (Coleridge, *Universal Dictionary of Knowledge*, 16). See also Blake, revolted by Bacon's reference to the King as 'a mortal god on earth' (Geoffrey Keynes, *Complete Writings of William Blake* (1966), 196–210). What Bacon actually said (**xi**, 266) was that the King's voice was 'not the voice of God', but 'the voice of God in man'.

43 Emerson, 'Lord Bacon', in *The Early Lectures*, i, 310–66. Emerson was inspired with 'a new courage and confidence in the powers of man at the sight of so great a work done under such great disadvantage by one scholar' (ibid., 335–6); but, like Coleridge, he was overwhelmed with 'the impossibility of welding together vice and genius' – vice being that his 'Archangel of knowledge' should be contaminated by the, to him, absolutely alien 'spirit of courts'.

44 Vivian C. Hopkins, 'Emerson and Bacon', *American Literature*, xxix, 4 (Jan. 1958), 408–30.

45 Essay, 'of Praise'. 'To suggest what a man should be under colour of praising what he is, was ever a form due in civility to the great,' *De Aug*, iv, 488.

46 See note 36 above.

47 'To the King', *AL*, **iii**, 262.

48 Essay, 'Of Ceremonies and Respects'. Bacon was not alone in his high hopes of the 'British

Solomon' during those years, but few had so strong a desire to influence the King at such a propitious time. As Michèle Le Doeuff put it, Bacon was attempting 'to capture, in a flattering mirror, the will of the real king' (*Francis Bacon, Du Progrès et de la promotion des savoirs (1605)*, 1991, p. lxi).

49 Advice to call a Parliament, 1615 (**xii**, 190). Bacon frequently employed this technique, e.g. in the Parliament of 1604 (**x**, 182); before presenting his strong protest against purveyance; and when protesting (13 Aug. 1613; **xi**, 386–7) against certain harsh instructions for the Irish Parliament ('But these things that I write are perhaps but my own simplicities. Your Majesty's wisdom must steer and ballast the ship'); or when tempting James to take on the role of codifier of the English law (1622, **xiv**, 361).

50 A 'teacher of kings', see below, chapter 27; Marwil (151–33) described this History as an ineffectual bid to 'revive the author's fortunes', see chapter 32.

51 Spedding, **xiv**, 302, and *History of Henry VII*, **vi**, 10ff. Bacon, wrote a contemporary (cited *BB*, 410) had 'perfectly put himself into the King's own garb and livery, giving as sprightly a view of certain secrets of his Council as if he himself had been President of it'.

52 B. to Bm, 18 Apr. 1623, **xiv**, 423.

53 Notes for advice to Bm, 25 Nov. 1623 to Jan. 1624, **xiv**, 442–7. See on the these notes, Ruigh, *Parliament of 1624*, 262–3. The same concern is visible here as in Bacon's letters to Essex three decades earlier (see above, chapter 22), and the same clear-sighted advice: 'win the Queen', which becomes, 'keep great with the Prince.'

54 Epstein, *Francis Bacon*, 120, 137, 181.

55 *ER*, ii, 365–6. The proclamation ordered the gentry of London to move into the country, but London had become so empty that it was not found necessary. Still it would do no harm, said James, and would show his 'care'.

56 Essay, 'Of Counsel'. At the end of his career, Bacon was convinced that he had been 'one that was never author of immoderate, no, nor unsafe or unfortunate counsel' (B. to Bm, 31 May 1621, **xiv**, 280).

57 Mac., 333.

58 See chapter 22 above.

59 Already in 1608 he had noted, in a general review of the nation's affairs, that if trouble did not start first in Scotland, he did not anticipate it at home (*CS*, 28 July).

60 Chapters 8 and 21 above.

61 Trevor-Roper, 'General Crisis', 56.

62 B. to Bm, 23 July 1620, **xiv**, 110.

63 *De Aug.*, **v**, 32, see G. R. Elton, 'Reform in an Age of Change', in *Studies in Tudor and Stuart Politics and Government* (1983), iii, 277–8. Epstein (*Francis Bacon*, 137) reproached Bacon with presenting no major programme of reform to the 1621 Parliament, but, as Elton saw it, no major reform was possible without a widespread recognition of the need for it, and above all, without royal support.

64 Trevor-Roper, 'General Crisis', 58.

65 Wormald, *Francis Bacon*, 210, 213.

66 Marwil, 114, also 25, 135, 201.

67 Hurstfield, 'Explaining James', letter to *TLS*, 23 May 1935. 'Men of deep wisdom are objects of jealousy to kings, as being too close observers' (*De Aug.*, **v**, 48).

68 James's remark, June 1616, later recalled by Bacon (B. to King, 18 Sept. 1612, **xi**, 311: his pages, said James, were 'no tricks nor novelties, but true passages of business'); Bm to B., 9 Sept. 1619, **xiv**, 43–4.

69 Epstein, *Francis Bacon*, 121–1; Zaller, 20; Derek Hirst: 'The good intentions he trumpeted seem to have produced little more than self-righteous and unsolicited advice . . .' (*Authority and Conflict: England, 1503–1658* (1986), 125).

70 Bm to B., 9 Sept. 1619, **xiv**, 44.

71 Text of the *Ordinances*, **vii**, 759–74 (see chapter 10 above), Zaller, 95. 'More needed to be done,' wrote Prestwich, 'but it was not Bacon's fault that he fell before he accomplished more' (281).

72 **xiii**, 182–93; Ritchie, *Cases Decided by Bacon*, Preface, pp. iii–iv and xvi–xviii; see the decision that a contract to procure a knighthood for money should not be enforced, as tending to make matters of knighthood venal and mercenary (ibid., 67). A similar one was made once again in 1925.

73 Prestwich, 280.

74 Coquillette, *Francis Bacon*, 200, and **xiv**, 100; 'This measure came to nothing', Spedding noted (**xiii**, 266–7), once again Bacon was too far ahead of his time. Spedding's analysis, well worth reading, is endorsed today by Coquillette, *Francis Bacon*, 215.

75 Chamberlain, 24 May 1617, ii, 70.

76 Epistle Dedicatory, *The Great Instauration* (1602), **iv**, 11.

77 B. to Bodley, Apr. 1605, **x**, 253.

78 'Proem', **x**, 85.

79 SS, **ii**, 576; *De Aug.*, **iv**, 404, and for more such 'quaeres', **iv**, 417; Roland G. Usher, 'Francis Bacon's Knowledge of Law French', *Modern Language Notes*, xxiv (1919), 28–32.

80 **iv**, 265–70.

81 *Catalogue of Particular Histories*, **iv**, 265.

82 B. to King, 6 Aug. 1612, **xi**, 314. As Bacon had written to Essex (Jan. 1595, **viii**, 345), 'the waters of Parnassus quench appetites and desires'.

83 *De Aug.*, **v**, 64 and 74. See *De Aug.*,

v, 74: 'the ablest persons both to improve their own fortunes and to assail the fortunes of others are those who have no public duty to perform, but are ever occupied in this study of advancement in life.'

Chapter 24 'With not a Trace of Pity for any Human Being'

The chapter title is from W. G. Thorpe, *The Hidden Lives of Shakespeare and Bacon, and their Business Connections* (1897), see chapter 31.

1 Mac., 320.

2 Abbott, *Bacon's Essays*, p. xxiii; Hugh Trevor-Roper, address given in St Michael's Church, St Albans, 22 Jan. 1961, publ. *Encounter* 18 (Feb. 1962): 75–7. 'His intellectual greatness', writes Trevor-Roper, 'was rendered purer' through being 'unentangled by any genial warmth of heart'. As Kuno Fischer, following this long tradition, had put it a century earlier, 'the degree of warmth belonging to his heart stood very close to zero' (*Francis Bacon of Verulam*).

3 See David Lloyd, *State Worthies*, chapter 2 above.

4 Trevelyan, *England under the Stuarts*, 115–18; Neale *Queen Elizabeth*, 343 ('What wisdom, what subtlety! What coldness of heart!'); Prestwich, 268; Pitcher, 24.

5 Mac., 329; Campbell, iii, 66. The only previous notice of Bacon as a torturer comes from the anti-Stuart historian, Lucy Aikin, who in 1822 had referred to his interrogation of Peacham as 'an indelible stain on his memory' (ii, 166).

6 Coquillette, *Francis Bacon*, p. viii and 285; Adrian Berry in the *Sunday Telegraph*, 19 Feb. 1995. On the abandonment of torture in the eighteenth century because of

the development of regular police forces, and on its recrudescence after World War II, and its present systematic, worldwide and far more refined use under the provocation of terrorism, see Peters, *Torture*, chapters 3 and 4.

7 'At the present day' – so a contemporary of Macaulay's could begin his study of the subject – 'when the practice of torture has wholly disappeared from the criminal procedure of every European nation . . .' (Jardine, 4). Meanwhile, however, England was transporting large numbers of convicts to Australia, where they received a hundred lashes for merely being seen to smile on a chain-gang. Smith, *De Republica Anglorum*, ii, 105; Hall, 'Some Perspectives on the Use of Torture in Bacon's Time and the Question of his "Virtue"', *Anglo-American Law Review*, 18.4 (1989), 296.

8 State Trials, i, 1338, cited James Heath, *Torture and English Law* (1982), 143; Coke's speech for the prosecution of Guy Fawkes, cited, Bowen, *Coke*, 223. See on Coke's expedition, in issuing a warrant, signing it and executing it himself, all in one day, Jardine, 46–7.

9 Warrant in the King's handwriting, Jardine, 47.

10 Reported Chamberlain, 2 Apr. 1606, i, 221.

11 Christopher Devlin, an account of Southwell's trial by Father Garnet and others, *The Life of Robert Southwell, Poet and Martyr* (1956), pp. 309–11. For Coke's orations as Attorney General, aimed at inciting those who (as they were to do with Floyd, chapter 15 above) might 'urge a more sharp death', and on his summings up, gloating over the details of the hanging, drawing and quartering awaiting the condemned, see Bowen, *Coke*, 223–4.

12 Hall, 'Some Perspectives on the Use of Torture', 304–5; see the Countess of Shrewsbury's case, Jardine, 65, and Hall, 'Bacon and the Legality of Torture', *Baconiana* 187 (1987), 30; Coke on the interrogation of Peacock in 1620, *Institutes*, iii, 35.

13 Mac., 329.

14 Jardine, 15; Hall, 'Some Perspectives on the Use of Torture', 305.

15 Ibid.; Langbein, *Torture and the Law of Proof*; Heath, *Torture and English Law* (1982).

16 Hall, 'Some Perspectives on the Use of Torture', 300ff.

17 Ibid., 297–9, and more fully, Jardine. (In James's reign exact figures are not available because some of the Council records are lost.) In particular the case of Felton, the murderer of Buckingham in 1628, discussed by Jardine (7, 11, 26, 40 and 55) and by Hall, 'Some Perspectives on the Use of Torture', 309–11, and 'Bacon and the Legality of Torture', 28–9. Macaulay's jibe that no legal sycophant would dare to defend the practice is another of his mistakes of fact. James consulted the judges as to the legality of applying the rack to Felton because this was not a case of treason, but of felony. They found that, except in cases of high treason, torture could not be applied under common law, i.e. without resorting to the prerogative. It had been applied twice in the two previous years, and would again be used in 1640, without discussion.

18 See on the two forms of prerogative, Hall, 'Some Perspectives on the Use of Torture', 306 and 309, and Coquillette, *Francis Bacon*, 287.

19 It was referred to as 'the ordinary torture', or 'the accustomed torture of the rack', Jardine, 15, 59 and 67. See Spedding, **xii**, 92.

20 Burghley published two pamphlets in 1583, claiming to have

racked Campion 'in as charitable manner as such a thing might be' (Paul Johnson, *Elizabeth, A Study in Power and Intellect*, 1974, 351).

21 Letter of the Papal Secretary of State, in Johnson, *Elizabeth*, 241.

22 'Letter of Advice to the Queen' (**viii**, 47–53), probably written for Burghley in 1584, in which Bacon anticipated a more humane version of the oath of loyalty imposed on Catholics (which would be adopted in 1606). For his views on the unnecessary severity of penal laws, see 'Pacification of the Church', **x**, 114 and 126. See also *In Felicem Memoriam*, **vi**, 314–15.

23 **viii**, 307–8.

24 Ibid., 309.

25 On Bacon's 'Tower employment', Spedding, **viii**, 302–5, 313–14, 316–20.

26 19 Dec. 1596, Feb. 1597 (a conspiracy to burn the Queen's ships), 13 Apr. 1597, 17 Apr. 1598, see Jardine, Appendix, 99–100. Heath found another case in which torture may have been used on 19 Oct. 1598 (*Torture and English Law*, 135).

27 14 Apr. 1597, John Gerard, *The Autobiography of an Elizabethan*, translated from the Latin original (*c.* 1609) by Philip Caraman (1951), 106; Hall, 'Some Perspectives on the Use of Torture', 318.

28 14 Apr. 1597, with Coke in charge (Gerard, *Autobiography of an Elizabethan* (1609, trans. Philip Caraman, 1951), 108, 124, and for the Gunpowder Plot, 200). Heath noted that after his session with Ward, Gerard was not further tortured (*Torture and English Law*, 129).

29 Rawley, i. 3. See **xii**, 316; **viii**, 137, also 'the poor commoners', **xiii**, 48; and see the tone of B. to Bm, praying that his Majesty may pardon a man who had 'retracted his wicked opinions ... because of the misery of the man' (Dec. 1619,

xiv, 67).

30 Full story, **xii**, 90–128 and *ER*, ii, 93–140; see Gardiner, ii, 274–80.

31 Cited Dick, introduction to *Aubrey's Brief Lives*, 122.

32 Knox and Cartwright, cited Anderson, *Francis Bacon*, 75 (commenting on Bacon's religious writings). Catholics, of course, were equally ferocious.

33 The intimidating came from the other side. Coke, only too happy to volunteer his opinion (as he was to do repeatedly, the year after, on the Overbury case) so greatly imposed on his fellow judges that they dared not opine against him. It was not an innovation for a king – the supreme Judge over all of them, when sitting in Parliament – to consult with his judges. ('Neither was there ever a King, I am persuaded,' Bacon declared in praise of James, 'that did so often confer with his judges,' **xii**, 143.) Though later, in his new role, Coke was to pronounce against extrajudicial consultation, here it was the '*auricular* taking of opinions, single and apart' – which prevented him from influencing the other judges – that Coke found 'new and dangerous' (**xii**, 107). Bacon approved both forms of consultation, 'for private opinion is more free, but before others it is more reverend' ('Of Counsel', 1612). Gardiner, Whig as he was, thought Bacon's wish to keep the judges in relative subjection to the throne had stood the test of modern experience (iii, 3 and n1). He quoted de Tocqueville on the dangers of allowing a single, unrepresentative body – in this case the Common Law judges – to override Statute Law.

34 Note in James's hand, preserved in Dalrymple's *Memorials* (1766), cited **xii**, 105–6.

35 Gardiner, ii, 279, Coke's opposi-

tion meant that the King did not
have the support of the whole
King's Bench. He maintained (**xii**,
120, contradicting his decision on
Ralegh, ten years earlier) that
defamation, importing that the
King was unworthy to govern,
was not treason if it did not 'disable his title'. Bacon feared that
an avalanche of seditious pamphlets might be expected if
Peacham's writings were not held
treasonable; but what he actually
advised is not known.

36 Warrant for the torture and proposed interrogatories, reproduced
xii, 92. Winwood, as Principal
Secretary and Senior Privy Councillor being doubly concerned in
the proceeding, was not at all disposed to delegate his powers, and
was not friendly to Bacon (see
chapter 23, n24 above). B. to King,
21 Jan., **xii**, 96.

37 B. to King, 28 Feb. 1615 and to
same 12 Mar., enclosing his report
on the interrogation of Peacham
(10 Mar.), countersigned by Crewe
and Yelverton, **xii**, 122–7.

38 Dalrymple's *Memorials*, 61, cited
Spedding, **xii**, 105; B. to King, 12
Mar., see preceding note.

39 Chamberlain, i, 612–16; xii, 120–22
and 127–8. The suspension of the
execution, Macaulay concluded,
arose out of the 'obvious futility'
of the charges and the supposed
'shame' of the Government.

40 21 Jan. 1615, **xii**, 96.

41 On Bacon's fainting fits, Rawley,
i, 17.

42 *De Aug.*, **iv**, 479.

43 B. to King, 5 Feb. 1620, on Peacock, a schoolmaster who claimed
to have affected the King's judgement by sorcery – something still
looked on at the time as a reality
and tantamount to assassination
(see Giordano Bruno's plan 'to
pull off an ultimate coup against
the popes by permanently enchanting Pope Clement VIII',

John Bossy, *Giordano Bruno* (1991),
154). And in 1662 a mother and
daughter were executed for
witchcraft on the word of an enlightened doctor, Sir Thomas
Browne, author of *Religio Medici*,
after he had condemned by an
upright judge, Sir Matthew Hale
(Montagu, *Life of Francis Bacon*, p.
clxxix). Bacon thought that the
evidence against witches should
not rashly be believed, for they
are 'themselves imaginative, and
believe oft-times that which they
do not' (*SS*, **vi**, 642). He was unconvinced in this case, as he had
been for Peacham, but conceded
to James that Peacock deserved it
'as well as Peacham did'.

44 On the present widespread use of
refined forms of torture, see n6
above.

45 **xii**, 93; Fuller, *Worthies*, 394; Isaac
Walton, *The Lives of John Donne,
Sir Henry Wotton, Richard Hooker,
George Herbert and Robert Sanderson*
(1640, ed., 1962), 127.

46 e.g. *Cymbeline*, V. v., and *Othello*,
V. ii.

47 See Hall, 'Some Perspectives on
the Use of Torture', 292.

48 'Here were three seminary priests
hanged and quartered the last
week, but what is one among so
many?' (Chamberlain, 26 Apr.
1602, i, 138–9, see editor's remark,
i, 19).

49 Ibid., 11 June 1612, i, 355.

50 Dick, Introduction to Aubrey, 23–
4.

51 Chief Justice Alfred Denning, see
below, chapter 32.

52 See above, chapters 2 and 5. A
protest to the RSC elicited a courteous reply. The author, who had
now left their staff, troubled that
she might have 'innocently
libelled a man she admires', was
certain she had found the information in books she had consulted, but no reference could be
supplied.

53 Peter Levi, *The Life and Times of William Shakespeare* (1988).

54 e.g. with Antonio Pérez, one-time Secretary to Philip II, see below, chapter 30.

55 Christopher Devlin, *Hamlet's Divinity and Other Essays* (1965), 65 (source traced with the author's kind assistance). Also, Devlin, *Life of Robert Southwell*, 254.

56 Examination of John Ballard, 16 and 18 Aug. 1586, in Pollen, *Mary Queen of Scots and the Babington Plot*, 137–8. Ballard was tortured, but not on this occasion, see Heath, *Torture and English Law*, 128.

57 'In Praise of Knowledge', the Second Counsellor's advice to the 'Prince of Purpoole', Gray's Inn Revels, Christmas 1592, **viii**, 125.

58 See chapter 4 above.

59 Devlin, *Life of Robert Southwell*, 254.

60 On Topcliffe, 'spy and sergeant, judge and counsel, warder and executioner, all in one', see among others, Devlin, *Hamlet's Divinity*, 62 (on his boasting that he had stretched one of Campion's companions a foot longer than God had made him), 65–9 (on his boast that he had the Queen's favour), and p. 364.

61 *De Aug.*, **iv**, 387; also **v**, 373 on the mitigation of pain. Compare Bacon's attitude to that of Giordano Bruno who, when he knew a man could not bear torture, coolly suggested he should be subjected to more (Bossy, *Giordano Bruno*, 99 and 159).

62 'Magnalia Naturae', **iii**, 167; see chapter 22 above.

Chapter 25   The Lukewarm Hater

1 Zaller, 90.

2 Amboise, Preface to *Histoire Naturelle*, 16, in which he speaks of Bacon as 'loved by the people and cherished by the great'; Aubrey, *Brief Lives*, ed. Clark, 67.

3 17 Feb, 1607, **x**, 325, see **viii**, 76; *NA*, **iii**, 136.

4 Mathew, *James I*, 176.

5 B. to Burghley, 6 May 1586, **viii**, 59, see Bacon's observations about himself, *CS*, **xi**, 52.

6 B. to TM (referring to spring 1619), Mar. 1621, **xiv**, 201.

7 Memorial of Henry, Prince of Wales, **vi**, 328; B. to Princess Elizabeth, Oct. 1625 (**xiv**, 535–6); see B. to Bm in 1623 (**xiv**, 450), urging him to do all he could for that 'excellent Lady, whose fortune is so distant from her merit and virtue'.

8 Rawley, i, 3–4.

9 B. to King, 1 Jan. 1609, **xi**, 114–15. Whenever he mentioned Elizabeth ('of blessed memory'), Bacon could not refrain from pausing to remark, 'a most prudent and admirable Queen' (1615, **xii**, 245), or 'comparable and to be ranked with the greatest of Kings' (1614, **xii**, 7), see Spedding, **vi**, 284, and **xi**, 107–110. De Thou, see below, chapter 34, n74.

10 B. to Essex on Egerton's recent appointment as Lord Keeper, 10 May 1596, **ix**, 30. Justice, he wrote, which had begun 'to shake and sink', was now 'mightily established'.

11 B. to Egerton, late summer 1597, **ix**, 62. It was to Egerton Bacon turned for help when seized in the street 'upon a despite' by a notorious goldsmith, who, like Shylock, rather than have his money, preferred to see him in prison (B. to Egerton, 24 Sept. 1598, **ix**, 107). On Bacon's fitness to succeed him, B. to Villiers (future Buckingham), 21 Feb. 1615, **xii**, 255. On their relations, B. to King, Jan. 1615 and Feb. 1616, **xii**, 112 and 249. Most of Bacon's official letters to James during that year included some anxious or

hopeful words about the Chancellor's condition, and showed his efforts to 'rouse and raise his spirits' (**xii**, 248).

12 Sackville, for whom Bacon wrote an 'account from the sweet air of the country' in 1625 (now lost), was the brother of Bacon's 'great admirer and friend', Richard, Earl of Dorset (Aubrey, 171); 'I find Sir Edward Sackville very zealous to do you service,' wrote the watchful Meautys to Bacon, 3 Jan. 1622, adding, on 7 Jan., that Sackville and Montgomery 'seemed to contend who should have most patience' in waiting at Court on his behalf. One of Bacon's few bequests to personal friends was to Sackville ('the ring with the crushed diamond which the Prince gave me', **xiv**, 228). On Pembroke, see Clarendon, i, 71–2; Bacon saw eye to eye with him over political issues, such as the war with Spain, and both men urged James not to make his tactless proclamation in the 1621 Parliament. After his fall Bacon wrote to him acknowledging 'the moderation and affection his Lordship showed in my business' (Sept. 1621, draft, **xiv**, 299, n2). On Falkland, see Bacon's letter of 11 Mar. 1622: 'It is the best accident amongst men, when they hap to be obliged to those whom naturally and personally they love, as I ever did your Lordship' (**xiv**, 344). Greville, Bacon's friend throughout (see their cordial and easy letters in 1594, **viii**, 292 and 359–60), had boldly defended him before his fall against a defamer (Mar. 1618, **xiii**, 307), and after it, warmly commended his *History of Henry VII* (3 Jan. 1623, **xiv**, 325–6). Bacon praised him as one who used 'his much access to Queen Elizabeth' so as to do 'many men good' (Apophthegm 235, **vii**, 158).

13 B. to Bristol, 18 Apr. 1623, **xiv**, 424–5.

14 See chapter 16 above. The good news was that certain abuses against the English Catholics were being checked, see further J. Loomie, 'Bacon and Gondomar: An Unknown Link in 1618', *Renaissance Quaterly* 21 (1968), 1–10.

15 B. to Lady Paulett, 23 Sept. 1593, Dixon, 76–7; see above chapter 24. For examples of the appreciation of his friends, see Francis Allen to AB (17 Aug. 1589, **viii**, 111) on some assistance he needed: 'your brother hath used me with great humanity'; or Henry Gosnold to AB (28 Nov. 1592, **viii**, 121) on the joy and sorrow he had given Bacon, 'your kind brother and mine especial friend', with some good news and bad (the sorrow was for Anthony's ill-health).

16 Mac., 337.

17 Campbell, iii, 92.

18 B. to Cecil, 9 Apr. 1601, **x**, 3–5. Further insults came from Coke, which Bacon, as he put it, 'answered with silence'. We have seen his quick anger on other occasions (chapter 16).

19 Aubrey, 171. The counteraction aroused Lady Bacon's mistrust (Lady B. to AB, 23 Jan. 1595, **viii**, 347), Anthony's conviction that there was underhand dealing on Cecil's part, and Bacon's own uncertainty as to where he stood with his cousin. But Cecil did assist him on occasion, and he once advanced £300 to get Bacon out of prison for debt. Bacon addressed him as 'one that I ever found careful of my advancement, and yet more jealous of my wrongs' (9 Apr. 1601, **x**, 3–5).

20 The briar image: Essay, 'Of Revenge'.

21 Notestein, *Four Worthies*, 79; Rowley, 'Francis Bacon', i, 15. See e.g. G. Walter Steeves, according to whom Bacon was so embit-

tered by Coke's promotion to Attorney General and so jealous of his marriage to Lady Hatton that, on attaining power himself, twenty-two years later, 'he at once deprived Coke of his office of Chief Justice' (*Francis Bacon*, (1910), 8).

22 *BB*, 398; speech at the trial of Lord Sanquhar, **xi**, 291; *Meditationes Sacrae*, **vii**, 246.

23 Northampton to Rochester, cited above, chapter 18, n5; Spedding, **i**, 11–12, and chapters 18 and 19 above.

24 Cecil's disposition towards Bacon should be seen in the light of his confession to Bodley (chapter 6 above) that he had done his best to block the advancement of Essex's friends. Charles Williams described the 'amiable breachless wall' which Cecil presented to Bacon for so many years (*Bacon*, 185).

25 Abbott, *Francis Bacon*, 177ff., and *Bacon and Essex*, 252–4.

26 Anne, to herself, in *Persuasion* (1818), chapter 21.

27 **xi**, 12; B. to King, 31 May 1612, **xi**, 279–81.

28 B. to King, 31 May 1612 and 18 Sept. 1612, **xi**, 279–81 and 313; B. to Cecil, Aug. 1602, **x**, 45, enclosing his paper, 'The Queen's Service in Ireland'.

29 Bacon recalled his remark and the King's answer in Apophthegm 9, **vii**, 175; Rawley, i, 15.

30 Hurstfield, *The Queen's Wards*, 349; Prestwich, 66. Others at the time shared Bacon's view of Cecil, including Chancellor Ellesmere (Jones, *Ellesmere and Politics*, 40), and Gardiner concluded that 'Bacon spoke truly of Salisbury' (ii, 144).

31 Chamberlain, 17 Dec. 1612, ii, 391. ('He paints his little cousin to the life.')

32 B. to King, 31 May 1612, **xi**, 279–81;

to King advising the calling of a Parliament in 1613, **xi**, 369–71, and again in 1615, **xii**, 185.

33 Toby Matthew, cited in full chapter 2 above. Marwil (143), contradicting Rawley's statement that Bacon was 'no defamer of any man to his prince', adduces a remark of Bacon's to the King (**xii**, 101–2) on the 'farming' of recusants' penalties – that Winwood was not 'versed much in these things'; but Bacon's objective review bears out Matthew. 'It is my Lord Treasurer and the Exchequer must help, if it is to be holpen,' he continued, and went on to praise Coke, who *was* 'versed' in those things.

34 Willson, *King James VI and I*, 178, and see chapter 19 above.

35 B. to King, 31 May 1612, **xi**, 279–81.

36 Notestein, *Four Worthies*, 78.

37 Jonson to Drummond of Hawthornden in 1619, *Works*, i, 162.

38 See chapter 9 above. Martin suggests that Coke's resentment was partly based on envy of Bacon's supernumerary status and favour as Queen's Counsel Extraordinary, whereby he bypassed Coke's own superior authority (*Francis Bacon*, 124).

39 Aubrey, 'Life of Sir Edward Coke', in Aubrey, 226.

40 B. to King, 22 Jan. 1616, **xii**, 232, and 12 Aug. 1617, **xiii**, 239.

41 So Marwil (78), referring to Chudleigh's Case, pleaded by Bacon in the Exchequer, Easter 1596 (**vii**, 617ff., esp. 618); Coquillette, *Francis Bacon*, 11 and 30.

42 Bacon told the King he expected to be judged by posterity as as good a lawyer for his *Rules and Decisions* as Coke was for his *Reports* ('Amendment of the Laws', 1616, **xiii**, 70); 27 Jan. 1615, **xii**, 234.

43 Anonymous letter of advice to Coke in 1616, see **xiii**, 122–7.

Bacon himself looked on Coke's overbearing ways as 'a kind of sickness of my Lord Coke's' (B. to King, 21 Feb. 1615).

44 B. to King, 27 Jan. 1615, **xii**, 102; B. to Bm, 13 Sept. 1619 on the sentence awarded to Suffolk and Lady Suffolk, **xiv**, 55; 'This I will say of him, and I will say as much to ages: that never man's position and his place were better met in a business than my Lord Coke and my Lord Chief Justice in the cause of Overbury' (charge against the Countess of Somerset, May 1616, **xii**, 302). See also the regrets expressed by the Chief of Shin Bet (Israeli Security Service) over the five bus-passenger victims of a bomb in August 1995: their lives could not be saved, he said, because Shin Bet had been prevented from using suitably 'extreme forms of interrogation' (*Weekly Guardian*, 29 Oct. 1995).

45 A seat on the Privy Council, **xi**, 379–82; Chamberlain, 14 Oct. 1613, i, 479, see **xi**, 379–82.

46 The fear that his customers might take their fees to other courts may have been a factor. Meanwhile, as Privy Councillor, the King complained, Coke insisted on 'running separate courses from the rest of the Council'. Rather than advise on what could be done, said James, he was always drawing attention to what should not be done; he made himself popular, not because he was liberal, affable or 'magnificent', but 'by design only, in pulling down the government'. Bacon, 'Remembrances of his Majesty's Narrative Touching the Lord Coke', Nov. 1616, **xiii**, 95.

47 B. to King, 21 Feb. 1616, **xii**, 249.

48 2 Oct. 1616 (lost, though the contents are clear from the King's reply, on 3 Oct.), and 6 Oct., **xiii**, 76–8, drafted by Bacon, and signed jointly by Bacon and Ellesmere.

49 Chamberlain, 26 Oct. 1616, ii, 29, see also 6 July, ii, 14, and 7 Dec., ii, 41, where Chamberlain reports that Bacon 'committed two of his own men to the Fleet' for giving orders for a process against Coke in his name.

50 *BB*, 398.

51 Rawley, i, 13.

52 Mac., 320.

Chapter 26 'Without Steady Attachments'

The chapter title is from Campbell, iii, 140.

1 *De Sap.*, **vi**, 706; on Bacon's care of his Cooke relations, particularly of his widowed aunt Anne, see Harold Hardy, 'Bacon's Warwickshire Relations', *Baconiana* 39 (July 1912), 134–43.

2 See dedication of the *Essays* to his brother-in-law in 1612: 'Missing my brother, I found you next, in respect of bond of near alliance, and of straight friendship . . . my contemplations ever found rest in your loving conference and judgement'; B. to Sir Thomas Lucy, 1598, a letter written on the marriage of his cousin William (mistakenly dated by Spedding in 1601), **ix**, 369.

3 Anne, daughter of his half-sister Anne Bacon. Caesar was called to Bacon's death-bed in Arundel House, see Edmund Lodge, *Life of Sir Julius Caesar Knt; with Memoirs of his Family and Descendents* (1810); Fuller, *Worthies*, 393–4.

4 Receipts and Disbursements, 24 June to 21 Nov. 1618, **xiii**, 327–36.

5 Last will and testament, **xiv**, 539ff. The poor of Twickenham were not forgotten, and Bacon's chambers at Gray's Inn were to be sold 'to bestow some little present

relief upon twenty-five poor scholars in both universities'.

6 Henry Wotton, *Reliquiae Wottonianae* (1641), 392; Meautys to B., 11 Sept. 1622, cited Chambers Bunten, *Sir Thomas Meautys and his Friends* (1918), 29, see also 18–35. Through Bacon's influence, Meautys was appointed Clerk of the Council in 1619, and entered Parliament for Cambridge in Jan. 1621 – in time to intervene there on his master's behalf (chapter 12 above). He married Bacon's great-niece fourteen years after Bacon's death.

7 See frontispiece, and chapter 2 above. In the inscription, *sic sedebat*: Jesus Christ 'sat thus' on the edge of the well, and when the woman of Samaria came to draw water, told her that he would give her 'living water' (Gospel according to St John, chapter 4, verses 6–14).

8 Aubrey, 171, 308, 313–14.

9 Arthur Wilson, *Annals of King James I* (1653, ed. 1706), ii, 734.

10 Aubrey, 173. According to his contemporary, John Ray (cited in Lawson Dick's introduction to ibid., 58), he was 'a little too inclined to credit strange relations' (such as that the 'crook-back Cecil' was one of the 'stallions' of Lady Mary Pembroke); Chamberlain, 24 Mar. 1621, ii, 356.

11 Mac., 320.

12 A summary description of Bacon, appended under his portrait, Johnson, *Elizabeth*, 10, see also 371.

13 A. L. Rowse, in *The Times*, 24 Apr. 1971.

14 David Holloway, reviewing *A Cornishman Abroad* by Rowse, in the *Daily Telegraph*, 1 Mar. 1976; Mac., 323; Lytton Strachey, *Portraits in Miniature* (1931), 177; J. Cotter Morison, *Macaulay* (1882), 55–9; Harriet Martineau, *Biographical Sketches*, 419.

15 See on D'Ewes, Thomas Hearne, *The History of Richard II* (1729), p. xxxvi, and *Niger Scacarii* (1728), p. x; Simonds D'Ewes, *Autobiography* (ed. 1729), 387.

16 Lady Bacon to AB, 17 Apr. 1593, **viii**, 244 (Antonio Pérez did not arrive in England until the summer). See e.g. the two austere 'companions of bed and board' (Richard Hooker and Bishop Jewell), described in Walton's *Lives*, 168. Bacon kept Henry Percy in his service, left him £100 in his will, and entrusted his manuscripts to him for delivery to his legatee (**xiv**, 540). Birch's misreading (Birch, i, 143) is explained by Spedding, **viii**, 245. On Pérez, see further chapter 30 below.

17 Daphne Du Maurier, *Golden Lads, A Story of Anthony Bacon, Francis and their Friends* (1975), 68. The tone of Anthony's friendships may be gathered from a letter addressed to him with youthful enthusiasm by his most faithful follower, Jacques Petit: 'I humbly kiss your poor sick hands . . . I have found in Anthony Bacon my Apollo and my oracle' (Christmas 1595, ibid., 147–8). But the trouble could have been serious. In 1631 a relation by marriage to the Bacons was to be executed for unnatural vice (Anon., *The Arraignment and Conviction of Mervyn Touchet, Earl of Castlehaven*, 1942).

18 AB to Essex, reporting on a conversation with his aunt, Lady Russell, Sept. 1596, Birch, ii, 132–7. In a letter to Dr Barker, 1597 (cited du Maurier, *Golden Lads*, 196–7), Anthony wrote: 'I have never been troubled by any venereal disease, because I have never had intercourse with anyone, and the doctors do not praise my abstinence.'

19 For some of her letters, see **viii**, 112–17, 243–4, 269–71, 300, 312 and 364.

20 B. to Lady B., 14 Feb. 1594, **viii**, 271.

21 AB to Lady B., 1594, cited du

Maurier, *Golden Lads*, 122.

22 Jan. to May 1592, 'In Praise of Worthiest Affection, Love', from 'A Conference of Pleasure', 17 Nov. 1592 (see Spedding, **viii**, 119–22), in *Northumberland MS*, 9–13.

23 B. to King, 25 July 1617, **xiii**, 233, and chapter 23 above. See Apophthegm 36, **vii**, 168, for Bacon's appreciation of Lady Hatton. The gift of seeds was noticed by du Maurier in Bacon's accounts (*Golden Lads*, 143).

24 *ER*, i, 106.

25 *NA*, **iii**, 152; B. to Cecil, 3 July 1603, **x**, 80, also **x**, 290–91; see Hurstfield, *The Queen's Wards*, 134, 143, 147, 154. Bacon settled £500 on his wife. If we may believe Dudley Carleton (2 Apr. 1606, cited **x**, 291 n5), on the wedding of Bacon with 'his young wench', a good deal of her portion went on purple and cloth of gold for the ceremony.

26 Rawley, i, 8.

27 B. to Sir Thomas Hoby, 4 Aug. 1601, **x**, 289. Bacon's mother-in-law, Lady Packington, that 'little violent woman', as Chamberlain called her, was always quarrelling with her second husband, and threatening to descend on Bacon. For Bacon's conciliating but firm attitude towards her, see **x**, 290. On his wife's suffering for him in Dec. 1621, see **xiv**, 321, and see a letter to her beginning 'It doth much grieve me', on the subject of her health, 8 Sept. 1615, **xiv**, 538 n3.

28 From a *bon mot* about Lady Derby and Lady St Alban, in Rawley's commonplace book, cited **x**, 291; **xiv**, 541 and 543; Aubrey, 174. The marriage ended in a judicial separation thirteen years later, on account of Underhill's jealousy of one Robert Thurrell, a member of her household (Chambers Bunten, *Life of Alice Barnham, 1592–1650*, 63–4). Gorhambury went to Meautys, see n6 above.

29 The 'love-sick' Edward II, dwelt on by Marlowe with evident pleasure, as he frolics with his 'sweet Gaveston', has no more parallel among Bacon's constant friends than he has among Shakespeare's protagonists.

30 *NA*, **iii**, 152–4, three pages expatiating on 'the depraved custom' of seeking other partners, and the loss of self-respect involved in all forms of lust; see also Essay, 'Of Love': 'Nuptial love maketh mankind, friendly love perfecteth it, but wanton love corrupteth, and embaseth it.'

31 **x**, 299, see further chapter 26 below.

32 Essay, 'Of Love', and see *De Sap.* (**vi**, 722): 'the sweets of marriage and the dearness of children commonly draw men away from performing great and lofty service to the commonwealth; being content to be perpetuated in their race and stock, and not in their deeds.'

33 *AL*, **iii**, 295; *NO*, **iv**, 27. The image of the 'happy match between the mind of man and the nature of things' is already in his Device, 'In Praise of Knowledge', 1592, **viii**, 125; *NO*, **iv**, 100; *AL*, **iii**, 295, see also 'that excellent book of Job' that 'will be found pregnant and swelling with natural philosophy': *RP*, F. *Phil.*, 126, and Plan of Work of the Great Instauration, **iv**, 29. Vivid images of a man's work as his child are frequent in Bacon, see **x**, 256, **xii**, 2, 179 and 234.

34 *TPM*, F. *Phil.*, 72, see esp. 133, addressing future generations.

35 B. to Casaubon, 1609, **xi**, 146–7.

36 B. to Father Baranzano, summer 1622, **xiv**, 377–8. Spedding thought Baranzano's premature death deserved 'to be recorded among Bacon's personal misfortunes'.

37 Aubrey, 'Life of Sir Kenelm Digby', in Aubrey, 256. Digby, Bacon remarked to their mutual

friend Toby Matthew, had 'much greatness of mind, a thing almost lost among men' (B. to TM, Mar. 1621, **xiv**, 210–11). In a letter to Digby (1625), Bacon regrets his departure to Madrid, but looks forward to his correspondence as a 'nutritive cordial', for 'those whom in absence we remember are truly present, when those we speak to are not here' (cited Blackbourne, in his edn of Bacon's *Works*, i, 58–9).

38 Rawley, i, 15.
39 Bodley to Bacon, soon after hearing from him on 18 Dec. 1577, in Bodley, *Reliquiae Bodleianae,* letter ccxxxii; B. to Bodley, Dec. 1607, **x**, 366.
40 Bodley to B., 19 Feb. 1608, in Bodley, *Reliquiae Bodleianae,* letter ccxxxiii. Bodley, who had himself withdrawn from public life, regretted that his old friend had entered politics, 'a study not worthy of such a student'; nevertheless, since his country was thereby 'roundly served', he concluded: 'I can but wish with all my heart, as I do very often, that you may gain a full reward to the full of your deserts, which I hope will come with heaps of happiness and honour.'
41 For their early friendship, from at least 1592, when Andrewes visited him at Twickenham, see **viii**, 117, and **ix**, 256; also B. to TM, sending him a copy of *AL* ('I have now at last taught that child to go, at the swaddling whereof you were'), addressing it to you 'who have more right to it than any man, except Bishop Andrewes, who was my inquisitor' (**x**, 255–6). In Sept. 1609 Bacon sent Andrewes *Cogitata et Visa*, asking him to mark whatever he found 'not current in the style, or harsh to credit and opinion . . . for no man can be judge and party' (**xi**, 141).

42 Hacket, *Scrinia Reserata*, i, 186; John Milton, elegy in Latin, cited in Engl. transl., Aikin, ii, 272.
43 B. to Andrewes, then Bishop of Winchester, summer 1622, **xiv**, 371–4. Among Bacon's other scholar friends, besides Selden (chapter 15 above) was the eminent jurist-poet, Sir John Vaughan, in whose house he stayed on his release from the Tower.
44 Aubrey, 171, and 'Life of Sir John Danvers', in Aubrey, *Brief Lives,* 240. Danvers, said Aubrey, 'gave his opinion what he misliked, which my Lord acknowledged to be true, and mended it'. Danvers married the mother of Bacon's friend George Herbert.
45 B. to TM, Dec. 1909, **xi**, 138–9.
46 Aubrey, *Brief Lives*, ed. Clark, 67; B. to Sir Thomas Hoby, 4 Aug. 1606, **x**, 298.
47 Another such friend was Cecil's secretary, Sir Michael Hicks, to whom Bacon wrote on his mother's death that if he could have his company for two or three days (though 'not if it is any trouble'), he 'should pass over this melancholy occasion with more comfort' (27 Aug. 1610, **xi**, 217–18).
48 Campbell, iii, 113; F. C. Montague, ed., *Critical and Historical Essays Contributed to the Edinburgh Review by Lord Macaulay* (1907), ii, 31–3 and n4.
49 'In Praise of Love', in *Northumberland MS*, 9–13.
50 Essay, 'Of Friendship' (1612).
51 Campion, Epigram 190, *Works*, 263 ('*tuus almus amor*' – 'your nourishing, beneficent love'); *The Misfortunes of Arthur*, in 1588.
52 See chapter 2 above.
53 Chamberlain, 19 Mar. 1617, ii, 67. See Jessop, *John Donne* (1897), 26–7 and 68–9; on Donne's admiration for Bacon, Aubrey, *Brief Lives,* ed. Clark, 68.

54 Walton, 'Life of George Herbert', in *Lives*, 273; *Ad Fr. Bacon, Cancell.*, 29 Jan. 1620, Letter 14, in *The Works of George Herbert*, ed. F. E. Hutchinson (1941), 467; 'Latin Poems', in ibid., 436.
55 Edmund Blunden, 'George Herbert's Latin Poems', *Essays and Studies by Members of the English Association* 19 (1933), 35–6. Blunden suggested that Bacon's biographer (as yet to come) should 'glance at the friendship' between him and Herbert as shown in their letters and poems: Bacon, Dedication of 'Translation of Certain Psalms' to Mr George Herbert (1625), **vii**, 275. See W. A. Sessions, 'Bacon and Herbert, an Image of Chalk', in *Too Rich to Clothe the Sunne, Essays on George Herbert*, ed. Summers and Pebworth (1980).
56 Sessions, 'Bacon and Herbert'; Walton, 'Life of Herbert', in *Lives*, 302; *NA*, **iii**, 155–6.
57 See Herbert's Elegy, chapter 2 above, trans. A. Sutton, in *Manes* 38; here unpublished trans. by Benjamin Farrington.
58 Rawley, i, 5; Aubrey, 174; AB to Essex, Oct. 1593.
59 Opinion 'vouchsafed' by the Queen 'in the presence of several persons', Birch, i, 125.
60 AB to Lady B., 16 Apr. 1593, **viii**, 243–4.
61 Lady B. to AB, Oct. 1596, Birch, ii, 61.
62 See du Maurier, *Golden Lads*, 61, 108 and 136. On another occasion Bacon writes (Birch, i, 486), 'I observe your intention of privateness; else I had visited you.' Gustav Ungerer, *Anglo-Spanish Relations* (1956).
63 B. to AB, Jan. 1595, **viii**, 349; AB's reply, 26 Jan., **viii**, 352; AB to Lady B., summer 1596, cited Dixon, 101. Anthony Bacon wrote Francis a consolatory letter, grounding his own comfort 'upon the good proof you have gener-

ally given of your Christian wise patience under more important accidents' (July 1594, cited Spedding, **viii**, 304 n1).
64 **vi**, 523.
65 See above, chapter 7, and B. to Burghley (spring 1597, **ix**, 53) asking him not to impute to him 'the errors of any other' (i.e. Anthony's bitter recriminations against their uncle, expressed to his aunt Russell, Sept. 1596, Birch, ii, 132–7), and his message asking Essex not to misinterpret his own recent approach to Cecil. There could well have been some unexpressed understanding between them, compatible with Anthony's total devotion to Essex and Francis's determination to remain loyal to the Crown, that they would protect each other from their respective positions in the two great factions of their day. Later, when it was safe – and prudent – to do so, Bacon told James (25 Mar. 1603, **x**, 63) that he had not been 'altogether a stranger' to the correspondence carried to him in Scotland by Anthony, 'though by design, as between brothers, dissembled'.
66 Du Maurier, *Golden Lads*, 257–60; B. to AB, 15 May 1601, **ix**, 368. It is addressed 'good brother', and signed, 'your entire loving brother', see chapter 7 above.
67 B. to TM, 18 June 1623, **xiv**, 344.
68 Harington, *Nugae Antiquae*, ii, 215.
69 A. H. Mathew, *The Life of Sir Tobie Matthew, Bacon's Alter Ego* (1907), 24, where Toby is described as 'one of a crowd of gallants whose time was spent feasting by day and in debauchery by night', and 158–9.
70 Ibid., 213.
71 B. to Burghley, Jan. 1592, **viii**, 108.
72 B. to TM, summer 1604, **x**, 216; B. to TM, then in Scotland with James's Court, Apr. 1603, **x**, 73–4; B. to TM, 1606 (Mathew, *Life of Sir*

Tobie Matthew, 49–60). These were what Bacon, writing to another friend, called 'letters of kindness', which, though they bring no news, are the more welcome (B. to Viscount Felton, 18 June 1617, **xiii**, 210).

73 B. to TM, Feb. 1608, **xi**, 10.
74 Toby Matthew, Aug. 1611, *Autobiographical Letter to Dame Mary Gage*.
75 Sir Dudley Carleton to Sir Thomas Edmondes, 11 July and 14 Oct. 1607, cited Mathew, *Life of Sir Tobie Matthew*, 22; ibid., 100–101; Chamberlain, 9 Aug. 1617, ii, 94. In the following years he continued his carping remarks to Carleton (ii, 104, 137, 518) about their mutual 'peremptorily and superstitiously Popish' ex-friend, caught sight of at the play on a fast day, or 'too gawdy in his attire', and finally knighted 'for what service God knows' (actually, his efforts to promote the Spanish marriage). Secretary Winwood too had received Matthew very coldly, not, he said, for want of affection, but because he considered it dangerous that any man who refused to take the oath should be countenanced or 'cockered' (Winwood to Carleton, 26 July 1617, cited Mathew, *Life of Sir Tobie Matthew*, 150).
76 B. to TM, Oct. 1609 to Feb. 1610, **xi**, 134–45. See also B. to TM, Mar. 1622, acknowledging his 'continual care', and promising 'to watch for you as you do for me' – and to find a 'little book' he had been asking for.
77 21 Aug. 1618, Mathew, *Life of Sir Tobie Matthew*, 157.
78 From Flanders, 1619, cited ibid., 161.
79 B. to TM, June 1621, **xiv**, 296–7.
80 B. to TM, Mar. 1622, **xiv**, 344.
81 *The Confessions of the Incomparable Doctour S. Augustine*, trans. Sir Tobias Matthew (1620).
82 Preface to the Italian translation of the *Essays*, 1618, see chapter 2

above; B. to TM, Mar. 1621, **xiv**, 211.
83 B. to Bm, 18 Apr. 1623, **xiv**, 423.
84 TM, as in note 82 above.

Chapter 27 The 'Meanest of Mankind'

1 Aubrey, 179 (data from Bacon's secretary, the future philosopher Thomas Hobbes).
2 Descartes, wrote his contemporary biographer, was much affected by the death of 'the Lord Chancellor Bacon' (cited Napier, *Lord Bacon and Sir Walter Raleigh*, 57 and 61). 'Le Chancelier Bacon, que j'estime guères moins que Pythagore . . .'; Jean Baudoin (preface to his translation of Bacon's *Essays* into French, 1619); Gassendi, *Opera* (1658), I, i, 90. We will find the same references to 'the late most wise Francis Bacon, Chancellor of England' all over Europe, see S. B. L. Penrose, 'The Reputation and Influence of Francis Bacon, in the Seventeenth Century', unpubl. thesis, New York (1934), 80–83.
3 In 1632, when Marshal of France, Effiat arranged for the publication of *De Augmentis* in French. The *Essays, AL, De Sap., History of Henry VII* and *Sylva Sylvarum* had already appeared. On Richelieu's patronage of Bacon's works, see De Mas, *Francis Bacon*, 36, and M. Le Doeuff, 'Bacon chez les grands au siècle de Louis XIII', *Francis Bacon, Terminologia e fortuna nel xvii secolo*, ed. Marta Fattori (1984), 155–8, see p. 175. On his portrait, Henry Bellasis, 'An English Traveller's First Curiosity', cited Marwil, 200 (the King's Librarian was Bacon's friend, Isaac Casaubon). Bacon himself had a portrait of Henri IV, dressed in armour, at Verulam (Aubrey, 177).

4 Jean Amos Comenius, *Physicae ad Lumen Divinum Reformatae*, or *Via Lucis*, a Synopsis of Physics (1668), Preface, 9. Comenius visited England in 1641, seeking to found that 'universal college' which Bacon had propounded to James (Introduction to *De Aug.*, **iv**, 286), dedicated to 'free and universal studies in the arts and sciences', and which took shape later, in a less utopian form, as the Royal Society.

5 Pierre Amboise's 'Life of Bacon' in his *Histoire Naturelle de Maître François Bacon* (1631), described by Gilbert Wats, editor of *AL* in 1640, as 'a just and elegant discourse upon the life of the author'; Le Doeuff notes that he was well informed about Bacon's life ('Bacon chez les grands', 170). See another French contemporary, 'the learned Mr Leclerc', cited Birch (ii, 277), expressing his resentment at the neglect of King James in deserting Lord Bacon. 'One cannot read, saith he, without indignation, that which is reported of the Chancellor of England, Francis Bacon, whom the King suffered to languish in poverty while he preferred worthless persons, to his dishonour.'

6 Boener, 'Life of Bacon'; see also P. Dibon, 'Sur la réception de l'oeuvre de F. Bacon en Hollande dans la première moitié du XVIIe siècle', in *Terminologia e fortuna*, 91–116.

7 'Crescit occulto velut Arbor aevo Fama BACONI', Wats, conclusion of a new issue of *Manes*, affixed to his edition of *De Aug.* in 1640.

8 *Manes* 30, an allusion Bacon would not have missed. When created Viscount St Alban, just before his fall, he had written to James (**xiv**, 168) that he could now 'without superstition be buried in St Alban's habit'.

9 Chamberlain, 27 May 1612, i, 351. Rawley did not include all the contributions offered in *Manes*, for, like some of Bacon's papers which he kept back from publication, he judged them 'to tread too near the heels of truth' (Tenison, 81).

10 1627, text in *Baconiana* 70 (Jan. 1937): 253, see chapter 16 above.

11 Jonson, *Works*, viii, 592; Mac., 355–6.

12 Milton, *Apology against a Modest Confutation of the Animadversions* (1642), 10; see Evelyn, Aubrey, Boyle and Joseph Glanvill, who proclaimed 'Solomon's House in the New Atlantis' as 'a Prophetic Scheam of the Royal Society' (Dedication of *Scepsis Scientifica* to the Royal Society, 1665), also Bishop Thomas Sprat, 'I shall only mention one great man, who had the true imagination of the whole extent of this enterprize', *History of the Royal Society* (1667), 35.

13 'Ode to the Royal Society', in *The Works of Abraham Cowley* (1668), 39.

14 Robert Hooke, *Cutlerian Lectures and other Discourses read at the meetings of the illustrious Royal Society* (1705).

15 Charles Mollay, *Resuscitatio of Francis Bacon* (1670), address to the Reader.

16 Thomas Powell, *The Attorney's Academy* (1623), dedicated to 'true nobility and tried learning'.

17 *The Mirror of State and Eloquence* (1656), anon., cited *Manes*, 31.

18 Joseph Addison on silence, *The Tatler*, no. 133, 13 Feb. and 23 Dec. 1710, repr. in *Works*, ed. Tickell.

19 Camden, *Annals of the Reign of King James*, ii, entry for Mar. 1621; Fuller, *Worthies*, 380, see above chapter 16.

20 Rushworth, *Historical Collections* (1659), i, 26; H. L., *The History of King Charles* (1656).

21 Carte, *General History*, iv, 73.

22 *BB*, 407, also 381, 383, 395 and 411.

23 Mallet, *Life of Bacon*, 113; *BB*, 411.

Mallet saw Bacon as a victim of 'the rapine and insolence of his domestics', and had no doubt that he had been made a scapegoat for Buckingham. Among others, Peter Shaw, in the 'Life' affixed to his edition of *The Philosophical Works of Francis Bacon* (1733), stresses Bacon's patience, pleasure in contemplation, backwardness in asserting, readiness in acknowledging error, and his 'application and address' in all posts of honour. See also Dugdale, *Baronage of England*, i, cited Tenison, 254–5.

24 Tenison, 17; *BB*, 411.
25 Hume, *The History of England*, **vi**, see index under 'The Fall of Bacon'.
26 Mac., 320. He was probably also influenced by his namesake, the strongly radical historian Catherine Sawbridge, known as Mrs Macaulay. A classic in her time (see below chapter 30), she had taken her views on Bacon, and her virulence, straight from the libellers.
27 Fuller, *Church History*, iii, 243.
28 Swift, *The Prose Works of Jonathan Swift*, ed. Davis (1941), x, 183; Addison, in *The Spectator*, 6 Aug. 1711, repr. in *Works*; Tenison, 15; *BB*, 393–5.
29 Weldon. 'I never read a more malicious-minded author, nor any who had such poor and mean observations,' wrote Bishop Goodman (*Court of James I*, i, 412), denouncing a number of statements he knew to be untrue; for the second remark, Bowen, *Coke*, 401. William Sanderson, Bishop of Lincoln, in *Aulus Coquinariae or A Vindication in Answer to a Pamphlet . . .* (1650) (i, 174), denounced 'some men who so delight in sin' that 'they will take much pain to scandal the dead'. It is these 'scurrilous histories', as Zaller noted (12) which perpetrated the false

tradition of a foolish James, duped by a knavish Gondomar.
30 Weldon, 9, 20, 37, 72, 77, 130–31, 136, 144, 165, 180 and 194.
31 Ibid., 116–32. On Cranfield's similar sentence, Weldon commented: 'The Bishops kept him also from degrading, which I do verily believe is one cause the gentry will degrade them.'
32 *BB*, 393.
33 Weldon, 121–5. An even more outrageous libel concerning Bacon's dealings with Ellesmere (ibid., 115) was refuted by Sanderson (ibid., 171).
34 *BB*, 394; Sanderson, *Aulus Coquinariae*, 171.
35 *BB*, 395 and 407; Mac., 340.
36 Wilson, *Annals of King James I*, ii, 661, and 'Observations of God's Providence in the Tract of my Life', in Peck, *Desiderata Curiosa*, 460–83. Wilson was a retainer of the son of Essex, the third Earl; like Weldon, he had been dismissed from his post at Court.
37 Sanderson, *Aulus Coquinariae*, 174. Thomas Hearne, *The History of Richard II*, p. xxxvi.
38 D'Ewes, *Autobiography*, 385.
39 Ibid.
40 See above, chapter 5.
41 *BB*, 375, see chapter 6 above.
42 D'Ewes, *Autobiography*, 385; Wilson, *Annals of King James I*, 158–9; Weldon, 111 and 123–4.
43 Mac., 398.
44 Anon., 'A Lover of Truth', *Great Merit Triumphant* (1749), 1.
45 *The Justice of Parliaments* (1725), 54–9, an attack on 'those two great delinquents, Cardinal Wolsey and Lord Bacon', by 'Britannicus' (the notoriously aggressive and sycophantic Benjamin Hoadley, Bishop of Hereford).
46 *London Journal*, 1 July 1732, repr. in *The Gentleman's Magazine* 2 (1732): 833. The author attributed Bacon's depravity to the lack of that knowledge of the human

passions which, in the eyes of his contemporaries, had been his principal merit – and was to be throughout the eighteenth century, see Joseph Warton, *An Essay on the Writings and Genius of Pope*, 1756, vol. i, 119, on 'the acuteness, comprehension and knowledge of man which so eminently distinguished that philosopher'.

47 Alexander Pope, *An Essay on Man* (1734), *The Twickenham Edition of the Poems of Alexander Pope* (1951), III, Ep. iv, p. 154, lines 231–2.

48 Church, *Bacon*, 177.

49 Pope, 'Advertisement' to the first 'Imitation of Horace' (Apr. 1735), *Epistles to Several Persons (Moral Essays)*, Twick. edn, III, ii, cited Bateson, editor, p. xxxviii. For himself Pope used a different criterion: he committed his morals to the testimony of his 'virtuous friends' (Pope to Swift, 28 May 1733, in *The Correspondence of Alexander Pope*, ed. Sherburn, 1956, iii, 372).

50 *BB*, 411.

51 A. B. Grosart, *Thoughts that Breathe and Words that Burn* (1893), Introduction.

52 Joseph Spence, *Observations, Anecdotes and Characters* (1735), ed. S. L. Singer, 1858. Bacon's 'Twickenham retreat', 'my pleasure and my dwelling' (**viii**, 315, and **ix**, 28), Pope's 'elegant retreat' (Maynard Mack, *Alexander Pope, A Life* (1985), 358ff.). On Bolingbroke and Bacon, see further chapter 32 below.

53 *The Dunciad*, V. iii. lines 213–16; *Imitations of Horace*, IV, Book II, Satire II, ii (the booby Lord was Grimston, into whose hands Verulam had fallen in 1700); *Moral Essays*, III. ii, Epistle v, line 60 ('To Mr Addison, Occasioned by his Dialogues on Medals'), see Mack, *Alexander Pope, A Life*, 280. See also, invoking Bacon as a master of language, 'Command old words that long have slept to wake, / Words that wise Bacon or brave Rawleigh spake' (II. ii. 168). Bacon headed the list of eighteen writers from whose works Pope planned to collect an authoritative English dictionary (he rejected Ralegh as too affected). Spence, *Observations, Anecdotes and Characters*, 235.

54 Pope, Twick. edn, V. iii. line 213.

55 Pope, *Essay on Criticism*, Twick. edn, I, line 215. The Baconian source of 'bear like a Turk no danger near the throne' (from the Epistle to Dr Arbuthnot, Twick. edn, IV, ii, line 328 – in Bacon, *De Aug.*, **iv**, 358) was noticed by Pope's editor, Joseph Warton, *The Works of Alexander Pope* (1797), ii, 304.

56 Pope, *Essay on Criticism*, Twick. edn, I, line 200, parallel noted by Warton (*Writings and Genius of Pope*, i, 136–7); Essay 'Of Beauty'.

57 Warton, *Writings and Genius of Pope*, i, 36 (his annotated copy is at the British Library, Stowe MS 964); dedication of the *Essays* to Buckingham, 1625 (**vi**, 373). Pope planned, after Bacon, a fuller 'advancement of learning', to study the extent and limits of human reason, arts and sciences, and note the misapplications of learning (*Essay on Man*, Twick. edn, III, i, Epistle ii, line 43, see Warton, *Writings and Genius of Pope*, ii, 143–4). Warton in Pope's time and Mack in ours both use Bacon to cast light on Pope's meaning (e.g. Warton, ibid., i, 118 and ii, 214), and cite many striking examples of likely influence, such as on 'wit oblique' that breaks 'the steady light of reason' (*Essay on Man*, Epistle ii, line 83); in Bacon, the mind 'that alters the rays of things' (Essay, 'Of Studies').

58 *AL*, **iii**, 411; Pope, *Essay on Man*, Twick. edn, III, i, Epistle ii, line 73.

59 Essay, 'Of Empire'; see *AL*, **iii**, 437–42 and 459–60. We must inform ourselves 'of the predominancy, what humour reigneth most, and what end is principally sought'; and on men's natures and ends, *De Aug.*, **v**, 63.

60 Pope, 'Epistle to Cobham', *Moral Essays*, Twick. edn, III, ii, lines 178 and 209–10.

61 Pope, *Essay on Man*, Twick. edn, III, i, ii, lines 167–8. On the dramatic presence of the ruling passion at the moment of death, Bacon 'Of Death', Pope, 'Epistle to Cobham', lines 262–3, see Warton, *Writings and Genius of Pope*, ii, 197. See Epistle ii, lines 75–80, 161–4, 183–4, and *AL*, **iii**, 437–42, 443–7.

62 Mack, Preface to Pope, *Essay on Man*, xxxvi ff., and lines 167–8; Pope, *Moral Essays* (Twick. edn, III, ii), p. xxii.

63 Montaigne, cited Mack, in Pope, *Essay on Man*, Twick. edn, III, i, Epistle ii, lines 167–8; 'Like Aaron's serpent, swallows up the rest', 'As Heav'n's blest beams turn vinegar more sowr', *Essay on Man*, Epistle ii, lines 131–1 and 147–8; in Bacon, **iv**, 290, and *SS*, **ii**, 637 on the vessels of wine 'placed in the noon sun to make the liquor sour'.

64 Could Pope have done this (Grosart regretfully asked) despite his earlier condemnation of 'all tricks to show the stretch of human brain'? (Twick. edn, III, ii, Epistle ii, line 47).

65 H. Kendra Baker, 'Pope and Bacon', *Baconiana* 85 (Jan. 1937): 1–24.

66 Pope, *Essay on Criticism*, Twick. edn, I, Part I, lines 195–6, and 'The Universal Prayer'.

67 B. to Dr Playfer, summer 1606, **x**, 301.

68 Mac., 359.

69 Pope, 'Argument of the Fourth Epistle', in *Essay on Man*, Twick.

edn, III, i, 127; Epistle iv, lines 51–2.

70 Only the virtuous enjoy felicity, but among the rich and talented we cannot tell who are the good. ('Who then but God can tell us who they are?', line 136). Compare lines 199–200 with Bacon, Apophthegm 255, **vii**, 161, and the 'loud huzzas', lines 255–6, with '*plaudites* are fitter for players than for magistrates', **xiii**, 211.

71 Pope, Twick. edn, III, ii, Epistle iv, lines 101 and 236, see for a bleeding Bacon earlier in this chapter.

72 Pope, Twick. edn, III, ii, Epistle iv, lines 259ff. and 281–2.

73 Spence, *Observations, Anecdotes and Characters*, 128 (cited Mack, *re* line 256). For Pope's inordinate admiration of Bolingbroke, who inspired him with the idea of the *Essay on Man*, see Warton (*Writings and Genius of Pope*, ii, 178), Spence (127) and Mack (*Alexander Pope, A Life*, 507 and 512). His praise of Bolingroke as man and writer is immediately followed by his remarks on Bacon as 'the greatest genius that England ever produced', and on the misfortunes of extraordinary geniuses. 'When a man is much above the rank of men, who can he have to converse with?' The thought was also Bacon's, see *History of Henry VII*, **vi**, 105.

74 'Who could imagine that Locke was fond of romances; that Newton once valued astrology; that . . . Elizabeth was a coquette and Bacon received a bribe?' Warton, *Writings and Genius of Pope*, ii, 186–7.

75 John Dennis, Preface to *Reflections Critical and Satirical on a Late Rhapsody called an Essay on Criticism* (1711).

76 Pope was notoriously unscrupulous in his choice of examples for his complicated arguments, as when he substituted Julius Caesar

for Peter the Great, and turned Caesar into a drunkard (Warton, *Writings and Genius of Pope*, i, 129–30, see also ii, 128, 138–9 and 445–6). Even Bacon was only a substitute for his original example: the Duke of Wharton. ('If parts allure thee, think how Wharton shin'd / Wharton, the shame and scandal of mankind,' see Mack, Twick. edn, *Essay on Man*, III, i, Epistle iv, 154). I am grateful to Geoffrey Plowden, author of *Pope on Classic Ground* (1984) for drawing my attention to this earlier, entirely inept example, since Wharton, without 'parts' or high-minded 'preheminance', was a mendacious profligate, qualified by Pope elsewhere as 'flagitious yet not great', and 'from no one vice exempt' (Epistle to Cobham, Twick. edn, III, ii, lines 180ff.). In switching from a worthless Wharton to a wise Bacon, had Pope carelessly chosen a more striking example, or one which was more consistent with his argument? A volte-face no greater than his change in the first lines of his poem, where he first described 'this scene of Man' as 'A Mighty maze of walks without a plan', and later as 'A mighty maze, but not without a plan' (Twick. edn, III, ii, Epistle i, line 6).

77 Benjamin Farrington, unpublished notes for a volume to be entitled *Bacon, Personality and Performance*, on the influence of Bacon over Herbert, Pope, Milton, Coleridge and other poets, which he did not live to finish.

Chapter 28 The Two-Souled Monster

1 *Essays Moral, Economical and Political* by Francis Bacon, edited

by 'A New Editor' (1913); *BB*, 411.
2 Aikin, i, 193–5 and ii, 203.
3 Henry Hallam, *The Constitutional History of England* (1827), i, 358–9.
4 Thomas Martin, *Character of Lord Bacon* (1835).
5 'Who can forbear to observe and lament the weaknesses and infirmity of human nature?' enquired Robert Stephens, in *Letters and Life of Bacon* (1701), pp. liv–v; and Mallet, *Life of Bacon*, 111: he 'had the misfortune to be made a memorial for the greatest and wisest, to take heed lest they fall'.
6 Mac., 320; Church, *Bacon*, 1.
7 Mac., 390.
8 Ibid., 397–8. These last lines were still quoted with approval by Quinton in 1980 (*Francis Bacon*, 7).
9 Mac., 338 and 355.
10 'Two souls, alas, dwell in my breast,' cited Walter Steeves, *Francis Bacon* (1910), 34.
11 Gardiner, *Introduction to English History* (1881), 224.
12 J. A. Froude, 'Lord Campbell as a Writer of History', *Westminster Review* (1854), 446–9, see p. 447. The seven-volume *Lives* sold 2,000 copies on the day of publication.
13 *Quarterly Review*, cited in 'A Railway Review, Companion to the Railway Edition of Lord Campbell's Life of Bacon' (published separately in paperback). This small volume, published in 1853, unsigned, is by Spedding. He cites a New York review of Campbell's 'Life of Bacon', pronouncing it 'a masterly review of Bacon's whole career', which should 'be studied and admired, now and hereafter, in the work on which it alone would have been sufficient to stamp the character of solid worth'.
14 Lord Alfred Denning, see chapter 32 below.
15 A contemporary (cited *DNB*)

attributed Campbell's tendency to denigrate his subjects to his habit of telling degrading stories about his predecessors in office. He presented Sir Christopher Hatton, for example, against all contemporary evidence, as an incapable profligate. Froude, with newly published letters, showed that many of his statements were false ('Lord Campbell as a Writer of History'), but Campbell, barring a few half-hearted minor corrections, left his misstatements untouched.

16 'A Railway Reader', 15.

17 Ibid., 33 and 44, see chapter 10 above. Campbell changed his version this time to 'Bacon made an evasive attempt to support the abuse of monopolies by pretending that the proper course was humbly to petition the Queen', thus, while withdrawing a false statement of fact, attributing to Bacon, more deviously, the same iniquitous intention.

18 Ibid., 74.

19 Campbell, iii, 42 (Bacon is then suspected of having prompted Essex's execution).

20 Campbell's 'great pain', ibid., 89 and 114; the threefold exclamation, ibid., 70. Weldon, see above, chapter 27. Among other blunders, see Campbell's vehement condemnation of Bacon for prosecuting, as Attorney General, the disreputable and seditious 'Black Oliver', who had accused the King of perjury 'more gross than that of Richard II'. Campbell mistook him for the eminent lawyer, Sir Oliver St John, later Chief Justice of England ('Life of Bacon', 62, and Spedding, **xii**, 131).

21 'A Railway Reader', 61–3. Campbell corrected this mistake by removing the word 'maiden' from Bacon's speech, but not the intoxication.

22 Campbell, iii, 77. See also on this

page the 'exquisite delight' with which Bacon is made to write Coke's dismissal.

23 Ibid., 1–2, 75–7, 94–6, 115 and 141, see Spedding, **xiii**, 122 and 129, and *ER*, ii, 271.

24 Campbell, iii, 72 and 134–6.

25 Sir Henry Taylor, cited G. S. Venables, Preface to Spedding, *ER*, i, p. xiv.

26 J. R. Green's widely read and translated *Short History of the English People* (1874, last reprinted 1960), 592. On its importance, see J. P. Kenyon, review of J. W. Burrow, *A Liberal Descent*, TLS, 4 Dec. 1981.

27 B. C. Lovejoy, *Francis Bacon, A Critical Review of his Life and Character* (1988), 54.

28 *Francis Bacon* was written for high school classes at the request of the historian J. R. Green (n26 above). Spedding conclusively refuted Abbott's first presentation of Bacon, introducing *Bacon's Essays* (1876), see Spedding, 'The Latest Theory about Bacon', *Contemporary Review* 28 (Nov. 1876); Lee, 'Francis Bacon', in his *Great Englishmen*, 259, and Robertson, *Pioneer Humanists*, 61.

29 Abbott, *Francis Bacon*, 191.

30 Abbott, *Bacon and Essex*, 175, also Introduction, p. xix. See chapter 21 above.

31 Abbott, *Francis Bacon*, 317.

32 Theobald, 'Bacon as Viewed by his Biographers' (1886).

33 Abbott, *Bacon and Essex*, 114, and *Francis Bacon*, 58 and 86. Spedding had already drawn attention to a couple of unimportant lapses of memory in Bacon as to dates, natural enough when writing years after the event (**x**, 162). Typically, Bacon used the same remark (that the Irish were not to be undervalued as enemies) as a challenge in the letter he wrote to encourage Essex on the eve of his departure (**ix**, 131) which, in the

Apology (**x**, 146), he claims to have used to discourage him in the early stages. For Abbott this showed his dishonesty throughout. For Judge Webb (chapter 31, n35), echoing him in 1902, the discrepancy proved that 'every word of this *Apology* can be shown to be untrue'; a century later, Marwil saw it, after Abbott, as 'a purposeful creation of Bacon's to build up and restore his own image' (*Trials of Counsel*).

34 Abbott, *Bacon and Essex*, 12.
35 Ibid., 106–7. All accounts agree, as Spedding pointed out (**ix**, 125) – Camden's, Fynes Moryson's and Essex's own – that it was by Essex's influence that Mountjoy's appointment was cancelled. Naunton was in no doubt that Essex 'utterly disliked' the Queen's plan to send Mountjoy to Ireland. He writes that Essex opposed it 'with many reasons and arguments of contempt, against his professed friend and familiar, so predominant were his words to reap the honour of closing up that war – and all other' (*Fragmenta Regalia*, 53).
36 *Apology*, **x**, 146 (the statement cannot be verified as there is no letter from this period); Abbott, *Bacon and Essex*, 347–9.
37 Lee, *Great Englishmen*, 227–8.
38 *Apology*, **x**, 153.
39 Abbott, *Bacon and Essex*, 173, and *Francis Bacon*, 62.
40 Lee, *Great Englishmen*, 228.
41 Jardine, *Criminal Trials*, i, 332.
42 'This melancholy discovery was made by my friend, Mr Jardine,' Campbell, iii, 41n.
43 Spedding, **ix**, 366–7.
44 Abbott, *Bacon and Essex*, 214–15, 238–42 and 211; *Francis Bacon*, 73–4.
45 Sidney Lee, article on Bacon in the *DNB*.
46 Abbott, *Bacon and Essex*, 230–3. As noted chapter 7 above, one of Essex's followers, unable to be-

lieve he had gone to such lengths in denunciation, wrote to Anthony Bacon describing the Rev. Ashton, Essex's chaplain, as 'base and mercenary', and implying that he had been got at by the Government. Even if it were so (clergymen were often requested to encourage the accused to confess), this does not invalidate Essex's confession to a man who was there at his own request. Feeling a strong need to unburden his soul (Essex to Southampton, in Birch, ii, 484), he had made it a condition of his surrender that he should be allowed the visits of Ashton as a man 'already familiar with his conscience' (**ix**, 234), and he afterwards thanked the Queen that it had 'pleased her to have this little man, Mr Ashton, my Minister, with me for my soul'. Following Abbott's lead, a later biographer, Robert Lacey, was to look upon Essex's confession as the outcome of 'manic religious depression' (see chapters 6 above and 32 below).
47 Abbott, *Francis Bacon*, 111, 237, 144.
48 Ibid., 22, 110 and 216.
49 Ibid., 327–8, 20–2, 168.
50 Ibid., 180, 265.
51 *AL*, **iii**, 456.
52 Abbott, *Francis Bacon*, 356 and 459.
53 *AL*, **iii**, 471–2. As Wormald noted in 1993 (*Francis Bacon*, 323), far from supporting Machiavelli's 'evil arts', Bacon explicitly excluded them.
54 Beckinsale, *Burghley*, 218ff.
55 *AL*, **iii**, 456. See R. Cochrane, 'Francis Bacon and the Architect of his Fortune', *Studies in the Renaissance* 5 (1958), 176–9, see pp. 182 and 186.
56 Bacon, 'Character of Julius Caesar', **vi**, 341–3; *AL*, **iii**, 279 and 472.
57 'A Letter and Discourse to Sir Henry Savill Touching Helps for the Intellectual Powers' (1596),

vii, 98; letter written by Bacon in the name of his brother Anthony, encouraging Essex to regain the Queen's favour by conforming and reforming (summer 1600), **ix**, 200. Solomon, as Bacon pointed out (**v**, 54), 'though he often takes notice of what is bad in human life, never enjoins it'.

58   Abbott, *Francis Bacon*, 132, 322, and 48.

59   Ibid., 176, also 18, 144, 223–4. See above, chapter 20.

60   Abbott, *Francis Bacon*, 458.

61   *AL*, **iii**, 456.

62   Abbott, *Francis Bacon*, 458.

63   Lee, *Great Englishmen*, 225. Abbott's other proof was a neutral remark, in 'Of Fortune': 'Extreme lovers of their country or masters were never fortunate, neither can they be,' since they place their thoughts 'outside themselves'. Disregarding many other statements on the subject, such as that 'wisdom for a man's self' is 'a depraved thing' – 'the wisdom of rats and crocodiles' – he took for granted that Bacon was supporting the fortune-seeker against unworldly devotion.

64   *CS*, published Spedding, 1868, **xi**, 39–94.

65   Marwil, 119. On a very abstruse piece of fault-finding of Abbott's, related to *CS*, see Spedding, 'The Latest Theory about Bacon', 824–5.

66   **xi**, 20.

67   Abbott, *Francis Bacon*, 150 and 131.

68   *AL*, **iii**, 419 and 432–5; *Meditationes Sacrae*, **vii**, 248.

69   *AL*, **iii**, 420 and 431; *Meditationes Sacrae*, **vii**, 245. See also, 'Whatever deserves to exist deserves to be known' (*NO*, **iv**, 106) and 'To the pure all things are pure' (**iv**, 258).

70   *Prayers*, **vii**, 255–9, see also *The Great Instauration*, **iv**, 20 and 33.

71   Mac., 330.

72   *AL*, **iii**, 285 and 459; Abbott,

Francis Bacon, 317–31.

73   Abbott, *Francis Bacon*, 318–19.

74   *De Aug.*, **v**, 63 (citing Cicero); Abbott, *Francis Bacon*, 319.

75   Abbott, *Francis Bacon*, 131.

76   Ibid., 330–31 and 111; Introduction to *Bacon's Essays*, pp. lv–lvi.

77   Burke, '"Lord" Bacon and the Cambridge Style'. A Bacon full of intellectual conceit, whose mind was 'majestic' though his character 'rotten to the core', fills the few pages of this article.

78   'In Praise of Knowledge', **viii**, 123, and *AL*, **iii**, 287; **iii**, 315–16; *De Aug.*, **iv**, 405.

79   Essay, 'Of Goodness and Goodness of Nature'.

Chapter 29   The 'Creeping Snake'

Chapter title from Macaulay, 'Francis Bacon', 330.

1   Church, *Bacon*, 1–2, 174–7. All Abbott's views as quoted here from *Francis Bacon* (1885), many verbatim, had already appeared in his introduction to *Bacon's Essays*, 1876, eight years before Church published his book.

2   Church, *Bacon*, 177–8, 4 and 171.

3   Abbott, *Francis Bacon*, 22. Wormald attributes the change in Gardiner to reading Bacon's diary (*CS*). If he did read *CS* now, it was clearly in the light of Abbott's comments. 'Bacon's character', writes Gardiner in *DNB*, 'is nowhere else depicted so completely as a whole, as in the loose jottings.' Abbott had written (*Bacon's Essays*, p. xlviii): 'We shall gain more knowledge of him from these few pages than from any of his other works.' See Gardiner's remarks in *DNB*, also from Abbott, on the marginal notes found in the *Declaration of Treasons*.

4   Gardiner, iv, 94 and 104.

5   Gardiner's only quarrel with Bacon in his *History of England* (iv,

105–7) had been, from the Whig standpoint, that he did not see 'the intolerable abuses which would necessarily spring from the powers which he claimed for the Crown'.

6   On Hurstfield's change of view after reading Abbott, chapter 18 above.

7   For Lee, chapter 28 above, and for both Lee and George Saintsbury, chapter 33 below.

8   Trevelyan, grand-nephew of Macaulay, of whom it is said that 'all his work was written as if he had a bust of Lord Macaulay upon his desk' (G. M. Trevelyan *England under the Stuarts* (1904), 1960).

9   C. D. Broad, *The Philosophy of Francis Bacon: An Address Delivered at Cambridge on the Occasion of the Bacon Tercentenary*, 1926.

10   R. A. Tsanoff, 'Francis Bacon and Philosophic Thought', University Extension Lectures on Francis Bacon in Observance of the Three Hundredth Anniversary of his Death, *Rice Institute Pamphlet* 13 (April 1926), 1; Samuel Glenn McCann, 'The Public Life of Francis Bacon', ibid., 34–7, 46 and 50; Stockton Axson, 'Francis Bacon as Man of Letters', ibid., 110–12.

11   James Rowley, 'Francis Bacon, his Public Career and Personal Character', 163–4.

12   Neale, *Essays in Elizabethan History*, 226.

13   Strachey, 205, 218, 243, 250 and 266–7 (see him on Essex, chapter 6 above). From a remark by Bishop Goodman (*The Court of King James the First*, i, 285) that Lady B., who died in 1610, was 'little better than frantic in her old age', Abbott deduced that 'Bacon inherited some abnormal characteristics, one of which took the shape of an excessive and even monstrous self-confidence.'

14   Strachey, 116, 24, 253, 45.

15   *AL*, **iii**, 280.

16   *De Aug.*, **iv**, 405, and **v**, 77; *AL*, **iii**, 430–31; *Meditationes Sacrae*, **vii**, 244.

17   Mac., 329–30.

18   Abbott, *Francis Bacon*, 319.

19   Bowen, *Francis Bacon*, 12.

20   Aubrey, *Brief Lives*, ed. Clark, 72 (though Aubrey may simply have noted Hobbes as his source). Of Hobbes's eye he wrote: 'When earnest in discourse there shone (as it were) a bright live coal within it', ibid., 28 (Aubrey, 174 and 314).

21   Strachey, 45.

22   See chapter 33 below.

23   Sprat, *History of the Royal Society*, 36; Hume, *The Philosophical Works of David Hume* (1702); Henry Hallam, *History of European Literature* (1837), iii, 217: 'He was more eminently the philosopher of human than of general nature. Hence he is exact as well as profound in all his reflexions on civil life and mankind . . .' In the eighteenth century it was for Bacon's achievements in 'knowledges of men', rather than his programme for nature, that Vico took him for his model in the *Scienza Nuova*, see Wormald, *Francis Bacon*, 338. On Bacon's 'incredible insight into human nature in action', see Whitaker, 'Francis Bacon's Intellectual Milieu'. As Whitaker sees him, 'he is always best in writing about man.'

24   T. C. Albutt, 'Palissy and the Revival of Natural Science', *Proceedings of the British Academy* (1913), vi, 14. Farrington ('On Misunderstanding the Philosophy of Francis Bacon', 444–6) refuted the notion also advanced by Albutt that Bacon spoiled what he (hypothetically) borrowed.

25   A. P. McMahon, 'Francis Bacon's Essay "Of Beauty"', *Modern Language Association of America*, 60

(1945), 716–59, see pp. 758–9 (recommended for further reading by Pitcher, 50). In the essay 'Of Youth and Age', Bacon gives the pro and contra, and the young men – to whom his works were dedicated – naturally come out best ('Imaginations stream into their minds better, and as it were more divinely'). See also 'Icarus', in *De Sap.*, **vi**, 754, and *History of Life and Death*, **v**, 318–19.

26 W. K. Jordan, *Philanthropy in England, 1486–1660* (1950), 285 n3, and *The Charities of London, 1480–1660*, 64–5. It was Farrington ('Francis Bacon, Personality and Performance', unpublished) who first protested against Professor Jordan's unwarranted sneers.

27 Aubrey, 'Life of Thomas Sutton', 452–3, and *DNB*; Chamberlain, 18 Dec. 1611, i, 323–4.

28 As found in his diary (*CS*), in the *Essays*, and even in his endowment of two university lectureships in his will (**xiv**, 544). In *De Aug.* (**iv**, 286) he attributes the dearth of men 'for business of state' to the lack of a collegial education 'designed for these purposes'. It was when the 1601 Parliament proposed to repeal an Act to prevent the misapplication of the revenues of charitable institutions – an Act which Bacon had sponsored in 1587, and called 'a Feast of Charity' (**x**, 37) – that he became so excited as to surprise some Members of the House. Inexplicably, Epstein remarked that his agitation suggests 'the egoism that was to reveal itself more and more' (*Francis Bacon*, 56). See also in *BB* (386 and note CC) Bacon's similar effort, for the same reasons, to oppose the actor Alleyn's charity, much as he appreciated it ('I like well that Alleyn playeth the last act of his life so well', 18 Aug. 1618, **xiii**, 324). He remained Alleyn's friend,

and attended the banquet celebrating the opening of his foundation.

29 'Advice to the King Touching Sutton's Estate', **xi**, 249–55.

30 Prince Charles awarded 'the lucrative post' of Master of Charterhouse school and hospital to one of his followers (Strong, *Henry, Prince of Wales*, 31).

31 Chamberlain, 10 June 1613, i, 456; Fuller, *Worthies*, i, 45. See David Cressy, 'Francis Bacon and the Advancement of Schooling', *History of European Ideas* 2 (1981), 65–74.

32 *BB*, 396; Rowley, 'Francis Bacon', 151–2.

33 Trevor-Roper, 'General Crisis', 54–5. See also by the same author, 'Thomas Sutton', *The Carthusian*, 15 (1948).

34 Letter to the New Zealand *Listener* from 'a Baconian', commenting on the recent broadcast programme about Bacon and Coke, cited *Baconiana* 123 (Apr. 1947): 113.

35 Abbott, *Bacon's Essays*, Preface, p. liv.

36 Read, *Lord Burghley and Queen Elizabeth*, 496. The tempting parallel is still generally made by both academic and popular writers. See Quinton, *Francis Bacon*, 5, and George Garrett's novelized Ralegh (*Death of the Fox*, 1972, discussed n67 below), where Coke, a 'deeper mind' than Bacon's, with 'the enormous power of simplicity', unlike Bacon (who merely tries to trick Ralegh), 'serves the Law of England' and thus 'serves England always' – and as a result, the future (ibid., 325); so that he 'has more shareholds in the colony of the future than Bacon can hope for'.

37 McElwee, *The Murder of Overbury*, 227, 245 and 256.

38 Irwin, *The Great Lucifer* (1960); Edward Leconte, *The Notorious Lady Essex* (1970), 56, 161, 114, 153

and 178. In Leconte's earlier biography of John Donne (1965), Bacon had already appeared with his 'viper's eye', as 'the meanest of mankind . . . for centuries labelled a hypocrite'.

39 Andrew Amos, *The Great Oyer of Poisoning* (1846). According to Professor Amos's thesis, too extravagant to be taken seriously (though it has been), the King was the real procurer of the murder of Overbury, out of fear that he might reveal the secret vices to which Overbury, Somerset and himself were allegedly addicted together. After which, fearing that Somerset might disclose the truth, he employed Bacon and Coke to 'get up' a case against the Somersets and ensure their conviction. 'The preliminary arrangements for the trial', wrote Amos, 'convict Bacon as one of the most wicked men in recorded history . . . Perhaps there is not to be found a more disgraceful course of conduct in our judicial annals than that which, under Bacon's own hands, we find he pursued with an express view to a preconcerted pardon.' See further **xii**, 342–6 and Gardiner, ii, 352 n1.

40 Campbell, iii, 72–3.

41 *BB*, 389; Montagu, *Life of Francis Bacon*, p. clxxxv.

42 B. to King, early 1611, **xi**, 242, and 12 Feb. 1615, **xii**, 242, see Spedding, **xi**, 393–5. 'Marry, his obligations are such', Chamberlain grumbled (23 Dec. 1613, i, 493), 'as well to his Majesty as to the great Lord . . . as he can admit no partner.'

43 **xii**, 283–4, and Gardiner, ii, 349. Bacon enjoined (**xii**, 285) that 'the matter itself being tragical enough, bitterness and insulting be foreborne'. For his arrangements, **xii**, 331; for his presentation of the evidence, chapter 25 above.

44 See Gardiner, ii, 333, 338 and 341.

Nevertheless, though critical, particularly of Coke's overconfidence (**xii**, 232), Bacon praised him for his collaboration with Chancellor Ellesmere over these trials (see chapter 25 above).

45 Gardiner, ii, 352; Spedding, **xii**, 275, and Bacon's charge against Somerset, **xii**, 317.

46 Mattingley, *Renaissance Diplomacy*; see Gardiner, ii, 349 and 360 n1, for two points of the evidence favourable to Somerset, overlooked by Spedding. For Somerset and the Spanish pensions, chapter 17 above.

47 B. to King, 28 Apr. 1616, **xii**, 277–8. On the confession that 'might open the gate of mercy', B. to King, May 1616, **xii**, 293.

48 **xii**, 335; Pitcher, 44.

49 'I find no reason why the Spanish ambassador should complain,' Ralegh to James, 24 Sept. 1618, cited Edwards, *Life of Walter Ralegh*, ii, 368.

50 Mac., 331–2; Adrian Berry in the *Sunday Telegraph*, 19 Feb. 1995. Napier, *Lord Bacon and Sir Walter Raleigh*. (The first part of this work is a study of Bacon's philosophical ideas, with no reference to his life.) See Spedding's exhaustive analysis, **xii**, 342–441 and Gardiner, iii, 44–60, 108–53; Charles Nicoll, *The Creature in the Map*, see Appendix.

51 Aubrey, 416; Ralegh, *History of the World* (1614), iv, 565.

52 Bacon, recalling a walk with Ralegh in the grounds of Gray's Inn, Apophthegm 37, **vii**, 68–9; for his plans about Ralegh, CS, **xi**, 63. Owing to a mistaken 'rough note' ('he and my Lord. Chllr') on Ralegh's reported remark about a conversation he had held with the Lord Chamberlain (Thomas Wilson's report of his conversations with Ralegh in 1618, *State Papers Domestic*, Public Record Office, James I, 14/99, folios 172–

3), Spedding thought (**xiii**, 347 n1), as Napier had done before him (*Lord Bacon and Sir Walter Raleigh*, 254) and many others after, that Ralegh referred to the walk Bacon recalled. Ralegh's biographers, e.g. Stebbing (*Sir Walter Raleigh*, 303–4), taking the mistaken attribution for granted, found it inconceivable that he should have been so 'intemperately rash' as to confide these thoughts to Bacon, the opponent of his principal backer, Secretary Winwood. Pembroke was a political ally. None the less, Ralegh was to denounce both of them, in a last attempt to escape execution (Gardiner, iii, 144 and Napier, *Lord Bacon and Sir Walter Raleigh*, 253).

53 Napier, *Lord Bacon and Sir Walter Raleigh*, 242–4.

54 **xii**, 396 and 432–3; Gardiner, iii, 141; Napier, *Lord Bacon and Sir Walter Raleigh*, 253, see Appendix to the present volume.

55 Gardiner, iii, 48. On Ralegh's and the King's motives, see Willson, *King James VI and I*, 370–74. Spedding pointed out (**xiii**, 439) that James's position was no different from that of Ralegh when, as he tells it in his *Apology*, he put in for water at Gomera, promising the Governor of the island 'by word of the King of Great Britain' that if any of his company took so much as an orange or a grape, he would 'make an example to the rest and hang him up in the market-place'.

56 Gardiner, iii, 148. On the antiquated sentence see Appendix below. We cannot test an early seventeenth-century verdict by twentieth-century rules, as Hurstfield pointed out ('Raleigh's Treason', *History Today*, vii, Jan.–Dec. 1957, 480); in Ralegh's time decisions were usually reached before the trial, which was principally an opportunity for public display, and in this case the examining judge, Chief Justice Popham, of known integrity, was satisfied with Ralegh's guilt.

57 As reported to Dudley Carleton, Nov. 1618, cited Edwards, *Life of Walter Ralegh*, i, 694, see Appendix below. Ralegh became the figurehead of commercial England, excluded from the American market by James's peace (see Hill, *Century of Revolution*, 32).

58 Bacon, 'Advice to Villiers', 1616, **xii**, 50; Council meeting on 21 June 1618, Gardiner, iii, 133.

59 Jardine, *Criminal Trials*, i, 520.

60 Irwin, *The Great Lucifer*, 245, 263, 292–3 (see also her wild and entirely unhistorical cloak-and-dagger tale, in which Bacon leaps out of bed at midnight to take over a hushing-up job (at which he is 'past-master') and appoints two servants to 'hoodwink' Somerset away from his trial). For the first letter, see above and n52. The second letter, from *Familiar Letters* (201) by James Howell – according to Carteret an author of 'vulgar tales mixed with many mistakes' (*BB*, 411) – and dismissed by Gardiner (iii, 131) as thoroughly unreliable, was never given credence by any serious historian. Howell's source was Ralegh's equally untrustworthy son Carew, who reported many years later that Ralegh, allegedly consulted by Bacon as to whether his commission for Guiana did not imply a full pardon, replied, 'upon my life, you have sufficient reason for all that is past already.' No Lord Keeper could have volunteered an implied pardon, and if he had, Ralegh would certainly have appealed to it in his *Apology* (Gardiner, iii, 47 n2). Napier concluded that such an opinion from Bacon was as improbable as that James would have acceded to it (*Lord Bacon and*

Sir Walter Raleigh, 235, see 257n). In fact he deliberately refused it so as to hold Ralegh to his good behaviour.

61 Irwin, *The Great Lucifer* 245 and 292–3; text of the Commissioners' letter, **xiii**, 260–63. Sir Henry Howard, writing to Essex, referred to 'Burghley's cub', Cecil, as 'tortuosum colubrum' (Aikin, ii, 441). Howard was himself repeatedly alluded to by Lady B. as 'that subtle serpent' (letters to AB, March, April and October 1595, see Dixon, 316, 322 and 330).

62 Rowse, *Ralegh and the Throgmortons*, 210. He could not, however, refrain from a passing dig at 'Cecil's jealous cousin'.

63 'Observations on a Libel', **viii**, 158. See Maurice Beresford, 'Habitation versus Improvement', in *Essays in the Economic and Social History of Tudor and Stuart England in Honour of R. H. Tawney*, ed. Fischer (1961), 40–49. Enclosure ruined the small man, and led to the eviction of tenants, but it allowed the occupier to experiment with rotation of crops and increase productive investment (Hill, *Century of Revolution*, 13). See **ix**, 79–83, chapter 21 above, and Edwards, *Life of Walter Ralegh*, i, 273–4. See further on this debate, Townshend, *Historical Collections*, (1680), 264 and 204. Ralegh also opposed Bacon in 1593 over the triple subsidy, see *Journals*, coll. D'Ewes, 478–515.

64 For Bacon's views on enclosures, see his *History of Henry VII*, **vi**, 94; for his action on them in Parliament, chapter 22 above.

65 Irwin, *The Great Lucifer*, 127–8. The Statute was ratified, with a proviso that it should not apply to Northumberland. See Neale, *Elizabeth and her Parliaments*, ii, 417.

66 Ibid., 93, 175, 286, 309, 378 and 415, see chapter 21 above. Bacon's 'defects of character', Neale writes (438), 'no doubt explain the rather ineffective role, verging on that of a busybody, that Bacon seems to have played in the House of Commons'. (Compare Carteret, in *BB*, 391, who saw him 'not as a busy and forward man, found thrusting himself into anything, but as an active and diligent servant to his prince'.) This was the Parliament at which Ralegh was exposed by Cecil for forcing the failure of a bill by holding back a Member by the sleeve. He confessed to having done it often (Handover, *The Second Cecil*, 260). On Ralegh's pro-slavery views, Napier, *Lord Bacon and Sir Walter Raleigh*, 222–3. 'None more cursed daily of the poor', wrote a contemporary complaining of his monopoly of broadcloth (cited Lacey, *Sir Walter Ralegh* (1973), 74).

67 George Garrett, *Death of the Fox* (1972), Bacon, it seems, was despised by Essex, distrusted by the Queen and doubted by James; 'Alas', he *'meddled'* (316, 318, 120, 322 and 346). Here in some thirty pages of monologue and dialogue Bacon shrugs and sneers – and finds himself 'unable to contain his laughter at the thought that Ralegh will die on the Lord Mayor's Day'.

68 Robert Nye, *The Voyage of Destiny* (1982), 19–25 and 356–63. In Lord Alfred Denning's *Landmarks in the Law* (1984), 4–16, Bacon is still the villain of Ralegh's piece.

Chapter 30 The Venomous Atheist, the Traitor and the Coward

1 Voltaire to Thiérot, 24 Jan. 1733, letter no. 12, *Lettres sur les Anglais* (1734), in Engl. edn, *Letters*

*Concerning the English Nation by Mr
de Voltaire* (1750), 68.

2 B. to Bishop Andrewes, summer
1622, **xiv**, 373.

3 Vico, *Scienza Nuova* (1713), 359.

4 Marin Mersenne, *La vérité des
sciences* (1628). On Bacon's widespread influence in France, where
most of his principal works
appeared between 1619 and 1639,
see Le Doeuff, 'Bacon chez les
grands de ce siècle', 155ff. There
were ten Italian editions of the
Essays between 1618 and 1629,
some in Venice, under the auspices of Sarpi's friend, Father
Fulgentio Micanzio (see chapter 2
above on his enthusiastic letter to
the Duke of Devonshire about
Bacon's works); others in Florence, prepared by Marcantonio
de Dominis, the apostate Bishop
of Spalato, whose sermons Bacon
attended when, in 1616, the
Bishop was a refugee at James's
Court (De Mas, *Scritti politici*, 101–
3, and *Francis Bacon*, 28–9).

5 Fray Benito Geronimo Feyjoó,
Teatro Crítico Universal (1726–30),
iv, Discurso 7, para. 40, and
Discurso 15, para. 37. Feyjoó was a
Benedictine encyclopedist, interested in mathematics, astronomy,
alchemy and medicine. He was
celebrated for his goodness and
serenity.

6 Bacon in *Encyclopaedia Universalis*
(Paris, 1985); Report of the
Convention of 25 Brumaire, III,
cited Michel Malherbe, 'Bacon,
L'Encyclopédie et la Révolution',
Les Etudes Philosophiques, July–
Sept. 1985, 401.

7 J. A. Naigeon, *Philosophie ancienne
et moderne* (1789–1810), i, 369 and
337 n1.

8 Antoine Lasalle, Preface to
Bacon, *Oeuvres*, 15 vols (1799–1803),
xi, 378. When Bacon drew 'wrong
conclusions', Lasalle blamed the
copyist, adding, whenever he saw
fit, a few words of his own, in

order to 'draw nearer' to Bacon's
meaning ('and to the truth'), or
simply to conclude Bacon's unfinished thoughts.

9 Joseph de Maistre, *Examen de la
Philosophie de Bacon* (written 1803,
published 1836), ii, 12, 40, 114, 117,
127–31. On the admiration of
Maistre for Bacon, see De Mas,
Francis Bacon, 86. Maistre's
reactionary views led him to defend the Inquisition and approve
of torture.

10 Maistre, *Examen*, ii, 94–7 and 131,
and by the same author, *Soirées de
Saint Petersbourg*, in *Oeuvres*, i, 317.
Condemnation sometimes sprang
from a terminological misunderstanding, e.g. translating Bacon's
'res publica' or 'common weal',
into 'république'.

11 J. A. de Luc, *Bacon tel qu'il est*
(1800), see De Mas, *Francis Bacon*,
83.

12 J. A. Emery, in *Le Christianisme de
François Bacon* (1799–1800), battled
with another of Bacon's trans-
lators, Alexandre Deleyre (see n22
below), an anti-Christian theist
who had also put large chunks of
his own invention into Bacon's
mouth in the form of additions to
the Essay 'Of Atheism', and other
writing (see De Mas, *Francis Bacon*, 71–2).

13 Mallet, *Life of Bacon*, see below,
n29; Emery, *Le Christianisme de
François Bacon*, pp. clxxv, clxxxxiv
and cxxiv, and 752–3, also p. cxvi.

14 Ibid., pp. cci, cxxiv and cxxxvii to
cxxix. The ref. is to the hint by
Arthur Wilson (chapter 27 above)
at Bacon's indulgence of his servants 'opening a gap to infamous
reports', which he put down as
calumnies, while dwelling on all
that Bacon 'raked in' to satisfy
those youths' craving appetites
with his 'putrid blood'. (Emery
cites the *New Atlantis* (**iii**, 52–3),
where Bacon 'paid his most
shining tribute to chastity'.)

15 Maistre, *Examen*, i, 326. The paper on Christian paradoxes, as shown by Grosart in 1864, was written by Herbert Palmer, and published in his *Memoirs of Godliness and Christianity* (1695).

16 De Mas, *Francis Bacon*, 83 and 87.

17 Catherine Macaulay, *History of England from the Accession of James I to that of the Brunswick Line, from 1603 to 1714* (1763–83, and in French, under the sponsorship of Mirabeau, 1791–2). It was largely based on contemporary tracts.

18 Catherine Sawbridge (aged fifty-six) had married Dr George Macaulay (twenty-one), a distant relation of Thomas Babington. The history by this 'Republican Virago', as Edmund Burke designated her, a widely read classic in its time, was eulogized by Pitt in the House of Commons. On her adventures in Paris (1775) and Washington (1785), where she was immortalized in a statue 'seated on Liberty's tribunal, meting out justice to kings', see Lucy Donnelly, *The Celebrated Mrs Macaulay* (1949), 202, and on her behaviour at the British Museum, Isaac D'Israeli (father of the statesman, Disraeli), 'Dissertation on Anecdotes', *Gentlemen's Magazine* 2 (1794): 685.

19 Catherine Macaulay, *History*, 99, 163–4 and 276.

20 J. A. Buchon, Preface, in *Oeuvres philosophiques de Bacon* (1836), 52–8.

21 J. B. de Vauzelles, *Histoire de la vie et des ouvrages de F. Bacon* (1833); A. F. Ozanam, *Deux Chanceliers d'Angleterre* (1836). The myth of Essex had been imported into France by Mallet's *Life of Bacon*, published in France by a highly unreliable translator of Bacon's works, Alexandre Deleyre, in *Analyse de la philosophie de Bacon* (1755), vol. 3. Thus Vauzelles could echo Mallet: 'never was any man

so long and so universally hated' (35–6).

22 Vauzelles, *Histoire*, 215, see *BB*, 393. (There are echoes of *BB*, 64 and 66; a refutation, pp. 236–7, comes from *BB*, 396). Another of Weldon's 'faithfully delivered tales' (116–17, see chapter 27 above) was now circulated in France (Vauzelles, *Histoire*, 68): When Bacon received the Seal, Buckingham told him that 'he knew him to be a man of excellent parts...fit to serve his master in the Keeper's place, but he also knew him of a base and ungrateful disposition, and an arrant knave'; so he warned him that if he found him ungrateful he would 'cast him down as much below scorn as he had now raised him high above any honour he could have expected'.

23 Apophthegm 6, **vii**, 175.

24 Vauzelles, *Histoire*, 68.

25 Ozanam, *Deux Chanceliers*, 63.

26 Ibid. It is sometimes overlooked that in Catholic countries there is no 'bloody Mary', only a 'bloody Elizabeth'. Ozanam was the more puzzled in that he saw in Bacon a poet, for whom everything was 'entrancing visions, intoxication of the soul' (ibid., 31).

27 Ibid., 59–60.

28 Weldon, 50. Ozanam may have misread Mallet (p. 37), who refers to events taking place in the next, not the previous reign. But we may wonder what Ozanam would have thought of Yelverton's exemplary behaviour, if it is true, as Weldon stated, that he endeavoured to protect his pretended patron by persuading the principal witnesses to conceal their evidence?

29 Ozanam, *Deux Chanceliers*, 32, 35, 50–51, 63, 71, 73–5, 84–6.

30 Charles de Rémusat, *Bacon, sa vie et son temps* (1857), 4–6, 77, 81–3. Bacon appears for the first time

in France, placing 'equivocation and torture...at the service of James's odious prejudice'.

31 Camoine de Vence, *La vérité, sur la condamnation du Chancelier Bacon* (1833), 52–8.

32 Gaston Sortais, *La philosophie moderne depuis Bacon jusqu'à Leibnitz* (1920), 271.

33 Gaston Bachelard, *La formation de l'esprit scientifique* (1938), see chapter 33 below; André Cresson, *Francis Bacon, Sa vie, son oeuvre* (1948).

34 Souky de Cotte, *La Reine vierge* (1938), 226 and 239.

35 Le Doeuff, 'Bacon chez les grands', 52–3.

36 Adam, Preface to his edition of Campanella's *Realis Philosophia Epilogistica* (1623); Kant, cited De Mas, *Francis Bacon*, 95; Humboldt, *Kosmos* (1845).

37 Fischer, *Francis Bacon of Verulam*, 6, 7 and 13. (See Hallam, a year later, on Bacon's 'incomparable ductility' in Parliament, *Constitutional History of England*, ii, 358–9.)

38 Justus von Liebig, *Über Francis Bacon von Verulam und die Methode der Naturforschung* (1863), see Preface by Pierre de Tchihatchef, translator of the French 1866 edn, p. xiii, and text, 43–6. Liebig had his Bacon from an editor of Bacon's *Works* (1846), Henry Bohn, who took his Bacon from Campbell. Liebig on *NO*, see De Mas, *Francis Bacon*, 98, 101.

39 Liebig, *Über Francis Bacon*, 125–7,

40 Ibid., 101, 126, 164; Bacon, *TPM*, F. *Phil.*, 71; Rawley, i, 11. De Mas (*Francis Bacon*, 99), overlooking Rawley's actual remark, took Liebig's misquotation, that Bacon drew most of his knowledge from books, at face value. For the crucial role played by 'the meanest mechanical practice' in Bacon's New Instrauration, see, among others, *Valerius Terminus*,

iii, 222. This was the 'despised weed', through which he worked, see his prayer, **xiv**, 230.

41 Liebig, *Über Francis Bacon*, 44–5, 126, 104–5.

42 Ibid., 164, translator's footnote.

43 Oskar Kraus, *Der Machtgedanke und die Friedensidee in der Philosophie der Engländer: Bacon und Bentham* (1926); J. Schick, cited Rudolf Metz, 'Bacon's Part in the Intellectual Movement of his Time' (1938), 24.

44 E. F. Litvinova, *Francis Bacon* (1891).

45 Benito Perez Galdós, *Torquemada en Purgatorio* (1894), chapter 12 (in *Obras Completas*, p. 1070).

46 *Enciclopedia Universal Europeo-Americana* (Espasa Calpe, Madrid, 1928).

47 Ballesteros, *Documentos inéditos* (see chapter 17 above), ii, 47–8 n1. 'El Canciller es persona de muy buen natural . . .' said Gondomar, reporting the regret expressed to him by Bacon over Ralegh's act of piracy. In this context Gondomar meant he was a man who could be trusted not to sacrifice his principles to support a criminal act, though he probably had in mind also the kindly disposed adversary, happy to give him good news about the Government's treatment of the Catholics, and to share a good joke with him (chapters 16 and 25 above). Ballesteros cites as his authority Israel Levine, whose *Francis Bacon* (1925) presented the same man, lacking all moral sense, the same 'checkered' life, 'problem' and 'solution' as Abbott had presented forty years earlier.

48 Gregorio Marañón, *Antonio Pérez, 'Spanish Traitor'* (1948, Engl. 1953), 54–5.

49 For the misreading of Lady Bacon's letter, which also led Rowse astray, see above, chapter 26, n16, and for text of the letter,

Spedding, **viii**, 244–5.

50 Marañón, *Antonio Pérez*, 56; Gustav Ungerer, *Anglo-Spanish Relations* (1956), 120–22.

51 For another such twinning of Bacon to a villain, see below, chapter 32.

52 Bacon, *Ensayos*, ed. L. E. Bareño (1961, this vol. bought in La Coruña, Spain, 1974), 9–11.

53 See TM to B., 1617 (cited Napier, *Lord Bacon and Sir Walter Raleigh*, 65), reporting the words of a friend in Florence that Galileo 'had answered your discourse concerning the flux and reflux of the sea, and was sending it unto me', but that he had hindered Galileo 'because his answer was founded on a false supposition', and would now be calling on Galileo himself. Antonio Pérez-Ramos, citing a study by Paolo Rossi in 1971, pointed out that Galileo elaborated his own theory of the tides, partly as a response to this work of Bacon's, written around 1616 (Pérez-Ramos, *Francis Bacon's Idea of Science*, 248 n11).

54 L. Negri, 'Campanella e i primi Lincei', *La Cultura* (1929), 542–8, cited De Mas, *Scritti politici, giuridici e storici*, 26 n19; De Mas, *Francis Bacon*, 29–31. The Accademia dei Lincei served as a model for Bacon's team of truth-seekers, the College of Salomon, which was looked on in turn as their model by the founders of the Royal Society (see Rémusat, *Bacon*, 388 n1).

55 De Mas, *Francis Bacon*, 127.

56 Mac., 346. This act of renunciation was seen with particular approval by Adolfo Levi, *Il pensiero di Francesco Bacone considerato in relazione con le filosofie della natura del Rinascimento e col razionalismo cartesiano* (1925).

57 De Mas, *Scritti politici*, 43–51.

58 *Scritti politici*, ed. in 2 vols by Francesco De Mas; *Scritti filosofici di Francesco Bacone*, ed. Paolo Rossi (1975 and 1986); Paolo Rossi, *Francesco Bacone: dalla magia alla scienza* (1957); and see among others the studies collected in *Terminologia e fortuna*.

59 De Mas, *Francis Bacon*, 94.

60 Ibid., 9–10; Abbott, see chapter 28 above.

61 Mario Manlio Rossi, *Saggio su Francesco Bacon* (1935), 150. De Mas, refuting his interpretations in 'La filosofia linguistica e poetica', concluded that Rossi was showing the prejudice of positivists, who see Bacon solely as a natural philosopher, but Rossi's misjudgements stem in great part from the oral condemnation he had taken over from Strachey.

62 Rossi, *Saggio su Francesco Bacon*, 12, 17, 42, 70, 75–6, 81, 92–3. Strachey's snake glides in (e.g., p. 20, as Bacon's 'serpentine soul'). Among the remarks that betray Rossi's distance from the reality is a curious description (p. 33) of an exclusively legalistic Bacon, who looked for his inspiration – as Linnaeus looked to the green beaches of England, and Kant to the starry sky – solely to 'the cold, dark walls of Gray's Inn' and its 'enormous, sad trees'. So Rossi saw them on his visit to London, but they were not enormous in Bacon's day, since he planted them himself – and surely not sad when he walked among them, discoursing with Ralegh or Lady Hatton, or with his 'private friend' Thomas Bettenham?

Chapter 31 *'England's One Scoundrel'*

1 Among others, Peter Quennell, *Shakespeare, The Poet and his Background* (1963), 232, and Rowse,

William Shakespeare, 345.

2 A. L. Rowse, in *The Spectator*, 26 Sept. 1970.

3 Lord Sydenham of Combe, 'The First Baconian', *Baconiana*, 80 (Feb. 1933), 143–50; S. Schoenbaum, *Shakespeare's Lives* (1970), 541ff.; Delia Bacon, *The Philosophy of the Plays of Shakespeare Unfolded* (1857), see Schoenbaum, *Shakespeare's Lives*, 529–41. Emerson, impressed by Delia Bacon's 'brilliant paradox', on which he had heard her lecture, thought seriously of founding a Shakespeare Society that might 'melt into one identity those two reputations', but, along with Hawthorne, he gave up the idea when she failed to produce the expected proof. See also, Benjamin Disraeli, *Venetia* (1837), 21–2; Freud to Zweig, 2 Apr. 1937, in *Letters of Sigmund Freud to Arnold Zweig*, ed. E. L. Freud (1970), 140; Henry James to Violet Hunt, 26 Aug. 1903, in *Letters of Henry James*, ed. Percy Lubbock (1920), i, 432; Mark Twain, *Is Shakespeare Dead?* (1909). Among historians of literature, W. C. Hazlitt, evidently influenced in his view of both Shakespeare and Bacon by his grandfather William, favoured a possible collaboration between the 'poetical philosopher' and the 'philosophical poet', *Shakespeare: Himself and his Work* (1902).

4 Georg Gottfried Gervinus, *Shakespeare Commentaries* (1849), trans. F. E. Bunnet (1863); David Masson, Essay V, in *Wordsworth, Shelley and Keats, and other Essays*, 1874, repr. from *North British Review*, 1853.

5 Gerald Massey, *The Secret Drama of Shakespeare's Sonnets* (1888), 392–3.

6 James Arther, 'The Royal Birth Theme', *Baconiana* 128 (summer 1948), 132.

7 Between 1617 and 1950 new acquisitions by the London Library included seventy-seven titles on Bacon, of which fifty-three dealt with his authorship of the plays, without counting the innumerable articles published in *Baconiana* from 1886 to date.

8 Toast proposed at 'The Ladies Guild of Francis St Alban', eulogizing its moving spirit, Alicia A. Leith (*Baconiana* 74 (June 1928): 322); see also the 'loyal' and 'whole-hearted' Baconians celebrated in *Baconiana* 32 (Oct. 1910): 246–9. 'There is something so foreign to British love of fair play in all this, that one feels it must be of alien origin', writes 'Veritas' in 'The Hidden Hand' (*Baconiana* 74 (June 1928): 205–8); it is pointed out that the Cecils, who 'hampered' Bacon's career, were foreigners, i.e. of Jewish origin, and that two of the principal critics of the Baconian heresy (Gollancz and Sidney Lee, born Solomon Lazarus Levi) were Jews.

9 As noted by Appleton Morgan, letter to the Editor, *Baconiana* 31 (July 1910), 183.

10 Donnelly, *The Great Cryptogram*, ii, 845–8.

11 Mrs Elizabeth Wells Gallup, *The Bi-literal Cypher of Sir Francis Bacon* (1900); *Un problème de cryptographie et d'histoire* (1938), by General Cartier, former Director of the Service du Chiffre. See *De Aug.*, iv, 445, for Bacon's description of the cipher, which, as a young man in Paris, he had elaborated out of a similar one by Blaise de Vigenère (*Traité des Chiffres*, 1587). Mrs Gallup inherited the outlines of her story from Dr Orville Ward Owen, a Detroit physician (*Sir Francis Bacon's Cipher Story*, 1893–5), who used at least six different, often contradictory ciphers. For some years his assistant, Mrs Gallup praised his remarkable achieve-

ment (pp. 2–4), in particular for 'being evolved entirely without the aid which Bacon had prepared in the biliteral cipher for its elucidation'. How this lady, whose sincerity and sanity were personally vouched for by her debunkers, managed to produce a translation in blank verse, while painfully making out a complicated cipher, remains a mystery. She died in poverty, almost blind from the strain of distinguishing minute differences of print, having deciphered with total conviction a tale of some 150,000 words (which included passages personally distasteful to her). Though strong arguments against the biliteral cipher were put forward by other Baconians (e.g. C. L'Estrange Ewen, 'The Gallup Decipher', *Baconiana* 83 (Oct. 1935): 66–79), and conclusive proof adduced against it (n14 below), it is still defended in *Baconiana* today.

12 An echo of the flies 'entombed and preserved for ever in amber, a more than royal tomb' (v, 320).

13 And believe that Bacon could spare the emotion, and the time, to feel that 'The sole relief doth come by making out a complete history of my wrong that doth so embitter my days.'

14 W. F. and E. S. Friedman, *The Shakespearian Ciphers Examined* (1957).

15 Parker Woodward, 'Shakespeare's Sonnets, 1609', *Baconiana*, 37 (Jan. 1912); as Donnelly explained, Bacon had often 'to enlarge, or even double the size of the original plays, rendering them useless for acting purposes, but priceless as conveying the secret history of his own times'.

16 The true authorship of the *Essais*, originally written in English, was first revealed by Mrs D. F. A. Windle – who had her infor-

mation direct from the spirit world – including the fact that Montaigne himself had never existed (see her *Report to the British Museum*, San Francisco, 1881, 18). The discovery was taken up by other Baconians, as noted by Schoenbaum, *Shakespeare's Lives*, 564–6.

17 Brig.-Gen. S. A. E. Hickson, 'Review of Bacon-Shakespeare-Cervantes', *Baconiana* 64 (Jan. 1923): 52, and *Baconiana* 65 (Apr. 1923): 143. Here Hickson explains that Cervantes's *La Galatea* (1584) was 'about some Arcadian league to prevent the marriage of Queen Elizabeth with a French Prince.' The suggestion of Baconian authorship was first made by Sir Edwin Durning-Lawrence, in 'Did Bacon Write "Don Quixote"?' *Baconiana* 47 (July 1914); see also Parker Woodward, 'Don Quixote', *Baconiana* 56 (Oct. 1916), 173–86, and R. Langdon-Down, 'Observations on Shelton's *Don Quixote*', *Baconiana* 143 (July 1952), 58–67.

18 Horace Nickson, 'The Authorship of "Don Quixote"', *Baconiana* 78 (Feb. 1931), 283.

19 See further, Schoenbaum, *Shakespeare's Lives*, 628.

20 A. E. Waite, *Real History of the Rosicrucians* (1888) and *Brotherhood of the Rosy Cross* (1924); W. F. C. Wigston, *Bacon and the Rosicrucians* (1889).

21 Constance Potts, *Francis Bacon and his Secret Society* (1891); the famous theosophist, C. W. Leadbeater (who referred to Bacon as 'the Head of all true Freemasons', *The Hidden Life in Freemasonry*, 1928), 15; H. Bayley, *New Light on the Romance and Lost Language of Symbolism* (1909); the communicant with Bacon was Ella M. Hornsey, 'Portrait of Francis Bacon', *Baconiana* 131 (spring 1949), 69.

22 On Bacon's Chaldean activities, 'Veritas', in 'The Hidden Hand',

Baconiana 74 (June 1928): 205; E. F. Udny, *Later Incarnations of Francis Bacon* (1925).

23 Waite, *Brotherhood of the Rosy Cross*, 32.

24 W. C. Arensberg, *The Burial of Francis Bacon and His Mother in the Lichfield Chapel House* (1924), cited Schoenbaum, *Shakespeare's Lives*, 529. The discovery by one James Morgan, in the early 1950s, that Bacon was a reincarnation of Edward VI was dismissed by a correspondent (*Baconiana* 142 (1952): 7) on the ground that it conflicted with the revelations of both the bi-literal and the Owen ciphers.

25 *SS*, **vi**, 641.

26 Among them the American doctor, Edwin Reed, who at the turn of our century gave a preview of the early authorship theory for Shakespeare's plays; the distinguished actor, Roderick Eagle, who contributed numerous items of interest to Shakespeare's life story, and the jurist, Sir John A. Cockburn, who did the same for Bacon at Gray's Inn. Following in the footsteps of R. M. Theobald, an early editor of *Baconiana*, Cockburn defended Bacon convincingly against some of the defamations studied in the present work.

27 Georg Brandes, *William Shakespeare* (1896), ii, 413.

28 B. J. A., 'The Humbug of Bacon', *New York Herald*, 5 Oct. 1874; *The Boston Literary World*, 21 Oct. 1882; Marie Corelli to the Editor, *Baconiana* NS 12 (Apr. 1903): 135.

29 Dover Wilson, 'Treasure in an Old Book', *Edinburgh English News*, 5 June 1943.

30 R. S. Jackson, Warden of the National Memorial to Shakespeare in London, in *The Atheneum*, 6 Nov. 1909.

31 G. K. Chesterton, in *The Eye Witness*, 12 Sept. 1912, repr. *Baconiana* 40 (Oct. 1912): 247–52. G. K. C. is following a Catholic trend, represented by Cardinal Newman, who declared that Bacon had the right to be the meanest of mankind: 'His mission was the increase of physical enjoyment and social comfort; and most wonderfully, most awfully has he fulfilled his conception and his design' (John Henry Newman, 'Discourses on University Education', *Newman, Prose and Poetry*, ed. Tillotson, 1957, 470–71).

32 George Greenwood, *Is There a Shakespeare Problem?* (1926), pp. xiv–xv.

33 B. to Greville, 27 May 1594, **viii**, 298, see above, chapter 4.

34 Pierre S. Porohovschikov (Judge at the High Court of Justice, St Petersburg), *Shakespeare Unmasked* (1940), cited Schoenbaum, *Shakespeare's Lives*, 619.

35 J. M. Robertson, *The Baconian Heresy, A Confutation* (1913); E. G. Harman, *Edmund Spenser and the Impersonation of Francis Bacon* (1914). Among the more vicious Baconian detractors, following Abbott, was a Dublin Professor, Judge Webb, in *The Mystery of William Shakespeare* (1902).

36 W. G. Thorpe, *The Hidden Lives of Shakespeare and Bacon, and their Business Connections* (1897), 57 and 64.

37 Joan Ham, 'Bacon's Belated Justice', *Baconiana* 173 (1973), 35–65, see 28; Bacon, *History of King Henry VII* (1622), **vi**, 145 and 221, but see 168. In his charge against Somerset for the murder of Overbury (May 1616) Bacon said 'Overbury is the first prisoner murdered in the Tower since the murder of the young princes by Richard the third, the tyrant' (**xii**, 290, and again 310).

38 Pierre Henrion, 'A Most Humorous Quixotic Quest', *Baconiana* 179 (1979), 13–26.

39 *Baconiana* 181 (1981): 101; suggestion made by Henrion to the

Chairman of the Bacon Society, as reported by him in *Baconiana* 186 (1986).

40 Alfred Dodd, *Francis Bacon's Personal Life-Story*, see review by Robin Robbins, *TLS*, 6 Mar. 1987.

41 Jean Overton Fuller, *Sir Francis Bacon, A Biography* (1981), 113, 176, 182, 190, 227. Ben Jonson, who in real life lost no opportunity to satirize the 'bare-breeched brethren of the Rose-Cross' (see *The Fortunate Isles*, 1624), is here made out 'one of the initiates of the Temple of Canonbury Tower'. Among articles citing incontrovertible historical evidence against the royal birth theory, see J. A. Cockburn, 'Reasons for Not Accepting the Biliteral Deciphering in Relation to Bacon's Parentage', *Baconiana* 73 (Dec. 1927), 95–9, and Roderick Eagle, 'Queen Elizabeth and Bacon's Birthday', *Baconiana* 152 (1955), 89–90.

42 W. A. Vaughan to the Editor, *Baconiana* 88 (Jan. 1938): 51. The Francis Bacon Research Trust, 'dedidated to showing how Bacon's work is based upon the Ancient Wisdom and Temple Science', founded in 1980, marks the birth of a new light, 'the Baconian Rosicrucian impulse of the Great Instauration, born of the "Virgin womb" of Elizabethan England and destined to "come of age" for the Golden Age of Aquarius'; it leads its followers in the mystic quest which Francis Bacon and his 'Knights' pursued. In 1992, aside from a pilgrimage to St Albans ('to a more recent martyr to truth'), four seminars were offered at Canonbury Tower to 'reveal the alchemical artistry and sublime wisdom of the Hermetic Master'.

43 Allan Campbell, 'A Talk to the Francis Bacon Society', 10–16, and N. M. Gwynne, 'Skeleton of a True Appreciation of the Occult Life, Works and Importance of Francis Bacon', both in *Baconiana* 191 (Dec. 1992).

44 Waite, *Brotherhood of the Rosy Cross*, 32.

45 John Churton Collins, *Studies in Shakespeare* (1904), 365–9; Edward Dowden, *Shakespeare, His Mind and Art* (1875), 18; Edgar I. Fripp, *Shakespeare, Man and Artist* (1938), ii, 622; Dover Wilson, reported by the Editor, *Baconiana* 128 (summer 1948): 122.

46 Levi, *William Shakespeare*, see above, chapter 24.

47 Every opportunity to link the two great writers is missed. Instead, already on p. 4, Bacon is placed with zealous torturers and those 'frantic to rise high'. We then find him (p. 216) seizing 'the opportunity to change sides' against Essex, and 'sourly' remarking that 'it is not good to stay too long in the theatre' (a disclaimer which actually disguised his eager interest in that subject, see below, chapter 33).

48 See above, chapter 24.

Chapter 32   The 'False Persona'

1 The uncovering was assisted by studies such as those collected in Vickers, *Essential Articles* (1964) and Sessions, *The Legacy of Francis Bacon* (1971).

2 R. H. Popkin, of the University of California, in *Philosophical Review* 73 (1964).

3 Max Patrick, 'Tribute to Bacon's 400th Anniversary', Writers and their Work, 7–10 and 13. Fortunately the year was also celebrated in America by Loren Eiseley (*The Man who Saw Through Time*, 26), who presented Bacon's real aims and efforts with penetration, and pointed out that the *canard* that he had aided in the fall of Essex had been repudiated by all his more able biographers.

G. P. V. Akrigg, *Jacobean Pageant* (1962), ii, 150, as noticed by Farrington, 'On Misunderstanding the Philosophy of Francis Bacon'.

4 Prestwich, 140–41, 168, 193, 289, 467. Similar contradictions are found in Neale (see chapter 29 above). He described Bacon as 'showing off' when intentionally introducing his proposals for law reform early in the 1593 Parliament (see chapter 29 above); yet when Bacon initiated the main legislative work in 1597 with his epoch-making bills against enclosures, Neale has nothing but approval.

5 Vickers, *Francis Bacon and Renaissance Prose*, 257.

6 Anderson, *Francis Bacon*; W. K. Jordan, see chapter 29 above.

7 Anthony Esler, *The Aspiring Mind of the Elizabethan Younger Generation* (1966), 181–91, kindly brought to my attention by Brian Vickers.

8 Lacey, 94, 106, 170, 217, 260, 311.

9 J. G. Crowther, *Francis Bacon, The First Statesman of Science* (1960), 324–8.

10 Bowen, *Francis Bacon*, 4, 14, 12 and 13.

11 Du Maurier, *Golden Lads*, 75; *The Winding Stair*, 76 and 35.

12 Jonson, *Works*, 582.

13 Johnston, *Francis Bacon, Selected and Edited*, 1, see chapter 3 above. Similarly, for Hugh Dick (*Selected Writings of Bacon*), Bacon, though a man of probity, remained 'an enigmatic figure'; Carlyle, cited Bowen, *Francis Bacon*, 13, though she herself did not reach that skin.

14 See Coquillette, *Francis Bacon*, 319. Among Epstein's mistakes (aside from the remark, p. 13, that Campbell was 'not vicious in his criticism of Bacon'): that Bacon met Essex through Anthony (p. 35); that James granted him a full pardon (p. 175, see chapter 1

above) and that, in order to 'spite Coke', Bacon left Lady Hatton a legacy in his will. The legacy was to Lady Cooke, the widow of his cousin and close friend, Sir William, her daughter Ann and son Charles (**xiv**, 542).

15 Epstein, *Francis Bacon*, 7, 12, 34, 39, 54, 100, 127, 155, 162; H. B. White, *Peace Among the Willows* (1968).

16 On Marwil's science, Brian Vickers, 'Francis Bacon and the Progress of Knowledge', *Journal of the History of Ideas* (1992), 500–501 (see further below chapter 33, n14). Marwil's declared aim in this book is to re-evaluate Bacon's *History of Henry VII*, a book 'early brooded' and responding entirely to Bacon's goals for History, as expressed in *AL* (see Wormald, *Francis Bacon*, 247–9, 260). For Marwil, Bacon's sole aim is to gain 'a ticket back to power' the easy way, by 'slip-shod scholarship'. But in denouncing Bacon's 'tinkering with History' this critic demonstrated his own ignorance of Renaissance historiography, as shown by Vickers. See also on Marwil's reductive and simplistic practices, Judith Anderson, *Biographical Truth, The Representation of Historical Persons in Tudor-Stuart Writing* (1984), chapter 10: 'Bacon's *Henry VII*', notes 34, 44, 53 and 65.

17 Like Abbott's, Marwil's Bacon is full of misplaced self-confidence, racked with the desire for self-aggrandisement, and is continually concealing from himself what Abbott and Marwil mysteriously know of his innermost motives. The trial of Essex, the *Declaration of Treasons* and Bacon's *Apology* ('every speech in that self-justifying brief is suspect') are undiluted Abbott.

18 Lee, *Great Englishmen*, 234 and 239. As noted in chapter 21 above, everything Marwil's Bacon did

was 'palpably designed to impress' royalty (p. 107). He used the law courts, as he did the House of Commons, for his advancement (p. 95); the draft proclamation for the 1621 Parliament which he had set his heart on was 'a ploy to gain attention' (p. 105), his pages on 'the true greatness of Britain' were a way 'to introduce his talents to the King' (p. 106). Even in his paragraphs on Orpheus in *De Sap.*, Bacon is 'once again' simply insisting on 'the distinction of his own mind' (p. 128).

19 Marwil, 71 and 117. He mentions Loren Eiseley, author of *The Man Who Saw Through Time* (124 and n50), as one of the deluded.

20 Marwil, citing Spedding, *ER*, i, 141 and **x**, 161–2.

21 Marwil, 63, 97 and n56, 211.

22 Ibid., 114, 111.

23 Ibid., 146; see remarks by Evelyn and Osborne in chapter 2 above.

24 Marwil, 223 n8; 'for too long have his words about men and events seemed the truth' (ibid., 13).

25 Ibid., 98. 'If a man will begin with certainties, he shall end in doubts,' wrote Bacon (**iii**, 293). For Marwil 'a passion for certitude' runs through all Bacon's writings, and his unflagging efforts to revise and improve on his texts – the sign, as Farrington, De Mas and Vickers saw it, 'of an intellectual horizon which is always expanding' – allegedly betray (p. 76) a rigid inability to grow (see Vickers, *Bacon and Renaissance Prose*, 203 and 231).

26 Marwil, 71, 120, 130, 152; Jonson, *Works*, viii, 592. Compare Rawley, who admired Bacon's 'masculine and clear' style (i, 11).

27 Marwil, 118, 95, 111–12, 166, 84, 108, 71. This partial qualifying is often another way of denigrating. Vickers, in his lecture on 'Francis Bacon and the Progress of Knowledge', saw it as an example of

Marwil's 'mastery of the sneer'.

28 Marwil, 93–4, 103.

29 Ibid., 93.

30 Ibid., 201–2 and 71.

31 Otto Friedrich, 'They Do Not Know It Is Wrong'. *Time* (15 Feb. 1985).

32 Wrenham was convicted on 5 May 1618, see **xiii**, 311 and Dixon, 346–51. A similar situation had arisen a few months earlier (**xiii**, 295–7, and Dixon, 347ff.) when the violent Sir Gervase Clifton, maddened by a decree against him in the Star Chamber, on hearing that Bacon was trying to solve his case by arbitration, threatened to stab him on the judgement seat. Bacon wrote (to Bm, 17 Mar. 1618) that a public censure was necessary as an example, but as for the punishment of Clifton, he hoped the King would remit it. He himself, he said, would 'not formally but heartily intercede for him'.

33 Cobbett, *State Trials*, i, 1064 and 1072. There was no bribery. After the trial was over, like many others who gave the Chancellor presents on his installation at York House, Wrenham's opponent, Fisher, gave him a set of hangings. The gift is set down by Gardiner (iv, 95) among the legitimate payments, according to the ideas of the time. See *Wraynam's Case or a Vindication of the Lord Chancellor Bacon* (1618, publ. 1725), 11 and 29.

34 Carteret (*BB*, 398), who noted that Bacon had been 'very much injured by this Wrenham' (see above, chapter 13). For 'though he was fully acquitted of blame on account of this matter, yet the effects of it stuck close to him, and in the end proved his ruin, the industry of Wrenham producing those complaints of which we shall hear enough hereafter.'

35 In 1933 the French Ambassador in

London described Toby Matthew as a man 'sans intéret particulier, qui ne travaille que pour l'honneur et pour sa passion', to succour the English Catholics (*DNB*).

36 Noonan, *Bribes*, 327, 338, 352 and 358.

37 Bacon, confession to the Lords, 22 Apr. (**xiv**, 243); memo for a conversation with the King, 6 Apr. 1621 (**xiv**, 238); *IM*, **iv**, 22, and Essay, 'Of Truth'.

38 Noonan, *Bribes*, 365. This is the hell of Paolo and Francesca, in Dante.

39 Lord Denning, *Landmarks in the Law* (1984), part 2: 'Torture and Bribery', 31–50. On Denning, see Iris Freeman, *Lord Denning, A Life* (1993) and *TLS* review by Louis Blom-Cooper, 14 Jan. 1994.

40 On Bacon's bride, B. to Cecil, 3 July 1603, **x**, 80, and on his marriage in 1606, chapter 26 above.

41 For the very different reality about Peacham, see above, chapter 24. The 'false fire' blunder was swallowed whole from Campbell, who refers to it (iii, 65, note k) as 'a new species of torture not to be found in his [Bacon's] records'.

42 Holdsworth, cited chapter 21 above.

43 Anthony Quinton, *Francis Bacon*. 'Past Masters Series' (1980).

44 Coquillette, *Francis Bacon*, pp. viii, 5–6, 32, 59, 222, 284, 295 and 314.

45 Adrian Berry, *Sunday Telegraph*, 19 Feb. 1995. See chapter 3 above for similar remarks by this author in 1982.

46 Aubrey, 179.

Chapter 33   The Sterile Philosopher

1 Liebig, *Über Francis Bacon*, and G. K. Chesterton, *The Eye Witness*, see chapters 30 and 31 above.

2 Rossi, *Saggio su Francesco Bacon*, 20, see chapter 30 above.

3 G. E. Aylmer, 'Downfall of a Chancellor', review of Marwil's *Trials of Counsel*. *TLS*, 15 Oct., 1976.

4 Paolo Rossi, 'Ants, Spiders and Epistemologists', *Terminologia e fortuna* (1984), 246.

5 Vickers, 'Bacon and the Progress of Knowledge'.

6 Contributors to *Manes* (1626), 44 and 42; Danby, *Shakespeare's Doctrine of Nature* (1948), 21; Lewis, *Surprised by Joy* (1954), 171; Stephens, *Francis Bacon and the Style of Science* (1975); Marwil, see chapter 32 above; and Charles Whitney, *Francis Bacon and Modernity* (1986), see below, n14.

7 Draper, *Intellectual Development of Europe* (1862, ed. 1902), ii, 260.

8 Lynn Thorndike, *A History of Magic* (1958), vii, 63 and 88; Edmund Cahn, 'Confronting Injustice', in *The Edmund Cahn Reader* (1966), 357–67, cited Coquillette, *Francis Bacon*, 15; Heer, *The Intellectual History of Europe* cited Quinton, *Francis Bacon*, 17.

9 George Saintsbury, *History of Criticism and Literary Taste* (1922), ii, 105, 190 and 195 n1, and *A History of English Literature* (1920), 207–11. Of Clarendon he could write that 'men's merits were their own, and their faults those of the time', but not of Bacon. (Curiously, his dismissal of Bacon follows just after his almost excessive praise of the poet Samuel Daniel, for taking exactly the same stand Bacon was taking in favour of English rhymes as opposed to classical measures.) Kant headed his *Critique of Pure Reason* with a passage from the *Instauratio Magna*; Nietsche, cited Rudolf Metz, 'Bacon's Part in the Intellectual Movement of his Time', 22.

10 Pitcher, 17–40. Percy B. Shelley, *A Defence of Poetry* (1820, edn 1891), 9.

See *De Aug.*, **v**, 17–20, where Bacon explains the need for a 'Treatise on the Inner Nature of Things', based on acquaintance with the evil in man's heart.

11 Pitcher, 24, 25 and 48; Brian Vickers, *Francis Bacon* in the series Writers and their Work (1978).

12 Pitcher, 25, see Jonson, *Works*, viii, 591.

13 Pitcher, 23, see Bacon, 'Antitheta', *De Aug.*, **iv**, 479.

14 On Marwil's ignorance of Bacon's science, see Vickers, 'Francis Bacon and the Progress of Knowledge', 500–501; on James Stephens (*Francis Bacon and the Style of Science*), see Vickers, 'Bacon among the Literati: Science and Language', *Comparative Criticism* 13 (1990), 256, where he demonstrates this critic's inability to grasp the simplest details of Bacon's philosophy; in the same article, pp. 258–9, on Charles Whitney (*Francis Bacon and Modernity*), Vickers shows among other blunders Whitney's absurd reading of Bacon's 'negative instances' as a 'displacement' of the mystical doctrine of the *via negativa*.

15 Vickers, 'Francis Bacon and the Progress of Knowledge', 511–18; Pérez-Ramos, *Francis Bacon's Idea of Science*, 38.

16 Liebig, see chapter 30 above; Harold Fisch, 'Bacon and Paracelsus', *The Cambridge Journal*, v, 12 (Sept. 1952), 758; Strachey, chapter 29 above. See also Lee (*Great Englishmen*): 'The great poetic faculty of imagination, which is mainly the fruit of emotion, was denied Bacon!'

17 Bacon, wrote another critic, 'had divided natural science from morality, with catastrophic results' (V. K. Whitaker, address in honour of Bacon's 400th anniversary, repr. in Vickers, *Essential Articles*, 47–8).

18 See Paolo Rossi in 1984, 'Ants, Spiders and Epistemologists', *Terminologia e fortuna*, 246–7, and see Anne Righter, 'Francis Bacon', *The English Mind, Studies in the English Moralists Presented to Basil Willey* (1964), 301–2. The same views had been expressed by R. F. Jones, *Ancients and Moderns* (1936), 88, and by C. S. Lewis in 1954, *English Literature in the Sixteenth Century*, 3, 14, and 525.

19 Rossi, 'Ants, Spiders and Epistemologists'. In 1992, noting that Rossi's was 'the best attempt to unravel the question of Bacon's putative utilitarianism', Pérez-Ramos showed up this charge as 'a gross conceptual distortion' of Bacon's ideas (*Francis Bacon's Idea of Science*, 157 n16, 291).

20 Brian Vickers, 'Bacon's So-called "Utilitarianism", Sources and Influence', *Terminologia e fortuna* (1984), 313; *AL*, **iii**, 327.

21 In *Corriere della Sera*, 12 May 1978.

22 Bacon contrasted a 'revealer of new things' to one who is 'mad about innovations', *RP*, F. *Phil.*, 117.

23 G. K. Chesterton, in *The Eye Witness*, 12 Sept. 1912; Fisch, quoting Matthew Arnold in 'Bacon and Paracelsus', 752.

24 *NA*, **iii**, 147; *NO*, **iv**, 17, 110 and 122. See Farrington, 'On Misunderstanding the Philosophy of Francis Bacon', and Paolo Rossi, 'Sul carattere non utilitaristico della filosofia di F. Bacone'. *Rivista critica di storia della filosofia*, 12 (1957), 22–41. *AL*, **iii**, 147; 'the very beholding of the light is itself a more excellent and a fairer thing than all the uses thereof' (**iv**, 115); 'Atalanta, or Profit', *De Sap.*, **vi**, 744; Preface to the *IM*, **iv**, 17.

25 L. C. Knights, 'Bacon and the Seventeenth Century Dissociation of Sensibility', *Scrutiny* 11, 1943, repr. in *Explorations* (1946), 94; Metz, 'Bacon's Part in

the Intellectual Movement of his Time', 30; Fisch, 'Bacon and Paracelsus', 752 and 758.

26 Preface to part III of the *IM*, **v**, 132–3; *De Aug.*, **iv**, 373; *NA*, **iii**, 156; *Valerius Terminus*, **iii**, 221. This work, central in Bacon's thought, is the first draft of his *Great Instauration*; a quarter of its text is devoted to the 'limits and ends' of knowledge. See also, **v**, 132–3.

27 See 'Erichtonius, or Imposture', *De Sap.*, **vi**, 736.

28 Ibid., 734–6.

29 *NO*, **iv**, 115. Sir Peter Medawar, 'On "The Effecting of all Things Possible"', presidential address to the British Association for the Advancement of Science. 3 September 1969, printed in *The Advancement of Science*, 26 (1969–70). Dismissing the 'acute sense of human failure and mismanagement' felt by many, Medawar insisted that 'there can be no contentment but in proceeding.'

30 *NA*, **iii**, 165; ibid., 166.

31 Abbott, *Francis Bacon*, p. xvii; *IM*, Plan of the Work, **iv**, 33. Bacon placed 'the incessant prayers and supplications' of the monastic orders not among acts of contemplation which, he thought, were reserved for God and the angels, but among the true works that 'cast their beams upon society' for the benefit of man (*AL*, **iii**, 422).

32 In particular by Benjamin Farrington, in 'The Christianity of Francis Bacon', *Baconiana* 165 (1965), 15–33, and 'Francis Bacon after his Fall', in *Legacy* (1971).

33 *AL*, **iii**, 296–7; Preface to part III of the *IM*, **v**, 132; *Valerius Terminus*, **iii**, 220–221.

34 *NA*, **iii**, 129, 135–7, 166; *De Aug.*, **v**, 117.

35 *The Tatler*, 23 Dec. 1710.

36 Lasalle, see above, chapter 30; Broad, *The Philosophy of Francis Bacon*, 19, endorsed by Quinton, *Francis Bacon*, 72; Metz, 'Bacon's

Part in the Intellectual Movement of his Time', 30; Crowther, *Francis Bacon* (1977), see above, chapter 32; Marwil, 92 and 112; Pitcher, 44–5.

37 Fisch, 'Bacon and Paracelsus', 752–8. Bacon (*CV*, F. *Phil.*, 101) declared himself always ready to hand over the work to people 'endowed with a deeper, more capacious understanding than his own'.

38 Article on Boyle in *DNB*; *NO*, **iv**, 110. 'And thus I conceive that I perform the office of a true priest of the sense, from which all knowledge in nature must be sought', *IM*, Plan of the Work, **iv**, 26, see *NO*, **iv**, 107.

39 *De Aug.*, **iv**, 362.

40 Fisch, 'Bacon and Paracelsus', 753. For Bacon as 'dissociator', see below.

41 *AL*, **ii**, 379 and 479. See Father Stanley Jaki, *The Relevance of Physics* (1960), 420–21. As a Catholic, Jaki thought Bacon went too far with what was nevertheless a wholesome distinction between 'those two sources of truth, nature and the Bible', and a justified attempt to free science from vain speculation.

42 *NO*, **iv**, 89, 236 and 324; Edwin Schroedinger, *What is Life?* (1944, ed. 1969), 91.

43 Rossi, 'Ants, Spiders and Epistemologists', 259.

44 Metz, 'Bacon's Part in the Intellectual Movement of his Time' (1938); in 1855 David Brewster decided that philosophy 'did not derive the slightest advancement from his precepts' (*Sir Isaac Newton*, ii, 402); for these views, held also by Alexandre Koyré, Karl Popper and others, see Rossi, 'Baconianism', in *Dictionary of the History of Ideas*, i, 172; Imre Lakatos, 1968, cited by A. Pérez-Ramos, 'Bacon in the Right Spirit', review of *A New Source* by

Graham Rees, *Annals of Science* 42 (1985): 604 n4.

45 Peter Urbach, *Francis Bacon's Philosophy of Science* (1987), cited Vickers, 'Francis Bacon and the Progress of Knowledge', 508.

46 Hobbes's correspondent, cited Anderson, *Francis Bacon*, 9; when the works of Bacon and Galileo came into the hands of Leibniz, 'il se crut transplanté dans un autre monde', see Leibniz, 'Introductio Historica', *Oeuvres*, ed. Erdmann (1840), 91–2; Darwin, cited Stephen Jay Gould, *The Panda's Thumb, More Reflections on Natural History* (1980), 54; Coleridge, *Coleridge on the Seventeenth Century*, ed. Brinkley (1955), 58.

47 B. to Father Baranzano at Annecy, June 1622 (**xiv**, 375–7), urging him to undertake a history of the heavens, complete with the instruments newly in use, and all known hypotheses, which Newton was to follow up.

48 See various 'Lives' and studies by Farrington from 1953, Fulton Anderson from 1962, Paolo Rossi from 1957, and Brian Vickers from 1968.

49 Pérez-Ramos, *Francis Bacon's Idea of Science; NO*, **iv**, 63 and 81.

50 Plan of the *Great Instauration*, **iv**, 25; *NO*, **iv**, 112. Bacon's logic was an 'immensely different' art, for which man was required to 'open and dilate the powers of his understanding' by submitting them to a natural world subtler 'many times over' than his own mind.

51 **iv**, 25, 47, 50, 56, 112, and the 'new mercies', **iv**, 20 and 33.

52 Urbach, cited Vickers, 'Francis Bacon and the Progress of Knowledge', 508.

53 Graham Rees, assisted G. Upton, *Francis Bacon's Natural Philosophy: A New Source* (1984).

54 Bacon's theory of spirits reached its final elaboration only in his later works, see Walker, 'Spirits in Francis Bacon'. He followed Democritus in *De Principiis atque Originibus* (1609), **v**, 465 and 492, and rejected him in *Thema Coeli* (1612) and in *NO* (1620), where he denied the vacuum and unchangeable matter. Mary Hesse suggested that he had learned new empirical facts on the existence of a subtle matter in space ('Francis Bacon's Philosophy of Science', *A Critical History of Western Philosophy*, ed. O'Connor, 1964, repr. *EA*, 136–8).

55 *De Aug.*, **iv**, 348–9 and 'Proserpina or the Spirit', *De Sap.*, **vi**, 758–61. The spirits of all animate bodies, Bacon believed, 'have a fine commixture of flame, and an aerial substance' linking them with that which fills all space, and 'which is to the stars what air is to flame', *SS*, **ii**, 528, see **v**, 533.

56 Rees, *Francis Bacon's Natural Philosophy*, 29. Bacon's 'spirits' are seen today as 'phenomena resembling chemical reactions', more meaningful to his 'maker's knowledge' and 'purely mechanical rules of impact', Pérez-Ramos, *Francis Bacon's Idea of Science*, 129.

57 Alan N. Whitehead, *Science and the Modern World* (1926). See also Adolfo Levi, *Il pensiero di Francesco Bacone*, 223 and 432.

58 T. S. Eliot, 'The Metaphysical Poets', in *Selected Essays* (1934, ed. 1951). Eliot described poetry as the act of 'amalgamating disparate experience that in the mind will form new wholes'.

59 See in particular Heisenberg, *Physics and Philosophy* (1956), 155.

60 Metz, 'Bacon's Part in the Intellectual Movement of his Time', 27.

61 Wolfgang Pauli, 'Die Philosophische Bedeutung der Idee der Komplementarität', *Experientia*, 6 (1950), as discussed in R. S. Westman, 'Nature, Art and Psyche',

Occult and Scientific Mentalities in the Renaissance (1984), 212.

62 De Mas, *Francis Bacon*, 77, citing Vico, *Scienza Nuova*, 1713. See also Coleridge: 'scarcely was the impulse given' by Bacon towards 'a true natural philosophy', based on observation and 'legitimate experience', when it was betrayed, in particular by Descartes, and the ascendency transferred to the science of mechanics, which, once placed 'on the philosophic throne', became 'the sole portal at which truth was allowed to enter' (*Coleridge on the Seventeenth Century*, 53–4). The recent view: Douglas Bush, 'English Literature in the Earlier Seventeenth Century', *The Oxford History of English Literature* (1945, ed. 1962), 280.

63 Heisenberg, *Physics and Philosophy*, 44–5. See also Fred Hoyle, *The Intelligent Universe* (1983), 204.

64 William James (who influenced both Pauli and Bohr), *The Principles of Psychology* (1890), cited Westman, 'Nature, Art and Psyche', 215.

65 **v**, 71, see chapter 20 above; *IM*, Plan of Work, **iv**, 25.

66 **iv**, 53.

67 *De Principiis atque Originibus*, **v**, 475, and *NO*, **iv**, 120; the Aphorisms of Heraclitus, cited Philip Wheelwright, *Heraclitus* (1959), Introduction. Bacon invoked eighteen different Aphorisms, some repeatedly. See on the influence of Heraclitus over Bacon, Wolff, *Francis Bacon und seine Quellen* (1913), i, 242–3.

68 'Grounded in nature', **iv**, 167, i.e. 'not accidental or merely apparent, much less superstitious or curious resemblances'; *AL*, **iii**, 349, 355; *NO*, **iv**, 58, 119–22, 164–7. 'Dwelling purely and constantly among the facts of nature', said Bacon, we must follow her 'knotted and tangled lines', withdrawing our intellect no further from them 'than may suffice to let the images and rays of things meet in a point, as they do in the sense of vision' (Preface to the *IM*, **iv**, 19). See Coleridge: 'The poet must likewise understand and communicate what Bacon called the *vestigia communia* of the senses, the latency of all in each, and more specially, by a magical *penna duplex*, the excitement of vision by sound' (*Coleridge on the Seventeenth Century*, 597).

69 Pérez-Ramos, *Francis Bacon's Idea of Science*, 259; Bacon, *The Interpretation of Nature*, **iii**, 218.

70 Shelley, *A Defence of Poetry*, 5. Shelley picked up Bacon's image of 'the same footsteps' to illustrate the quality of poetic association.

71 William Hazlitt, 'Lectures on the Age of Elizabeth' (delivered in 1804), in *Works*, ed. Howe (1901), ii, 124–5, and 'Character of Bacon's Works', in ibid., Lecture 7, published 1820; 'The Eloquence of the British Senate', speech in Parliament 1807, in *Works*, i, 147. See also De Mas, 'La filosofia linguistica e poetica di Francesco Bacone' (*Filosofia* 14, 1963), on Bacon's search for a way of 'speaking in images' so as not to replace the object by a verbal formula.

72 Saintsbury, *History of Criticism and Literary Taste*, 192.

73 Eliot, 'The Metaphysical Poets', in *Selected Essays*, 286–7; Knights, 'Bacon and the Seventeenth Century'.

74 Coleridge, *Coleridge on the Seventeenth Century*, 54.

75 Knights, 'Bacon and the Seventeenth Century', 96, 100–101, 105–7, 109. The link between Hazlitt, Eliot and Knights was noticed by Jeanne Andrews, 'Bacon, Hazlitt and the "Dissociation of Sensibility"', *Notes and Queries* 199 (Nov. and Dec. 1954), 484–6 and 530–32.

76 Vickers, *Francis Bacon and Renaissance Prose*, 142, 154, 164, 169–70, 174–5, 200 and 206. See also J. L. Harrison, 'Bacon's View of Rhetoric, Poetry, and the Imagination', *The Huntington Library Quarterly* 20 (1957), 268, and Michael Kiernan, *Sir Francis Bacon: The Essayes* (1985), pp. xliii–xlvii.

77 Quinton, *Francis Bacon*, 77–8; Whitney, *Francis Bacon and Modernity*, 165–9, see Vickers, 'Bacon among the Literati', 266.

78 Pitcher, 43–5, a notion which recalls the electroshock treatment recommended by Crowther (chapter 29 above) to bring together the allegedly separate areas of Bacon's brain.

79 Ibid., 51–2.

80 John Carey, 'English Poetry and Prose, 1540–1674', in *Sphere History of Literature in the English Language*, ed. Ricks (1970), 396–7.

81 Bush, 'English Literature in the Earlier Seventeenth Century', 197, 281 and 529.

82 C. S. Lewis, *English Literature in the Sixteenth Century*, 537–8.

83 G. W. von Leibniz, *Opera Omnia*, ed. Dutens (1768), vi, 303; *De Aug.*, **iv**, 482.

84 *AL*, **iii**, 295; 'Proserpina or Spirit', *De Sap.*, **vi**, 759; *De Principiis atque Originibus*, **v**, 471, and among numerous other such images, natural history as 'a granary', **iv**, 255; see also above, chapter 23, and see Vickers, 'Bacon's So-called "Utilitarianism"', in *Terminologia e fortuna*, 286.

85 Mac., 390; Abbott, *Bacon's Essays*, p. xxiv.

86 Sidney Lee, *Great Englishmen*, 246; Knights, 'Bacon and the Seventeenth Century', 104–5; Brian Vickers, 'Bacon's Use of Theatrical Imagery', *Legacy* (1971), 189.

87 E.g. Vico in the seventeenth century, who considered that he was following Bacon when he gave poetry precedence over science, and Benedetto Croce, who observed in 1941 that poetry acted for Bacon as a mediator between science and art, because of the unique role he attributed to fables as witnesses (De Mas, 'La Filosofia Linguistica e poetica', 517, 528 and 540 n17). In Italy only Mario Rossi, after reading Strachey (chapter 30 above) concluded that Bacon knew nothing of the art of poetry (*L'estetica nel empirismo inglese* (1944), 107 and 124, and *Saggio su Francesco Bacon*, 150).

88 Tenison, 73, also Bishop Sprat on his 'strong, clear and powerful imaginations' (*History of the Royal Society*, 35–6); Addison, in *The Tatler*, 15 Dec. 1709; 23 Dec. 1710. Emerson thought Bacon was 'possessed by an imagination as despotic as Shakespeare's' (in *Early Lectures*, i, 322).

89 Campion, Epigram 190, in *Works*, 263; Thomas Randolph, 'On the Death of Lord Francis Bacon, Baron Verulam, Late Chancellor of all England', *Manes*, 47; see C. D., of King's College, and Dean Williams, in ibid., 44 and 41, and others chapter 2 above.

90 Edmund Waller, *Poems* (1645), Dedication to Queen Henrietta Maria. The mutual friend was Viscount Falkland, whose son, Lucius Cary, was the guiding light of the 'Great Tew Circle', through which Bacon influenced a new generation.

91 Stow, *Annales*, 811; Bacon (probably as the best known in France) headed a list of English poets from the Renaissance to the Civil War made by the French critic Adrien Baillet, which included Donne, Shakespeare, Herbert and Milton ('Des Poètes Anglais', in *Jugement des Savants* (1685), cited J. J. Jusserand, *Shakespeare in France* (1899), ii, 328–9).

92 Aubrey, 172; B. to Lord Henry

Howard, Dec. 1599, **ix**, 161; B. to the lawyer poet Sir John Davies, a good friend of the other poet, John Davies, who had addressed a sonnet to Bacon as himself a poet (see above, chapter 2), 28 Mar. 1603, **x**, 65. In the tenth elegy of *Manes,* Bacon is called *reconditarum et gemma pretiosa Literarum,* 'the precious gem of concealed literature', R. C. and T. C., 41.

93 Poem cited in full by Aubrey, 172–3; see a study of this poem by Paul Fussell Jr, *Poetic Meter and Form* (1965), chapter 8.

94 Shelley, *A Defence of Poetry*, 9.

95 *AL*, **iii**, on the 'excellent dew' Bacon imbibed from *the poet*. He also liked to quote Pindar, whose 'peculiar gift', he wrote, was 'to surprise the mind with a striking expression, as with a magic rod' (**v**, 246, and **v**, 31). See Vickers, 'Bacon's Use of Theatrical Imagery', *Legacy*, 216 and 214. On one of the masques Bacon produced, Chamberlain, 18 Feb. 1613, i, 425–6.

96 See **iv**, 317–18, 327, 336 and 406, and Preface to *De Sap.*, **vi**, 694–9. Campion, see n99 below; George Sandys, *Ovid's Metamorphoses Englished* (1632), 18. On the 'lights he received from Bacon's interpretation of the myths', Lee T. Percy, *The Mediated Muse* (1935). Carteret (*BB*, 382) thought none 'was better acquainted with their beauties, or had pierced deeper into their meaning'. Today's disparager: Stephens, *Francis Bacon and the Style of Science*, see Vickers, 'Bacon among the Literati', 258.

97 C. W. Lemmi, 'Mythology and Alchemy in *The Wisdom of the Ancients*', in *The Classic Deities in Bacon: A Study in Mythological Symbolism* (1933), 8; 'Pan, or Nature', *De Sap.*, **vi**, 708–10.

98 Maistre, *Examen de la Philosophie de Bacon*, i, 121.

99 Baudelaire and Rimbaud, see Le Doeuff, 'Bacon chez les grands de ce siècle', 155–6; J. L. Borges, on Bacon's images, like his own, interweaving 'the wakeful intellect with myth and dream', in *La Cifra* (1981). Campion thanking Bacon for 'this enchanting book' (*De Sapientia Veterum, Of the Wisdom of the Ancients*), 'many are the writings that bring you fame, but this is the one in which I can truly taste your wisdom' (Epigram 189, in Campion, *Works*, 263). Herbert, see Sessions, 'Bacon and Herbert'; Milton welcomed the *Great Instauration* as a challenge, when he was still at Cambridge, in his *Prolusiones*, see Milton, *Private Correspondence and Academic Exercises* (1625–32). Farrington, in 'Bacon, Personality and Performance' (unpubl.) had already traced many links between Bacon and Herbert, and had studied the influence of Bacon on Milton.

100 Coleridge, *Coleridge on the Seventeenth Century*, 116, 396, 545; Shelley, Preface to *The Banquet of Plato*, p. vi. See W. O. Scott, 'Shelley's Admiration for Bacon', *Publications of the Modern Language Association* 73 (1958), 228–36 (parallels also noticed by Farrington in 'Bacon, Personality and Performance').

101 Lee, *Great Englishmen*, 243; Bowen, *Coke*, 375; Lecomte, *The Notorious Lady Essex*.

102 Lee, *Great Englishmen*, 243; Strachey, 44–6.

103 Kocher, 'Francis Bacon and his Father', *Huntington Library Quarterly* 21 (1958), 133–57, 143–4, 151.

104 Marwil, 201; Quinton, *Francis Bacon*, 7.

105 19 Dec. 1621, **xiv**, 321.

106 B. to Bm, 4 June 1621, on his release from the Tower, **xiv**, 281; B. to Bm, 5 Mar. 1621, **xiv**, 341; *De Aug.*, **v**, 9.

107 B. to Arundel, Apr. 1626, **xiv**, 550;

Meditationes Sacrae, **vii**, 250; Essay, 'Of Death'.

108 The 'living life', in 'The Hermit's Speech', revels of Gray's Inn, Christmas 1594, **viii**, 378–80, see B. to Gondomar, 6 June 1621, **xiv**, 285; Tenison, 255.

109 *AL*, **iii**, 427; *SS*, **ii**, 661 and 630; Essay, 'Of Beauty'; *Valerius Terminus*, **ii**, 230.

110 *AL*, **iii**, 413. See Bacon on stones 'that have in them fire spirits'; and 'clear pools do greatly comfort the eyes and spirits,' especially 'when the moon shineth'.

111 *AL*, **iii**, 265–6.

112 *De Aug.*, **iv**, 475–6; *RP*, F. *Phil.*, 104.

113 *De Aug.*, **iv**, 375; 'Pan, or Nature', *De Sap.*, **vi**, 712–13; *AL*, **iii**, 296, 299; **iv**, 325. He suggested that the 'tops or summits of human nature', and its highest powers and virtues both in mind and body, should be collected in a volume which should serve for a 'Register of the Triumphs of Man'.

114 Liebig, *Über Francis Bacon*, 95–6, see Bacon's *Historia Vitae et Mortis* (1603, **v**, 213–335), in which he discussed ways of preserving life by keeping the 'spirits' from oozing away.

115 Bachelard, *La formation de l'esprit scientifique*, see chapter 30 above.

Chapter 34 The Secret of their Success

1 Johnson, cited Iris Origo, *A Need to Testify* (1984), 3.

2 *AL*, **iii**, 435.

3 Gardiner, iv, 94.

4 *Apology*, **x**, 141–2; **xiv**, 229–31; see chapter 16 above.

5 Gardiner, iv, 103.

6 Gondomar, in Ballesteros, *Documentos inéditos*, ii, 47–8, see above, chapter 30, n48.

7 Amos, *The Great Oyer of Poisoning*, see above, chapter 29, n39;

Campbell, iii, 75–6 and 144–5; Liebig's French translator, see chapter 30 above; Abbott, *Francis Bacon*, see chapter 28 above; Thorpe, *Hidden Lives*, 57 and 64; Seccombe and J. W. Allen, *The Age of Shakespeare: 1579–1631* (1903), Introduction; R. S. Jackson, Chairman of the National Memorial to Shakespeare, in *The Atheneum*, 6 Nov. 1909.

8 Pitcher; Noonan, *Bribes*, see chapter 32 above.

9 e.g. Pitcher, and Strachey, never out of print.

10 A situation deplored by Vickers, *Francis Bacon and Renaissance Prose*, 257.

11 See chapter 3 above.

12 e.g. Quinton, see chapter 32 above.

13 J. A. Guy, *The Public Career of Thomas More* (1981).

14 Charles Ross, *Richard III* (1981).

15 Bacon, *History of Henry VII*, **vi**, 168, see p. 88 on the people's love of Richard, and p. 220 on his guilt.

16 Churchill, *Marlborough*, i, 379–80; Handover, in *The Second Cecil*, as noticed by Hurstfield, who added that she had made *amende honorable* in her book on Arabella Stuart (review in *EHR*).

17 Abbott, *Bacon's Essays*, p. xliii. Items Abbott could have noticed: 'I love birds, as the French King doth' (Notes, Dec. 1623, **xiv**, 444); his express dislike of aviaries, unless they were spacious and filled with plants and bushes 'that the birds may have more scope and natural nestling', for which he made a model, sparing no cost (Essay, 'Of Gardens'); his own expensive aviary at York House (Aubrey, 172). See also the 'great pride and delight' the people of the New Atlantis took in 'the feathers of birds', their ancestors having been 'invited unto it by the infinite flights of birds that came up to the high gardens' (*NA*,

iii, 143).

18 Campbell, see chapter 28. When rewarding his follower for five years' unpaid service with a modest piece of land, wrote Campbell (iii, 37), he was showing him 'a friendship not exceeded by any mentioned in history or fiction'. Never, wrote Vauzelles (in *Histoire*) 'was any man so long and so universally hated', see above, chapter 30 n22.

19 Mac., 388 and 390. So portentous were these feats, Macaulay believed, that 'the devil must be in him.'

20 Abbott, *Bacon's Essays*, pp. xlv, lii, lxiii, xxxv, xxxix, liii and lv, cited Spedding, in *CR* (June – Nov. 1876): 655–6.

21 From Mac. (312) to Campbell, and from Church, *Bacon*, to Abbott, *Francis Bacon*, see chapter 28 above.

22 Abbott, *Francis Bacon* – his first version was already an improvement on Macaulay's (313); Lee, *Great Englishmen*, see above, chapter 28.

23 While Bacon, having 'backed the wrong horse', secures his own advancement by abandoning Essex, Mountjoy, insinuating himself into 'an absolute dependency' on Cecil, and, estranging himself from all Essex's friends (Fynes Moryson, *An Itinerary* (1617), Pt II, Bk i, chapter 1, 89), is wisely giving up his 'flirtation with Essex' and preparing a logical escape route (Strachey, 205–18, Lacey, 170–71, 318).

24 *Video meliora, proboque; Deteriora sequor* ('Georgics of the Mind', *AL*, iii, 410); on the architect of his fortune, chapter 28 above.

25 *AL*, iii, 280. When he spoke of the 'corrupter sort of mere politiques' (Marwil, 119), 'it hardly needs saying that Bacon was here responding to charges he had often heard levelled at himself.' (Marwil does

not say when or by whom.)

26 J. Cotter Morison (*Macaulay*, 83) could not help 'regretting that he never saw the propriety or even the necessity of either answering or admitting the grave reflections on his truthfulness' made in 1840 by Barwell Impey, in *Memoirs of Sir Elijah Impey* (the author's father, much maligned by Macaulay). Venables (*ER*, i, p. xxiv) thought that Macaulay 'justly calculated on the general indifference' with which Impey's book was received; as, in publishing a new edition of his essay after Jardine had refuted his remarks on torture in England, he 'boldly relied on the improbability that his readers should have consulted Mr Jardine's treatise'.

27 Campbell, see above chapter 28, Noonan and Denning, see chapter 32.

28 Church, *Bacon*, 2–3. Epstein, though he spoke with admiration of Spedding's 'monumental work', made many statements showing his ignorance of it.

29 Lee on Bacon in *DNB*, see above, chapter 28 and n28 there; Pitcher, 52.

30 Campbell, see chapter 28 above; Epstein, *Francis Bacon* (for some of his mistakes, see chapter 32, n14, above). Two biographers took Bacon to task for prosecuting a disreputable political agitator, known as 'Black Oliver' – a prosecution, said Gardiner, no one would have noticed had Coke or Hobart been Attorney General (Spedding, **xii**, 131, who cites Gardiner, and Dixon, 252–3). They mistook the accused, in one case for a Lord Chief Justice, a friend of Bacon's, and in the other for a distinguished Irish peer of the same name.

31 Marwil on Spedding's view of the *Apology*, chapter 32 above; on D'Ewes, chapters 26 and 27.

32 Epstein, *Francis Bacon*, 7.
33 See chapter 33 above.
34 Mac., 397, 338 and 355; Campbell, iii, 77 and 141. In France Rémusat declared in *Bacon*, 71, that 'not a day went by' without his returning 'with passionate pride and enthusiasm' to the 'great cherished idea that dominated his writings'; not one of his days as Minister was honoured by 'a noble counsel, a dignified resistance, a generous initiative' (ibid., 87).
35 The false persona, see Marwil, chapter 32 above; Bacon as a 'dark saying', 'dark and dangerous', Pitcher, 7. See James Stephens in 1975, in whose book, as Vickers pointed out ('Bacon among the Literati', 269), 'the *New Atlantis*, that triumphantly clear and cogent exposition of a fully organized research institute, is said to be delivered in a "dark and enigmatic manner"' (*Francis Bacon and the Style of Science*, 164).
36 **vi**, 21–2.
37 Spedding, see above, chapter 28.
38 *Life and Letters of John Lindgard* (1912), cited John Kenyon, *The History Men* (1983), a reference to Macaulay's doubtful sources, erratically used, and never critically examined; see chapter 3 above.
39 See Kenyon, *The History Men*, 68–76.
40 Lindgard, cited Kenyon, *The History Men*, 68.
41 Melbourne, cited Firth, *A Commentary on Macaulay's History of England*, 54.
42 Chorus of voices: Firth, ibid., 289; John W. Burrow, *A Liberal Descent, Victorian Historians in the English Past* (1981), 82; Kenyon, *The History Men*, 67–9; John Clive, *Thomas Babington Macaulay, The Shaping of a Historian* (1973), 195–6. For Macaulay's defamation of historical characters and their historians – including among others Warren Hastings, Clive and

Horace Walpole – see, e.g., his attack on the editor of Mackintosh's *History of the Revolution* which nearly led to a duel (Kenyon, *The History Men*, 67), and his charges against William Penn, the founder of Pennsylvania, one of which rests on a confusion of identity, while another is only made to seem plausible by a series of perversions of the facts (Firth, *Commentary*, 269–72). W. E. Foster, in *Brief Observations on the Charges made in Mr. Macaulay's History of England against the Character of William Penn* (1849), remarked on the way 'the very virtues of a man are thus twisted into grounds for the most injurious attacks' (p. 32). Although his well-told story 'has bewitched the ears of the public', Foster concluded, it can but rank as 'a most attractive historical romance'. Macaulay's review of a new edition of Boswell's *Johnson* by the Tory J. W. Croker, pouring sarcasm on mostly imaginary errors, was 'a massacre' (Clive, 195–6). It was 'so damaging', writes Jonathan Clark (*TLS*, 14 Oct. 1994) because it was a projection of Macaulay's polemic with Croker in the Commons, over the Reform Bill.
43 On the libels, a jumble of mistakes and anachronisms, which Macaulay rejected on all but Marlborough', see Paget, 'Lord Macaulay and the Duke of Marlborough', Firth, *Commentary*, and Churchill, *Marlborough*, i, 534, 64, 363, 433–4.
44 Foster, *Brief Observations*, 42.
45 Martineau, *Biographical Sketches*, 419–25; Gardiner, iv, 104; *Letters of Lord Acton to Mary, Daughter of the Right Hon. W. E. Gladstone*, 1 Sept. 1883, p. 173; Churchill, *Marlborough*, i, 46; Rowse, *The English Spirit*, 231.
46 Quinton, *Francis Bacon*, 7.
47 Rowse, *The English Spirit*, 231. Few

works, he wrote, exclaiming on its 'immense readability...have been so severely criticized or shown to have more serious errors than Macaulay's *History*'.

48 Mac. to Napier, cited Morison, *Macaulay*, 162. After the publication of his *History* (Kenyon, *The History Men*, 71), he 'preened himself on a success as resounding as Sir Walter Scott's', and (as he wrote of himself to Napier) 'when he spotted a copy of Hume in a bookseller's window, reduced to two guineas, with a notice saying "highly valuable as an introduction to Macaulay"', he 'laughed so convulsively that the other people who were staring at the books took me for a poor demented gentleman'.

49 Clive, 104; Joseph Hamburger, *Macaulay and the Whig Tradition* (1976), 163; Kenyon, *The History Men*, 68–72.

50 Kenyon, *The History Men*, 68; Morison, *Macaulay*, 309.

51 Firth, *Commentary*, 35.

52 Churchill, *Marlborough*, i, 306; *ER*, i, 203–12.

53 Kenyon, *The History Men*, 71; Clive, 76; Matthew Arnold, *Friendship's Garland* (1871), 71.

54 Rowse, *The English Spirit*, 228. His inaccuracy is so habitual, wrote Spedding, 'that it has grown to be unconscious'; he attributed Macaulay's 'obstinacy in refusing to correct his mistakes' to his marvellous memory: 'the youthful accumulation of knowledge had become stereotyped in recollection' (*ER*, pp. xxiv and i, 11). Firth (*Commentary*, 272) thought Macaulay was 'mentally incapable' of seeing that any of his charges had been disproved.

55 Clive, chapter 10: 'Hannah and Margaret', esp. 262–3; Firth, *Commentary*, 74, 268 and 273; Morison, *Macaulay*, 113 and 175; Burrow, *A Liberal Descent*, 82. The 'evil

passions', Herbert Butterfield, *The Englishman and his History* (1944), 2. As Morison put it (*A Liberal Descent*, 71 and 173), Macaulay was content to look at the past 'through the wrong end of the telescope'; in attacking Strafford and Laud (or Bacon), in defending Pym and Cromwell, he was attacking the Tories of his own time, and defending the Reform Bill.

56 So wrote E. H. Carr in *What is History?* (1961), 38.

57 Acton to Gladstone, 21 June 1876, *Letters of Lord Acton to Mary*, cited Clive, 492.

58 Firth, *Commentary*, 37, and Kenyon, *The History Men*, 56. G. M. Trevelyan (cited Churchill, *Marlborough*, i, 144) was surely echoing his illustrious great-uncle's views when he excused his vilification of Marlborough's early life on the ground that it was necessary 'in order by contrast to make the glories of his great period stand out more vividly'.

59 Carlyle, cited H. A. L. Fisher, 'The Whig Historians', *The Ralegh Lecture on History*, Proceedings, vol. iv (1928), 192.

60 *De Aug.*, **iv**, 448–9.

61 David Mallet, see above, chapter 1.

62 *ER*, Preface, p. xxi.

63 Among others, D. G. James (*The Dream of Learning*, 1), setting off to explore Bacon's works 'with considerably more excitement' than he would have felt on a more dramatic quest.

64 *IM*, Plan of the Work, **i**, 137, in Farrington's more literal translation, 'On Misunderstanding the Philosophy of Francis Bacon', 444.

65 *RP*, F. *Phil.*, 107. As Vickers noted in 'Bacon among the Literati' (p. 250), 'the peculiar feature of Bacon's work, compared to that of other writers who excelled in a

variety of genres, is that so many paths that begin from apparently different positions turn out to cross each other, and to converge.' Spedding (*ER*, i, 253) had seen the 'many seeming inconsistencies' in Bacon as 'in fact only the natural branches and development of one consistent purpose'.

66   *RP, F. Phil.*, 109.

67   Arnold (1889), Carlyle (1848), Stuart Mill (1854) and Gladstone (1876), cited Clive, 492. For Bacon's suspect mental complication, see Bowen, *Coke*, 292, with reference to the royal prerogative: 'he was entirely sincere – if sincerity can inhabit an imagination so flexible.'

68   Essay, 'Of Truth'.

69   Vickers, 'Francis Bacon and the Progress of Knowledge'.

70   *NO*, **iv**, 56 and 58.

71   Buckingham himself (now a sharer in the feast) had written in Sept. 1617 (**xiii**, 252) to Bacon, then temporarily out of favour, of the 'detracting speeches' he had heard about him, 'which made me rather regret the ill nature of mankind, that, like dogs, love to set upon him that they see once snatched at'.

72   So Macaulay's biographer, Morison, *Macaulay*, 159.

73   Among those who, like Macaulay, 'blushed' for Bacon: Mac., 314–17, 338 and 397; Campbell – 'I must again be pained by pointing out instances of weakness and meanness by which he still tarnished his fame' (iii, 116); Abbott (*Francis Bacon*, 330), contemplating Bacon's life 'with sorrow rather than with pity or unmixed contempt'; Church, cited chapter 19 above; Bowen, *Coke*, 14; Matheson, cited chapter 3 above. We have seen a number of biographers (chapter 33) enjoying his 'pitiable failure',

and noted the various hells in which Abbott (see chapter 28), Noonan, Pitcher and Denning (chapter 32) placed him. By a curious coincidence, the last two, both in 1984, independently used Bacon's own image in his translation of Psalm 1 'like the chaff of the summer threshing floors. . . the wind carried them away' (Denning, *Landmarks in the Law*, 32, Noonan in *Bribes*, cited in chapter 32 above).

74   Jacques Auguste de Thou, *Histoire Universelle* (privately circulated 1620, publ. 1734, French edn 1739); *BB*, 337. Quite a few writers (e.g. Campbell, iii, 48, Marwil, 126, Quinton, *Francis Bacon*, 4) have been 'amused', with Macaulay (Mac., 322), at Bacon's assumedly grievous disappointment in being dubbed a knight with three hundred others, because he had written to Cecil (July 1603, **x**, 80–81) that he would like 'this almost prostituted title of knight' to improve his image after a recent disgrace for debt, now that he was planning to marry; but preferably in a manner that might grace him, 'not gregarious in a troup'. As late as 1995, Alvin Kernan (in *Shakespeare, the King's Playwright: Theater in the Stuart Court, 1603–1613*, 155–6 and 189) dwells at length on Bacon's assumed 'devastation' at an allegedly 'irreparable loss': 'Never did Bacon experience more painfully the truth of his mot, "rising into place is laborious"', Kernan writes of a mishap to the masque he produced with Gray's Inn and the Inner Temple for the wedding of Princess Elizabeth, 'The Marriage of the Thames to the Rhine'. But let us hear Chamberlain: their 'show by water' he wrote, was 'very galant', with its 'infinite store of lights very curiously set', was delayed by the tide until

James was too sleepy to see it, and the effect of surprise was lost. Bacon, as usual, passed off the setback lightly, hoping his Majesty 'would not as it were bury them quick', and indeed the King 'gave them very good words, and appointed them to come again on Saturday'; when, 'nothing discouraged', they 'performed their parts exceeding well and with great applause and approbation both from the King and all the company'. The next night they were feasted in the new marriage-room, each and all of them warmly received, and 'much graced with kissing his Majesty's hand' (18 and 25 Feb. 1613, i, 426 and 431).

75 Montagu, *Life of Francis Bacon*, p. clxxv; see also Bacon's French translator, Lasalle (*Oeuvres Complètes*, p. lxii): 'What lowers them raises us.'
76 Abbott, *Francis Bacon*, 330; Strachey, 206. An extreme case was Maistre, who admired Bacon as much as he hated him.
77 Lee, *Great Englishmen*, 219.
78 Epstein, *Francis Bacon*, 121. ('While his behaviour as Chancellor was less than admirable, it is not hastily to be condemned.')
79 Churchill, *Marlborough*, i, 64 and 124.
80 See above, chapter 26.
81 Mac., 330; Clive, 73 and 255.
82 Campbell, iii, 77; Michael Holroyd, 'Looking back at Bloomsbury', *The Times*, Mar. 1980.
83 Morison, *Macaulay*, 77.
84 See above, chapter 4.
85 Shelley, *A Defence of Poetry*, 43.
86 Letter from Spedding cited in Sir Henry Taylor's *Autobiography* (1885), i, 236–8; *ER*, i, 225.
87 *AL*, **iii**, 279; Stanley Jones, *Hazlitt: A Life* (1991), 22.
88 Sir James Stephen in *DNB* article on Spedding; Fitzgerald, cited

Bowen, *Francis Bacon*, 13; Venables, Preface to *ER*, pp. xix and xx.
89 Montagu, *Life of Francis Bacon*, 12 (also the friend of Wordsworth); Dixon in *DNB*; Gardiner, see Kenyon, *The History Men*, 214–15; Hazlitt in *DNB*; Aikin, see P. H. Le Breton, *Memoirs of the Late Lucy Aikin* (1864), 152–3; Addison, see Samuel Johnson, *Lives of the Most Eminent English Poets*, ii, 106–8, 241; 'God bless thee dear old man!' – so Coleridge saluted the shrewd, humourous, kindly historian of Church and lay 'worthies' (Fuller in *DNB*).
90 Article on D'Ewes in *DNB*.
91 Article on Abbott in *DNB*.
92 Pitcher, 7.
93 Bacon on History, see above, chapter 20; among the recent scholarly works on Bacon, those of Pérez-Ramos and Wormald.
94 Article on Carteret in *DNB*. Swift, referring to his six years as Lord Lieutenant of Ireland, thought 'he had a genteeler manner of binding the chain of the kingdom than most of his predecessors'.
95 Michael Holroyd, *Lytton Strachey: a Biography* (1967–8, rev. edn 1979); John Rothenstein's review of it, in the *New York Times*, cited on the jacket of Holroyd's book, see pp. 915, 919, 926, and 44, 48, 63.
96 Whitney, *Francis Bacon and Modernity*, 161, see Vickers, 'Bacon among the Literati'.
97 Benedetto Croce, *History as the Story of Liberty*. (Engl. trans. of *La Storia*, by S. Unwin, 1941).
98 C. R. Cammell, *The Great Duke of Buckingham* (1940), 127. 'The fall of Bacon', wrote Cammell, 'is one of the greatest spiritual tragedies in the history of mankind. To blame such a being is childish; all censure is impertinence . . .'
99 Origo, *A Need to Testify*, 22 and 31.
100 Fuller, *Worthies*, 380.

Bibliography

The major editions of Bacon's works are *The Works of Francis Bacon*, collected and edited by James Spedding, Robert L. Ellis and Douglas D. Heath, 7 vols (1861–74), and *The Letters and the Life of Francis Bacon, Including all his Occasional Works*, edited with commentary by James Spedding, 7 vols (1861–74) (repr. together in 14 vols by Friedrich Frommann Verlag, Stuttgart, 1963). See further p. xii above, Principal Writings of Bacon Referred to Here, and below under the names of the following editors: Abbott, Bareño, Baudoin, Blackbourne, De Mas, Dick, Durning-Lawrence, Farrington (abbrev. F. *Phil.*), Johnston, Kiernan, Lasalle, Le Doeuff, Matheson, Montagu, Pitcher, Reynolds, Rossi, Tenison, Thou and Wats. See also, in the press, *Francis Bacon, A Critical Edition of the Major Works*, ed. Brian Vickers, Oxford.

The place of publication is London unless otherwise stated.

Abbott, Edwin A., *Bacon's Essays*, 2 vols, 1876.
——*Bacon and Essex*, 1877.
——*Francis Bacon*, 1885.
Acton, Lord, *Letters of Lord Acton to Mary, daughter of the Right Hon. W. E. Gladstone*, 1904.
Adam, Charles F., *La Philosophie de Francis Bacon*, Paris, 1890.
Adams, S. L., 'Foreign Policy and the Parliaments of 1621 and 1624', in Kevin Sharpe, ed., *Faction and Parliament*, 1978.
Addison, Joseph, *The Works of the Right Hon. Joseph Addison*, ed. Mr Tickell, 6 vols, 1804.
Aikin, Lucy, *Memoirs of the Court of King James the First*, 2 vols, 1822.
Akrigg, G. P. V., *Jacobean Pageant*, 1962.
Albutt, T. C., 'Palissy, Bacon and the Revival of Natural Science', *Proceedings of the British Academy* 6 (1913–14): 1–15.
Amboise, Pierre, *Histoire Naturelle de Maitre François Bacon*, Paris, 1631.
Amos, Andrew, *The Great Oyer of Poisoning*, Chicago, 1846.
Anderson, Fulton, *Francis Bacon: His Career and Thought*, Los Angeles, 1962.
Anderson, Judith, *Biographical Truth: The Representation of Historical Persons in Tudor-Stuart Writing*, New Haven, 1984.

Bibliography

Andrews, Jeanne, 'Bacon, Hazlitt and the "Dissociation of Sensibility"', *Notes and Queries* 199 (Nov. and Dec. 1954): 484 and 530–32.

Anon., *Wraynham's Case, or A Vindication of the Lord Chancellor Bacon for the Aspersion of Injustice cast upon him by Mr Wraynham*, 1618, publ. 1725.

Anon., 'A Lover of Truth', *Great Merit Triumphant*, 1749.

Anon., *The Arraignment and Conviction of Mervyn Touchet, Earl of Castlehaven*, 1942.

Arensberg, W. C., *The Burial of Francis Bacon and his Mother in the Lichfield Chapel House*, Pittsburgh, 1924.

——*Francis Bacon, William Butts, and the Pagets of Beaudesert*, Pittsburgh, 1929.

Arnold, Dennis, *Monteverdi, the Master Musician*, New York, 1963.

Arnold, Matthew, *Friendship's Garland*, 1871.

Arther, James, 'The Royal Birth Theme', *Baconiana* 31 (July 1948).

Aubrey, John, *Brief Lives*, deposited at the Ashmolean 1694, ed. Andrew Clark, 1898.

——*Aubrey's Brief Lives*, ed. Oliver Lawson Dick, Harmondsworth, 1972.

Augustine, Saint, *Confessions of St. Augustine*, trans. E. B. Pusey, 1907.

Austen, Jane, *Pride and Prejudice*, 1813.

——*Mansfield Park*, 1814.

——*Persuasion*, 1818.

Axson, Stockton, 'Francis Bacon as Man of Letters', in Rice Institute Pamphlet 13, Houston, 1926, 93–112.

Aylmer, G. E., *The King's Servants: The Civil Service of Charles I*, 1961.

——'Downfall of a Chancellor', Review of *Trials of Counsel* by J. Marwil, *TLS*, 15 Oct. 1976.

Bachelard, Gaston, *La formation de l'esprit scientifique* (1938), Paris, 1963 edn.

Bacon, Delia, *The Philosophy of the Plays of Shakespeare Unfolded*, 1857.

Bailey, Nathaniel, *Etymological Dictionary*, 1926.

Baillet, Adrien, *Jugement des savants*, Paris, 1685.

Baker, H. Kendra, 'Pope and Bacon: The Meaning of the Meanest', *Baconiana* 85 (Jan. 1937).

Ballesteros y Beretta, Antonio, ed., *Documentos ineditos de la historia de Espana*, 4 vols, Madrid, 1936–45.

Barcroft, J. H., 'Carleton and Buckingham: The Quest for Office', in H. G. Reinmuth Jr, ed., *Early Stuart Studies, Essays in Honour of D. H. Willson*, Minneapolis, 1970.

Bareño, L. Escolar, ed., *Bacon, Ensayos* (1961), Buenos Aires, 1974 edn.

Barrington, Daines, *Observations on the more Ancient Statutes from Magna Carta to the Twenty-First of James*, 1766.

Barroll, Leeds, 'A New History for Shakespeare and his Time', *Shakespeare Quarterly* 39 (1988), 441–65.

Baudoin, Jean, *Essais de Mr François Bacon*, Paris, 1619.

Bayrou, François, *Henri IV, le roi libre*, Paris, 1990.

Beckinsale, Bernard, *Burghley, Tudor Statesman, 1520–1598*, 1967.

Beier, A. L., *The Problem of the Poor in Tudor and Early Stuart England*, Lancaster Pamphlets, 1983.

Belloc, Hilaire, *A History of England in Seven Volumes*, 1931.

Beresford, Maurice, 'Habitation versus Improvement, the Debate on Enclosure by Agreement', in F. J. Fischer, ed., *Essays in the Economic and Social History of Tudor and Stuart England, in Honour of R. H. Tawney*, Cambridge, 1961.

Bindoff, S. T., *Tudor England* (1950), Pelican edn., 1965.

Bindoff, S. T., Hurstfield, J., and Williams, C. H., eds, *Elizabethan Government and Society, Essays Presented to Sir John Neale*, 1961.

Biographia Britannica, or the Lives of the Most Eminent Persons who Have Flourished in Great Britain and Ireland, ed. A. Kippis, 6 vols, 1747–66.

Birch, Thomas, *Memoirs of the Reign of Queen Elizabeth, from the Year 1581 till her Death*, 2 vols, 1754.

Black, J. B., *The Story of the Reign of Elizabeth, 1558–1603*, Oxford, 1936.

Blackbourne, John, ed., *Works of the Lord Bacon*, 1730.

Blake, William, *Complete Writings of William Blake*, ed. Geoffrey Keynes, 1966.

Blunden, Edmund, 'George Herbert's Latin Poems', *Essays and Studies by Members of the English Association* 19 (1933).

Bodley, Thomas, *The Life of Sir Thomas Bodley, the Honourable Founder of the Publique Library in the University of Oxford, Written by Himselfe* (1609), Oxford, 1647.

——*Reliquiae Bodleianae*, 1648.

Boener, Peter, 'Life of Bacon', prefixed to the Dutch edition of Bacon's *Essays* (Leyden, 1647), trans. J. d'A. de Bonzowill, *Atheneum*, 10 June 1871.

Borges, J. L., *La Cifra*, Madrid, 1981.

Bossy, *Giordano Bruno*, New Haven, 1991.

Bowen, Catherine D., *The Lion and the Throne: The Life and Times of Edward Coke*, 1957.

——*Francis Bacon, the Temper of a Man*, 1963.

Bowyer, Robert, *The Parliamentary Diary of Robert Bowyer, 1606–7*, ed. David H. Willson, Minneapolis, 1931.

Brandes, Georg, *William Shakespeare*, 2 vols, 1896.

Brewster, David, *Memoirs of the Life, Writings and Discourses of Sir Isaac Newton*, 1855.

Broad, C. D., *The Philosophy of Francis Bacon: An Address Delivered at Cambridge on the Occasion of the Bacon Tercentenary*, Cambridge, 1926.

Buchon, J. A., *Oeuvres philosophiques de Bacon*, Paris, 1836.

Bullough, Geoffrey, 'Bacon and the Defence of Learning', in *Seventeenth-Century Studies Presented to Sir Herbert Grierson*, Oxford, 1938 (*Northumberland MS*).

Burgoyne, F. J., ed., *Collotype Facsimile and Type Transcript of an Elizabethan Manuscript Preserved at Alnwick Castle, Northumberland*, 1904.

Burke, J. B., '"Lord" Bacon and the Cambridge Style', *The Outlook*, 19 Mar. 1910.

Burrow, John W., *A Liberal Descent, Victorian Historians in the English Past*, Cambridge, 1981.

Burton, Robert, *The Anatomy of Melancholy*, 1621.

Bush, Douglas, 'English Literature in the Earlier Seventeenth Century, 1600–1660', in *The Oxford History of English Literature*, vol. 5 (1945), rev. edn, 1962.

Bushell, Thomas, *Abridgement of the Lord Chancellor's Philosophical Theory in Mineral Prosecutions*, 1659.

Butterfield, Herbert, *The Whig Interpretation of History*, 1931.

——*The Englishman and his History*, 1944.

Cahn, Edmund, 'The Lawyer as Scientist and Scoundrel', in *The Edmund Cahn Reader*, Boston, 1966.

Camden, William, *The History of Elizabeth, the Late Queen of England, Annales*, iii and iv, 1617, ed. Thomas Hearne, 1635.

——*Annals of the Reign of King James*, Latin 1635, Engl. 1703.

Cammell, Charles R., *The Great Duke of Buckingham*, 1939.

Campanella, Tommaso, *Realis Philosophia Epilogistica*, Frankfurt, 1623.

Campbell, Allan, 'A Talk to the Francis Bacon Society', *Baconiana* 181 (1992).

Campbell, John, 'Life of Lord Bacon', in *Lives of the Lords Chancellors* (1845–7), 1868 edn in 10 vols, vol. iii, 1–146.

Campion, Thomas, *The Works of Thomas Campion*, ed. Percival Vivian, Oxford, 1967.

Carey, John, 'English Poetry and Prose, 1540–1674', in Christopher Ricks, ed., *Sphere History of Literature in the English Language*, 1970.

Carleton, Dudley, *Dudley Carleton to John Chamberlain*, ed. Maurice Lee Jr, New Brunswick, 1972.

Carr, E. H., *What is History?*, 1961.

Carte, Thomas, *A General History of England from the Earliest Times*, 4 vols, 1747–55.

Carteret, John, Earl Granville, 'Francis Bacon', in *Biographia Britannica*, ed. A. Kippis, 6 vols, 1747–66.

Cartier, General, *Un problème de cryptographie et d'histoire*, Paris, 1938.

Chamberlain, John, *The Letters of John Chamberlain*, 2 vols, ed. N. E. McClure, Westport, Conn., 1939.

Chambers, Bunten A., *Life of Sir Thomas Meautys, Secretary to Lord Bacon, and his Friends*, 1918.

——*Life of Alice Barnham, 1592–1650*, 1919.

Chambers, R. W., *William Shakespeare*, 2 vols, Oxford, 1930.

Chapman, George, *Georgics of Hesiod . . . Translated Elaborately out of the Greek*, 1618.

Chesterton, G. K., in *The Eye Witness*, 12 Sept. 1912.

Church, R. W., *Bacon*, 1884.

Churchill, Winston S., *Marlborough, His Life and Times*, 6 vols, 1934.

Churton Collins, John, *Studies in Shakespeare*, 1904.

Clare, John, *Letters*, ed. M. Storey, Oxford, 1986.

Clarendon, Edward Hyde, Earl of, *The History of the Rebellion and Civil Wars in England* (begun 1641), ed. Dunn Macray, 6 vols, Oxford, 1888.

——'The Difference and Disparity between the Estates and Conditions of George, Duke of Buckingham and Robert Earl of Essex . . . by the Earl of Clarendon in his younger days', in Henry Wotton, *Reliquiae Wottonianae*, 1672.

——*A Brief View and Survey of the Dangerous and Pernicious Errors to Church and State in Mr. Hobbe's Book Entitled Leviathan*, 1673.

Clark, P., Smith, A. G. R., and Tacke, N., *The English Commonwealth 1547–1640, Essays in Politics and Society presented to Joel Hurstfield*, Leicester, 1974.

Clarkson, William, *Memoirs of the Private and Public Life of William Penn* (1813), 1849 edn.

Clive, John, *Thomas Babington Macaulay, the Shaping of a Historian*, 1973.

Cobbett, William, ed., *Parliamentary History, 18 James 1620 and 19 James 1621* (1776), 1806–26 edn.

——with T. B. Howell, *State Trials*, 1806–26.

Cochrane, R. C., 'Francis Bacon and the Architect of his Fortune', *Studies in the Renaissance* 5 (1958).

Cockburn, John A., 'Reasons for Not Accepting the Biliteral Deciphering in Regard to Bacon's Parentage', *Baconiana* 73 (Dec. 1927).

Coke, Edward, *Institutes of the Laws of England*, parts II–IV (written 1628), 1644.

Coleridge, Samuel T., 'The Friend', in *Essays*, 1818.

——*Universal Dictionary of Knowledge*, 1845.

——*A Treatise on Method* (1848), ed. A. D. Snyder, 1934.

——*Coleridge on the Seventeenth Century*, ed. R. F. Brinkley, Durham, N.C., 1955.

Comenius, Jean Amos (Komensky), *Physicae ad Lumen Divinum Reformatim*, or *Via Lucis, a Synopsis of Physics*, Engl. transl., 1668.

Coquillette, Daniel, *Francis Bacon*, Edinburgh, 1992.

Coward, Barry, *The Stuart Age, A History of England in 1603–1714*, 1980.

Cresson, André, *Francis Bacon, sa vie, son oeuvre, avec un exposé de sa philosophie*, Paris, 1948.

Cressy, David, 'Francis Bacon and the Advancement of Schooling', *History of European Ideas* 2 (1981): 65–74.

Croce, Benedetto, *History as the Story of Liberty*, transl. of *La storia come pensiero e azzione*, 1938 by Sylvia Unwin, 1941.

Crowther, J. G., *Francis Bacon, The First Statesman of Science*, 1960.

——'Nature to be Commanded must be Obeyed', *New Scientist*, 1977.

Danby, John, F., *Shakespeare's Doctrine of Nature*, 1948.

Davies, John, *Scourge of Folly*, 1610.

Delayre, Alexandre, *Analyse de la philosophie de Bacon*, Paris, 1755.

De Mas, Enrico, 'La filosofia linguistica e poetica di Francesco Bacone', *Filosofia* 14 (1963): 495–542.

——*Scritti politici, giuridici e storici de Francesco Bacone*, 2 vols, Turin, 1971.

——*Francis Bacon*, Florence, 1978.

Denning, Alfred, *Landmarks in the Law*, 1984.

Dennis, John, *Reflections Critical and Satirical on a Late Rhapsody called an Essay on Criticism*, 1711.

Devereux, Walter, B., *Lives and Letters of the Devereux, Earls of Essex, in the Reigns of Elizabeth, James I and Charles I*, 2 vols, 1853.

Devlin, Christopher (S. J.), *The Life of Robert Southwell, Poet and Martyr*, 1956.

——*Hamlet's Divinity and Other Essays*, 1965.

D'Ewes, Simonds, *The Journals of all the Parliaments of Queen Elizabeth, both of the House of Lords and House of Commons*, collected by Sir Simonds D'Ewes, ed. Rev. Paul Bowes, 1682.

——*Autobiography*, 1729 edn.

——'Extracts from the Manuscript Journal of Sir Simonds D'Ewes', in *Biblioteca Topografica Britannica*, vi, 1790.

Dibon, F., 'Sur la réception de l'oeuvre de F. Bacon en Hollande dans la première moitié du XVIIe siècle', in *Terminologia e fortuna*, 1984.

Dick, Hugh G., ed., *Selected Writings of Bacon*, New York, 1955.

Disraeli, Benjamin, *Venetia*, 1837.

D'Israeli, Isaac, *Curiosities of Literature*, 1791.

Dixon, C. J., *A Preface to Bacon*, Hutchinson Educational, 1963.

Dixon, W. Hepworth, *Personal History of Lord Bacon from Unpublished Papers*, 1861.
——*The Story of Lord Bacon's Life*, 1862.
Dodd, Alfred, *Francis Bacon's Personal Life-Story* (1949), expanded 1987 edn, 2 vols.
Doleman, R. (= Robert Parsons = Cardinal Allen), *A Conference about the Next Succession to the Throne*, 1595.
Donnelly, Ignatius, *The Great Cryptogram*, 2 vols, 1888.
Donnelly, Lucy, *The Celebrated Mrs Macaulay*, 1949.
Dover Wilson, John, 'Treasure in an Old Book', *Edinburgh English News*, 5 June 1943.
Dowden, Edward, *Shakespeare, His Mind and Art*, 1875.
Draper, John William, *Intellectual Development of Europe* (1862), 1902 edn.
Driver, Olive W., *The Bacon Shakespearean Mystery*, Northampton, Mass., 1960.
Dryden, John, *Poems and Fables*, ed. J. Kinsley, 1962.
Dugdale, William, *Baronage of England*, 3 vols, 1675.
Du Maurier, Aubéry, *History of Holland*, 1680.
Du Maurier, Daphne, *Golden Lads, A Story of Anthony Bacon, Francis and their Friends*, 1975.
——*The Winding Stair: Francis Bacon, His Rise, and Fall*, 1976.
Durning-Lawrence, Edwin, 'Bacon's *Promus*', in *Bacon is Shakespeare*, 1910.

Eagle, Roderick L., 'Bolingbroke and Essex', *Baconiana* 139 (spring 1951).
——'Queen Elizabeth and Bacon's Birthday', *Baconiana* 152 (1955).
Edwards, Edward, *The Life of Walter Ralegh Together with His Letters*, 2 vols, 1868.
Eiseley, Loren, *The Man Who Saw Through Time*, rev. and enlarged edn of *Francis Bacon and the Modern Dilemma*, New York (1961), 1973 edn.
Eliot, George, *Middlemarch* (1871), Everyman edn, 1930.
Eliot, T. S., *Selected Essays*, 1934.
Elsing, Henry, Clerk of the Parliaments A.D. 1621, *Notes of the Debates in the House of Lords*, ed. S. R. Gardiner, Camden Society, 1870.
Elton, Geoffrey R., 'Reform in an Age of Change', in *Studies in Tudor and Stuart Politics and Government*, 1983.
Emerson, Ralph Waldo, *Ten Lectures on English Literature*, Boston, 1885.
——*The Complete Works of Ralph Waldo Emerson*, centenary edn in 12 vols, ed. E. W. Emerson, and W. E. Forbes, Boston, 1903–4.
——'Lord Bacon', in *The Early Lectures of Ralph Waldo Emerson*, vol. 1: *1833–1836*, ed. S. E. Wicher and R. S. Spiller, Princeton, 1959.
Emery, J. A., *Le Christianisme de François Bacon, ou pensées et sentiments de ce grand homme sur la religion*, Paris, 1799–1800.
Epstein, Joel J., *Francis Bacon: A Political Biography*, Athens, Ohio, 1977.
Esler, Anthony, *The Aspiring Mind of the Elizabethan Younger Generation*, Duke University Press, Durham N.C., 1966.
Essex, Robert Devereux, Earl of, *An Apologia*, 1597.
Evelyn, John, *Numismata, A Discourse of Metals Antient and Modern*, 1697.
——*Diary of John Evelyn*, ed. William Bray, 2 vols, 1966.

Faolain, Sean, *The Great O'Neill*, 1942.
Farrington, Benjamin, 'On Misunderstanding the Philosophy of Francis Bacon', in

E. Ashworth, ed., *Science, Medicine and History, Essays Written in Honour of Charles Singer*, 1953.

—— *The Philosophy of Francis Bacon, An Essay on its Development from 1603 to 1609 with New Translations of Fundamental Texts*, Liverpool, 1964.

—— *The New Atlantis of Francis Bacon*, tenth lecture of the New Atlantis Foundation, Lymington, 1964.

—— 'The Christianity of Francis Bacon', *Baconiana* 165 (1965): 15–33.

—— 'Francis Bacon after his Fall', in W. A. Sessions, ed., *The Legacy of Francis Bacon*, Atlanta, 1971.

—— *Francis Bacon, Philosopher of Industrial Science*, 1973.

Feyjoó y Montenegro (Fray) Benito Gerónimo, *Teatro Crítico Universal*, 1726–40.

Firth, Charles H., *A Commentary on Macaulay's History of England*, 1938.

Fisch, Harold, 'Bacon and Paracelsus', *Cambridge Journal* 5.12 (Sept. 1952): 752–8.

Fischer, H. A. L., 'The Whig Historians' (Raleigh Lecture on History), *Proceedings of the British Academy* 4 (1928).

Fischer, Kuno, *Francis Bacon of Verulam* (Berlin, 1856), Engl. transl. by John Oxenford, 1857.

Foley, Henry, ed. *Records of the Society of Jesus*, 1877.

Foster, Elizabeth Read, 'The Procedure of the House of Commons against Patents and Monopolies, 1621–24', in W. A. Aiken and B. D. Henning, eds, *Conflict in Stuart England, Essays in Honor of Wallace Notestein*, New Haven, 1960.

Foster, Genevieve, *The World of Captain John Smith*, New York, 1959.

Foster, W. E., *Brief Observations on the Charges Made in Mr. Macaulay's History of England against the Character of William Penn*, 1849.

Fowler, Thomas, *Francis Bacon*, 1884.

Freedman, Sylvia, *Poor Penelope*, 1983.

Freud, Siegmund, *Letters of Sigmund Freud to Arnold Zweig*, ed. E. L. Freud, 1970.

Friedman, W. F. and Friedman, E. S., *The Shakespearian Ciphers Examined*, 1957.

Friedrich, Otto, 'They Do Not Know It Is Wrong', *Time*, 15 Feb. 1985.

Friis, Astrid, *Alderman Cockayne's Project*, Copenhagen and London, 1927.

Fripp, Edgar, I., *Shakespeare, Man and Artist*, Oxford, 1938.

Froude, James A., 'Lord Campbell as a Writer of History', *Westminster Review* (1854): 446–9.

Fuller, Thomas, *Worthies of England* (1652), ed. J. Freeman, 1943.

—— *Church History of Great Britain* (1655), ed. James Nichols, 1868.

Fussell, Paul Jr, *Poetic Meter and Form*, New York, 1965.

Galdós, Benito Pérez, *Torquemada en Purgatorio* (1894), in *Obras completas*, Madrid, 1942.

Gallup, Elizabeth Wells, *The Bi-literal Cypher of Sir Francis Bacon*, Detroit, 1900.

Gardiner, Samuel R., *History of England from the Accession of James I to the Outbreak of the Civil War, 1603–1642*, vols ii to iv, 1863–9.

—— 'On Four Letters from Lord Bacon to Christian IV', *Archaeologia* 41 (1867).

—— *Introduction to English History*, 1881.

Garrett, George, *Death of the Fox*, 1972.

Gassendi, Pierre, *Opera*, 6 vols, Lyons, 1658.

Bibliography

Gerard, John, *What Was the Gunpowder Plot?* 1897.

—— *The Autobiography of an Elizabethan* (written *c.* 1609), transl. from the Latin by P. Caraman, 1951.

Gervinus, Georg Gottfried, *Shakespeare Commentaries* (Heidelberg, 1849), Engl. transl. by F. E. Burnet, 1863.

Gladstone, W. E., article in *Quarterly Review*, July 1879.

—— *Gleanings*, 1879.

Glanvill, Joseph, *Scepsis Scientifica*, 1655.

Gohorry, John, 'Acts of Merit', *Encounter*, Sept.–Oct. 1984.

Gooch, G. P., *Political Thought in England from Bacon to Halifax*, 1914.

Goodman, (Bishop) Godfrey, *The Court of King James the First* (*c.* 1650), ed. J. S. Brewer, 1939.

Gosse, Edmund, *The Life and Letters of John Donne, Dean of St Paul's*, 2 vols, 1899.

Gough, J. W., *The Superlative Prodigal: A Life of Thomas Bushell*, Bristol, 1932.

—— *Fundamental Law in English Constitutional History*, Oxford, 1955.

Gould, Stephen Jay, *The Panda's Thumb, More Reflections on Natural History* (1980), Penguin edn, Harmondsworth, 1990.

Green, J. R., *Short History of the English People*, 1874.

Green, M. A. E., ed., *Calendar of State Papers, Domestic Series*, 1858.

Greenwood, George, *Is There a Shakespeare Problem?*, 1926.

Grice, Elizabeth, 'Common Battleground Divides Peer and Commons', *Sunday Times*, 26 July 1981.

Grosart, A. B., *Thoughts that Breathe and Words that Burn*, 1893.

Guy, John A., *The Public Career of Sir Thomas More*, Lectures in Modern British History, Bristol, 1980.

Gwynne, N. M., 'Skeleton of a True Appreciation of the Occult Life, Works and Importance of Francis Bacon', *Baconiana* 191 (1992).

Hacket, (Bishop) John, *Scrinia Reserata, A Memorial Offered to the Great Deservings of John Williams*, 1693.

Hall, Clifford, 'Heath on Bacon in Steward's Case, Through a Glass, Darkly', *Baconiana* 184 (1984).

—— 'Francis Bacon, a "Landmark in the Law"?', *Baconiana* 186 (1986).

—— 'Then and Now, Francis Bacon and Law Reform', *Baconiana* 187 (1987).

—— 'Some Perspectives on the Use of Torture in Bacon's Time and the Question of his "Virtue"', *Anglo-American Law Review* 18.4 (1989): 289–321.

—— 'Bacon and the Legality of Torture', *Baconiana* 188 (1989).

—— 'From Little Acorns: How Bacon Lost "Friends" but Influenced People in 1593', *Baconiana* 189 (1990).

Hallam, Henry, *The Constitutional History of England from the Accession of Henry VII to the Death of George II* (1827), 1881 edn.

—— *History of European Literature*, 1837.

Ham, Joan, 'Bacon's Belated Justice', *Baconiana* 173 (1973).

Hamburger, Joseph, *Macaulay and the Whig Tradition*, 1976.

Handover, P. M., *The Second Cecil, The Rise to Power 1563–1604 of Sir Robert Cecil, later First Earl of Salisbury*, 1959.

Hardy, Harold, 'Bacon's Warwickshire Relations', *Baconiana* 39 (July 1912): 134–43.

Harington, John, *Nugae Antiquae*, 1769.

Harman, E. G., *Edmund Spenser and the Impersonation of Francis Bacon*, 1914.

Harris, R. W., *Clarendon and the English Revolution*, 1983.

Harrison, G. B., *Shakespeare at Work*, 1933.

——*The Life and Death of Robert Devereux, Earl of Essex*, 1937.

——ed., *The Elizabethan Journals, Being a Record of Those Things Most Talked of during the Years 1591–1603* (1933), rev. edn, 1938.

Harrison, John L., 'Bacon's View of Rhetoric, Poetry and the Imagination', *Huntington Library Quarterly* 20 (Feb. 1957): 107–25, repr. in Brian Vickers, ed., *Essential Articles for the Study of Francis Bacon*, Hamden, Conn., 1968.

Hazlitt, William, *Works*, ed. P. P. Howe, 1901.

Hazlitt, W. C., *Shakespeare: Himself and his Work*, 1902.

Hearne, Thomas, *Niger Scacarii*, 1728.

——*The History of Richard II*, 1729.

Heath, F. C., 'Origins of the Binary Code', *Scientific American* 227.2 (Aug. 1972).

Heath, James, *Torture and English Law*, Westport, Conn., 1982.

Heer, Friedrich, *The Intellectual History of Europe*, New York, 1968.

Heisenberg, Werner, *Physics and Philosophy: The Revolution in Modern Science* (1956), Engl. transl. 1959.

Henrion, Pierre, 'A Most Humorous Quixotic Quest', *Baconiana* 179 (1979).

Heraclitas, see below under Wheelwright.

Herbert, George, *George Herbert's Latin Poems*, ed. Edmund Blunden, 1933.

——*The Works of George Herbert*, ed. F. E. Hutchinson (1941), rev. edn, Oxford, 1945.

——*The Latin Poems of George Herbert*, ed. M. McClosky and P. R. Murphy, 1965.

——*The English Poems of George Herbert*, ed. C. A. Patrides, 1974.

Hesse, Mary, 'Francis Bacon's Philosophy of Science', in D. J. O'Connor, ed., *A Critical History of Modern Philosophy*, New York, 1964, repr. in Brian Vickers, ed., *Essential Articles for the Study of Francis Bacon*, Hamden, Conn., 1968.

Heylin, Peter, *Examen Historicum*, 1659.

——*Cyprianus Anglicus* (a life of Archbishop Laud), 1661.

Hickson, S. A. E., 'Review of Bacon-Shakespeare-Cervantes', *Baconiana* 64 and 65 (Jan. and Apr. 1923).

Hill, Christopher, *Intellectual Origins of the English Revolution*, Oxford, 1965.

——*The Century of Revolution, 1603–1714*, 1980.

Hirst, Derek, 'Court, Country and Politics before 1629', in Kevin Sharpe, ed., *Faction and Parliament*, 1978.

——*Authority and Conflict: England 1503–1658*, 1986.

Hoadley, Benjamin (Bishop), alias 'Britannicus', *The Justice of Parliaments*, 1725.

Hoffer, P. C., with N. E. H. Hull, *Impeachment in America, 1635–1805*, New Haven, 1984.

Holden, W., 'Bacon's Association with Gray's Inn', *Baconiana* 141 (autumn 1951).

Holdsworth, William S., *A History of English Law*, 1909.

——'The Elizabethan Age in English Legal History', *Iowa Law Review* (1927).

Holloway, David, Review of *A Cornishman Abroad*, in *Daily Telegraph*, 1 Mar. 1976.

Holroyd, Michael, *Lytton Strachey: A Biography* (1967–8), rev. edn, 1979.

——'Looking Back at Bloomsbury', *The Times*, 1 Mar. 1980.

Hooke, Robert, *Cutlerian Lectures and Other Discourses Read at the Meetings of the Illustrious Royal Society*, 1705.

Hopkins, Vivian C., 'Emerson and Bacon', *American Literature* 29.4 (Jan. 1958): 408–30.

Hornsey, Ella M., 'Portrait of Francis Bacon', *Baconiana* 131 (spring 1949).

Hotson, Leslie, *Shakespeare's Sonnets Dated*, 1950.

Howell, James, *Epistolae Ho-Elianae, Familiar Letters Domestic and Foreign* (1650), 1678 edn.

Hoyle, Fred, *The Intelligent Universe*, 1983.

Hughes, Robert, *The Fatal Shore*, 1986.

Humboldt, Alexander von, *Kosmos*, 1845.

Hume, David, *The History of England*, 8 vols, 1770.

——*The Philosophical Works of David Hume*, 1926 edn.

Hurstfield, Joel, *The Queen's Wards*, 1958.

——'The Succession Struggle in Late Elizabethan England', in S. T. Bindoff, J. Hurstfield and C. H. Williams, eds, *Elizabethan Government and Society*, 1961.

——Review of *Arabella Stuart* by P. M. Handover, *English Historical Review* 76 (Jan. 1961): 150.

——Review of *Francis Bacon* by Fulton Anderson, *English Historical Review* 79 (July 1964): 603.

——*Freedom, Corruption and Government in Elizabethan England*, 1973.

——'Raleigh's Treason', *History Today*, 7 (1957): 480.

——'The Essex Rebellion', in *History of the English Speaking Peoples* (1970): 1536–8.

Hussey, Vincent, Letters in *CSPD 1598–1601*.

Huygens, Constantijn, *De Jeugt van Constantijn Huygens door hemzelf beshreven* (The author's youth described by himself) (1629–31), trans. from the Latin by A. H. Kan, The Hague, 1946.

Impey, Barwell, *Memoirs of Sir Elijah Impey*, 1840.

Irving, Henry, 'Shakespeare and Bacon', lecture delivered at Princeton University, 19 Mar. 1902, repr. *Baconiana* 103 (Apr. 1942).

Irwin, Margaret, *The Great Lucifer*, 1960.

Jackson, R. S., in *The Atheneum*, 6 Nov. 1909.

Jaki, Stanley L., *The Relevance of Physics*, 1966.

James I, *The Trew Law of Free Monarchies*, 1598.

——*Correspondence of King James VI of Scotland with Sir Robert Cecil and Others*, ed. John Bruce, 1861.

James, D. G., *The Dream of Learning*, Oxford, 1951.

——*The Dream of Prospero*, 1967.

James, Henry, *Letters of Henry James*, ed. Percy Lubbock, 1920.

James, William, *The Principles of Psychology*, 1890.

Jardine, David, *Criminal Trials*, 1832.

——*Use of Torture: A Reading on the Use of Torture in the Criminal Law of England Previously to the Commonwealth*, 1837.

Jenkins, Elizabeth, *Elizabeth and Leicester*, 1972.

Jessop, A., *John Donne*, 1897.

Johnson, C. W., *The Life of Sir Edward Coke, with Memoirs of his Contemporaries*, 2 vols, 1837.

Johnson, Paul, *Elizabeth, a Study in Power and Intellect*, 1974.

Johnson, Robert C., 'Francis Bacon and Lionel Cranfield', *Huntington Library Quarterly* 23.4 (1960): 301–20.

Johnson, Samuel, *Lives of the Most Eminent English Poets* (1779), 1801 edn.

Johnston, Arthur, *Francis Bacon, Selected and Edited*, New York, 1965.

Jones, R. F., *Ancients and Moderns*, 1936.

Jones, Stanley, *Hazlitt: A Life*, 1991.

Jones, W. J., *Ellesmere and Politics, 1603–1617*, Alberta, 1967.

Jonson, Ben, *Volpone*, 1607.

——'Conversations with Drummond' (1618–19), in vol. i of *Works*, 1925.

——*Works*, ed. C. H. Herford and Percy and Evelyn Simpson, 11 vols, Oxford, 1925–52.

Jordan, W. K., *Philanthropy in England, 1486–1660*, Chicago, 1959.

——*The Charities of London, 1486–1660*, Chicago, 1960.

Joseph, B. L., *Shakespeare's Eden, The Commonwealth of England 1558–1629*, 1971.

Jusserand, J. J., *Shakespeare in France*, 1899.

Kahn, C. H., ed., *The Art and Thought of Heraclitus*, Cambridge, 1979.

Kenyon, John, *The History Men, The Historical Profession in England since the Renaissance*, 1983.

Kernan, Alvin, *Shakespeare, the King's Playwright: Theater in the Stuart Court 1603–1613*, New Haven, 1995.

Keynes, Geoffrey, 'William Blake and Sir Francis Bacon', *TLS*, 8 Mar. 1957, 152.

Keynes, John Maynard, *Essays in Biography*, 1933.

Kiernan, Michael, ed., *Sir Francis Bacon, The Essayes, or Counsels, Civill and Morall*, Oxford, 1985.

Klibansky, Raymond, with Erwin Panovsky and Fritz Saxl, *Saturn and Melancholy*, 1964.

Knights, Lionel C., 'Bacon and the Seventeenth-Century Dissociation of Sensibility', *Scrutiny* 11 (1943): 268–86, repr. in Knights, *Explorations*, 1946.

Kocher, Paul, 'Francis Bacon on the Science of Jurisprudence', *Journal of the History of Ideas* 18 (1957): 3–26, repr. in Brian Vickers, ed., *Essential Articles for the Study of Francis Bacon*, Hamden, Conn., 1968.

——'Francis Bacon and his Father', *Huntington Library Quarterly* 21 (1958), 133–57.

——'Francis Bacon on the Drama', in R. Hosley, ed., *Essays on Shakespeare and Elizabethan Drama in Honor of Hardin Craig*, Columbia, Mo., 1962.

Kraus, Oskar, *Der Machtgedanke und die Friedensidee in der Philosophie der Engländer: Bacon und Bentham*, Leipzig, 1926.

Lacey, Robert, *Robert, Earl of Essex, An Elizabethan Icarus*, 1971.

——*Sir Walter Ralegh*, 1973.

Langbein, John, *Torture and the Law of Proof*, Chicago, 1977.

Langdon-Down, R., 'Observations on Shelton's *Don Quixote*', *Baconiana* 143 (July 1952).

Lasalle, Antoine, ed. and trans., Bacon, *Oeuvres Complètes*, 15 vols, Dijon, 1799–1803.

Leadbeater, C. W., *The Hidden Life in Freemasonry*, 1928.

Lecomte, Edward, *The Notorious Lady Essex*, 1970.

Le Doeuff, Michèle, 'Bacon ches les grands au siècle de Louis XIII', in *Terminologia e fortuna*, 1984.

——*Francis Bacon, du progrès de la promotion des savoirs (1605)*, Paris, 1991.

Lee, Sidney (Simeon Lazarus Levi), *Great Englishmen of the Sixteenth Century* (1904), 1925 edn.

Leibniz, Gottfried Wilhelm von, *Opera Omnia*, ed. Dutens, Geneva, 1768.

——'Introductio Historica', in *Oeuvres*, ed. Erdmann, Berlin, 1840.

Leishman, J. B., *The Monarch of Wit: Donne, the Man*, 1951.

Lemmi, C. W., *The Classical Deities in Bacon*, Baltimore, 1933.

Levi, Adolfo, *Il pensiero di Francesco Bacone considerato in relazione con le filosofie della natura del Rinascimento e col razionalismo cartesiano*, Turin, 1925.

Levi, Peter, *The Life and Times of William Shakespeare*, 1988.

Levine, Israel, *Francis Bacon*, 1925.

Lewis, C. S., *English Literature in the Sixteenth Century, Excluding Drama*, Oxford, 1954.

——*Surprised by Joy* (1955), 1984 edn.

Liebig, Justus von, *Über Francis Bacon von Verulam und die Methode der Naturforshung*, Munich, 1863, transl. Pierre de Tchihatchef, Paris, 1866.

Lingard, John, *Life and Letters of John Lingard*, ed. E. Bonney and M. Haile, 1912.

Litvinova, E. F., *Francis Bacon*, St Petersburg, 1891.

Lloyd, David, *State Worthies, or the Statesmen and Favourites of England since the Reformation, their Prudence and Policies, Successes and Miscarriages, Advancements and Falls, Henry VIII to Charles I*, 1665.

Lloyd, Howell A., *The Rouen Campaign*, Oxford, 1973.

Lloyd Williams, Norman, *Sir Walter Raleigh*, 1962.

Lockyer, Roger, *Buckingham, The Life and Political Career of George Villiers, First Duke of Buckingham 1592–1628*, 1981.

Lodge, Edmund, *Life of Sir Julius Caesar, Knt, with Memoirs of his Family and Descendents*, 1810.

——Portraits of Illustrious Personages of Great Britain, 1894.

Loomie, J. (S. J.), 'Bacon and Gondomar: An Unknown Link in 1618', *Renaissance Quarterly* 21 (1968): 1–10.

Lovejoy, B. C., *Francis Bacon, A Critical Review of his Life and Character*, 1888.

Luc, Jean André de, *Bacon tel qu'il est*, Berlin and Paris, 1800.

Macaulay, Catherine Sawbridge, *The History of England from the Accession of James I to that of the Brunswick Line, 1603–1714*, 1763–83 (transl. into French, 1791–2).

Macaulay, Thomas Babington, 'Francis Bacon', *Edinburgh Review* (July 1837), repr. in Macaulay, *Critical and Historical Essays*, Everyman edn, 1961, vol. 2, 280–398.

——*The Letters of Thomas Babington Macaulay*, ed. Thomas Pinney, Cambridge, vol. iii, 1976, and vol. vi, 1981.

MacCaffery, William T., 'Place and Patronage in Elizabethan Politics', in Bindoff et al., eds, *Elizabethan Government and Society*, 1961.

McCanles, Michael, 'Myth and Method in the Scientific Philosophy of Francis Bacon', in *Dialectical Criticism and Renaissance Literature*, Los Angeles, 1975.

McCann, Samuel G., 'The Public Life of Francis Bacon', in Rice Institute Pamphlet 13, Houston, 1926, 23–55.

McElwee, William, *The Murder of Thomas Overbury*, 1952.

McEwan, J. M., *The Riddell Diaries, 1908–1923*, 1986.

Mack, Maynard, *Alexander Pope, A Life*, New Haven, 1985.

Maclean, Hugh N., 'Reliquiae Bodleianae: Letter ccxxxii', *Bodleian Library Record* 6 (1960): 537–501.

McMahon, A. Philip, 'Francis Bacon's Essay "Of Beauty"', *Publications of the Modern Language Association of America* 60 (1945): 716–59.

Madariaga, Salvador de, *On Hamlet*, 1948.

Mair, G. H., *A Short History of English Literature*, 1911.

Maisse, A. H. de, *Journal* (1597), trans. B. G. Harisson and R. A. Jones, 1931.

Maistre, Joseph de, *Examen de la Philosophie de Bacon* (written 1803), 2 vols, Brussels, 1836.

——*Soirées de Saint Petersbourg*, in *Oeuvres Complètes de Joseph de Maistre*, Lyons, 1882.

Malherbe, Michel, 'Bacon, *L'Encyclopédie* et la Révolution', *Les Études Philosophiques* (July–Sept. 1985): 387–404.

Mallet, David, *The Life of Bacon, Lord Chancellor of England*, 1740.

Manes Verulamiani, in Memory of the Greatly Honoured Lord Bacon, Baron Verulam, Viscount St Alban (1626), ed. W. G. C. Gundry, 1949.

Marañón, Gregorio, *Antonio Pérez, 'Spanish Traitor'* (Madrid, 1948), trans. C. D. Ley, 1954.

Martin, Julian, *Francis Bacon. The State and the Reform of Natural Philosophy*, Cambridge, 1992.

Martin, Thomas, *The Character of Lord Bacon*, 1835.

Martineau, Harriet, *Biographical Sketches*, 1869.

Marwil, Jonathan L., *The Trials of Counsel, Francis Bacon in 1621*, Detroit, 1976.

Massey, Gerald, *The Secret Drama of Shakespeare's Sonnets*, 1888.

Masson, David, *Essays Biographical and Critical*, 1853.

——Essay V, in *Wordsworth, Shelley and Keats, and Other Essays*, 1874, repr. from *North British Review*, 1853.

Matheson, P. E., and Matheson, E. F., eds, *Francis Bacon: Selections, with Essays by Macaulay and S. R. Gardiner* (1992), Oxford, 1964.

Mathew, Arnold H. and Calthrop, Annette, *The Life of Sir Tobie Matthew, Bacon's Alter Ego*, 1907.

Mathew, David, *James I*, 1933.

Mathews, N., 'Francis Bacon Upside Down', *Baconiana* 179 (1979): 61–71.

Matthew, Toby, *Autobiographical Letter to Dame Mary Gage* (1611), ed. Edward Dowden, 1904.

——Dedicatory letter to the Grand Duke of Tuscany, prefixed to Matthew's transl. of Bacon's *Essays*, Florence, 1618.

—— transl. from the Latin, *The Confessions of the Incomparable Doctour S. Augustine*, St Omer, 1618.

——*A Collection of Letters made by Sir Tobias Matthew Kt, to which are added many Letters of his own*, 1660.

Mattingley, Garrett, *Renaissance Diplomacy*, 1955.

Medawar, Peter, 'On "The Effecting of all Things Possible"', *The Advancement of Science* 26 (1969–70).

Mersenne, Marin, *La vérité des sciences*, Paris, 1628.

Metz, Rudolf, 'Bacon's Part in the Intellectual Movement of his Time', trans. Joan Drever, in *Seventeenth-Century Studies Presented to Sir Herbert Grierson*, Oxford, 1938.

Milton, John, *Private Correspondence and Academic Exercises* (1625–32), transl. from the Latin and introd. by P. B. Tillyard and E. M. W. Tillyard, 1932.

——*An Apology against a Pamphlet called 'A Modest Confutation of the Animadversions'*, 1642.

Mollay, Charles, *Resuscitatio of Francis Bacon*, 1670.

Montagu, Basil, *Life of Francis Bacon*, appended to *Works of Francis Bacon, Chancellor of England*, 16 vols, 1825–34.

Montague, F. C., ed., *Critical and Historical Essays Contributed to the Edinburgh Review by Lord Macaulay*, 3 vols, 1907.

Morgan, Appleton, letter to the Editor, *Baconiana* 31 (July 1910).

Morison, J. Cotter, *Macaulay*, 1882.

Moryson, Fynes, *An Itinerary*, 1617.

Munden, R. C., 'James and "the Growth of Mutual Mistrust"', in Kevin Sharp, ed., *Faction and Parliament*, 1978.

Naigeon, J. A., *La Philosophie ancienne et moderne*, Paris, 1789–1810.

Napier, Macvey, *Lord Bacon and Sir Walter Raleigh*, Cambridge, 1853.

Naunton, Robert, *Fragmenta Regalia, or Observations on the Late Queen Elizabeth, her Times and Favourites* (1630), ed. E. Arther, 1895.

Neale, J. E., *Queen Elizabeth*, 1934.

——*Essays in Elizabethan History*, 1958.

——*Elizabeth and her Parliaments*, vol. 1: *1559–1581*, 1953; vol. 2: *1584–1601*, 1957.

Negri, L., 'Campanella e i primi Lincei', in *La Cultura*, 1929.

Newman, John Henry, 'Discourses on University Education', in *Newman: Prose and Poetry*, ed. Geoffrey Tillotson, 1957.

Nichol, John, *Francis Bacon, His Life and Philosophy*, 2 vols, 1888–9.

Nicholl, Charles, *The Creature in the Map: A Journey to El Dorado*, 1995.

Nichols, John, *The Progresses and Public Processions of Queen Elizabeth*, 1788–1807.

Nickson, Horace, 'The Authorship of "Don Quixote"', *Baconiana* 78 (Feb. 1931).

Noonan, John T. Jr., *Bribes*, New York, 1984.

Notestein, Wallace, *Four Worthies*, 1956.

——*The House of Commons 1604–1610*, New Haven, 1971.

Notestein, Wallace, Relf, Frances, and Simpson, Harttey, eds, *Commons Debates 1621*, New Haven, 1935.

Nye, Robert, *The Voyage of Destiny*, 1982.

Origo, Iris, *A Need to Testify*, 1984.

Osborne, Francis, *Advice to a Son* (1656), 1673 edn.

——*Historical Memoires on the Reigns of Queen Elizabeth and King James*, 1658.

——*A Miscellany of Sundry Essays*, 1659.

Overton Fuller, Jean, *Sir Francis Bacon: A Biography*, 1981.

Owen, Orville Ward, *Sir Francis Bacon's Cipher Story*, 5 vols, Detroit, 1893–5.

Ozanam, A. F., *Deux Chanceliers d'Angleterre*, Paris, 1836.

Paget, J., 'Lord Macaulay and the Duke of Marlborough', *The New Examen* 1 (1861).

Palmer, Herbert, *Memoirs of Godliness and Christianity*, 1695.

Parry, Graham, *The Golden Age Restored: The Culture of the Stuart Court, 1603–1642*, Manchester, 1981.

Patrick, J. Max, 'Tribute to Bacon's 400th Anniversary', *Writers and their Work* 131 (1961).

——'Hawk versus Dove, Francis Bacon's Advocacy of a Holy War by James against the Turks', in W. A. Sessions, ed., *The Legacy of Francis Bacon*, 1971.

Pauli, Wolfgang, 'Die Philosophische Bedeutung der Idee der Komplimentarität', *Experientia* 6 (1950).

Pawlisch, Hans, *Sir John Davies and the Conquest of Ireland: A Study in Legal Imperialism*, Cambridge, 1985.

Pearcy, Lee T., *The Mediated Muse*, 1985.

Peck, ed., *Desiderata Curiosa*, 1732.

Peck, Linda L., 'Corruption at the Court of James I: The Undermining of Legitimacy', in B. C. Malament, ed., *After the Reformation, Essays in Honour of J. H. Hexter*, Manchester, 1980.

——*Northampton, Patronage and Policy at the Court of James I*, 1982.

Peltonen, Markku, 'Politics and Science: Francis Bacon and the True Greatness of States', *Historical Journal* 35.2 (1992): 279–305.

Penrose, Stephen B. L. Jr, 'The Reputation and Influence of Francis Bacon in the Seventeenth Century', Ph.D. thesis, Columbia University, New York, 1934.

Percy, Lee T., *The Mediated Muse*, 1935.

Pérez-Ramos, Antonio, *Francis Bacon's Idea of Science and the Maker's Knowledge Tradition*, Oxford, 1988.

Peters, Edward, *Torture*, Oxford, 1985.

Pitcher, John, ed., *Francis Bacon: The Essays*, 1985.

Pitt, M., *The Cries of the Oppressed*, 1691.

Plowden, Geoffrey, *Pope on Classic Ground*, Athens, Ohio, 1984.

Pollen, John H., the Younger (S. J.), *Mary Queen of Scots and the Babington Plot*, Edinburgh, 1922.

Pope, Alexander, *An Essay on Man* (1734), ed. Maynard Mack, Twickenham Edition of the Poems of Alexander Pope, gen. ed. John Butt, III, i, 1951.

——*Epistles to Several Persons (Moral Essays)*, Twick. ed., III, ii, 1951.

——*Essay on Criticism*, Twick. ed., I, 1961.

——*The Correspondence of Alexander Pope*, ed. George Sherburn, Oxford, 1956.

Popkin, R. H., Review of *Francis Bacon, His Career and Thought* by Fulton Anderson, *Philosophical Review* 73 (1964).

Porohovschikov, Pierre S., *Shakespeare Unmasked*, 1940.

Potts, Constance, *Francis Bacon and his Secret Society*, 1981.

Powell, Thomas, *The Attorney's Academy*, 1623.

Prestwich, Menna, *Cranfield, Politics and Profits under the Early Stuarts, The Career of Lionel Cranfield, Earl of Middlesex*, Oxford, 1966.

Pryme, Abraham de la, *Memoirs of Thomas Bushell taken from the MS Diary of A. de la Pryme*, ed. W. Harrison, 1878.

Quennell, Peter, *Shakespeare, the Poet and his Background*, 1963.

Quinton, Anthony, *Francis Bacon*, Oxford, 1980.

Ralegh, Walter, *History of the World* (1614), Edinburgh, 1820 edn, 6 vols.

——*The Prerogative of Parliaments in England*, 1628.

Randolph, Thomas, 'On the Death of Lord Francis Bacon, Baron Verulam, Late Lord Chancellor of all England', in *Manes Verulamiani* (1626), ed. W. G. Gundry, 1950.

Rawley, William, *Life of the Honourable Author*, introducing *Resuscitatio*, his edition of Bacon's works, 1657; see Spedding et al., eds, *The Works of Francis Bacon*, **i**, 3–18.

Read, Conyers, *Mr Secretary Walsingham and the Policy of Queen Elizabeth*, 1925.

——*Mr Secretary Cecil*, 1955.

——*Lord Burghley and Queen Elizabeth*, 1960.

——'William Cecil and Elizabethan Public Relations', in Bindoff et al., eds, *Elizabethan Government and Society*, 1961.

Rebholz, Ronald, A., *The Life of Fulke Greville, First Lord Brooke*, Oxford, 1971.

Rees, Graham, 'Francis Bacon's biological ideas', in *Occult and Scientific Mentalities*, 1984.

——(assisted by Christopher Upton), *Francis Bacon's Natural Philosophy: A New Source*, British Society for the History of Science, 1984.

Rémusat, Charles de, *Bacon, sa vie et son temps*, Paris, 1857.

Reynolds, Samuel H., ed., *The Essays, or Counsels Civil and Moral, of Francis Bacon, Lord Verulam, Viscount St Alban*, Oxford, 1890.

Righter, Anne, 'Francis Bacon', in Hugh Sykes Davies and George Watson, eds, *The English Mind, Studies in the English Moralists Presented to Basil Willey*, Cambridge, 1964, repr. in Brian Vickers, ed., *Essential Articles for the Study of Francis Bacon*, Hamden, Conn., 1968.

Ritchie, John, ed., *Reports of the Cases decided by Francis Bacon in the High Court of Chancery (1617–1621)*, 1932.

Roberts, Clayton, *The Growth of Responsible Government in Stuart England*, Cambridge, 1966.

Robertson, J. M., *Pioneer Humanists*, 1907.

——*The Baconian Heresy, A Confutation*, 1913.

Ronsard, Pierre de, *Oeuvres complètes*, ed. P. Laumonier, Paris, 1914.

Roskell, J. S., *The Impeachment of Michael de la Pole, Earl of Suffolk, in 1386*, 1984.

Ross, Charles, *Richard III*, 1981.

Rossi, Mario, M., *Saggio su Francesco Bacon*, Bologna, 1934.

Rossi, Paolo, 'Sul carattere non utilitaristico della filosofia di F. Bacone', *Rivista critica di storia della filosofia* 12 (1957): 22–41.

——'Per una bibliografia degli scritti su Francesco Bacone, 1800–1956', *Rivista critica di storia della filosofia* 12 (1957): 75–89.

——*Francesco Bacone: dalla magia alla scienza*, Bari, 1957 (Engl. transl., 1968).

——'Venti, maree, ipotesi astronomiche in Bacone e Galilei', in *Aspetti della rivoluzione scientifica*, Naples, 1971.

——'Baconianism', in *Dictionary of the History of Ideas*, 4 vols, New York, 1973.

——'Ants, Spiders and Epistemologists', in *Terminologia e fortuna*, 1984.

——ed., *Scritti Filosofici di Francesco Bacone*, Turin, 1986.

Rowley, James, 'Francis Bacon, his Public Career and Personal Character', in *Wordsworth and Other Essays*, Bristol, 1927.

Rowse, A. L., *The English Spirit*, 1944.

—— *Ralegh and the Throgmortons*, 1962.

—— *William Shakespeare, A Biography*, 1963.

—— *Shakespeare's Southampton*, 1965.

—— *Court and Country*, 1987.

Ruigh, Robert E., *The Parliament of 1624, Politics and Foreign Policy*, Cambridge, Mass., 1971.

Rushworth, John, *Historical Collections*, 1659.

Russell, Conrad, *Parliaments and English Politics 1621–1629*, Oxford, 1979.

—— *The Causes of the English Civil War*, Ford Lecture (1987), Oxford, 1990.

—— 'John Bull's Other Nation', *TLS*, 12 Mar. 1993.

Rymer, Thomas, *Foedera*, ed. R. Sanderson, 20 vols, 1704–32.

Saintsbury, George, *A History of English Literature*, 3 vols, 1920.

—— *History of Criticism and Literary Taste*, 1922.

Salisbury Papers, Calendar of the Manuscripts of Salisbury Preserved at Hatfield House, Historical Manuscripts Commission, 1892.

Sanderson, (Bishop) William, *Aulus Coquinariae, or A Vindication in Answer to a Pamphlet intitulated The Court and Character of King James the First*, 1650.

Sandys, George, *Ovid's Metamorphoses Englished*, 1632.

Sayers, Dorothy, *Gaudy Night*, 1935.

Schoenbaum, S., *Shakespeare's Lives*, Oxford, 1970.

Schreiber, Roy E., *The Political Career of Sir Robert Naunton, 1589–1635*, London Royal History Society, 1981.

Schroedinger, Edwin, *What is Life?* (1944), Cambridge, 1969.

Schweitzer, Albert, *The Philosophy of Civilization* (1923), trans. C. T. Campion 1924.

Scott, William O., 'Shelley's Admiration for Bacon', *Publications of the Modern Language Association* 73 (1958): 228–36.

Seccombe, Thomas, and Allen, J. W., *The Age of Shakespeare*, 2 vols, 1903.

Seeley, John, *History of England, 1603–1642*, 1911.

Sessions, William A., 'Bacon and Herbert, An Image of Chalk', in C. J. Summers and T. L. Pebworth, eds, *Too Rich to Clothe the Sunne, Essays on George Herbert*, Pittsburgh, 1980.

—— 'Recent Studies in Francis Bacon', *English Renaissance* 17 (1987).

—— ed., *The Legacy of Francis Bacon*, Studies in the Literary Imagination, iv, 1, Atlanta, Georgia, April 1971.

Sewell, Elizabeth, *The Orphic Voice, Poetry and Natural History*, New Haven, 1960.

Sharpe, Kevin, ed., *Faction and Parliament, Essays on Early Stuart History*, 1978.

Shaw, Peter, *The Philosophical Works of Francis Bacon*, 1733.

Shaw, W. A., *The Knights of England, A Complete Record from the Earliest Time to the Present Day of the Knights of all the Orders of Chivalry in England, Scotland and Ireland*, 2 vols, 1906.

Shelley, Percy B., *A Defence of Poetry* (1820), 1891 edn.

—— *The Banquet of Plato and Other Pieces* (1887), 1905 edn.

Sidney, Philip, *An Apology for Poetry* (1595), 1965 edn.

—— *Sidney Papers, Letters and Memorials of State*, 2 vols, written and collected by

Bibliography

Henry Sydney and others and transcribed by A. Collins, 1746.

Slaughter, J. W., 'Francis Bacon and the Ideal Commonwealth', in Rice Institute Pamphlet 13 (1926): 56–72.

Smedley, W. T., 'The Mystery of Francis Bacon', *Baconiana* 33 (Jan. 1911).

Smith, Alan G. R., 'Crown, Parliament and Finance: The Great Contract of 1610', in P. Clark, A. G. R. Smith and N. Tacke, eds, *The English Commonwealth*, Leicester, 1974.

Smith, Logan Pearsall, *The Life and Letters of Sir Henry Wotton*, 2 vols, 1907.

Smith, Thomas, *De Republica Anglorum* (1583), ed. Alston, Cambridge, 1906.

Solzhenitsyn, Alexander, *Cancer Ward*, Engl. transl. New York, 1969.

——*A Documentary Record*, ed. L. Labedz, 1970.

Sortais, Gaston, *La philosophie moderne depuis Bacon jusqu'à Leibnitz*, 2 vols, Paris 1922.

Spedding, James (unsigned), 'A Railway Reader, Companion to the Railway Edition of Lord Campbell's Life of Bacon', 1853.

—— *The Letters and the Life of Francis Bacon, Including all his Occasional Works*, ed. with commentary by J. Spedding, 7 vols (1861–74).

—— *The Works of Francis Bacon*, collected and ed. J. Spedding, R. L. Ellis and D. D. Heath, 7 vols (1861–74).

——'Lord Macaulay's Essay on Bacon Examined' and 'The Latest Theory about Bacon', *Contemporary Review* 27 and 28 (June–Nov. 1876).

——*Evenings with a Reviewer (ER)*, 2 vols, privately circulated 1848, pub., 1881.

Spence, Joseph, *Observations, Anecdotes and Characters of Books and Men Collected from Conversation* (1735), ed. S. L. Singer, 1858.

Sprat, (Bishop) Thomas, *History of the Royal Society* (1667), 1772 edn.

Stebbing, William, *Sir Walter Ralegh, A Biography*, Oxford, 1891.

Steeves, G. Walter, *Francis Bacon*, 1910.

Stephen, James, Article on James Spedding, in *DNB*.

Stephens, James, *Francis Bacon and the Style of Science*, Chicago, 1975.

Stephens, Robert, *Letters and Life of Bacon*, 1701.

Stone, Laurence, 'The Fruits of Office, The Case of Robert Cecil, First Earl of Salisbury, 1596–1612', in F. J. Fisher, ed., *The Economic and Social History of Tudor and Stuart England, Essays in Honour of R. H. Tawney*, Cambridge, 1961.

——*The Crisis of Aristocracy*, Princeton, 1965.

——*Family and Fortune, Studies in Aristocratic Finance in the Sixteenth and Seventeenth Centuries*, Oxford, 1973.

Stopes, C. M., *The Third Earl of Southampton*, 1922.

Stow, John, *Annales, a General Chronicle of England from Brute until the present year of Christ 1580*, 1580; continued Edmund Howes, 1615.

Strachey, Lytton, *Eminent Victorians*, 1918.

——*Elizabeth and Essex*, 1928.

——*Portraits in Miniature*, 1931.

Strong, Roy, *Henry, Prince of Wales, and England's Lost Renaissance*, 1986.

Swift, Jonathan, *The Prose Works of Jonathan Swift*, ed. Herbert Davis, Oxford, 1941.

Sydenham (Lord, of Combe), 'The First Baconian', *Baconiana* 80 (Feb. 1933).

Taylor, Henry, *Autobiography*, 1885.

Tenison, (Archbishop) Thomas, *Certain Remains of Sir Francis Bacon, Baron of Verulam and Viscount of St Alban*, 1679.

Theobald, R., 'Bacon as Viewed by his Biographers', *Journal of the Bacon Society* (1886).

Thorndike, Lynn, *A History of Magic and Experimental Science*, vol. 7, New York, 1958.

Thorpe, W. G., *The Hidden Lives of Shakespeare and Bacon, and their Business Connections*, 1897.

Thou, Jacques Auguste de, *Historia mei Temporis, 1553–1617* (written 1604–20), privately circulated 1620, published 1734; in French, *Histoire Universelle*, 1739.

Tite, Colin G. C., *Impeachment and Parliamentary Judicature in Early Stuart England*, 1974.

Tittler, Robert, 'Sir Nicholas Bacon and the Reform of the Tudor Chancery', *University of Toronto Law Journal* 23 (1973).

——*Nicholas Bacon, The Making of a Tudor Statesman*, 1976.

Townshend, Hayward, *Historical Collections, or Exact Account of the Proceedings of the Last Four Parliaments of Q. Elizabeth, etc.*, 1680.

Trevelyan, G. M., *England under the Stuarts* (1904), 1960 edn.

Trevor-Roper, Hugh, 'Thomas Sutton', *The Carthusian* 15 (1948).

——'The General Crisis of the Seventeenth Century', *Past and Present* 16 (Nov. 1959).

——Address on Francis Bacon, 22 Jan. 1961, *Encounter*, Feb. 1962.

——'Reputations Revisited', *TLS*, 21 Jan. 1977.

——*From Counter-Reformation to Glorious Revolution*, 1992.

Tsanoff, R. A., 'Francis Bacon and Philosophic Thought', in Rice Institute Pamphlet 13, Houston, 1926, 1–22.

Twain, Mark (Samuel C. Clemens), *Is Shakespeare Dead?*, 1909. Copyright 1970, the Mark Twain Company.

Udny, E. Francis, *Later Incarnations of Francis Bacon*, Wheaton, Ill., 1925.

Ungerer, Gustav, *Anglo-Spanish Relations*, Berne, 1956.

Urbach, Peter, *Francis Bacon's Philosophy of Science*, La Salle, Ill., 1987.

Usher, Roland G., 'Francis Bacon's Knowledge of Law French', *Modern Language Notes* 24 (1919): 28–32.

Vaughan, W. A., Letter to the Editor, *Baconiana* 88 (Jan. 1938).

Vauzelles, J. B. de, *Histoire de la vie et des ouvrages de F. Bacon*, 2 vols, Paris, 1833.

Venables, G. S., Preface to James Spedding, *Evenings with a Reviewer*, 1881.

Vence, Camoin de, *La vérité sur la condamnation du Chancelier Bacon*, Paris, 1886.

Vickers, Brian, *Francis Bacon and Renaissance Prose*, Cambridge, 1968.

——'Bacon's Use of Theatrical Imagery', in W. A. Sessions, ed., *The Legacy of Francis Bacon*, 1971.

——'Francis Bacon and the Progress of Knowledge', address delivered at the Francis Bacon Library, Claremont, to commemorate the 428th anniversary of Bacon's birth, 25 Jan. 1989, publ. in part in *Journal of the History of Ideas* (1992).

——'Bacon among the Literati: Science and Language', *Comparative Criticism* 13 (1990).

——ed., *Essential Articles for the Study of Francis Bacon*, Hamden, Conn., 1968.

——ed., *Occult and Scientific Mentalities in the Renaissance*, Cambridge, 1984.

Bibliography

Vico, Giambattista, *Scienza Nuova*, Bari, 1713.

Vigenère, Blaise de, *Traité des Chiffres*, Paris, 1587.

Voltaire, *Lettres sur les Anglais* (1734), Engl. transl., *Letters Concerning the English Nation by Mr Voltaire*, 1750.

Waite, A. E., *Brotherhood of the Rosy Cross*, 1924.

——*Real History of the Rosicrucians*, 1988.

Walker, D. P., 'Spirits in Francis Bacon', in *Terminologia e fortuna*, 1984.

Waller, Edmund, *Poems*, 1645.

Walton, Izaak, *The Lives of John Donne, Sir Henry Wotton, Richard Hooker, George Herbert and Robert Sanderson* (1640), Oxford, 1962 edn.

Warton, Joseph, *An Essay on the Writings and Genius of Pope*, 1782.

——ed., *The Works of Alexander Pope*, 9 vols, 1797.

Wats, Gilbert, Preface to *The Advancement and Proficience of Learning*, his translation of Francis Bacon, *De Dignitate et Augmentis Scientiarum*, Oxford, 1640.

Watts, Jonathan, 'Lionel Cranfield, Earl of Middlesex', in Timothy Eustace, ed., *Statesmen and Politicians of the Stuart Age*, 1985.

Webb, (Judge), *The Mystery of William Shakespeare*, 1902.

Webster, Charles, *The Great Instauration, Science, Medicine and Reform, 1626–1700*, 1975.

Weldon, Anthony, *The Court and Character of King James*, 1651.

Westman, Robert S., 'Nature, Art and Psyche: Jung, Pauli and the Kepler-Fludd Polemic', in Brian Vickers, ed., *Occult and Scientific Mentalities in the Renaissance*, Cambridge, 1984.

Wheelwright, Philip, *Heraclitus*, Princeton, 1959.

Whitaker, Virgil, K., 'Francis Bacon's Intellectual Milieu', Address delivered at the William Andrews Library, Los Angeles, 16 Nov. 1961, celebrating the 400th anniversary of Bacon's birth, repr. in B. Vickers, ed., *Essential Articles for the Study of Francis Bacon*, 1968.

White, Howard B., *Peace Among the Willows*, The Hague, 1968.

White, Stephen D., *Sir Edward Coke and the Grievances of Commonwealth*, Manchester, 1979.

White, William, *A Criticism of Macaulay's Essay*, 1900.

Whitehead, Alan N., *Science and the Modern World*, 1926.

Whitney, Charles, *Francis Bacon and Modernity*, New Haven, 1986.

Wigston, W. F. C., *Bacon and the Rosicrucians*, 1889.

Williams, Charles, *Bacon*, 1933.

Williams, C. H., 'In Search of the Queen', *Elizabethan Government*, 1961.

Willson, David, H., *The Privy Councillors in the House of Commons, 1604–29*, Minneapolis, 1940.

——*King James VI and I*, 1956.

Wilson, Arthur, *The Annals of King James I* (1653), 1706 edn.

Wilson, Thomas, 'The State of England, Anno Dom. 1600', *The Camden Miscellany* 16, 1936.

Windle, D. F. A., *Report to the British Museum*, San Francisco, 1881.

Winwood, Ralph, *Memorials of the Affairs of State in the Reigns of Queen Elizabeth and King James the First*, 3 vols, 1725.

Wolff, Emil, *Francis Bacon und seine Quellen*, 2 vols, Berlin, 1913.

Woodward, Parker, 'Shakespeare's Sonnets, 1609', *Baconiana* 37 (Jan. 1912).

——'Don Quixote', *Baconiana* 56 (Oct. 1916).

Wormald, B. H. G., *Francis Bacon, History, Politics and Science, 1561–1616*, Cambridge, 1993.

Wotton, Henry, *Reliquiae Wottonianae*, 1641.

Yates, Frances A., *The French Academies of the Sixteenth Century*, 1947.

——*Astraea, The Imperial Theme*, 1975.

——*The Occult Philosophy in the Elizabethan Age*, 1979.

Zaller, Robert, *The Parliament of 1621, A Study in Constitutional Conflict*, Berkeley, 1971.

Zolla, Elemire, *Storia del Fantasticare*, Milan, 1964.

Note on Primary Sources

Since the published sources for the period are plentiful, it was not generally found necessary to resort to unpublished material. The principal manuscript consulted was, at the Public Record Office, James I, 14/99, folios 172–3, a note made by Thomas Wilson of Ralegh's report to him about a conversation he had held with the Lord Chamberlain, Pembroke (erroneously read until now as the Lord Chancellor, i.e. Bacon), in which he had confessed his intention of seizing the Spanish Plate fleet. In Chancery the *Decree Book*, 1618, C33, was examined to estimate the number of decrees awarded by Bacon during his four years of service. See also at the Public Record Office, State Papers 14/90, folio 113, Lovelace to Carleton, 16 March 1617, on the bills expected to be brought against Chancellor Ellesmere in the Star Chamber.

Index